1/98

D0205986

CROSSING SWORDS

CROSSING SWORDS

POLITICS AND RELIGION
IN MEXICO

Roderic Ai Camp

VILLA JULIE COLLEGE LIBRARY
STEVENSON, MD 21153

New York   Oxford
OXFORD UNIVERSITY PRESS
1997

Oxford University Press

Oxford   New York
Athens   Auckland   Bangkok   Bogota   Bombay
Buenos Aires   Calcutta   Cape Town   Dar es Salaam
Delhi   Florence   Hong Kong   Istanbul   Karachi
Kuala Lumpur   Madras   Madrid   Melbourne
Mexico City   Nairobi   Paris   Singapore
Taipei   Tokyo   Toronto

and associated companies in
Berlin   Ibadan

Copyright © 1997 by Oxford University Press, Inc.

Published by Oxford University Press, Inc.,
198 Madison Avenue, New York, New York 10016

Oxford is a registered trademark of Oxford University Press

All rights reserved. No part of this publication may be reproduced,
stored in a retrieval system, or transmitted in any form or by any means,
electronic, mechanical, photocopying, recording, or otherwise,
without the prior permission of Oxford University Press.

Library of Congress Cataloging-in-Publication Data
Camp, Roderic Ai.
Crossing swords : politics and religion in Mexico / Roderic Ai
Camp.
    p.   cm.
    Includes bibliographical references and index.
    ISBN 0-19-510784-5
    1. Catholic Church—Mexico—History—20th century.
2. Christianity and politics—Catholic Church—History—20th
century.   3. Church and state—Catholic Church—History—20th
century.   4. Church and state—Mexico—History—20th century.
5. Mexico—Church history—20th century.   6. Mexico—Politics and
government—1988–   I. Title.
BX1428.2.C27   1997   96-838
261.7′0972—dc20

9 8 7 6 5 4 3 2 1
Printed in the United States of America
on acid-free paper

Acknowledgments

It would be impossible to undertake a project as comprehensive as this without the assistance and encouragement of many individuals. I began the research in 1986, and the documentary searches took me to many libraries and individuals. I have been particularly impressed with the collegiality and supportiveness of Mexican religious scholars, many of them clergy, who are engaged in efforts to deepen our knowledge of the contemporary Church. Among those who have made special efforts to keep me apprised of ongoing research and make invaluable sources available, I owe special thanks to a group of professors and graduate students of religious studies at Ibero-American University. These include Enrique Luengo González, who directed a number of graduate students in one of the most important projects on the views of priests anywhere in the hemisphere, Oscar Aguilar Ascencio, who has repeatedly provided me with unpublished materials and answered my probing questions, Eduardo Sota García, who went well beyond professional courtesy to make an entire set of back issues of a critical documentary source available by mail, and Roberto Blancarte, of the Colegio Mexiquense, who recommended other important sources.

I also owe a debt to Miguel Basáñez, who provided the basis for much of the original data in chapter 5, allowing me to pose religious questions in some of his national polls, and making other information available to me in his own polls for *Este País*. Also, Enrique Alduncin gave me the raw data related to religion for his national surveys at the National Bank of Mexico. I also am indebted to Manuel Carrillo Poblano and Miguel Basáñez for arranging numerous interviews and facilitating the interview process. In Puebla, José Alarcón Hernández brought me into contact with many interesting priests, and with Archbishop Rosendo Huesca, a cleric of many insights about the contemporary Church. In Jalisco, Javier Hurtado and Pedro Humberto Garza Gómez not only arranged my conversations with many clergy, but Pedro drove me into the countryside to visit rural parishes. María Emilia Farías, long interested in the Church, loaned me her prolific collection of clippings and materials, and José Luis Gaona, who covered the Church as part of his journalistic beat, sent me copies of every article he had published. Finally, the staffs at the Colegio de México, Ibero-American University, Bancroft Library,

Georgetown University Library, and Harvard University Divinity Library were extremely helpful.

I also owe thanks to many students in my seminar on Church and Politics in Latin America at Tulane University who have challenged my thinking and stimulated exploration of new interpretations. Scott Pentzer and Meg Mitchell carried out numerous interviews with priests throughout Mexico in 1993, adding further depth and diversity to my own interview schedule. Shannan Mattiace, under the auspices of a National Endowment for the Humanities stipend, did field research in Chiapas and Yucatán, adding numerous insights about Mexican ecclesiastical base communities.

I received generous financial support from the Howard Heinz Foundation, the Tinker Foundation, and the Roger Thayer Stone Center for Latin American Studies at Tulane. These funds allowed me to conduct the most extensive interviews in which I have ever engaged for a Mexican research project, and over a time period ideal for a study of politics and religion in Mexico: before, during, and after the unexpected constitutional reforms.

I also want to express my thanks to Edward Cleary, Daniel C. Levy, Kenneth Coleman, Carol Ann Drogus, Eduardo Sota García, and Scott Mainwaring for comments and suggestions on various parts of the manuscript, at different stages of completion.

New Orleans, Louisiana   R. A. C.
December 1995

Contents

1   Church and State: Foundations of Analysis   3
      Conditions Favoring a Secular Role   4
      Obstacles to Church Influence   7
      Analytical Choices—A Theoretical Argument   8
      Notes   19

2   Historical Underpinnings and Reform: Two Decades in Brief Repose   24
      Pre-1910 Themes Found in Mexican Religious History   24
      Post-1910 Themes Found in Mexican Religious History   26
      1968: A Turning Point in Church-State Relations?   29
      *Constitutional Reforms: Closing the Gap between Theory and
          Practice*   31
      The Reforms   34
      Reactions to and Consequences of the Reforms   37
      Notes   41

3   Issues Facing the Church: Politics, Partisanship, and Development   50
      Partisanship and Parties   54
      Election Fraud, Voting, and Chihuahua   60
      Social Justice   67
      Conclusions   69
      Notes   70

4   Issues Facing the Church: Moral and Spiritual Challenges   79
      Human Rights   79
      Vatican II, Medellín, and Liberation Theology   85
      Protestantism   94
      Conclusions   97
      Notes   99

5 Religion, Politics, and the Laity 109
    Mexican Religiosity 111
    Determinants of Religious Intensity 113
    Social and Political Consequences of Religiosity 116
    Conclusions 124
    Notes 126

6 Becoming a Priest: Why Mexicans Enter the Clergy 135
    Family Environment 136
    Religious Kinship 143
    Educational Influences 145
    Impact of History 146
    Personal Revelations 148
    Conclusions 149
    Notes 150

7 Educating the Clergy: From Priest to Bishop 154
    Careers and Education 154
    Seminarians, Teachers, and Students 158
    Montezuma: Priests in Exile 166
    A Roman Passage: Studies at the Gregorian University 170
    Conclusions 173
    Notes 174

8 Who Are the Bishops?: Consequences of Family and Place 180
    Consequences of Birth 180
    The Influence of Social Origins 191
    Conclusions 197
    Notes 199

9 Church-State Interlocks: Informal Relations 202
    Personal Linkages: Social, Familial, and Educational 203
    National and Local Structural Relations 209
    Local and State Linkages: Presaging New National Patterns? 212
    Presidential Friendships 215
    Conclusions 220
    Notes 222

10 Structure and Decision Making: International and National Actors 228
    Intervention or Nonintervention: The Papal Nuncio 229
    National Structures: Linking the Dioceses to the Episcopate 233
    Extranational Influences, Finances, and Personnel 241

Conclusions   249
Notes   251

11   Structure and Decision Making: The Bishop in His Diocese   259
    Governing the Diocese: The Autonomous Bishop   259
    Choosing a Successor: Who Selects the Bishop?   263
    Priest and Bishop: Dissension in the Ranks?   267
    Divisions in the Church: Origins, Tendencies, and Consequences   271
    Conclusions   274
    Notes   276

12   The Church Viewed through Political and Clerical Lenses   283
    How Politicians View the Catholic Church   284
    How Bishops View the Church's Role   288
    Priests and the Church: Views of the Rank and File   295
    Notes   302

Appendix: Mexican Bishops   309

Bibliographic Essay   319

Index   327

CROSSING SWORDS

Church and State

Foundations of Analysis

S ocial scientists have proffered numerous methodological strategies in pursuit of understanding the secular role of religion in society. This literature, much of it originally advanced by political historians, focused on institutional analysis, as did the study of politics in general. That emphasis led to an examination of religious and secular society's two major institutional representatives, church and state. As the discipline developed, scholars reached out for broader and deeper topics, exploring issues involving mass religion and politics—in short, how popular religious beliefs affect a citizen's political behavior. North American and European scholarship led the way because religious affiliation was deemed a significant variable in political partisanship in societies where a diversity of religious beliefs and institutions prevailed.

Most examinations of religion and politics are drawn to the topic on the assumption that religious beliefs or behavior confront the political status quo, leading to conflicts between religious and political institutions.[1] As Daniel Levine has argued, "[C]oncern with 'politization of religion' works from a false premise: that 'politics' is only (or principally) a matter of challenges to established arrangements."[2] It is often forgotten that religion forms an integral component of a society's culture, including its political culture, and that religious institutions historically, more often than not, were allies of, not vocal challengers to, the state. Religion and religious institutions are important vehicles for granting legitimacy to other, more "political" structures and agents.[3] Typically, the Catholic Church has been viewed as a legitimizing agent of the state, and of the existing order in Mexico, despite periods of deep, historical antagonism.[4]

Religion and politics in Mexico today are of particular interest to American scholars and the general reader. Mexico is a country that has witnessed the assassination of a cardinal (of which there are fewer than 150 worldwide), that has seen the government reverse perhaps the most stringent constitutional restrictions on religion present in the 1990s of nearly any country, that boasts a flowering of civic action groups with religious origins or affiliations working for social and political change, and that faces a major political crisis in southern Mexico, where the Catholic Church is both an actor and mediator.

Mexican Catholicism is different in many ways from its counterparts elsewhere in the region, in Europe, or in the United States. At the same time, the Latino population in the United States, among the fastest growing minorities, is predominantly Catholic. The largest single group from that Spanish-speaking minority is Mexican, and they bring their specific religious and political values with them to their northern neighbor. Among Catholics generally, Mexico is one of the largest members in the world community. Mexico's future, and the impact Mexicans have and will continue to exercise on the United States, are deeply intertwined with religion and religious behavior. For these and many other reasons, therefore, it is essential to understand the interactions between religion and politics and the nature of Mexican Catholicism.

Conditions Favoring a Secular Role

Religion plays a potential and actual role in many facets of society. In Mexico specifically, what is religion's potential role beyond its spiritual scope? Obviously, religion would not be a topic of major interest to social scientists unless society itself was religious. The focus of this study is on one religion, Catholicism, and one religious institution, the Catholic Church, and their respective impact on society and political institutions. Mexico, like most of Latin America, is a Catholic culture. But how religious is Mexico? And how important is Catholicism among the religious in Mexico?

Over time, Mexico has been characterized by an increasing growth in secularism, a pattern shared by most contemporary societies. Nevertheless, secular influences, measured by levels of atheism, remain quite limited, affecting fewer than 3 percent of Mexicans. Organized beliefs other than Catholicism and Protestantism were essentially nonexistent at the turn of the 20th century, and only approximately 2 percent of the population now share such views. The largest group of non-Catholics, however, have been Protestants, especially evangelicals, who accounted for 5 percent of all Mexicans in 1990 (Protestants claim 10 percent) but were fewer than 1 percent in 1940. As the century comes to a close, despite increased religious competition and the growth of secularism, Mexico remains a predominantly Catholic country, in which nine out of 10 Mexicans consider themselves Catholic, even if only nominally (see Table 1-1).

Catholicism's most important influence in Latin America occurs in the realm of values. Christianity is deeply embedded in the culture, and even nominal Catholics retain strong emotional ties to the Church.[5] The most sophisticated nonbelievers are affected "culturally" by Catholic traditions. As Carlos Fuentes, one of Mexico's leading intellectuals, revealed to the *Los Angeles Times,* "I am a nonbeliever, but I am a Catholic in the sense that I belong to a Catholic culture. I can't get away from it. It impregnates everything—my world view, my view of politics, my view of women, of education, of literature."[6] The Church's critics admit that a potential source of its influence is the depth of Catholicism in Mexican society

Table 1-1. Religious Beliefs of the Mexican Population

Year	Catholic	Percentage of Total Population	Protestant	Other	None
1895	12,517,518	99.09	44,214	—	63,162
1900	13,519,655	99.36	53,066	2,721	19,049
1910	15,330,076	99.16	68,839	13,328	20,015
1930	16,179,667	97.74	130,322	65,768	175,180
1940	18,977,585	96.56	177,954	47,255	443,671
1950	25,329,498	98.00	330,111	131,408	—
1960	33,692,503	96.50	578,515	237,958	192,963
1970	46,380,401	96.20	876,879	199,510	768,448
1980	60,236,263	92.60	2,400,724	589,629	1,993,557
1990	63,285,027	90.28	3,447,507	1,079,244	2,288,234

Source: Adapted from Enrique Luengo González, *La religión y los jóvenes de México: El desgaste de una relación* (Mexico City: Ibero-American University, 1993), 113.

and the persistence of its values, which form the predominant social code.[7] Religious institutions can alter societal patterns by challenging the religious individual's underlying cultural norms affecting his or her world view.[8]

Ironically, one of the dominant features of Mexican political culture, attributed to Catholic tradition, is the character of the state and its relationship to the economy and society. As Douglas Bennett convincingly argues, the organic-statist tradition, derived from Catholicism, "legitimizes the state's playing a much larger and more tutelary role than in liberal-capitalism society. Catholic-derived values provide a key underpinning of the contemporary Mexican regime."[9]

In addition to the statist values originating from the Catholic tradition, many scholars attribute general authoritarian values to Catholicism. It has been suggested that the Church indirectly fosters a certain style of political education by disseminating values learned in the interaction between laity and ecclesiastical authorities, including deference, obedience, and respect for hierarchy.[10] It also has been argued that these values support the status quo institutions by discouraging participation at the bottom of the hierarchy, reducing the inclination of individuals to blame the system for social inequalities.[11] In her detailed case study of a Mexican entrepreneurial family, Larissa Lomnitz concluded that

> [i]t may be said that religion and family are the primary ideological leitmotifs of the Gómez kin. Other aspects of their ideology, including economics and politics, are imbedded in the concepts of religion and family and derive their validity and cohesion from these principal concepts. Such issues as family morality, the position of individuals within the family, authority, economy, and political ideology can only be properly understood and explained in terms of Catholicism.[12]

Some scholars would even argue that the Church's actual position as a real or potential political actor can be explained through its formation of dominant, societal values.[13] The Church is a significant source of what Demerath labels "cultural power," the capacity to use cultural resources to affect political outcomes. Such resources include symbols, ideologies, moral authority, and cultural meanings.[14]

Latin American societies, including Mexico, steeped in religious traditions, will continue to be spiritual symbols.[15] Indeed, analysts of radical elements among Catholic pro-life groups in Mexico City in recent years believe that manifestations against individual rights and freedom of speech are products of dogmatic, cultural principles whose origins can be found in Catholicism.[16]

A second source of Church influence in Mexican society stems from its potential role as a social mobilizer. The Catholic Church has not used its potential for political mobilization in a direct way since the 1930s, rather it exists as a possible form of pressure.[17] Social mobilization does not refer to the large numbers of Mexicans that the pope can individually attract on short notice.[18] Rather, the Church's mobilization potential relies on the network of voluntary organizations it generates. In the United States, churches representing all religions account for the most extensive network of such groups, reaching perhaps two-thirds of the adult population.[19] In Mexico, nearly 60 percent of all citizens are not members of any organization, religious or secular. Of those who do belong to a group, 25 percent belong to a religiously affiliated organization, followed in importance by secular charitable groups and labor unions.[20] The Church has built up a sizable network of educational, religious, and charitable agencies at the parish level. This organizational network creates their mobilization potential, the essential ingredient in the Church's political capital.[21] Some scholars argue that no other institution in Mexican society can compete with the Church's "convoking capacity, mobilization, and organizational network."[22] Nevertheless, as the following chapters make clear, individual Mexicans, organized or not, are not a captive audience of the Church. As the government's own Institutional Revolutionary Party (PRI) cautions, the Church's ability to manipulate people is greatly exaggerated.[23]

The Church offers additional sources of potential societal influence beyond its basic values and its ability to mobilize sympathetic laity. Elements within the Church always have established formal educational tasks. Elite education, through preparatory and university institutions, reaches a small but influential leadership community.[24] Indeed, Jesuits and Franciscans educated many of Mexico's future politicians. Although the Church can reinforce some of its values through educational formation, largely at the pre-university level, no empirical evidence exists to support a connection between a citizen's parochial education and his or her ideological tendencies. It is true, as one might well expect, that parochial students share higher levels of religiosity than their public school counterparts.[25]

The fourth and potentially most disruptive role the Church can play in society, infiltrating religion into more explicit secular affairs and consequently conflict with the state, is a result of increased participation. Participation involves many facets. Religious teachings borrowed indirectly from the consciousness-raising tenets emphasized by liberation theology in the 1960s and 1970s may threaten the status quo, encouraging larger numbers of Mexicans to expand their political demands. These consequences have been somewhat overdrawn. Recent scholarship makes clear that members of ecclesiastical communities primarily are driven by religious motivations, typically are politically neutral, taking on a political character only as specific issues arise.[26] Perhaps the more important consequence, and therefore potential influence, is that these numerous communities, wherever they exist, enhance civic participation's prestige and legitimacy. Increased participation affects not only the process of politics but its ideology as well. The Church's influence has been ranked as second only to socioeconomic development in moving Latin America toward democracy in the 1980s.[27] In Mexico, until the August 1994 elections, even an increased voter turnout was viewed as threatening to the government party's fortunes.[28] Not only does Catholicism or specific Catholics become a potential source of radical political action, but the Church itself may provide an institutional shield for dissent.[29] For example, its potential role as a defender of human rights is likely to influence its actions well into the future.

Finally, the Catholic Church's potential influence relies heavily on the laity's perception of its institutional representative, the parish priest. Priests are sometimes viewed by secular leaders as threatening, largely because of their potential ability to impose their values, presumably different from the political leadership's, on their parishioners. It is well to remember, however, that clergy generally express the norms and values of societal groups they lead, not solely their personal, private values. Their ability to represent laity depends largely on the population's respect for their profession.[30] Priests receive a high level of respect in Mexican society, well above that of police, politicians, and judges, and more importantly, parish residents actually personally know their priests.[31]

Obstacles to Church Influence

Every institution offers strengths and weaknesses that enhance and detract from the potential role it might play in society. Mexico's Catholic Church retains many characteristics that might inhibit its potential or actual role beyond spiritual matters. Despite the population's level of religiosity, the importance of Catholicism, and even the prestige of priests, clergy are very much underrepresented in Mexican society, as they are elsewhere in the world. A revealing study of religious workers elsewhere suggests many consequences for religion in general. As Table 1-2 indicates, the percentage of religious workers as part of the economically active population remained stable, although in Mexico they have declined substantially during the same period. More important, whereas religious workers were an

Table 1-2. Growth of Religious and Knowledge Workers

Type of Worker	1870	1910	1950	1970	1984
Religious workers as % of EAP*	.37	.32	.36	.32	.34
Religious workers as % of knowledge workers	13.20	6.70	4.20	2.20	2.20
Knowledge workers as % of EAP	2.80	4.70	8.40	14.50	15.70

Source: Adapted from James Davison Hunter, "Religious Elites in Advanced Industrial Society," *Comparative Studies in Society and History* 29 (April 1987): 361.

* Economically active population

important proportion of knowledge workers generally, especially prior to 1950, they have ceased to be significant within this occupational category. In short, knowledge workers are an extremely important group in today's society, but religious workers are a declining, tiny minority of knowledge workers. The importance of these figures is accentuated by the fact that few Mexican Catholics are well educated religiously; in fact, priests ranked four-fifths of their parishioners as having little or very little religious training. No priests thought any of their parishioners were well trained.[32] This can be explained by deficiencies in Catholic religious structures and also by the fact that Catholic schools educate only 6 percent of the population.[33] Mexican bishops also lament the fact that few Mexican intelligentsia profess and express their Catholic values in the mass media.[34] In short, Catholic spokespersons, lay or clergy, are in short supply, decreasing their potential contact with laity.

Another explanation for why Catholicism specifically, as well as religion generally, exerts limited influence in the secular world is the separation between public and private spheres of behavior. Scholars have described differing patterns of behavior between private and public spheres in Catholic cultures. N. J. Demerath argues that "religion is less likely to wield 'public power' than 'private power,' where the former refers to actions on the part of the government itself and the latter refers to the actions of citizenry as individuals. Although this boundary differs from society to society, it is rarely absent and rarely without a constraining influence on religion's legitimacy as a social force."[35]

One of the strengths of the institutional Church, its regional leaders' autonomy, can become a weakness when making pronouncements concerning temporal matters. Critics long have charged that the Church's positions on important issues is inconsistent. This is explained by the fact that each bishop responds to his diocese's necessities, and that the hierarchy is divided among differing theological viewpoints. These regional differences are further complicated by a centralized, extra national influence: the Vatican.[36]

Finally, since 1992, the Catholic Church, while strengthening its constitutional position and its relationship to the state, potentially risks compromising its legitimacy if it is identified too closely with the state. It has to pursue a very careful course so as not to be viewed as supporting state policies or as an ally of the state. Even such cosmetic actions as attending presidential inaugurations might be seen as giving added credibility to the government while detracting from the Church's prized and valued prestige.[37]

Analytical Choices—A Theoretical Argument

A survey of the major works on religion and politics indicates the development of some important theoretical arguments, especially recently, on the religious sources of secular beliefs and behavior and on differences promoted by religious beliefs. The exploration of the Catholic Church as an institution, however, has not kept pace with the level of analysis devoted to religious beliefs, except for the association between lay activism and formal religious institutions and their representatives. In the Latin American case especially, much of the attention devoted to religion in politics has focused on popular religious groups, especially ecclesiastical base communities and their descendants. It has been argued, however, that the focus of scholarship has returned to that of church versus state, but that the issues confronting their relationship have shifted to a different emphasis, including human rights, justice, and the role of popular classes.[38]

Strangely, however, one searches in vain for broad country studies that examine and integrate the relationship between church and state, the influence of religion on politics, the internal structure of the Church, the sociology of religious leadership, the views of the rank and file, the religious beliefs and attitudes of secular elites, and the importance of religion in society.[39] David C. Bailey, who devoted his entire professional career to examining the Mexican Catholic Church, concluded shortly before his death that while mounds of literature existed on religious themes, almost no work examined the Church's internal, institutional condition, including its structure, government, and ideological shifts.[40] One explanation for this failure is the difficulty of doing research within the Church.[41]

To capture these themes under the umbrella of a single analysis it is necessary to borrow from some broad, theoretical literature from which church-state or religion and politics components can be effectively sketched.[42] One of the most important theoretical contributions to church-state analysis is that of state theory, and state-group relations, which identify structural variables determining various groups's influence on the state, including actors within the state. A number of general variables have emerged as significant in state-group relations, all of which offer some degree of utility in explaining Mexico's church-state relationship. However, the danger of borrowing from this literature is that it may lead one to be predisposed to believe that the Church is a typical pressure or interest group "with eminently political goals."[43] Important peculiarities distinguish the Catholic Church and Mexican clergy from other institutional forces in society.

This work seeks to examine a number of important theoretical issues that are laid out in some detail as 14 premises. Nevertheless, the theoretical framework of this research is informed by three major, interrelated arguments. First, and most important, the relationship between religion and politics, and more specifically church and state, in a society is affected strongly by the foremost structures representing leading religious and political actors. In the Mexican case, the Catholic Church and the post-1920s political model, dominated by a dynamic yet continuous elite, provide the structural variables essential to this relationship. Contrary to popular impression, it is the decentralized qualities of the diocesan structure that influence Catholic decision making, leadership, and policy preferences. This decentralized authority structure produces numerous characteristics of the domestic institution and, consequently, is of primary significance in determining Church behavior toward the state. Equally important, the semiauthoritarian structure of the Mexican government, and the formation of professional politicians within its hierarchical, political model, molds political actors' perceptions of Church organizational features and the informal rules by which Church decision making is accomplished. Politicians' misperceptions, largely a product of ignorance, not only have affected their views of the political and social role the Church might play, but have unnecessarily complicated church-state relations and emphasized external actors representing the Vatican, whose influence might otherwise be limited.

Second, beyond the peculiar structural variables characterizing these institutions is a shared cultural-historical context that affects both the religiosity of society and its elite actors, secular and religious. Whereas most studies place religious-political interactions within the larger context of a society's historical experience, it is remarkable, particularly in the Latin American context, how few analyses have actually examined the level of religiosity in the society, the impact of religion on political behavior in general, and, most notably, religious and secular elite's perceptions toward each other. In short, the religious and cultural formation of the actors themselves, who are products of the political and religious ambience of their respective cultures, must be assessed to offer a complete understanding of elite interactions, as well as interactions on the mass level. This milieu explains why the Church will be a political actor, but also why it will largely serve as a voice of the laity, not as its leader.

Third, because any analysis of religion and religious actors must consider spiritual qualities in their assessment of rank-and-file as well as elite behavior, the socialization and recruitment of priests and bishops, the Church's most significant representatives, are essential ingredients in such an examination. Why such individuals have chosen a clerical profession, when and where they made such decisions, which type of clergy rose to leadership positions, and how they emerged in such responsible tasks all explain more completely the Church's strengths and weaknesses. These qualities in turn can be compared to those of other leadership groups in Mexican society. As will be argued, Mexico's Catholic clergy share significant characteristics, especially in relation to their potential political role, which are not encountered among other elite groups.

The forces that describe and construct a relationship between the state and any institutional actor are structural, historical, and psychological. Historical experience is a significant explanatory variable in establishing the larger setting of institutions in society: their prestige, their legitimacy, and their level of compatibility with state institutions. As the next chapter demonstrates, the Mexican Catholic Church's historical underpinnings have not helped to foster a positive relationship. Mexico shared the experiences of the Latin American Church, although to an exaggerated degree, in that it competed politically with the government for many decades, but only recently has it competed religiously (against Protestant sects).[44] These 19th and early 20th century experiences forced the Catholic Church into a defensive posture, excluding it altogether as an integral ingredient of secular, political rhetoric. Indeed, if Catholicism or the Church were mentioned, typically it occurred in a pejorative light. The 1917 Constitution, the product of a social, revolutionary phase, including an anti-Church posture, incorporated some of the severest restrictions against religion ever included in an official political document.

Historical experiences contribute two essential ingredients for understanding as well as developing some broader arguments about Mexican church-state relations. The Catholic Church has operated in a political world that, for the most part, has been hostile, if not overtly, at least in terms of its culture, its premises, and its rhetoric. This ambience, in which it has evolved and functioned quite success-fully, nevertheless, produced certain psychological consequences affecting both clergy and politicians. The Catholic Church, long assigned an inferior status by the state, is not entirely comfortable with and has not felt confident in its relations with the state. In terms of general theory on state-group relations, clergy share some similarities with Mexican entrepreneurs, who expressed obvious concerns with what they considered to be their second-class status vis-à-vis their excluded position in the dominant political organization, the Institutional Revolutionary Party (PRI).[45]

The second component of the historical setting, which explains the behavior of institutional actors, clergy and politicians, and the religious population's political behavior, is the absorption of those personal and societal experiences through familial and educational socialization processes. The Mexican public educational system since the 1930s, which schooled most Mexicans, generally has been de-scribed in secular, 19th-century Liberal terms, passing on the rhetoric of the post-revolutionary governments. On this basis alone, one might expect Mexican society to have rejected religious influences. Inside the family, from the lowliest peasant to cabinet minister, most Mexicans received formative religious influences, typi-cally from their mothers. All domestic agents of Mexican church-state relations, clergy, politicians, and laity, are products of integrated Liberal/Catholic cultural influences.[46] Thus, contemporary Mexican bishops and priests, offshoots of a Lib-eral heritage and a strong sense of nationalism, share much in common with their secular, political counterparts. A tendency exists to paint priests and seculars as having two distinct value systems.[47]

These two historical contributions of state-group relations can be expressed more precisely in theoretical terms. Premise 1: The personal tone of the relation-ship between the state and any single actor is often more strongly determined by the historical ambience than by actual practice. In the case of Mexican church-state relations, although priests and bishops were allowed to vote before 1992, in violation of the constitution, clergy never overcame their suspicions of the state, nor could they, similar to entrepreneurs, easily establish high levels of trust in government officials. Therefore, their relationship, while generally positive since 1970, was nevertheless tenuous.

Premise 2: An important bridge between the representatives of any institution vis-à-vis the state is their formation in the historical experiences and values of society. Mexican bishops are a joint product of Liberal and Catholic influences, just as politicians are products of Catholic and Liberal values. Their differences are ones of degrees, not completely opposing value systems. Today, priests in Mexico are Liberals, and Liberals in Mexico are Catholics. "Modern" Mexican Liberalism is no longer anti-Church. Their sharing of Liberal influences, for exam-ple, make bishops as accepting of the principle of separation of church and state as politicians are its advocates.

Most institutions that deal with the state are attempting to exercise influence over its allocation of public resources, or in some cases, to limit its influence in their realm of activities. Normally, however, they are competing against other groups and institutions for funds, or funding projects of interest to their constituencies. The Catholic Church in Mexico is not an interest group in this sense. It generally does not seek governmental funds but instead competes with government for the population's values and orientations. In its crudest sense, the Church is a competitor for the minds of the population. This role—indeed the very perception of the Church performing such a task—is strengthened by the peculiar circumstance of the Mexican political model, in which a fluid leadership and its electoral vehicle PRI have dominated politics for seven decades. The characteristics of a political system, including its level of authoritarianism, not only determine practical, day-to-day relationships between institutions and the state but assign a role to the Church no other institution can play.

In the Mexican case, the Catholic Church is a highly autonomous actor, even during most of the period under study, when restrictive constitutional prohibitions remained in force.[48] Since political parties were not challenging secular leadership's monopoly, some of its opponents and supporters perceived the Catholic Church as playing this role. This is not to suggest that Church leadership wished to perform such a function, but the political vacuum created by a semiauthoritarian political structure, given the Church's institutional legitimacy and financial autonomy, increasingly thrust it into such activities or clothed it in the ability to threaten such a role.

The differing conditions of a political model alter and enhance its relationship to various political and nonpolitical actors. Premise 3: The Catholic Church is more likely to be drawn into a successful "political" role in Mexican church-state relations because of the deficiencies or qualities inherent in the Mexican political model than because of internal, theological changes. The loss of political space and legitimacy by the government encourages the Church to fill the void, explaining its increased involvement after 1985.

The clergy is a hesitant actor in the secular role pushed on it by the political model and societal concerns. Despite an occasional exception, Catholic leadership typically does not initiate, nor has it recently sought out, controversial secular matters. As Cornelia Butler Flora suggests, "[M]ore often than acting directly to bring about change or forging links with marginal groups, the Church has been a reactive mechanism."[49] It has taken numerous public positions since the 1970s, but generally in reaction to societal conditions and often in response to implicit or explicit pressures from its constituencies. The Catholic Church has not been very successful in molding the views of Mexican society, especially when those views are not held by the middle classes.[50] On controversial politically and socially charged issues, the Church is very successful in consolidating, directing, and representing consensual views, but it is not so adept at changing them.

To capture these views, an analysis is required of both what the Church says and what it does. Both the popular and scholarly perceptions see the Catholic Church as hierarchical. Indeed, most institutions, or at least their bureaucracies, are hierarchical. This description of the Catholic Church is misleading. It draws most heavily on the Pope's ideological control and on personnel linkages between the Pope and the bishops. In reality, not only is the Catholic Church peculiar to Mexico, as distinct from all other Catholic churches worldwide, but there exists as many Catholic churches in Mexico as there are dioceses. These dozens of autonomous units have only tenuous ties to any concept of a national, Mexican Church, and the ties are more theological than structural.

The reality of the Mexican Catholic Church is that it is a decentralized structure in which each diocese or archdiocese operates with extraordinary autonomy. Within the diocese, however, strong hierarchical traditions may prevail. It is therefore ironic, as Kenneth Wald points out, that despite the apparent growth worldwide in religiously based political conflict, scholars have paid little systematic attention to the most likely source of religious influence on citizens: the local church.[51] The nature of the Mexican political model, and the manner in which it channels its relations with other important institutional actors, encourages a perception that the state's relationship to the Catholic Church can be managed as a unified, hierarchical institution. Premise 4: The state's misperception of the Catholic Church as a *nationally* unified, hierarchically controlled organization has caused it to misunderstand its motivations and to deal with the Church in ways that have exacerbated differences among the clergy and accentuated the level of difficulty in church-government relations.

No institution is homogeneous despite perceptions to the contrary. But the formal structure of the Catholic Church and its own internal governance, prescribed under canon law and in practice, establishes clear, decentralized decision making, making more complex an assessment of its motives and values. It is very important to identify and evaluate carefully the positions of these "regional" churches and their leaders, who are products of local historical and social experiences, which differ in degree and intensity from those patterns general to Mexico as a whole.[52]

According to Church leaders, bishops largely are a product of diocesan environments, either those in which they were personally formed and educated or those they came to serve in as priests and bishops. A sociological analysis of Church leadership and their career paths illuminates significant structural differences between Catholic and governmental institutions. The Mexican political model consists of a highly centralized, executive-dominated structure that in turn has emphasized national recruitment and career experiences among its leadership. Given structural differences between Church and government, the origins and experiences of their leadership could not be more different. Premise 5: Structural characteristics in the construction of governmental and group institutions dramatically affect the nature of state-group relations, especially when differences produce a nationally versus a regionally formed leadership.

Elite theories are very important in capturing other features of institutional leadership in terms of understanding not only differences between that leadership and its rank-and-file agents but also between leaders of two or more institutions operating in society. In Mexico, an examination of the backgrounds of top government and clerical figures reveals substantial differences that may explain their respective institutions' distinct views, value systems, and perceptions. Geographic and social origins may also suggest the degree to which leaders are representative of their constituencies and their potential for closer ties to them.

In Mexico, the geographic origins and the social composition of bishops' parents differ greatly from those of politicians. Indeed, Mexican clergy are more representative, geographically and socially, of the average Mexican than are politicians. The origins of Catholic leadership typically are the product of local historical experiences, the importance of the Catholic Church in the region, and the significance of religion or religious values within the immediate family. Premise 6: Catholic clergy share stronger roots in their communities and are more representative of those communities socially and regionally than are national politicians and consequently suggest a greater potential for representing accurately the typical Mexican's views. In his work on religion in the United States, Kenneth Wald hypothesized that the more interaction that occurs socially in a church or local religious community, the higher its level of political cohesion.[53]

The role or potential role of any institution in society cannot be accurately assessed without understanding the context in which that institution operates. The degree to which it might influence the state is largely determined by how society perceives it, its representatives, and its functions. The general literature abounds with studies of religion and the impact religious views have on political and social values. Rarely, and nearly nonexistent in Latin American studies, do we find an analysis of how society views Catholicism combined with an exploration of the Church, its leadership, and its relationship to the state. Separating the study of leadership, institutional characteristics, and religion is artificial and counterproductive to understanding the Church's role.

Religion is an extremely important value in Mexican society. Its importance enhances the Church's potential influence as an institution since it too is seen in a very positive light by the typical Mexican who is Christian and Catholic. But the Catholic laity also has specific views of the role it believes the Church is playing, or should play, and that may or may not limit the Church's pastoral and temporal activities. Contrary to educated and popular assumptions, Catholicism has little to do with partisan politics in Mexico. Support for various parties, including a party that has drawn some of its important ideological principles from Christian democratic and Catholic encyclicals, cannot be attributed to Catholicism per se. Premise 7: Empirical, survey research demonstrates that religion, Christianity, Catholicism, and the Catholic Church are held in high esteem by the vast majority of Mexicans, and that these beliefs give the Church the potential to perform an important role in society in secular affairs, especially as a representative for the laity on nonspiritual matters. The potential influence of the Church and the possibility for increased tensions with the state are associated strongly with the declining legitimacy of governmental institutions.

Much of the historical analysis of the Catholic Church, especially in Mexico, was accomplished by religious scholars. Most recent research is by social scientists. While the individual who is religious first and a scholar second potentially carries intellectual baggage with many biases, the social scientist, in attempting objectivity, often ignores a quality that sets clergy apart from nearly any other group having a relationship to the state: its spiritual component. Clergy who make decisions in the Church and represent it in their dealings with the state are governed by the same motivations that govern all other leadership groups, including self-preservation and selfish ambition. At the same time, they incorporate a strong moral, spiritual foundation on which most of their other values are built. This can never be forgotten in attempting to assess the clergy's motivation or potential in taking a specific posture on a temporal issue. Morality can motivate individuals to pursue positions not in their self-interest or in the interest of the institution they represent. As Scott Mainwaring concluded, "[A] church will renounce financial benefits, prestige, institutional expansion, and other interests if it feels that its religious mission compels it to do so. Forgetting this point is tantamount to eliminating the religious element from the study of the Church."[54]

These moral threads are no better illustrated than among the issues now confronting the Mexican Catholic Church. Although some of these have to do with self-preservation, such as the challenge of Protestantism, or its internal theological principles, including integrating liberation theology, the Church is most likely to confront the Mexican state on two primary themes: democratization (specifically, electoral fraud) and human rights. As Levine argues, democratization trends might initially give the impression of reducing pressures for political action. In reality, churches and religion will continue to be important to the formulation of political issues and phenomena because the joining of democracy and Catholicism provides a new discourse on justice and equality.[55] Church leadership, including papal teachings and diocesan documents, has established the principle of the Church teaching civic responsibility. Christian principles and the basic moral precepts of Catholicism clearly define their posture on basic, human rights. Premise 8: Tensions between the Church and the state in Mexico are most likely to develop over the Church's posture on clean elections and human rights, two positions on which there exists firm, unified agreement among the various dioceses and representatives of the hierarchy, regardless of other ideological preferences. The Church will publicly express its views on these two issues even when a bishop's personal posture typically is one of silence or aloofness. These two issues and the hierarchy's views have widespread support among the laity, and the clergy simply reflect societal perceptions on these questions.

Only a handful of studies attempt to characterize the Catholic Church's leadership in North and Latin America compared to dozens analyzing political leadership. Most studies of bishops are more interested in their views than in their composition. But as Edward Cleary notes, the naming of bishops is the most effective way to change the Church's orientation.[56] To comprehensively understand the institutional Church, it is essential to view differences among the rank-and-file actors, priests, and clerical leadership. There are at least three elements to such an analysis. First, what type of Mexican goes into the clergy? After all, in a population of 90 million only 12,000 individuals practice this profession. Second, what type of priest becomes a bishop? As is true among politicians and military officers, what distinguishes a leader from the typical professional? Such qualities are very revealing about leadership and what the institution itself values among its leaders. Finally, what differences exist between clerical and political leaders, and do they produce consequences in values and behavior that affect the relationship between the two groups and institutions?

Even though the Catholic Church does not have a national hierarchy or a career training ground in national, centralized agencies, priests who eventually become bishops and archbishops share many similarities in their career tracks. The Catholic Church, similar to many contemporary secular institutions, has increasingly placed greater emphasis on its intellectual and staff careerists, just as politicians have emphasized bureaucratic types in the national executive branch, and military leaders have emphasized administrative officers as distinct from field commanders. The Catholic Church has moved away from priests with practical, pastoral experience in rural and urban parishes to those who largely make their careers in seminary teaching and administration in metropolitan diocesan settings.

The Church, by duplicating other institutions' leadership selection processes, places at risk important qualities setting it apart from its secular peers, reducing its institutional uniqueness. The Church retains the important distinction of producing clergy who are locally formed, both in education and experience. Of those priests, it increasingly promoted clergy with the least pastoral experience. Premise 9: The Church, while retaining the strongest roots among its constituency of any major institutional player in the political arena, has encouraged a more elitist trend, removing future leadership away from the practical, pastoral, and spiritual problems of parishes to those heavily focused on the institutional preparation of its priests. This pattern generates a potential for greater divisions between rank-and-file priests who carry out the tasks demanded of most parish assignments, as well as distancing the bishop from the practical concerns of the diocese. The opposing qualities are those that have strengthened the Church in temporal matters, giving it greater cohesiveness and societal legitimacy.

Priests who are likely to be promoted to bishops typically demonstrate their leadership abilities and become known to their resident bishops as talented seminarians. Interestingly, just as politicians-cum-professors recruit the best and the brightest of their students into political careers, seminary teachers and administrators, who most often are likely to become the select members of the episcopate, bring potential future bishops to the attention of incumbent bishops in their dioceses. Unlike politicians, who are educated in a variety of large, public institutions and, more recently, smaller, private schools, whose student peers seek many professional futures, successful priests typically remain within the confines of seminary education, beginning after the age of 12, and occasionally younger, for most of their training. The significance of this is that priests, somewhat similar to military officers, are primarily educated in their own schools, operated and controlled by clergy.

The consequence of a closed, educational environment is that it tends to produce a more caste-like mentality where priests associate with other priests rather than with diverse, secular representatives. Similarly, the exclusive training environment of Mexico's military officers produced a significant separation between civilian politicians and the officer corps, resulting in numerous negative consequences for their mutual understanding and perceptions. Most seminary students do not become priests. Consequently, the students who do become priests and who maintain friendships with former classmates are welcomed into many secular groups in society. But very few educational companions among politicians end up as priests. This fact, combined with a politician's familial environment being less receptive to formal religion and religious activism, affects relations between the two groups. Premise 10: The historic environment in Mexico exaggerating the separation between religion and politics, and the separate formation of clergy and politics educationally and familially, produced a political leadership woefully ignorant of Church structures, misinformed about decision-making processes within the Church, and lacking in personal relations with influential clergy. In contrast, clergy are much better informed about politics and politicians. This lack of information on the part of politicians leads to misinformation and closed channels of communication, as well as to their reliance on a select group of political go-betweens to provide necessary linkages.

All political systems rely heavily on informal channels to carry out political functions, especially governmental relations to important institutions and interest groups. The personal quality of relationships in Mexico is a well-established and overriding characteristic of the political culture. It is also an essential ingredient in decision making, both within the executive branch, which overwhelmingly controls the process in Mexico, and between it and other agents of society. Constitutional prohibitions in Mexico and the antireligious rhetoric of the political regime generated a situation in which the state developed no formal structures to channel Church communications. Instead, the government had to rely almost exclusively on informal contacts to facilitate its relationship with the Church.

Given the informal nature of such contacts, the relationship between church and state at the national level has taken on the imprint of an incumbent president, who often sets the tone of their linkage and uses personal friends to facilitate his contacts with the episcopate. Yet by focusing attention on the national level, scholars may be missing the more extensive relationships at the local and state level, built on much greater personal knowledge and contact between priests and bishops and their secular counterparts. Premise 11: The decentralized and autonomous nature of Catholic dioceses and the relationship between the diocese and secular authorities are generally quite positive, and more important, may differ qualitatively from the national relationship. The national patterns obscure linkages among individual dioceses, conflictual or positive, suggesting more diversified patterns that collective assessments of the institutional relationship at the national level ignore.

Decision-making theory also makes an important contribution to the examination of the Catholic Church and of its relationship to the state. Decision-making analysis identifies a number of variables that must be taken into account in assessing the role and influence exerted by each institutional actor. One of the distinguishing characteristics of the Church within the Mexican domestic political context is that it incorporates an international component, both within the Catholic structure and in the relationship between the state and external Catholic actors, such as the Vatican. The presence of an international variable, the Pope as the superior to all bishops, and the papal nuncio as the Vatican representative to the Mexican government, affects internal decision making within the Mexican Church and between the Mexican Church and government. The source of funding, domestic versus international, can also introduce an additional structural variable in the equation of church-state relations.

An activist papal delegate or nuncio, who has characterized the Mexican scene since the mid-1970s, expanded the importance of the international variable on the relationship between church and state. Premise 12: The presence of an activist papal nuncio representing a papal agenda differing in emphasis and tone from the Mexican episcopate and willing to negotiate with the state for the Vatican's agenda in lieu of the episcopate's complicated church-state relations, increased nationalism within the episcopate, accentuated divisions within the natural, ideological wings among the hierarchy, and misled the state to dialogue with a centralized representative, ignoring a multifaceted Church.

Recruitment theory is also important to facilitating a clearer image of episcopal leadership and that characterizing the Church in the foreseeable future. Few institutions in society are governed by such a small, long-lasting set of leaders over time. The career duration of bishops, often 30 or more years, establishes a level of continuity in both leadership and ideology. Thus, how bishops are selected and the type of priests who will become future bishops will have long-lasting consequences on the episcopate's pastoral positions.

Ideologically, the Mexican Catholic Church, as is true elsewhere in the region, represents many postures, most of which have been discussed in the general literature on Latin American Catholicism. An attempt to classify these differences into wings, categories, or tendencies in the popular press has led to greater obfuscation rather than clarity in understanding differing viewpoints. As is so often the case in efforts at model building, where ideological labels become a distinction, few such categories are all-encompassing. A traditionalist on religious matters, or even on the social pastoral Church role, may be equally progressive on democratization as his more non-traditional counterpart. Premise 13: A more lucid understanding of the issues facing the Catholic Church and bishops' individual positions on those issues can be facilitated by assessing the points on which the episcopate is unified rather than on those which generate widespread and diverse opinions. It is the unified positions on which the Church will exert considerable influence as a national institution and in the local diocese. These are the same issues that will establish the boundaries, ideologically speaking, of its relationship to the state.

Methodologically, an important ingredient in the theoretical growth of church-state literature is the need to focus on and explore, through personal interviews, the four primary actors in the relationship: hierarchy, priests, laity, and politicians. This has been accomplished for laity through broad survey research, reported in some detail in chapter 5. Interview data with priests and brothers, bishops and archbishops, and national political figures appear throughout the text. It seems extraordinary that in previous examinations of church-state relations no effort has been made to compare the experiences, religious formation, and views of national secular and religious leaders about the social, economic, and political issues facing their societies, including the role the Church does or should play. A comparative examination of the views of the primary actors in the relationship, excluding the laity, demonstrates their differences and, potentially, the source of those differences. Premise 14: A comparison of views among priests, politicians, and bishops suggests a level of agreement on some important issues and identifies significant differences, and implicitly the origins of those differences, explaining the potential for future tensions and conflict. Such an examination moves well beyond understanding the source of tensions within the Mexican Catholic Church to understanding those which exist not only between the Church and the government, but among other groups and government as well.

NOTES

1. In fact, the emphasis on the political implications of recent change within the Catholic Church is so strong that its pastoral orientation—its focus on evangelization, bringing people into a relationship with God, Christ, and the Church—is largely ignored. Thomas G. Sanders, "The Puebla Conference," *American Universities Field Staff Reports,* no. 30, 1979, 6.

2. Daniel H. Levine, "From Church and State to Religion and Politics and Back Again," *World Affairs* 150 (Fall 1987): 94.

3. As Brian Smith concluded two decades ago: "Classic studies of the impact of religion on society, written in the latter part of the nineteenth and early twentieth century, arrived at the same general conclusion: Religion is predominantly an integrating and legitimizing force for the prevailing values and structures in society and is not a motivating force for social change." "Religion and Social Change: Classical Theories and New Formulations in the Content of Recent Developments in Latin America," *Latin American Research Review* 10 (1975): 4.

4. Octavio Rodríguez Araujo, "Iglesia, partidos and lucha de clases en México," in *Religión y política en México,* Martín de la Rosa and Charles A. Reilly, eds. (Mexico City: Siglo XXI, 1985), 262; Soledad Loaeza, "Notas para el estudio de la Iglesia en el México contemporáneo," *Religión y política en México,* 49.

5. Brian H. Smith, "Church and Human Rights in Latin America," *Journal of Inter-American Studies and World Affairs* 21 (February 1979): 118.

6. *Los Angeles Times,* April 19, 1992.

7. Soledad Loaeza, "La Iglesia católica mexicana y el reformismo autoritario," *Foro Internacional* 25, no. 2 (October–December 1984): 142. I am not suggesting, however, that Catholicism necessarily provides a strong, cultural unity in Latin America or Mexico.

8. Carol Ann Drogus, "Religious Change and Women's Status in Latin America: A Comparison of Catholic Base Communities and Pentecostal Churches," Kellog Institute for International Studies, University of Notre Dame, 1993, 3.

9. Douglas C. Bennett, "Catholicism, Capitalism, and the State in the Development of Mexico," in *Global Economics and Religion,* James Finn, ed. (New Brunswick, N.J.: Transaction Books, 1983), 139.

10. Charles L. Davis, "Religion and Partisan Loyalty: The Case of Catholic Workers in Mexico," *Western Political Quarterly* 45 (March 1992): 276. Indeed, elsewhere, Kenneth Coleman and Charles L. Davis argue that modes of interaction between citizens and religious authorities may have been extended to political authority structures, favoring Mexican elite behavior. "Civil and Conventional Religion in Secular Authoritarian Regimes: The Case of Mexico," *Studies in Comparative International Development* 13, no. 2 (Summer 1978): 57.

11. Kenneth P. Langton, "The Church, Social Consciousness, and Protest," *Comparative Political Studies* 19 (October 1986): 327.

12. Larissa Adler Lomnitz and Marisol Pérez-Lizaur, *A Mexican Elite Family, 1820–1980* (Princeton: Princeton University Press, 1987), 204.

13. Soledad Loaeza, "Continuity and Change in the Mexican Catholic Church," in

Church and Politics in Latin America, Dermot Keogh, ed. (New York: St. Martin's, 1990), 273–275. Loaeza carries this to an extreme, however, suggesting that because social values derived from the Church persist, secularization in Mexican society has not been completely achieved. The assumption that secular societies ultimately cleanse themselves of their religious influences is unfounded.

14. N. J. Demerath, "Religious Capital and Capital Religions," *Daedalus* 20, no. 3 (Summer 1991): 31.

15. Brian H. Smith, "Religion and Social Change: Classical Theories and New Formulations in the Content of Recent Developments in Latin America," 24.

16. Marta Eugenia García Ugarte, "Las posiciones políticas de la jerarquía católica, efectos en la cultura religiosa mexicana," in *Religiosidad y política en México,* Carlos Martínez Assad, ed. (Mexico City: Ibero-American University, 1992), 95. Ugarte concluded that they "were not without convulsive expressions of a culture . . . which continues to be nurtured by dogmatic and moral principles of the Catholic Church."

17. Blanca Heredia, "Profits, Politics, and Size: The Political Transformation of Mexican Business," in *The Right and Democracy in Latin America,* Douglas A. Chalmers, et al., eds. (New York: Praeger, 1992), 286.

18. As Roberto Blancarte points out, even the same people involve themselves for entirely different reasons, and thus the Pope's ability to attract these people should not automatically be considered social influence. Some three million people gathered in Mexico City for the 1979 visit. "La Iglesia católica en México desde 1929: introducción crítica a la producción historiográfica (1968–1988)," *Cristianismo y Sociedad* no. 101 (1989): 40.

19. Kenneth D. Wald, D. E. Owen, and S. D. Hill, Jr., "Churches as Political Communities," *American Political Science Review* 82, no. 2 (June 1988): 532.

20. Taken from raw data provided by Enrique Alduncin in his 1987 survey and Luis Narro Rodríguez, "Qué valoran los mexicanos hoy?," in *Como somos los mexicanos,* Alberto Hernández Medina, et al., eds. (Mexico City: Centro de Estudios Educativos, 1987), 34.

21. Soledad Loaeza, "Continuity and Change in the Mexican Catholic Church," 283.

22. Oscar Aguilar and Enrique Luengo González, "Iglesia y gobierno en el D.F.," in *D.F.: gobierno y sociedad civil,* Pablo González Casanova, ed. (Mexico City: El Caballito, 1987), 198.

23. Partido Revolucionario Institucional, "Memorandum sobre las relaciones estado-iglesia católica," unpublished manuscript, November 1988, 21.

24. Claude Pomerlau, "The Changing Church in Mexico and Its Challenge to the State," *Review of Politics* 43, no. 4 (October 1981): 548.

25. In their study of religion and partisanship, for example, Charles Davis and Kenneth Coleman found parochial students were less likely to support the National Action Party, often identified in the popular Mexican mind with the Catholic Church, than were public school children. "Discontinuous Educational Experiences and Political and Religious Nonconformity in Authoritarian Regimes: Mexico," *Social Science Quarterly* 58, no. 3 (December 1977): 494.

26. This is reflected in the excellent work of Carol Ann Drogus, "Popular Movements and the Limits of Political Mobilization at the Grassroots in Brazil," in *Conflict and Competition: The Latin American Church in a Changing Environment,* Edward L. Cleary and Hannah Stewart-Gambino, eds. (Boulder, Colo.: Lynne Rienner, 1992), 63–86. It is important to remember, however, that it is the perception of the Church's potential role, not its actual behavior, which often determines a political response.

27. Edward L. Cleary, "Politics and Religion—Crisis, Constraints, and Restructuring," in *Conflict and Competition,* 203.

28. The Church considers voting, in a democracy, as an essential civic responsibility, viewing it as sinful not to participate. In Mexico, increased voter turnout generally has favored the opposition parties. This was not the case, however, in the August 1994 presidential elections. For example, see the comment on this by Otto Granados Roldán, later President Salinas's press secretary, in "La iglesia católica mexicana como grupo de presión," (Mexico City: UNAM, Departamento de Humanidades, 1981), 52–53.

29. Daniel H. Levine, *Religion and Politics in Latin America, The Catholic Church in Venezuela and Colombia* (Princeton: Princeton University Press, 1981), 28.

30. Gerhard Lenski, *The Religious Factor: A Sociological Study of Religion's Impact on Politics and Family Life* (Garden City, N.Y.: Doubleday, 1963), 11.

31. For example, in the case of Tijuana, 73 percent of 22,000 Mexicans interviewed knew their local priest. Catholic Church, *Plan pastoral, 1989–1994, hacia una iglesia nueva* (Tijuana: La Diocese, 1989), 233; and Mori de México, *Encuesta Semanal,* December 4, 1992.

32. José María Díaz Mozaz and Vicente J. Sastre, "Una encuesta de opinión al clero mexicano, aproximación a la realidad socio-religiosa mexicana," *Vida Pastoral,* 2, no. 11 (August 1976): 14, based on a survey of 234 priests from all regions and ages. An earlier study by the Social Secretariat of the Catholic episcopate discovered a high level of ignorance about the Catholic Church in Mexico City. See Secretariado Social, "Informe acerca de las actividades del Secretariado Social, 1961–1967," unpublished manuscript, n.d., 4.

33. Jorge Adame Goddard, *La libertad religiosa en México, estudio jurídico* (Mexico City: Porrúa, 1990), 45.

34. Grupo Consultor Interdisciplinario, "Carta de política mexicana, las otras iglesias, las razones del cambio y lo que viene," March 20, 1992, 4.

35. N. J. Demerath, "Religious Capital and Capital Religions," 31–32.

36. Such criticisms have been leveled at the Church in Latin America by Brian Smith, "Religion and Social Change," 10; and specifically in Mexico by the Jesuits at the Instituto Regional of Chihuahua and Estudios Sociales in the capital. See José Luis Gaona Vega, *Punto,* September 22, 1986, 10.

37. Claude Pomerlau warned, even as early as the late 1970s, that the frequent negotiations between the Church and the government "gives more legitimacy to the government than benefits to the Church." "The Catholic Church in Mexico and its Changing Relationship to Society and the State," Unpublished manuscript, December 1980, 9.

38. Daniel H. Levine, "From Church and State to Religion and Politics and Back Again," 97.

39. Michael Fleet and Brian Smith included several of these same elements in their recommendations for scholarly appraisals of the contemporary Latin American Church, arguing that an approach must incorporate the ideology of the hierarchy, the ecclesiastical base, and civil society in dynamic interaction. "Rethinking Catholicism and Politics in Latin America," Paper presented to the Latin American Studies Association, Miami, 1989, 3.

40. David C. Bailey, unpublished notes for an article in *Americas* (March 1975), n.p.

41. Enrique Luengo González, "Los párrocos: una visión," Unpublished manuscript, Department of Political and Social Sciences, Ibero-American University, December 1989, 20.

42. Robert Wuthnow is highly critical of three broad theoretical approaches—critical, modernization, and world systems theories—chiding them for the lack of credit they give to the shaping power of religious leaders and the role of faith in motivating people to take political action. See his "Understanding Religion and Politics," *Daedalus,* 29, no. 3 (Summer 1991): 2, 3, 8–9, 14.

43. Roberto Blancarte, *El poder salinismo e iglesia católica, una nueva convivencia?* (Mexico City: Grijalbo, 1991), 77–78.

44. As Philip E. Hammond concludes, in contrast, churches in the United States, because of the doctrine of religious liberty, have always competed religiously, but never politically, that is, over the rules governing competition. "The Conditions for Civil Religion: a Comparison of the United States and Mexico," in *Varieties of Civil Religion*, Robert W. Bella and Philip E. Hammond, eds. (New York: Harper and Row, 1980), 68.

45. For evidence of this, and its consequences among businessmen, see Roderic Ai Camp, *Entrepreneurs and Politics in Twentieth-Century Mexico* (New York: Oxford University Press, 1989), 125.

46. As Michael Parenti suggests, "religious belief systems possess both the inspirational and the durable traditional qualities and through much of history have played a key role in the determination of moral and normative codes." "Political Values and Religious Cultures: Jews, Catholics, and Protestants," *Journal for the Scientific Study of Religion* 6 (1967): 260.

47. A broader, theoretical argument has been offered, although not applied to seculars and priests, in explaining differences between Latin and North American culture. Basically, the argument is that Latin Americans do operate in two different value systems, religious and political. Catholic cultures follow a two-track moral system that distinguishes their private behavior from their public lives. Specifically, Catholic-Christian values govern their private, familial behavior, whereas a different set of secular, less attractive, and socially responsible values govern their public careers. If Glen Dealy is correct in his assumptions about two ethical worlds in Latin America and Mexico, a strong potential for conflict emerges among religious and secular figures. Although he does not examine them specifically, the argument could be made that priests, whose lives personally *and professionally,* are governed by Christian principles, are not as likely to share this ethical duality. Politicians, on the other hand, who practice these same ethics at home, are not as likely to do so in governmental careers, thus generating a basic value conflict between the two groups. *The Latin Americans, Spirit and Ethos* (Boulder, Colo.: Westview Press, 1992), 11–13. Kenneth Coleman and Charles Davis, however, offer an explanation that may moderate such differences. They believe that the routines of patron-clientelism may explain why conventional religion is psychologically compatible with secular, authoritarian politics. See their "Civil and Conventional Religion in Secular Authoritarian Regimes: The Case of Mexico," *Studies in Comparative International Development* 13, no. 2 (Summer 1978): 60.

48. Ivan Vallier, in his ground-breaking work, assigned the Church to a category he described as separate from the state with low autonomy. Theoretically his description was correct, especially in the late 1960s, but in reality the Church did exercise its independence, in nearly all areas, in directing its own affairs. As we have suggested, the constitutional restrictions rarely were applied. *Catholicism, Social Control, and Modernization in Latin America* (Englewood Cliffs, N.J.: Prentice-Hall, 1970), 35.

49. Cornelia Butler Flora and Rosario Bello, "The Impact of the Catholic Church on National Level Change in Latin America," *Journal of Church and State* 31, no. 3 (Autumn 1989): 529.

50. For evidence, see the case study in Vikram Khub Chand's unpublished Ph.D. dissertation, "Politics, Institutions, and Democracy in Mexico: The Politics of the State of Chihuahua in National Perspective," Harvard University, May 1992.

51. Kenneth D. Wald, D. E. Owen, and S. D. Hill, Jr., "Churches as Political Communities," 532.

52. As Fleet and Smith conclude, it "is extremely important to distinguish among Catholics with different exposures to Catholic values and culture at the local level, and to focus

and political mobilization in the parish neighborhood. Such contextual factors are important in shaping Catholic lay attitudes on both religious and political issues and need closer examination." Michael Fleet and Brian Smith, "Rethinking Catholicism and Politics in Latin America," n.p.

53. Kenneth Wald, Dennis E. Owen, and Samuel S. Hills, "Political Cohesion in Churches," *Journal of Politics* 52, no. 1 (February 1990): 213. Rodney Stark also discovered that the level of religiosity in a community determines the extent to which religion is an effective variable in governing social behavior. See his excellent study on teenagers, "Religion and Conformity: Reaffirming a Sociology of Religion," *Sociological Analysis* 45 (1984): 275.

54. Scott Mainwaring, *The Catholic Church and Politics in Brazil, 1916–1985* (Stanford: Stanford University Press, 1986), 10. Others making this same argument include Thomas G. Sanders, "The Politics of Catholicism in Latin America," *Journal of Inter-American Studies and World Affairs* 24, no. 2 (May, 1982): 255.

55. Daniel H. Levine, "Religion and Politics, Dimensions of Renewal," *Thought* 59, no. 233 (June 1984): 117; "From Church and State to Religion and Politics and Back Again," 104.

56. Edward Cleary, "Politics and Religion—Crisis, Constraints, and Restructuring," in *Conflict and Competition, The Latin American Church in a Changing Environment* (Boulder, Colo.: Lynne Rienner, 1992), 201.

2

Historical Underpinnings and Reform

Two Decades in Brief Repose

In contrast to the lack of literature analyzing religion, religious institutions, and the Church's political role in recent decades, historians have provided a far more complete picture of the institution during various periods prior to the 1970s. It is not the purpose of this work to go over ground well cultivated by others, or to provide a historical narrative, readily available and detailed in other works. Although references to specific historical circumstances, national and international, occur throughout the remaining chapters, it is useful to summarize briefly some important internal conditions that have a specific relevance to religion and politics, and more narrowly, church and state, at the end of the 20th century.

Pre-1910 Themes Found in Mexican Religious History

One of the most important themes underlying the historical roots of church-state or religion-politics tensions in Mexico is the symbiotic relationship between civil and religious authorities, or the lack of separation between church and state in the colonial period. Throughout the Spanish colonization, the Church was an active but sometimes recalcitrant ally of secular institutions. This alliance, whatever its fundamental characteristics, brought the Church and Catholicism squarely into secular and political affairs. It was never the case, however, that the Spanish crown could count on the Church to pursue its goals rather than the Church's, potentially undercutting royal interests.[1] It is equally important to stress that the two institutions never behaved as equals in the relationship since the Church operated as the subordinate partner. According to Ivan Vallier, their subservient role actually contributed to the Church involving itself more deeply in politics, while at the same time reducing its ability to influence extrapolitical values.[2] Nevertheless, despite decades of anticlericalism characterizing Mexico in both the 19th and 20th centuries, the Mexican state demonstrated a willingness, even before the advent of constitutional reforms in 1992, to elicit the Mexican episcopate's active support for secular policy matters if it believed the Church could play a useful, influential role.[3]

After independence, the Catholic Church, similar to other colonial institutions, struggled to retain its strength, autonomy, and stature in Mexican society. Within the larger context of political uncertainty, and as an actor contributing to societal instability, the Church involved itself overtly in political life. Thus, a second well-established thread of the Mexican heritage is Church involvement, often direct, in politics. As one scholar concluded, "The active political participation of ecclesiastics—from the archbishop to the lowliest seminarian, including members of the regular orders—was a natural part of public life in early independent Mexico until the Constitution of 1857 and the War of the Reform ended the practice. Before that turning point, the clergy remained active in political affairs, including matters that did not directly affect the Church."[4]

Mexican Liberalism provided a counterpart to this religious theme in direct reaction to the Church's secular political alliances. Among its strongest, orthodox principles, Liberalism sought to remove all aspects of religious control—cultural, economic, and social—from Mexican life. This Liberal heritage, in terms of its anticlericalism, reached an apex legislatively in the constitutions of 1857 and 1917. As part of this heritage, the Church is portrayed as antirevolutionary and conservative.[5] Mexicans, as noted repeatedly in subsequent chapters, are products of this dual, conflicting Liberal/Catholic tradition. The conflict between the two traditions, beginning in the early 19th century, led to a broader historical legacy: a slanted, unchanging portrayal of the Church in the public, secular culture. As the newly elected head of the Mexican episcopate in 1995, Sergio Obeso Rivera confessed, "I am saying this as a person, a Mexican, and a bishop, that it is very unfortunate that we are always noted as totally negative elements in our country, because . . . the official history . . . the presence of the Church in Mexico . . . is accursed."[6]

A fourth theme dominating the historical literature on the Catholic Church is Catholicism's monopoly and its lack of religious competition for most of the country's early history. It can be argued that given Catholicism's dominant position in society, religiously and culturally, the Church was free to compete with the State rather than focus its competitive spirit against other religions. Although Protestants have had some presence in Mexico since the mid-19th century, they were never threatening to Catholicism until the 1960s.[7] Scholars of American politics have argued that United States politicians "have felt little ambivalence toward the church because, unlike the Catholic church in Mexico, the various U.S. churches have competed not with the state but only with one another. Politicians are therefore free to deal in religious symbols."[8]

The independence of Mexico from Spain raised an issue that both clergy and politicians referred to frequently: the difference between lower clergy, many of whom favored the independence movements, and higher clergy, who continued to support the crown. The existence of a division between lower and higher clergy on the major political issue of the day, as well as the inability of secular authorities to understand fully differing positions within the Church, repeats itself again during the 1910 Revolution and later in the Cristero rebellion in the 1920s. A fifth theme that characterizes the Church's civil image in Mexico is the continued perception of it as a centralized, hierarchical institution. The Church has long harbored pastoral and theological differences among and between the episcopate and clergy, differences that many priests identify as the institution's strength.

Any analysis of the contemporary Mexican Church, especially since the application of anti-Church provisions in the 1917 Constitution, points to a large gap between theory and reality. The national authorities' unwillingness to apply the laws and the degree of resistance among those for whom the laws apply extend well back to the colonial period. More recently, the legal relationship between Church and State is evident in the pattern established under Porfirio Díaz (1884–1910), who "reverted to the practices of the late Juárez years, with the central government intervening to insure compliance only when there were reports of blatant or frequent violations without an adequate response by local or state officials."[9] Although scholarship on the church-state relationship emphasizes state intolerance toward the Church, in practice, tolerance has long been apparent in the relationship, even as early as the 1870s. As one bishop, who believes it a crucial ingredient in the relationship suggested, "[W]e have learned to live for many years in a situation I would describe as tolerant, and this situation has existed approximately since 1940."[10] Prominent politicians agreed. As president Luis Echeverría admitted, "[T]here is one essential value, tolerance. This value is the key to accomplishing a positive relationship."[11]

An important heritage affecting church-state relations in Mexico about which almost nothing has been written is the role of the *mayordomo*. The impact of the mayordomo, a figure whose roots extend back to the colonial period, is significant at the local level, which may explain his omission from these broader religious themes. Nicéforo Guerrero, who for many years represented the national government in Church affairs, considers his role crucial to internal disputes, sometimes extending into the larger community.[12] The mayordomo is a secular figure responsible for organizing major fiestas in small communities throughout Mexico and is generally in charge of, or financially responsible for, the local saints. These individuals often represent the parishioners before the parish priest. Conflicts may sometimes arise between mayordomo and priest or between mayordomo and parishioners.

Post-1910 Themes Found in Mexican Religious History

The most important events influencing the pattern of church-state relations in the 20th century are the Mexican Revolution of 1910 and the 1917 Constitution, a document codifying the eclectic values emerging from that violent conflict. The framers of the Constitution of 1917 attacked the Catholic Church for many reasons. But according to a student of the constitutional debates on the religious provisions, the most constant theme was "to destroy the ideological domination of the church."[13] It is interesting that the revolutionaries should return to a prominent 19th-century Liberal theme—the Church's influence over the socialization of values. The other explanation for these provisions and the constitution's virulent anticlerical tone stems from the Church joining Victoriano Huerta in 1913 in opposing the revolution. As one prominent historian concluded: "The Catholics compromised themselves by choosing the wrong side when Huerta ousted the Maderistas. . . . [T]he Catholics seemingly feared radicalism more than they feared dictatorship."[14] The Church sealed its fate in the post revolutionary era by immediately rejecting the document and more importantly calling on Catholics to fight for its abolition.[15]

A second, less common view explaining the tone of the 1917 Constitution toward the Church is offered by other scholars who argue that during the first decade of the 20th century, the Mexican clergy took to heart Pope Leo XIII's socially liberal encyclical *Rerum Novarum,* establishing peasant cooperatives, workers' unions, and technical institutions well in advance of governmental authorities. This interpretation argues that the Church "represented not a reactionary force that had to be crushed in order for the revolution to continue, but rather its chief competitor for the leadership of the movement for social change."[16] In short, the state would not tolerate any rivals.[17]

Interestingly, however, during the revolutionary decade the episcopate did not encourage identification with the fledgling Partido Católico Nacional (PCN), the only time a Catholic political party functioned in this century. Although the archbishop of Mexico participated in its founding, other bishops prohibited their clergy from allying with any party, specifically the PCN.[18] Regardless of the state's motivation for suppressing the Catholic Church, limiting its religious influence, the primary heritage emerging from this era was state supremacy over the Church, and monopolization of secular values.

The anticlerical provisions in the constitution created the legal and secular, cultural environment in which the Church operated from 1917 to 1992. Many of its long-term consequences on church-state relations are elaborated elsewhere. An insightful, if brief, summary of its impact on the Church suggests that

> [t]he 1917 Constitution damaged their ability to express public convictions, which also produced an invasion into private religious rights. It placed the citizen in a terrible dilemma of respecting civil authority or their conscience. This wound provoked the Cristero revolt—absurdly obligating the government to take up arms against its own citizens. It forced the Catholic Action to form secret societies. It also created a group of people who still believe that anything connected to the government is corrupt. I know one of these individuals, who told me out of personal honor that he has never set foot in the national palace.[19]

The revolutionary rhetoric codified in the 1917 document did not deter religiously predisposed Mexicans from accepting the Church as their spiritual guide while adopting the political elite as their secular leaders.[20]

If the 1917 Constitution conveyed extreme anticlericalism in words, the Cristero war of 1926–1929 did so in deeds. According to its leading scholar, this violent conflict between Catholics and clergy and the government explains many of the differences between the Mexican Catholic Church and Catholic institutions in the rest of the region. The Cristero rebellion fostered a unique set of conditions on

Mexican Church-state behavior, leaving a significant residue of mutual distrust and resentment on the part of clergy, secular elites, and the officer corps. For example, Jean Meyer suggests that it is this specific heritage that led to a Church much slower to implement post-Vatican-II-era reforms.[21] In part, the confrontation can also be seen as a consequence of a state "determined to broaden the scope of its authority."[22] Yet, it is also important to emphasize, as is the case of other sources of church-state conflict, that the Catholic hierarchy never accepted the Cristero movement completely, essentially because they did not fully control it.[23]

Revisionist history argues that 1929 is a benchmark year in church-state relations. Previous interpretations have presented a picture of continued conflict between the two institutions, after political and Church leaders achieved an informal, orally negotiated peace. Peter Reich discovered that "broad-based compromise took place at the national, regional, and local levels," and that this pattern explains many of the contemporary linkages and behavior.[24] No better public illustration of the cooperative posture between the two exists than President Lázaro Cárdenas's 1938 decision to expropriate oil, which the Church supported politically and financially.[25] Other analysts suggest that the Catholic hierarchy moved away from its involvement in secular matters to encouraging laity to take a more active role during this era.[26] For example, in 1934, one bishop urged the episcopate to advise Catholics to take an active role in the next election in opposition to socialist education provisions in the constitution.[27] The Pope himself echoed this view when he stated in a special encyclical on the "Religious Situation in Mexico" in March 1937 that lay Catholics should "continue to exercise their political and civil rights and obligations in defense of personal and Church rights" while cautioning the "Church, clergy and Catholic Action against involvement in any type of Catholic political party."[28]

The compromises that were taking place quietly after 1929 received public exposure in 1940, a date universally seen by historians as signifying new church-state relations. This was symbolized in the oft-cited example of newly elected President Manuel Avila Camacho declaring, "I am a believer." Clergy were completely surprised by the president's declaration, believing it to have had a profound effect on the citizenry and to have contributed to social peace.[29] Avila Camacho's actions established the concept of conciliation as an acceptable public policy in the political arena, generating a climate favorable to a more open implementation of the conciliation strategy. The president went well beyond a symbolic statement, making it clear through numerous actions that secularization was no longer an explicit administration goal. Moreover, the values the Church traditionally supported—unity, order, and social peace—appeared to coincide with those adopted by the political leadership.[30] In 1945, Avila Camacho allowed the Church to hold a massive religious celebration to commemorate the coronation of the Virgin of Guadalupe, even permitting a religious broadcast over national radio. Most important, his administration abolished the controversial socialist provisions in Article 3 of the constitution.[31]

His successor, Miguel Alemán (1946–1952), continued Avila Camacho's conciliatory pattern, implementing a policy of collaboration repeated by successive administrations. For example, Alemán used the clergy to help improve agricultural development, specifically in his campaign to control hoof and mouth disease. Similar to Luis Echeverría in the 1970s, Alemán appropriated funds for the restoration of the Basilica of Guadalupe.[32] Although a Mason, Alemán raised his own children in an environment respectful of religion, and before reaching the presidency, he reopened churches when he was governor in his home state of Veracruz.[33]

The level of cooperation between church and state in the 1950s and 1960s did not obviate their differences nor compromise the autonomy of the Church. Although important patterns of cooperation were established during these decades, the period provides equally important indications of the Church's more open, critical posture in the 1980s and 1990s. For example, its pastoral letter on *Rerum Novarum*'s 60th anniversary was one of the first to criticize Mexico's development model.[34] According to one scholar, some clergy began to interfere more directly in politics, recommending that Catholics vote specifically for National Action Party candidates in the 1955, 1958, 1961, and 1964 elections.[35] Members of the hierarchy launched a campaign to urge Catholics to exercise their civic responsibilities and to vote their religious convictions.[36]

The 1960s provide a transitional period in church-state relations. Naturally, the single most influential event for the Catholic Church internally, and subsequently for Church involvement in politics, was the Second Vatican Concilium in 1962. This episcopal reunion and the Conference of Latin American Bishops (CELAM) regional meetings were seminal events, whose consequences are analyzed from a Mexican perspective in chapter 4.

Political events in Cuba, with the rise of Fidel Castro and the suppression of Catholicism, also spurred new forms of Catholic political change elsewhere in the region.[37] In Mexico, Christian democracy strongly influenced the National Action Party, but it never was translated into electoral victories, nor was the Church itself an active participant in party affairs. Nevertheless, Cuba introduced reverberations in Mexico prompting the episcopate to approve a statement outlining the dangers of Communism, offering to help the government oppose this threat on the one hand, while on the other, offering strong criticisms of the government's economic policies, allowing liberation theology to establish a foothold.[38] The majority leader of the Chamber of Deputies, Alfonso Martínez Domínguez, anticipating President Salinas's gesture 20 years later, invited Bishop Sergio Méndez Arceo of Cuernavaca and the canon of the Mexico City cathedral to a 1967 session of congress.[39] Although theological differences abounded within the Mexican episcopate throughout these decades, the common thread in Church behavior was open criticism of economic and social failures tempered by a reserved posture on political matters.

1968: A Turning Point in Church-State Relations?

The violent suppression of the student movement in Mexico City in the fall of 1968 did more to change the societal context of Mexican politics than to influence Church behavior. In fact, what is most surprising is that while this social violence marked a critical departure in the evolution of the Mexican political model, affecting an entire generation, it produced little reaction from the Mexican episcopate. Clergy who spoke out publicly against the massacre of Tlatelolco were in the minority, although a group of priests issued a statement in support of the students' position before the suppression occurred.[40] The only member of the hierarchy to express strong, public criticism was the bishop of Cuernavaca, Sergio Méndez Arceo, a leading advocate of Vatican II principles. He tried, unsuccessfully, to get the Mexican Conference of Bishops to explore the affair.[41]

Nevertheless, the events of 1968 did have an impact on the Catholic Church, most notably on the Mexican Social Secretariat, which parted company with the hierarchy, criticizing it publicly for its indecisiveness in responding to the student massacre.[42] More important, a schism appeared among the most progressive priests and the hierarchy. It marks a crisis in the social control within the institution, particularly in the increasing internal conflicts of authority and the breakdown of ideological homogeneity, stable since 1929.[43] The serious questions that the government's actions raised about the legitimacy and effectiveness of the political model came at a time when the Church leadership already had begun, early in 1968, to reflect on its social responsibilities, questioning Mexico's economic and political characteristics, specifically deriding administrative corruption and the lack of civic development.[44]

The Church's statements mirrored international trends manifested at the second meeting of the Council of Latin American Bishops in Medellín, Colombia, that same year.[45] As Daniel Levine argues, 1968 marked the beginning of the openness of the Latin American hierarchy to change and "a new critical discourse about society and politics."[46] It can be argued that a coincidence of internal political events, the Church's historic relationship with the state, and international Catholic theological trends in the region conspired to rejuvenate the Mexican Church, but unlike its counterparts elsewhere in Latin America, Mexico's episcopate concentrated more strongly on its internal revival than on translating its newly acquired perspectives into a secular, pastoral arena.[47] It was only at the end of the 1970s, 10 years after the progressive movements had peaked in Latin America, that Mexico's hierarchy began to focus on external political and economic issues.

A strong case can be made that 1979, not 1968, marks a significant turning point in Mexican church-state relations. During this year, the Pope visited Mexico and the third Conference of Latin American Bishops took place in Puebla. The Puebla conference was far more important to the Mexican hierarchy than was its more notable predecessor, which exerted tremendous influence on Latin American clergy.[48] As one scholar suggests, particularly after Puebla, the episcopate began "to feel the fuller impact of the Vatican council."[49] Numerous Mexican bishops personally were involved in this meeting, and unlike the Medellín reunion, the bishops themselves, not their experts (many of whom were liberation theologians), wrote the working documents.[50] The crucial issue on which Puebla focused was the means or process by which the clergy could deliver its religious message, including a Christian vision of social and political realities.[51] As one Mexican bishop recalled, his interest in the "social project of evangelizing" grew with new force after this meeting.[52] Although the bishops explicitly denied their competence to speak on politics or economics, emphasizing their evangelical role, they did claim the authority "to provide moral criticism and guidelines for those who share Catholic values in making specific decisions on social and political questions."[53]

The Pope's visit reinforced the ability of the bishops to transfer moral into political and social statements. John Paul II's public appearance symbolized the resurgence of Church involvement in Mexican political life.[54] Indeed, it has been argued that his overt violations of the Mexican constitution, with permission of public authorities, contributed to the secretary of government's resignation.[55]

The relationship between Presidents Echeverría (1970–1976), López Portillo (1976–1982), Miguel de la Madrid (1982–1988), and Salinas to the Mexican episcopate, and specific occurrences drawing the Church into political activities, are detailed in subsequent chapters. The interaction between social movements and the Church during these decades is well documented.[56] But by the early 1980s, three broad changes in the Mexican political context established conditions favorable to introducing constitutional reforms: successive electoral reforms in the late 1960s, 1970s, and early 1980s and their consequential increase in political opposition; the declining legitimacy of the political leadership and established political institutions; and the rapid expansion of Church-affiliated popular groups in the wake of the 1985 earthquake in Mexico City.[57] The Church acquired additional prestige because it was the only major civil organization that reacted immediately to the disaster, using its network of organizations to receive foreign donations and distribute them to those who needed the help. Moreover, hundreds of church-based groups emerged in the aftermath of the earthquake, demonstrating a talent for negotiating assistance and gaining "confidence in their ability to handle 'secular' affairs" and creating an organizational model in the social arenas.[58]

As political reforms gave greater voice to opposition parties on the right and left, it generated greater potential for political competition and realistic consequences of exercising civic responsibilities. In some cases, in their desire to promote pluralism, some opposition parties such as the Mexican Communist Party expressed the view that clergy should have the right to vote.[59] The very societal changes that inserted the Church into a more active role in social and political affairs also worked to lessen support favorable to changing the status quo.[60] When the Church began to voice concerns about major political deficiencies such as electoral fraud, governmental restrictions began to tighten, and Liberal politicians sought to block its secular influence.

Constitutional Reforms: Closing the Gap between Theory and Practice

Carlos Salinas Gortari accepted the presidential sash on December 1, 1988, but not a single analyst anticipated that he would introduce a new agenda for church-state relations. A representative of the Mexican hierarchy conceded it was "Salinas who really initiated this new period by inviting us to the Chamber of Deputies [for his inauguration] and more directly later, establishing a public forum for creating a dialogue between Church and State."[61] Salinas's invitation to representatives of the hierarchy to attend his inauguration, the first president to do so in modern times, generated tremendous opposition from congressional deputies.[62] Yet even as late as August 1989, Salinas's secretary of government informed the press that his administration was not contemplating any modifications in Article 130 of the constitution, central to church-state relations, and that "the spirit of the Laws of the Reform" would remain in force.[63]

In 1988, government officials, at least within the party, viewed the Church's power as having grown considerably in the last few years.[64] The Catholic hierarchy's spokesman, shortly before Salinas's inauguration, claimed his peers would "demand and open and frank dialogue to arrange Church-State relations."[65] For his part, the Vatican delegate described their relations as analogous to an unmarried couple living together, a *matrimonio salvaje,* arguing that it should receive legal sanction.[66]

The question uppermost in the minds of most observers—clergy, politicians, and intellectuals alike—is what motivated the new president to make public the dialogue between Church and state and then, within two years, in his November 1, 1991, State of the Union address, to propose major reforms to the constitutional status of the Church and other religious institutions.[67] At least five credible interpretations can be offered to explain the president's decision.

The first and most complex is that the president and his advisers developed a grand political strategy for reformulating Mexico's traditional political alliances, specifically those between the state and major interest groups. One could argue that Salinas only had to look at one of his most skillful political predecessors, Porfirio Díaz, to find an appropriate model. According to Don Coerver, "Díaz wanted to deemphasize politics in favor of promoting economic development; such an approach required a conciliatory policy toward former opponents whether political, military, or clerical."[68] There is absolutely no question that Salinas made economic neoliberalism his fundamental priority, and that political liberalization would be subordinate to and follow its implementation.[69]

Federico Reyes Heroles, son of the former government secretary and a leading intellectual, recalls that Salinas told him that "the relationships between business, the Church, and the government had to be changed," confirming this broader strategy of altering interest group–state relations.[70] Reyes Heroles believed the president hoped to rebuild a new set of constituencies. This is a convincing argument, and the president demonstrated in his relationships with other groups that some were strengthened and others weakened in what became a broad constituency involving the Church, the middle classes, the entrepreneurial class, the military, and the United States.[71] His most important political opponents give credence to this interpretation. Cuauhtémoc Cárdenas, the greatest political threat to Salinas, viewed this strategy as a means of reducing the Democratic Revolutionary Party's political space.[72]

Some politicians have suggested that Salinas wanted to open up government relations with various groups, lessening traditional, corporatist ties. They argue that the changes, while genuine, suggest a "strategic" not a concrete, alteration in which the state was attempting to improve its image with the Church, not alter its substantive posture.[73] This, too, is a convincing caveat to the broader rationale for

Salinas's decision and may well express his actual intentions, which are difficult to assess in the small number of years elapsed since 1992. What this argument ignores, however, is whether or not the president's goal was intentional. Given the extraordinary negative rhetorical and legal bashing the Church has suffered, image itself produces substantive alterations in the relationship.

The second explanation attributes the burden of influence to the Church, asserting that Catholic leadership sought out an altered relationship, specifically major legal changes in its status, constitutional and otherwise.[74] Evidence exists to suggest that as early as November 1982, bishops were sending a clear signal that "they intended to seek major modifications in Article 130, perhaps even its abolition.[75] The government official in charge of Church relations under Salinas, Arturo Núñez Jiménez, revealed that the episcopate indeed made a formal proposal to the president concerning constitutional changes, specifically an article-by-article description, in 1989, a year before the president announced his desire to entertain possible legal revisions.[76] However, it is important to emphasize that the hierarchy did not undertake such a request until *after* Salinas indicated the government's good intentions by opening up a public forum with the clergy. Clergy also have revealed secondhand that since 1982, at the beginning of de la Madrid's administration, certain Church officials at the highest levels were engaged in a calculated effort to reformulate their relationship.[77]

The third view of Salinas's radical departure from his predecessors explains the president's decision as responding to public, not interest group, pressures. Some members of the hierarchy also support this interpretation.[78] Public opinion poll data in chapter 5 make clear that many Mexicans believed that the legal restrictions on the Church, specifically the prohibition against priests voting, was anachronistic and a violation of human rights, a highly visible agenda of issues affecting all Mexicans. Yet a counterpoint to this from the government's viewpoint was a revealing sentence in a PRI document in September 1988, which implied that Salinas already was planning to change the relationship, and that the most important aspect of his strategy was to prepare public opinion for the necessity and desirability of such a change.[79]

The fourth explanation, strongly associated with the first view, is that the president, who arrived in office at a low point in Mexican political history, with Mexico's presidency and governmental leadership lacking legitimacy, viewed improved relations with the Church and, consequently, improved relations with the broad constituencies it represented as a viable path toward improving his political standing and strengthening his personal and institutional presidency.[80] Undoubtedly, the president and his collaborators had selfish motives in making such a change. There is no question that, in retrospect, Salinas benefited from his decision. But it is critical to remember that at the time he made it, against the advice of all of his close advisers, who perceived little public pressure for him to do so and great risks in altering the established pattern, negative political fallout was far more likely than any alleged benefits.[81]

The final explanation for Salinas's decision rests on the view that the president, as was true of many members of his generation, found the contradiction between the theory and reality, the constitutional provisions and practices, to be outdated and inappropriate.[82] As one priest expressed it, the constitution created in Mexicans a distorted conscience, a collective lie that harmed the nation.[83] On principle alone, ignoring the issue of violating Church rights, the statutes were contrary to an open and participatory society.[84] Salinas expressed his reservations about this gap in theory and practice as bringing the relationship in line with modern societies. Thus, the restrictions on the Church contradicted his view of modernization. While this is probably the case, a much more politically motivated, selfish rationale also can be offered. Salinas's view of economic and social "modernization" was linked strongly to incorporating Mexico into the international economic community through its association with the United States and Canada. Some bishops and analysts viewed Salinas's efforts as a pragmatic attempt to present Mexico in the best possible light, from a human rights perspective, in anticipation of United States congressional debates over the North American Free Trade Agreement.[85]

The Reforms

A brief examination of how the changes came to be proposed not only reveals important features of the decision-making process at the highest levels but also suggests how government officials viewed the church-state issue and the Catholic Church. The Conference of Mexican Bishops (CEM), the formal representative of the Mexican hierarchy, evaluated several specific proposals, including two from members knowledgeable about canon law and the issues of religion and politics. But the CEM never formally presented a document to the Mexican congress or to any of the political parties.[86] Other church representatives did meet with legislators.[87] Most of the decision-making process was handled informally, repeating past patterns in the relationship between the Church and government officials, as evidenced later in the book.

The actual negotiations over the content of these reforms took place among representatives of the Church hierarchy and the Mexican government in 1989 and 1990. Antonio Roqueñi, legal counsel to the cardinal archbishop of Mexico, functioned as the bridge between the bishops and the politicians.[88] Many of the exchanges occurred in the Vatican delegate's private residence, and in addition to the delegate, a major actor, the cardinal and other leading members of the CEM were involved.[89] According to one source, at least 30 clergy expressed their views before government representatives, including the majority leader of the Chamber of Deputies, Fernando Ortiz Arana. One of the important features of the negotiating process is that representatives of non-Catholic faiths were not included.[90] In fact, when Salinas actually announced the proposed reforms in his third State of the Union address on November 1, 1991, he invited only three non-Catholic representatives. On December 18, the Chamber of Deputies approved changes to the Constitutional Articles 3, 4, 24, 27, and 130, after a short debate (published in the *Diario Oficial* on January 28). The fundamental legal changes, however, were not in the constitution but in the implementing legislation, not approved until July 15, 1992.

Strangely, the agency primarily responsible for and most knowledgeable about the Catholic Church, the secretariat of government, played no role in the formulation of the proposed legislation.[91] Instead, the presidential Office of Coordination grasped those responsibilities for itself. Important figures other than congressional leaders included José Córdoba, its director and the president's chief of staff and most influential adviser; Mariano Palacios Alcocer, the former governor of Querétaro; and Juan Rebolledo, from Córdoba's staff. The secretariat of government's exclusion from the decision-making process can be explained in part by the fact that the secretary, Francisco Gutiérrez Barrios, opposed the reforms, as did some other officials in the agency. Equally important, throughout Salinas's administration a tendency existed to centralize significant decision making on political matters in the hands of a few close associates. Although the secretariat of government worked out its own version of the bylaws, detailing the explanation and enforcement of constitutional provisions, it ultimately exercised no influence in writing the law. The legislative branch produced a revised version in which Senator José Luis de la Madrid and Mariano Palacios Alcocer played major roles in crafting the document.[92] The ultimate version, however, came from the presidency, not the party.[93] Opposition parties also presented draft bills and amendments, and some of these modifications were incorporated into the final document.[94]

In the case of both the government and the clergy, internal conflicts affected the pace, direction, and actors in the decision-making process. Within the episcopate, the Vatican delegate and the bishops favored different goals. Equally important, some bishops and most religious order leaders and lay groups wanted a public debate of the proposed reforms.[95] On the government side, congressional representatives believed they should be responsible for the final version. What the process actually demonstrates is both groups' preference to negotiate through a small circle of influential leaders.

According to analysts, six basic principles in constitutional church-state relations can be identified in Salinas's reforms proposed on January 28, 1992:

1. Preserve state sovereignty
2. Retain public, secular education
3. Establish a clear demarcation between civil and ecclesiastical affairs
4. Respect freedom of religion
5. Maintain equality among all churches and religious groups
6. Recognize the legal personality of religious groups.[96]

The first four principles were already codified in the 1917 Constitution. It is the last two that are most strongly affected in the new legislation. The symbolic and actual significance of these reforms is suggested by the fact that of 380 modifications to the Constitution of 1917 prior to 1991, none altered Articles 24 and 130.[97] The actual reforms appeared in the *ley reglamentaria,* or bylaws, on July 15, 1992, where specific legal provisions can be found, rather than in the brief, abstract principles in the constitutional document approved seven months earlier. The enabling legislation contains 36 sections. It fundamentally alters Article 130. The original bylaws, published on January 18, 1927, include the following significant provisions:

1. Only state legislatures have the ability to determine, according to local necessities, the maximum number of religious ministers.
2. The law does not recognize any personality of church dominated religious groups.
3. Religious publications, whatever their program or title, may not comment on national political affairs or comment on the acts of the country's authorities.
4. The prohibition of any political group who has ties or relations with any religious beliefs.
5. Any religious minister must be a Mexican by birth to practice in Mexico.[98]

The most politically significant tenets of the 1992 bylaw, known as the "Law of Religious Associations and Public Cults," include the following:

Number 7: Those desirous of registration as religious associations must:
    Part II: have realized religious activities in Mexico for at least 5 years and *have notable roots in the community* [emphasis added].
    Part III: have sufficient resources to complete its objectives.

Number 12: Religious associations must notify the secretariat of government who they have designated as clergy.

Number 14: Clergy from whatever cult have the right to vote. . . . They cannot run for elective public office, nor may they serve in higher public offices without having left formally, materially, and definitively the clergy for five years in the first case, and three years in the second, before the day of election or acceptance of a post.[99]

The new bylaws did not change Article 3 of the Constitution, which is a major article devoted to education and the tenet of secular (public), primary education. This surprised many observers.[100] The Council of Mexican Bishops publicly expressed their desire to alter this article so that parents could educate their children in their chosen beliefs.[101] A leading representative from the National Action Party, which often endorsed religious freedom in education, concluded that the Church, having acquired legal recognition, should use its new-found status to increase educational opportunities since only a small minority, 4 percent of the school children, can attend private secular or parochial schools.[102] According to a member of the congressional committee responsible for discussing this legislation, the Catholic hierarchy erred in its political strategy:

The Church representatives made a big mistake. They were much too outspoken before the statutes were changed. The political class was offended by this. The clergy kept harping on all the things they wanted, and spoke about obtaining control over radio and television stations. Those demands created the circumstances in which the statutes were written. The atmosphere was extremely tense. I ran into Archbishop Adolfo Suárez [president of the CEM] on a flight to Monterrey. I advised him to tell his colleagues to tone down their public remarks, and to stop making these statements. He agreed with me, but threw up his hands in despair, saying he couldn't do anything about it.[103]

The primary changes occurred in constitutional Articles 24 and 130. Under Article 24, which includes restrictions on religious activity, the reforms allow special acts to be celebrated outside of churches to be governed by the new bylaws. In addition to the changes in Article 130 mentioned above, clergy may not associate themselves with political goals and proselytize against or in favor of any political party or candidate, nor can they make public statements against the laws. Also, they may not inherit property from those individuals to whom they administer spiritually.[104] The government also removed prohibitions in Article 5 against the establishment of monastic orders and, more important, in Article 27, against owning property. The Church may now own property *"indispensable"* (emphasis added) to its tasks within the limitations of the bylaws.[105] The bylaws are far more important than the phrasing in Article 130 or the changes made elsewhere in the constitutional document. These are the laws that actually govern Church behavior and, consequently, its institutional relationship with the state. The constitutional reforms were approved after a brief 25 hours of debate in the Chamber of Deputies on December 18, 1992.[106]

The Vatican delegate sought the reestablishment of Vatican relations with Mexico as the primary change within the larger reform package. Most clergy who were interviewed prior to 1992 did not consider this an important issue but saw it as a task assigned to the delegate. One could make the argument that initially Salinas purposely avoided relations with the Vatican in recognition of the antagonism between Girolamo Prigione, the delegate, and certain sectors of the episcopate. On the other hand, the case could be made that the president left out recognition initially to gain something more from the Church. Manuel Carrillo, a former analyst for the secretariat of government, whose responsibilities included church-state relations, believes the president wanted to test public receptiveness to the constitutional changes before taking additional political risks.[107] This is the most convincing argument given the fact that there existed little public pressure for formal relations. Only 43 percent of all Mexicans thought such relations would be good in September 1992, when relations formally were established.[108]

Reactions to and Consequences of the Reforms

The passage of the constitutional reforms and their bylaws produced immediate reactions from clergy and public figures.[109] Public figures and clergy also speculated on their long-term consequences. Formally, the Council of Mexican Bishops publicly expressed a moderate posture on the legislation. Nevertheless, it specifically criticized government sanctions on possible violators of specific provisions and, more important, criticized the reforms for their failure to extend religious liberty into education.[110] Others suggested that the restrictions, some of which apply to other groups, unfairly singled out the Catholic Church.[111] Three months later, during the CEM's November meeting, bishops critical of the legislation proposed rejecting the bylaws altogether.[112]

Many bishops publicly and privately questioned specific provisions of the bylaws. For some, the definition of a "religious association" was ambiguous since it required groups to have well-known roots in the community and sufficient resources to meet their needs. Clergy charged that no one could define these two requirements or decide if they had been met. Granting the Church ownership of "indispensable" property also raised similar questions.[113] A prominent reporter discovered in a series of interviews that all of the clergy with whom he spoke were upset with these provisions and the authority of the secretariat of government to define a religious association.[114] Ironically, the officials in the government secretariat assigned to implement the laws were equally disturbed with the wording. Since they played no role in actually writing the legislation, they did not comprehend the rationale behind some of the terminology and they found the legislation difficult to implement.[115]

Representatives of the secretariat of government viewed the requirement that "religious associations" register as the most important change in the bylaws. The Church's response to this requirement illustrated a fundamental conflict within the leadership. The Vatican delegate made a request in the name of the Roman Catholic Apostolic Church of Mexico. Government and clerical experts both criticized the delegate for such a request, which was legally incorrect. Each individual diocese, as a legal entity, must request recognition, since each bishop is an autonomous actor within Mexico. The delegate's actions placed government officials in a difficult situation. The archdiocese of Mexico, representing Cardinal Ernesto Corripio Ahumada, sent lawyers to oppose the delegate's request, arguing that the Roman Catholic Apostolic Church of Mexico had no patrimony nor personnel, and that the delegate, as a foreigner, had no legal standing to make such a request. The secretariat of government settled the dispute between the bishops and the Vatican delegate by allowing legal recognition for a single Mexican Church but requiring that the president of the Mexican Conference of Bishops and the cardinal sign the request.[116] A long-term consequence of its newly acquired legal status, as one bishop argued, is that the Church is not only a Mexican but also a universal institution, and Mexican clergy must respond to universal patterns among laity and clergy, not to those apparent only within Mexico.[117]

Structurally, the reforms also provoked a change within the government itself. Prior to 1988, religious affairs were handled informally by various presidential representatives and by secretaries of government, not by an established, federal agency. Realizing the magnitude of the registration problem and the issues raised by requirements in the legislation, the government reorganized its government division within the secretariat, establishing a directorate general–level department to handle religious affairs. This new agency included several divisions and numerous department heads.[118]

Others, particularly lower clergy, criticized the entire reform process, viewing it as a significant distraction from many of their primary tasks. These clergy viewed the focus on reform as refocusing emphasis away from serious theological debates on pastoral issues to less important, institutional relationships. In particular, bishops representing the progressive tendency within the hierarchy, including Arturo Lona Reyes, bishop of Tehuantepec, and Samuel Ruiz, bishop of San Cristóbal de las Casas, believed the debate over church and state distracted Church priorities away from the poor.[119] Many clergy actually opposed the reforms altogether, viewing them as putting at risk the Church's primary tasks, specifically its evangelizing role.

Some hierarchy, representing a variety of theological tendencies, expressed concern at the level of controls over religious associations granted to the government. Although supporters of the reforms strongly expressed interest in the Church's legal personality so it could freely voice its politically oriented positions in defense of human rights, many raised a question offered by a Jesuit: "We ask ourselves how we would work better in a legality that will tie our hands or in an illegality that allows us to do as we want."[120] Repeatedly, priests and even some bishops argued that by eliminating the gap between the law and practical realities, the Church would be placed under closer scrutiny. Some clergy even went so far to argue that the government would now exercise influence over bishops' selection.[121] Moreover, to all priests working on day-to-day parish matters, even the most radical, the reforms made little difference.[122]

The only reforms that reached the parish level directly affected fiscal matters. According to well-informed clergy, the Church always produced two sets of books in response to their previous status. The new civil law, in effect, is forcing them to comply with fiscal requirements within canon law because the treasury department exercises more coercive powers over parish fiscal matters than do bishops. Having legal recognition, then, requires each church to keep records similar to a small business. The most important immediate conflict, however, has risen as a consequence of a traditional Church practice to evade its lack of legal status while owning property. The Church asked its most loyal laity to hold property in their own names, known in Mexico as *prestanombres*. It appears, from several cases reported in the media, that various bishops are having some difficulties in persuading these individuals to transfer property back to the Church.[123]

Even if the reforms did not reach down to affect priests' daily routines, many bishops viewed it as initiating a contextual change advancing relations between the two institutions. One cleric believed that the reforms indicated that both politicians and bishops learned more about each other, and although he could not speculate as to where this improved understanding might lead, he remained convinced it would help Mexico in the future.[124] A more pessimistic view suggested that legislation alone would not alter the relationship between church and state, that a state of inertia had characterized it far too long. Nevertheless, as Archbishop Rosendo Huesca of Puebla revealed, the Church would

> have to learn anew how to function in this [legal] context. I work closely with the CEM on the education committee. I have the conviction that it just isn't a legal agreement, but that the state has offered us some new space, and we need to take advantage of this space to benefit all human beings. When we will achieve these benefits, I can't say. We have to begin, however, and if we don't take the first step, there will never be a last one.[125]

Abel Vicencio, a former president of PAN, agreed with Huesca, making an even broader argument that the reforms advanced not only a more civilized environment for church-state relations but, more important, the culture of law in society.[126]

Another interpretation within the clergy is that the reforms essentially left un-changed the relationship between church and state, primarily benefiting the state. This interpretation supports the earlier view that Salinas introduced the changes to increase the state's legitimacy. Some clergy who pursue this line of thought extend it even further, suggesting that the Church has compromised its own prestige to enhance that of the state. These priests argue that the Church is losing credibility among the people, and this is the price it has paid for legal recognition.[127] Indeed, an interesting twist on this is suggested by Manuel Carrillo, who concluded that the "Church has lost its image as a victim. . . . It benefited from that image in terms of its rights being suppressed, just like other Mexicans."[128] The contrary argument is that these reforms, rather than legitimizing the political system, helped to open it up to more diverse opinions and behavior. Moderates, such as Bishop Mario Gasperín Gasperín, view both institutions, government and Church, benefiting from the constitutional reforms.[129]

The most unexpected consequence of the reforms is their impact on the Protes-tant churches, and on the relations between Catholics and Protestants. As César Pérez of the Methodist Church remarked, the reform sparked a new social con-sciousness within the churches.[130] This has led to a stronger emphasis among some Protestants toward human rights issues and a desire to establish their own organizations.[131] An unpleasant consequence, however, is increasing tensions be-tween the two faiths. Many Protestants viewed the reforms as initiated and formu-lated between the Catholic Church and the government, placing on the margin participation and recognition of Protestant faiths. Some observers view the process of reform and the legal recognition of churches as encouraging the Catholic Church to take a more aggressive posture toward Evangelical Protestants in their proselytizing.[132]

The most important potential consequence of the reforms, having the greatest impact on the broader relationship, is the impact of legal recognition on the ability and desire of the Church to involve itself in nonevangelical matters. Many clergy and Liberal politicians are worried that the reforms generated greater, not fewer, risks in the relationship. Given their outstanding differences on the level of de-mocratization, the role of private education, human rights abuses, and abortion, to name just a few issues, the potential for conflict is significant. Some clergy, such as progressive Bishop Samuel Ruiz, believed that the reforms would not affect the relationship because the Church would define itself in the same way regardless of state actions.[133] Other bishops, including the late cardinal and arch-bishop of Guadalajara and former CEM leader, Juan Jesús Posadas, recognized that these reforms would definitely create tensions with the government but that the Church had an obligation to proceed.[134] The bishop of Querétaro explains why:

I think the Church should always be somewhat of a bother to the state because its views don't coincide with the state's views or methods. This is part of a divine view of man. Anthropologically speaking, there are always going to be points of conflict, such as our differing vision of human beings and human rights. They play the role of a critical conscience for the state and society, not to confront it, but because it is part of its natural, institutional responsibilities. However, acting maturely and creating bridges for dialogue with the State are included in this responsibility.[135]

The actual results, in a political sense, in the period since the implementation of the reforms have been mixed, as anticipated by Arturo Núñez Jiménez, who concluded that the law would encourage clergy who wished to exert greater influence politically over laity, whereas others would moderate their efforts in this direction. Those who expected increased politization among the clergy could point to their involvement in the Chiapas rebellion in early January 1994 and in the subsequent mediation efforts as evidence of greater involvement, but San Cristóbal de las Casas, the primary diocese where the rebellion took place, has long maintained an active, aggressive posture in defense of Indian rights. Nevertheless, individual cases of clerical involvement in politics led the otherwise reserved former president in 1994, Miguel de la Madrid, to break his silence and express concern with Church intervention in politics.[136]

NOTES

1. Margaret E. Crahan, "Church and State in Latin America: Assassinating Some Old and New Stereotypes," *Daedalus* 120, no. 3 (Summer 1991): 131.

2. Ivan Vallier, *Catholicism, Social Control, and Modernization in Latin America* (Englewood Cliffs, N.J.: Prentice-Hall, 1970), 46.

3. This is a point made by Soledad Loaeza, "La iglesia y la democracia en México," *Revista Mexicana de Sociología* 47, no. 1 (January–March 1985): 161–168, but of course, this justification has always been a factor in Mexican church-state relations.

4. Anne Staples, "Clerics as Politicians: Church, State, and Political Power in Independent Mexico," in *Mexico in the Age of Democratic Revolutions, 1750–1850,* Jaime Rodríguez, ed. (Boulder, Colo.: Lynne Rienner, 1994), 240. Benito Juárez, believing Protestants could help them, actually invited representatives to Mexico. Personal interview with César Pérez, Methodist Church of Mexico, Mexico City, July 14, 1993.

5. Miguel Concha Malo, "Tensiones entre la religión del pueblo y las CEB's en México con sectores de la jearquía: implicaciones eclesiológicas," *Ciencia Tomista* 114 (May–August 1987): 20.

6. Oscar Hinojosa, "La misión evangélica ordena dejar la sacristía, afirma Obeso Rivera," *Proceso,* September 8, 1986, 12. Obeso also admits in the same interview that the activities of the Church in Mexican history have been unfortunate, but that the attitudes of the past cannot be judged by the criteria of the present.

7. For evidence of this, see Jean-Pierre Bastian's excellent *Los disidentes, sociedades protestantes y revolución en México, 1872–1911* (Mexico City: Fondo de Cultura Económica, 1989).

8. Philip E. Hammond, "The Conditions for Civil Religion: a Comparison of the United States and Mexico," in *Varieties of Civil Religion,* Robert W. Bella and Philip E. Hammond, eds. (New York: Harper and Row, 1980), 71. Hammond also argues that in the separation of church and state in the United States, the Church lost its monopoly on religious symbols, sharing them with civil agencies, therefore allowing the government to use religious symbols. *Varieties of Civil Religion,* 68.

9. Don M. Coerver, "From Confrontation to Conciliation: Church-State Relations in Mexico, 1867–1884," *Journal of Church and State* 32 (Winter 1990): 72.

10. Personal interview with Bishop Jorge Martínez Martínez, Mexico Archdiocese, Mexico City, May 28, 1987.

11. Personal interview with President Luis Echeverría, Mexico City, August 2, 1992.

12. Personal interview with Nicéforo Guerrero, Mexico City, June 19, 1989.

13. Richard Roman, "Church-State Relations and the Mexican Constitutional Congress, 1916–1917," *Journal of Church and State* 20 (Winter 1978): 79.

14. Robert E. Quirk, *The Mexican Revolution and the Catholic Church, 1914–1929* (Bloomington: Indiana University Press, 1973), 38. The Protestants pursued a different path. See Deborah J. Baldwin, *Protestants and the Mexican Revolution: Missionaries, Ministers, and Social Change* (Urbana: University of Illinois Press, 1990).

15. Soledad Loaeza, "Continuity and Change in the Mexican Catholic Church," in *Church and Politics in Latin America*, Dermot Keogh, ed. (New York: St. Martin's, 1990), 277.

16. Dennis M. Hanratty, "The Political Role of the Mexican Catholic Church: Contemporary Issues," *Thought* 59 (June 1984): 166.

17. Donald J. Mabry, "Mexican Anticlerics, Bishops, *Cristeros,* and the Devout during the 1920s: A Scholarly Debate," *Journal of Church and State* 20, no. 1 (1978): 88. This argument has been further substantiated in recent research extending to the 1920s, where the National Catholic Labor Union stood in the way of the Regional Confederation of Mexican Labor (CROM) absorbing all labor groups, and the Church became an obstacle to "Calles' related goal of subjecting rival forces to the state." See Scott Hanson Randall, "The Day of Ideals: Catholic Social Action in the Age of the Mexican Revolution, 1867–1929," unpublished Ph.D. dissertation, Indiana University, 1994.

18. Karl M. Schmitt, "Catholic Adjustment to the Secular State, 1867–1911," *Catholic Historical Review* 48 (July 1962): 202. Michael C. Meyer, a student of Victoriano Huerta, also demonstrates that clergy and Catholic politicians operated independently of each other at the time. See his *Huerta, a Political Portrait* (Lincoln: University of Nebraska Press, 1972), 167–170.

19. Personal interview with Julio Faesler, Mexico City, February 12, 1993.

20. James W. Wilkie, "Statistical Indicators of the Impact of National Revolution on the Catholic Church in Mexico, 1910–1967," *Journal of Church and State* 12, no. 1 (Winter 1970): 103.

21. Jean Meyer, *Historia de los cristianos en América Latina, siglos xix y xx* (Mexico City: Vuelta, 1989), 243.

22. Soledad Loaeza, "Continuity and Change in the Mexican Catholic Church," 279.

23. Roberto Blancarte, *El poder salinismo e iglesia católica, una nueva convivencia?* (Mexico City: Grijalbo, 1991), 94.

24. Peter Reich, "Mexico's Hidden Revolution: The Catholic Church in Politics since 1919," unpublished Ph.D. dissertation, UCLA, 1991, 197. This is one of the best works on the period from 1929 through 1940.

25. Elwood Rufus Gotshall, "Catholicism and Catholic Action in Mexico, 1929–1941," unpublished Ph.D. dissertation, University of Pittsburgh, 1970, 144–145. This is all the more remarkable given Cárdenas's public posture as anti-Church. Nevertheless, Cuauhtémoc Cárdenas, his son, reveals that the president held individual clergy in high regard, and that when he directed the Papaloapan Commission, he gave workers a day off out of respect for the death of the bishop of Ciudad Guzmán. Personal interview, Mexico City, May 6, 1992.

26. Elwood Rufus Gotshall, "Catholicism and Catholic Action in Mexico, 1929–1941," 154.

27. Stanley E. Hilton, "The Church-State Dispute over Education in Mexico from Carranza to Cárdenas," *The Americas* 21 (October 1964): 179–180.

28. Elwood Rufus Gotshall, "Catholicism and Catholic Action in Mexico, 1929–1941," 143.

29. Personal interview with Father Alberto Aguirre, Seminary of the State of México, Toluca Diocese, Toluca, México, June 9, 1988.

30. Soledad Loaeza, "Notas para el estudio de la Iglesia en el México contemporáneo," in *Religión y política en México,* Martín de la Rosa, et al., eds. (Mexico City: Siglo XXI, 1985), 47–48.

31. Hugh Gerald Campbell, "The Radical Right in Mexico, 1929–1949," unpublished Ph.D. dissertation, University of California, Los Angeles, 1974, 393. Silvia Bénard has argued that the Catholic leadership did not support PAN electorally in the 1940s, preferring its well-established working relationship with president Avila Camacho. "The Relationship between Church and State in Mexico: An Analysis of the Pope's Visit in 1979," unpublished M.A. thesis, University of Texas, Austin, 1986, 40.

32. Hugh Gerard Campbell, "The Radical Right in Mexico, 1929–1949," 394, and citing Franchon Royer, "Mexico's New Deal," *Catholic World* 125 (April 1952): 32.

33. Alemán's father, General Miguel Alemán González, was a nonpracticing Catholic and an important member of the Veracruz Masonic Lodge. His mother, Tomasa, was an evangelical. Alemán, like Avila Camacho, was a "believer." Personal interview with Miguel Alemán, Jr., Mexico City, July 30, 1992.

34. Roberto Blancarte, *Iglesia y estado en México: seis décadas de acomodo y de conciliación imposible* (Mexico City: Instituto Mexicano de Doctrina Social Cristiana, 1990), 21.

35. Silvia Bénard, "The Relationship between Church and State in Mexico," 40.

36. Roberto Blancarte, *El poder salinismo e iglesia católica, una nueva convivencia?,* 55.

37. Daniel H. Levine, "From Church and State to Religion and Politics and Back Again," *World Affairs* 150 (Fall 1987): 97.

38. Dennis M. Hanratty, "The Political Role of the Mexican Catholic Church," 168.

39. Otto Granados Roldán, "La iglesia Católica mexicana como grupo de presión," *Cuadernos de Humanidades,* no. 17 (Mexico City: UNAM, Departamento de Humanidades, 1981), 39.

40. Dennis M. Hanratty, *Change and Conflict in the Contemporary Mexican Catholic Church,* unpublished Ph.D. dissertation, Duke University, 1980, 150.

41. Roberto Blancarte, *El poder salinismo e iglesia católica, una nueva convivencia?,* 220. Méndez Arceo spoke out repeatedly against the student massacre and the imprisonment of political dissenters. David C. Bailey, "The Church since 1940," in *Twentieth-Century Mexico,* W. Dirk Raat and William H. Beezley, eds. (Lincoln: University of Nebraska Press, 1986), 240. Surprisingly, this issue has never been well researched. A contributing factor may have been president Gustavo Díaz Ordaz's close relations with archbishop Miguel Dario Miranda and with the Vatican delegate, Luigi Miranda. Pedro Moctezuma Díaz, father of president Zedillo's first secretary of government, served as the president's personal emissary in Church matters. See Oscar Hinojosa, "Dejarán de ser en la noche los encuentros con funcionarios mexicanos: Prigione," *Proceso,* December 12, 1988, 9.

42. Dennis M. Hanratty, "Change and Conflict in the Contemporary Mexican Church," 150–152.

43. Miguel Concha Malo, "Tensiones entre la religión del pueblo y las CEB's en México con sectores de la jerarquía," 16.

44. Claude Pomerlau, "The Changing Church in Mexico and Its Challenge to the State," *Review of Politics* 43, no. 4 (October 1981): 554, and *Carta pastoral del episcopado mexicano sobre el desarrollo e integración del país* (Mexico City: CEM, 1968), 15.

45. John B. Housley, "The Role of the Churches in U.S.–Latin American Relations," in *Prospects for Latin America,* David S. Smith, ed. (New York: International Fellows Policy Series, Columbia University, 1970), 3.

46. Daniel H. Levine, "From Church and State to Religion and Politics and Back Again," 100.

47. I am indebted to Archbishop Rosendo Huesca for capturing this emphasis on internal affairs, an era of reconstruction stemming from the repression of the Cristiada and a reopening of seminaries. Personal interview, Puebla Archdiocese, Puebla, Puebla, July 16, 1993.

48. Edward L. Cleary, *Crisis and Change: The Church in Latin American Today* (Maryknoll: Orbis Books, 1985), 47. As Cleary concluded, the episcopate was influenced by movements from below and by Mexican intellectual circles.

49. Edward L. Cleary, "Politics and Religion—Crisis, Constraints, and Restructuring," in *Conflict and Competition: The Latin American Church in a Changing Environment,* Edward L. Cleary and Hannah Stewart-Gambino, eds. (Boulder, Colo.: Lynne Rienner, 1992), 24.

50. Shannan Mattiace, "The Social Role of the Mexican Catholic Church: The Case of the Yucatán Base Community," senior honors thesis, Central University of Iowa, 1990, 19.

51. Daniel H. Levine, "Religion, Society, and Politics: States of the Art," *Latin American Research Review* 16, no. 3 (Fall 1981): 189.

52. Jorge Martínez Martínez, *Memorias y reflexiones de un obispo* (Mexico City: Editorial Villicaña, 1986), 132.

53. Thomas G. Sanders, "The Puebla Conference," *American Universities Field Staff Reports,* no. 30, 1979, 2–3. The document approved at the conference states: "[I]t is christian to evangelize all human existence, including politics, and the church should be present in realities, personal and professional." Conferencia General del Episcopado Latinoamericano, *La evangelización en el presente y en el futuro de América Latina* (Mexico City: CEM, 1979), 131.

54. Roberto Blancarte, "La Iglesia católica en México desde 1929: introdución crítica a la producción historiográfica (1968–1988)," *Cristianismo y Sociedad* no. 101 (1989): 31.

55. Allan Metz, "Church-State Relations in Contemporary Mexico, 1968–1988," in *The Religious Challenge to the State,* Matthew C. Moen and Lowell S. Gustafson, eds. (Philadelphia: Temple University Press, 1992), 114. The then secretary of government, Jesús Reyes Heroles, author of a widely read historical work on Liberalism, was adamantly opposed to the Pope's visit. Mexico's cardinal and Vatican delegate personally carried a message from the episcopate to Reyes Heroles informing him of the expected visit, of which, of course, he was already well aware. When they handed the secretary their letter, he opened it, read it, refolded it, and set it down. He then ordered his aide to bring him a copy of the constitution. Opening up the document, he read out loud the articles referring to the Catholic Church. He then lectured them briefly on the relationship between church and state and told them the supreme law in Mexico was the constitution, after which he terminated the interview. Naturally, the two clergy were insulted, which suggests the level of Reyes Heroles's anticlericalism. Personal interview with Fausto Zerón Medina, one of Luis Echeverría's representatives to the Catholic Church, Mexico City, May 29, 1987. Reyes Heroles also tried to prohibit the faithful from attending the Basilica of Guadalupe

(Our Lady of Guadalupe is Mexico's most popular patron saint) in Mexico City during the Pope's visit, but relented when told by the Vatican delegate that such a prohibition would lead to violence. Personal interview with Archbishop Jirolamo Prigione, Vatican delegate, Mexico Archdiocese, Mexico City, June 2, 1987.

56. See the excellent case studies by Víctor Muro González, *Iglesia y movimientos sociales en México, 1972–1987, los casos de Ciudad Juárez y el Istmo de Tehuantepec* (Zamora: Colegio de Michoacán, 1994).

57. Soledad Loaeza has argued that the Catholic Church was one of the primary beneficiaries of political reforms between 1965 and 1985. "La iglesia y la democracia en México," 166.

58. This point has been made most strongly in Dennis Goulet, "The Mexican Church: Into the Public Arena," *America* 160, no. 13 (April 8, 1989): 318, and in Soledad Loaeza, "El fin de la ambiguedad, las relaciones entre la Iglesia y el Estado en México, 1982–1989," in *La participación política del clero en México*, Luis J. Molina Piñero, ed. (Mexico City: UNAM, 1990), 148. For example, FAC, a church organization assisting the homeless, signed a contract with the Department of the Federal District even though it had no legal recognition. *Unomásuno*, December 12, 1988, 5.

59. Otto Granados Roldán, "La iglesia Católica mexicana como grupo de presión," 56. A decade later, shortly before Salinas took office, Pablo Gómez, the coordinator of the Mexican Socialist Party and former leader of the Unified Socialist Movement of Mexico, revealed his intention to "modernize" church-state relations by publicly speaking in favor of an open dialogue between church and state but announced it should be among all priests and religious organizations, not just the hierarchy. *La Jornada*, September 12, 1988, n.p. In 1987, the secretary general of the PRD also published a statement favoring new relations.

60. Analysts have speculated on why president Miguel de la Madrid, who improved relations on a personal level with the Church and the Vatican especially, did not introduce such formal changes. Guillermo Floris Margadant suggests that the resistance of the then governor of Michoacán, Cuauhtémoc Cárdenas, seen as an inheritor of his father's posture on church-state relations, explains the president's hesitation. *La iglesia ante el derecho mexicano, esbozo histórico-jurídico* (Mexico City: Miguel Angel Porrúa, 1991), 209. The president, however, offers his own explanation: "I advised the Catholic Church that given the present social and economic crisis in Mexico, it was not an opportune time to make constitutional changes. I recommended that we wait for a better climate in order to alter our dialogue. I wanted to achieve a national consensus about this issue, and study it carefully, but not to make changes during my administration." Personal interview with President Miguel de la Madrid, Mexico City, February 22, 1991. Nevertheless, the president favored changing the law and expressed such a view privately to a group of prominent Mexicans before Salinas became president. Personal interview with Antonio Martínez Báez, a constitutional expert consulted about the legal changes, who attended the private session with de la Madrid. Personal interview, Mexico City, August 1, 1992.

61. Personal interview with Archbishop Manuel Pérez Gil, Tlanepantla Archdiocese, Tlanepantla, México, February 18, 1991. Pérez Gil noted that president Miguel de la Madrid, despite several highly visible confrontations with the Church, had established a study group focused on problems in church-state relations, which reported its findings to the president and established a basis for dialogue and contact between clergy and government officials. However, as was true of his predecessors, this dialogue was never made public.

62. Deputies from various parties expressed concern over public violations of the constitution and demanded that the chamber's leadership be removed. For example, see *Unomásuno*, December 3, 1988, n.p., and *Mexico Journal*, December 19, 1988, 7. The following

year, the Popular Socialist Party filed a suit against the state government of Querétaro for allowing an outdoor ceremony in the consecration of a bishop. Allan Metz, "Mexican Church-State Relations under President Carlos Salinas de Gortari," *Journal of Church and State* 34, no. 1 (Winter 1992): 117.

63. Rodrigo Vera, "En secreto, negociaciones entre funcionarios públicos y herarcas católicas," *Proceso,* August 7, 1989, 6. Ironically, the explanation for this precise, public declaration according to Roberto Blancarte, one of Mexico's leading historians of the Catholic Church, was that Manuel Camacho, the then head of the Federal District Department and later pre-presidential candidate, nearly derailed the entire process by sending his own representative to the Vatican without the knowledge of the secretaries of government or foreign relations to demonstrate to the president that he could accomplish major policy goals. Instead, it led to internal chaos on this issue. Personal interview, Mexico City, February 20, 1991.

64. Partido Revolucionario Institucional, "Memorandum sobre las relaciones estado-iglesia católica," unpublished manuscript, November 1988, 2.

65. *Proceso,* October 25, 1988, n.p.

66. Rodrigo Vera, "Prigione, a un paso de culminar su misión de trece años," *Proceso,* March 11, 1991, 8.

67. *Christian Science Monitor,* November 4, 1991, 3. For the text of the address and the specific wording of the president's statement, see *El Nacional,* November 2, 1991, 3.

68. Donald M. Coerver, "From Confrontation to Conciliation: Church-State Relations in Mexico, 1867–1884," *Journal of Church and State* 32 (Winter 1990): 71.

69. For evidence of this, see Roderic Ai Camp, "Political Liberalization: The Last Key to Economic Modernization in Mexico?," in *Political and Economic Liberalization in Mexico,* Riordan Roett, ed. (Boulder, Colo.: Lynne Rienner, 1993), 17–34.

70. Personal interview with Federico Reyes Heroles, Valle de Bravo, México, May 3, 1992.

71. Support for this view can also be found in *Mexico Report,* May 18, 1992, 5. Ricardo Pascoe, a leader of the Democratic Revolutionary Party (PRD), described his constituencies as including the State Department, capitalists, the Church hierarchy, and a sector of the bureaucracy, believing it to be a mistaken strategy, emulating South American countries. Personal interview, Mexico City, May 5, 1992. Some might include the National Action Party (PAN) as part of this new political constituency. PAN, which historically has called on reforms related to religion and education, was not actively pressuring the president on church-state relations. In fact, as late as 1989, the president of PAN, Luis H. Alvarez, who strongly favored continued separation of church and state, was not convinced that diplomatic relations with the Vatican were urgent but did believe that all clergy should be able to vote, though not run for office. *Mexico Journal,* June 12, 1989, 4.

72. Personal interview with Cuauhtémoc Cárdenas, Mexico City, May 6, 1992.

73. This view is presented most convincingly by Nicéforo Guerrero, one of Mexico's most well informed public figures on the Catholic Church. Personal interview.

74. Other interest groups were also making demands favorable to changing the constitutional provisions regarding the Church. Such was the case of entrepreneurs and their representatives in the media. See Silvia M. Bénard, "The Relationship between Church and State in Mexico," 114.

75. Dennis M. Hanratty, "The Political Role of the Mexican Catholic Church," 179.

76. Personal interview with Arturo Núñez Jiménez, Mexico City, February 12, 1993. This is confirmed by Grupo Consultor Interdisciplinario, "Carta de política mexicana, las relaciones estado-iglesias," February 21, 1992, 5, which says the letter came from the presidency of the Mexican Conference of Bishops on June 5, 1989.

77. Personal interview with Luis Narro Rodríguez, director of the Center of Educational Studies, Mexico City, June 28, 1989.

78. Personal interview with Bishop José Pablo Rovalo, Mexico Archdiocese, Mexico City, February 21, 1991.

79. Partido Revolucionario Institucional, "Memorandum sobre las relaciones estado-iglesia católica," 4.

80. One scholar who agrees strongly with this interpretation is Manuel Ceballos Ramírez, who argues that "[w]ithout a doubt, it was the Mexican state that initiated the dialogue with the Church. This step was taken by Mexican politicians not to weaken themselves but, on the contrary, to complete some proposed objectives and to augment the degree of state maturity and legitimacy." "Iglesia, estado y sociedad en México, una visión histórica del presente," in *Religiosidad y política en México,* Carlos Martínez Assad, ed. (Mexico City: Ibero-American University, 1992), 123. Complementary to this view, and associated with the interpretation that it was Church initiated, is the argument that the Church wanted the state as an ally in its battle with evangelical sects over the faithful. See Marta E. García Ugarte, "Las posiciones políticas de la jerarquía católica, efectos en la cultura religiosa mexicana," in *Religiosidad y política en México,* Carlos Martínez Assad, ed. (Mexico City: Ibero-American University, 1992), 100.

81. One highly placed collaborator, who confirmed the president's attitude, also indicated that every Catholic politician the president consulted told him it was too risky, but he decided to do it anyway. Personal interview with Father Antonio Roqueñi, Mexico Archdiocese, Mexico City, July 14, 1993.

82. Even some older members of Mexico's political leadership, where support for such changes would generally be found lacking, favored changes in the legal status of the Church, finding it inexplicable that the state could regulate an institution it did not legally recognize. Personal interview with Rodolfo González Guevara, a former prominent member of PRI who joined PRD and who was involved in anti-Catholic protests in his student days. Mexico City, February 21, 1991. Such circumstances have produced bizarre legal situations in Mexico. For example, Father Xavier González, director of the National Choir of Mexico, received an estate in a woman's will, and relatives tried to abrogate it on the grounds that it was left to a priest and a religious organization with no legal standing. The priest, on the other hand, took the legal position that the relatives must prove he was a priest since the state maintains no records on clergy. Matt Moffett, "In Catholic Mexico, a Priest's Power Is Limited to Prayer," *Wall Street Journal,* December 6, 1989, n.p.

83. Dennis Goulet, "The Mexican Church," 320.

84. Luis Rubio, "La Iglesia, el estado y los mexicanos," *La Jornada,* April 5, 1991, n.p., and personal interview, Mexico City, February 13, 1991.

85. Personal interview with Bishop Samuel Ruiz, San Cristóbal de las Casas Diocese, Lago de Guadalupe, Cuiutatlán, México, April 20, 1992. George Grayson, who analyzed the Church at the time of the reforms, believed the changing status of the Church would add to the legitimacy of his economic initiatives. "Mexico's Salinas Shrewd to Play His Papal Card," *Houston Chronicle,* May 9, 1990, n.p.

86. Grupo Consultor Interdisciplinario, "Carta de política mexicana, la ley de asociaciones religiosas, un estatuo transitorio," August 28, 1992.

87. Some even presented their own versions to members of congress. For example, the Methodists suggested the concept of conscientious objectors to the PRI, which did not understand that idea. Personal interview with César Pérez.

88. Personal interview with Antonio Roqueñi.

89. For background on this, also see George Grayson, *The Church in Contemporary Mexico,* 83–85.

90. Grupo Consultor Interdisciplinario, "Carta de política mexicana, las relaciones estado-iglesias."

91. Personal interview with Manuel Carrillo Poblano.

92. This version can be found in the Comisión de Gobernación y Puntos Constitucionales, "Proyecto de decreto que reforma y adiciona los articulos 5, 24, 27 y 130 de la Constitución Política de los Estados Unidos Mexicanos," Cámara de Diputados, Mexico, 1992.

93. Personal interview with Arturo Núñez Jiménez, former Director of Political Development, 1989–1991, and Subsecretary of Government, in charge of church-state relations, 1991–1993, Mexico City, February 12, 1993.

94. See Roberto Blancarte, "Religion and Constitutional Change in Mexico, 1988–1992," *Social Compass* 40, no. 4 (1993): 555–569, for a brief but excellent overview of the chronology of events.

95. Roberto Blancarte, *El poder salinismo e iglesia católica, una nueva convivencia?*, 204.

96. Instituto Mexicano de Estrategias, "Relaciones estado-iglesia, nuevo marco jurídico," Executive Report, December 31, 1992, 2–3.

97. *Crónica Legislativa,* 1, no. 1 (April 1992): 32.

98. These can be found in the *Ley reglamentaria del Artículo 130 de la Constitución Federal* (Mexico, 1988), 389, 390, 411.

99. *Diario Oficial,* "Ley de asociaciones religiosas y culto público," July 15, 1992, 39, 40, 44.

100. An excellent discussion of the changes and their potential ambiguity can be found in Raúl González Schmal, "El nuevo marco jurídico en materia religiosa," *Umbral XXI* no. 11 (Spring 1993): 42–46.

101. *El Nacional,* March 23, 1990, 7.

102. Personal interview with Abel Vicencio Tovar, former president of PAN, Mexico City, July 13, 1993.

103. Personal interview with Agustín Basave, federal deputy from Monterrey, Nuevo León, Mexico City, August 4, 1992.

104. *Diario Oficial,* "Decreto por el que se reforman los articulos 3, 5, 24, 27, 130," January 28, 1992, 3–4.

105. *Crónica Legislativa,* 38–39.

106. "25 horas de debate bastaron para cambiar la situación legal de las iglesias," *Proceso,* December 23, 1991, 24. According to César Pérez, who attended all of the sessions of congress, it could not be described as a debate since only the Popular Socialist Party opposed the reforms. Personal interview.

107. Personal interview with Manuel Carrillo Poblano, Mexico City, August 4, 1992.

108. MORI de México, *Encuesta Semanal,* September 25, 1992. Formal relations were announced on the 14th.

109. Detailed discussions of these issues from the hierarchy's point of view can be found in *La Iglesia católica en el nuevo marco jurídico de México* (Mexico City: CEM, 1992).

110. "Declaraciones de los obispos mexicanos sobre el nueva ley de asociaciones religiosas y culto público," Conference of Mexican Bishops, Plenary Assembly, August 13, 1992, 3–4.

111. For example, most public figures who become political candidates must resign their positions several months before the election. Yet, as the new bylaws illustrate, priests, depending on their status, are required to do so years in advance.

112. Personal interview with Arturo Núñez. Among those who opposed the legislation at the CEM meeting were Luis Cervantes Reynoso, Carlos Quintero, and Alberto Almeida.

113. See, for example, David Clark Scott, "Mexicans Debate the Structure of New Church-State Relations," *Christian Science Monitor,* May 19, 1992, n.p.

114. Personal interview with David Scott Clark, *Christian Science Monitor,* Mexico City, August 1, 1992.

115. Personal interview with Carlos Mainero, Mexico City, August 4, 1992.

116. Personal interview with Arturo Núnez Jiménez.

117. Personal interview with Bishop Raúl Vera López, bishop of Ciudad Altamirano, Mexico City, May 3, 1992.

118. Personal interview with Father Antonio Roqueñi; Instituto Mexicano de Estrategias, "Relaciones Estado-Iglesia," 11.

119. Rodrigo Vera, "La visita del Papa a Salinas, arranque de las nuevas relaciones," *Proceso,* January 1, 1990, 8.

120. Allan Metz, "Mexican Church-State Relations under President Carlos Salinas de Gortari," 119.

121. Personal interview with Father Servando García, Acatlán de Juárez Parish, Acatlán de Juárez, Jalisco, Mexico, July 6, 1993.

122. Personal interview with Father José Alvarez Franco, Tateposco Parish, Tonala, Jalisco, July 7, 1993, who ministers without the official sanction of the Catholic Church; interviews by Scott Pentzer and Meg Mitchell with priests from Guanajuato, Zacatecas, San Luis Potosí, and Morelos, July, 1993.

123. See, for example, Rodrigo Vera and Francisco Castellanos, "Cara simulación: sus testaferros, quitan a la Iglesia 'mas bienes que Juárez,' " *Proceso,* April 5, 1993, 27–29, and Rodrigo Vera, "El obispo de Iguala, en guerra con sus prestanombres," *Proceso,* April 12, 1993, 29–30.

124. Personal interview with Bishop Mario Gasperín Gasperín. The then secretary general of the Mexican Conference of Bishop, Ramón Godínez, auxiliary bishop of Guadalajara, concurred that the future of the relationship would depend on the efforts of both groups, but that the reforms provided a "basis for more respect and collaboration." Personal interview, Mexico Archdiocese, July 16, 1993.

125. Personal interview with Archbishop Rosendo Huesca.

126. Personal interview with Abel Vicencio Tovar.

127. Personal interview with Father Salvador Tello Robles, Madre de Dios Parish, Guadalajara Archdiocese, Guadalajara, Jalisco, Mexico, July 6, 1993.

128. Personal interview with Manuel Carrillo Poblano.

129. Personal interview with Mario Gasperín Gasperín, Querétaro Diocese, Querétaro, Mexico, July 12, 1993.

130. Personal interview with César Pérez.

131. Personal interview with Mariclaire Acosta, president, Mexican Commission for the Defense and Promotion of Human Rights, Mexico City, August 3, 1992.

132. Personal interview with Cuauhtémoc Cárdenas, presidential candidate of the Democratic Revolutionary Party, who held this view, as did church scholar Roberto Blancarte, who told David Clark Scott that prior to the law, "It all comes down to the clarity of the law which is supposed to grant religious liberty but may end up persecuting or creating an inequity between the churches." "Mexicans Debate the Structure of New Church-State Relations," *Christian Science Monitor,* May 19, 1992.

133. Personal interview with Bishop Samuel Ruiz.

134. Personal interview with Archbishop Juan Jesús Posadas, Archdiocese of Guadalajara, Conference of Mexican Bishops, Mexico City, February 20, 1991.

135. Personal interview with Bishop Mario Gasperín Gasperín.

136. "Entre el poder y la gloria," *El Financiero,* May 15, 1994, 64.

3

Issues Facing the Church

Politics, Partisanship, and Development

R eligion performs numerous functions for individuals, institutions, and societies. Normally, one conceptualizes religion performing spiritual functions,
and indeed that is the primary responsibility and expectation of Catholicism and
most other religions. Religion, as a depository of values, also interacts with society, creating a composite culture that mixes religious and secular principles. Over
time, secular values, having their origins in religion, may be indistinguishable
from the religious. Latin American scholars repeatedly point to the impact of
Catholicism on the region's culture, as distinct from its narrow traditional spiritual influences.

Religion also extends beyond the values it imparts to society because in society's absorption of certain values, religion may well contribute to behavior. As
Daniel Levine argues: "[R]eligion shapes actions through images of itself, and of
good and proper behavior in general, which are expressed in the daily life of the
religious community."[1] When a set of religious beliefs comes in conflict with
secular laws, or the views of other groups in society, it produces consequences
for the religious community and for society. These potential consequences take on
added importance in Mexico because of the overwhelming dominance of Catholicism and Christianity in the lives of its citizens, as evidenced in chapter 5.

It is relatively easy to identify a religious teaching and point to the potential
conflict it might raise in the larger society. For example, the Church's teachings
on birth control and abortion are indisputable. Yet it is not necessarily the case
that most Catholics agree in practice with the Church's dogma on these issues.
Nevertheless, if the government were to pass a law contradicting these religious
precepts, the Church would be forced to challenge the state's legislation, and these
challenges would naturally be expressed in the political arena. The Church could
pursue various strategies including using informal channels among elites, creating
interest group pressures, or persuading laypersons to challenge the legislation electorally. Typically, these sorts of issues prompt conflict in American politics, but
they are much less significant in the Mexican context.

The primary issue in church-state relations in Mexico is the Church's actual role; that is, what is its larger responsibility to society and how should it function outside of its religious, spiritual responsibilities involving faith and family? If the Church believes it has responsibility to speak up on a broad range of social, moral, and economic issues—including human rights abuses or maldistribution of wealth—it enters the political arena because these and other such concerns are not confined to religion but raise basic temporal "issues of power, authority, legitimacy, and distribution."[2]

The Catholic Church has made it clear in Mexico since the early 1970s that it is uninterested in temporal power. In short, it does not seek political power directly or attempt to manipulate political parties or organizations, as might a secular interest group. The Mexican episcopate, even at the high point of the socially progressive liberation theology's influence, makes this distinction:

> The salvation activity of the People of God does not seek either the acquisition or exercise of political power, nor the determination of the system of government, nor entering in the democratic game of political parties. With this we are not saying that those who promote the faith or conversion should not act, even isolated or associated, in politics or should be absent from it. On the contrary, it is hoped that all men converted to the truth of God and to the betterment of their brothers would act openly and forcefully for the realization of a political community that facilitates the integral transformation of all men.[3]

Not only does the Church argue that the basic values it teaches require laypersons and clergy to both defend and advocate those values within the secular and, if necessary, political world, but also the Church hierarchy conceptualizes the "Church" in very broad terms. Politicians are likely to think of the Church in narrow, institutional terms, represented by bishops and priests. Adolfo Suárez Rivera, archbishop of Monterrey and leader of the Mexican episcopate in the 1990s, offered a contrasting view in his important pastoral letter on politics: "Nevertheless, 90 percent of Mexicans form part of this Church and very few belong to the hierarchy. It is clear that 'the church' defined in this way, actively participates in Mexican politics. Moreover, many militants of political parties and no small number of government functionaries recognize, publicly or privately, their membership in the Church."[4]

Critics have charged that since the 1960s the Catholic Church has increasingly used the pulpit for political ends. Although they provide little evidence of such use,[5] it is clear that since the mid-1980s Church leadership has become more deeply involved in political matters. What explains the perceived and actual level of involvement in politics? As the Mexican episcopate's pastoral letter of 1973 suggests, the Church never renounced a political role.[6] Most Mexicans, and politicians specifically, were unaware of the leadership's position on politics.[7] Even Mexico's Vatican delegate for the last two decades, who promoted a cautious Church role in church-state affairs and influenced the selection of a series of traditionally oriented bishops in numerous dioceses, argues that the Church at all times and in all places must be able to preach its faith with authentic liberty, to teach its doctrine regarding society, to exercise its mission among people without interference, and to pronounce its moral judgment, even on matters referring to political order.[8] Some analysts believe that the profound social and political changes in Mexico after 1968, and increasingly in the 1980s, encouraged the politization of religion, particularly religion's extension into the secular values of laypersons, rather than limiting it to a small circle of Church leadership.[9]

If one thinks of the Church as an institution representing most of Mexican society, the argument can be made that the clergy's interest, or lack of interest, in politics is merely a reflection of societal concerns in general. A leader of the Methodist Church, for example, believes a general lack of interest in politics characterizes most Mexicans before the 1980s, and the Catholic Church mirrored that societal posture.[10] Contemporary priests are interested in political affairs, although they are not necessarily well informed about politics.[11] But the pressure for this changing posture among the clergy appears to be coming from parishioners, especially in those regions were social conflict is intense or where electoral fraud and competition are strong. Most priests and bishops believe their constituencies are pressuring church leadership to take public positions.[12]

A representative of the hierarchy contributed to the trend in the early 1970s toward a different pattern in the clergy's political participation when Bishop Sergio Méndez Arceo handed his famous "Letter of Anenecuilco" to President Luis Echeverría, requesting, among other suggestions, that the future president end the fictional arrangement of church-state relations.[13] However, revisions in the constitutional restrictions, most of which were not altered until 1992, would not necessarily change the Church's attitude toward political involvement. Many observers seem unaware or forget that the Church's own canon law establishes strict restrictions on clergy's participation in politics and their eligibility for public office.[14]

Another element contributing to religion's increased political role originates from public life. Strongly Catholic political leaders have, for the first time, spoken publicly at Masses. Carlos Medina Plascencia, the PAN governor of Guanajuato, addressed local youth in a Mass at the Church of Christ the King of the Cubilete Cerro in January 1992, receiving strong criticism in the media and from other political figures.[15] He defended his actions by saying he spoke as a private citizen and a Catholic, not as a politician. The Vatican took the official position that political speeches during Church acts were not approved.[16]

The Catholic Church has come into conflict in Mexico in the political realm not because it associates itself with a particular political party or urges Mexicans to vote for one party versus another (two issues we will explore in considerable detail), but because it feels compelled to intervene on moral matters, which may, on occasion, bring it into direct confrontation with the state on purely temporal, political questions. Many politicians, of course, believe Church leadership desires a new distribution of political power, and this motivation explains priests' political intervention.[17] It can be argued that the Church's primary role is to provide the entire community with a broad set of moral values. Such a task requires it to retire from the political arena and any other area that compromises its essential role in establishing a moral framework.[18]

Such a task is all well and good, but the shaping of general moral values has direct political implications. Morality does affect the population's political consciousness. It may well be that the 1992 changes in the constitution freed some clergy from linking religion to local or national politics for fear of violating informal norms of the church-state relationship.[19] In fact, since the 1970s Mexican bishops have strongly praised the crucial importance of politics in the lives of Mexicans and the importance of family, cultural institutions, and education in instilling and developing political values.[20] Bishops argue that they "may criticize political actions or activities contrary to Christian values but would not involve themselves in political party platforms or mythologies that are the exclusive domain of those who do not belong to the clergy."[21]

Two of the most important politically associated values that the Church may teach as part of its general moral framework are tolerance and nonviolence. One way to measure a religion's tolerance is to question the degree to which it would permit others to attack it or to support unpopular secular ideologies such as communism and fascism. For example, in the United States, a study of clergy and laity revealed that Catholics were very intolerant of supporting someone's constitutional right to attack religion and even more intolerant of protecting fascists and communists.[22] Catholic clergy were not much better in their level of tolerance. Many Mexican priests and bishops believe the Church should actively convey the morality of tolerance. As one Yucatán priest suggested, the Catholic Church is a church of love, not violence, and dialogue comes first. The Church's responsibility is to care for the lives of all people; its primary job is to bring people together.[23] A bishop expressed it differently, as "a need to develop a sense of community in each parish. I just don't want the priests or the parish or organizations to be service agencies for religion. I believe that our people are very religious and they ask for lots of services to respond to realities, but we need to develop a strong sense of identity and community."[24]

José Pablo Rovalo put into practice this strong sense of moral commitment by taking the unusual step of resigning as bishop of Zacatecas to help young people. He articulated this concern most effectively:

> The most important part of a person's attitude is in being a human being. In my youth, I traveled throughout Mexico. I'm not going to be totally changed by where I live in terms of the values that formed me, but what is important is the need to listen to people, and that's what bishops must do in their diocese.[25]

An issue that has brought the Church, or more specifically certain sectors of the Church, in conflict with civil authorities in Latin America in the 1960s, 1970s, and 1980s is their position on the use of violence. In Latin America, violence may be necessary to achieve social justice.[26] In Mexico, the Church is unequivocally opposed to the use of violence.[27] So is the laity. Even in the 1994 uprising in Chiapas, in which most Mexicans identified positively with indigenous demands, few agreed violence was an acceptable tool. However, a tremendous reservoir of support exists for violent protest as a means of last resort, even among the clergy. Enrique Luengo discovered that over half of all priests (53 percent) agreed with the statement that violent protest is justified as a last resource to defend the people's interest against abusive civil authorities.[28]

Partisanship and Parties

The Catholic Church's relationship to political parties is both a moral and pragmatic political issue. Mexico's touchy history of church-state relations from the
19th century through the Revolution, when the Church identified itself explicitly,
or in some cases allied itself directly, with political factions on the losing side of
civil conflict further restricts the Church from playing such a role and places in
doubt its motivations. Yet as liberation theologians and others have argued, institutional silence is translated into a partisan role when an authoritarian government
is in charge or when a dominant one-party system maintains an established political leadership. As some of these critics charge, a dual standard is often applied to
Church involvement:

> Is the Church fulfilling a purely religious role when by its silence or friendly relation-
> ships it lends legitimacy to a dictatorial and oppressive government? We discover . . .
> that the policy of non-intervention in political affairs holds for certain actions which
> involve ecclesiastical authorities, but not for others. In other words, the principle is
> not applied when it is a question of maintaining the status quo, but it is wielded when,
> for example, a lay apostolic movement or group of priests holds an attitude considered
> subversive to the established order.[29]

Although this criticism was applied specifically to Latin American dictatorships
during the 1970s and 1980s, the same principles are apparent in Mexico. Thomas
Sanders suggested that even in Latin America, by 1979, most bishops were convinced that political partisanship was a misguided role for the Church, and instead
it needed to concentrate on forming a renewed Christian community, especially
among the poor.[30]

In the Mexican case, the historic and legal context has given much greater
encouragement to both priests and bishops to shy away from any action or posture
that might be perceived as politically threatening. The Mexican episcopate explicitly expressed its position on the role priests should play in sociopolitical affairs:

> Temporal autonomy limits the exercise of priests' rights to seek, even with legitimate
> means, political power; it limits, furthermore, the right to have an option through
> political parties because priests are leaders and models and instruments of community
> unity, and so the exercise of their rights and the completion of their obligations should
> be animated by their pastoral mission as promoters of a faithful community.[31]

Although priests are specifically restricted by both the Church and the state from
participating in political activities, they are not shielded from the political arena
and may take actions that ultimately have political consequences. Even priests
themselves understand or believe that the Church exercises considerable influence
in Mexican society and that no political party has the opportunity to substantially
increase its impact among diverse social groups without some Church influence.
In other words, one-third of Mexico's priests actually believe what politicians fear
most: the Church could affect the strength and appeal of political organizations.[32]
Some Mexican analysts also imply that the Church might seek ties with specific
parties in order to maintain broad, widespread support.[33]

The Roman Catholic Church, from the Pope on down, tried to establish a clear distinction between partisanship, or specifically favoring a political party, and playing a political role, justified in Church doctrine. Recently, the Pope repeated this distinction, saying that although the Church does not identify with specific parties or even political systems, it "does not mean that the church has nothing to say to the political community, to enlighten it with the values and common sense of the Gospel." He continued, "In fact, it is easy to see that many social and even political problems have roots in the moral order that is the object of the church's evangelizing and educational role."[34] Jirolamo Prigione, Mexico's papal nuncio, is even more specific about what the Church cannot do: "We cannot afford to be identified with any party. I have told several friends who are National Action Party leaders to continue their electoral battles, but not to expect any help from us."[35]

It is equally clear, however, that bishops and priests alike do see Catholics, distinct from clergy, as exercising an important influence among Mexican parties. The former cardinal archbishop of Mexico, Ernesto Corripio, recommends that Catholic laypersons are the people who should participate in politics, having the liberty to exercise their personal actions.[36] The Mexican episcopate as a whole agrees with the cardinal's philosophy, but they are more precise about the nature of this participation. On one hand, while the laity should actively participate, they "do not represent us nor the voice of the Church; they are involved under their own responsibility as Catholic, Mexican citizens."[37] On the other hand, the episcopate recently argued that while it is citizen groups who must become involved in partisan politics, "Catholics should intervene to form, direct and participate in political parties *which are inspired by values of the Gospel*" (emphasis added).[38]

Bishops also believe, however, that the media and political representatives misrepresent the Church's posture on politics, in part because of semantic misunderstandings over the word "Church" and the Church's responsibility to orient their flocks to values producing political and social consequences. The broad concept of the Church, on which most clergy agree, is that it incorporates laity and clergy. Therefore, someone discussing what the Church should or should not do needs to distinguish among its various components. Most bishops and priests believe the clergy should use their position and knowledge only to help clarify the major issues confronting society, making clear the options available to their parishioners.[39] They admit that room for abuse exists on the part of individual clergy to analyze these problems unfairly, interjecting personal biases. Bishops give particular emphasis to their responsibilities on human rights.[40] At the same time, they also recognize the practicalities of a situation in which the political system is in flux, thus making it understandable that the public might identify the Church with a party if it speaks out on issues that are politically related.[41]

The problem of speaking up about controversial, politically tainted issues is that priests have found it more difficult to carry out in practice than in theory. Because priests are looked up to by the Mexican population, as the next chapter demonstrates, they are called upon to serve as mediators, often voluntarily playing that role. One priest in the diocese of Mérida, where the National Action Party is very active, describes his own experiences. The PRI was having some difficulties that began affecting many members of his parish. He offered to arbitrate the dispute, but some people interpreted his actions as showing a preference for one side, resulting in members representing the opposing view refusing to attend Church meetings. Many parishioners are not well educated, and they may assume that anything the priest says is indicative of partisan politics.[42] Experiences like these encourage priests to remain neutral.

To what degree has the Church actually involved itself in partisan politics, defined here as supporting a specific political party or candidate? As I have suggested elsewhere in this book, many Mexicans, analysts, and politicians have identified the Catholic Church with the National Action Party. For example, Alan Knight, the distinguished historian, describes PAN as a political quadruped, resting on four unequal legs, one of which is a traditional Catholic constituency, strong in San Luis Potosí and Jalisco.[43] As Soledad Loaeza argues, however, the Catholic Church "does not seem ready to engage itself permanently with the PAN . . ., even though the party has made the Church's demands its own."[44] Priests have frequently suggested, however, that Mexican Catholics belong to all parties. The data in the following chapter bear out the belief that Catholic laity are not more prone to support PAN than the PRI. In fact, to assess partisan prejudices as well as the complexity of priests' ideology, it is revealing to report the results of a question Enrique Luengo posed to clergy he surveyed. When asked which party they thought represented the views of the majority of Mexicans, only 23 percent identified leftist parties, and only 20 percent chose the National Action Party. In fact, nearly one-third thought no party represented the majority of Mexican interests.[45]

The clergy, nevertheless, has been identified strongly with PAN because PAN is often the only viable opposition to the incumbent party in many regions. The PRI leadership is in a defensive position because any criticism of government, the state, or the status quo is a criticism of the PRI. For example, in 1983, the archbishop of Chihuahua sent a pastoral letter calling on his diocese to vote responsibly, to vote a Christian orientation, to vote for change, and to analyze the parties' ideologies. A vote for change, however, automatically was seen as a vote for PAN, given the PRI's permanent incumbency.[46] The same accusation has been leveled against the ex-bishop of Mexicali, Manuel Pérez Gil, who allegedly told his priests in various homilies that the political system could be blamed for the economic disaster in the mid-1980s and that, consequently, they needed a change. PAN propaganda could be found posted around his church.[47]

PAN also has benefited from the Church, even if the Church typically has no desire to associate itself with it. The hierarchy's criticism of corruption, authoritarianism, and Marxism helps flavor similar platform statements from PAN.[48] Ideologically, elements of PAN's party platforms closely parallel Catholic reforms in such papal encyclicals as those of Pope John XXIII and Pope Paul VI, a claim that the PRI cannot make.[49] Many priests or bishops might naturally have a favorable image of PAN given its long support for basic religious principles and rejection of constitutional restrictions on the Church. For example, as early as 1946, PAN called for the reform of Article 3, which excluded religious teachings in early education, violating basic human rights and other norms elsewhere in the constitution. In 1970, it called for the elimination of constitutional provisions against the Church and strongly supported full religious liberty in practice. In 1988, PAN specifically supported the Church's right to engage in public religious acts and to acquire whatever private property was necessary to carry out its goals.[50]

Another linkage between the Catholic clergy and PAN occurs through lay organizations, most notably the Acción Católica de la Juventud Mexicana (ACJM), the oldest and strongest Catholic lay organization, which for many years recruited youngsters among the most brilliant and wealthy Catholics, many of whom eventually became prominent Panistas.[51] A number of prominent PAN leaders obtained their first social experiences in the ACJM.

An increasing pattern of direct or perceived Church involvement in partisan politics has been evidenced since 1979. Officially, during elections themselves, the Socialist Workers Party issued most of the formal complaints. In all cases, they have accused the Church of supporting either PAN or the far more conservative, Catholic-oriented Mexican Democratic Party (PDM). In 1979, the parties made two complaints and in the 1982 presidential election, eight complaints. Eleven complaints were filed in the hotly contested local and congressional elections of 1985.[52] Given the large number of parishes in Mexico, even if such numbers are valid, they are hardly indicative of widespread abuse.

Nearly all of the accusations against the Church showing partisan preference for PAN have occurred in the North, where PAN is typically strongest. The earliest incident of an alleged alliance between PAN and the Church that received national attention took place in Hermosillo, Sonora, April 1983, when the bishop of Hermosillo met with PAN's candidate for governor, representatives of the American embassy, and several businesspeople. Mexican analysts assumed this signified a new electoral alliance among the United States, the Catholic Church, the business community, and PAN.[53] A more balanced assessment of Bishop Quintero's role suggests that his constant references to the state's political situation and the need for Christians to be actively involved politically subjected him to accusations of intervening in politics and promoting PAN.[54] Much stronger evidence of partisanship has been directed against several priests. Concrete evidence has been presented in cases in the dioceses of Ciudad Juárez and Huajuapan.[55]

The studies of priests in multiple dioceses by Luengo and a specific case study of Zacatecas, a state that could be described as representative of a "typical" diocese in Mexico with no strong pro- or antihistorical posture vis-à-vis the Catholic Church, reveal that the majority of priests have no notion of party identification. In her study of Zacatecas, Lucía Alonso Reyes did find some priests sympathetic to PAN, expressing their sympathy contrary to Church policy in their sermons. She found other priests sympathetic to other opposition parties, including the left. Still other priests were critical implicitly or explicitly of the official party.[56]

The clergy's most explicit political activity, which extends beyond their motivation of others to vote for specific views and political parties, is to become political candidates. Canon law prohibits any member of the clergy from holding public office. In the case of PAN, several ex-priests did become candidates in 1990 in the third and sixth state legislative districts in San Luis Potosí. Both lost the election.[57] Much earlier, a Franciscan, Edmundo Avalos Covarrubias, opposed both by religious and political authorities, actually became mayor of Penixtlahuaca, Oaxaca, in 1969, before his bishop removed him from office.[58]

Despite the fact that little evidence exists linking clergy directly to PAN, except in unusual instances of individual priests or bishops, politicians and others continue to perceive the hierarchy's posture on other issues as partisan. The most important source of potential conflict, analyzed in considerable detail in the next section, is elections, specifically voting and electoral fraud. The most significant single event tying some Church leadership to PAN were bishops' declarations concerning the controversial 1986 Chihuahua state elections.[59] The then head of the Mexican episcopate, Archbishop Sergio Obeso Rivera, had this to say about his fellow bishops' declaration: "[W]e are not making party politics nor do we favor any party. This is not our intention. It is not just to link the bishops of Chihuahua with PAN. We did not make nor are we making propaganda in favor of this party."[60] Nevertheless, despite these and other statements clarifying the position of these bishops, who were acting independently of the episcopate, the then president of Mexico, Miguel de la Madrid, later confessed:

> In 1986, the bishops of Chihuahua took a very strong political stand, and *expressed an attitude which I frankly perceived as open sympathy for the National Action Party,* especially among bishops Talamás and Almeida. When they made these statements *I perceived them acting as Panistas, rather than as bishops.* I have always supported the view that the Church should not participate in politics, especially in party political affairs. [emphasis added][61]

Some analysts also have suggested that certain types of Catholics, especially traditional and rural Catholics in specific regions, have given support to the conservative Mexican Democratic Party (PDM), for many years the party to the far right of the Mexican political spectrum.[62] This party evolved from a core of supporters and leaders of the National Sinarquista Union, a movement emerging from Catholics whose roots extended back to the Cristero rebellion. Miguel Alemán, Jr., son of President Alemán and a prominent PRI figure in the 1990s, suggested that in the 1980s the PDM identified itself with some priests when it asked them to bless their candidates in special ceremonies. When some of these priests moved from blessing to supporting candidates and parties, they antagonized government officials.[63]

A potential does exist for the Catholic Church to be identified more closely with specific political parties, at least ideologically. Although PAN borrowed heavily from papal encyclicals during earlier eras, Mexico never produced a Christian Democratic Party similar to those found in Chile or Venezuela. After President Salinas began moving toward a more formal and open relationship with the Catholic Church, some Mexicans in 1990, including the niece of his personal envoy to the Pope, began organizing the Partido Demócrata Cristiano (PDC), but it never obtained official registration.[64] However, Guillermo Schulenburg, for many years abbot of the Basilica of Guadalupe, Mexico's most revered shrine, announced in a 1992 speech to students at the Ibero-American University that if the people so desired, they could organize a Catholic Party, a nonconfessional party.[65] The Mexican episcopate was quick to respond that it was not interested in the creation of such a party, but rather it expressed more interest in human rights and poverty.[66]

Catholic clergy have been publicly identified as having partisan preferences not just for PAN or the PDM but also for and against far leftist parties. However, since the 1970s the Mexican episcopate has not emphasized an active posture on Marxism; instead, that has fallen to the purview of individual bishops. During the period of electoral reforms in 1976 and 1977, opposition parties on the left, specifically the Mexican Communist Party (PCM), began courting the Church, making a formal proposal in the Chamber of Deputies that the constitution be amended to allow priests to become political party members.[67]

The most celebrated case of a public Church position on this issue, although not associated with a specific political party, can be found in the remarks by six members of the Mexican episcopate's permanent council on March 9, 1978. They issued a statement condemning comments attributed to Cuernavaca bishop Sergio Méndez Arceo implying that holding Marxian views was a necessary ingredient to achieve salvation.[68] These bishops did not represent the episcopate, nor did they fully understand Méndez Arceo's original remarks.

The clearest case of important clergy making an open statement against a specific party was that directed against the short-lived Unified Socialist Party of Mexico (PSUM), a coalition of small leftist groups including the Mexican Communist Party. When this alliance made a concerted effort to appeal to voters sympathetic to Catholic liberation theology during the 1982 presidential elections, Cardinal Ernesto Corripio Ahumada of the Mexico archdiocese, in association with his auxiliary bishops, distributed 10 million pamphlets entitled *Cristianos por un partido marxista,* stating that a vote for a party supporting Marxist principles was a vote against Christianity and that it was not possible to be a Marxist and a Christian.[69] Their declaration denounced economic liberalism as well.[70] Nevertheless, individual priests and bishops have also identified with progressive groups or parties, sometimes publicly.[71] Bishop Lona pointed to a coincidence of interests between the Catholic Church and COCEI, an independent group of students, workers, and peasants that won the mayorship of Juchitan, Oaxaca, in the 1980s.[72]

Clergy partisan preference for opposition parties, specifically the PAN, receives media attention, and the clergy and opposition parties are linked in the popular mind. However, clergy can also be identified with strong partisan postures against the PRI and, in some cases, for the PRI. Such priests identify the political party, the PRI, rather than the government generically as responsible for the average Mexican's economic and social woes. For example, the bishop of Huejutla, Hidalgo, was quoted by the press as saying that the "PRI in this moment is not the best electoral option because of its black history."[73] On the other hand, documented cases of individual priests openly favoring the PRI exist, and one scholar claims, without much evidence, that Catholic clergy supported a conservative PRI offshoot, the Mexican Civic Front for Revolutionary Affirmation (FCMAR).[74]

Church leadership also has been subjected to pressures from local and national political leaders affiliated with the PRI. In fact, it is apparent from an interview with Archbishop Adalberto Almeida Merino that a high-ranking party representative asked him shortly before the disputed 1986 elections in Chihuahua to announce himself personally in favor of the PRI's gubernatorial candidate, Fernando Baeza. Almeida told the official that "in no manner could we [Catholic clergy] intervene in party politics."[75]

This unusual incident is illuminating because it demonstrates that government officials have a distorted perception of Church neutrality. Some government officials must believe that the Church is favorably inclined, at the highest levels, toward the establishment elite and the PRI. This belief may have been based on the interpretation that before 1992, a strong state provided the stability necessary to maintain the informal modus vivendi between it and the government. According to David C. Bailey, one of the few American scholars to have studied the Mexican Church in considerable detail, "The higher clergy knows this, and most of the bishops would be alarmed at the prospect of the PRI's losing national power. For this reason, the upper clergy have a dislike, bordering on contempt, for the National Action Party (PAN), despite its popular reputation of being proclerical."[76] Today Bailey's statement appears exaggerated, but it provides a sense, from an informed source, of why higher clergy might have supported the status quo leadership for many decades.

Finally, clergy may also involve themselves in partisan issues through political action organizations unaffiliated with any political party. The broader implications of such activities are more fully drawn and analyzed in the discussion of base community organizations later in this chapter, but nongovernmental organizations flowered in Mexico, especially since the 1985 earthquake. For example, a veteran of the base community movement, Father Camilo Daniel Pérez, helped found the Democratic Electoral Movement (MED), which launched a civil disobedience campaign, organized rallies, occupied public buildings, and staged a sit-down strike on the bridge linking El Paso, Texas, to Ciudad Juárez.[77]

Election Fraud, Voting, and Chihuahua

The issue most likely to bring the Catholic Church into the partisan political arena is government-perpetrated election fraud. There are three fundamental reasons why the Church has become strongly involved in this issue. First, the episcopate has offered a clear position on the issue of political liberalization, specifically democracy, of which free elections are integral. Second, the hierarchy takes an especially active position historically on civic responsibility, urging people to vote. Third, given the respect a typical parish priest engenders among residents in his diocese, he is often sought out to solve disputes or represent his parishioners' frustrations to civil authorities.

Of all the temporal issues on which the Church is united, few draw more universal support than the right to vote.[78] As one analyst argues, "[T]he Catholic church sees its task as encouraging participation, the integral development of individuals, and greater pluralism in highly conflictual societies."[79] The Church goes well beyond the right to vote, charging Mexican citizens with the responsibility to vote. Its position is founded on historic precedence in Church doctrine extending back to Pope Pius XI's exhorting Mexican Catholics to vote and to form political

parties. At least since the late 1930s, clergy have encouraged the faithful to participate.[80]

The Mexican episcopate first laid out the Church's responsibility in elections in
recent times in a 1956 document entitled "Seven Civic Duties of Catholics."[81]
Twenty years later, in the episcopate's statement on Christian political options,
the bishops requested that all Catholics "faithfully complete their temporal duties,
guided by evangelical spirit," referring specifically to participating in political decisions (voting).[82] In 1991, in a specific statement on elections entitled "Free
and Democratic Elections: A Challenge for Mexico's Destiny," the episcopate
encouraged the faithful to carry out four responsibilities: be familiar with the ideas
of each political party; be aware of the governmental program that the candidate
proposes to carry out; examine the ability and moral prestige of each candidate;
and harbor a reasonable trust that those elected will seek the interests of all citizens before private and party interests.[83]

The Mexican episcopate has criticized its citizenry for its low social and political participation.[84] Some bishops have gone beyond this criticism, suggesting to
their parishioners that a failure to vote, without reasonable cause, is a sin because
you are committing an injury against the common good.[85] Bishops and archbishops who have been labeled conservative, traditional, progressive, and moderate
all have taken similar positions on this issue, both in their pastoral statements and
in their personal activities. Some of the diocesan statements and activities included
the following:

> The church . . . feels it has a right and responsibility to be involved in this field of
> reality [voting in local elections] because Christianity should evangelize the totality of
> human existence.[86]

> In Zacatecas the bishop recirculated a document entitled "para votar" to the entire
> diocese. Citizens have the obligation to participate in politics.[87]

> In more than 500 churches, priests and members of religious orders invited people,
> during mass, to actively participate in elections next Sunday, on instructions of arch-
> bishop Rosendo Huesca Pacheco of Puebla, Puebla.[88]

> Bishop Luis Reynoso [Cuernavaca Diocese, Morelos] votes and other priests have
> performed functions in polling places.[89]

> The citizens have the right and obligation not only to vote at election time, but to
> organize, unite, work, so that in our society a real democracy exists that permits the
> development of diverse political options with real opportunities to obtain power.
> —Bishops of Hidalgo[90]

Interestingly, political authorities rarely have intervened against the Church's
exhortations to vote. It was easy for them to take this position because for many
decades increased voter turnout, most of which went to the governing party,
helped to legitimize the government. In fact, the government began the process of
electoral reforms, guaranteeing opposition parties increased representation, only
when they perceived voter apathy and cynicism were at such high levels that the
PRI and the electoral system had lost legitimacy. Historically, the PRI delayed
female suffrage largely based on the belief that women were deeply religious,

were controlled by the parish priest, and would vote for PAN. The 1955 elections, the first in which women voted nationally, sharply disproved that political myth. As Roberto Blancarte concludes, not until 1986, when the northern bishops spoke out against electoral fraud in Chihuahua, did a new concept of a separate Catholic vote reemerge.[91]

The Church also maintained a special interest, extending beyond the early foundations of Catholic dogma, in encouraging citizens to vote. The clearest human rights violation present in the Mexican constitution was the prohibition against priests voting. In fact, it may well have been the most violated constitutional provision of church-state relations openly permitted by authorities. Since clergy did not have a legal right to vote, they acquired both an emotional and pragmatic interest in other Mexicans exercising this crucial privilege. Their interest in voting rights for the clergy intensified in the mid-1980s.[92]

A variable that is complementary to the Church's interest in civic responsibility is democracy. Mexicans are somewhat confused about its status since although a majority favor moving strongly in a democratic direction, some are opposed to such an option, others believe democracy already exists in Mexico, others are neutral, and some have no opinion on the issue.[93] The Church's position on political participation in general and voting in particular is much clearer than its position on democracy. Some analysts suggest that the typical Mexican Catholic has learned little from the clergy about democracy. They imply that priests express less interest in democracy and more interest in opposition to the government.[94] The democracy issue within the Church is more complex. It can be argued that the Church frequently does not specify a political model in the Mexican case because theoretically the model is allegedly democratic. By encouraging participation, and by criticizing the model's authoritarian abuses, the Church implicitly supports democracy. As one episcopate document argued when conceptualizing the Church's democratic vision, it involves equality of all men and women and sociopolitical participation.[95]

It is not so much a question of the clergy's support for democracy as, Daniel Levine suggests, a question of their support for democratization. He argues that it is more difficult to advocate democratization because it calls on Church leadership and rank-and-file "Catholics to legitimate new concepts of equality and to implement new models of democratic governance in the heart of traditionally hierarchical and authoritarian institutions. Democratization thus means building and sustaining spaces within these institutions where the practice of democracy can be valued, nurtured, and expressed in day-to-day affairs."[96] Clergy have been critical of these weaknesses in political institutions, particularly the lack of a competitive party structure and the inability of the government to respond to the democratic aspirations of the people.[97]

Given the Church's strong interest in participation and in a healthy multiparty system, it is not surprising that the clergy becomes most embroiled in politics and in conflict with the state on the issue of election fraud. The clergy's perception of electoral fraud is a natural reflection of citizen attitudes, which can be described as cynical as well as uninformed about electoral procedures.[98] Four out of 10 Mexicans have little or no confidence in the electoral process, 46 percent have some confidence, and only a tiny minority, 14 percent, have much confidence in it.[99] Clergy believe they must take a public position on fraud not only because it represents their constituents' demands but also because denunciations of electoral fraud will never produce positive consequences if the Church and prominent social institutions do not condemn it.[100]

Some analysts believe that both the Church and business groups increased electoral activities after the 1977 political reforms.[101] Priests' and bishops' statements and Church literature on political affairs indeed were abundant during the July 1979 elections.[102] But the benchmark date for the Church activist posture on electoral fraud was not until 1986, following several years in the early 1980s under Miguel de la Madrid's administration (1982–1988), when the president briefly made clean elections a reality, resulting in many local victories among opposition parties. The pattern of Church involvement continued through the 1990s when bishops increasingly began issuing condemnations of fraudulent elections, largely affecting individual dioceses:

> We cannot remain silent when political-civic events have occurred in some entities of the country and today in our state of Oaxaca, as a result of the lost elections.
> —Huajuapan de León Diocese, Oaxaca[103]

> The violation by means of fraud or repression, of the right to vote, is more serious and harmful than any economic fraud.
> —Monterrey Archdiocese, Nuevo León[104]

> Our beloved Durango has been offended. The vote was not respected; physical, psychological, and material pressures were made. . . . [N]o one accepts a silent Church.
> —Durango Diocese, Durango[105]

In other cases where fraud was allegedly excessive, such as the highly disputed 1989 Michoacán local and state elections, the Church remained silent. Some observers believe the Church's silence in Michoacán is predicated on the diocese's lack of sympathy for the PRD, PRI's primary opposition in the region.[106] A more likely explanation is that the archbishop of Morelia, who is a traditionalist on political activism, is not known for public statements on politics.

The episcopate itself, however, did not become involved in the issue of electoral fraud until 1988. The presidential election, in which the government declared its candidate, Carlos Salinas de Gortari, to be the winner over Cuauhtémoc Cárdenas, was the most disputed in decades. Immediately prior to the election on August 15, 25 bishops or archbishops spoke out, asking that the vote be respected, and announced that the Church would not tolerate fraud. The hotly disputed electoral results produced a delicate political situation, and the Mexican episcopate called a meeting just eight days following the election. They issued a statement, published in several national dailies, concluding that the people had demonstrated a clear commitment to pluralism, that they wanted an authentic, democratic political process, and that they wished to participate in the country's decision making.[107] The bishops did not specifically denounce the 1988 elections as fraudulent. Before the intensely contested off-year congressional elections in August 1991, the episcopate published *Free and Democratic Elections,* calling on public authorities "to guarantee and assure truly free and democratic elections, offering the same opportunities to each party and respecting the citizen's vote."[108] They went on to charge that those who commit electoral fraud commit a civic-political sin. Cardinal Posadas, who was very active in the Mexican episcopate, although not speaking for his colleagues, publicly suggested that the PRI's gubernatorial candidate in San Luis Potosí should consider resigning since most residents thought he obtained his post through electoral fraud.[109]

No single Church action politically compares to what happened in Chihuahua in the summer of 1986 and the consequences that ensued.[110] As suggested above, opposition parties, particularly the National Action Party, initially made considerable inroads on the local level during Miguel de la Madrid's moral renovation policy in electoral practices. By the third year of his administration, PRI officials, taking note of numerous losses, reversed this trend, deciding to resort to traditional practices to sustain their election victories. Several months before the July 6, 1986, elections in Chihuahua, local bishops issued a pamphlet, "Church and Politics," reaffirming their right to "enlighten, with the light of faith, the arena of political reality."[111]

Charges of massive fraud were widespread immediately following these elections, closely watched by members of the media, intellectuals, and other political observers. Chihuahuan bishops, led by Archbishop Almeida, waited only three days before making a statement, citing the following: (1) they found fraudulent actions, including stuffed ballot boxes before voting began; (2) they wanted all participants to conduct themselves within the law; (3) they supported the people in anything that was just, including the right to defend their vote under the law; (4) they were not attacking any party in particular, since fraud could be committed by any party; (5) the people should not permit the imposition of candidates because they have the right to select them; and (6) civil disobedience will be used when the people do not have the opportunity to defend themselves through other means.[112]

The bishops' statement on electoral fraud drew widespread support from 15 other bishops and archbishops, including the then head of the Mexican episcopate, Sergio Obeso Rivera, his successor, Monterrey archbishop Adolfo Suárez Rivera, the Jesuit order, the Diocesan Committee of Laity, and the head of the Mexican Social Secretariat.[113] Despite tremendous popular support, civil authorities did not respond to their charges of electoral fraud. Archbishop Almeida then decided to pursue an extraordinarily radical strategy.[114] In his July 13 homily, he announced that he would close all Masses in his diocese to protest the fraud and the intransigence of the authorities. This declaration produced immediate results.[115]

The then secretary of government, Manuel Bartlett, considered Almeida's threat extremely serious, remembering that 60 years earlier, under strongly anti-Catholic president Plutarco Elías Calles, the government shut down all Masses, contributing to civil violence and the Cristero rebellion. Differing interpretations exist as to what happened next and how Almeida was persuaded to rescind the boycott of Chihuahuan Masses. The details of what occurred are important because they demonstrate how Mexican political leadership perceives the structure of the Church, how interaction occurs between the Vatican, the episcopate, and civil authorities, and how individual bishops operate autonomously from national authorities.[116]

The government took the first initiative. Instead of approaching the individual bishops or the Mexican episcopate, the logical national Church body, Manuel Bartlett sought out the Vatican delegate, an individual with whom he had excellent personal relations. According to Almeida, Prigione urged Bartlett to speak directly to the archbishop,[117] but Bartlett insisted that Prigione carry his message. He warned the Vatican delegate that in his opinion such a boycott could produce violent reactions. Prigione admonished Bartlett that what the government "did in Chihuahua wasn't worth their efforts. They could have won by any amount, even a small percentage of votes, as long as the election itself was clean. They can't continue with this policy. . . . [T]hey won the battle but not the war."[118]

Prigione's own position on the matter is clear. He agreed not only with the bishops' right to take a public position on the electoral fraud but also with the Chihuahuan bishops' perception of fraud:

> In the case of Chihuahua, I believe that the bishops had every right to express their opinions publicly to the press. But to close the churches was a dangerous and counter-productive policy. I advised the Vatican and asked for instructions, because I wanted to avert what happened in 1926. . . . I find that the Mexicans have a tendency to polarize their beliefs, to make a confrontational choices.[119]

Prigione obviously did not agree with the bishops' strategy. He then arranged a meeting between Bartlett and the Mexican episcopate, represented by the six-member presidency of the permanent council consisting of bishops from all of the pastoral regions. Bartlett once again repeated his concerns, alleging that "if next Sunday the churches are closed, blood will run in Chihuahua. Who will be responsible? Think about it carefully." The presidency decided to send Father Ricardo Cuéllar, their executive secretary, to speak to Almeida. Almeida, however, refused to withdraw the boycott, saying, "[I]t is too late for this; the Pope should order me" to stop.[120] Under canon law, the Pope is the archbishop's only superior. Prigione recalls that when Cuéllar reported Almeida's response, he seized upon these words, interpreting them as Almeida's desire to find a way out. The Mexican episcopate asked Prigione to call the Vatican and explain the situation.[121] Cardinal Achille Silvestrini, an official in the secretariat of state, responded: "Tell Monsignor Almeida that he cannot do this, that it is not permitted by the canon law code. The Eucharist cannot serve as an instrument of political repression. Other means exist." The Pope was not consulted before this oral message was conveyed.[122] The Vatican followed up this oral command with a letter from Cardinal Agustin Casaroli, Vatican secretary of state, specifying that despite the civil rights situation in this diocese, it "does not justify the measure that would deprive the Catholic people of their right to participate in the weekly Mass."[123]

Almeida, faced with the Vatican's request, called off the boycott. He did not, however, back down from criticism of electoral fraud. Indeed, he raised the visibility of the issue nationally and internationally. The Chihuahuan bishops' statements produced numerous consequences involving the Church, the political-electoral arena, and social mobilization.

When Almeida first announced the Church boycott on July 13, the federal government responded with a media campaign against the Church, using radio and television to air images of the Pope speaking against priests intervening in politics.[124] The archbishop actually hardened his stance, admonishing Catholics that if "a candidate who is Catholic is elected during fraud," he is obligated "to not accept an illegitimate position."[125] Finally, on August 7, Almeida, Bishop Manuel Talamás of Ciudad Juárez, and Bishop José A. Llaguno Farías of the Tarahumara issued a statement entitled "A Moral Judgment."[126]

This statement appeared the following week in the *Washington Post* as evidence of extensive Mexican electoral fraud. It is important to cite this document in detail because it contains all of the elements defining the Church's posture on voting and elections since that date:

> To the civic authorities, to all Mexican citizens, and especially to all the Catholics in our diocese: . . . Vatican Council II teaches us that "it is with justice that the Church may at all times, in all places, preach the faith with complete freedom, teach its social doctrine, fulfill its mission among men free of any hindrance, and issue its moral judgment, even in matters of a political nature, whenever the fundamental rights of individuals do not exist or for the salvation of their souls, utilizing every means in accord with the Gospel and for the good of all" *(Gaudium et Spes)*. . . .
>
> We emphatically reject any accusation of political partisanship that could be made of our statement, since the dissatisfaction that reigns among a large majority of the people of Chihuahua has gone beyond the limits of a confrontation between political parties and is now located in the realm of human rights and moral principles affecting all of us.
>
> We therefore declare that, in our firm and clear view, the irregularities evident in the electoral process of July 6 and in the activities preceding it, were so numerous and of such magnitude that they affected the process seriously and persuaded the people in general that it was invalid.
>
> That is the way the people of Chihuahua expresses itself daily with increasing force. This is the way it is seen by the most qualified group of intellectuals in Mexico. This is the way it is perceived and experienced by our brothers who have been committing their lives in a prolonged fast, *demanding respect for fundamental human rights, particularly the right of all Mexicans to vote.*
>
> We bishops also believe that the best means of attaining peace is to void the July 6th elections, and pledge to hold new ones. [emphasis added][127]

The Chihuahua bishops' position on the elections generated important repercussions in the intellectual community, which published a similar petition in the national media. Until 1986, only rarely can one encounter a coincidence of interests between Mexican higher clergy and prominent intellectual leaders. This pattern repeated itself again when leading intellectuals joined with the archbishop of Oaxaca, Bartolomé Carrasco, in denouncing election fraud in his state.[128] The unification of intellectuals and Church officials is an important precedent and could be repeated again under similar circumstances.

The Vatican delegate, as in other situations, has been accused of dismantling the Chihuahuan bishops because of their outspoken posture on election fraud. Almeida and Manuel Talamás retired in 1992 because they reached the maximum age. José Alberto Llaguno died, and his temporary replacement was considered Prigione's, not Llaguno's, choice.[129]

The political ramifications, however, were most direct. In broad terms, some analysts believe that Chihuahua confirmed for PRI officials that a Catholic, non-partisan middle class would increasingly vote for PAN in the absence of a more attractive organization.[130] Other politicians were deeply concerned that priests would increase their political involvement, taking a cue from the Chihuahuan bishops. Their concerns led to changes in the electoral law.

The final version of the 1987 Federal Electoral Code, specifically Article 343, that emerged from the Mexican legislature differed from the version the executive originally introduced. Specifically, the code, which went into effect February 13, imposed heavy fines and four-to-seven-year prison sentences on any priest or minister who induced a citizen to vote in favor of a certain candidate or party or who encouraged abstention. It further stipulated that clergy might not engage in any political activities in places of worship or in any other location.[131]

Mexico's legislature, dominated by the executive branch, rarely alters executive-initiated legislation, so radical changes in Article 343 suggest some important disagreements within national political leadership. It also demonstrates that the Catholic Church itself can become a political football in the hands of various political interests. The most careful analyst of this law, Oscar Aguilar, suggests that the changes were a consequence of battles being fought among different *camarillas* in the presidential succession. What is most remarkable, however, as Aguilar suggests, is that no debate took place in the chamber concerning this article, at least none is recorded in the *Diario de Debates*. In short, it seems incredible that no member of PAN or any other party spoke up about the proposed changes affecting the Church, and that any article having this level of influence on church-state relations could get through the chamber of deputies without argument.[132]

The Mexican episcopate, unaware of the proposed restrictions until after it became law, publicly condemned Article 343. In their words, "As persons, as Mexican Catholics, and as pastors of the people of God, we publicly express our disagreement with the mentioned article (343) as an expression of hostility, illegality, and injustice."[133] Twenty bishops signed a letter opposing the law as a violation of human rights, specifically the 1981 United Nations Declaration of Human Rights to which Mexico is a signatory, as well as articles in the Mexican constitution. They also described it as violating liberty of expression and opinion and discouraging the hope of a democratic opening. Specifically, the Mexican episcopate sought an *amparo*, a legal writ to stop the law's implementation.[134]

Social Justice

The Church's posture on issues of social justice, extending beyond the realm of political authoritarianism, corruption, and fraudulent elections, concentrated largely on economic issues, specifically distribution of wealth and human rights. In the years since 1970, human rights have taken on much greater importance, particularly in the 1980s and 1990s. The distribution of wealth issue is linked to internal conflicts over pastoral strategies related to the influence of liberation theology in Mexico in the 1960s and early 1970s. The larger impact of liberation theology as a significant issue confronting the Church and church-state relations will be taken up in the next chapter.

Pastoral statements on purely economic themes, however, are rare. During the controversial years in the 1960s and 1970s, the Mexican Social Secretariat, an agency of the episcopate then strongly influenced by progressive priests, published three important statements: "Mexican Integration and Development" in March 1968, "Justice in Mexico" in 1971, and "Christian Social and Political Options" in October 1973. The earliest of the three documents, which appeared before the 1968 student massacre in Mexico City, announced that it was urgent for citizens to accept innovative and audacious transformations if they did not wish to augment indefinitely the influence of the wealthy and the servitude of the poor.[135] The 1971 statement provided a complete analysis of Mexican society.[136] The first version, a working paper circulated in 1970, has been described as liberationist in tone and actually criticized the Church. Among other things, it charged that corruption was institutionalized, and that the Church was an active accomplice of the Mexican oligarchy. It was so controversial that the bishop in charge of the Social Pastoral Committee that produced it, Adalberto Almeida Merino, was forced to resign.[137] The episcopate never formally considered the revised document, and neither version appears in published collections of episcopal statements.[138]

The 1973 episcopal document on Christian social and political options has been the source of many important political principles for the Catholic hierarchy. This pastoral document also states specifically that priests, "as all men, should denounce social, economic, and political injustice and contribute to seek new forms of social organizations and legitimate means of making their decisions effective."[139] The Conference of Latin American Bishops in Puebla in 1979 reinforced the Mexican view because it made clear that while politicization of the Christian message was unacceptable, the Church did have a responsibility to use its influence to improve society and bring about structural changes.[140] As is the case in the purely political realm, this does not signify that social issues are the center of Church preoccupations, nor are the Church's actions motivated by social objectives.[141] What it does imply, simply, is that the Church is willing to take public stands on social-economic issues and to criticize those responsible.[142] In short, as Bishop Sergio Obeso, then head of the Mexican episcopate suggested, the "Church has come out of the sacristy."[143]

Although election fraud has received most of the attention, bishops have given increasing interest to the distribution of wealth, especially as the gap accentuates between rich and poor in the 1990s. As Bishop Raúl Vera López of Ciudad Altamirano, Guerrero, a diocese in one of Mexico's poorest, less-developed states, concluded: "The structures and organization of scarce resources need to be better utilized and to influence the level of investment and income in this zone. The Church should encourage individuals to make greater investments without just thinking of larger profits."[144]

Interestingly, the Church assumed an extremely strong position on Mexico's foreign debt and its implication for poor people, supporting the government's request for debt relief. On the other hand, the Church disassociated itself from the jewel of Carlos Salinas's economic strategy, the North American Free Trade Agreement (NAFTA). The Mexican episcopate's Social Pastoral Committee, according to *La Jornada,* said that the free trade agreement "was negotiated 'behind the backs' of the Mexican people," and that it "attends the interests of large corporations and not those of medium and small businesses."[145] In April 1993, at the episcopate's 54th assembly, Cardinal Juan Jesús Posadas read a statement authored by the head of the episcopate, Archbishop Adolfo Suárez Rivera, that if NAFTA did not attend to internal markets and demand, Mexico would pay high social costs as poverty reached alarming levels.[146]

Conclusions

An institution as large and influential as the Catholic Church incorporates many views of its broader role in society. But a careful examination of the Mexican Church's posture on political activity, political development, and elections makes clear, especially at the highest levels, that bishops have little desire to support specific parties or candidates. Although some bishops would prefer to take no public position on developmental issues—political, social, and economic—the consensus is that they have an obligation, indeed, a moral responsibility, to engender a sense of civic responsibility among their parishioners.

The major explanation for why the Catholic Church has become embroiled in political controversy since the mid-1980s is the declining legitimacy of the government party, the PRI, and the fact that one-party dominance for so many years shifts the Church's public criticisms of governmental failures automatically to the shoulders of the PRI. Bishops and priests alike sense an obligation to help channel their constituents' frustrations in Mexico's transition to democracy. Mexico's recent constitutional reforms both discourage and encourage a more activist Church role. Even if the Church were to pursue a course similar to its strategy prior to 1992, the reforms themselves highlight the Church's visibility, bringing it increased influence while opening it up to severe criticism.

Pragmatism also explains why most bishops agree with their colleagues that the Church cannot ignore electoral fraud. Even if the Church wishes to remain on the political sidelines, it could not do so on the issue of electoral fraud. Mexicans have chosen free and fair elections as the primary path toward political development. This issue demonstrates the broader principle, as in the case of Chihuahua, that when the Church identifies strongly with public opinion, support from many sectors is immediately forthcoming. The legitimacy of elections is so widely questioned by most Mexicans that the Church risks losing its own institutional prestige and credibility if it ignores citizen demands when fraud is committed. A loss in legitimacy for the Church not only affects its ability to convey important spiritual and temporal values but also weakens its battles against the encroachments of competitive religions, especially evangelical Protestants.

President Salinas gave new emphasis to the Church as a social and political actor in the 1990s. His reforms, in the short run, benefited the state, borrowing the Church's legitimacy for the state's own ends, and strengthened religion's legal and political position in the constitution and in the minds of ordinary Mexicans. But if the president and his advisers believed they could co-opt the Church into their new political alliance, they were mistaken. The Church, like all well-established institutions, has its own agenda and responsibilities, formed within Mexico's historical and cultural context. If the clergy has learned anything in the liberal 20th century, it is that it must remain independent of the state, it must not ally with any political faction, and it must support the majority of the population. Mexico's bishops will continue to pursue their civic obligations, while maintaining a fine balance between responsible exercise of political rights and partisan, political favoritism.[147] It will be an increasingly difficult tightrope for the Church to tread, as Mexico encounters numerous obstacles on the path to political development.

NOTES

1. Daniel H. Levine, *Religion and Politics in Latin America: The Catholic Church in Venezuela and Colombia* (Princeton: Princeton University Press, 1981), 13.

2. Daniel H. Levine, *Religion and Politics in Latin America*, 26.

3. Conferencia del Episcopado Mexicano, *Compromiso cristiano ante las opciones sociales y la política* (Mexico City: Edición Senal, 1973), 23.

4. Adolfo Suárez Rivera, "Instrucción pastoral sobre la dimensión política de la fe," Monterrey Archdiocese, Monterrey, Nuevo León, March, 1987, 6.

5. A typical example can be found in Pablo González Casanova, *Democracy in Mexico* (New York: Oxford University Press, 1965), 40.

6. For example, the Mexican episcopate also stated in 1973 that both bishops and priests have the responsibility to defend liberty and rights and denounce their abuse whenever they are present. Conferencia de Episcopado Mexicano, *Compromiso cristiano ante las opciones sociales y la política,* 24–26. This pastoral letter also refers to the earlier episcopal statement on "Development and Integration of the Country," which criticized internal colonialism and unequal development, statements that would have brought it into direct confrontation with political elites had it been publicized. The traditional point of view was expressed by Luis Reynoso Cervantes, later bishop of Cuernavaca, who stated unequivocally that politics is excluded from the Church's responsibilities. Sociedad Teológica Mexicana, *La evangelización en México, sexta semana de estudios teológicos* (Mexico City: Ediciones Paulinas, 1975), 209.

7. Soledad Loaeza, "La Iglesia católica mexicana y el reformismo autoritario," *Foro Internacional* 25, no. 2 (October–December 1984): 147.

8. Dennis Goulet, "The Mexican Church: Into the Public Arena," *America* 160, no. 13 (April 8, 1989): 320, quoting Jirolamo Prigione. Prigione further stated that "[t]he Church does not take political positions. It only defends principles, orients moral sentiments; but it does not take sides in favor or against anyone. It never says: this is the truth [in political matters]." *Unomásuno,* August 7, 1982, 18.

9. Soledad Loaeza, "La iglesia y la democracia en México," *Revista Mexicana de Sociología* 47, no. 1 (January–March 1985): 166.

10. Personal interview with César Pérez, Mexican Methodist Church, Mexico City, July 14, 1993.

11. See Enrique Luengo, "Los párrocos: una visión," Ibero-American University, un-

published manuscript, December 1989, which concluded that 87 percent of priests were interested in politics but only 32 percent knew their federal legislator.

12. Scholars believe Church involvement in political activity includes the necessity of the hierarchy to legitimate itself before its own social bases. Bernardo Barranco and Raquel Pastor, "La presencia de la iglesia católica en el proceso de sucesión presidencial 1988," *Análisis Sociales* no. 2 (1988): 50.

13. Roberto Blancarte, *El poder salinismo e iglesia católica, una nueva convivencia?* (Mexico City: Grijalbo, 1991), 196.

14. *Proceso,* February 19, 1990, 16.

15. Francisco Ortiz Pinchetti, " 'Hablaré cada vez que me lo pidan,' responde Medina Plascencia a las críticas por su discurso en el Cubilete," *Proceso,* February 10, 1992, 15–16.

16. Declaration by delegate Jirolamo Prigione, *El Nacional,* February 5, 1992.

17. Roberto Blancarte, "La Iglesia católica en México desde 1929: introdución crítica a la produción historiográfica (1968–1988)," *Cristianismo y Sociedad* no. 101 (1989): 39.

18. Michael Macaulay makes just such an argument for the Peruvian Catholic Church in his "Ideological Change and Internal Cleavages in the Peruvian Church: Change, Status Quo, and the Priest: The Case of ONIS," unpublished Ph.D. dissertation, Notre Dame University, 1972, 11.

19. Charles L. Davis makes this argument before the reforms were in place, in his "Religion and Partisan Loyalty: The Case of Catholic Workers in Mexico," *Western Political Quarterly* 45 (March 1992): 291–292.

20. Conferencia de Episcopado Mexicano, *Compromiso cristiano ante las opciones sociales y la política,* 19.

21. Javier Lozano Barragán, in an address to all priests, nuns and parishioners in his diocese. "Relaciones Iglesia-Estado, Instrucción Doctrinal," Zacatecas Archdiocese, Zacatecas, Zacatecas, 1992, 9. Lozano Barragán is an important member of the episcopate and active in its committees.

22. Gerhard Lenski, *The Religious Factor: A Sociological Study of Religion's Impact on Politics and Family Life* (Garden City, N.Y.: Doubleday, 1963), 278.

23. Personal interview between Shannan Mattiace and Father Carrillo, Mérida Archdiocese, Mérida, Yucatán, April 18, 1988.

24. Personal interview with Bishop Manuel Samaniego Barriga, Cuautitlán Diocese, Cuautitlán, México, February 13, 1991.

25. Personal interview with Bishop José Pablo Rovalo, Episcopal Vicariate, Fifth Zone, Mexico Archdiocese, Mexico City, February 21, 1991.

26. Frederick Sontag, "Liberation Theology and Its View of Political Violence," *Journal of Church and State* 31, no. 2 (Spring 1989): 285–286.

27. Conferencia de Episcopado Mexicano, *Compromiso cristiano ante las opciones sociales y la política,* 17.

28. Enrique Luengo, "Los párrocos: una visión," 97.

29. Brian Smith, "Religion and Social Change: Classical Theories and New Formulations in the Content of Recent Developments in Latin America," *Latin American Research Review* 10 (1975): 13, citing Gustavo Gutiérrez's classic *A Theology of Liberation* (Maryknoll: Orbis Books, 1975), 65.

30. Thomas G. Sanders, "The Politics of Catholicism in Latin America," *Journal of Inter-American Studies and World Affairs* 24, no. 2 (May 1982): 256.

31. Conferencia del Episcopado Mexicano, *Compromiso cristiano ante las opciones sociales y la política,* 26.

32. Enrique Luengo, "Los párrocos: una visión," 100.

33. Soledad Loaeza argues, for example, that the Church "has avoided identifying itself with any one particular political party, because doing so would belie its pretensions to represent the majority of Mexicans. By being tied up with a particular party, the Church would limit its own political freedom and lose its appeal to the groups that do not identify with that party. It is crucial for the Church to keep the flexibility needed to maintain support in a diverse society. That is why, while the bishops in the North support PAN, those to the South have adopted positions closer to leftist parties, and many others support the PRI." While Loaeza's rational for nonsupport is correct, her implication that some central authority has encouraged different bishops to support different parties in some concerted way is incorrect. It is the product of natural, regional issues, problems, and constituencies, having nothing to do with what "the Church" wants. "Notas para el estudio de la Iglesia en el México contemporáneo," in *Religión y política en México,* Martín de la Rosa et al., eds. (Mexico: Siglo XXI, 1985), 47.

34. *New York Times,* May 12, 1990, 1.

35. Personal interview with Archbishop Jirolamo Prigione, Vatican Delegate to Mexico, Mexico Archdiocese, Mexico City, June 2, 1987.

36. Manuel Robles, "En las elecciones, la Iglesia 'no dará sino orientaciones': Corripio," *Proceso,* August 17, 1987, 14.

37. Adolfo Sánchez Rebolledo, "Los motivos de la Iglesia, entrevista con Genaro Alamilla Arteaga," *Nexos* no. 141 (September 1989): 27. Alamilla was president of the committee for social communication, or the official spokesperson of the episcopate, and auxiliary bishop in the Mexico Archdiocese.

38. Conferencia de Episcopado Mexicano, "Free and Democratic Elections: A Challenge for Mexico's Destiny," Mexico Archdiocese, March 21, 1991, 10, cited in *The Other Side of Mexico,* March–April, no. 20 (1991): 10.

39. As Father Márquez remarked, "The Church should have the opportunity to clarify the issues which these parties raise. They should make clear an honest analyses of the issue so that the ordinary person understands his options." Personal interview, Mexico Archdiocese, Mexico City, May 29, 1987.

40. Personal interview with Bishop Manuel Samaniego Barriga. "The bishops have to try to illuminate and clarify without any kind of political partisanship the conditions in Mexico, especially human rights."

41. See, for example, the comments of Bishop Manuel Talamás Camandarí, of Ciudad Juárez, in "El Clero confía en que CSG corrija errores," *Excélsior,* December 30, 1988, n.p.

42. Personal interview between Shannan Mattiace and Father Pedro of the Church of San Cristóbal, Mérida Archdiocese, Mérida, Yucatán, Mexico, April 12, 1988.

43. Alan Knight, "Historical Continuities in Social Movements," in *Popular Movements and Political Change in Mexico,* Joe Foweraker and Ann L. Craig, eds. (Boulder, Colo.: Lynne Rienner, 1990), 86.

44. Soledad Loaeza, "Notas para el estudio de la Iglesia en el México contemporáneo," 47.

45. Enrique Luengo, "Los párrocos: una visión," 99.

46. Luis Guzmán García, "También en la Iglesia hay corrientes," in *La sucesión presidencial en 1988,* Abraham Nuncio, ed. (Mexico City: Grijalbo, 1988), 385.

47. Oscar González, "Batallas en el reino de este mundo," *Nexos* no. 78 (June 1984): 23.

48. R. Bruce McColm, "Mexico: the Coming Crisis," *Journal of Contemporary Studies* (September 1984): 20.

49. Joseph Klesner, "Changing Patterns of Electoral Participation and Official Party

Support in Mexico," in *Mexican Politics in Transition*, Judith Gentleman, ed. (Boulder, Colo.: Westview Press, 1987), 102.

50. María Elena Alvarez de Bernal Vicencio, ed., *Relaciones iglesia estado: cambios necesarios, tesís del Partido Acción Nacional* (Mexico City: Epessa, 1990), 9, 19–21.

51. Abraham Nuncio, *El PAN, alternativa de poder o instrumento de la oligarquía empresarial* (Mexico City: Editorial Nueva Imágen, 1986), 38.

52. Sylvia Gómez Tagle, who has devoted years to studying election fraud and illegal participation, does suggest that the PPS's and PST's motives may be questionable. "Democracy and Power in Mexico: The Meaning of Conflict in the 1979, 1982, and 1985 Federal Elections," in *Mexican Politics in Transition*, Judith Gentleman, ed. (Boulder, Colo.: Westview Press, 1987), 167.

53. Carlos Martínez Assad, "State Elections in Mexico," in *Electoral Patterns and Perspectives in Mexico*, Arturo Alvarado, ed. (La Jolla, Calif.: Mexico-U.S. Studies Center, UCSD, 1987), 36, 39.

54. Graciela Guadarrama, "Entrepreneurs and Politics: Businessmen in Electoral Contests in Sonora and Nuevo León, July, 1985," in *Electoral Patterns and Perspectives in Mexico*, Arturo Alvarado, ed. (La Jolla, Calif.: Mexico-U.S. Studies Center, UCSD, 1987), 102.

55. *El Universal de Juárez*, June 15, 1988, and Enrique Marroquín, "El conflicto religioso en Oaxaca," in *Religiosidad y política en México*, Carlos Martínez Assad, ed. (Mexico City: Ibero-American University, 1992), 294.

56. Lucía Alonso Reyes, "Función social de la iglesia en Zacatecas," in *Memorias, segundo informe de investigación sobre el estado de Zacatecas* (Zacatecas, 1989), 196.

57. *El Nacional*, March 26, 1990, 37; August 6, 1990, 3.

58. Enrique Marroquín, "El conflicto religioso en Oaxaca," 293.

59. For their actual statement, which cites Vatican II's *Gaudium et Spes*, no. 76, see "Juicio moral sobre el proceso electoral del 6 de julio '86 en el estado de Chihuahua," August 7, 1986, in *Documentación e Información Católica*, August 1986, 550–551.

60. Oscar Hinojosa, "La misión evangélica ordena dejar la sacristía, afirma Obeso Rivera," *Proceso*, September 8, 1986, 11.

61. Personal interview with Miguel de la Madrid, Mexico City, February 22, 1991.

62. Joseph Klesner, "Changing Patterns of Electoral Participation and Official Party Support in Mexico," 101–102, 108.

63. Personal interview with Miguel Alemán, Jr., Mexico City, July 30, 1992.

64. Rafael Rodríguez Castañeda, "La relación con el Papa riesgoso acto pragmático en busca de popularidad," *Proceso*, February 26, 1990.

65. *La Jornada*, October 1, 1992, 1, 12.

66. *El Nacional*, October 3, 1992, 3.

67. George Philip, *The Presidency in Mexican Politics* (New York: St. Martin's, 1992), 106.

68. Dennis M. Hanratty, "Change and Conflict in the Contemporary Mexican Catholic Church," unpublished Ph.D. dissertation, Duke University, 1980, 256.

69. For background on this statement, see Abraham Nuncio, *El PAN, alternativa de poder o instrumento de la oligarquía empresarial*, 98–99; Dennis M. Hanratty, "The Political Role of the Mexican Catholic Church: Contemporary Issues," *Thought* 59 (June 1984): 172; and Oscar González et al., "Batallas en el reino de este mundo," *Nexos* no. 78 (June 1984): 25.

70. Carlos Fazio, *La cruz y el martillo* (Mexico City: Joaquín Mortíz, 1987), 225.

71. Olga Aragón Castillo, "No le interesa al Estado un acercamiento con la Iglesia," *El Sol de México*, January 6, 1989, n.p., concluded that the majority of priests in the Chihua-

hua archdiocese were not sympathetic to the PRI but leaned politically toward the left and the right. Similar to PAN, an ex-priest ran as a candidate of the Party of the Democratic Revolution (PRD) for governor of Querétaro. Grupo Consultor Interdisciplinario, "Carta de política mexicana, la relación estado-iglesia, nuevos espacios para conflictos," March 6, 1992, 7.

72. George Grayson, *The Church in Contemporary Mexico* (Washington: CSIS, 1992), 58.

73. José Luis Gaona Vega, "Los candidatos presidenciales tras el apoyo de obispos," *Punto*, June 27, 1988, 12.

74. Silvia Marcela Bénard Calva, "The Relationship between Church and State in Mexico: An Analysis of the Pope's Visit in 1979," unpublished M.A. thesis, University of Texas, Austin, 1986, 41; Enrique Marroquín, "El conflicto religioso en Oaxaca," 296.

75. The official was Manuel Gurría Ordóñez, general delegate of the National Executive Committee of the PRI in Chihuahua. *Proceso*, July 21, 1986, 14–15.

76. David C. Bailey, "The Church since 1940," in *Twentieth Century Mexico*, W. Dirk Raat and William H. Beezley, eds. (Lincoln: University of Nebraska Press, 1986), 239. This was Bailey's last published interpretation of the Catholic Church.

77. George Grayson, *The Church in Contemporary Mexico*, 60.

78. Julio Faesler, who heads one of the most important NGO umbrella organizations on democracy in Mexico, believes priests are divided on electoral issues related to democracy. As he noted, "I spoke to Bishop Manuel Talamás, who told me he was very interested in democracy, but that if he speaks out, the newspapers will accuse him of being a PRD supporter. But he was willing to instruct his priests to tell the people of their obligation to vote, and to insist on fair elections." Personal interview, Mexico City, February 12, 1993.

79. Margaret E. Crahan, "Church and State in Latin America: Assassinating Some Old and New Stereotypes," *Daedalus* 120, no. 3 (Summer 1991): 137.

80. Soledad Loaeza, "La Iglesia católica mexicana y el reformismo autoritario," 144.

81. Alejandro Gálvez, "La iglesia mexicana frente a la política exterior e interior del gobierno de Adolfo López Mateos," in *Religión y política en México*, Martín de la Rosa and Charles A. Reilly, eds. (Mexico City: Siglo XXI, 1985), 66–67. A controversy arose over this document because in the seventh point the episcopate stated that the "prelate or confessor must determine how imperative is the obligation of citizens to participate in the elections according to moral principles and teachings," which critics charged meant the priest would determine for whom the person would vote. The archbishop of Puebla, speaking for the episcopate, clarified this shortly after publication. See also Silvia Marcela Bénard Calva, "The Relationship between Church and State in Mexico," 40.

82. Conferencia del Episcopado Mexicano, *Compromiso cristiano ante las opciones sociales y la política*, 19.

83. Conferencia del Episcopado Mexicano, "Free and Democratic Elections: A Challenge for Mexico's Destiny," 10.

84. Conferencia del Episcopado Mexicano, *Presencia de la iglesia en el mundo de la educación en México, instrucción pastoral* (Mexico City: CEM, 1988), 30.

85. Rodrigo Vera, "Ante las elecciones, los obispos católicos claman: a votar y a no dejarse defraudar," *Proceso*, August 5, 1991, 11, 13.

86. Abraham Nuncio, *El PAN, alternativa de poder o instrumento de la oligarquía empresarial*, 99.

87. *La Jornada*, April 22, 1993, 3; Lucía Alonso Reyes, "Función social de la iglesia en Zacatecas," 195; Javier Lozano Barragán, "Relaciones iglesia-estado, instrucción doctrinal," 2.

88. *El Nacional*, November 6, 1992, 7. Other bishops, in pastoral letters on elections,

have offered specific statements on this issue. For example, Javier Lozano Barragán of Zacatecas made clear his opposition to any party relying on Marxist-Leninist principles, which he defined as destructive of individual dignity. "Ante las futuras elecciones," *Documentación e Información Católica*, April 1985, 313–314.

89. Oscar Hinojosa and Rodrigo Vera, "Política de dos caras ante el problema religioso," *Proceso*, August 14, 1989, 20.

90. *Documentación y Información Católica* 15 (January 29, 1987): 50.

91. Roberto Blancarte, *El poder salinismo e iglesia católica, una nueva convivencia?*, 55.

92. David Torres Mejía, "El regreso de la iglesia," in *Política y partidos en las elecciones federales de 1985* (Mexico City: UNAM, 1987), 24–25.

93. MORI de México, *Encuesta Semanal*, December 11, 1992, n.p.

94. Bernardo Barranco and Raquel Pastor, "La presencia de la iglesia católica en el proceso de sucesión presidencial 1988," *Análisis Sociales*, no. 2 (1988): 59.

95. Conferencia del Episcopado Mexicano, "Free and Democratic Elections," 10.

96. Daniel H. Levine, "Religion and Politics: Dimensions of Renewal," *Thought* 59, no. 233 (June 1984): 117.

97. *Documentación y Información Católica* 15 (January 22, 1987): 29, citing "Catholics and Democracy," Parts 1–2, which accuses the government of a "party dictatorship, revealing a marked contrast between a democratic image which it presents abroad and the limitations it imposes on its own citizens."

98. The Church itself lays the blame on the political system. For example, cardinal archbishop of Mexico, Ernesto Corripio Ahumada, suggested that "[t]he 'indifference and disinterest' of Mexicans in social problems are the fruit of the deformed image of politics that has been created in our country." Manuel Robles, "En las elecciones, la Iglesia 'no dará sino orientaciones': Corripio," 12.

99. Ricardo de la Peña and Rosario Toledano Laguardia, "Capitalinos: el 55%, insatisfechos con nuestra democracia," *Etcétera*, February 11, 1993, 20, based on a survey of Federal District residents.

100. Sixty-six percent of the priests Enrique Luengo interviewed agreed with this statement. "Los párrocos: una visión," 97.

101. Soledad Loaeza, "Cambios en la cultura mexicana: el surgimiento de una derecha moderna (1970–1988)," *Revista Mexicana de Sociología* 51, no. 3 (July–September 1989): 227.

102. Otto Granados Roldán, *La iglesia católica mexicana como grupo de presión*, Cuadernos de Humanidades Series, no. 17 (Mexico City: UNAM, Departamento de Humanidades, 1981), 52.

103. Guillermo Correa, "Une a intelectuales e iglesia, la lucha contra la imposición electoral," *Proceso*, September 1, 1986, 28.

104. *Denver Post*, July 2, 1988, n.p.

105. Manuel Olimón Nolasco, *Tensiones y acercamientos, la iglesia y el estado en la historia del pueblo mexicano* (Mexico City: Instituto Mexicano de Doctrina Social Cristiana, 1990), 54.

106. John J Bailey, "The PRI and Liberalization in Mexico," *Journal of International Affairs* 43, no. 2 (Winter 1990): 291–312.

107. Miguel Concha, "La iglesia y las pasadas elecciones," *Análisis Sociales* no. 2 (1988): 69–70.

108. Rodrigo Vera, "Ante las elecciones, los obispos católicos claman," 12.

109. Joe Keenan, "Showdown in San Luis Potosí," *El Financiero Internacional*, September 30, 1991, 14.

110. By far the most comprehensive bibliography on the event, and an outstanding source, is María Cristina Bernal, "Relaciones Iglesia-Estado en México: Las elecciones de 1986 en Chihuahua," *Cuadernos Políticos* (1989): 48–68.

111. Dennis Goulet, "The Mexican Church: Into the Public Arena," *America,* April 8, 1989, 319. Almeida offered an early warning when he told Enrique Krauze that the people were tired of these deceptions and that violence would occur if the vote was not respected. See his "Chihuahua, Ida y Vuelta," *Vuelta* no. 115 (June 1986): 37. The northern pastoral region, including Almeida, already had issued a comprehensive statement addressed to laity who were party activists. See *Documentación e Información Católica* 14 (April 1986): 209–214. The most insightful case study of this incident and the historical antecedents in Chihuahua can be found in Vikran Khub Chand's excellent Ph.D. dissertation, "Politics, Institutions, and Democracy in Mexico: The Politics of the State of Chihuahua in National Perspective," Harvard University, May 1991, 183–262. Among other findings, Chand demonstrates that Almeida and Manuel Talamás, key players in the pastoral declarations, were present at all four sessions of Vatican II and at the Medellín Conference. He also demonstrates clearly that unlike the social justice issues of the 1970s, which were too radical for the populace, electoral reform in the 1980s struck a sharp, sympathetic chord among Chihuahuans, priests, and bishops. For another case study of the Church's role in democratization, see Víctor González Muro's excellent analysis of Ciudad Juárez, *Iglesia y movimiento sociales en México, 1972–1987* (Zamora: El Colegio de Michoacán, 1994).

112. Javier Contreras Orozco, *Chihuahua, trampa del sistema* (Mexico City: EDAMEX, 1987), 63–64.

113. *La Jornada,* November 17, 1988, 4; Víctor Gabriel Muro González, "Iglesia y movimientos sociales en México, 1972–1982, los casos de Ciudad Juárez y el istmo de Tehuantepec," unpublished Ph.D. dissertation, Colegio de México, August 1991, 278. *Proceso,* August 18, 1986, 16, provides a complete list of the bishops that cuts across all wings of the Church, suggesting how uniform higher clergy's attitudes are toward election abuse.

114. Almeida has not been described as an extremist. Porfirio Muñoz Ledo, a prominent government official and former PRI president in 1986, knew the archbishop well and considers the situation to have been very special. Personal interview with Porfirio Muñoz Ledo, president of the PRD, Mexico City, February 21, 1991. Another former government official from an important 19th-century Liberal family agreed: "I'm one of those who believes that the announcements by the bishops in northern Mexico are exceptional, and that they do indeed have a responsibility, just as Father Hidalgo, to express themselves." Personal interview with Sealtiel Alatriste, Mexico City, June 3, 1988.

115. One of the peculiar consequences is that a representative of the National Institute of Anthropology and History suggested to the Mexican media that the bishops could not carry out their threat because the churches are national property, specified in Article 27, part II, of the pre-1992 constitution. Javier Contreras Orozco, *Chihuahua, trampa del sistema,* 67. The homily can be found in *Documentación e Información Católica* 14 (July 1986): 503–504.

116. The general outlines can be found in George Grayson, *The Church in Contemporary Mexico,* 60.

117. Jaime Pérez Mendoza, "Por petición de Bartlett El Vaticano ordenó que hubiera misas en Chihuahua," *Proceso,* August 4, 1986, 7.

118. Personal interview with Archbishop Jirolamo Prigione, Vatican Delegate, Mexico City, June 2, 1987.

119. Personal interview with Archbishop Jirolamo Prigione.

120. Rene Delgado, "Delegado Prigione: notas autobiográficas," *Este País,* June 1991, 23.

121. This is a major point of contention. Almeida continues to believe that Prigione, at Bartlett's insistence, spoke to the Vatican rather than acting on the orders of the Mexican episcopate. See Rodrigo Vera, "La visita del Papa a Salinas, arranque de las nuevas relaciones," *Proceso,* January 1, 1990, 10. Prigione, during my interview, personally took credit for averting the boycott, never mentioning that the Mexican episcopate asked him to take these actions.

122. Jaime Pérez Mendoza, "Por petición de Bartlett El Vaticano ordenó que hubiera misas en Chihuahua," 6.

123. *Unomásuno,* December 14, 1988, n.p.

124. Víctor Gabriel Muro González, "Iglesia y movimientos sociales en México, 1972–1982," 277–278.

125. Francisco Ortiz Pinchetti, "El caso Chihuahua transita al ámbito religioso," *Proceso,* July 6, 1987, 8.

126. Dennis Goulet, "The Mexican Church; Into the Public Arena," 319.

127. *Washington Post,* August 13, 1986, A9.

128. Guillermo Correa, "Une a intelectuales e Iglesia," 28.

129. Francisco Ortiz Pinchetti, "Con nuevos obispos se desmantela la Iglesia contestataria de Chihuahua," *Proceso,* March 9, 1992, 30.

130. Rafael Segovia, "Modernization and Political Restoration," in *Sucesión Presidencial: The 1988 Mexican Presidential Elections,* Edgar W. Butler and Jorge A. Bustamante, eds. (Boulder, Colo.: Westview Press, 1991), 68.

131. Allan Metz, "Church-State Relations in Contemporary Mexico, 1968–1988," in *The Religious Challenge to the State,* Matthew C. Moen and Lowell S. Gustafson, eds. (Philadelphia: Temple University Press, 1992), 117; *Hispano Americano,* March 10, 1987, 69; Dennis Goulet, "The Mexican Church: Into the Public Arena," 321; Luis Guzmán García, "También en la Iglesia hay corrientes," 395.

132. Oscar Aguilar and Ismael Martínez, "La Iglesia católica mexicana como factor del riesgo para la estabilidad del sistema político mexicano," unpublished manuscript, May 1987, 6, 16–17, and Annex.

133. José Luis Gaona Vega, "La Iglesia quiere influir en la sucesión presidencial," *Punto,* March 2, 1987, 9.

134. *Documentación e Información Católica,* 15 (May 14, 1987): 365; Conferencia del Episcopado Mexicano, "Consideraciones acerca Articulo 343 del CFE," February 18, 1986; *Excélsior,* February 25, 1987, 11A; *Documentación e Información Católica* 15 (March 5, 1987): 143–144. Father Domingo Arteaga Castañeda actually took the president, the secretary of government, and the chamber of deputies to court, alleging that Article 343 violated his constitutional rights and those found in international agreements signed by Mexico. See Allan Metz, "Church-State Relations in Contemporary Mexico," 117.

135. Conferencia del Episcopado Mexicano, "Carta pastoral del episcopado mexicano sobre el desarrollo e integración del país," (Mexico City: CEM, 1968), 10.

136. Jean Meyer, "Las organizaciones religiosas como fuerzas políticas de substitución: el caso mexicano," *Christus* 41 (December 1976): 34.

137. Almeida, whose posture is non-Marxist but socially responsible, has a long history of supporting progressive statements, politically and socially, as both this and the Chihuahuan incident illustrate. His sympathies can be explained in large part by his extensive involvement in the Conference of Latin American Bishops and Vatican II and his active participation as an adviser to numerous Catholic Action organizations. *Enciclopedia de la*

iglesia católica en México (Mexico City: Enciclopedia de México, 1982), 197; *Proceso,* August 4, 1986, 8; Rubén Rocha Chávez, *Obispos de la Nueva Vizcaya, en la histórica conmemoración, 1620–1991* (Chihuahua, 1991), 71–74.

138. Dennis M. Hanratty, "Change and Conflict in the Contemporary Mexican Catholic Church," 164, 173, 199–200.

139. Conferencia del Episcopado Mexicano, *Compromiso cristiano ante las opciones sociales y la política,* 26.

140. Thomas G. Sanders, "The Puebla Conference," *American Universities Field Staff Reports,* no. 3, South America, 1979, 4.

141. Roberto Blancarte, "La Iglesia católica en México desde 1919," 38.

142. For example, the Church leadership took a position on the much debated Laguna Verde nuclear power plant in Veracruz. Cardinal Corripio toured it, claiming that it offered no threat to humans. On the other hand, in two pastoral letters seven regional bishops, including Sergio Obeso Rivera, president of the Conference of Mexican Bishops, opposed continued construction and supported public demonstrations and awareness of the risks. Allan Metz, "Mexican Church-State Relations under President Carlos Salinas de Gortari," 121.

143. Dennis Goulet, "The Mexican Church: Into the Public Arena," 319.

144. Personal interview with Bishop Raúl Vera López, Ciudad Altamirano Diocese, Guerrero, Mexico City, May 3, 1992. In 1988, the bishop of Zacatecas accused the government's economic solidarity pact of not functioning, implying the sacrifices of the working classes were too great. Lucía Alonso Reyes, "Función social de la iglesia en Zacatecas," 194.

145. *Miami Herald,* September 4, 1992, n.p.

146. *La Jornada,* April 20, 1993, 8. This critical line of thinking has been continued publicly by the new cardinal of the Mexico archdiocese, Norberto Rivera, who in a 10th anniversary homily on the devastating 1985 earthquake, argued that the present economic crisis was more significant and that it was economic, political, and moral, calling for a "change in the current course toward neo-liberal capitalism." This provoked criticism from PRI legislators and again suggests the lines of future conflict. *El Financiero International,* September 25, 1995, 2.

147. This posture can be clearly seen in the episcopate's message, "Por la justicia, la reconciliación y la paz en México," *Signo de los Tiempos* 10, no. 55 (March–April 1994): 31–34.

4

Issues Facing the Church

Moral and Spiritual Challenges

The primary issues facing the Mexican Catholic Church cannot easily be separated into temporal and spiritual or political and nonpolitical issues. Most of the significant problems for the Church since the 1970s have important, secular implications, often of a political nature. Nevertheless, the Church's posture on human rights, liberation theology, and Protestantism, which are grouped together for reasons of convenience rather than for scholarly logic, do share stronger theological foundations than the more temporal political issues such as elections and voting analyzed in chapter 3. One of the most important moral issues, one that places the Church squarely in the political arena in Mexico, is that of human rights.

Human Rights

Human rights and the clergy's role first received attention in South and Central America. In the region south of Mexico, where repressive military regimes dominated during most of the 1970s, many bishops and clergy were sensitized to the "close relationship between the existing unequal arrangement of economic and political power and the systematic violation of civil rights of individuals and groups." [1]

Mexico's Catholic Church, with some exceptions, came much later to this realization, at least publicly. Compared to Latin American human rights abuses frequently identified in the popular and scholarly literature, Mexico's were largely ignored. Despite its low-key image on human rights, its record is poor at best. According to recent observers, Mexico is increasing the potential for violence. In 1989, the Jesuit Center for Human Rights Miguel Agustín Pro Juárez recorded a 400 percent increase in human rights abuses in urban areas. [2] Americas Watch, the major international organization with a specific Latin American focus, confirms these conditions and offers a pessimistic assessment of Mexico's future human rights picture. [3]

The Catholic Church can take little comfort in its civil rights posture at the beginning of the 1970s, following its questionable behavior during the 1968 student massacre in Mexico City. The episcopate addressed the military repression on October 9 through Archbishop Ernesto Corripio, then president of the Mexican episcopate, saying only that it opposed violence and favored authentic dialogue.[4] Priests who were members of the episcopate's social secretariat, as well as Jesuits from the Ibero-American University, protested the repression against students and bystanders. A year later, a group of nuns and priests attempted to celebrate Masses for those killed, but the cardinal archbishop of the Mexico City Archdiocese prohibited their efforts in all but one church.[5] Leaders of the social secretariat and Bishop Sergio Méndez Arceo assisted imprisoned students and leaders, essentially political prisoners, in the days and months following the events at Tlatelolco Plaza.[6] When the episcopate assembled in January 1970, Méndez Arceo informed his fellow bishops of the condition of the political prisoners. The episcopate, however, made no references to the massacre itself or to the outcome.[7]

Although the Church took a weak stance in denouncing government repression and in helping its victims, these events affected the Church internally. The student massacre strongly influenced the attitudes of many individual clergy and the episcopate's social secretariat, the agency designed to oversee ecclesiastical social action policy.[8] The events of 1968, according to Mexican Jesuits, contributed to their decision to shift from elite education to social action programs among the urban poor.[9]

The Puebla conference and the Pope's visit in 1979 continued to reinforce a positive, activist stance on human rights but did not stimulate any overt activity among the higher clergy. Although the Puebla conference indicated no retreat from the Church's earlier position on human rights,[10] the Pope, rather than stressing general human rights, urged Mexicans to speak out against attacks on their fellow citizens' religious liberty.[11]

A strong case can be made for the interpretation that the Mexican Church's limited legal status under severe constitutional restrictions deflected an interest away from general human rights abuses toward those involving the clergy or the issue of religious rights. In the early 1980s, for example, the episcopate called for an open debate on Article 130 of the constitution on whether its educational provisions complied with the United Nations' Charter on Human Rights.[12] Again, in the mid-1980s, the episcopate made the same request about all religiously related articles in the constitution.[13] In 1987, much of the bishops' criticism of the electoral law focused on human rights issues. As Sergio Obeso Rivera, then president of the episcopate, remarked, it "opened the way to the violation of basic human rights, rights which Mexico supported at an international level," a position the episcopate advertised in the media.[14] Following the highly disputed 1988 presidential elections, the episcopate conference, held in Guadalajara in November, argued that fundamental human rights were being violated.[15]

Mexico's gradual evolution to a stronger, more vociferously expressed posture on human rights seems to have followed a pattern found elsewhere in the region. The basis of Church interest is not rooted in politics but is a moral judgment found in the Christian faith in the completion of preaching the gospel.[16] Although the concrete foundation for a temporal, activist posture extends back to the 1968 Medellín, Colombia, conference, as Brian Smith notes, Church human rights programs basically were reactive strategies responding to unforeseen crises in secular society. He argues that promoting human rights did not become a conscious policy in any national Latin American Catholic hierarchy until it was stimulated to act by rank-and-file laypersons or priests or by groups outside the Church.[17]

The religious orders, not the diocesan clergy, took the lead in Mexico's Catholic human rights movement. The Dominicans founded the first Centro de Derechos Humanos "Fray Francisco de Vitoria" to provide legal assistance to victims and to document the abuses. In February 1988, the Jesuits established their organization to defend human rights and to promote the fundamental objectives of defending human rights and the political rights of organizations to fight for structural change.[18] The Jesuit-run Miguel A. Pro Human Rights Center has taken the most active posture nationally of any Church-related group. In February 1990, it issued a scathing critique of the Mexican government's human rights record for 1989, "citing scores of murders, kidnappings and incidents of torture by the police, the armed forces and PRI loyalists. The report accused the government of widespread fraud in state elections, and criticized economic austerity measures that are hurting the poor. It was the third time that the . . . Center had issued a report on the government, but the first time it had given the study to the news media."[19] After *Proceso* cited the report, the secretary of government called in the Jesuits, warning them that the president was upset.

On the regional level, such organizations as the San Cristóbal de las Casas diocese's Friar Bartolomé de las Casas Human Rights Center, founded by Bishop Samuel Ruiz, have focused specifically on abuses against indigenous peoples, confronting local authorities on more than one occasion.[20] Importantly, Ruiz's efforts among the indigenous people strengthened his contacts with Protestants, especially the Methodist Church. As César Pérez concludes, government authorities, led by the then governor of Chiapas, Patrocinio González Blanco Garrido, whose administration was repeatedly accused of human rights abuses, tried to promote divisions among various church groups to strengthen his own position. The Methodists made a declaration supporting Ruiz's defense of Indian rights and in 1993 gave serious consideration to establishing jointly with other Protestant churches their own human rights commission.[21] The Methodist proposal has significant potential consequences for collaboration among the various religious groups and in changing the traditionally narrow temporal focus of Protestants and evangelicals to encompass broader human social issues. Similar to Catholic clergy, such interests will connect them with political activities and tensions at the state and local levels.

The collective Catholic hierarchy, however, has not adopted the sharply critical Jesuit view as its own. Individual bishops, or groups of bishops, have offered criticisms of government or military abuses on par with those of the Jesuits.[22] More typically, higher clergy have presented a moderate position on human rights. Mexican bishops appear to be responding to several themes in their evolving role on this issue: establishing a balance between evangelization versus humanization, achieving a clear understanding of its relation to the state, and establishing an authority to confront such injustice.[23] In other Latin American countries, the Catholic Church relied heavily on international linkages, both financial and material, to support its efforts.[24] In Mexico, however, the hierarchy has not made a similar use of such ties. In fact, representatives of the hierarchy actually rejected the Inter-American Commission on Human Rights' participation in Mexican electoral affairs.[25] In some cases, individual bishops also resisted collaborating with secular, domestic human rights groups.[26]

Since 1990, however, Church leadership began moving decisively and coherently in the rapidly changing political context. The leadership shifted cautiously on this issue for the same reason that it presented a similar stance on electoral fraud and voting: fear of being accused of partisanship. Archbishop Rosendo Huesca explains the Church's dilemma:

> It is certain that the Church plays a formative role as a force for human rights, and it has done that in the past. But today, in Mexico, there is great risk about it becoming politicized. In this country the system is seen as the aggressor, therefore, any accusations against these abuses are pounced on by opposition parties, who then claim support for the human rights institutions. This is very difficult situation for us because we cannot become identified with the political parties themselves. I am a freelancer, I want to defend human rights on my own, but I don't want political parties supporting me or taking advantage of my position. On the other hand, if we don't pursue these goals, we will lose our own legitimacy.[27]

Other bishops agreed with Huesca's explanation but also were convinced that despite the risks, the Church must pursue an active defense of human rights. As the bishop of Cuautitlán, México, argued, "When you deal with human rights, although there are risks for the Church in taking a stand in this area, it is my opinion that the hierarchy must take a position on this and must carry out its obligations in dealing with human rights abuses."[28]

Despite the Church's caution, it is receiving mixed messages from the government and other sectors of society. Ironically, in April 1991, the Mexican episcopate met with Jorge Carpizo, then director general of the governmental National Human Rights Commission. During a three-hour, closed meeting, Carpizo told the bishops that they should take a more active, direct role in the defense of human rights.[29] The fact that Carpizo urged the bishops to pursue such a mission takes on added significance given his appointment in January 1994 as secretary of government, Mexico's national security cabinet agency. Leaders from nongovernmental organizations also are encouraging the Church to heighten its visibility on human rights issues. Julio Faesler, prominent ex–public official who presides over the Acuerdo Nacional para la Democracia (ACUDE), a leading civic organization monitoring electoral abuses, believes the Church should use the pulpit more frequently to focus attention on human rights and to promote social responsibility among the citizenry.[30]

Mexican bishops received a threatening, contrary message from another source. Their strong and unified interest in human rights was translated formally in 1992 into a diocesan organization in the Mexico City archdiocese. The newly appointed director of that human rights office, Teresa Jardi, received death threats. Some analysts charged that details contained in these threats suggest that they came from security forces and the police, groups responsible for most reported violations.[31] Those holding this view suggest that the Mexican state, or more likely, certain elements within the state, were sending a different message to the Catholic Church: that its newfound freedom under the constitution did not extend to human rights. Some priests even believe that Cardinal Posadas, murdered in 1993, may have been killed because of his outspoken posture on human rights, especially in denouncing numerous deaths resulting from the Pemex explosion in Guadalajara.[32]

By the summer of 1992, the Mexican episcopate had taken the unequivocal position that "the promotion and defense of human rights, particularly religious liberty, has to be one of our principle tasks."[33] The view of the laity corresponds with that of bishops. Among Mexicans who thought they should involve themselves more in Church activities, human rights ranked only behind education in importance.[34] Interviews with individual bishops confirm the developing consensus among the higher clergy during this period, as do interviews with lower clergy.[35]

> All bishops, in my opinion, believe that it is the obligation of the Church to protect human rights. Many times these abuses are contrary to our constitution, and these too have to be regularized in terms of theory versus practice. . . . I don't think there's any bishop who doesn't believe in these rights.
>
> —Cardinal of Guadalajara[36]

> When we defend human rights we are defending liberty and human dignity independently of the posture of political parties. This is part of the Church's mission, because he who doesn't encounter God in man will not encounter him anywhere. We are the children of God, we are brothers, and to attack the dignity of man is to offend God. For this reason, the Church, with complete rights, is completing its mission, entering into the defense of human rights.
>
> —Archbishop of Chihuahua[37]

> I think the role of the Church in this area of human rights is definitive. They are defending the rights of God in the realization of human welfare against the abuses and excessive behavior of others. Our position would be firm on the moral issues, but in politics, no.
>
> —Bishop of Texcoco[38]

> I think the motivation for human rights is stronger today, but it always has been a traditional role of the Church in the past. The right of association, social justice, and other concepts, these are part of the evangelical function. We are now cooperating with other civil institutions and the United Nations' organizations. We must help people in a transcendental sense to focus on all human values.
>
> —Bishop of Aguascalientes[39]

Within the clergy elsewhere in Latin America, human rights efforts produced significant conflict. It has been suggested, however, that divisions occurred not over the Church's responsibility in the human rights arena but over the means the Church might employ in their defense.[40] This appears to be true in Mexico, especially when human rights become directly involved in partisan political issues. Of course, human rights abuses involving the government are automatically placed squarely on a political agenda. As Archbishop Huesca suggested, although most bishops would like to avoid their stance being labeled partisan, it is difficult. Another bishop suggested that the potential conflict had more to do with the concept of liberty, with how leaders defined those who should share liberties and those who, for whatever reasons, were excluded.[41]

The Mexican clergy, unlike their Latin American counterparts, appear to have avoided becoming subjects of government physical abuse. For example, out of 6,813 reported human rights violations between 1971 and 1986, only 12 priests were victims, including three who were murdered.[42] However, since clergy number only 12,000 out of a population of 70 to 80 million during that period, they were 10 times more likely than the typical Mexican to be a victim. The Church appears to have treated human rights issues involving its own members similarly to its average parishioner. For example, when Father Rodolfo Escamilla was murdered in his office in Mexico City in April 1977, the hierarchy made no public declaration. They took the same position in the murder of Father Rodolfo Aguilar Alvarez in Chihuahua a month earlier.[43] These and other cases have been linked to state and federal police and have never been solved. The PRI itself links these deaths to local political bosses.[44]

Two human rights–related cases in the 1990s focused attention on the issue and on clergy as victims. The case most directly linked to human rights is that of Father Joel Padrón, who repeatedly denounced violations in the San Cristóbal de las Casas diocese, the same site as the 1994 indigenous uprising.[45] State authorities arrested Padrón and kept him incommunicado. His local bishop complained, and the Mexican episcopate sent its secretary general, Manuel Pérez Gil, to see the governor of Chiapas.[46] The most notorious case, about which the motivations remain unclear, was Cardinal Posadas's murder in Guadalajara in 1993. Priests and bishops do not believe the government's account of these events. Many also believe police authorities were involved in his assassination. Their interpretations associate his murder with his denunciation of drug trafficking and his protests against the government cover-up in the deadly Pemex explosion in a residential Guadalajara neighborhood.[47]

Mexican clergy's comparative lack (compared to their Latin American peers) of direct physical involvement as human rights victims may explain why they have been slower to emphasize this issue in Mexico. Blancarte believes, however, that the explanation also lies in the fact that they did not carefully analyze the institutional causes of or the state's responsibility for human rights violations.[48]

Strangely, an issue sometimes couched in human rights terminology but more narrowly focused within the confines of Catholic religious dogma is abortion.[49] Abortion has involved many religious groups in the United States, although religiously affiliated lay groups rather than the institutional Church typically are agents in the social and political arena. The same is true in Mexico, but abortion, a significant political issue in the United States, has not provoked nearly as much attention as other themes, including other human rights issues. In Mexico, a Pro Vida (pro-life) group was founded in 1978 in opposition to the Mexican Communist Party's proposal to legalize abortion. It consists of 140 religious, educational, and secular groups, with about 27,000 members and 3,000 active volunteers. They first seriously raised the abortion issue in the February 1980 legislative session.[50]

The pro-life groups have shifted their demands specifically to the political arena by not only opposing proposed legislation or government family planning programs but more specifically calling on voters to withdraw support from parties or candidates supporting legalized abortion.[51] For example, in 1991 they criticized the candidacy of Miguel Alemán Velasco as senator of Veracruz.[52] Pro Vida has not yet successfully prevented any individual politician's electoral victory. Its greatest success occurred at the state level in Chiapas and on a tangentially related issue in the Federal District. The local Catholic Church succeeded in temporarily suspending a Chiapan abortion law passed in December 1990, threatening legislators with excommunication.[53] The Pro Vida group broadened its support beyond a single diocese by obtaining the episcopate's and Mexico City archdiocese's backing in removing Rolando de la Rosa's work from the Museum of Modern Art in January 1988. The group considered his paintings to be irreverent. Although the episcopate made a public statement favoring Pro Vida, widespread disagreement existed within the higher clergy on what they considered an issue of censorship, not human rights.[54]

Vatican II, Medellín, and Liberation Theology

The ideas presented in the Second Concilium of Bishops at the Vatican (popularly known as Vatican II) have their origins in earlier papal encyclicals and Church documents. The history of this is well known and described in detail elsewhere. Some observers of the Catholic Church consider Vatican II to be of paramount importance in the last four centuries, a critical revision of Church thinking. The most important document produced by 3,000 bishops at the concilium was *Gaudium et Spes* (The Church in the Modern World). What is unique about this statement is that its methodology is as important as its substance. Edward Cleary explains succinctly, in general theological terms, why this is so: "The methodology used in the document turns traditional theory on its head. Instead of proceeding in the time-honored fashion, discussing theological or biblical principles and then applying them to a present-day situation, *Gaudium et Spes* reverses the process: it begins with a careful analysis of the de facto situation, then turns to sacred scripture and theology for reflection on that situation, and finally, as a third step, makes pastoral applications."[55]

Mexican bishops, as did their colleagues throughout the world, attended this rare Vatican council. Adolfo Hernández Hurtado, who was only 38 years old when he became bishop of Tapachula, Chiapas, in 1958, remembers the concilium with considerable awe:

> There was nearly complete unity, and the results of the vote were almost immediate. Vatican II incorporated many interesting themes, but the most important for me was the integration of all classes, social groups, ethnic backgrounds into one group of human beings. It was an incredible experience to be in St. Paul's.[56]

For Latin American bishops, the practical consequences of Vatican II's philosophy, interpreted in a very progressive manner, appeared within the documents produced at the 1968 Latin American Bishops Conference (CELAM) in Medellín, Colombia. In effect, the Medellín conference exposed Latin America to the results of Vatican II. CELAM's statements argued that tyranny did not apply to individual dictators alone but was equally applicable to unjust social structures.[57] Even the Church's position on sin shifted; sin was seen as a structural situation having origins in social oppression and injustice rather than personal behavior and morality.[58] Vatican II also increased the role of women in the Church.[59] Finally, by switching the liturgy and ritual from Latin to local languages, the Church encouraged Bible study as a central religious practice.[60]

Mexican bishops view the impact of Vatican II and the Medellín conference from a variety of perspectives. Even those unsympathetic to liberation theology per se, foreshadowed by Vatican II, found interpretations and concepts with which they could identify, believing that much of Vatican II was later misinterpreted by those strongly sympathetic to liberation theology. Moderates, who represent the mainstream within the Mexican episcopate, argue that Vatican II reinvigorated and revived the Church's important role in determining social values without the use of violence. They also see it as linking together development and evangelization.[61]

Geography and historical experiences, however, altered the impact of Vatican II and CELAM in Mexico in the 1970s and 1980s. Although Mexican clergy were involved in the first CELAM conference in the late 1950s, they remained on the margin of the Medellín conference.[62] In the first place, priests most sympathetic to applying Vatican II's methodology, including its potential social and political consequences, only accounted for approximately 15 percent of the episcopate and 20 percent of the clergy. About 15 percent of the more than 50,000 sisters also favored this progressive current.[63] A clear indication of the progressive faction's minority status among the bishops is illustrated in the episcopate elections held in October 1973. Out of their 18 presidential council and commission directorships, only one, dealing with indigenous issues, went to a bishop openly sympathetic to this new social direction.[64]

Despite its limited reach among both bishops and priests, Mexican clergy, high and low, agree unanimously that Vatican II and the Medellín conference introduced many significant influences in Mexico. For example, changing the language of the liturgy, what might appear a minor, technical alteration, provoked little resistance in Mexico. José Garibi Rivera of the Guadalajara Archdiocese, although personally favoring retention of Latin, implemented this change immediately.[65] Other priests recall the establishment of numerous, small communities, a by-product of the changing language and of Bible study.[66]

The Catholic Church's expanding focus on a sense of community marked a second consequence in Mexico related to the first. As one bishop suggested, Vatican II not only generated a sensitivity among bishops and the Pope, "but everyone in the Church played an important role."[67] Garibi's successor, José Salazar López, established an active, consulting body in the diocese, an element of decentralization Vatican II indirectly emphasized.

An expanded conception of the Church's social role introduced a third consequence in Mexico. Bishops believe that the Mexican laity itself pursued a more activist phase.[68] Unlike some Latin American dioceses in which priests and bishops often filled these new social roles personally, few Mexican priests or bishops actively sought such functions, believing it was their responsibility to foster such perceptions among the laity.[69] Moderate, influential bishops, such as Archbishop Sergio Obeso Rivera of Jalapa, head of the Mexican episcopate in the 1980s, believe the Mexican clergy's expanded participation in secular affairs would not have been possible without Vatican II, long before the 1992 constitutional changes.[70] Others link the Church's recent active criticism and resistance to drug trafficking to Vatican II.[71]

A fourth consequence in Mexico involved melding together indigenous religious practices with Christianity. The most important of these beliefs, in the Mexican case, includes reverence for individual saints. As one bishop has noted, although the post–Vatican II policy has not been to remove the physical presence of the saints, "there has been a tendency to try to lessen the emphasis which the Mexican Church places on saints, and to create a much stronger figure in the symbol of Christ. The idea is to educate the people to have a strong faith in Christ."[72]

Another important consequence in Mexico occurred within the Church structure, specifically, in the seminary curriculum. Some priests who were seminarians during this era describe the changes as too rapid, reducing seminary discipline, shifting emphasis to secular universities, and opening preparatory programs to outsiders, including women.[73] In the 1980s, the seminaries recovered their equilibrium, restoring an emphasis on some of the earlier, positive features, while retaining useful elements introduced in the late 1960s.

In the longer run, the Mexican hierarchy expects two consequences of Vatican II to influence future Church activities. For the progressives, Vatican II and Medellín advanced many fresh ideas about the Church's potential and actual role, but Mexico has yet to fulfill their original goals. Moreover, because of the Church's ambiguous legal and political position prior to 1992, Medellín's impact never was clear in Mexico.[74] For moderate traditionalists, Vatican II defined two religious models—what one bishop labeled as ecclesiastical (traditional) and republican (post–Vatican II).[75] Although they confronted each other, sometimes rather aggressively, most Mexican bishops now realize that both models must play a role, and a greater consensus exists as to what each can contribute to the clergy.

Although these and other consequences are apparent in the Latin American literature in the post–Vatican II era, why were the effects of Vatican II and Medellín in Mexico limited? Mexican clergy offer a number of interpretations to explain the differing influences of these international and regional documents. All of them emphasize, to one degree or another, the importance of geographic, cultural, economic, and social variables in explaining significant patterns in their religious development.

Bishops and priests repeatedly stress differences between Mexican and Latin American history.[76] In the first place, nearly all of those interviewed point to the Mexican Revolution of 1910. As is true in the evolution of so many other Mexican institutions, both structurally and ideologically, including the armed forces and the government party, the revolution is essential in explaining their characteristics and behavior. Archbishop Manuel Pérez Gil, who attended the Medellín conference, believes that the problems that many South American bishops perceived as new in 1968 were already part of the post-1920s Mexican heritage. In particular, they believe the social distance between Mexican bishops and their flocks, a point stressed in a following chapter, and between many South American bishops and their parishioners was crucial. As Pérez Gil argues:

> I remember that we [Mexican bishops attending CELAM] felt somewhat strange in the Colombian environment because our own experiences were so different from that of the Colombians. We found it to be a Church quite different from the Mexican Church. We also found other differences in the style of the Argentineans and Chileans and even the Brazilians. Since we had lived under a long period of persecution, and had been close to the poor during those years, I don't think Medellín had the same impact on me that it had on other bishops who might not have had this kind of personal contact.[77]

A second explanation, also linked to the revolution, although not exclusively, is the anti-Church environment generated by the revolution, both in the Constitution of 1917 and in the immediate postrevolutionary Cristero rebellion of the 1920s. In short, Mexican priests see the revolution as creating an ambience of "cultural schizophrenia" rather than a "culture of freedom," in which a Catholic country does not allow its priests or ministers to speak out on political issues.[78] Thus, despite the deeper authoritarian control in Latin America in the 1970s and 1980s, the Church in certain respects exercised more freedom there than in Mexico.

A third explanation for the rejection of deeper Vatican II/Medellín influences stems from a belief that Mexico's problems, compared to those of Latin America, can be more accurately described as political rather than socioeconomic. Although this is not offered as universally as the first and second explanations, many priests believe that while social-economic conditions are terrible for numerous Mexicans, they are better than such conditions in many other countries in the region. For many of these priests, therefore, the essential problem is that Mexico is characterized by a corrupt and authoritarian system, by alienation, and by political frustration.[79] While they see democratic change as a means of altering this pattern, they do not see social upheaval and structural change as essential.

The most progressive elements of Vatican II and Medellín were blended together into a religious/secular philosophy popularly known as liberation theology. The origins of what is now considered liberation theology find strong roots in the British Reformation, which also describes a God who sides with the poor.[80] Liberation theology takes on many different features, conceptualized as including the following significant elements. First, liberation involves freedom from the bondage of ignorance, alienation, poverty, and oppression. Second, liberation is neither spiritual nor secular but a unique combination of religious and political freedom.[81] Third, the theology of liberation implies that citizens must participate fully in shaping their own lives. Fourth, social structures must be reordered to encourage human cooperation. Fifth, liberation theologians stress the value of equality, making it inseparable from freedom.[82] Sixth, its advocates pay close attention to the external causes of oppression and poverty and see external and internal colonialism as intertwined.[83] Seventh, liberation theology borrows conceptually from Marxist sociology, such as in its stress on mass participation, but does not believe such reliance jeopardizes its religious roots and commitment.[84] Eighth, it alters the Church's mission from a spiritualist redemption of the human race to an ethical duty to denounce injustice.[85] Ninth, it reinterprets symbols that determine the relationships between the individual and the community, the private and the public, and the political and the religious, challenging the ethics of public and private behavior.[86] Tenth, liberation theology attempts to view issues through the eyes of the poor, to share their lives, and to alter the relationship between the Church and the ordinary parishioner.[87] Eleventh, the tone of liberation theology may incite retaliation and hatred toward local and international oppressors, whereas traditional Catholicism preaches love.[88] And finally, it is assumed implicitly that the presence of these conditions will produce a stronger and more influential Church than the traditional, apolitical institution.[89]

A careful examination of these concepts makes clear why widespread application of liberationist ideas would be threatening to political institutions, as well as to many groups within the Church. Higher clergy most opposed to liberation theology, however, objected to its association with Marxism. Archbishop Manuel Castro Ruiz of Mérida, Yucatán, who is often identified in the traditionalist camp, cannot be simply categorized:

> When there is a Marxist element, liberation theology cannot be accepted. The danger in liberation theology is this Marxist element, but the positive part of liberation theology is its option for the poor. I'm very much in agreement with this and, as part of this option for the poor, helping the poor to better their lot in life. When liberation theology expounds on these themes, the Church in Mexico is in agreement.[90]

In Mexico, not only did Vatican II's general flavor not pierce traditional practices as deeply or widely as occurred elsewhere in Latin America, but its most threatening concepts to traditionalists, incorporated in liberation theology, did not achieve the same level of influence in Mexico as they did elsewhere in the region. Indeed, the Church's own comprehensive survey of regular attenders at Mass discovered that only 53 percent considered themselves well informed about it in 1986.[91] The conditions inhibiting Vatican II's influence also blocked liberation theology's influence. In addition to these adverse qualities, others were also present. Some analysts have long argued that liberation theology is strongest in those regions where state-led violence is most prevalent, a situation not present, comparatively speaking, in Mexico.[92] Others believe that a weak theological tradition of praxis characterized Mexico—that is, interpreting the secular reality—as was happening in Brazil.[93] In fact, students of the movement in Mexico describe it as having few organic origins.[94] A third element is the minor presence of foreign clergy in Mexico, a group that played a significant role in countries accepting liberation ideology.[95] A fourth explanation for Mexico's lower interest in liberation theology stems from the relatively small number of religious orders, those groups most receptive to this progressive thought.[96] In fact, the Latin American Conference of Religious (CLAR), composed of some 160,000 members from orders and congregations, supports a far more liberal posture than that of CELAM.

Furthermore, the Mexican episcopate has criticized its affiliate to this group, the Conference of Religious Institutes of Mexico.[97] Finally, John Paul II tried, since his first visit in 1979, to encourage bishops to spurn this doctrine. In May 1990, he energetically condemned liberation theology before 102 bishops in Mexico.[98]

The vehicles through which liberation theology has been applied, generating the most controversy, are the *comunidades eclesiales de base,* base ecclesiastical communities. Originally, these communities developed as a response to Church concerns for pastoral care and evangelism, especially in Brazil. They drew on the French pastoral theology emphasizing small, tightly knit Christian groups and strong lay participation and training.[99] In Latin America, sufficient priests did not exist to respond to laypeople's needs, but no specific link existed between political participation, liberation theology, and the communities. Bishops viewed these communities in 1979 as

> a small group which, by reading the Bible, participating in the sacraments, and discussing common concerns and action, will internalize a new awareness of Christianity. In the CEBs, the individual is expected to find "new interpersonal relations in the faith, deepening of the Word of God, participation in the eucharist, communion with the pastors of the particular church, and a greater commitment with justice in the social reality around them."[100]

The third CELAM conference in Puebla, Mexico, in 1979, joined base communities and liberation theology in an authentically complementary way.[101] This led to a much stronger emphasis on their social mission. As Hewitt explains, they met not only to celebrate their faith but also to translate that faith into social action, to solve the material problems affecting them, and to help the poor and oppressed to achieve justice and equality.[102] It is very important to emphasize, however, that although all CEBs are involved in Bible study, they are by no means homogenous across Latin America, nor within individual countries. "The way they link spiritual understandings and group life to social and political issues ranges across the entire gamut of alternatives."[103]

Base ecclesiastical communities offer new opportunities for small groups of ordinary citizens and pose a potential for numerous religious, social, and political consequences. Contrary to the widespread impression that all of these groups are lower class, evidence demonstrates the presence of middle-class groups who are developing an awareness of their poorer counterparts' needs.[104] In a broader sense, CEBs provide an opportunity for Latin Americans to create a sense of community, to develop friendships, to share experiences, and to talk with one another. More specifically, they give individuals the opportunity to participate in a society that discourages their participation, they create new channels for making demands, and they focus on problem solving and practical local issues.[105] In the longer term, even if their direct political linkages decline, they will continue to promote new sources and styles of leaders, who in turn will affect the larger society.[106] Specifically, they have had a tremendous influence on resocializing women, who provide the majority of participants in most such communities. Not only have CEBs affected how women view their traditional roles, but they have encouraged women to take up new social roles, generating an interest in politics where none existed before.[107]

CEBs, as a representation of the new Church theology in the late 1960s, created a limited yet significant path in Mexico. They began in 1967 with the pastoral efforts under Bishop Sergio Méndez Arceo in the Cuernavaca diocese.[108] By the 1970s, CEBs existed throughout Mexico, 70 percent operating in rural regions, and the remainder in working-class urban neighborhoods.[109] In Mexico, a typical community consisted of eight to 10 people and, as is true elsewhere in Latin America, although they share common characteristics, they are quite heterogeneous.[110] It is also true in the Mexican case that the vast majority of these communities are composed of lower, not middle, classes. The CEB founders, including Bishop Méndez Arceo, agree, without empirical data, that the majority of community leaders were religious order members.[111]

Although a sizable minority of bishops initially provided support for this movement or were neutral, the two Mexicans receiving the most attention as proactive CEB supporters were Sergio Méndez Arceo and Samuel Ruiz García, head of the San Cristóbal de las Casas diocese since 1960. Méndez Arceo generated considerable controversy in his diocese as a symbol of liberation theology. He represents to his supporters all that was positive about a Church of the Poor. To his worst detractors, he was known as the "Red Bishop," a scandalous sympathizer of socialism.[112] Indeed, Méndez Arceo publicly declared his support for socialism, arguing in 1970 that Christianity and socialism could coexist. Two years later, he was the only member of the episcopate to attend the Christians for Socialism conference.[113] He also attracted criticism because in 1970 he encouraged President Echeverría to form a committee of notable citizens to examine Mexico's most serious social and economic problems.[114] Echeverría himself viewed Méndez Arceo as Mexico's foremost proponent of liberation theology and favored his emphasis on redistribution of wealth and on the poor. He also believed that the clergy could help Mexicans learn the best means of organizing themselves in a capitalist society. Interestingly, both the president and Méndez Arceo considered labor unions essential to the success of base community organizing, but heavy state-controlled labor organizations limited their penetration.[115]

Méndez Arceo never was able to expand his individual influence or that of the base communities beyond a small proportion of Mexican dioceses. By becoming too controversial, he lost a sense of collegiality important to Mexican bishops and the episcopate. Expressed differently, many bishops told Dennis Hanratty that Méndez Arceo lacked sufficient commitment to the institutional Church.[116] Since Méndez Arceo's retirement in 1983, the Vatican delegate used his influence to select unsympathetic bishops who reversed Méndez Arceo's impact. His initial successor, Juan Jesús Posadas Ocampo, replaced 25 priests in two months.[117] Nevertheless, 10 years later, nearly half of the priests in the dioceses were still Méndez Arceo's followers.[118] Although many critics charged that Méndez Arceo politicized his diocese and its base communities, implying that its members opposed the government party, empirical evidence suggests no such support; indeed, religiosity in Cuernavaca is associated with increased PRI support.[119]

Samuel Ruiz replaced Méndez Arceo as the most reviled bishop by certain elements in Mexican society. The three-time head of the episcopate's indigenous affairs committee, Ruiz participated in both Vatican II and CELAM. Yet Ruiz, despite his role as the symbolic leader of liberation theology, heartily denies an interest in this philosophy. As he has stated repeatedly, "I do not have any interest in liberation theology as a theory; I am interested in liberation. It's the word of God that we must listen to. The reality that exists is not a theory, it is a Christian commitment. As baptized people we have a responsibility to deal with the reality."[120] He takes the following position on base communities:

> I myself would not encourage the formation of base communities. If they're base communities, by definition they emerge from the very bottom. As bishop I would not order their commencement or support these base communities. People will have to do that on their own. I do not think of myself as being part of a progressive Church. I only respond to the problems that are around me; I don't look behind or in front of me, I just respond to problems I see.[121]

Ruiz's defense of indigenous rights has embroiled him in many controversies in his diocese. With the uprising of the Zapatista Army of National Liberation in January 1994, his stature as a cleric sympathetic to the Church of the Poor received national and international attention.[122] Nevertheless, he long recognized the tremendous pressure on him and an attempt to portray him as a stereotype of a certain type of Latin American bishop, a portrait from which he has attempted to distance himself since the late 1980s.[123]

By the 1990s, about 20 percent of Mexico's bishops openly supported base ecclesiastical communities, and another 5–10 percent tolerated their presence.[124] Yet the influence of base communities may be more extensive in Mexico than is generally believed. For example, it has been asserted that no CEBs exist in the Mérida, Yucatán, archdiocese, whose archbishop is a traditionalist. Despite this perception, grassroots organizations perform functions typical of CEBs elsewhere in Mexico. These organizations were introduced in the Yucatán as *comunidades parroquiales* (parish communities). The archbishop opposed the language of liberation theology but not some of its essential concepts.[125]

In Mexico, activists and analysts alike agree that all CEBs, whatever their differences, typically focus on issues of social equality, social justice, and economic development rather than political democracy. In fact, generally they have little interest in political parties or partisan voting. Priests take the same posture. Overwhelmingly, they have told interviewers that poverty is a far more important issue than elections. Priests and nuns organize these grassroots groups, but unless they remain actively involved over long periods of time, the groups cease to function.[126] Although some observers predicted that committed priests would replace teachers as important local community leaders, sufficient Mexican clergy are not available to perform such functions even if every priest were willing.[127]

In reality, how do community-based organizations operate in Mexico? According to priests and nuns in Chiapas, central to their success are weekly meetings with catechists *(animadores),* who then return to their communities to deal with local issues. The groups initially started out discussing economic and social problems, combining it with analyzing the word of God and the Bible. Some members of these groups reportedly join other organizations such as peasant federations. Active clergy and religious believe, as does Bishop Samuel Ruiz, that it is essential that change occur among the people from the bottom up.[128] Indeed, some of the priests who now educate Chiapan residents in the goals and methodology of grassroots organizations are themselves products of the region's earliest base communities.

Priests and sisters in other parts of Mexico, when initially introducing the concept of base ecclesiastical communities, encounter resistance from parishioners who think of the Church only as a place for prayer, not work. They have found, however, that once they develop a sense of trust and respect, Mexicans quickly adopt new behaviors based on a pastoral philosophy described as "ver, pensar, actuar (to see, to think, to act)."[129]

Base communities are prohibited in many dioceses. Support from some bishops also appears to be conditional, based on the CEBs' political behavior or associations. Support among priests is more widespread. In Luengo's study, administered in dioceses containing few actual CEBs, one-fifth of the priests favored such community groups.[130] In the minds of some priests, a relationship exists between the growth of community organizations and the lack of priests. For example, many priests choose not to come to Chiapas, where social and political issues are very much part of the problems confronted daily in the diocese. Their decision, in turn, positively affects the growth of Chiapan CEBs that substitute for traditional parish priests and diocesan lay organizations.[131]

Over the last 20 years, Mexican priests and bishops have viewed CEBs positively and suspiciously. In the mid-1970s, less than 10 years after CEBs first arrived in Mexico, one-third of priests attending a conference in central Mexico (of all ages and from all regions) believed these communities were necessary to evangelize. About the same percentage agreed that Christianizing should include the promotion of justice.[132] By the mid-1980s, the president of the Mexican episcopate attended the CEBs' national meeting, symbolizing the hierarchy's general endorsement.[133] The increasingly positive reception of CEBs could also be attributed to the role they played in relief efforts immediately following the 1986 earthquake.[134] This open endorsement may stem in part from the hierarchy's perception that CEBs may be the Catholic Church's strongest defense in the fierce competition against evangelical groups.[135] Northern bishops addressed this issue in their pastoral letter, stating, "[T]he witness of your lives and your missionary zeal is an evangelizing force that helps to dispel the confusion and division fostered by the Protestant sects. . . . Let the CEB help the people not to lose, or to recover their Christian historical consciousness."[136]

One bishop sagely noted that CEBs in Mexico are not well understood and that clergy often are for or against them without comprehending their actual functions. He reports that many of his colleagues openly show their lack of confidence in the vocabulary of liberation theology and likens their posture to one of ideological warfare.[137] A generation of younger priests have been influenced generally positively by the presence of such organizations. In Brazil, for example, priests under

35 typically defined the people as the poor or oppressed.[138] In Mexico, half of all priests interviewed thought CEBs were the best form of living Catholicism. Only one-fourth disagreed with that statement.[139]

Bishops throughout Latin America, and Mexico specifically, have the same reservations about religious grassroots communities as they do about political activities in general. They fear being drawn into potentially dangerous political confrontations through popular group activities, they fear the growing salience of class-based groups and demands diluting the spiritual and religious mission of the Church, they fear undercutting the authority of bishops and clergy by legitimizing such groups, and they are afraid that redefining the Church's base according to social class precludes all classes from receiving the message of salvation.[140] Clergy who are critical of this position charge that the hierarchy does not engage sufficiently in self-criticism and has not concerned itself adequately with the option for the poor.

Protestantism

One of the most dynamic social changes in Latin America in the 1970s and 1980s is the growth of evangelical Protestantism. Mainline Protestants, such as the Methodists, have not shared in this growth. Although Mexico nationally is not in the forefront of this growth, certain regions have witnessed increasingly rapid expansion among certain Protestant faiths. This has led some analysts to claim that the major challenge to the Catholic Church's influence is not the state but competition from other religions.[141] The secretariat of government received 1,206 requests from Protestants to obtain legal recognition from 1940 through 1964. From 1968 through 1988, when President Salinas took office, the requests increased sixfold, to 8,199. By 1990, the states with the highest percentage of Protestants were Chiapas (16 percent), Tabasco (15 percent), Campeche (14 percent), and Quintana Roo (12 percent).[142]

Mexicans have converted to Protestantism for many of the same reasons that can be found elsewhere in Latin America. First, some observers suggest that activist Catholics have strayed too far from their pastoral responsibilities, leaving a spiritual void filled by the Protestant sects. This is a rather questionable assumption in the Mexican case. A better argument can be made for the widespread deficiencies in Catholic evangelization, extending back to the conquest, a weakness the hierarchy recognizes.[143] Second, spouses have encouraged many men to join these sects to eliminate their alcoholism and the abusive behavior it often entails.[144] Third, the typical individual who joins the evangelicals is religiously unaffiliated rather than a practicing Catholic who converts to Protestantism. Those states with the highest percentage of increase among the evangelicals, Baja California del Sur, Chiapas, Colima, México, Oaxaca, Querétaro, and Quintana Roo, have the highest percentage of religiously unaffiliated.[145] Fourth, Protestant converts tend to come from lower socioeconomic backgrounds.[146] Fifth, Mexicans who covert to the sects are individuals who practice their religion intensely, value home- and neighborhood-centered religious environments, are literal in their dogma, and see religion as a route to personal salvation. In particular, they are especially attracted to an organizational structure that is small and emphasizes a strong sense of community.[147] Sixth, laypersons themselves believe that Protestant groups are attractive because of the material assistance they provide, a view shared among some bishops.[148]

The increased growth of evangelical Protestants and the assertiveness of these various faiths in seeking converts engenders a conflictual and tense environment among Catholic and Protestant clergy and parishioners. In fact, the level of tension between the two religions is higher than at any other point in the last three decades.[149] The Mexican population as a whole, which remains predominantely Catholic, views these Protestant sects negatively. Many Mexicans see these new religious groups as insidious, foreign influences that are infiltrating and destroying their national religious culture and unity.[150] This view predominates despite the historical fact that on occasion Catholic clergy have cooperated with various Protestant faiths, including the Pentecostals.[151] Typically, however, Catholic bishops have been uncooperative with Protestants.[152]

Catholic clergy, including the hierarchy, echo the same sentiments as the typical layperson. Interestingly, important parallels exist in how government leaders and Church leaders respond to competition. Because both have controlled their respective secular and spiritual constituencies for so long, essentially without effective competition, they confuse threats to their sovereignty and legitimacy with threats to the state and religion. This explains why representatives of the Mexican episcopate can claim that defending the Catholic religion is an issue of national security. Specifically, they charge the sects with threatening Mexico's national sovereignty.[153] Some Mexican bishops have even publicly considered the possibility of the sects being linked to United States intelligence agencies.[154] According to Dennis Hanratty,

> The church's position is that the uncontrolled proliferation of sects in Mexico is an issue which threatens not only Catholicism but the nation as well in that the sects disrupt social peace and divide communities. Perceiving the source of the threat to be the United States, the hierarchy has not hesitated to employ anti-American language.[155]

Another interpretation, however, suggests that both the government and Church leaders respond with claims of nationalism because the Protestants are introducing new values neither institution knows how to manipulate.[156]

In fairness to the Catholic perception that these sects have introduced a destabilizing element in the culture, it is true that frequent conflicts on the local level, typically in rural villages, occur between Protestant and Catholic adherents. As one scholar concluded, "The appearance of Protestant communities sometimes provokes bloody feuds with neighboring Catholic villages, and it is still dangerous to be a Protestant in many parts of Mexico."[157] Catholic priests also view Protestant groups as aggressive, as divisive, and as producing social dissolution. Some priests perceive the Protestants not only as spreading and practicing their religion but also as attacking Catholicism.[158]

The Catholic hierarchy's suspicion toward the evangelical Protestants and their view of Catholicism as the dominant religion have influenced their perceptions of the 1992 constitutional reforms. As Cardinal Posadas remarked, "[I]t would be an injustice to give equal recognition to religious associations without taking into account the historic weight and number of members of each church and denomination." Or as the Vatican representative suggested less diplomatically, "[O]ne doesn't receive an elephant the same as an ant." [159] Some Mexicans believe that the Protestants have benefited most from the constitutional revisions because they were least likely to operate in the informal limbo during the pre-1992 church-state relationship.

A number of suppositions about the Protestant impact, based on the experience of evangelical Protestant growth in Central America and Brazil, have been suggested. In the first place, it is not true that Catholicism declines as Protestantism advances. Most Protestant converts, as suggested above, are nominal Catholics or unaffiliated. Thus Catholicism is enjoying a rebirth simultaneously with Protestantism's growth. [160] The Catholic Church, until the development of the CEBs, was not well equipped to counter the sects' influence. Because CEBs stress the same grassroots sense of community sought by those who join the sects, they provide the Catholic Church with an effective alternative. An important indirect consequence of CEBs within the Catholic Church is their ability to lay the groundwork for local democratic institutions. [161] A potentially more effective counterweight to evangelical Protestantism is the Catholic charismatic movement, which takes on many of the same features as the sects. On the other hand, at least in the case of Chihuahua, the charismatic movement establishes its own posture independent of the bishops. [162]

Originally, many theorists argued that Latin Americans were converting from Catholicism to Protestantism to avoid becoming victims of military repression. More broadly speaking, analysts made the argument that Protestants were perceived by the poor as a nonpoliticized, religious alternative. The level of converts to Protestantism potentially dampened liberation theology's most radical consequences: Catholic social activism. It would therefore be to the state's advantage to encourage evangelical growth. In Mexico, this is not a convincing argument since only in selected regions such as Chiapas did CEBs function as aggressively as grassroots political and human rights advocates. Recent research, however, contradicts the politically neutral Protestant interpretation. Andrew J. Stein discovered, for example, in examining Central American Protestants, that they are no more socially passive than their Catholic counterparts and that evangelicals attend other organizations and civic groups in numbers equal to Catholics. He also concluded that their level of support for the government does not differ from Protestants. However, among both Catholics and Protestants, those who are the least fundamental in their beliefs demonstrate lower levels of support for political systems. Protestants also vote in greater proportions than do the religiously nonaffiliated. [163]

In general terms, do Catholics and Protestants differ on broad social and political issues? In other countries, evangelical Catholics, distinguished from mainstream Catholics, share positions consistent with their Protestant counterparts. [164] A difference that does exist between Catholics and Protestants who share similar methodological and substantive religious beliefs stems from the importance of authority and obedience in the Catholic faith. Catholic clergy stress the importance of obedience, ranking it well ahead of intellectual autonomy.[165] As we will see in chapter 5, however, this does not mean that laypeople follow Church directives. What it does indicate, however, at least in the United States, is that Catholic evangelicals, if their leadership has spoken strongly on a moral-political issue, are more likely to support that interpretation than are Protestant evangelicals.[166] Studies also demonstrate that contrary to myth, Catholics in both the United States and in Europe are more politically tolerant than Protestants.[167]

The presence of Protestant groups in Mexico does expand the number of potential social actors. Although Protestants prior to 1992 were not closely linked to the government, did not establish close ties with local politicians, and were more reluctant than priests to violate constitutional norms,[168] they provide a tremendous political potential. As one of the leaders of the Democratic Revolutionary Party, a product of an Anglican heritage, argued, "[T]he Protestant church is a dissident church, but as an institution, it reflects the dissidence of society generally. Protestantism must be looked at not in theological terms, but as a choice stemming from the frustrations about typical social conditions."[169] Some scholars believe these new Protestant converts might be important sources of democratic values because they favor egalitarian political values. One of the few scholars of Mexican Protestantism concluded that Protestants do involve themselves in politics on the local level and are directly or indirectly threatening to local bosses.[170] The Protestant churches as institutions, regardless of their posture on temporal issues, exercise somewhat greater potential than does the Catholic Church because their faithful attend church twice as frequently as do Catholics.[171]

Conclusions

Liberation theology and the ecclesiastical base communities have already made their mark on the Mexican clergy and hierarchy. Whatever their influence, base communities as such are not likely to expand rapidly in the next decades. Rather, these influences have been incorporated into the diocesan structures of the Church, and the emphasis on the Church of the Poor is now incorporated in the visions of many priests and bishops, moderated by subsequent religious debates in the 1970s and 1980s.

Protestantism as an issue pushing the Church into the political arena is tangential to more direct influences. It will only become a significant temporal issue to the Church if the tensions between the evangelicals and the Catholics increase to such an extent that the state is forced to mediate between them, in the same way the Church mediated the conflict between the government and Chiapan Indians in 1994. Protestantism could also become a prickly issue if nationalism increases its importance on the political agenda in the wake of the North American Free Trade Agreement and closer economic ties between the United States and Mexico. Mexican politicians and the populace increasingly could perceive these sects associated with United States institutions, fearing threats to their national cultural sovereignty. A greater likelihood exists in the immediate future for a wave of negative reaction toward the United States as part of a longer pattern in their bilateral relations, a dispute into which the Church might easily be drawn.

A more significant issue on a day-to-day basis, and one more likely to place the Church squarely in conflict with the state and its political leadership, is its activist posture on human rights. Human rights poses a broader set of issues than Protestantism. It directly involves more secular groups, it is fundamentally rooted in Catholic dogma, and it is gaining importance as political instability and electoral violence increase. As has been demonstrated above, the Church moved away from its passive response to human rights violations not only by establishing its own institutions to monitor such abuses but also through its numerous pastoral letters and public statements. The fact that the Church increasingly is confronting the state on this issue and that widespread unanimity exists among bishops of all ideological preferences in taking a strong position ensures that the Church's posture will have political consequences. If Protestant churches that are considering the establishment of human rights organizations also emulate the Catholics, the voice of religious spokespersons is further strengthened.

That the Mexican Catholic Church will confront the state on human rights is not in question because the government itself is the primary source of such abuses. What remains to be seen is how far the state will go to force the Church to step back from its protective posture on human rights. Increasingly, the Church is linked to extranational organizations as well as domestic secular human rights groups. These ties make it more difficult for the state to manipulate Church spokespersons and to ignore critical statements emanating from individual dioceses. An excellent example of these forces coming together can be found in the indigenous guerrilla uprising in Chiapas, where the government reversed its repressive military strategy amid media accusations of summary executions and human rights abuses.

Less visible, but possibly more important, are the indirect influence of base ecclesiastical communities. These grassroots organizations and their differently named counterparts indirectly contribute to laypeople's growing awareness of social and economic issues. They clearly teach people how to organize and articulate their ideas on spiritual and nonspiritual issues. Most nongovernmental organization leaders still believe that religiously affiliated groups have not yet bridged the gap between focusing on important local social and economic issues and forging a broader political strategy for reform. Yet even their involvement in prodemocracy umbrella organizations, which have taken on the role of observing elections, introduces an entirely new civic responsibility to the average Mexican. As Daniel Levine aptly notes, in order to have any long-term impact beyond their diocese, grassroots groups need to transcend local boundaries, forging ties with other allies.[172]

The secular and religious challenges to the Catholic Church have received, as one might expect, a moderate response, but a response well grounded in many of the spiritual and political trends sweeping the region. The gradual introduction of these changing values and orientations should not be misinterpreted. Although the pace of change is gradual, the Church, long reinforcing the authoritarian culture through its own religious authoritarianism, is contributing just as importantly to breaking down those traditions. As Mexico faces new political and economic challenges on its developmental path, the Church's contributions are likely to expand rather than be withdrawn.

NOTES

1. Brian H. Smith, "Church and Human Rights in Latin America," *Journal of Inter-American Studies and World Affairs* 21 (February 1979): 117.

2. Comisión Mexicana de Defensa y Promoción de Derechos Humanos, *Report on Human Rights* (Mexico City: CMDP, 1992), 43; Rafael Rodríguez Castañeda, "Antidemocracia y violación de derechos humanos, en aras de salvaguardar el proyecto económico," *Proceso,* March 26, 1990, 14.

3. Americas Watch, *Unceasing Abuses: Human Rights in Mexico One Year after the Introduction of Reform* (New York: Americas Watch, 1991), 5.

4. Patricia Arias et al., *Radiografía de la iglesia católica en México* (Mexico City: UNAM, 1981), 14.

5. Martín de la Rosa, "La Iglesia católica en México, del Vaticano II a la CELAM III," *Cuadernos Políticos* 19 (January–March 1979): 94.

6. Dennis M. Hanratty, "Change and Conflict in the Contemporary Mexican Catholic Church," unpublished Ph.D. dissertation, Duke University, 1980, 158.

7. Martín de la Rosa, "La Iglesia católica en México," 95.

8. Allan Metz, "Church-State Relations in Contemporary Mexico, 1968–1988," in *The Religious Challenge to the State,* Matthew C. Moen and Lowell S. Gustafson, eds. (Philadelphia: Temple University Press, 1992), 107.

9. Personal interview with Father Ernesto Menenses Morales, former president of the Ibero-American University, Mexico City, June 6, 1988.

10. Carolyn Cook Dipboye, "The Roman Catholic Church and the Political Structure for Human Rights in Latin America, 1968–1980," *Journal of Church and State* 24 (Autumn 1982): 522–223.

11. Allan Metz, "Church-State Relations in Contemporary Mexico," 117.

12. Article 4 of the Universal Declaration of Human Rights contains the following: "All states shall adopt effective means of preventing and eliminating all discrimination based on religion or beliefs in the recognition, the exercise, and the enjoyment of human rights and fundamental liberties in all aspects of civil, economic, political, social, and cultural life." See Luis Reynoso, "Planteamiento del problema entre la iglesia y la comunidad política," in *La participacíon política del clero en México,* Luis J. Molina, ed. (Mexico City: UNAM, 1990), 171. For evidence of the debate, see George Grayson, *The Church in Contemporary Mexico* (Washington: CSIS, 1992), 58.

13. *Proceso,* May 13, 1985, 16.

14. Allan Metz, "Church-State Relations in Contemporary Mexico, 1968–1988," 119.

15. *Proceso,* November 28, 1988, 18.

16. Carolyn Cook Dipboye, "The Roman Catholic Church and the Political Structure for Human Rights in Latin America, 1968–1980," 513.

17. Brian H. Smith, "Church and Human Rights in Latin America," 116.

18. Comisión Mexicana de Defensa y Promoción de Derechos Humanos, *Report on Human Rights* (Mexico City: CMDP, 1992), 55–57, 72.

19. Marjorie Miller, "Mexico Church-State Relations: Stepping Out from the Shadows," *Los Angeles Times,* April 29, 1990, n.p.

20. For example, the center came under considerable criticism for protecting Indians accused of murdering two army officers. Bishop Ruiz was trying to prevent the authorities from torturing them in the interrogation process, not to protect the murderers from justice. Rodrigo Vera, "Samuel Ruiz, objeto de todos los ataques," *Proceso,* April 19, 1993, 6–7.

21. Personal interview with César Pérez, Methodist Church of Mexico, Mexico City, July 14, 1993.

22. For example, bishops in Chihuahua alleged that "under the pretext of fighting drug trafficking, there have been repeated violations of human rights among the poorest, among other Indians and peasants." *El Universal,* December 9, 1988, n.p.

23. Carolyn Cook Dipboye, "The Roman Catholic Church and the Political Structure for Human Rights in Latin America, 1968–1980," 497.

24. Brian Smith, "Church and Human Rights in Latin America," 116.

25. According to the Grupo Consultor Interdisciplinario, "Carta de política mexicana, las relaciones estado-iglesias," February 21, 1992, 6, Cardinal Juan Jesús Posadas and Archbishop Carlos Quintero argued that Mexicans were sufficiently mature to resolve these issues themselves.

26. Mariclare Acosta Urquidi, president of the Mexican Commission for the Defense and Promotion of Human Rights, explained the difficulties she had in obtaining an interview, along with the Americas Watch representative, with the archbishop of Acapulco. The archbishop nevertheless issued a pastoral letter condemning violence in Guerrero, opened his churches to Party of the Democratic Revolution partisans and their families, permitted victims of human rights abuses to stage a hunger strike, and gave homilies praising political tolerance. Personal interview, Mexico City, August 3, 1992.

27. Personal interview with Archbishop Rosendo Huesca, Puebla Archdiocese, Puebla, Puebla, July 16, 1993.

28. Personal interview with Bishop Manuel Samaniego Barriga, Cuautitlán Diocese, Cuautitlán, México, February 13, 1991.

29. Rodrigo Vera, "La violación de los derechos humanos en el país es norma de conducta," *Proceso,* April 15, 1991, 17, and *El Nacional,* April 12, 1991, n.p. Carpizo also explained that his commission would not intervene in the violation of political and labor rights, which the bishops criticized as a severe limitation.

30. Personal interview with Julio Faesler, president of the Acuerdo Nacional para la Democracia (ACUDE), Mexico City, February 12, 1993.

31. *Mexico Report,* November 4, 1992, 5.

32. Personal interview with Father Servando García, Acatlán de Juárez Parish, Jalisco, July 6, 1993.

33. Conferencia del Episcopado Mexicano, "The Declaration of Mexican Bishops Concerning the New 'Law of Religious Associations and Public Worship,' " Plenary Assembly of the CEM, August 13, 1992, 4; *Mexico Report,* November 4, 1992, 5.

34. *Este País,* May, 1994, 28.

35. As three priests suggested to me, although they disagree on many issues, they concur on the need for the Church to take a strong position and believe that it will become increasingly involved in these issues. Personal interview with Fathers Rafael Tapia, Abelardo Hernández, and Humberto Vargas, Puebla Archdiocese, Puebla, Puebla, July 16, 1993.

36. Personal interview with Cardinal Juan Jesús Posadas Ocampo, Guadalajara Archdiocese, Guadalajara, Jalisco, Mexico City, February 20, 1991.

37. Jaime Pérez Mendoza, "Por petición de Bartlett El Vaticano ordenó que hubiera misas en Chihuahua," citing Archbishop Adalberto Almeida Merino.

38. Personal interview with Bishop Magín Camarino Torreblanca Reyes, Texcoco Diocese, Texcoco, México, July 12, 1993.

39. Personal interview with Bishop Rafael Muñóz, Aguascalientes Archdiocese, Aguascalientes, Aguascalientes, Mexico City, July 15, 1993.

40. Carolyn Cook Dipboye makes this argument in "The Roman Catholic Church and the Political Structure for Human Rights in Latin America," 514.

41. Personal interview with Bishop Luis Mena, auxiliary bishop of Mexico City, Mexico Archdiocese, Mexico City, July 13, 1993.

42. Miguel Concha Malo, "Las violaciones a los derechos humanos individuales en México (periodo: 1971–1986)," in *Primero informe sobre la democracia, México 1988,* Pablo González Casanova, ed. (Mexico City: Siglo XXI, 1988), 171.

43. However, according to the late Bishop Sergio Méndez Arceo, numerous changes occurred within the dioceses where the murder took place. He noted that the diocese was restructured and the bishop retreated from some of his more progressive positions. Personal interview with Sergio Méndez Arceo, bishop emeritus of Cuernavaca Diocese, Morelos, Mexico City, June 21, 1989.

44. *Documentación e Información Católica,* 2, no. 29 (July 18, 1974): 299–300; *Unomásuno,* January 6, 1989, n.p.; *Proceso,* May 13, 1985, 20; Patricia Arias et al., *Radiografía de la iglesia católica en México,* 59. For the Partido Institucional Revolucionario's version, see PRI, "Memorandum sobre las relaciones estado-iglesia católica," November 1988, 17.

45. Extensive documentation of government abuses in the region and United States tolerance of such infractions can be found in "Mexico: The New Year's Rebellion," *Human Rights Watch—Americas* 6, no. 3 (March 1, 1994): 24–26.

46. Rodrigo Vera, "El gobierno de Chiapas fija condiciones políticas para liberar al padre Joel Padrón," *Proceso,* October 14, 1992, 18–21.

47. As one bishop argues, "[T]he problem is not just in the explanation, but in the things that haven't been said." Personal interview with Bishop Mario de Gasperín, Querétaro Diocese, Querétaro, Querétaro, July 12, 1993. Heberto Castillo, a leader of the PRD, suggested that the killers may have hoped to shoot Jirolamo Prigione, the Vatican delegate, who was meeting Posadas at the Guadalajara airport, where the assassination occurred. He believes their motive was to destabilize the country, a theory gaining more credibility since the Chiapan uprisings and the assassination of the PRI's presidential candidate, Luis Donaldo Colosio, in the early months of 1994. Personal interview, Mexico City, July 12, 1993. Bishop Luis Reynoso Cervantes, identified with the Prigione faction, also doubts Posadas's murder was a case of mistaken identity (the official version) because he was shot at a distance of only four to five feet. *Gaceta Oficial Diocesana* 6, no. 4 (July–August 1993): 11.

48. Roberto Blancarte, *El poder salinismo e iglesia católica una nueva convivencia?* (Mexico City: Grijalbo, 1991), 220.

49. For example, the bishop of Tuxtla Gutiérrez, Chiapas, denounced a state abortion law as "a violation of human rights." The Church was never consulted on the law. *Proceso,* December 24, 1990, 29.

50. Otto Granados Roldán, *La iglesia católica mexicana como grupo de presión,* Cuadernos de Humanidades, no. 17 (Mexico City: Departamento de Humanidades, 1981), 54.

51. In Chiapas, the three bishops indicated that "if we respect the life of the unborn as human beings who have all the rights to exist, we cannot support with the vote those who would involve themselves" in supporting the elimination of innocent beings. Rodrigo Vera, "Ante las elecciones, los obispos católicos claman: a votar y a no dejarse defraudar," *Proceso,* August 5, 1991, 13.

52. Ibid., 13; Marjorie Miller, "Tradition, Poverty Shape Mexico Abortion Debate," *Los Angeles Times,* April 9, 1989.

53. *Proceso,* December 24, 1990, 27; Allan Metz, "Mexican Church-State Relations under President Carlos Salinas de Gortari," *Journal of Church and State* 34, no. 1 (Winter 1992): 128.

54. Bernardo Barranco Villafan and Raquel Pastor Escobar, *Jerarquía católica y modernización política en México* (Mexico City: Palabra Ediciones, Centro Antonio de Montesinos, 1989), 55–58; Rodrigo Vera, "El respeto al pudor detiene la promoción de los condones," *Proceso,* June 17, 1989, 19.

55. Edward L. Cleary, *Crisis and Change: The Church in Latin America Today* (Maryknoll: Orbis Books, 1985), 60–61.

56. Personal interview with Auxiliary Bishop Adolfo Hernández Hurtado, Guadalajara Archdiocese, Guadalajara, Jalisco, July 7, 1993.

57. David E. Mutchler, *The Church as a Political Factor in Latin America* (New York: Praeger, 1971), 124.

58. Larissa Adler Lomnitz and Marisol Pérez-Lizaur, *A Mexican Elite Family, 1820–1980* (Princeton: Princeton University Press, 1987), 207.

59. Katherine Anne Gilfeather, "Coming of Age in Latin America," in *The Church and Women in the Third World,* John Webster and Ellen Low, eds. (Philadelphia: Westminister Press, 1985), 71.

60. Daniel H. Levine, "Assessing the Impacts of Liberation Theology in Latin America," *Review of Politics* 50 (1988): 244.

61. Personal interviews with Bishop José Melgoza Osorio, Nezahualcóyotl Diocese, Nezahualcóyotl, México, May 27, 1987, and Archbishop Manuel Pérez Gil, Tlanepantla Archdiocese, Tlanepantla, México, February 18, 1991.

62. Ricardo Cuellar Romo discovered that Latin American bishops were preoccupied with Mexico's lack of active involvement in the organization. He suggests that the main reason CELAM was held in Puebla in 1979 was to strengthen Mexico's role and symbolize its involvement. By the late 1980s, Mexican clergy were well represented in the CELAM leadership (Adolfo Suárez Rivera, archbishop of Monterrey, and Javier Lozano Barragán, bishop of Zacatecas). Personal interview, Mexico City Archdiocese, May 25, 1987.

63. Father Baltazar López, a longtime supporter of the progressive interpretation of Vatican II and Medellín in the Cuernavaca Diocese under Bishop Sergio Méndez Arceo, provided these estimates. Personal interview, Cuernavaca Diocese, Cuernavaca, Morelos, June 3, 1988.

64. Dennis Hanratty, "Change and Conflict in the Contemporary Mexican Catholic Church," 253.

65. Personal interview with Salvador Tello Robles, parish priest, Madre de Dios Parish, Guadalajara Archdiocese, Guadalajara, Jalisco, July 6, 1993.

66. For example, Father José Alvarez Franco, one of Mexico's most radical priests, who is no longer recognized by the Church, was then a member of the archdiocese's liturgy committee. He recalls working more closely with the people and celebrating Masses more openly. Personal interview, Tateposco Parish, Tonala, Jalisco, July 7, 1993.

67. Personal interview with Ramón Godínez, auxiliary bishop of the Guadalajara Archdiocese and secretary general of the Mexican Episcopate, Mexico City, July 16, 1993.

68. Personal interview with Bishop Raúl Vera López, a Dominican priest, Ciudad Altamirano Diocese, Guerrero, Mexico City, May 3, 1992.

69. Examples of specific bishops and numerous priests do, however, exist. In April 1972, Archbishop Adalberto Almeida Merino of Chihuahua met with 40 priests in San Luis Potosí to establish a group called "Priests for the People," which published a statement "stressing their desire for a Church committed to transforming society, to struggling for

justice, and responding to division already existing within the Church." Dennis M. Hanratty, "Change and Conflict in Contemporary Mexican Catholic Church," 220.

70. Oscar Hinojosa, "La misión evangélica ordena dejar la sacristía, afirma Obeso Rivera," *Proceso,* September 8, 1986, 12.

71. Personal interview with Ramón Godínez, July 16, 1993.

72. Personal interview with Bishop Abelardo Alvarado Alcantara, who at one time was in charge of all of the Comunidades de Bases in Mexico, Mexico Archdiocese, Mexico City, June 2, 1987.

73. Personal interview by Scott Pentzer and Meg Mitchell with Father Jesús López Larra de Castañeda, Zacatecas Diocese, Zacatecas, Zacatecas, July 19, 1993.

74. Bishop José Pablo Rovalo, Mexico Archdiocese, a Brother of Mary and an activist among national Catholic youth groups in the 1970s, took that position. Personal interview, Mexico City, February 21, 1991.

75. Personal interview with Bishop Mario de Gasperín, Querétaro Diocese, Querétaro, Querétaro, July 12, 1993.

76. For example, Bishop Jorge Martínez Martínez, who attended the CELAM conference in Puebla, Mexico, in 1979, suggested "the hierarchy in Mexico didn't respond to the Medellín recommendations in the same way because of their attitudes and interpretations of the conditions that existed here in Mexico. Of course, the other reason is more obvious and has to do with our historical experience." Personal interview, Mexico Archdiocese, May 28, 1987.

77. Personal interview with Archbishop Manuel Pérez Gil, Tlanepantla Archdiocese, Tlanepantla, México, February 18, 1991. Sergio Méndez Arceo, one of the Mexican bishops most influenced by CELAM, recalls an interesting incident in which the then bishop of Puebla told him and Pérez Gil that Medellín was for South America only, not Mexico. Personal interview with Sergio Méndez Arceo, Mexico City, June 21, 1989.

78. Personal interview by Scott Pentzer and Meg Mitchell with Father Carlos González Martínez, Guanajuato Diocese, Guanajuato, Guanajuato, July 10, 1993.

79. Personal interviews by Scott Pentzer and Meg Mitchell with Father Rafael Montejano Aguiñago, San Luis Potosí Diocese, San Luis Potosí, San Luis Potosí, July 13, 1993, who grew up during the Cristero rebellion, and Father Tranquilino Romero, Zacatecas Diocese, Zacatecas, Zacatecas, July 19, 1993, who was ordained in 1971, at the height of this influence.

80. John H. Yoder, "The Wider Setting of 'Liberation Theology,' " *Review of Politics* 50 (1988): 291.

81. Daniel H. Levine, *Religion and Politics in Latin America: The Catholic Church in Venezuela and Colombia* (Princeton: Princeton University Press, 1981), 46.

82. Michael Dodson, "The Christian Left in Latin American Politics," *Journal of Inter-American Studies and World Affairs* 21 (February 1979): 53.

83. Edward L. Cleary, *Crisis and Change: The Church in Latin America,* 55.

84. Daniel H. Levine, "Assessing the Impacts of Liberation Theology in Latin America," 246.

85. Cornelia Butler Flora and Rosario Bello, "The Impact of the Catholic Church on National Level Change in Latin America," *Journal of Church and State* 31, no. 3 (Autumn 1989): 532.

86. Claude Pomerlau, "The Catholic Church in Mexico and Its Changing Relationship to Society and the State," unpublished manuscript, December 1980, 17.

87. Daniel H. Levine, "Assessing the Impacts of Liberation Theology in Latin America," 243.

88. Frederick Sontag, "Liberation Theology and Its View of Political Violence," *Journal of Church and State* 31, no. 2 (Spring 1989): 286.

89. Hannah W. Stewart-Gambino, "New Approaches to Studying the Role of Religion in Latin America," *Latin American Research Review* 24, no. 3 (1989): 198.

90. Personal interview between Shannan Mattiace and Archbishop Manuel Castro Ruiz, Mérida Archdiocese, Mérida, Yucatán, August 21, 1989.

91. Comisión Episcopal para el Apostolado de los Laicos, *Qué piensan los laicos mexicanos del sínodo '87* (Mexico City: CEM, 1986), 17.

92. See, for example, Penny Lernoux, *Cry of the People: The Struggle for Human Rights in Latin America—The Catholic Church in Conflict with U.S. Policy* (New York: Penguin, 1982).

93. Dennis Goulet, "The Mexican Church: Into the Public Arena," *America,* April 8, 1989, 322.

94. Martín de la Rosa, "La Iglesia católica en México," 102.

95. Shannan Mattiace, "The Social Role of the Mexican Catholic Church: The Case of the Yucatán Base Community," senior honors thesis, Central University of Iowa, 1990, 29.

96. Personal interview with Brother Jesús Vergara Aceves, Mexico City, June 29, 1989.

97. George Grayson, *The Church in Contemporary Mexico,* 31–32, also notes that several of the most important religious research centers in Mexico City, such as the Jesuit Reflexión Teológica or the Dominican Estudios Dominicanos, favor liberationist themes, as do important religious publications such as *Christus* and *Cencos.*

98. *El Nacional,* May 13, 1990, n.p.

99. Brian Smith, "Religion and Social Change," 9.

100. Thomas G. Sanders, "The Puebla Conference," 7.

101. John H. Yoder, "The Wider Setting of 'Liberation Theology,' " *Review of Politics* 50 (1988): 286.

102. W. E. Hewitt, "Christian Base Communities (CEBS): Structure, Orientation, and Sociopolitical Thrust," *Thought* 63, no. 249 (June 1988): 164.

103. Daniel H. Levine, "Religion and Politics: Dimensions of Renewal," *Thought* 59, no. 233 (June 1984): 132; Thomas C. Bruneau, "Basic Christian Communities in Latin America: Their Nature and Significance, Especially in Brazil," in *Churches and Politics in Latin America,* Daniel Levine, ed. (Beverly Hills: Sage Publications, 1980), 226; W. E. Hewitt, "Christian Base Communities (CEBS)," 173–174.

104. W. E. Hewitt, "Christian Base Communities (CEBs)," 174.

105. Thomas C. Bruneau, "Basic Christian Communities in Latin America: Their Nature and Significance, Especially in Brazil," 227, 235.

106. Daniel H. Levine, "From Church and State to Religion and Politics and Back Again," *World Affairs* 150 (Fall 1987): 104.

107. Carol Ann Drogus, "Religious Change and Women's Status in Latin America: A Comparison of Catholic Base Communities and Pentecostal Churches," unpublished paper, Kellogg Institute for International Studies, University of Notre Dame, 1993, 3, 7, 21–22; Katherine Anne Gilfeather, "Coming of Age in a Latin Church," 69. Gilfeather reports that 66 percent of women working in slum areas showed a marked tendency to reinterpret doctrinal affirmations.

108. Claude Pomerleau, "The Changing Church in Mexico and Its Challenge to the State," *Review of Politics* 43, no. 4 (October 1981): 554.

109. Miguel Concha Malo, "Tensiones entre la religión de pueblo y las CEB's en México con sectores de la jearquía: implicaciones eclesiologicas," *Cience Tomista* 114 (May–August, 1987): 309; Martín de la Rosa, "Iglesia y sociedad en el México de hoy," in

Religión y política en México, Martín de la Rosa and Charles A. Reilly, eds. (Mexico City: Siglo XXI, 1985), 279.

110. Matilde Gastalver and Lino F. Salas, *Las comunidades eclesiales de base y el movimiento popular en México* (Mexico City: Ibero-American University, 1983), 4.

111. Personal interviews with Sergio Méndez Arceo and Miguel Concha.

112. This label was often used in the press during the 1980s. Yet when I interviewed a leading entrepreneurial figure in 1992, he criticized the "terrible damage" the "Red Bishop" Méndez Arceo, allegedly a Communist, introduced in his diocese. Personal interview with Antonio Madero Bracho, Mexico City, August 7, 1992.

113. Lauro López Beltrán, *Diocesis y obispos de Cuernavaca, 1875–1978* (Mexico, 1978), 284.

114. Personal interview with Sergio Méndez Arceo.

115. Personal interview with ex-president Luis Echeverría Alvarez, Mexico City, August 2, 1992.

116. Dennis Hanratty, "Change and Conflict in the Contemporary Mexican Catholic Church," 255.

117. Enrique Maza, "En su compromiso con los pobres, don Sergio preferió ser parte y no juez," *Proceso,* February 10, 1992, 8.

118. Rodrigo Vera, "La jerarquía en combate contra seguidores de Méndez Arceo y su obra en Morelos," *Proceso,* April 3, 1989, 18.

119. Charles L. Davis, "Religion and Partisan Loyalty: The Case of Catholic Workers in Mexico," *Western Political Quarterly* 45 (March 1992): 280.

120. Personal interview between Shannan Mattiace and Bishop Samuel Ruiz García, San Cristóbal de las Casas Diocese, San Cristóbal de las Casas, Chiapas, August 15, 1989; personal interview with Bishop Samuel Ruiz García, Lago de Guadalupe, Cuautitlán, México, April 20, 1992.

121. Personal interview with Shannan Mattiace.

122. For example, an advertisement in *El Nacional,* written by Gustavo de Anda, condemns Ruiz as an international agitator who used his position to obtain funds to support the Zapatistas. "El Verdadero Samuel Ruiz," *El Nacional,* July 19, 1994, n.p. President Salinas asked Cardinal Corripio to denounce the Zapatistas on January 4, 1994. Corripio flatly turned down his request. See Michael Tangeman, *Mexico at the Crossroads: Politics, the Church, and the Poor* (Maryknoll: Orbis Books, 1994).

123. His self-description squares with that of a sister who has worked many years in his diocese as a base-community organizer. She described him as follows: "He experienced a great personal change at Medellín when he realized the plight of the poor and the social situation that he was facing as bishop of San Cristóbal. . . . Bishop Ruiz walks in the jungle with the people. He lives with them, sleeps where they do, and doesn't presume anything for himself or take personal credit. Ruiz gives all the credit to religious and lay people who work with the poor . . . He just animates the clergy and gives them support, but it's their job." Personal interview between Shannan Mattiace and Sister Efigenia Vásquez, San Cristóbal de las Casas Diocese, San Cristóbal de las Casas, Chiapas, August 15, 1989.

124. Cindy Anders, "No Power, No Glory," *Proceso,* June 15, 1989, 20.

125. Shannan Mattiace, "The Social Role of the Mexican Catholic Church," 40–41.

126. W. E. Hewitt, "Christian Base Communities (CEBs)," 174; Edward L. Cleary, *Crisis and Change: The Church in Latin America,* 142.

127. Soledad Loaeza citing Pablo González Casanova in "La iglesia y la democracia en México," 163.

128. Personal interview between Shannan Mattiace and Sister Efigenia Vásquez.

129. Personal interview by Scott Pentzer and Meg Mitchell with Father Ochoa Aguilar and layworker Ms. Faviola Díaz Elías, San Luis Potosí Diocese, July 14, 1993.

130. Enrique Luengo, "Los párrocos: una visión," 62.

131. Personal interview between Shannan Mattiace and Father Ramón Castillo Aguilar, San Cristóbal de las Casas Diocese, San Cristóbal de las Casas, Chiapas, August 14, 1989.

132. José María Díaz Mozaz and Vicente J. Sastre, "Una encuesta de opinión al clergo mexicano, aproximación a la realidad socio-religiosa mexicana," *Vida Pastoral* 2, no. 11 (August 1976): 14, 16.

133. Dennis M. Hanratty, "The Church," in *Prospects for Mexico,* George W. Grayson, ed. (Washington: Center for the Study of Foreign Affairs, 1988), 116.

134. Michael Tangeman, *Mexico at the Crossroads: Politics, the Church, and the Poor,* 119.

135. Dennis M. Hanratty, "Church-State Relations in Mexico in the 1980s," *Thought* 63, no. 250 (1988): 212.

136. *Documentacion e Información Católica* 13 (June 13, 1985): 429–430. David L. Clawson, in his case study of a Mexican village, also has remarked that the only way for the Catholic Church to compete against the Protestant faiths is to develop a small church ambience duplicating the sense of community among the Protestant churches. He believes CEBs could conceivably perform such a function. "Religion and Change in a Mexican Village," *Journal of Cultural Geography* 9, no. 2 (1989): 69.

137. Bishop Jorge Martínez Martínez's diary is full of significant insights. *Memorias y reflexiones de un obispo* (Mexico: Editorial Villicaña, 1986), 27, 36.

138. David Lehmann, *Democracy and Development in Latin America: Economics, Politics, and Religion in the Postwar Period* (Philadelphia: Temple University Press, 1990), 138.

139. Enrique Luengo, "Los párrocos: una visión," 90.

140. Daniel H. Levine, "Religion and Politics: Dimensions of Renewal," 134; Daniel H. Levine, "Religion, Society, and Politics: States of the Art," *Latin American Research Review* 16, no. 3 (Fall 1981): 199; Daniel H. Levine, "Assessing the Impacts of Liberation Theology in Latin America," 259.

141. Bernardo Barranco Villafan and Raquel Pastor Escobar, *Jerarquía católica y modernización política en México* (Mexico City: Palabra Ediciones, Centro Antonio de Montesinos, 1989), 29.

142. Grupo Consultor Interdisciplinario, "Carta de política mexicana, las otras iglesias, las razones del cambio y lo que viene," March 20, 1992, 2, 4. See also Secretaria de Gobernación, "Catalogo Nacional de Cultos Religiosos en México," unpublished manuscript, 1991, n.p., which lists the number of Protestant churches in each state. This is deceptive because large numbers of churches are not indicative of the percentage of residents who are Protestant. For example, Tamaulipas and Baja California have more Protestant than Catholic churches.

143. *El Nacional,* July 8, 1992, 11.

144. Personal interview with Manuel Carrillo, former adviser to the subsecretary of government (in charge of church-state affairs), Mexico City, August 4, 1992.

145. Rodolfo Casillas and Alberto Hernández, "Demografía y religión en México: una relación poco explorada," *Cristianismo y Sociedad* no. 105 (January–April 1990): 80.

146. Edwin Eloy Aguilar et al., "Protestantism in El Salvador: Conventional Wisdom versus the Survey Evidence," in *Rethinking Protestantism in Latin America,* Virginia Garrard Burnett and David Stoll, eds. (Philadelphia: Temple University Press, 1993), 9.

147. Ibid., 16; David L. Clawson, "Religion and Change in a Mexican Village," 61.

148. Catholic Church, Diocese of Tijuana, *Plan pastoral, 1989–1994, hacia una iglesia nueva* (Tijuana: La Diocese, 1989), 245.

149. Chris Woehr, "Catholic, Protestant Tensions Rise," *Christianity Today* 34 (March 19, 1990): 44.

150. Rolf Lahusen, "The Encounter between Church and Marxism in Mexico," in *The Encounter of the Church with Movements of Social Change in Various Cultural Contexts, Part 2,* Gerd Decke, ed. (Geneva: Department of Studies, Lutheran World Federation, 1977), 111.

151. For an example as early as 1914, see Guillermo Floris Margadant, *La iglesia ante el derecho mexicano, esbozo histórico-jurídico* (Mexico City: Miguel Angel Porrúa, 1991), 196.

152. An excellent example was provided by Eduardo Bustamante, secretary of government properties under President Adolfo López Mateos (1958–1964). The president's wife was a Protestant. "She had many close ties with Protestant groups in the United States. Once she went to a meeting in Oaxaca with a large group of Protestants, and during this meeting it came out that they wanted to bring gifts for needy children for Christmas. They asked her to come and present the children with the gifts, but the president's wife did not want to do this because she might have offended Catholics in the state. Instead, she called the Catholic bishop and asked him to give out the toys. However, the bishop adamantly refused because the toys were coming from Protestants rather than from Catholics." Personal interview, Mexico City, May 29, 1987.

153. Marta Eugenia García Ugarte, "Las posiciones políticas de la jerarquía católica, efectos en la cultura religiosa mexicana," in *Religiosidad y política en México,* Carlos Martínez Assad, ed. (Mexico City: Ibero-American University, 1992), 98; Allan Metz "Protestantism in Mexico: Contemporary Contextual Developments," *Journal of Church and State* 36, no. 1 (Winter 1994): 65–66.

154. Their assertions have some basis in historical fact. For evidence of this, see Gerard Colby and Charlotte Dennett, *Thy Will Be Done: The Conquest of the Amazon—Nelson Rockefeller and Evangelism in the Age of Oil* (New York: HarperCollins, 1995).

155. Dennis M. Hanratty, "Church-State Relations in Mexico in the 1980s," 211. Father Gabriel Medina Mavallanes told Scott Pentzer and Meg Mitchell that the Protestants were a "noxious U.S. import," that Catholicism and Mexican nationality were inseparable, and that the United Nations was plotting to destroy Mexican families with disinformation about birth control, sex education, and women's roles. Personal interview, Zacatecas Diocese, Zacatecas, Zacatecas, July 19, 1993. Catholic officials in Zacatecas, including Bishop Javier Lozano Barragán, have declared publicly that the sects threaten national sovereignty and that they are an attack against Mexican culture. See Lucía Alonso Reyes, "Función social de la iglesia en Zacatecas," *Memorias, segundo informe de investigación sobre el estado de Zacatecas* (Zacatecas, 1989), 192.

156. This has been suggested by Julio Faesler, personal interview.

157. Mario Méndez Acosta, "Belief and Unbelief in Mexico," *Free Inquiry* (Winter 1986–1987): 28.

158. Personal interview between Scott Pentzer and Father Rafael Ramírez Díaz, abbot of the Basilica of Guanajuato, Guanajuato Diocese, Guanajuato, Guanajuato, July 9, 1993.

159. David Scott Clark, "Mexicans Debate the Structure of New Church-State Relations," *Christian Science Monitor,* May 19, 1992, n.p.

160. Edward L. Cleary, "Politics and Religion—Crisis, Constraints, and Restructuring," in *Conflict and Competition: The Latin American Church in a Changing Environment,* Edward L. Cleary and Hannah Stewart-Gambino, eds. (Boulder, Colo.: Lynne Rienner, 1992), 215.

161. Ivan Vallier, "Religious Elites, Differentiations, and Developments in Roman Catholicism," in *Elites in Latin America,* Seymour Martin Lipset, ed. (New York: Oxford University Press, 1968), 196; Anthony J. Gill, "Rendering unto Caesar?: Religious Competition and Catholic Political Strategy in Latin America," paper presented at the Latin American Studies Association, Los Angeles, September 1992, 27.

162. See Vikram Khub Chand, "Politics, Institutions, and Democracy in Mexico: The Politics of the State of Chihuahua in National Perspective," unpublished Ph.D. dissertation, Harvard University, May 1991, 247–261.

163. Andrew J. Stein, "Religion and Mass Politics in Central America," paper presented at the New England Council of Latin American Studies, Boston University, October 1992, 25–26; Timothy Steigenga and Kenneth Coleman, "Protestantism and Politics in Chile, 1972–1991," paper presented at the New England Council of Latin Americanists, Boston, October 1992, 21.

164. Michael Welch and David Leege, "Dual Reference Groups and Political Orientations: An Examination of Evangelically Oriented Catholics," *American Journal of Political Science* 35, no. 1 (1991): 45.

165. Gerhard Lenski, *The Religious Factor: A Sociological Study of Religion's Impact on Politics and Family Life* (Garden City, N.Y.: Doubleday, 1963), 270.

166. Michael Welch and David Leege, "Dual Reference Groups and Political Orientations," 51.

167. John L. Sullivan et al., *Political Tolerance and American Democracy* (Chicago: University of Chicago Press, 1982), 136; Andrew M. Greeley, *The Catholic Myth: The Behavior and Beliefs of American Catholics* (New York: Collier Books, 1990), 51.

168. Susan Eckstein, "Politics and Priests: The 'Iron Law of Oligarchy' and Interorganizational Relations," *Comparative Politics* 9 (July 1977): 470.

169. Personal interview with Ricardo Pascoe, secretary of communications, Party of the Democratic Revolution, Mexico City, May 5, 1992.

170. Jean-Pierre Bastian, "Disidencia religiosa en el campo mexicano," in *Religión y política en México,* Martín de la Rosa and Charles A. Reilly, eds. (Mexico City: Siglo XXI, 1985), 190–192.

171. Edwin Eloy Aguilar, "Protestantism in El Salvador," 12.

172. Daniel H. Levine, "Assessing the Impacts of Liberation Theology in Latin America," 259; "Religion and Politics: Drawing Lines, Understanding Change," *Latin American Research Review* 20, no. 1 (1985): 199, where he further argues that the future path of change lies less with their ideas than with what they actually practice.

5

Religion, Politics, and the Laity

The role of the Catholic Church and clergy is strongly affected by the importance of religion in society and how religion affects the behavior and attitudes of individual Mexicans.[1] Empirical evidence exists to support a linkage between religiosity, however measured, and sociopolitical attitudes.[2] A larger premise of this study is that priests have the potential for affecting citizen values, if not their receptiveness to specific public policies.[3] Clergy have numerous opportunities to communicate social and political messages through such channels as Masses, pastoral letters, lay education classes, poster displays, and Church publications.[4] Since Catholic religious groups account for the largest number of social organizations in the country, the relationship between religion and the laity takes on added significance.[5]

Church Masses are perceived by many observers and politicians alike as having the potential for influencing partisan political choices in Mexico and Latin America. As Kenneth Wald argues, "[C]hurches do indeed promote distinctive political orientations. . . . [T]he extent of theological traditionalism prevailing in a congregation moves individual members to more conservative preferences on social issues and makes them more disposed to identify themselves as political conservatives."[6] More important, the nature and depth of people's religious beliefs may well affect how they define their church's role. For example, in El Salvador, active Catholics are twice as likely (51 percent) as Protestants (24 percent) to endorse a role for the Church in resolving conflicts.[7]

Since the mid-1980s, the Church's potential political influence among the laity has taken on much greater importance. This is true for several reasons. In the first place, the overall political environment in Mexico is increasingly contentious, especially since the 1988 presidential elections. As the intensity of political opposition has increased, so has electoral fraud.[8] Church leadership has been drawn directly into party conflicts as an institutional channel for criticizing regime fraud, especially in the North, South, and West, strongholds of an activist church.[9] The peasant uprising in Chiapas and the assassination of the PRI's candidate during the 1994 elections highlighted increasing political difficulties faced by the government. The Church, through Bishop Samuel Ruiz, served as a crucial mediator in the negotiations between the Zapatista army in Chiapas and the Mexican government. The Church is likely to increase its mediation functions as political disputes increase.

Secondly, as chapter 2 suggests, President Salinas himself emphasized the Church's importance as part of his political modernization program, implying through public statements and actions that the legal constructs that severely limited religious autonomy in Mexico were outmoded, a carryover from the 19th-century civil-religious conflict. Notable among those restrictions were constitutional prohibitions on the right of priests and nuns to vote and the Church's lack of legal status in its relationship to the state.[10] The 1992 changes in the constitutional restrictions on the Church increase the Church's legitimacy as a religious institutional and societal actor.

A third reason for increased Church influence among the laity is the National Action Party's (PAN) success in the North and West and its victory in the hard-fought 1989 gubernatorial election of Baja California (the first officially recognized opposition election at this level in some 60 years) in Chihuahua in 1992, in Guanajuato and Jalisco in 1995, and again in Baja California in 1995. These victories have a special relevance for the Church. As several authors suggest, PAN has drawn some ideological influence from Catholic thought and papal encyclicals.[11] PAN electoral victories were also important to the Church because its 1988–1994 platform called for numerous constitutional changes in the church-state relationship, changes specified in earlier party platforms.[12] PAN's election victories indirectly reinforce the legitimacy of some of the Church's pastoral messages.

Fourth, and finally, the Church itself, from the point of view of its constituencies and its own leadership, is in the midst of redefining its role.[13] Most Catholics in Mexico believe the Church responds well to spiritual necessities, moral problems, and family conflict, but only a minority (29 percent) believe the Church sufficiently responds to social and economic problems.[14] It is younger parishioners, however, who believe that this role is not adequately fulfilled.[15]

The Church's potential for influencing Mexican life more broadly in nonspiritual ways, particularly in relation to politics, can be examined from a variety of perspectives.[16] As recent studies of the Church in Latin America suggest, comprehensive analyses must examine the perspective of the hierarchy, the priests, lay organizations, and the laity itself. Most projects have examined the institutional church and its leadership, whereas others since the 1970s have explored the impact of the theology of liberation and the influence of *comunidades de base* (base communities).[17] Strangely, the area most neglected in Latin American and Mexican analyses is work on the laity.[18] Yet Church analysts consider changes affecting the laity to be the most significant, especially for the effect on politics and society.[19] Very little is known about the religiosity of the people, the importance of religion in their lives, the degree to which they are active Christians, and most important of all, the effects of religious intensity on political and social attitudes, voting, and partisan politics.

This chapter explores some empirical data on *national* Mexican religious values and their potential impact on the Church's political influence. Such comprehensive data has become available only recently.[20] It is logical to assume that the Church undoubtedly is an institution that could influence public opinion given the fact that a sizable body of Mexicans of voting age compose their audiences from one Sunday to the next. Although only 34 percent of Mexicans thought politics to be very important, among the 11 percent who considered religion very important, 55 percent rated politics as significant. It is necessary, however, to examine more closely Mexican religious values before accepting the notion that the Church does influence its parishioners.[21]

Mexican Religiosity

A variable that might positively affect the Church's position in any society is organized religion's importance to that culture's values. Mexicans value religion very highly. The average Mexican ranks family, work, and religion most important to his life and considers it far more significant than politics. In fact, seven out of 10 Mexicans regard themselves as religious and 85 percent claimed they received a religious education in their homes.[22] When asked the importance of religion, without comparing it to other values, 84 percent of Mexican respondents considered it very important or important, while only a meager 3 percent believed it had no importance in their lives.[23]

More specifically, Mexicans also expressed an overwhelming belief in a Christian god. In a 1982 study in which 92 percent of all Mexicans claimed to believe in a religion, an even higher percentage, 97 percent, believed in God and nine out of ten considered God important in their lives. God's significance to each Mexican did vary from one region to another, with the Center and North finding it most important and the Federal District, least important.[24] Nearly 80 percent of Mexicans, regardless of their educational backgrounds (public, religious, or private secular), believed God created the earth, plants, animals, and human beings.[25]

Even in the Federal District, where religion appears least influential comparatively, it has strong influences. For example, 79 percent claim to be Catholic and another 11 percent believe in God. Only 6 percent of Mexicans residing in the capital are atheists. When asked if they consult their religion before making an important decision, 58 percent of Mexico City respondents replied that they asked God.[26]

Strong religious beliefs only provide a receptive environment for active commitments to organized religion.[27] Traditionally, Mexicans have been overwhelmingly Christian and Catholic. At the beginning of the 20th century, Catholics accounted for nearly 99 percent of the population. By 1980, that figure had declined to 95 percent of the population.[28] In the last decade, however, the level of Catholicism has declined further, to somewhere between 81 and 88 percent. The level of Catholicism, not surprisingly, is stronger in rural Mexico than in metropolitan centers.[29]

Contrary to common beliefs, younger Mexicans are slightly more Catholic than older people.[30] This contradicts the often-repeated suggestion that older people are more Catholic and that Protestant sects are making inroads among the young in

Mexico.[31] Since the young form such a large proportion of the Mexican population, their interest in religion is likely to make them more receptive to Church influence too.[32]

It is also important to understand how Catholics in general and Mexican Catholics in particular conceptualize God. This perception is significant in evaluating the laity because an individual's devotional style and closeness to God are the strongest links to sociopolitical beliefs.[33] Catholics' conceptualization of God has been described best by Andrew Greeley:

> The Catholic tends to see society as a "sacrament" of God, a set of ordered relationships, governed by both justice and love, that reveal, however imperfectly, the presence of God. Society is "natural" and "good," therefore, for humans their "natural" response to God is social.[34]

Greeley goes on to suggest that Catholics picture God in two ways, either as a mother, spouse, friend, and lover or as a father, master, judge, and king. He discovered that among American Catholics the first of these two perceptions, on what he labeled the GRACE scale, correlated strongly with social and political attitudes and behaviors. For example, they were less likely to vote for Ronald Reagan in 1980 and 1984.[35] We know less about Mexican Catholics' image of God, but a study of Mexican and American students concluded that Mexicans perceived God as a strong figure, stressing affective qualities in being helpful, fair, and friendly.[36]

Regardless of potential linkages between religion and politics, many individuals draw a distinction between their religious beliefs and the institution that represents those beliefs. As Larissa Lomnitz argues in her study of an extended, successful Mexican entrepreneurial clan, "[F]amily members never fail to make a clear distinction between the Eternal Religion on the one hand and the Church as a temporal institution on the other. . . . Such attitudes are not uncommon among other Catholic groups."[37] In a rare case where an interviewer asked respondents (from Ciudad Juárez, one of Mexico's largest cities, bordering El Paso, Texas) whether or not they should obey certain institutions, 52 percent said they would obey the presidency and 49 percent said they would obey the Catholic Church. This same population evaluated the Church as a good or very good institution, slightly below the family in prestige. This led the author to conclude "that the level of acceptance which an institution enjoys is not an indicator of its symbolic force and its capacity to mobilize; this signifies that a rational-legal element plays a determinant role in political behavior."[38] Although many Mexicans make such a distinction, that author's data suggest that a sizable percentage, without specifying the directive to be followed, would be inclined to follow *some* Church leadership.

To what extent, therefore, do Mexicans universally praise the Church as an institution? In the 1990 World Values Survey, 46 percent of all Mexicans interviewed expressed great confidence in the Church, and an additional 30 percent had some confidence in this institution. Only 9 percent of Mexicans had no confidence in the Church, and, among all institutions, secular and nonsecular, none matched the Church in esteem. Expressed differently, in a comparative context, 37 percent of Mexicans believed the Church more than the government, 26 percent thought both institutions equally credible, and only 8 percent were inclined to take the government's word over the Church's. Slightly more than one out of four Mexicans doubted the word of both institutions.[39]

Some idea of the importance of religion in the average Mexican's general value system is suggested by the degree to which the typical parent wants his or her child to have a religious education. Nationally, more than two-thirds of all respondents in a 1990 survey said they desired such an education; only 17 percent rejected it. The responses varied somewhat geographically, with much higher favorable responses in Guadalajara in the West and Monterrey in the North.[40] Religious vows are also taken more seriously in marriage than might be expected given constitutional prohibitions on the legal validity of religious sacraments and the percentage of Mexicans living in common-law relationships.[41] One study of Mexico City found seven out of 10 marriages in the Federal District to have religious approval.[42]

The level of respect Mexicans have for various institutions in their social, political, and religious cultures stems largely, it can be argued, from their attitudes toward the organization's representative. Typically, Mexicans evaluate institutions on a level equal to their representatives, although some exceptions exist. Priests and teachers are highly respected in Mexican culture. After parents, teachers and priests appear at the top of the list, whereas politicians and military officers rank at the bottom.[43] In fact, in a recent poll, priests scored higher than teachers in prestige.[44] These data suggest the probability that priests, as distinct from the institution they represent, may have considerable influence on society. Of course, given their acceptance of the separation of church and state, many Mexicans might reject priests exercising broad social and political influence. Also, religious authority is probably only transferable to certain types of Catholics, typically the most traditional or "sacramental." Nevertheless, the data also suggest why the government might feel threatened by both the Church and its clergy. By comparison, the legitimacy of both is much higher than secular political institutions and their representatives.[45]

Determinants of Religious Intensity

Citizens' attitudes toward religion, the Church, and ordinary clergy suggest Mexicans might be receptive to the Church's guidance on some issues. It is one thing to describe yourself as religious, or in this case Christian, but it is quite another to practice your respective faith literally. Students of Latin American religion have always made the case that the decline of the Church's influence through the 1960s was accompanied by a decline in church attendance.[46] Furthermore, frequency of attendance is correlated with certain political and social attitudes.[47] Consequently, church attendance statistics provide a practical measure of the level of contact between the parish priest or the religious community and the secular constituency.[48] Moreover, many assertions have been made about the qualitative makeup of church attenders, that they are female, young or old, and disproportionately from certain social strata.

The chronology of Mexican church attendance over time, even when confined to recent decades, follows the expected pattern. From 1940 to 1960, attendance varied widely in the records of 34 dioceses: 4–25 percent in 12 dioceses, 30–60 percent in 16 dioceses, and 75–98 percent in 6 dioceses.[49] According to Barrett, 70 percent of Mexican Catholics attended church weekly in 1959.[50] In 1982, only 54 percent partook of Mass once a week or more, and 21 percent claimed monthly attendance.[51] In 1988, 44 percent attended once or more weekly, and 9 percent twice a month.[52] Most recently, two different surveys found that 44–45 percent attended church weekly or more often, 14–19 percent monthly, 26–32 percent rarely, and 9–11 percent never. A small percentage of Catholics, 3 percent, attended church daily.[53]

Who attends Mass and why they attend is also a determining variable in their religious attitudes and secular values. Michael Fleet and Brian Smith, careful students of Latin American religion and politics, concluded that three types of rank-and-file Catholics exist. They argue convincingly that "a full understanding of the different elements within the Catholic community requires closer attention to their divergence in religious and socio-political views, and to the factors contributing to these divergences."[54] They go on to describe three types of Catholics: *organizationals,* who actively participate in one or more church-sponsored group (a majority attend Mass regularly too); *sacramentals,* who attend church fairly regularly but do not participate in other activities; and *culturals,* who are not involved religiously or organizationally with the Church but have and acknowledge Catholic values.

Unfortunately, we do not have survey data on Mexican Catholics according to these precise categories, but we can identify certain characteristics of those who attend regularly and those who do not. In fact, if we assume an association between an individual's strength and/or intensity of religious beliefs and frequency of attendance, a measure commonly used by religious pollsters, certain attributes become clearer.[55] Although attendance alone is not the best variable to measure the relationship between religion and political attitudes, a statistically significant relationship between the two exists in other studies.[56]

A common assumption is that gender determines religiosity measured by attendance. Among the tiny percentage of Mexicans who attend church more than once a week, women account for two-thirds of those individuals. On a weekly basis, women also attend more frequently than men. Men are also more likely than women to never attend church. Several explanations can be provided for the greater frequency of female church attendance.[57] One of the more important explanations in the Mexican case, however, is that women (51 percent) find much greater consolation in religion than do men (36 percent).[58] A second reason is that women are most commonly the official and unofficial pastoral agents of the Mexican Church. Over 90 percent of the leaders of small base communities and 80 percent of the traditional educational leaders are lay women or religious sisters.[59]

Not surprisingly, education plays a significant role in the level of religiosity and church attendance in Mexico, as it does elsewhere in the world. However, care has to be taken to distinguish between the effects of education on Mexican religious beliefs in general and among acknowledged Catholics. Those who are avowedly Catholic drop from 90 to 82 percent when controlling for preparatory education or higher. A second major distinction occurs between Mexicans with postgraduate education and all other Mexicans, of whom only 62 percent consider themselves Catholics. Educational levels also play a role in religious intensity. Thus, as educational levels increase, church attendance declines. For example, among the most intensely religious Mexicans (those who attend church more than once a week), one-third have only a primary education and one-fifth, no formal education. More than one-half of this intensely religious minority have little or no formal education. Religion becomes somewhat less important among Catholics as educational levels increase, but differences are not significant from secondary levels on up.[60]

Income and occupational data on church attendance and religious intensity offer somewhat contradictory conclusions. However, if we apply what we know about gender and education, the importance of occupation and income makes more sense. In the first place, those small number of Mexicans who attend church more than once a week are heavily dominated by marginals (unemployed and underemployed with minimal incomes) and housewives. Among housewives, nearly two-thirds attend Mass at least weekly. On the other hand, one study reported Mexicans with the highest incomes (seven or more times the minimum wage) attended weekly Mass more frequently than other citizens.[61] Although this study is not as comprehensive as the Alduncin, Hernández, and Basáñez surveys, Alduncin found in his 1987 survey that company owners, among all occupational groups, gave the greatest importance to religion, significantly above the national average.[62] Blue-collar workers, on the other hand, expressed religious interests well below the national average. This may be one explanation why the percentage of blue-collar workers who attend church weekly is significantly lower than the percentage for other occupational groups. Basáñez's survey results confirmed Alduncin's findings. Not surprisingly, atheists most commonly are well educated and intellectual: journalists, writers, artists, students, professionals, and teachers.

Finally, urbanization and geography play a role in the pattern of Mexican religious beliefs. Regionalism and religion interest political analysts since they may explain differences in the voting population's support for parties with religious associations.[63] Such relationships are highlighted by the fact that in industrialized societies "the best single predictor of party vote are the religious affiliation and religious activities of the citizen."[64] Interestingly, Mexico, which has a long, turbulent history of regionalism affecting political leadership and behavior well into the 20th century, does not illustrate a significant connection between broad regions and religious intensity. Attendance figures are fairly unified geographically, although in more than one survey the Central region scores highest. However, if we control for cities as distinct from regions, then significant anomalies from the norm appear.[65] The data on cities suggest that capitals are most unique.[66] Mexico City, the most cosmopolitan center of intellectual and economic activity, is one of the least religious places. In the 1980s, three different surveys consistently reported that only slightly more than one-third of all Mexico City Catholics regularly attended church.[67] The city with the lowest attendance record of those surveyed was Tijuana, which borders San Diego along the California frontier.

Those cities with significantly higher-than-average attendance included León,

Guanajuato (Central-West), Guadalajara, Jalisco (West), and Oaxaca, Oaxaca (South). The first two might be explained by the fact that the Church maintained a strong colonial presence, that both cities boasted a major Catholic seminary, and, most important, that they significantly supported the intense religiously motivated rebellion in the 1920s, the Cristero revolt, against the Mexican government. Oaxaca's large Indian population also attracted a strong colonial presence, and religion remains important to contemporary residents. Although significant differences can be found from one city to another, generally no significant variations appear among attendance records for Catholics in all cities over 2,500 people.[68]

Social and Political Consequences of Religiosity

These data provide us with a clear sense of the level of religiosity in Mexico, the accessibility of clergy to Mexicans, and the type and location of Mexicans most receptive to the Church. What is most interesting to explore, however, is the extent to which religious beliefs affect Mexican perceptions of various social and political issues, issues directly relating to church and state, the political role of the Church, and partisan politics.

Different variables, in association with religion, may of course exert more influence over political and social values. However, in their recent study of South America, Fleet and Smith found that even such significant determinants of values as class may be autonomous from religion in shaping personal attitudes. As they suggest, it is important to distinguish among Catholics with different exposures to Catholic values and culture and to focus on such qualities as type of leadership and the level of political mobilization in the local church and community.[69] In the United States, it is clear that the content of religious values is more important than intensity of commitment in influencing political outlooks. Even more important, the collective outlook of each individual church or parish is more important than the world view of the individual member.[70]

Religiosity, defined by church attendance, nevertheless, does have certain measurable effects on Mexican Catholic values. For example, not surprisingly, the more frequently an individual attends Mass, the higher his or her esteem for the priest. Attendance alone might make an individual more receptive to a priest's views since, to some degree, a self-selection process occurs among those Mexicans who attend church regularly. Equally important, those who attend church daily—fewer than 5 percent of all Mexicans—are significantly intolerant of other religions compared to other Catholics (see Table 5-1). This pattern is not peculiar to Catholics, or to Mexican Catholics, and Catholics compared to other religions rank somewhere in the middle. Frequent attendance generally increases intolerance, and individuals with no religious affiliations are most tolerant as a group.[71] In Mexico, when asked if they should accept all religions or only Catholicism, 58 percent replied "all," 12 percent suggested "it depends," and 26 percent said "Catholic only."[72]

The most dramatic findings in the collective survey data concerning the effects of religiosity on political values is, however, related to the question of change. In the first place, one's Catholicism is not linked to membership in political organiza-

Table 5-1. Social and Political Views of Catholics

Variable	Intense Catholics	Moderate Catholics
Religious intolerance	46.9%	29.5%
Political change	31.5	21.4
Poor leadership	14.0	8.1

Source: From Mori de Mexico, "Encuesta nacional de opinión pública, iglesia-estado," 1990 (religious intolerance), and from "Encuesta nacional del proceso electoral, 1988" (political change and poor leadership).

Note: Intense Catholics are those who attend church more than once a week; moderate Catholics are those who attend weekly, monthly, or rarely. Religious intolerance refers to those respondents who answered the question, "Some people believe that in Mexico we should accept all religions and others think that we should only accept the Catholic religion. What is your opinion?," with the response, "Catholics only." Political change refers to those respondents who gave a positive response to the question, "In your opinion, should we change things completely?" Poor leadership refers to those who answered the question, "What is your opinion of the government of Miguel de la Madrid?," with the response, "very bad."

tions. More important, a 1988 poll revealed clearly that those Mexicans with the most intense religious beliefs identify least with the present political system (see Table 5-1). These individuals are the most critical of Mexico's leadership, in proportions twice the norm. In addition, instead of fitting a conservative stereotype, intense Catholics strongly favor radical political change. They may well be socially or morally traditional, but politically they do not favor conserving the present structure. The potential for this group having political influence is severely moderated by their small membership, their lower levels of education, their relative ignorance of politics, and their lower voter turnout.[73]

When specific issues focusing on church and state in contrast to general political attitudes are identified, some distinct citizen views emerge. From 1989 to 1992, two major church-state issues were openly debated on the public agenda: a general redefinition of church-state relations involving legal recognition of the Church and diplomatic recognition of the Vatican; and the right of priests to vote, prohibited by the constitution until late 1992. Mexicans, in their schooling and at home, are typically raised in a contradictory social milieu that on the one hand indoctrinates young people in 19th-century Mexican liberalism and on the other hand provides them with moral references within the dominant, Catholic-Latin culture.

Despite high levels of religiosity and Catholicism, religion seems not to have altered contemporary Mexican views of church-state history. As empirical survey data make clear, two-thirds of all Mexican's interviewed favored Benito Juárez's (major Liberal president) controversial decision to break relations with the Church in the mid-19th century, while only 15 percent thought it a bad policy. To reduce the Church's influence, Liberal leaders eliminated its control over birth registration and marriages, which remains codified in the present constitution. Although most Mexicans want their marriages sanctified by the Catholic Church, they are unwilling, in proportions of 55 to 29 percent, to return those decisions back to the Church.[74] The Liberals, determined to replace clerical influence with a secular, positivist educational philosophy, severely attacked the Church's educational role. Mexicans are still opposed to the Church reviving its educational role, although about one in five said it depended on the circumstances. On the other hand, when confronted with the acceptability of other laws or common practices regarding the Church, Mexicans responded differently. For example, announcements over the airwaves concerning the Pope's visit in 1990, legally prohibited but ignored by the government, were viewed quite favorably.

The most fundamental issue of church-state relations critical to the institution was, of course, reestablishment of formal church-state relations. Editorial opinion among a wide range of Mexican dailies favored new church-state relations by a wide margin.[75] Although the majority of Mexicans were not sure about the actual state of the relationship (that is, whether it was broken or not), most polls found the population evenly divided over reestablishing relations. The majority favored President Salinas's decision to appoint his own personal representative to the Vatican.[76] Not surprisingly, intensely religious Mexicans favored new relations most strongly, and those rarely attending were most opposed. One government poll also found that an overwhelming percentage of Mexicans (80 percent) favored constitutional changes granting the Church legal status.[77] Only one institutional issue involving church and state, whether church and state should be separated, showed no correlation with intensity of religious beliefs.

When we move from the plane of institutional relationships to the more personal level of individual rights, Mexican perceptions differ considerably. When asked specifically whether or not priests should have the right to vote, three polls in 1990 revealed a range of 55 to 68 percent favoring such a constitutional change.[78] Mexicans were much more favorably inclined to giving priests the right to vote because they could relate personally to this denial of a basic human right. Many Mexicans, while exercising their right to vote, indicated that their own rights had been violated through state-sponsored electoral fraud. Also, since most priests who wanted to vote actually exercised their right contrary to the law, custom, instead of law, became the norm.

Of all of the specific issues tied to the church-state relationship, the most significant one for Mexicans is the role of the Catholic Church in secular affairs, specifically, politics. One of the difficulties in assessing citizen attitudes toward the Church's role in politics is evaluating the meaning of the question, "Should the Church participate in politics?" To many individuals, it signifies a direct political role for the church and for priests, including supporting parties and holding office. A survey of the Tijuana diocese received the following responses to a question about what role the Church should have in politics: to orient Catholics (54 percent), to orient democratic participation (6 percent), to promote organizing the people (7 percent), or to form political parties (1 percent).[79] When asked in this context if Catholics would support priests playing nonreligious roles, the then head of the Mexican Council of Bishops replied, "No, they wouldn't support it. It isn't that we have done a survey. . . . My opinion is based on the following fact: they and all of us have been formed in years and years of a Liberal mentality and for many this has become the norm."[80]

The bishop understood his flock rather well. In a series of surveys from 1983 through 1990, as few as two-thirds and as many as 74 percent said the Church should not participate in politics. In 1983, nearly 24 percent thought the Church should participate all the time, sometimes, or occasionally. By 1990, that figure dropped to 16 percent.[81] Importantly, even among Catholics who attended Mass regularly, political participation by the Church was firmly rejected. Although the most uneducated Mexicans and those attending more than once a week expressed stronger feelings on this issue, their responses did not differ significantly on Church participation. For example, in 1989, 74 percent of all Mexicans believed the Church should refrain from political activity.[82] Among intense Catholics, the figure was 67 percent; among weak Catholics, it was 86 percent. Seventy-two percent of atheists agreed with this position. When asked more specifically whether priests should hold public office, 72 percent of all Mexicans responded negatively. The lack of significant variation among various groups according to religious intensity suggests a firmly held principle on this issue. Some variation does occur on the basis of region, party preference, occupation, and social activism.[83]

Not surprisingly, Mexicans most supportive of Church political participation are those who are members of the Mexican Democratic Party (PDM), a descendant of a Sinarquista movement, a fanatically proreligious organization from the 1930s. Four times as many Mexicans (16 percent), self-identified as PDM partisans, favored Church participation in politics, compared to only 4 percent for all Mexican respondents. What is interesting is not their greater sympathy for Church political involvement, but the fact that such a small percentage of this conservative, pro-Catholic party actually favored such a role. More significantly, respondents whose political sympathies were with other small, leftist parties, before the Democratic Revolutionary Party's (PRD) founding in 1989, also strongly favored Church political involvement, an unexpected finding. It can be argued that in the early 1980s, leftist opposition parties viewed the Church as a potential ally in breaking the government Institutional Revolutionary Party's (PRI) political stranglehold and, therefore, were more willing to see it actively involved in the electoral arena.

With the exception of respondents from Mexico City, geography plays little role in Mexicans' evaluations of Church political involvement. One variable that stands out among other possible influences is membership in an independent organization. This suggests, as Fleet and Smith argued above, that an activist social posture, measured in terms of organizational involvement, may affect attitudes toward religion and Church. For example, they discovered in Chile that wealthier Catholics, if they participated regularly in Masses and/or church organizations, were not opposed to a socially committed Church.[84] The other group that stands out from the norm were Mexicans indicating a strong preference for the National Action Party (PAN), an opposition party associated in the public mind and in Mexican political mythology with the Catholic Church.[85] Those favoring Church participation increased from 5 percent for ordinary PAN sympathizers to 10 percent for the most committed partisans.

It can be argued that those Mexicans who have been more subject to the "Liberal" socialization process in their familial environment, formal education, and workplace philosophy would express the strongest attitudes against Church involvement in politics. The higher a respondent's level of education, the greater his or her opposition to Church political involvement. Similarly, professionals who are well-educated public sector careerists, such as bureaucrats, politicians, and interest group leaders, are most opposed to Church political activity.

Naturally, the political question that interests analysts most is religion's effect on voting for a particular party or issue. In its crudest form, many Mexicans assume that the Church can transfer its authority directly to the secular political arena, and that parishioners will follow the lead of clergy in supporting specific parties and candidates.[86] This might well have been true in earlier eras, especially given the clergy's level of influence over formal education. It is evident that those children who attend religious preparatory schools are more likely to find religion more important in their lives and attend Mass more frequently.[87] On the other hand, religious versus secular education is translated into very little difference on a range of important issues, from respecting authority to civic responsibility.[88]

Before testing this relationship, it is valuable to understand the political values of the Catholic versus the non-Catholic Mexican. On this score, very little difference exists between the two (see Table 5-2).[89] Mexicans, as a whole, are not particularly interested in politics. Most respondents, 43 percent, are not interested in politics, 21 percent express some interest, but no more than in other subjects, and 32 percent are interested in politics but do not participate actively. According to the Church's own 1986 survey, 52 percent of regular attenders at Mass were not interested in politics, and as Christians, only 2 percent thought politics was their mission.[90] Only 4 percent of Mexicans are actively involved. They are disproportionately young, male, lower middle class, have completed at least a sixth-grade education, and reside in Mexico City.[91]

Because most authors have implied a connection philosophically and otherwise between the Catholic Church and the National Action Party, the latter largely without substantiating evidence,[92] it is assumed that strong Catholics will vote disproportionately for this party and its leading candidates. The relationship between religious intensity and self-described party sympathy is revealing. In 1989, 5 percent of Mexicans described themselves as strong PAN supporters, exactly the same percentage of strong Catholics. Seven percent of Mexicans described themselves as strong supporters of Cuauhtémoc Cárdenas's PRD, a populist, left-

Table 5-2. Political Preferences of Catholics and Non-Catholics

Ideology	Catholics	Non-Catholics
Extreme left	5%	4%
Left	6	5
Center	29	33
Right	25	27
Extreme right	26	28

Source: Based on a 1982 national survey of 1,837 respondents adapted from Ivan Zavala, "Valores políticos," in *Como somos los mexicanos*, Alberto Hernández Medina, ed. (Mexico City: Centro de Estudios Educativos, 1987), 102.

Note: Respondents who did not specify a preference or who did not answer this question are not included here. Therefore, responses do not add up to 100 percent.

of-center opposition party, compared to 6 percent of strong Catholics. For the PRI, 16 percent of Mexicans described themselves as strongly sympathetic, as did 18 percent of strong Catholics.[93]

In fact, if we examine other polling data from the late 1980s, the only relationship we can find between religious intensity and party sympathy is among that small percentage of intense Catholics, 3.4 percent, who attend Church daily (see Table 5-3).[94] This group differs from the rest of the population in the intensity of its support for PAN, 18 percent compared to 11 percent of the general population, or about 64 percent higher. This small group also voted in larger percentages for Manuel Clouthier, the charismatic PAN presidential candidate in the 1988 elections.

All other Mexicans, however, on the basis of Church attendance, do not indicate any significant difference in their party preferences, suggesting that Catholicism, contrary to common myth, has little or nothing to do with party sympathy in Mexico. In fact, among those Mexicans attending church daily, only 12 percent supported PAN, .5 percent above the national average.[95] Actually, PAN receives its strongest support religiously from those who do not attend church at all.[96] These findings are corroborated by Charles Davis in his examination of worker religiosity and partisanship from 1979–1980 data. He concluded that "secular workers are also slightly more likely to support rightist opposition parties than are religious workers. Clearly, Catholic workers in the survey are not generally attracted to the two right-wing parties, the National Action Party (PAN) or the Mexican Democratic Party (PDM)."[97]

In the most highly competitive election in modern times, the 1988 presidential election, religiosity and voting patterns support the contention above that the intensity of Catholic beliefs generally is not translated into partisan political support. For example, Manuel Clouthier, PAN's candidate, did no better among various religious groups with the one exception mentioned above. Cuauhtémoc Cárdenas, on the other hand, did much better among the nonreligious or atheists voters, a pattern found elsewhere in the region,[98] and Salinas received the lowest support among Protestants.[99]

A connection exists, of course, between atheism and level of education in Mexico. Independent parties tend to attract the better educated and nonreligious voters, students and intellectuals. These two educated groups account for the largest percentage of atheists. For example, in May 1990, in a survey in the Federal District, 42 percent of all respondents said they would vote for the PRI. Yet 60 percent of the uneducated opted for the PRI, while 67 percent of those with graduate educa-

Table 5-3. Religious Intensity and Partisanship

Party	Intense Catholic	Moderate Catholic	General Population
National Action Party (PAN)	18.2%	9.5%	11.4%
Party of the Democratic Revolution (PRD)	2.0	6.5	6.3
Institutional Revolutionary Party (PRI)	19.2	25.1	24.8

Source: Raw data, in Mori de Mexico, "Encuesta nacional de opinión pública, iglesia-estado," 1990.
Note: Questions asked: "Do you sympathize with any political party? Which one?"

tions would have cast their ballot for the PRD, favored by only 19 percent of all respondents.[100] Therefore, while it is true that religious versus no religious beliefs may influence voting behavior, among Catholics, who account for approximately 86 percent of the population, strong differences based on religious intensity have little connection to voting preferences. In the 1988 elections, PAN actually did less well among fanatic Catholics and only slightly better than the PRI and other parties among weekly attenders. Religious intensity was not related to voting for PAN in 1988, nor did Catholics as a group vote more for PAN and less for the PRI or Cárdenas's party in 1988.[101] Cárdenas, as an individual presidential candidate, did obtain larger numbers of votes from nonpracticing Catholics.

Joseph Klesner argued that "religiosity is correlated with voting for the right in Mexico," but his conclusions were based on regional voting preferences over time.[102] In other words, if one controls for region, a certain consistency of opposition support, including that for parties of the right (PAN and the PDM), appears in specific states, especially those where the Cristero rebellion was strongest. This is because, in part, some of these same regions have a higher percentage of intense, practicing Catholics, but the percentage of non-Catholics is evenly distributed throughout Mexico. As our data make clear, historical experience and religious beliefs combined, and not religious beliefs alone, may explain some voting patterns.

Allegations have been made that individual Mexican priests have encouraged their parishioners to vote for specific parties. While evidence exists to support isolated cases of this locally, this has been exceptional behavior in recent decades.[103] If, however, clergy were to suggest to their constituencies that they vote for specific candidates, parties, or policies, how would Mexicans respond? The evidence is very clear that Mexican Catholics, raised in a strong environment of church-state separation, are not favorably inclined toward Church political indoctrination.[104] The state in Catholic societies worldwide typically provoked the rupture with religious authorities, as in Mexico.[105]

Taking their lead from the state, Mexicans definitely separate Church positions on public policy issues from spiritual teachings. Contrary to widespread suspicions, Mexicans support policy issues and vote on the basis of their individual consciences. For example, when asked if they agreed with the Church's opposition to an AIDS prevention program, 71 percent said no compared to 17 percent who supported the Church's position. On the issue of family planning, which the Church opposes, 74 percent of Mexicans interviewed favored such a program, 19 percent said they thought it depended on the situation, and only 6 percent were opposed. More important, another study found that only 13 percent of those opposed gave religion as the reason.[106]

Even on abortion, the most highly politicized social issue with major religious ramifications, only 47 percent were opposed, in contrast to 42 percent who believe it depends on the case and 8 percent in favor.[107] Specifically, in one regional poll, when respondents who favored Church participation in politics were asked if they should vote for a candidate suggested by the Church, only 9 percent responded favorably and of those, more than two-thirds were women. In fact, that author discovered that 84 percent of the voters in Nuevo León were not influenced by suggestions to vote for a particular candidate. Among the most important agents making these suggestions were unions, clergy, and employers.[108]

Do these findings mean that the Church exerts, or potentially might exert, very little political influence? The answer to this question is no if one thinks of Church influence as much more subtle and broad. A far more critical issue for the politization of the population from the point of view of religious influence is the extent to which the Church's posture on important social and economic questions affects political attitudes and behavior. In other words, the Church is more likely to influence the formation of values and promote awareness of issues having political consequences than to specifically orchestrate citizen voting responses. Mexicans with Catholic religious values tend, overall, to be much less critical politically than atheists. Indeed, Mexican atheists are twice as critical as Catholics of political leadership and, to a lesser extent, of the president himself.[109]

Mexican Catholics, while not desirous of a politically active Church in the traditional meaning of the phrase, are much more interested in redefining the Church's role socially. Their conceived redefinition of the Church's role has serious, long-term implications for the Church as an institution, for Mexican political life, and for the indirect political role of the Church. When asked the principal function of the Church, not quite half, 45 percent, define it as religious. More than half see its principal activities as political, social, moral, economic, or something else.[110] A large percentage of Mexicans, therefore, do not conceptualize Church activities in a narrow, traditional, religious sense. More important, those who see the Church as having a broader set of responsibilities are not satisfied with the Church's performance. During the early 1980s, the more sophisticated and urbanized the region, for example, Mexico City and the border towns, the more critical they were of the Church's response to social and economic needs. Among those interviewed under age 34, 75 percent were unsatisfied, but even 52 percent in the oldest age group (55–72) were not pleased.[111] In 1990, levels of satisfaction continued at similar levels. In the Church's more traditional function of addressing spiritual problems, family life, and moral problems, Mexicans ranked the Church's answers adequate 74, 59, and 59 percent of the time, respectively. For social problems, 46 percent categorized the Church's response as inadequate.

Interestingly, Mexicans believe the Church should openly discuss Third World problems. Support for such a posture implicitly suggests a strong feeling that the Church actively take public positions and voice its opinions on controversial social and economic issues. For example, 59 percent of Mexicans interviewed thought the Church should discuss such problems compared to 31 percent who believed it was outside of Church responsibilities. Although the 1990 World Values Survey shows overwhelming support for discussing significant developmental issues, it also makes clear that Mexicans do not want the Catholic Church to evaluate government performance. In other words, they appear to separate criticism of government actions from discussing the merits of policy issues. Criticism for the majority is unacceptable (60 versus 30 percent), but discussing specific issues is acceptable to a nearly equally large percentage, depending on the issue.[112] The depth of this commitment is also measured by the fact that many Mexicans are sympathetic toward a Church of the poor. Thirty-nine percent believe the Church should most favor that group, conceptually a significant philosophical underpinning of liberation theology.

Conclusions

From a theoretical view of the political role of religion and the Catholic Church among the laity, these findings are most revealing. In the first place, the argument of scholarship on American religion and politics suggests that local religious communities exercise considerable influence on the political orientations of their members.[113] These studies, and those of Fleet and Smith, suggest the importance of refocusing our inquiry on the political influence of religion toward the local environment. Our data clearly suggest that the greatest differences in religiosity and the potential influence of religious intensity on partisan political sympathies stem from differences among cities and states. Further exploration of smaller religious communities, specifically parishes, would likely reveal stronger differences yet.

Secondly, recent work on Latin America argues that religious activism, specifically participation in lay groups, is a more important measure of religious commitment and related values than attendance alone. Attendance figures can only distinguish among regular churchgoers, intensive attendance, and nonattendance. The intensive churchgoers, 3–5 percent, are such a small group that their political and social views would have few consequences on Catholic behavior in general or the political community at large. Additional measures of religious commitment, in relation to partisanship, need to be examined.

Third, some of the most important differences occur between those who are religious and those who are not, and occasionally between Protestant and Catholics. Again, however, those who profess no religion are an extremely small group in Mexico. Thus, although they support populist leftist parties in greater numbers than Catholics, their likely influence on the electorate is marginal. Furthermore, their higher levels of education, a universally important variable in political partisanship, are probably more significant than lack of religious beliefs in determining political partisanship.

Fourth, Mexicans, religious or otherwise, are very sophisticated about the source of their views and their partisan political behavior, more so than observers have suggested. They can distinguish between various issues, and they do not automatically transfer strong loyalties and respect for Catholicism, priests, or the Church in favor of the Church's public views on social and political issues. Moreover, their views reflect an interesting blend of 19th-century Liberalism combined with a Christian, moral education.

Finally, Mexican Liberalism, which incorporates a heavy dose of anti-Church principles, socialized Mexicans since the Revolution. These secular principles fashioned a high level of acceptance among Mexicans for separation between church and state. Nevertheless, Mexicans, while steeped in this peculiar Liberal tradition, reject some of its more notorious elements, especially those infringing on individual versus institutional rights. Their rejection paved the way for a political context favorable to the 1992 constitutional reforms.

In the 1980s, there is no question that the Catholic Church became a more visible voice in social and political matters. Its leadership, confronted within the Mexican Church and abroad with the issue of pastoral versus social and political responsibilities, realized that it must represent the interests of its constituents if the Church was to survive. In recent years, some clergy, despite constitutional prohibitions, increasingly adopted public political positions. In July 1983, for example, the Bishop of Chihuahua, Manuel Talamás Calamandari, openly invited citizens to vote for the party of change and criticized PRI candidates.[114] In 1985, a spokesperson for the bishop of Monterrey, the 1991–1993 head of the Conference of Mexican Bishops, explained that the Church would not limit itself to "saying the rosary" as some would prefer but supported a multiparty system for the healthy expression of political ideas.[115] In 1986, after widespread electoral fraud in Chihuahua, a northern state, several bishops took out an advertisement demanding a vote recount, threatening to shut down Masses in protest.[116] In 1991, the archbishop of Guadalajara publicly requested that the newly elected governor of San Luis Potosí should consider resigning.[117]

These individual incidents by no means indicate universal attitudes among Mexican hierarchy or clergy. Nevertheless, they do indicate the level of internal discussion and even dissension on Church policies. While religion and the Church both serve as a moderating influence over radical, violent change, an alternative not widely entertained in Mexico, they also promote a steady pressure on democratization and redefining state-group relations along the lines of the North American model, in which churches often oppose and publicly criticize government policy. Indeed, the cooperation between various bishops, especially from the North, with Catholic dioceses and other United States religious institutions, only encourages Mexican clergy to take the broader view of Church responsibilities entertained by its northern neighbor.

The institutional Church is in the midst of responding to competing roles. Most bishops agree on their spiritual functions. An increasingly larger group of moderate bishops, however, see their pastoral functions from a broader perspective. Those administering urban dioceses are particularly concerned with the same issues confronting U.S. cities, specifically the consequences of drug and alcohol abuse. Individual bishops, and the episcopate collectively, are outspoken about this issue and its societal consequences. With the exception of the June 1993 episcopate statement on drug trafficking and the role of the military, public criticism of the government remains oblique. The episcopate has criticized more frequently and openly two important issues: election fraud and human rights abuses. Election fraud often brings together progressive and conservative bishops. Moreover, the Church has created important regional councils, structurally enhancing the voice of individual dioceses. Moderates also realize that the Church will lose parishioners' respect if it does not convey their electoral frustrations to the government. Finally, in the long run, given the extensive evidence of government responsibility in human rights abuses, this issue more than any other will draw the

Church into politically tainted activities. Human rights issues appeal to a broader group of bishops because of their clearer moral implications.

Neither the hierarchy nor the Mexican people see the Church as playing a direct political role, but a redefinition of its responsibilities, socially and economically, would have important political repercussions on the political process at a time of dynamic change. An awareness of this influence on the part of public figures has encouraged increasing criticism of the Church among those who suspect its motives. Mexicans themselves may take greater interest in political outcomes as these same issues confront Church authorities and laity alike.

NOTES

1. A shorter, different version of this chapter appeared in the *Latin American Research Review* 29, no. 3 (1994): 69–100.

2. David C. Leege, M. R. Welch, and T. A. Trozzolo, "Religiosity, Church Social Teaching, and Socio-Political Attitudes," *Review of Religious Research* 28 (1986): 118. The authors note, however, that the relationship is stronger when concerned with family life and sexuality than with economic and political matters.

3. In a comprehensive survey of some 14,000 regular attenders at Mass, nearly three-quarters said laity and priests worked together, and an equal number described their priest as a friend or as someone very close. Comisión Episcopal para el Apostolado de los Laicos, *Que piensan los laicos mexicanos del sínodo '87* (Mexico City: CEM, 1986), 33.

4. Kenneth D. Wald, D. E. Owen, and S. D. Hill, Jr., "Churches as Political Communities," *American Political Science Review* 82, no. 2 (June 1988): 533.

5. The most comprehensive survey of the literature on the relationship between religion and politics in the United States, which offers the strongest theoretical underpinnings, is Kenneth D. Wald, *Religion and Politics in the United States* (New York: St. Martin's, 1987), especially "The Religious Dimension of American Political Behavior," 61–101.

6. Kenneth D. Wald, D. E. Owen, and S. D. Hill, Jr., "Churches as Political Communities," 543–544.

7. Edwin Eloy Aguilar et al., "Protestantism in El Salvador: Conventional Wisdom versus the Survey Evidence," *Latin American Research Review* 28, no. 2 (1993): 19.

8. See, for example, the numerous essays in Edgar Butler and Jorge A. Bustamante, eds., *Sucesión Presidencial: The 1988 Mexican Presidential Election* (Boulder, Colo.: Westview Press, 1991), and Judith Gentleman, *Mexican Politics in Transition* (Boulder, Colo.: Westview Press, 1987).

9. Oscar Aguilar and Ismael Martínez, "La iglesia católica mexicana como factor de riesgo para la estabilidad del sistema político mexicano," unpublished paper, May 1987; Guillermo Correa, "Une a intelectuales e iglesia, la lucha contra la imposición electoral," *Proceso*, no. 513, September 1, 1986, 28–29; David Torres Mejía, "El regreso de la iglesia," in *Política y partidos en las eleciones federales de 1985* (Mexico City: UNAM, 1987), 20–25; Dennis Goulet, "The Mexican Church: Into the Public Arena," *America*, April 8, 1989, 318–322.

10. Marjorie Miller, "Mexico Church-State Relations: Stepping Out from the Shadows," *Los Angeles Times*, April 29, 1990; "Iglesia y estado: los puntos del conflicto," *Nexos*, no. 141 (September 1989): 19–23.

11. Joseph Klesner, "Changing Patterns of Electoral Participation and Official Party

Support in Mexico," in *Mexican Politics in Transition,* Judith Gentleman, ed. (Boulder, Colo.: Westview Press, 1988), 102; Donald Mabry, *Mexico's Acción Nacional: A Catholic Alternative to Revolution* (Syracuse, N.Y.: Syracuse University Press, 1973), 99ff; Franz A. von Sauer, *The Alienated "Loyal" Opposition* (Albuquerque: University of New Mexico Press, 1974), 13ff.

12. See María Elena Alvarez de Vicencio, ed., *Relaciones iglesia estado: cambios necesarios, tesís del Partido Acción Nacional* (Mexico City: Epessa, 1990), 20–21.

13. Adolfo Suárez Rivera, "Instrución pastoral sobre la dimensión política de la fe," Archdiocese of Monterrey, Nuevo León, March 1987, 6.

14. Luis Narro Rodríguez, "Qué valorán los mexicanos hoy?," in *Como somos los mexicanos,* Alberto Hernández Medina et al., eds. (Mexico City: Centro de Estudios Educativos, 1987), 36.

15. Alberto Hernández Medina, "Religión y moral," in *Como somos los mexicanos,* Alberto Hernández Medina et al., eds. (Mexico City: Centro de Estudios Educativos, 1987), 126.

16. For problems of general theory building, see Robert Wuthnow, "Understanding Religion and Politics," *Daedalus* 20, no. 3 (Summer 1991): 1–19.

17. Daniel H. Levine, *Church and Politics in Latin America* (Beverly Hills: Sage Publications, 1980), and *Religion and Conflict in Latin America* (Chapel Hill: University of North Carolina Press, 1986).

18. The work on the laity tends to focus on base community members. For example, see Thomas C. Bruneau and W. E. Hewitt, "Patterns of Church Influence in Brazil's Political Transition," *Comparative Politics* 22, no. 1 (October 1989): 39–61.

19. Edward L. Cleary, *Crisis and Change: The Church in Latin America Today* (Maryknoll: Orbis Books, 1985), 126. As Hannah Stewart-Gambino argues, survey research "could raise important questions for researchers, who have tended to concentrate primarily on attitudes and beliefs of church officials or church-state relations rather than on the far more complex relationships between church and society or church and individual. This development could be especially significant for studies analyzing the church's potential role in achieving such desirable sociopolitical goals as (re)democratization, social justice, and equitable distribution policies in Latin America." Hannah W. Stewart-Gambino, "New Approaches to Studying the Role of Religion in Latin America," *Latin American Research Review* 24, no. 3 (1989): 195.

20. In 1988, I commissioned the Centro de Estudios de Opinión Pública (CEOP), a leading, independent firm associated with WAPOR and the Roper representative in Mexico, directed by Miguel Basáñez, to include several religious questions in a series of national polls (1988–1992), all meeting international standards of polling methodologies. I am deeply indebted to Miguel Basáñez, who out of intellectual curiosity and friendship included these questions in other surveys. The questions, which in combination with many other political, economic, and social variables made cross-tabulations possible, were: What religion are you, how frequently do you attend church, and should the church participate in politics? Because I will be citing numerous polls, detailed information about the methodology, sample size, and margin of error will be omitted in the text. Unless otherwise noted, all polling data come from these polls. "Encuesta Nacional del Proceso Electoral," July 1988, of 4,414 respondents, available from UCLA or the Roper Center, partial results and methodology published in *Los Angeles Times,* November 2, 1989, n.p.; "Encuesta Nacional de Opinión Pública, Iglesia-Estado," April 1990, 3,606 respondents, partial results published in *Excélsior,* May 6, 1990, A1. Two additional national surveys, conforming to the same methodological rigor, were made available to me in their entirety. The first of these polls, referred to as the World Values Survey poll (1990), under the direction of Ronald

Inglehart, is available from the Survey Research Center at the University of Michigan. The Mexican poll for this international study was carried out by CEOP. The other two polls, sponsored by the economic studies division of the National Bank of Mexico, under the direction of Enrique Alduncin, also met similar international methodological standards. I am indebted to Enrique Alduncin for cross-tabulating the raw data for this study. His first project, based on a national survey in December 1981, included 3,543 respondents. Some of the data, including a detailed methodological section, are published in his *Los valores de los mexicanos, México: entre la tradición y la modernidad* (Mexico City: Fomento Cultural Banamex, 1986). The second study, completed in December 1987, included 3,750 respondents. Alduncin provides an excellent overview of national value surveys in Mexico, as well as the data and methodology of this second national survey, in *Los valores de los mexicanos,* vol. 2, *México en tiempos de cambio* (Mexico City: Fomento Cultural Banamex, 1991).

21. Enrique Garza Ramírez, *Nuevo León 1985* (Monterrey: Universidad Autónomo de Nuevo León, 1985), 105.

22. Centro de Estudios de Opinión Pública, *World Values Survey, Mexico* (May 1990). The World Values Survey project conducted by Ronald Englehart provides comprehensive data on changing attitudes in 40 countries, replicating a study done in 1980–1981.

23. Enrique Alduncin Abitia, cross-tabulations of his December 1987 survey, which can be compared with his 1981 study, *Los valores de los mexicanos, México entre la tradición y la modernidad.*

24. Luis Narro Rodríguez, "Qué valorán los mexicanos hoy?," 36–37; Alberto Hernández Medina, "Religión y moral," 120. This comprehensive, national survey interviewed 1,837 individuals based on a Gallup of London questionnaire and field study design. Its methodology is discussed and compared with other surveys in Enrique Alduncin, *Los valores de los mexicanos,* 2:9–14, 19. Enrique Luengo found in a study of college students attending the Jesuit-run Ibero-American University that 36 percent in the Federal District were practicing Catholics, compared to 49 percent from León (in the heart of West Central region) and 46 percent from Puebla (with a strong, colonial religious heritage). "La religiosidad de los estudiantes de la UIA," *Umbral XXI* no. 9 (Summer 1992): 40.

25. Nashiki Gómez and Martín de Jesús Díaz Vázquez, "Educación e iglesias," in "Política," *El Nacional,* April 16, 1991, 8.

26. Ricardo de la Peña and Rosario Toledo, "Encuesta: religiosos y satánicos," *El Nacional,* November 3, 1991, 4.

27. It is the "underlying religious world view" that explains variation in political ideologies, but unfortunately these data are, for the most part, unavailable for Mexican respondents. See Michael Welch and David Leege, "Religious Predictors of Catholic Parishioners' Socio-Political Attitudes: Devotional Style, Closeness to God, Imagery, and Agentic/Communal Religious Identity," *Journal for the Scientific Study of Religion* 27 (December 1988): 538.

28. David B. Barrett, *World Christian Encyclopedia* (New York: Oxford University Press, 1982), 487.

29. "Encuesta nacional de opinión pública, iglesia-estado," April 20–29, 1990, based on 3,606 individual interviews in 97 locales. Some of these results were published in *Excélsior,* May 6, 1990, A1. As Carol Ann Drogus suggests, designating oneself Catholic does not necessarily indicate the level of a person's religious beliefs nor their contact with the Church. Other studies note that rural residents do display greater religiosity than their urban counterparts, and that rural religious beliefs tend to have a more conservative tone. See Paul H. Chalfant and Peter L. Heller, "Rural/Urban versus Regional Differences in Religiosity," *Review of Religious Research* 33, no. 1 (September 1991): 76.

30. One explanation for this, and a characteristic that may distinguish Mexico from some European countries and the United States, is that the older generation were youngsters during the late 1920s and early 1930s, when the state carried out its most repressive measures against the Catholic Church. Andrew Weigert also discovered that Mexican students had stronger beliefs about biblical miracles and Jesus as the Son of God than did Catholics in the United States, Puerto Rico, and Germany. Andrew J. Weigert and Darwin L. Thomas, "Secularization and Religiosity: A Cross-National Study of Catholic Adolescents in Five Societies," *Sociological Analysis* 35, no. 1 (Spring 1974): 6. Another explanation is that younger Mexicans, while forming a higher percentage of Catholics, may be practicing their faith less than their older peers. Enrique Luengo found among Ibero-American University students a 20-year decline from 1970 to 1990. "La religiosidad de los estudiantes de la UIA," 40.

31. "Encuesta nacional del proceso electoral, 1988," June 6–17, based on 4,414 interviews, some results of which appear in *La Jornada,* July 5, 1988, n.p.

32. Mexicans may also be more interested in religion and the Church because of their perception of moral values in society. In his second national opinion survey, Alduncin found that three-quarters of all Mexicans agreed that a decline in moral values is one of the gravest problems Mexico faces. See his "Los valores de los mexicanos, crisis, modernidad y enajenación, pérfil sociopsicológico de los mexicanos en 1987," paper presented at the first National Reunion on Cultural Roots in Mexico, San Miguel de Allende, October 1989, 17.

33. Michael R. Welch and David C. Leege, "Religious Predictors of Catholic Parishioners' Socio-Political Attitudes: Devotional Style, Closeness to God, Imagery, and Agentic/Communal Religious Identity," 538.

34. Andrew Greeley, *The Catholic Myth: The Behavior and Belief of American Catholics* (New York: Collier Books, 1990), 45.

35. Ibid., 42.

36. Rogelio Díaz-Guerrero and Lorand B. Szalay, *Understanding Mexicans and Americans: Cultural Perspectives in Conflict* (New York: Plenum Press, 1991), 113. The World Values Survey also demonstrates that Mexican Catholics, compared to Protestants or Evangelicals, value friends more highly and consider family more important than Protestants.

37. Larissa Adler Lomnitz and Marisol Pérez-Lazaur, *A Mexican Elite Family, 1820–1980* (Princeton: Princeton University Press, 1987), 209.

38. Marco Antonio Bernal, "Ciudad Juárez, 1983 y 1985: Las dificultades de la democracia," in *La vida política mexicana en la crisis,* Soledad Loaeza and Rafael Segovia, eds. (Mexico City: El Colegio de México, 1987), 165–166.

39. "Encuesta nacional de opinión pública, iglesia-estado," 1990.

40. *Exámen,* 1, no. 8 (January 15, 1990): 6.

41. James Wilkie discovered no change in Church-sanctioned marriages at the high point of the Cristero movement in 1930, compared to the succeeding 30 years. The figures remained at two-thirds during the three decades. "Statistical Indicators of the Impact of National Revolution on the Catholic Church in Mexico, 1910–1967," *Journal of Church and State* 12, no. 1 (Winter 1970): 95.

42. Oscar Aguilar and Enrique Luengo G., "Iglesia y gobierno en el D.F.," unpublished paper, Ibero-American University, January 1986, notes, later published in *D.F.: Gobierno y sociedad civil,* Pablo González Casanova, ed. (Mexico City: El Caballito, 1987), 197–215.

43. Enrique Alduncin Abitia, *Los valores de los mexicanos,* 175.

44. "Encuesta nacional de opinión pública, iglesia-estado," 1990.

45. Interestingly, the only political figure in recent years who is rated at a comparable

level is president Carlos Salinas. Researchers have not specifically asked Mexicans about the presidency, although most observers believe its legitimacy declined precipitously since 1968. However, Mexicans appear to make a distinction between the presidency, the administration, and the individual president, consistently giving Salinas high marks since taking office until the end of his administration. Those ratings changed drastically after he left office.

46. John Considine, *The Church in the New Latin America* (New Orleans: Fides Publishers, 1964). For Mexico specifically, see Manuel González Ramírez, *La iglesia mexicana en cifras* (Mexico City, 1969).

47. John L. Sullivan, *Political Tolerance and American Democracy* (Chicago: University of Chicago Press, 1982), 135–139, discovered a negative correlation between frequency of church attendance and levels of tolerance toward unpopular minorities. U.S. Catholics were slightly more tolerant than U.S. Protestants.

48. Some informal measures of religious intensity through attendance also exist. For example, Bishop Mario de Gasperín of Querétaro noted that 65,000 people were making the eight-day pilgrimage from his diocese to the Virgin of Guadalupe in 1993, and the number increased each year. They were in their 103rd year, and some of the participants had gone 50 successive years. Personal interview with Bishop Mario de Gasperín, Querétaro Diocese, Querétaro, Querétaro, July 12, 1993.

49. Enrique Luengo, "Tendencias actuales y perspectivas futuras de la religión en México: el caso de los jovenes universitarios," Ph.D. dissertation, Ibero-American University, 1992, 96. Interestingly, in the only American study focusing on residence and church attendance, in strongly Catholic Rhode Island, the authors found no relationship between residence and attendance, even when controlling for other variables. Leon F. Bouvier and Robert H. Weller, "Residence and Religious Participation in a Catholic Setting," *Sociological Analysis: A Journal of the Sociology of Religion* 35, no. 4 (Winter 1974): 279.

50. David B. Barrett, *World Christian Encyclopedia,* 187. The archdiocese of Mexico found 78 percent of women and 71 percent of men attending Mass weekly in 1966. In certain dioceses, however, according to Church records, attendance was much lower. For example, in Tijuana, a dynamic, growing border city, attendance was only 25 percent at regular Masses in 1970 and 20 percent in 1987. Catholic Church, Diocese of Tijuana, *Plan pastoral, 1989–1994, hacia una iglesia nueva* (Tijuana: La Diocese, 1989), 131–132.

51. Luis Narro Rodríguez, "Qué valorán los mexicanos hoy?," 37. This compares favorably with the Archdiocese of Mexico's own surveys, showing half of all Catholics were practicing in 1985.

52. "Encuesta nacional del proceso electoral," 1988.

53. *World Values Survey,* 1990, and "Encuesta nacional de opinión pública, iglesia-estado," 1990. Ricardo de la Peña and Rosario Toledo, "La cultura política en el DF," *El Nacional,* May 10, 1990, 5, reported that, in the Federal District in 1990, 39 percent attended weekly and 16 percent during religious holidays.

54. See their "Rethinking Catholicism and Politics in Latin America," paper presented at the Latin American Studies Association Meeting, Miami, Florida, 1989, 3.

55. As Charles Davis argues, "Research shows that political behavior and attitudes tend to be affected more by active involvement in an organized religion than by simply an identification with a religion or agreement with a particular religious point of view." See his "Religion and Partisan Loyalty: The Case of Catholic Workers in Mexico," *Western Political Quarterly* 45 (March 1992): 275–297. Most analyses of American politics distinguish among various religious faiths, notably Catholic, Protestant, and Jewish, rather than differences between intensity of religious beliefs and voting behavior. Of course, in a cul-

ture dominated by a single religion, this approach has little utility. Intensity, as measured by Church attendance, between Protestant and Catholics does have a bearing on partisanship. This was found to be the case during the Kennedy–Nixon race in 1960. See William Flanigan and Nancy H. Zingale, *Political Behavior of the American Electorate,* 7th ed. (Washington: Congressional Quarterly Press, 1991), 76–77.

56. David Leege et al., "Religiosity, Church Social Teachings, and Socio-Political Attitudes," *Review of Religious Research* 28 (1986): 118–128, identified a low but statistically significant relationship between the two.

57. Noelle Montiel, "Las mujeres, instrumento de la iglesia institucional para mantener las estructuras de dominación," in *Religión y política en México,* Martín de la Rosa and Charles A. Reilly, eds. (Mexico City: Siglo XXI, 1985), 160ff.

58. Data for gender come from Enrique Alduncin Abitia, "Los Valores de los Mexicanos," 1987, "Encuesta nacional de opinión pública, iglesia-estado, 1990, and "Encuesta nacional del proceso electoral," 1988; and Alberto Hernández Medina, "Religión y moral," 144. Carol Ann Drogus suggests that the traditional Catholic tends to view religion as a source of solace but is generally not interested in applying this to broad social issues. Personal correspondence, May 3, 1992.

59. Claude Pomerlau, "The Catholic Church in Mexico and Its Changing Relationship to Society and the State," unpublished manuscript, December 1980, 28.

60. Data on education and church attendance come from "Encuesta nacional del proceso electoral," 1988, and Enrique Alduncin Abitia, "Los valores de los mexicanos," 1987.

61. *Examen* 1, no. 8 (January 15, 1990): 6.

62. Ralph Carleton Beals also concluded in a 1965 study that self-identification as Catholic increased with social class standing. "Bureaucratic Change in the Mexican Catholic Church, 1926–1950," unpublished Ph.D. dissertation, University of California, Berkeley, 1966. Kenneth Coleman and Charles L. Davis also noted that "[a]s religiosity increases in the upper class, so does a generalized sense of trust in political leaders. . . . [F]aith in the structure of political leadership *is* a direct function of upper-class conventional religiosity." "Civil and Conventional Religion in Secular Authoritarian Regimes: The Case of Mexico," *Studies in Comparative International Development* 13, no. 2 (Summer 1978): 69.

63. One explanation for geographic distinctions in religiosity is that regional cultural differences lead to differential social learning, thus leading to differences in patterns of religiosity and levels of participation in religious activities. Paul H. Chalfant and Peter L. Heller, "Rural/Urban Versus Regional Differences in Religiosity," 77.

64. Kenneth Wald et al., "Political Cohesion in Churches," *Journal of Politics* 52, no. 1 (February 1990): 197, citing Gabriel Almond and G. Bingham Powell, Jr., *Comparative Politics: Systems, Process, and Policy* (Boston: Little, Brown, 1978), 92.

65. Even more significant comparisons could be made among parishes. Unfortunately, no such survey data on Mexico is available. As David Leege notes, "[D]ifferences from parish to parish, often within the same region, suggest that 'the Catholic viewpoint' is not well tapped by descriptions that rely on national survey data alone. Instead of 'the Catholic viewpoint' there are many Catholic viewpoints, and these differ often by the parish one calls home." David C. Leege and Joseph Gremillion, *The People, Their Pastors, and the Church: Viewpoints on Church Policies and Positions,* Notre Dame Study of Catholic Parish Life, Report no. 7 (Terre Haute, Ind.: University of Notre Dame, 1986), 10.

66. Enrique Luengo demonstrates in his dissertation that among Ibero-American University students in four cities, figures for those who said their religious beliefs affected party preferences ranged from 19 to 30 percent. "Tendencias actuales y perspectivas futuras de la religión en México," unpublished Ph.D. dissertation, Ibero-American University, 1992.

67. In addition to the data from the Hernández study, and the raw data "Los valores de los mexicanos," 1987, the unpublished data from the "Encuesta nacional," 1989, is revealing.

68. Unpublished data from a poll taken October 28–November 4, 1986, for the *New York Times,* involving a sample of 1,875 respondents. Some of the results of that survey were published in the *Times* on November 16, 1986, 1, 16, and November 17, 1986, A8.

69. Michael Fleet and Brian Smith, "Rethinking Catholicism and Politics in Latin America," 25.

70. Kenneth D. Wald, D. E. Owen, and S. D. Hill, Jr., "Churches as Political Communities," 534, 545.

71. Kathleen Murphy Beatty and Oliver Walter, "Religious Preference and Practice: Reevaluating Their Impact on Political Tolerance," *Public Opinion Quarterly* 48 (1984): 319–323.

72. Mori de México, *Encuesta Semanal,* September 25, 1992.

73. Data for the effects of religiosity on general values are from the "Encuesta nacional de opinión pública, iglesia-estado," 1990, "Encuesta nacional del proceso electoral," 1988, and two state-level polls CEOP conducted, "Encuesta Electoral sobre Michoacán and Baja California," September 1989.

74. "Encuesta nacional de opinión pública, iglesia-estado," 1990.

75. From a survey done of major Mexico City papers, published in *Estrategias Actuales* 1, no. 3 (March 1990): 1.

76. Even the government's own poll, financed by its official newspaper *El Nacional,* agreed with these results. See the "Política" section, July 5, 1990, 13.

77. *El Nacional,* March 25, 1990, 15.

78. For these figures, see *El Nacional,* "Política," May 10, 1990, 13; George Grayson, "Courting the Church in Mexico," *Christian Science Monitor,* May 17, 1990, 19; and "Encuesta nacional de opinión pública, iglesia-estado," 1990.

79. Catholic Church, Diocese of Tijuana, *Plan pastoral, 1989–1994, hacia una iglesia nueva,* 260.

80. Oscar Hinojosa, "La misión evangélica ordena dejar la sacristía, afirma Obeso Rivera," *Proceso,* September 8, 1986, 13.

81. See Miguel Basáñez, "Elections and Political Culture in Mexico," in *Mexican Politics in Transition,* Judith Gentleman, ed. (Boulder, Colo.: Westview Press, 1987), 184; and *El Nacional,* "Política," May 10, 1990, 13.

82. Perhaps Mexicans are transferring their own personal attitudes toward political participation onto the Church and its representatives. In the survey completed by the Tijuana Diocese, 74 percent, exactly the same percentage, said they should do nothing in response to the question: In what form should you be active as a Catholic in politics? Only 3 percent thought they should try for political office, 10 percent would become a party member, and another 10 percent would join an electoral committee. Catholic Church, Diocese of Tijuana, *Plan pastoral, 1989–1994, hacia una iglesia nueva,* 245.

83. Data are from "Encuesta Nacional," 1989.

84. Michael Fleet and Brian Smith, "Rethinking Catholicism and Politics in Latin America," 25.

85. For evidence of philosophical ties, see Donald Mabry, *Mexico's Acción Nacional: A Catholic Alternative to Revolution* (Syracuse, N.Y.: Syracuse University Press, 1973).

86. In fact, this influence more than any other discouraged establishment politicians from granting Mexican women the right to vote. See Ward Morton, *Women Suffrage in Mexico* (Gainesville: University of Florida Press, 1962).

87. Enrique Luengo, "Tendencias actuales y perspectivas futuras de la religión en Méx-

ico," 226, found that 63 percent of Ibero students who had attended religious high schools attended Church weekly compared to only 37 percent of those who had attended secular schools. About the same percentages found religion important in their lives.

88. In fact, this comprehensive survey of Mexico on the basis of public, private, and religious education concluded, "[A]lthough religious students score higher in accepting propositions about the goodness of God and his treatment of human beings, they are not substantially different from most responses by private and public school students." Elvia S. Palomera et al., *Valores en la comunidad educativa mexicana* (Mexico City: Instituto de Proposiciones Estratégicas, 1990), 92.

89. This finding is confirmed by Andrew Stein in his study of Catholics and Protestants in Central America, where he discovered little difference in their support for government or in left/right voting. What he did find is that fundamentalism, conceptualized as a "belief in the Bible or the literal word of God," does illustrate a stronger correlation with center/right parties. Stein and others demonstrate that fundamental religious beliefs and religious subcategories are far more revealing than traditional differences among Catholics, Protestants, and Jews. "Religion and Mass Politics in Central America," paper presented at the North Central Council of Latin Americanists, Boston University, October 1992, 24–25.

90. Comisión Episcopal para el Apostolado de los Laicos, *Que piensan los laicos mexicanos,* 32–33.

91. Ivan Zavala, "Valores políticos," 96.

92. Carlos Martínez Assad, "State Elections in Mexico," in *Electoral Patterns and Perspectives in Mexico,* Arturo Alvarado, ed. (La Jolla, Calif.: UCSD, Mexico–United States Studies Center, 1987), 36.

93. Raw data, *Los Angeles Times* poll, August 1989.

94. The first evidence of no relationship between party choice and religiosity, in Mexico City only, appeared in Kenneth Coleman's pioneering effort, "The Capital City Electorate and Mexico's Acción Nacional: Some Survey Evidence on Conventional Hypotheses," *Social Science Quarterly* (1975).

95. One explanation for this is offered by Enrique Garza Ramírez, who notes correctly that most Mexicans who vote for a political party are unaware of their ideology. In his study of Nuevo León in the mid-1980s, this was true for 79 percent of PAN and 83 percent of PRI voters. *Nuevo León 1985,* 138.

96. Miguel Basáñez, "Encuesta nacional de opinión pública estado-iglesia," cross-tabulations of raw data.

97. Charles L. Davis, "Religion and Partisan Loyalty: The Case of Catholic Workers in Mexico," 8. Kenneth Coleman and Charles L. Davis have concluded that the PRI would be embarrassed to acknowledge that the most religious segments of Mexican society are a political resource and are anxious to hide the fact since it often portrayed PAN as a reactionary tool of the Church. Of course, this posture has changed since the constitutional reforms. "Civil and Conventional Religion in Secular Authoritarian Regimes," 58.

98. In their excellent preliminary findings, Timothy J. Steigena and Kenneth M. Coleman reported that the religiously nonaffiliated in Chile tend to favor left-wing political views. "Protestantism and Politics in Chile, 1972–1991," paper presented at the New England Council of Latin Americanists, Boston University, October 1992.

99. Edgar Butler et al., however, found a significant correlation between non-Catholic voters and support for the PRI and a negative correlation to PAN. Of course non-Catholics include atheists and other religions. "An Examination of the Official Results of the 1988 Mexican Presidential Election," in Edgar W. Butler and Jorge A. Bustamante, *Sucesión presidencial: The 1988 Mexican Presidential Election* (Boulder, Colo.: Westview Press, 1991), 33.

100. Ricardo de la Peña and Rosario Toledo, "La cultura política en el DF," *El Nacional,* "Política," May 10, 1990, 10.

101. "Encuesta nacional del proceso electoral," 1988.

102. Joseph Klesner, "Changing Patterns of Electoral Participation and Official Party Support in Mexico," 108.

103. Oscar González et al., "Batallas en el reino de este mundo," *Nexos,* no. 78 (June 1984): 23.

104. In fact, Andrew Weigert and Darwin L. Thomas's comparative study concluded that Mexican high school students from the religiously conservative city of Mérida, Yucatán, did not follow priests' wishes in voting, nor were they any less independent than their European and U.S. students. "Secularization and Religiosity: A Cross-National Study of Catholic Adolescents in Five Societies," 12.

105. Gabriel Zaid, "Intelectuales," *Vuelta,* November 1990, 22.

106. Enrique Luengo, "Tendencias actuales y perspectivas futuras de la religión en México: el case de los jovenes universitarios," 114–115.

107. "Encuesta nacional de opinión pública, iglesia-estado," 1990.

108. Enrique Garza Ramírez, *Nuevo León 1985,* 106, 158.

109. In their earlier study of urban Mexico, Kenneth Coleman and Charles Davis concluded that "secular authoritarian regimes benefit from the propensity of those who are more conventionally religious" and that "PRI attracts a greater percentage of its support from the most conventionally religious elements of urban Mexico" than PAN. "Civil and Conventional Religion in Secular Authoritarian Regimes: The Case of Mexico," *Studies in Comparative International Development* 13, no. 2 (Summer 1978): 59.

110. *El Nacional,* "Política," May 10, 1990, 13.

111. Alberto Hernández Medina, *Como somos los mexicanos,* 126.

112. "World Values Survey," 1990. For example, the episcopate has been critical of the North American Free Trade Agreement.

113. Kenneth D. Wald et al., "Church as Political Communities," *American Political Science Review* 82 (June 1988): 531–548.

114. Enrique Garza Ramírez, ed., *Nuevo León,* 102.

115. Graciela Guadarrama, "Entrepreneurs and Politics: Businessmen in Electoral Contests in Sonora and Nuevo León, July 1985," in *Electoral Patterns and Perspectives in Mexico,* Arturo Alvarado, ed. (La Jolla, Calif.: UCSD, Center for U.S.-Mexican Studies, 1987), 102.

116. Javier Contreras Orozco, *Chihuahua, trampa del sistema* (Mexico City: EDAMEX, 1987), 63–66.

117. Joe Keenan, "Showdown in San Luis Potosí," *El Financiero Internacional,* September 30, 1991, 14. The governor did resign two weeks into his administration, on October 9, 1991. I am not implying, however, that it was in response to the archbishop's statement.

6

Becoming a Priest

Why Mexicans Enter the Clergy

A primary theme of this book is to explain how Church leaders and prominent politicians view each other. I believe that the experiences that form both politicians and bishops contribute to their attitudes and values in general and to their social, political, and religious beliefs in particular. One of the variables that explains some personal qualities is why an individual chooses to make a life career out of one profession versus another. Comparisons between politicians and bishops are especially revealing because these two groups of individuals exercise, or have the potential for exercising, enormous influence over society, and despite their obvious differences of emphasis, share many leadership skills.

Not much information exists in religious studies as to why individuals choose the priesthood. The most comprehensive study, that of Joseph H. Fichter, surveyed priests and brothers in the United States. Fichter discovered five chief reasons, categorized according to the two religious groups:

Priests	*Brothers*
Priestly work	Do good in life
Salvation	Salvation
Vocational sense	Educated by brothers
Love of God	Attraction to brothers' work
Salvation of others	Salvation of others [1]

Fichter also discovered that most men make a decision to become priests in high school, at an average age of 17. This is interesting because it is the age at which most future Mexican politicians have shown a strong interest in student politics, from which they will build a base to pursue a national political career. It is also the age when most military officers join the Heroic Military College as cadets. The reasons given in the Fichter study suggest, with the exception of brothers, that most U.S. priests reach their decisions internally, motivated by elements in their personal values.

Mexican priests, however, in contrast to their U.S. counterparts, place a higher emphasis on external actors influencing their decisions. Several of these agents of influence were also apparent in a study by Andrew Greeley. Greeley reported that the most important influences in the decision to become a priest were another priest (mentioned by more than two-fifths of his respondents) and the priest's own mother (mentioned by an additional third).[2]

If we combine elements discovered in the Fitcher and Greeley studies, several broad categories exercising a potential influence on an individual's choice to become a priest become apparent. One category is the family, whether it is a parent, a relative, or the general family environment. A second category is contact with a priest, nun, or other member of the clergy. A third element is entirely personal, stemming from the individual's self-examination of his values, personal and spiritual. In fact, in a conversation with three priests, all of whom represented different facets of the Catholic Church, each seemed to fall into one of these three categories: the first spoke of an especially kind and thoughtful priest who impressed him, a second believed it was his family environment, and a third considered it a spiritual decision involving his desire to help people.[3] A fourth category, which appeared only among North American brothers, is the influence of educational experiences. Teachers, usually brothers or priests, encourage their leanings toward the priesthood. A fifth category, which does not appear in the studies of U.S. priests, is the impact of historic events. In the same way that the Depression or a presidential campaign influenced numerous Mexicans to pursue political careers, a major historical event, the Cristiada, affected an entire generation of priests.

Family Environment

Of all the categories, family environment is by far the most important in affecting a Mexican's desire to become a priest, not only because of a future priest's parents' behavior, but because parental values often determine the extent to which their children become religiously active, whether or not they attend a parochial school, or the degree to which they might come in personal contact with other religious models such as priests or nuns. It is revealing, therefore, to examine some of the individual testimony of bishops as to how their families affected these choices, and at the same time to compare family backgrounds of equally influential politicians, looking for differences.

Bishop Francisco María Aguilera González, who grew up in Guanajuato in the 1920s, offers an insightful view:

> I have often asked myself that same question, why I became a priest, but I think it was due to the religious environment of my family. I think this was really the most important reason. But what I mean by religious environment is how my parents seem to face life, their values, their attitude towards justice, and the way they ran their business (in which I was involved, since I worked for them). I had a good upbringing in literature and history. I had an opportunity to study these subjects, and this com-

bined with the intellectual environment and their serving as a model for me, plus the fact that my mother had to resign her teaching job because of the antireligious situation in Mexico, made me decide to become a priest.[4]

Aguilera González mentions familial religious environment, but what he is really emphasizing is family values, perhaps even Christian values, without associating them directly to religion and religious practices. Many other Mexican priests have also emphasized family values in general and their parents as models, rather than their specific religious attitudes. For example, a priest from Jalisco with a reputation for radical pastoral strategies talks about his parents, who immigrated to California and then returned to his birthplace in Irapuato, Guanajauto. He describes them as poor, with little formal education, but they both could read and discussed many subjects with their son. For him, they set a wonderful personal example.

Many top church leaders, including the Vatican delegate, Archbishop Jirolamo Prigione, believe that young men not only join the clergy because of their family environment, but that their family environment strongly affects their values. This effect is translated not only into personal values but also into values affecting their behavior within the Church. It is no accident, for example, that what Bishop Samuel Ruiz, who has made a strenuous effort to help the indigenous poor, most remembers from his childhood "is my father and mother going out and helping people, regardless of their social class, and I often accompanied them," a task he has institutionalized in his Chiapas diocese.[5]

A second familial environment is the degree to which religion plays a role in parents' and grandparents' beliefs, a variable that distinguishes most future priests from future politicians. Over and over again various priests and bishops emphasize the continuity of the religious values among their parents and their antecedents. For example, Father Baltazar López, a disciple of Bishop Sergio Méndez Arceo of Cuernavaca, describes himself as "the son of a very Catholic father, from a traditional Catholic environment. My father originally was from Guanajuato where the Cristeros were part of the lifestyle of our village. He was very religious and he wanted me to be a priest. My grandparents were Spanish peasants, also very strongly religious."[6] An older parish priest, Father Fernando Glagoaga, recalls a similar heritage: "[M]y family was religious, I don't know very much about my grandparents' history; but my paternal grandfather went far enough in his education that he was at the point of being ordained a priest. My maternal grandparents were also religious, not 100 percent, but they maintained close ties with the Church, affecting me the most religiously."[7]

Some parents, as in the case of Father López, pushed their children into the priesthood. Most, however, only provided a serious, religious ambience. Many of these parents were also products of religious education. For example, one priest noted that although his family came from peasant origins, his father had the opportunity to study under the Jesuits and his mother explored Catholicism under nuns' watchful eyes.[8] Consequently, some priests may have been raised in families with higher levels of religious sophistication.

Other priests learned about the importance of religious values through grandparents' or parents' experiences. For example, a Jesuit describes his parents' religious practices as nothing unusual but remembers his grandparents celebrating Masses with representatives of various religious orders in violation of the law. He recalls that the state governor, a family friend, would inform them ahead of time if it was alright to hold these illegal, private Masses.[9] Other future priests, similar to politicians, were children of activist parents. Bishop José Pablo Rovalo, a member of the Brothers of Mary order, resigned from his diocese in Zacatecas to spend eight years traveling with young Catholic activists as their adviser. His parents, who were very religious, were involved actively in the Catholic Action organization, and his father became its president. Rovalo describes him as "a wonderful model because he always took his faith seriously and didn't make a distinction between practice and belief."[10]

Still other Mexicans became priests because their families, in implementing their religious beliefs, regularly took their children to Mass. In the United States, many who entered the priesthood began serving in some capacity in the Mass as a young child. A close examination of the backgrounds of future Mexican priests and bishops suggest a similar pattern. One bishop reported:

> My interest in the priesthood extends back to when I was 11 years old, when I began serving as an acolyte in the Guadalajara diocese. It was the Church's environment which affected my decision. I would say its impact extends to my soul as a layperson since I served the Virgin in the Santisimo Chapel each Saturday. I would have to say that serving as an acolyte for each of these services provided an influential example, affecting me deeply in my heart.[11]

Mexican Catholicism has developed along very unique and peculiar lines, not only in the relationship between religion and the state, but also in how other prominent groups view Catholicism, politics, and Church behavior. The Mexican population, including its priests, are products of a unique 19th-century Liberal hybrid of Catholicism on the one hand and state domination of religion on the other. For example, Juan Bazdresch, a Jesuit who teaches at the Ibero-American University, describes his father's family as classical Liberals and his great grandfather as a public figure in Benito Juárez's administration. His mother was a practicing Catholic, so all of the children were baptized. As is true of many Mexicans, but more so of parents of secular rather than religious leaders, the father was Catholic but never practiced his faith.[12] Leading public and cultural figures, even from non-Catholic religious backgrounds, have been affected by this dichotomous, parental pattern. Among active Catholic laity, nearly one-half mentioned a mother who strongly expressed and practiced Catholic beliefs.[13] It is important to examine these familial experiences in order to comprehend how religion and Catholicism specifically are perceived in Mexican culture.

When the same questions were put to prominent Mexican public and cultural figures from all political persuasions, some interesting comparative patterns emerged. Many of Mexico's leading politicians were from self-described Catholic families and, in some cases, were also educated in Catholic schools. President Miguel de la Madrid is very forthcoming in his description of his familial religious environment and his childhood formation in Catholic schools:

I was born in a Catholic family. My father was a traditional Liberal and my mother was very religious without being overly addicted to her beliefs. She practiced her religion, she was faithful, and she took Catholicism seriously. On my father's side it was a Liberal family in the Mexican sense, respectful of religion, not persecutors of religion; and the same was true of my grandfather, governor of the State of Colima, who was also a Liberal but respected religion.

I was basically raised in Catholic private schools from the third year of primary through my preparatory education in La Salle institutions, specifically the Cristóbal Colón school. I think in the first place that my family education, my formal education, never produced a fervent Catholicism, but my beliefs did develop a respectful attitude toward the Catholic religion. In school, I had the opportunity to study Catholic religion, and I believe in its fundamental teachings. I think I have certain disagreements with the faith, and there are discrepancies between what I believe and what the Church advocates.

I did my legal studies at the National University, and the university provided a very important contrast to my previous schooling because it did encourage a different set of values. I never received a strong dose of anti-Catholicism or antireligion from the law school; rather I obtained a Liberal influence, a belief in religious rights and against any form of intolerance. I am basically in agreement with essential Liberal principles on the church/state question, especially those dealing with the separation of church and state.[14]

The experiences of Miguel de la Madrid, a hybrid of religious and Liberal familial influences, are duplicated repeatedly among leading figures in the Mexican political establishment, including other former presidents. One of the dominant characteristics of Mexican politicians' families is the mother's strong religious beliefs, which probably explains why among priests it is typically the mother who influences a child to pursue a religious career. President Luis Echeverría Alvarez described his mother as very religious and his father as secular and Liberal, a norm he ascribes to most Mexican families. He believes among his generation (1920s) that the maternal side was most strongly influenced by Catholicism, and that the pattern found among his grandparents was similar.[15]

Among public figures, fathers seem to be more significant in passing on their spiritual beliefs than mothers. President José López Portillo, de la Madrid's predecessor, describes some similar features:

My great-grandfather on my mother's side was very religious. I was educated as a Catholic and baptized, but I lost my faith a little bit after I was 14. I'm a freethinker now. I won't return to religion from fear, but I do maintain an amount of respect for the mystery and doubt concerning faith. My parents were very religious; in fact my father was so religious that when public officials were requested to denounce their faith, he resigned rather than do so. His action penalized us greatly, resulting in a heavy economic hardship on my parents. But he remained steadfast in his refusal to take an anti-Catholic oath. To me, tolerance is the most important quality we need today.[16]

In the case of López Portillo, it is also important to note that he comes from two generations of political figures—both his grandfather and father were prominent in political life. His father, obviously holding strong religious beliefs, also was molded in the Liberal philosophy, not only meaning separation of church and state but also tolerance of religious beliefs, a principle he adamantly defended. Most young men who enter the clergy never had familial connections with politicians, as in the cases of the last four presidents.[17]

Among nonestablishment politicians most closely identified in the popular mind with Catholicism and religion are leaders of the National Action Party, which ideologically borrowed many elements of Catholic Christian Democratic thinking at various points of its evolution.[18] Abel Vicencio Tovar, who joined the party in 1951, serving as its president and representing PAN in the Chamber of Deputies on four occasions, did not draw his religious principles from his family, which shares more in common with other politicians' backgrounds, including establishment figures, but from lay religious activities:[19]

> My parents weren't religious. My father is what you would call a Liberal, and my mother was typically religious for her era. My father died when I was four; he was president of the Supreme Court. My mother wasn't strongly religious, and our religious training was more of an environmental circumstance than anything intentional. When I was 12, however, some friends invited me to join the Mexican Catholic Action Youth (ACJM). This was very interesting because it involved me in public and political debates in 1938. I joined the regular ACJM at 16, and eventually I became its president. I remained active for many years, participating in numerous protests against the church-state articles. . . . My religious values were influenced by my ACJM experiences.[20]

Mexican politicians who have made their mark with parties on the left share familial experiences similar to those of other politicians, whether they are part of the establishment or leaders of the National Action Party. For example, Heberto Castillo, president of the Mexican Workers Party and later a leader of Cuauhtémoc Cárdenas's Democratic Revolutionary Party, born in a village in the Huasteca region of Veracruz, without any church, described his parents as believers but not active Catholics. "We lived in a very violent region; in fact, the priest wore a pistol. As a youth I did not accept religion. I was very much a rebel then, and I just could never believe in it."[21] But Castillo never became anti-Church, suggesting, like many other Mexican politicians, that he did not believe in any dogma. In fact, he fondly recalls the visits of Bishop Sergio Méndez Arceo when he was imprisoned as a leader of the 1968 student movement. Another political figure, Rodolfo González Guevara, a prominent leader of the populist wing of the Institutional Revolutionary Party and its secretary general before joining the PRD in 1991 describes another typical family:

> I was born in Mazatlán in 1918, the son of Antonio J. González, a completely committed Liberal without any religious tendencies whatsoever. My mother was a very deeply Catholic woman, but I didn't receive any influences from her because she died when I was four, and my father, who had to educate five children, took us to live in Guadalajara. . . . I lived in Guadalajara with two aunts, who were both teachers, one Aurelia, a strong Liberal without any religion, who was in charge of the household, and the other Alicia, who like my mother was deeply Catholic. Since Aurelia was respon-

sible for our educational orientation, we were raised as very strong Liberals. During the Cristiada, all of the members of my family opposed the Cristeros and were strong and faithful supporters of the government.[22]

Some Mexican politicians and intellectual figures incorporate a third variable, Protestantism, in the traditional Liberal-Catholic heritage. Protestant influences among their parents' generation were part of small, traditional Protestant groups, typically Methodist or Anglican, not contemporary evangelical groups. Ricardo Pascoe, PRD communications secretary, has one of the most unusual religious backgrounds:

> My great-grandfather was the first Anglican bishop, a discreet negotiator between President Cárdenas and the American embassy, and very intense in promoting his religious beliefs. He encouraged his workers to become Protestant, causing a tremendous conflict with the Catholic Church, especially with the local priest. . . . My grandfather converted Francisco Múgica [one of the leading advocates of the religious restrictions at the 1917 Constitutional Convention], whose last wife was a Protestant. My father was a practicing Catholic, rejecting his parents' religious beliefs. He actually became a Quaker. I would describe my mother as a typical Protestant. There was nothing unusual about her religious upbringing, a normal Anglo-Saxon.
>
> I believe I joined the opposition because of my Protestant religious upbringing. Protestantism, as you know, is a minority religion, thus it forms part of the religious opposition.[23]

A small but important group of Mexicans in public life have acted as a bridge between the Catholic Church and the clergy and the state and politicians.[24] Surprisingly, in the early 20th century, during the Revolution, when anticlerical sentiments ran high, many politicians received important religious influences, exposing them to the clergy, allowing them to develop social relationships necessary to the informal contacts that sustain the actual church-state relationship. Antonio Martínez Báez, member of President Miguel Alemán's generation (born in the 1900s), which introduced many features of contemporary Mexican politicians, describes his upbringing in the heart of Michoacán, in West Central Mexico:

> My grandfather Ramón Martínez Aviles, a lawyer and author of many religious hymns, who I knew personally, lived in Guadalajara on a pension as organist of the Cathedral of Michoacán. My father, Manuel, a doctor and botanist, directed the Colegio de San Nicolás de Hidalgo, the same school in which Father Morelos [a distinguished independence leader] studied. My father studied preparatory at the Conciliar Seminary of Morelia because his father was deeply involved in the Catholic Church. My father was dedicated to the natural sciences, a man with advanced Liberal ideas, and his studies produced conflicts with his parents, who were so religious. . . . My mother was from a traditional Catholic family of middle-class farmers. She studied and became a teacher at the Colegio Terciano. I was formed in a familial environment in which my father, a Liberal who believed in Darwin but was never a Mason, earned the respect of Jesuit scientists, his fellow botanists. He never attended Church, yet he baptized all of his children.[25]

Many important figures in Mexican public life attended seminaries before the 1920s, and many fathers of postrevolutionary politicians attended conciliar seminaries. Recent generations of public figures have attended public or parochial schools, often where religious fathers or nuns taught, but they have not been, without exception, costudents of future priests.

A key figure in Mexican public life who provided an important link between the Church and politicians during the administration of Luis Echeverría and José López Portillo was Fausto Zerón Medina. His family, extending back to his great-grandparents, came from Los Altos, Jalisco, a stronghold of Catholic traditionalism and a region serving as a basis of Agustín Yáñez's dark, religiously influenced novels.[26] His grandparents sent Fausto's father to the conciliar seminary, after which he became active in politics. But because he attended one of Mexico's most important seminaries, he met many future Church leaders, including Bishop Pasquel Díaz. One of his father's teachers, Bishop Miguel de la Mora, was involved in the Cristero rebellion.[27] Fausto remembers playing in his grandfather's house, meeting many national politicians who figured prominently in Mexico's history, including Gilberto Valenzuela, a candidate for the presidency in 1929 who left his personal affairs in the hands of Zerón's grandfather.

Among younger generations of Mexican politicians, stronger Catholic backgrounds are more common. These similar familial religious environments are likely to help bridge the separation between future clergy and public figures. Agustín Basave, an important PRI ideologue and federal deputy from Monterrey, participated in the 1992 congressional debates on religious reforms, serving on the congressional advisory committee. His personal formation and experiences were tied deeply to his father's religious and spiritual values:

> My paternal grandfather was a religious man, a strong Catholic, who late in life, through the influence of his intellectual friends, passed through a crisis of faith but in the end remained a strong Catholic. I was four when he died. My father and my grandmother were tremendously profound believers, and if you recall the chapter in [José] Vasconcelos's memoirs describing his mother's mysticism, that is how I would describe their religious beliefs. My father is a Catholic, but also a Catholic philosopher. He is an adviser to the Pope, a member of a group of selected thinkers chosen by the Vatican, and of his 30 some books, most are about philosophy or religion. . . . Moral values are the most important thing for him. He taught me to respect his values above anything else. Even though I now have my own religious crisis, because I am very close to agnosticism, I still retain those religious values. What I admired most is that he defended his views, risking his life in the 1960s as dean of the School of Philosophy at the University of Nuevo León, the last administrator who was openly anticommunist during this period. . . . It was his religious beliefs which made him oppose these groups. They threatened his life repeatedly, they threw a bomb in my bedroom, they threatened to kidnap us, and they would call my mother and tell her they had killed my father. . . . I was eight years old then, and I remember seeing a sign which said, "death to Basave," and I asked my mother why someone wanted to kill me. She explained it was my father, not me.[28]

Many of Mexico's leading intellectuals have unusual religious origins as well, sometimes Catholic-Protestant-Liberal or a more unusual religious flavor, Jewish or Greek Orthodox. Mexican intellectuals, because they lack a strong Catholic upbringing, have not been enthusiastic advocates of Catholicism or religious values in their writings, Basave's father notwithstanding. For example, Mariclaire Acosta Urquidi, president of the Mexican Committee for the Defense and Promotion of Human Rights, has familial roots extending back to Independence and the Reform. On her mother's side, her family was strongly anticlerical but Catholic and Liberal and supported Benito Juárez. Her maternal grandmother, mother of Víctor Urquidi, one of Mexico's leading economists and intellectuals, was an English Anglican, raising Mariclaire's mother as an Anglican. Her father's relatives were typically Catholic of Spanish origin but practiced their religion "Mexican style," believing strongly in religious values but not the Church. Mariclaire Acosta was baptized a Catholic but only because, she discovered, they didn't want her to have trouble later on or when she was ready to marry, not because they wanted her to practice her Catholicism.[29] Today, she remains a Catholic.

Gabriel Zaid, one of Mexico's leading poets and essayist for *Vuelta,* an influential intellectual monthly, is of Greek Orthodox origin. Although Zaid's parents were Middle Eastern immigrants and his father was sufficiently religious to bring him from Monterrey to Mexico City to baptize him in a Greek Orthodox church, Zaid was educated in a private, Protestant, secular-oriented school in Monterrey.[30] Another prominent intellectual figure, political economist Luis Rubio, was raised in a secular environment by nonpracticing Jewish parents. Although he briefly attended Hebrew school, most of his education took place in private institutions run by anticlerical Spanish Republicans.[31]

Religious Kinship

As some of the descriptions of public figures or of those Mexicans having ties between the religious and political communities demonstrate, personal contact with models from either community were common. Nearly one-third of prominent Mexican politicians in the 20th century came from politically active families.[32] Children are strongly influenced by parental behavior, especially by example. Mexican politicians and priests are not alone in this quality. In the United States, 70 percent of seminary students reported close family members in religious orders. In Latin America, a study of seminary students found that 32 percent claimed similar religious relatives. It should be remembered, however, that the percentage of priests with family members in the Church is likely to be much higher than among seminary students in general since most seminary students drop out before becoming priests.[33] If military cadets are any measure of the importance of family ties, those who persist have much higher percentages of military kin than those who enroll.[34] Future priests, like future military officers, are more likely to understand their choice of a military or religious career and the sacrifices it means if they come from a familial environment both familiar with and supportive of such professional choices.

For clergy, regardless of socioeconomic background, the presence of priests or nuns in the immediate family seems a typical thread in their family origins. Among recent bishops, Sergio Méndez Arceo, noted for his controversial influence in Cuernavaca, claimed four uncles as archbishops, bishops, canons, or priests. His biographer attributes a switch in his interest from engineering to the priesthood to a speech his uncle gave about the scarcity of priests in Mexico.[35] Many short comments from priests and bishops support this belief:

[W]e were 15 brothers and sisters in that family. Three of my brothers entered the Church, and my oldest brother has a son who is also a priest.[36]

—Parish priest

I wouldn't say religion was anything special in my family, but I did have a brother who was a priest. We are the only ones in the family. We did have close friends who were priests, and my father's sister entered a nunnery, but left before taking her vows.[37]

—Jesuit priest

My grandfather served on the diocese committee in Huajuapan, Oaxaca; in fact, for many years he was in charge of the tithing funds; a very honest man. . . . My uncle Lucio became a priest in the diocese of Puebla, where he became rector of the seminary and later bishop of San Cristóbal de las Casas, Chiapas [1947–1954]. In 1959, he became bishop of Durango. . . . In 1938 [when he was 11, after his father died], my uncle came to get me and took me to Puebla.[38]

—Bishop of Texcoco

In 1933, all the churches were closed, and my mother had a brother who was a priest in Juilquilpan, Michoacán. I didn't know this uncle, but I was sent to visit him. A month later he became a priest in Zamora; I entered the seminary at 13.[39]

—Auxiliary bishop of Mexico City

Many future priests mention other priests as significant, without being related to them through members of their own family. In fact, it is likely that most future priests pattern themselves after a priest with whom they have had some contact. Thus, the religious attitude of the parents are often crucial since they typically provide the means of contact through which a young man associates with the family priest. The common thread that links the priests as a decisive model to future priests is the parents' encouragement in bringing the child into contact with the priest and the child's image of the priest's pastoral activities. Future Mexican bishops who were influenced by such a figure recalled the following characteristics:

My parents were fairly religious, and they wanted to encourage me to frequent the church since the age of ten, to learn more about religious dogma and songs and rituals of the Church. One day the priest invited me to accompany him on his visit to rural areas, which I did. I had many conversations with rural people and I learned to understand their problems. It occurred to me that this would be a wonderful occupation, doing what the priest was doing on these visits.[40]

—Bishop of Nezahualcóyotl, México

I was a student at the National Autonomous University of Mexico in chemical engineering. I graduated in this program, but I got to know several Dominican fathers who were the first in Mexico to establish a university parish and were located nearby. They strongly influenced my decision to become a priest. . . . Father Agustín was originally from a Dominican group in France. He personally had the greatest influence on my formation. Interestingly, he too was a chemist before becoming a priest.[41]

—Bishop of Ciudad Altamirano, Guerrero

I always thought of my parents as being very helpful in making it possible for me to choose such a career. But they never put any personal pressure on me to become a priest. A priest whose name was José María Chávez had a lot to do with my decision and he also helped in the seminary. I thought of him as a heroic figure because of his posture during the Cristero period.[42]

—Bishop of Cuautitlán, México

I think it was my family's life and the figure of the village priest which convinced me. With the religious persecution, the Oaxacan seminary closed, so they sent one of the priests from the seminary to my small town. He was very cultured, intelligent, and impressed me greatly with his education and knowledge.[43]

—Archbishop of Puebla, Puebla

Educational Influences

Studies of politicians elsewhere in the world have shown that a large percentage attribute their interest in politics and a political career to their educational experiences, whether it is peer influence, teachers, or curricular materials. Among Canadian party officials, for example, 40 percent linked their interest to school.[44] Mexican politicians also were strongly influenced in their choice of careers by professors and students.[45] Mexican politicians in the past have attended specific schools that have encouraged their ideology and their political activism. Among older generations of politicians who dominated public life during the 1960s and 1970s, public preparatory schools, specifically the National Preparatory School, were most common. In more recent years, particularly among those politicians born after the 1940s, private schools, specifically religious parochial schools, have become more common in politicians' educational backgrounds. Most Mexicans completed their preparatory education in their mid- to late teens.

The type of school and its specific political and social environment have affected Mexico's leaders. When Rodolfo González Guevara began preparatory school in the 1930s, he joined the Western Socialist Student Organization (FESO), a group that defended President Cárdenas's reforms, especially educational, against Catholic groups. González Guevara actually became the leader of this student organization and led attacks against the nearby Catholic-controlled Autonomous University of Guadalajara.[46] Porfirio Muñoz Ledo, president of the PRD, began to examine his religious and political beliefs seriously at preparatory school, during which time he too became a student leader, ultimately resolving his personal religious beliefs before leaving college at age 22.[47] Arturo Núñez, contemporary of President Carlos Salinas, who became deeply involved in the church-state constitutional reform negotiations, was a product of preparatory education in Tabasco, probably the most anticlerical environment in Mexico, even in the early 1960s, which he describes as strongly Liberal.[48]

Among future priests, almost without exception, most attended seminary as their equivalent of high school. The typical priest or bishop enrolls in seminary at the age of 12 or 13. This same pattern occurs elsewhere in Latin America, at least in Columbia and Venezuela.[49] This age is significant because the future priests are exposed to priests as teachers long before most public figures or military officers are exposed to their professionals as teachers. This experience is also significant because while most seminary students do not become priests, it is a semiclosed educational ambience where clergy are the sole educators.[50]

As is true among future politicians, future priests can be influenced by the seminary ambience alone. For example, Bishop Abelardo Alvarado Alcántara attributes his interest in the priesthood to attending seminary, during which he developed a strong desire to serve other people.[51] Other priests may have been influenced educationally at even earlier periods, in primary schools. One priest from Zacatecas describes his education in the 1930s as occurring in a clandestine school operated by a nun to avoid the "terribly anti-Christian" schools of his day. He claims fellow Mexicans then referred to the secretariat of public education as the "ministerio de prostitución pública."[52]

Impact of History

People are products of their individual and collective experiences. When those experiences occur in a specific historical context, they can result in strong influences on the individual, depending on the person's relationship to historical events. For example, among Mexican politicians, nearly one-fourth claimed that some historical event, political activity, or social context strongly affected their values and their interest in politics.

For Mexican clergy, the single most important event among recent generations is the Cristero rebellion. This rebellion and the general suppression of open religious activity during the late 1920s and early 1930s flavored the lives of strongly religious families. This antireligious context influenced some individuals only indirectly, that is, as younger priests reading about these events. Samuel Morín Suárez actually became interested in the priesthood in the most unusual of environments, the Military Medical School preparatory program, when he began reading books on the history of the Cristeros and the priests who were killed during the movement. As he recalls, "[T]heir lives and religion became very important to me," so he dropped out of school and enrolled in a seminary.[53]

Most bishops influenced by the Cristiada experienced it personally, typically as young children or as seminary students. Some of the parents of these future priests were extremely active as religious laypersons, giving refuge to priests and nuns. Others were members of lay organizations actively opposed to religious suppression, such as the Acción Católica de la Juventud Mexicana (ACJM). Still others had parents who lost their jobs or were forced to move because these events came too close to home. On rare occasions, among this generation of priests, they might have actively participated in the Cristeros, such as Bishop Genaro Alamilla, a long-time spokesperson for the Mexican Episcopate, who cheerfully admitted running guns for the Cristeros as a teenager.[54] The recollections that follow are some of the most vivid among priests who were witnesses to religious persecution.

The first recollection I have of my childhood was that of a persecuted Catholic Church. . . . The only thing which influenced me to become a priest, if anything at all, because it wasn't a person or some experience, was the environment of the religious persecution itself. I remember the death of some priests, and the repression of others, and in our home we actually hid persecuted priests who were fleeing from the authorities, as well as having secret Masses in the house. I think for my generation this was by far the single most important event of our lives.[55]

—Archbishop of Tlanepantla, México

From my personal experience, I remember as a child going into private homes in Veracruz for Masses. I remember a priest being shot by the authorities in the confessional inside his own parish church, which is now where the cathedral of Veracruz is located.[56]

—Jesuit priest

I just recalled something else important in my formation. A nun sought refuge with my grandfather in the 1930s. I remember talking to her. This had a great impression on me—all of those childhood memories.[57]

—Bishop of Texcoco, México

Both my parents were very religious. You have to remember that this was the period of religious persecution, and my father was an active member of the ACJM. My mother was a catechist and of course I absorbed during my childhood my parents' attitudes and experiences during state repression against the Church. The Cristero movement was very strong where my parents lived. In fact, when the priest was driven out of the community, because my mother was the catechist, she substituted for him in providing religious education.[58]

—Bishop of Cuautitlán, México

I am a child of the Revolution and a product of the persecution of the Church in that region [Morelia, Michoacán]. We had to practice our studies secretly after these events took place, and eventually I had to travel to Querétaro because they seized the seminary in 1934, and I had to abandon the state a year later.[59]

—Parish priest

During my schooling, I left Morelia because of governor Lázaro Cárdenas's influence. We went to various homes and humble villages to study. I went to live with an aunt who had a guest house. I came in contact with many seminary students who also lived with my aunt, and then I moved to a small town in Michoacán, a very beautiful place, where I remained for four years. I returned to complete my studies in Morelia from 1942 to 1943.[60]

—Cardinal of Guadalajara, Jalisco

These experiences for future priests are comparable to the revolutionary experiences of an older generation of Mexican political leaders. The increased activist suppression of the Church and religious activity not only encouraged young men to consider the priesthood but also inspired others who were taking seminary classes to stay the course, to become priests. Adversity often generates a special esprit de corps, a sense of shared experience. Some of the young men who went through the religious persecution believe it reinforced their spiritual and personal goals. This experience also may have affected strongly this generation's beliefs concerning their role as priests and the institution's mission. Carlos Escandón Domínguez indicates that he knew "many older clergy who had brothers, uncles, or relatives killed during the Cristero revolt. They don't want to be politically active because they don't want to bring about the violence which they remembered from their youth."[61] This is a significant point because Mexican politicians who grew up during the Revolution, reaching positions of influence in the mid-1940s, gave great priority to peace and to nonviolent solutions to policy issues.[62]

The only chronologically comparable events that the same generation of prominent politicians shared with bishops, in which the state was also the repressive agent, were the 1927 and 1929 presidential campaigns, which in addition to the older Alemán generation (1900–1910) influenced the Adolfo López Mateos (1910–1920) cohort. This group of students supported José Vasconcelos in 1929, the Cuauhtémoc Cárdenas of his era, and suffered repression and election fraud at the hands of the political establishment. They decided to enter political life to take over the leadership and institute reforms.[63]

Future politicians and clergy reached the apex of their institutions, products of violent episodes in Mexican history that both separated and joined them together. Although younger priests and bishops today believe the Cristero events no longer affect their peers, who are exposed to it only in history books, in some regions of Mexico, people are still likely to remember its consequences.[64]

Personal Revelations

In most professions, individuals can explain their career choice by pointing to many of the agents mentioned here. It is true, however, that becoming a priest is not analogous to choosing a secular profession. Making such a choice also involves deep spiritual and religious beliefs, accentuated not just by broad political and social events, but by personal, individual experiences. For example, one man entered the priesthood in 1939 at the age of 31 after having caused the death of a friend in a hunting accident.[65]

The choice to enter the priesthood also has been attributed to an act of God or merely an accident of fate, with no definitive explanation. For example, Bishop Samuel Ruiz, recognized nationally for a strongly defined pastoral philosophy, cannot attribute his choice to anything influencing him personally. As he suggests:

> I became a priest accidentally. Truthfully, I don't know why. I have a very good memory, and I can recall many details, but for the life of me I cannot pinpoint exactly when I decided to become a priest. When I asked my mother some years later, she told me that she and my father prayed that if they only had one son, God should take him to serve his needs. So, perhaps it was some sort of divine providence. Whatever the reason, in my own mind it remains a mystery.[66]

Other future bishops made this choice after more direct exposure to religious teachings but without any preconceived interest in the priesthood. José Pablo Rovalo, former bishop of Zacatecas, attributed his decision to spiritual intervention:

I really considered my joining the Church as a gift of God. Let me explain why. In the sixth grade, the Brothers of Mary invited me to become a priest. My parents approved of this choice, but I had no interest in joining at that time. . . . I decided to pursue a career in medicine. I chose my courses because of the teacher rather than the schedule, and I had a lot of free time on my hands. During that free time I came in contact with a priest who I asked for advice about a career. He simply advised me to search for whatever I wanted in life, so I enrolled in the seminary, and after a week, I knew my career was not in medicine, but in religion.[67]

Conclusions

When Mexican priests and politicians are allowed to speak for themselves about their religious upbringing, they reveal certain similarities attributable to most Mexican families. These attributes, collectively a hybrid of Catholic and Liberal influences, are important to identify because they suggest a dual heritage as the social setting for most Mexicans. Therefore, whatever values may characterize Mexican priests, they are also, for the most part, products of a Liberal heritage, the same influences affecting all other Mexicans, politicians included.

In Mexico, being Liberal and Catholic is not contradictory. While Liberalism does not mean being antireligious, for some Mexicans it may suggest a certain level of anti-Catholicism. But as so many prominent politicians indicated in their comments, even they are believers, and if not, they rarely express any antireligious or anti-Catholic sentiments.

What distinguishes a future priest's family environment from that of a future politician is the strength of the family's religious beliefs or the importance of religion in the extended family. Future priests were often encouraged to enter the seminary, and ultimately the priesthood, not only by their parish priest but often by a family member already associated with religious life. For many future priests, the regularity of church attendance established their familiarity with and positive inclination toward a spiritual life.

Families expressing a more positive appraisal of Catholicism were much more likely to allow or initiate their children's enrollment in seminary schools. These schools themselves, either through their broader educational environment or through the examples and influence of teaching priests and brothers, steered many young men into the priesthood.

Occasionally, history itself intervenes as a formative agent in the values and choices of a generation. For Mexican clergy in the late 20th century, no single event produced as many consequences for their spiritual values, their personal experiences, or their decisions to enter or remain in the priesthood as the religious conflict in the late 1920s and the persecution of the Church. The Cristiada, as well as local experiences or religious persecution from one region or state to another, repeatedly is recalled in the minds of priests who were youngsters or seminary students during those years. Rather than discouraging young men from entering the priesthood, the adversity of these events only encouraged their resolve to pursue a religious profession.

The violence and persecution they witnessed, whether affecting strangers or their own families, flavored these Mexicans in such a way that they followed a strategy of cooperation with the state, not confrontation, wishing to avoid repeating the violence and suppression characterizing their youth. In the same way, the political generations who passed through the Revolution as children hoped to avoid future violent conflicts, strongly believing that pragmatism and compromise were the most viable paths to political stability and development, whether in secular or religious affairs. This philosophy, in part a product of dual historical experiences, led both politicians and priests to resolve their potential conflicts in a reasonable, practical manner.

NOTES

1. Joseph H. Fichter, *Religion as an Occupation: A Study in the Sociology of Professions* (Terre Haute, Ind.: University of Notre Dame, 1961), 23.

2. Andrew M. Greeley, *Priests in the United States: Reflections on a Survey* (New York: Doubleday, 1972), 19.

3. Personal interviews with Fathers Rafael Tapia, Abelardo Hernández, and Humberto Vargas, Puebla Archdiocese, Puebla, Puebla, July 16, 1993.

4. Personal interview with Bishop Francisco María Aguilera González, Mexico Archdiocese, Mexico City, June 1, 1987.

5. Personal interview with Bishop Samuel Ruiz, Mexican Episcopate, Lago de Guadalupe, Cuautitlán, México, April 30, 1992.

6. Personal interview with Father Baltazar López, Cuernavaca Diocese, Cuernavaca, Morelos, June 3, 1988.

7. Personal interview with Father Fernando Glagoaga, Church of Our Lady of the Unprotected, Toluca Diocese, Toluca, México, June 9, 1988.

8. Personal interview with Father Samuel Morín Suárez, secretary to the bishop of Toluca, Toluca Diocese, Toluca, México, June 9, 1988.

9. Personal interview with Luis Narro Rodríguez, director of the Center for Educational Studies, Mexico City, June 28, 1989.

10. Personal interview with Bishop José Pablo Rovalo, Archdiocese of Mexico, Mexico City, February 21, 1991.

11. Personal interview with Auxiliary Bishop Adolfo Hernández Hurtado, Guadalajara Archdiocese, Guadalajara, Jalisco, July 7, 1993. Another bishop who attributes his service in the Church as crucial to his decision to follow the priesthood is Magín Camarino Torreblanca Reyes, who served as an acolyte in the Concepción Church under the guidance of Father Guzmán before entering the seminary in 1942. He believes many acolytes in this period became priests. Personal interview with Bishop Magin Camarino Torreblanca Reyes, Texcoco Diocese, Texcoco, México, July 12, 1993.

12. Personal interview with Father Juan Bazdresch, Ibero-American University, Mexico City, June 20, 1989.

13. Instituto Mexicano de Estudios Sociales, *Encuesta a los agentes laicos* (Mexico City: Archdiocese of Mexico, 1992), 19.

14. Personal interview with Miguel de la Madrid, Mexico City, February 22, 1991.

15. Personal interview with Luis Echeverría Alvarez, Mexico City, August 2, 1992.

16. Personal interview with José López Portillo, Mexico City, February 19, 1991.

17. Luis Echeverría Alvarez, whose father was a paymaster, came in contact with important political-military officers and married into an influential revolutionary family from Jalisco. José López Portillo's grandfather served as secretary of foreign relations, and Miguel de la Madrid came from an influential family of politicians in his grandfather's generation in Colima. Carlos Salinas de Gortari is the son of a cabinet member from the 1950s.

18. Donald Mabry, *Mexico's Acción Nacional: A Catholic Alternative to Revolution* (Syracuse, N.Y.: Syracuse University Press, 1973).

19. Some priests also were influenced by lay activities, including the Acción Católica de la Juventud Mexicana (ACJM), which was very active during the Cristero movement, or involvement in prayer groups, such as Adoración Nocturna. Personal interview between Scott Pentzer and Father Rafael Ramírez Díaz, abbot of the Basilica of Guanajuato, Guanajuato, July 9, 1993.

20. Personal interview with Abel Vicencio Tovar, Mexico City, July 13, 1993.

21. Personal interview with Heberto Castillo Martínez, Mexico City, July 12, 1993. Porfirio Muñoz Ledo, president of the PRD, also describes his family as typically Mexican, middle-class schoolteachers; his father was a moderate Jacobin, a Juárez Liberal, and mother, a moderate Catholic, with strong Catholic roots from Veracruz. His father also had strong Catholic antecedents from the Bajío region. Personal interview, Mexico City, February 21, 1991.

22. Personal interview with Rodolfo González Guevara, Mexico City, February 21, 1991.

23. Personal interview with Ricardo Pascoe, Mexico City, May 5, 1992.

24. These individuals play a role similar to that of bankers in the relationship between the state and Mexico's entrepreneurial class. See Roderic Ai Camp, *Entrepreneurs and Politics in Twentieth Century Mexico* (New York: Oxford University Press, 1989).

25. Personal interview with Antonio Martínez Báez, Mexico City, August 1, 1992.

26. Agustín Yáñez is one of the few Mexicans to reach prominent political office, including secretary of education and governor of his home state, who was actively involved with groups, including the ACJM, strongly supporting the Cristero movement. See Roderic Ai Camp, "An Intellectual in Mexican Politics: The Case of Agustín Yáñez," *Relaciones* 2 (Summer 1981): 137–162.

27. Personal interview with Fausto Zerón Medina, Mexico City, May 29, 1987.

28. Personal interview with Agustín Basave, Mexico City, August 4, 1992.

29. To illustrate this, she revealed, "My mother took me to some Irish nuns to educate me religiously, preparing me for my first communion. She chose them because she believed foreign nuns would be more open in their instruction. She took me to see the Mother Superior, bluntly telling her that she didn't want the sisters to fill my head with stupidities."

30. Personal interview with Gabriel Zaid, Mexico City, June 7, 1988.

31. Personal interview with Luis Rubio, Mexico City, February 13, 1991.

32. Roderic Ai Camp, *Political Recruitment across Two Centuries: Mexico, 1884–1991* (Austin: University of Texas Press, 1995).

33. Gustavo Pérez Ramírez and Yván Labelle, *El problema sacerdotal en América Latina* (Madrid: FERES, 1964), 77.

34. Roderic Ai Camp, *Generals in the Palacio: The Military in Modern Mexico* (New York: Oxford University Press, 1992), 159. Half of all generals graduating from the Higher War College had fathers in the military. Children of United States military officers also have lower attrition rates. R. F. Schloemer, "Making It at the Air Force Academy: Who Stays? Who Succeeds?," in *The Changing World of the American Military*, Franklin D. Margiotta, ed. (Boulder, Colo.: Westview Press, 1978), 321–344.

35. Lauro López Beltrán, *Diócesis y obispos de Cuernavaca, 1875–1978* (Mexico City,

1978), 248, identifies the four as José Mora y del Río, the influential archbishop of Mexico; Jenaro Méndez del Río, bishop of Tehuantepec; Antonio Méndez Rodríguez, canon of the Zamora Cathedral; and Efrén Arceo, parish priest.

36. Personal interview with Luis Gambino Botello, Precious Blood of Christ Church, Mexico City Archdiocese, Mexico City, June 10, 1988.

37. Personal interview with Brother Reuben Murillo, Ibero-American University, Mexico City, June 20, 1989.

38. Personal interview with Bishop Magín Camarino Torreblanca Reyes.

39. Personal interview with Auxiliary Bishop Luis Mena, Mexico Archdiocese, Mexico City, July 13, 1993.

40. Personal interview with Bishop José Melgoza Osorio, Nezahualcóyotl Diocese, Nezahualcóyotl, México, May 27, 1987.

41. Personal interview with Bishop Raúl Vera López, Ciudad Altamirano Diocese, Guerrero, Mexico City, May 3, 1992.

42. Personal interview with Bishop Manuel Samaniego Barriga, Cuautitlán Diocese, Cuautitlán, México, February 13, 1991.

43. Personal interview with Archbishop Rosendo Huesca, Puebla Archdiocese, Puebla, Puebla, July 16, 1993.

44. For example, Allan Kornberg, Joel Smith, and David Bromley, "Some Differences in the Political Socialization Patterns of Canadian and American Party Officials," in *Socialization to Politics,* Jack Dennis, ed. (New York: Wiley, 1973), 444.

45. Roderic Ai Camp, *The Making of a Government: Political Leaders in Modern Mexico* (Tucson: University of Arizona Press, 1984), 18.

46. Personal interview with Rodolfo González Guevara.

47. Personal interview with Porfirio Muñoz Ledo.

48. Personal interview with Arturo Núñez, former subsecretary of government, Mexico City, February 12, 1993. Núñez describes himself as a respectful but nonpracticing Catholic.

49. Robert H. Levine discovered that nearly all of the bishops in both countries started out in minor seminaries at the age of 11 or 12. However, he reported that minor seminaries are in decline in these two countries. *Religion and Politics in Latin America: The Catholic Church in Venezuela and Colombia* (Princeton: Princeton University Press, 1981), 103.

50. Father Rubén Murillo reports that when he was a child, the Jesuits had schools that would train a boy as young as eight to become a missionary. He read many novellas about Jesuit missionaries and decided he wanted to become one, but his parents would not let him enter this program, which was offered at a boarding school, telling him he could become a priest, if he still wanted to, when he was older. Murillo did enroll in the Jesuit seminary at age 13, joining the Jesuits six years later in 1942. Personal interview with Rubén Murillo.

51. Personal interview with Auxiliary Bishop Abelardo Alvarado Alcántara, Mexico Archdiocese, Mexico City, June 2, 1987.

52. Personal interview between Scott Pentzer and Meg Mitchell with Father Jesús López Larra de Castañeda, Zacatecas Diocese, Zacatecas, Zacatecas, July 19, 1993. The same characteristic may also be true of mainline Protestant ministers. According to César Pérez, a leader of the Mexican Methodist Church, he was always involved in Methodist Youth Groups and was educated in Protestant schools in Querétaro before studying in the Methodist seminary in Mexico City. Personal interview with César Pérez, Mexico City, July 14, 1993.

53. Personal interview with Father Samuel Morín Ruiz. Morín Ruiz did not come from a family that strongly emphasized religion, nor did he have any personal contact with a priest.

54. Larry Rohter, "Pope, in Mexico, Preaches Harmony," *New York Times,* May 9, 1990, n.p.

55. Personal interview with Archbishop Manuel Pérez Gil, Tlanepantla Archdiocese, Tlanepantla, México, February 18, 1991.

56. Personal interview with Ernesto Domínguez Quiroga, ex-president of the Ibero-American University, Mexico City, June 13, 1989.

57. Personal interview with Bishop Magín Camarino Torreblanca Reyes.

58. Personal interview with Bishop Manuel Samaniego Barriga.

59. Personal interview with Father Luis Gamino Botello.

60. Personal interview with Cardinal Juan Jesús Posadas Ocampo, Guadalajara Archdiocese, Mexico City, February 20, 1991.

61. Personal interview with Carlos Escandón Domínguez, Ibero-American University, Mexico City, May 25, 1987.

62. Roderic Ai Camp, *The Making of a Government,* 40, 62.

63. See Roderic Ai Camp, "La campaña presidencial de 1929 y el liderazgo político en México," *Historia Mexicana* 27 (Fall 1977): 231–259.

64. Larry Rohter, in reporting on the Pope's 1990 visit to Mexico for the *New York Times,* discovered the people at the San Juan de los Lagos Basilica in Jalisco, located in the heart of the Cristero rebellion, shouting the battle cry of the Cristeros: "Long Live Christ the King." Andrew J. Stein, in his "The Prophetic Mission: The Catholic Church and Politics—Nicaragua in the Context of Central America," unpublished Ph.D. dissertation, University of Pittsburgh, 1995, chap. 6, provides empirical evidence of pre- and post-Sandanista generational differences in values among priests.

65. Personal interview between Shannan Mattiace and Father Fernando Avila Alvarez, Mérida Archdiocese, Mérida, Yucatán, August 17, 1989.

66. Personal interview with Bishop Samuel Ruiz.

67. Personal interview with Bishop José Pablo Rovalo.

7

Educating the Clergy

From Priest to Bishop

Well-developed institutions, regardless of purpose or profession, generate for-mal and informal patterns for selecting and promoting future leaders. In Mexico, informal qualities such as kinship ties or personal friendships often exer-cise greater influence in both the choice and progress of future public leaders. Formally, education plays a significant role, not just in terms of level and quality of education but where it occurs. A politician's education, therefore, brings that individual in contact with present and future public figures.[1] Among Mexican entrepreneurial elites, family is overwhelmingly the determining variable in arriv-ing at the post of chief executive officer of a major corporation.[2] In the Mexican military, which shares more similarities with the Church, given its in-house train-ing structures, than do the private and public sectors, educational experiences establish lifelong linkages among officers, and certain levels have become a sine qua non for achieving the rank of general.[3]

The clergy, while sharing some similarities with each of these groups, differs substantially, generating credentialing processes peculiar to its structure and mis-sion. It is much easier to identify and measure formal credentials among a leader-ship group. It is more difficult to determine what informal criteria enter into an individual career trajectory, both in its pace and the level reached. Education informally and formally exercises a crucial influence on the careers of bishops and archbishops.

Careers and Education

Although we are examining bishops from the 1960s through the 1990s, the oldest generation of priests who provided most of the leadership through the 1960s re-veals changing professionalization patterns occurring within the Church after the 1910 Revolution. Among those bishops born prior to 1900 who served after 1960, about one in four devoted most of their clerical career before selection as a bishop in pastoral activities, typically as parish priests or vicars. One out of three served in a variety of administrative positions in their local dioceses, although an occasional future bishop performed duties in the Mexico City archdiocese or with national or international organizations. The remainder, slightly more than one-third, spent most of their early careers as seminary teachers and administrators. These data, when compared with the activities of priests in general, clearly demonstrate that a career as a parish priest typically does not lead to recognition as bishop material. Among priests who do not become bishops, 88 percent carry out pastoral responsibilities.[4]

As Table 7-1 illustrates, the career patterns of bishops have shifted over time. Contrary to what many individuals might expect, and what would be encountered in the Mexican military, serving in staff positions is not the usual track leading to a bishop. In the past, 26 percent of priests functioned primarily as church administrators prior to becoming bishops, but only 8 percent of recent bishops (born since 1920), one-third their predecessors' numbers, served in this capacity. Priests who perform the Church's primary pastoral tasks, devoting themselves directly to a parish, also declined, but not significantly, to approximately 24 percent. In contrast to priests who become bishops, most priests work in the parish or as advisers to various religious groups and movements. The most striking shift among future bishops are the increasing numbers who involve themselves in a diocesan seminary, teaching for many years and serving in a variety of educational positions, including rectorships. Mexican clergy often function simultaneously as ancillary parish priests while performing other tasks, including teaching, but they are categorized here by their primary career responsibilities.

The classic pattern from priest to bishop in Latin America is through the seminary. In the case of Chile, for example, the most certain path to bishop was through a seminary rectorship in Santiago. Thomas Sanders suggests that the seminary provides a valuable testing ground for a future bishop as an administrator, intellectual, and pastor.[5] In Colombia, often labeled the most Catholic of South American countries, priests typically follow a similar pattern to the hierarchy, primarily as professors or seminary rectors. A large minority also rise through the curia or church bureaucracy, often as a bishop's private secretary, vicar general of the diocese, or an episcopate official.[6]

Table 7-1. Career Experiences of Mexican Priests and Bishops

Year of Birth	Pastoral	Teaching	Curia
Bishops			
Pre-1900	36%	29%	36%
1900–1919	26	51	23
1920–	24	62	14
Average	26	55	19
Priests	88	9	3

Source: This and all tables with data on bishops are from the author's own data set of 138 cases.

Since the 1970s, a priest becoming a bishop in Mexico typically was recruited at a very young age, usually from a minor seminary. Recruits were sent to the Montezuma, New Mexico, seminary (before the 1960s) or to Rome, where they lived in the Colegio Pio Latino América and studied at the Jesuit-operated Gregorian University. After returning to Mexico, typically with brief or absolutely no pastoral experience, they were assigned to seminaries as instructors or administrators, often in the diocese from which they were recruited, and received initial seminary training. Generally after careers of 15 years or so in the seminary, they were assigned to diocesan administrative tasks. An examination of first-time positions of Mexican bishops over time illustrates why educational careers typically dominated (see Table 7-2). More than half of all future bishops began their priestly careers as educators; few ever leave that post to become parish priests.

Some changes in the classic career pattern seem to be occurring among recent Mexican priests selected as bishops. In the first place, larger percentages are characterized as having pastoral experiences. Although the data in Table 7-2 suggest little change in the percentage of bishops who began their careers in the parish, a significant increase has occurred among those born after 1940, with a corresponding decrease among those who initially teach. In the second place, the number of bishops who studied in Rome versus in Mexico is declining. In the third place, large numbers of bishops are continuing to teach in the major seminaries, serving as models to young priests and higher clergy alike. All of these changes, if they persist, introduce significant consequences. They suggest an increasing emphasis on producing an organic bishop, a priest formed and trained in Mexico rather than abroad. These patterns also suggest a perception that among the episcopate a vigorous, attractive Church requires closer ties to the faithful, including practical experience at the parish level.[7]

The importance of educators becoming bishops implies several significant characteristics about the Mexican episcopate. It suggests the value that higher clergy place on advanced seminary education and on their peers' intellectual training. Second, it suggests that these educational experiences typically bring future priests into closer contact with those who are most likely to recommend them as possible bishops. Third, the importance of educational careers in the backgrounds of Mexican bishops reinforces the significance of educational credentials in priests' ordination and preparation to teach in diocesan seminaries.

Future Mexican bishops appear to fall into four common career categories, and the educational preparation for each varies. These can be described as the *generalist,* the *specialist,* the *pastoralist,* and the *administrator.* The generalist fits the classic pattern of Church recruitment. An example is José Melgoza Osorio, a native of Michoacán, who entered the seminary in 1928 at the age of 16. Two years later he was sent to Mexico City to study in the major seminary, where he concentrated on Latin and philosophy. As he himself recalls:

[I]n my third year, I went to Rome where I continued to study philosophy. In 1940, I was ordained and I returned to Mexico and became a seminary professor in Jalapa, Veracruz. I remained at the seminary until 1962, at the beginning of Vatican II. I was invited to accompany the Mexican representatives to the Concilium in Rome. After I

Table 7-2. Initial Career Assignments of Mexican Bishops, by Generation

Initial Post	1880–1899	1900–1919	1920–1949	Average
Seminary	31	50	46	45
Parish	31	37	38	37
Other	19	8	7	9
Unknown	19	5	9	9

remained there during Vatican II, Church authorities asked me to return to Mexico and explain its principles in meetings and seminars throughout Mexico. For the next four years that is actually what I did, focusing particularly on the liturgy and pastoral work in Vatican II.[8]

Several years later in 1970, he was selected as bishop of Ciudad Valles, San Luis Potosí. Melgoza Osorio represents the typical bishop whose first post was in a seminary and who remained in that assignment for more than a decade—in his case, 22 years. It is very important to again stress, however, that many bishops whose early careers concentrated in the seminary also were exposed directly to pastoral issues and problems.[9]

The second type of Mexican bishop shares many similarities with the career of Melgoza Osorio but obtains higher and more specialized education. A *specialist,* who might be described as the Church's equivalent of a technocrat, often obtains advanced education in a specialty area such as canon law or something more secular. A number of religious order brothers fit this category and become professional educators, continuing a long-established intellectual tradition of such orders at the Jesuits. Bishop Luis Reynoso Cervantes, bishop of Cuernavaca, who obtained a Ph.D. in canon law, is a diocesan version of the specialist. He cofounded the Parroquia Universitaria and directed the graduate seminary at the San Pio X University. He taught public religious law at the National University for many years and played an important role in the negotiations between church and state under President Salinas. Father Antonio Roqueñi, dean of the ecclesiastical tribunal, the judicial body that resolves priests' legal problems, obtained very specialized advance secular and religious education, giving him the credentials for his specialized role as legal counsel to the Mexico Archdiocese.[10]

The third type of bishop, the *pastoralist,* represents the other major career pattern: priests who spent their lives primarily in pastoral activities, initially in parishes, and later as advisers to various religious groups. Bishop Manuel Samaniego Barriga, a native of San Francisco Pangamacutiro, Michoacán, began seminary at age 12, in 1942, after completing primary in a Catholic school. Most of his seminary education was in Morelia, a leading seminary in producing future bishops. As he recalls:

I completed my studies at age 23 and was ordained young, at 23. I served five years as a vicar in a Morelia parish from 1954 to 1959, and then from 1959 to 1969 I was an assistant to the Mexican Catholic Action Youth organization. I also taught at various Catholic schools and was involved in other activities in the Morelia archdiocese. In 1969, without any warning, the archbishop, for the Pope, asked me to become auxiliary bishop of Saltillo. I never taught at the seminary.[11]

Finally, a small but persistent group of priests continue to become bishops from the curia's administrative ranks, typically on the local level, although some future bishops become known through contacts at the Mexican episcopate or even at international or regional meetings such as CELAM. For example, Bishop Javier Navarro Rodríguez knew Cardinal Posadas long before becoming his auxiliary bishop in 1992, having met his superior in Mexico City at the Mexican episcopate 10 years prior to his designation.[12] A tiny minority of priests become bishops through service in the Vatican diplomatic corps but remain outside the Mexican episcopate. Such is the case of Luis Robles Díaz, a native of El Grullo, Jalisco, who graduated from the diplomatic academy in Rome and became the representative to the Red Sea region in 1969 and bishop in 1985.[13]

Seminarians, Teachers, and Students

Priests who become bishops typically received some preseminary education in religious grammar schools. In fact, over half of future bishops attended parochial schools before enrolling in seminary.[14] A large minority of bishops (one-fifth) also attended schools associated with seminaries prior to secondary school, at which time most priests enroll in lower seminary education. The Mexican episcopate recognizes the importance of this education and its role as a formative agent of influence on priests' values.[15] Another group (nearly one-fourth) attended mostly public, and infrequently secular, private schools.

Bishops began seminary schools at a young age. This is a phenomenon true in many parts of the Catholic world. Age is a critical issue because it determines where priests attend seminary, usually in their diocese of birth, and the degree of contact they will have with other priests and their local bishop. This is borne out by the fact that Mexican bishops make it their task to interview lower seminary students in their sixth year.[16] A typical priest will spend four to five years in the lower seminary and seven or more years in upper seminary. For example, in Colombia and Venezuela, Daniel Levine only encountered four out of 60 bishops who began their careers as adult vocations. The rest initiated their clerical careers at age 11 or 12, in minor seminaries.[17] In Latin America most priests generally enrolled in the seminary at a slightly higher age of 14–16, although nearly one-fourth were 13 or younger. Only 14 percent embarked on priestly careers after age 20.[18] Luengo discovered a similar pattern among Mexican priests: 21 percent, ages 10–12; 35 percent, ages 13–15; and 22 percent, ages 16–18. The largest percentage of Mexican priests (41 percent) joined the seminary at 14–16. Given the average age of Mexican priests who enrolled in the seminary, most joined before completing preparatory studies. In the United States, the vast majority of priests, nearly two-thirds, completed their preparatory studies and then joined the seminary.[19]

Access to education is more evenly distributed among future bishops compared to most other future elites. In other words, all priests have equal access to higher education once they are enrolled and performing well in lower seminary schools.

We have demonstrated that a priest's social origins does affect his level of education somewhat and, more important, his choice of a career track, especially in seminary education. However, when a priest is admitted to the seminary and decides to seek the priesthood, his college-level education is essentially guaranteed.

Future bishops may be distinguished from ordinary priests in both their desire and their ability to pursue their education, often outside of Mexico, beyond a basic seminary degree. Among Mexican bishops, more than 40 percent are known to have obtained doctorates, and 17 percent received two or more doctorates, generally in law, philosophy, and theology. Among priests, only 9 percent obtained any kind of postgraduate education. Thus, bishops are four times more likely to have postgraduate training and even more likely to obtain doctorates. In terms of educational levels, Mexican bishops are comparable to their Venezuelan peers, but in Colombia, where the socioeconomic makeup of bishops differs, bishops obtained even higher levels of doctorates.[20]

Among the older generation of Mexican bishops, a doctorate was extremely important, since twice as many of these bishops (81 percent) received that level of training. Today, although bishops are more likely than priests to have doctoral level work behind them, it is not a necessity. Indeed, among younger bishops, having a doctorate is less common than at any other time in the last 60 years.[21] Among those youngest bishops in our study born after 1940, none have earned doctorates. However, among the highest ranking members of the Mexican episcopate, archbishops and cardinals, a stronger relationship exists between achieving their position and having a doctorate. Nearly 60 percent of this episcopal elite received doctorates, evenly divided between single and multiple degrees. Having a doctorate, however, is also important to the career pattern one chooses within the Church. Of the bishops receiving a doctorate, 57 percent of those made teaching a career, the same percentage who initiated their careers as seminary professors or administrators.

The location where priests received their education is significant for several reasons. Not only is the educational career track most important among future bishops, but even among future bishops who fall into other career categories, a sizable percentage teach at some point in their careers. In fact, since this is true of 85 percent, seminary teaching is probably one of the most universal experiences of all future Mexican bishops. This experience, however, seems to be in decline, since 89 percent of those born in the 1920s taught, versus 79 percent and 69 percent of those born in the 1930s and 1940s, respectively.

The Catholic Church has no national educational center, unlike the Mexican Army, which relies on the Heroic Military and the Higher War Colleges to give future officers a preparatory education and college degree, respectively, or Mexican politicians, who have used the National University as a centralized, unofficial training ground.[22] Its educational structure, similar to other important institutional characteristics, is molded by the diocese. The diocesan pattern, true of bishops' geographic origins, decentralizes their education and recruitment throughout the republic. The same pattern is found in the United States. Thomas Reese discovered that two-thirds of all American bishops began their ecclesiastical careers by entering high school seminaries where they lived. Since World War II, about a third of U.S. bishops attended Catholic University in Washington, D.C., the closest equivalent to a national school.[23]

The Catholic Church operated 31 seminaries in Mexico by the 1980s. Some of these institutions, many of them with lengthy histories and traditions, produce a disproportionate percentage of Mexico's episcopate. In 1945, when Mexico's bishops totaled 42, the Guadalajara Seminary accounted for 21 percent of the bishops, the Morelia, Michoacán, seminary ranked second with 14 percent, and Mexico City was third with 12 percent. An even larger percentage of bishops at the end of World War II either taught at these three seminaries or held administrative positions.[24]

If we examine bishops' higher seminary education in Mexico, the first characteristic that becomes apparent is that they received a sizable proportion of their religious education in a Mexican regional or diocesan seminary. Only one of the 38 bishops examined did not receive some or all of his primary seminary education from Mexican Catholic institutions. Second, several institutions or dioceses dominate bishops' education, and their influence has remained unaltered for many decades. Third, the dominant Mexican seminaries typically are located in dioceses and states producing the largest percentage of bishops and priests.

As Table 7-3 shows, the two leading seminaries in Mexico are Guadalajara and Morelia. As chapter 8 will suggest, Jalisco and Michoacán are to bishops what the Federal District is to politicians. More than 40 percent of Mexico's bishops and archbishops claim those states as birthplaces, and approximately the same percentages attended the seminaries, in their respective dioceses located there. The same pattern is true among priests. According to Luengo's study, 41 percent of priests served in the same state where they attended lower seminary, and 44 percent did so in the state where they attended their major seminary.[25] Three other diocesan seminaries, with notable histories extending back to the colonial period, are Puebla and Mexico City, each accounting for approximately an additional 10 percent of seminary students, and Zamora, producing 5 percent of Mexico's bishops. No other Mexican seminary can claim more than 3 percent of Mexico's future bishops.

The Catholic Church does maintain, however, what might be considered a cen-

Table 7-3. Seminary Education of
Mexican Bishops

Seminary	Bishops
Guadalajara	17%
Mexico City	7
Monterrey	2
Morelia	15
Puebla	8
Zamora	5
Other Mexican seminaries	32
Foreign	11
Unknown	3

tral seminary, the Gregorian University in Rome, which will be analyzed in detail below. For historical reasons, the Mexican Church also maintained another such institution established during its years of persecution in Montezuma, New Mexico, also considered to be interdiocesan, recruiting priests from multiple dioceses throughout Mexico. Only a minority of priests continue beyond their basic seminary education, most of them outside of Mexico. About one-third of this group studies in Mexico City, a larger percentage in Europe, followed by Latin America and the United States.[26]

The educational influence of the Gregorian University and the Montezuma Seminary, when a bishop's higher education is analyzed, can be seen from the data in Table 7-4. Very few bishops finish their education at a Mexican seminary, yet most priests do complete their education in Mexico. In fact, only 18 percent of the priests Enrique Luengo examined studied in Rome. By comparison, most future bishops have been sent to Rome to study with priests from all over the world and, for a long period, to Montezuma, where Mexican priests lived, worked, and studied together. Mexican bishops differ from some of their Latin American counterparts, for example Chileans, who rarely have studied in Europe.[27]

It is apparent from the data in Table 7-4 that being selected to go to Rome and, for a brief historical period, Montezuma, was a significant first step on the path to becoming a bishop. As Dennis Hanratty concludes:

> The first step for an aspiring seminarian is to achieve high academic honors in his theology and philosophy courses such that he will be recommended for advanced study in these subjects in Rome. Upon returning from Rome, this new priest is immediately installed as a professor in the diocesan seminary. If he shows considerable promise, he may move up the chain of command in the seminary, finally achieving the coveted post of Rector.[28]

The decline in Mexican bishops' attendance at the Gregorian University and a comparable increase in attendance at both Mexican seminaries and the New Mexico seminary is the most striking pattern revealed in Table 7-4. In fact, bishops born since 1930 accounted for nearly half of all bishops educated only in Mexico. One reason for this is fairly straightforward. Many future bishops were chosen to attend the seminary in Rome but were prevented by World War II from reaching Europe. For example, this is why Adolfo Hernández Hurtado, bishop at Tapachula, Chiapas, completed all of his seminar education at the Guadalajara Seminary from 1939 to 1943.[29]

Table 7-4. Higher Seminary Education of Mexican Bishops

Year of Birth	Mexico	Montezuma[a]	Gregorian[b]	U.S. European
Pre-1900	19%	0%	75%	6%
1900–1919	10	15	73	3
1920–	23	29	42	6

[a] Montezuma also includes several graduates who received part of their higher education in Europe and at the seminary in Castroville, California.

[b] Gregorian also includes bishops who received part of their higher education in Mexico, Europe, and the United States.

A very small percentage of priests and bishops receive secular academic training. In fact, some do not even attend seminary. Among 8,000 priests in the 1960s, 119 graduated from college and 7 obtained Ph.Ds.[30] In Mexico in 1989 two bishops out of 106 active and emeriti had no ecclesiastical training, only secular college degrees. An additional bishop, Raúl Vera López, studied chemistry at the National University, then decided to become a priest. Bishop Vera believes that it is much more common in Mexico in the 1990s to complete a college degree and then enter the seminary.[31] Antonio Roqueñi, an important adviser to Cardinal Corripio, is a classic example of this new generation of priests who opt for a religious career in young adulthood, usually in college. As he describes his experience:

> I finished primary school in a Jesuit institution, and my secondary was in public schools. I pursued a law degree at UNAM, and it was there that I began to have serious religious questions. They were so important after my law degree that I received a fellowship to study in Rome, in canon law, at Saint Thomas Aquinas College, the school which graduated the Pope. I received a Ph.D. in canon law. At the same time, I also began my priestly studies. I studied the first year of theology, and after three years received my doctorate in Christian philosophy and theology in Rome; then I spent another three years in Spain, where I obtained a Ph.D. in civil law and completed the last three years of seminary. I was ordained in Madrid in 1963.[32]

It is interesting that since the constitutional reforms, some major universities, including the public University of Guadalajara, approved for the first time secular equivalency for seminary degrees.[33]

Seminary education in Mexico is designed to create a sense of loyalty to the Church and to the hierarchy. It also tries to encourage an individual's personal development so as to enhance personality traits that make a future priest more appealing.[34] The educational system, similar to that of the military, incorporates built-in weaknesses. When the seminaries began reopening in the 1930s and 1940s, they reflected the prevailing conditions of the time, having suffered through years of persecution.[35] Philosophically, therefore, they shut themselves off from other intellectual currents in society, which explains why further education in Rome or the United States were crucial to the formation of future bishops. "The tendency to listen to news, listen to music, to read newspapers was punished; life was closed from the rest of the world in a manner preventing contact with social issues, ideology, and human relations."[36]

In an insightful study conducted in 1973, researchers discovered that Mexican seminarians believed their institutions reinforced paternalism, authoritarianism, clericalism, and dependency.[37] Although clergy do not openly discuss this, potential priests, similar to potential military officers, are washed out of seminaries, forced to leave. Pomerlau claims 50 such cases of men who were expelled in 1979 for "rebellious attitude toward authority," a code expression he translates as excessive zeal for social ministry, popular religion, and service to the poor.[38] However, a significant difference between military and Catholic socialization is that numerous seminaries exist, allowing potential priests to join another seminary with a different philosophical emphasis. This again explains an important source of diversity within the Catholic Church and a means of recruiting, nurturing, and sustaining different philosophical currents.

In the 1970s, most Mexican priests were unsatisfied with their seminary education. Ten years later, a smaller survey revealed similar levels of dissatisfaction with the seminary curriculum.[39] The length of time priests spend in the seminary system appears to have little connection to their philosophic biases in Mexico or elsewhere; rather it is the seminary location that plays a crucial role in their socialization. The 1970s were a period of confusion in the formation of future cadres of priests, specifically on the issue of Church authority and personal liberty. Older generations of bishops recognized that the diversity of theological interpretations, combined with seminarians' changing attitudes toward authority, created a difficult educational environment.

Students of Mexican religious education believe that differences exist among the various seminaries. They are generally in agreement that the differences are not qualitative but rather focus largely on the theological methodology to be used in a priest's educational formation. As one Jesuit educator suggested, "[T]he essential difference in the seminaries was based on the definition of what their pastoral role should be, rather than the basic quality of the religious or theological training. For example, in those dioceses where the indigenous population was influential, the impact on the pastoral role was greatest. . . . In Durango, for example, their seminary continues to maintain a very orthodox type of attitude in their training."[40] Narro also believes that seminaries can be distinguished on the basis of psychological differences, illustrated by differing emphases conceptualizing modernization and the role of the Church in such issues as personal and familial development.

Other priests believe a qualitative difference exists among the seminaries based on availability of resources. Those that are well financed, relatively speaking, produce better-trained clergy. They also obtain the largest percentage of faculty trained in Rome. These same institutions are those recognized as leading institutions in the backgrounds of future bishops: Guadalajara, Puebla, Mexico City, and Morelia.[41] Also, many priests believe that most seminaries are products of their geographic environment and history. Different individuals attributed the institution's social or intellectual environment to these local differences. The reason for this is that in most instances seminaries are under the bishop's direct control,[42] thus the flavor of the seminary represents his philosophic biases or interpretations. For example, it was suggested that Morelia provided a stronger theological emphasis in its curriculum, which explains why so many of its graduates went on to Rome and also to become bishops.[43] Its recent episcopal leadership has been categorized as traditional or moderate.

Mexican priests and bishops who are members of religious orders received most of their education in religious training centers separate from the diocesan seminaries. Each of the major orders have their own educational institutions. Some of these orders have not changed their primary philosophy in a century.[44] However, individual orders began moving away from organized institutional instruction in the 1970s. For example, the Jesuits in Mexico City train future brothers within small, ecclesial communities, which integrate intellectual formation with pragmatic social and policy issues faced by the ministries. According to Claude Pomerlau, other dioceses, such as San Cristóbal de la Casas, have adopted this decentralized, less formal approach.[45]

A large percentage of the bishops who dominated the Mexican episcopate in the 1970s and 1980s were products of seminary training during the late 1920s and 1930s, differing completely from the environment since the 1970s. The persecution of the Church, and of seminarians, led to extreme conditions under which their institutions operated. Most survived on donations from the faithful. Even in Mexico City, students did not drink milk or eat meat.[46] Many enrolled and attended classes in secrecy. One priest, who studied in León, Guanajuato, in 1939, recalls passing through a cryptic interview in a private residence before being admitted to a secret classroom, where 10–15 young men were preparing for the seminary.[47]

One of the most striking recollections of the conditions of seminary education from this period comes from Manuel Pérez Gil, a native of Michoacán and a graduate and professor at the seminary:

> I did my primary studies at a nonreligious school, but I began my seminary studies at age 12. I took all of my humanities classes in Morelia, but under very special circumstances. My first 2½ years were fine, and we studied in the facility in the capital. But in 1934, after completing the first semester exams, the vice rector came to speak to all of us, saying, "We have an order to give this building to the government, and therefore we must complete our exams elsewhere." We actually finished the exams in the square out in the street, holding our papers on our knees. After that, we shifted to various halls, where we met and studied. Then the rector told us that if we wanted to continue our work as a priest, we would need to enroll in other seminaries; the one in Morelia had been shut down. This is when I decided to pursue my vocation as a priest. I traveled to numerous places, including Salamanca, El Alto, and other towns in Guanajuato, to continue my seminary studies. We operated under very difficult conditions. Sometimes I slept on the floor with a blanket; we didn't have beds, we had very limited and simple food, and of course given my background [wealthy] I was used to a completely different lifestyle. This took place from 1934 to 1936, and we traveled around the Bajío region. I studied, played soccer, and changed locations frequently, often by burro, sometimes on very rough roads or by train. We did this so we wouldn't create any suspicions by remaining permanently in one place. In those days, there were Cristeros, thieves, and government soldiers, and you never knew which you would encounter next.[48]

Educationally, the Catholic Church's greatest problem is no longer the suffering imposed on a persecuted institution. The conditions that many of Pérez Gil's colleagues experienced reinforced strong bonds of friendship, often important to their later careers. These conditions also winnowed out all but the most committed. But even without laboring under a repressive cloud, or being removed from the seminary for challenging authority, most prospective priests drop out of their own volition and are never ordained. Completion figures have never been high. For example, Cardinal Posadas Ocampo, who studied in the Morelia seminary during World War II, finished his seminary training with 11 companions, six of whom had started out together out of a total class of approximately 80.[49] The percentage of individuals completing seminary declined further. In the late 1950s and 1960s, Father Tranquilino Romero was one of 95 students in a class in Zacatecas. Only he and five others became priests. Most of the rest of his class remained in the state in other careers and professions.[50] By the 1970s, another priest described himself and his best friend in the class ahead of him as the only individuals to be ordained in classes of 53 and 57 students, respectively.[51]

These declining completion figures have led to a personnel crisis within the Church: a lack of priests during an era in which Mexico's population has expanded exponentially. It also has led to a critical situation where the average age of priests is reaching 50, closer than ever before to that of bishops. In 1960, the typical Mexican priest was only 38.[52] Not only does this have the potential for exacerbating generational differences between parishioners (half the population in Mexico is under 20) and priests, but it is difficult for the Catholic Church to retain some of its faithful and compete against Protestant sects. Although the Church has relied increasingly on laypersons to perform many religiously related services, except Masses, some individuals will no longer attend local parish churches because they are offended by the lack of priests.[53]

The declining class size and small initial classes have certain advantages, creating an excellent environment for developing close ties and friendships. Mexican politicians benefited from similarly small preparatory and law classes for many years, and numerous classmates can be found in presidential administrations, having helped each other's political careers as mentors and disciples. The most important reason that priests who are seminary teachers are more likely to become bishops than any other careerist within the Mexican Catholic Church is that each year bishops initiate these courses and typically have frequent contact with seminary professors, more so than with regular parish priests, especially those living some distance from the bishop's church.

Seminarians who obtain the educational credentials that increase their potential to become bishops typically are chosen by the bishop of the diocese in which they are students. Bishops seek out special qualities in students in addition to their scholarship. Sending a young man to Rome or to Montezuma does not assure that he will become a bishop, since most do not. Nevertheless, some bishops who are astute judges of personal qualities might identify a future peer regardless of the priest's formal educational credentials. This early identification is illustrated in an unusual story of a priest following a rocky path to bishop:

This friend, who later became an important bishop, told me that his bishop brought him into his office from the seminary and asked him to go to Rome. My friend said that he didn't want to go to Rome because he just wanted to be an ordinary priest, not a theologian. . . . The bishop was incensed with my friend and sent him back to the seminary. Six months later, he called my friend again and began talking with him about going to Rome. During this conversation he removed his hat, a symbol of being a bishop, and placed it on the head of my friend. My friend didn't understand what this meant, and the bishop explained, "I'm telling you that some day you too will be a bishop." He told my friend to complete his studies and sent him away. My friend worked for four years as a priest, encountering many difficulties, and his bishop became a cardinal. After four years, he went to visit the cardinal and asked him if he could now go to Rome. The cardinal was so upset with his original refusal to go to Rome that he denied him the privilege of studying abroad. However, you could say that the cardinal's judgment was right because eventually my friend became the bishop of Altamirano.[54]

Many future bishops, similar to public officials, make lasting friendships at the seminary with peers or professors. For example, Rosendo Huesca Pacheco, archbishop of Puebla, began his studies in the Puebla Palafoxian Seminary in 1943, remaining there until he attended the Gregorian University in 1954. When he returned to Mexico in 1960, he became a professor and prefect of discipline at his alma mater under Bartolomé Carrasco Briseño, later archbishop of Oaxaca. Carrasco, who was a professor at the seminary since 1948, became rector before Huesca's return. In 1963, he appointed Huesca, a former student and professor, as his vice rector, and Huesca succeeded him as rector the following year.

The educational linkage among bishops in Mexico is so powerful that some observers describe groups of them, who may be identified together for ideological reasons, as products of particular seminaries. For example, Cardinal Corripio and bishops Genaro Alamilla, Arturo Antonio Szymanski, and Lorenzo Cárdenas form the "Tampico Mafia," all of them former administrators of the Tampico seminary. Their careers have been strongly intertwined. Both Szymanski and Corripio were vicars of the Tampico Cathedral (their first positions), both were vice rectors of the seminary, and both became bishop of Tampico. Szymanski served as rector of the seminary when Corripio was bishop. Bishop Lorenzo Cárdenas first served in the Tampico diocese as a priest under Corripio and later held numerous posts at the seminary, including rector. Genaro Alamilla, for many years the cardinal's spokesperson and cofounder of the seminary with Corripio in the 1940s, later became vice rector, preceding Cárdenas as bishop of Papantla.[55]

Montezuma: Priests in Exile

Each diocesan seminary has produced a group of bishops similar to that of Tampico, especially the leading seminaries of Morelia, Puebla, Guadalajara, and Mexico. But future bishops can be drawn from much larger pools at two institutions: Montezuma and the Gregorian University. The Montezuma seminary experience is peculiar to Mexico, a product of Mexican church-state history and the persecution of priests. In 1936, Mexico's bishops sent a collective letter to various countries, including the United States, asking help for their seminaries. They eventually received a response from the U.S. Catholic hierarchy, offering them a half million dollars.[56]

The Inter-diocesan Seminary of Montezuma was founded on September 23, 1937, in the mountains of Montezuma, New Mexico. The Mexicans purchased an old resort hotel built in an isolated, scenic region at the turn of the century and converted it into dormitories and classrooms. The seminary, under the direction of the Jesuits, continued to train future priests and bishops until 1972, when it moved to Tula, Mexico, as a regional seminary, closing by the end of the decade. The original class of seminarians in 1937 included 353 students from 30 Mexican

Table 7-5. Seminary Rectors Who Became Mexican Bishops, 1961–1994

Seminary Directed	Seminary Attended	Bishop	Diocese
Aguascalientes	San Luis Potosí	Rafael Gallardo	Linares
Monterrey	Monterrey	Fortino Gómez	Oaxaca
Chihuahua	Zamora	Antonio Guízar	Chihuahua
	Chihuahua	Manuel Talamás	Ciudad Juárez
C. Juárez	Guadalajara	Juan Sandoval	Ciudad Juárez
Jalapa	Unknown	Emilio Abascal	Jalapa
	Montezuma	Guillermo Ranzahuer	San Andrés Tuxtla
León	León	Renato Ascencio	Ciudad Juárez
Guadalajara	Guadalajara	Ignacio de Alba	Colima
	Guadalajara	José Salazar López	Guadalajara
	Guadalajara	José G. Martín	León
México	México	Abelardo Alvarado	México
	México	Francisco Orozco	México
Acapulco	Montezuma	Rafael Bello	Acapulco
Durango	Unknown	Juan Caballero	Huejutla
	Durango	Héctor González	Campeche
Tampico	Unknown	Lorenzo Cárdenas	Papantla
Puebla	Puebla	Bartolomé Carrasco	Huejutla
	Puebla	Rosendo Huesca	Puebla
	Puebla	Luis Altamirano	Huajuapan
	Puebla	Lucio Torreblanca	Chiapas
León	León	Samuel Ruiz	Chiapas
Morelia	Morelia	Manuel Castro Ruiz	Yucatán
	Morelia	Carlos Suárez Cazares	Zamora
	Morelia	Juan Navarro	Altamirano
	Morelia	Fernando Ruiz	Yucatán
	Morelia	José Tirado	C. Victoria
Saltillo	Spain	Fernando Romo	Torreón
Tacámbaro	Tacámbaro	Luis G. Cuara	Tuxpan
Tampico	Montezuma	Arturo Szymanski	Tampico
Toluca	Toluca	Felipe Arizmendi	Chihuahua
Zacatecas	Montezuma	José E. Robles	Tulancingo
Zamora	Zamora	José L. Anezcua	Campeche

dioceses and 31 students from Morelia alone. The seminary boasted a staff of 13 priests and three unordained priests as teachers. The curriculum was based on studies at the Gregorian University as well as important European schools, where many of its professors were trained. Mexican bishops were allowed to visit their seminary students in Montezuma, and the rector provided a report three times a year to each of the bishops.[57]

The student-to-ordination rate at Montezuma was particularly high, which explains to some extent why it became so influential among the Church hierarchy. Between 1937 and 1962, 2,124 students passed through its classrooms, and of those, 67 percent actually became priests. Montezuma is a significant seminary in Mexican Catholic history for several reasons. It served as a key source of revival of Mexican clerical training and intellectual ideas eliminated by the Revolution and the anti-Catholic suppression in the 1920s and 1930s. It was the first Mexican seminary in that era to extend well beyond the diocese or regional boundaries, truly a seminary of national scope. It provided a unifying force for recent generations of Mexican clergy. Alumni agree that because they were Mexicans living in a foreign culture, it brought them closer together. Third, it has been seen as an integrating institution for a Church undergoing structural and intellectual change.[58]

Montezuma also provided stronger ties and greater comprehension between the U.S. and Mexican churches, and many priests and bishops from both countries came to know each other during this era. Although their physical isolation made it difficult to have regular contact with the U.S. clergy, graduates nevertheless believe an important positive consequence of living and studying in New Mexico was getting to know some North American bishops, especially from border dioceses. When graduate Manuel Pérez Gil became bishop of Mexicali in 1966, he cooperated with the U.S. Catholic hierarchy in joint projects, believing his earlier contacts with U.S. bishops encouraged this type of activity.[59]

The importance of Montezuma as a recruitment center for future bishops can be suggested by enrollment data. Of its graduates before 1962, 300 priests (approximately one-fourth of the graduates) had taught or served in various Mexican seminaries. Of those, 10 became seminary rectors elsewhere in Mexico. Four of the 10 rectors became bishops. In 1989, 34 of 106 diocesan bishops (37 percent) had attended the Montezuma seminary. In contrast, 50 or 54 percent had studied at the Gregorian University in Rome. The 13 bishops from religious orders studied in their own institutions, usually abroad. Generally these bishops are better represented in the prelatures, the missionary dioceses, rather than in the typical, mainstream diocese. Only 15 percent of Mexico's bishops at that time had not studied outside of Mexico.[60]

Table 7-6 suggests the chronological limitations of Montezuma's influence. Although the seminary continued to operate until 1972, its influence as a major center for future members of the hierarchy was already over by the late-1950s. The last bishop known to have graduated from Montezuma started his studies there in the mid-1950s. These figures also suggest that the important Mexican seminaries, which had supplied many of the best students, were back on their feet by the early 1950s and were once again producing leading clerical figures.

What is most remarkable about the data in Table 7-6 is the fact that of the 353 seminarians who began their studies in the 1937 class, 11 became bishops, probably the largest group of Mexican bishops from a single seminary and generation in this century. What is even more remarkable is that of the 31 of those students who were from the Morelia diocese, seven became bishops. This reflects the extraordinary influence of Morelia seminary students, even after leaving the direct patronage of their diocese and seminary. Of the 47 dioceses in Mexico in 1962, all but one counted Montezuma seminary graduates among their priests.[61] The majority of its priests ended up in fast-growing regions or in dioceses where evangelization was never very thorough. In fact, in 1962, shortly before the impact of Vatican II, Montezuma graduates actually accounted for more than half of all priests in the Tepic, Chiapas, Tulancingo, Zacatecas, Saltillo, Cuernavaca, and Campeche dioceses. It is also worth noting that this includes two dioceses, Cuer-

Table 7-6. Bishops from the Interdiocesan Seminary
of Montezuma*

Year	Bishop	Diocese Ordained
1937	Genaro Alamilla	Tampico
	Estanislao Alcaraz	Morelia
	Victoriano Alvarez	Morelia
	Rafael Ayala	Puebla
	Sabas Magaña	Morelia
	Fidel Cortes	Morelia
	Alfonso Sánchez	Morelia
	Manuel Pérez Gil	Morelia
	Juevenal Porcayo	Acapulco
	Rogelio Sánchez	Zamora
	Alfredo Torres	Morelia
1938	J. Esaul Robles	Zacatecas
1941	Arturo Szymanski	Tampico
	José María Hernández	Morelia
1943	Rafael Bello Ruiz	Acapulco
1944	Guillermo Ranzahuer	Jalapa
1947	Rafael Muñóz	Guadalajara
1948	Alfonso H. Robles	Guadalajara
	Adolfo Suárez	Chiapas
1949	Magín Torreblanca	Puebla
1950	José Fernández	Tulancingo
	Arturo Lona Reyes	Huejutla

Note: Other bishops whose exact generation is unknown include Salvador Martínez Pérez, Efrén Ramos Salazar, Benjamín Jiménez Hernández, Vicente García Bernal, Francisco Javier Chavolla Ramos, and Ramón Calderón Batres.

navaca and Chiapas, renowned for their receptivity to CEBs in the 1970s and 1980s, although their bishops were not graduates.

Bishop Manuel Pérez Gil, who was a member of the first Montezuma generation in 1937, sheds some light on the attitudes of the time and on why Morelia was so well represented. He lived with Bishop Fidel Cortes Pérez in Morelia and at Montezuma and traveled with other Morelia students, including Victoriano Alvarez Tena, bishop of Apatzingán, who became a very close friend. They often loaned money to each other to help their companions through difficult periods:

> In 1937, the bishop decided that our situation could not continue and negotiated for something to replace the seminary in the United States. This, of course, led to the establishment of the Montezuma seminary in New Mexico. I remember that many of us were hesitant about going, thinking that we were going to become converted to gringos. The bishop decided that not several, but all of us would go to Montezuma simultaneously so that we would have a large nucleus of members, and that we would reinforce each other's Mexican identity.[62]

The experience at Montezuma in the 1940s and 1950s continued to be formative for many priests and bishops during the heyday of its influence. Future bishops saw it as unique because they were involved in intellectual and work-related activities with a diverse group of faculty and students. Rafael Muñoz, later bishop of Zacatecas and Aguascalientes, attended Montezuma from 1947 to 1951 as a fellow of Catholic Action, after spending eight years at the Guadalajara seminary. He remembers his experiences in the following light:

> In my opinion, it was the best possible time to be there. We had outstanding professors, people who were much stronger in theology than here in Mexico, and even professors from the Gregorian University. I think Montezuma provided an experience different from the typical Mexican seminary, first because we came from many different dioceses of the republic. I see it as an opening, a beautiful experience. I believe the fact that we were all away from Mexico was equally important. It established a strong sense of family and community among students and teachers. All of the students had to work, whether it was manual labor or office tasks. This work experience was critical to their formation; having to live and work together created strong bonds, ties we have retained all these years.[63]

Other bishops who also attended the seminary during the early 1950s agree with Muñoz's assessment, suggesting that it provided a different set of values and amplified their vision of life and events. It opened these students up to many other experiences, enriching their lives.[64] By the 1960s, Montezuma's curriculum took on a more open, progressive bent. One graduate, an extreme example of a progressive priest, received his prior education in Guadalajara's distinguished seminary but found Montezuma more receptive to ideas associated with liberation theology.[65]

Montezuma lost its raison d'être when it became increasingly expensive to send students to the United States, and the regional seminaries fully recovered their operating status. Nationalism also became a significant issue because the Catholic hierarchy did not want future priests exposed to and possibly absorbing North American influences. Greater receptivity to liberation theology may also explain why Montezuma declined in importance.

A Roman Passage: Studies at the Gregorian University

If Montezuma was the most important seminary for Mexican bishops in the Western hemisphere, the Gregorian University exceeded even its influence in producing future bishops, having a well-established history, hundreds of alumni in Mexico, and a distinguished international reputation. As the secular state grew in influence in the 19th century, many Western European seminaries began to close. The Gregorian University came to serve as the primary academic locus for various national colleges located in Rome.[66] As one influential American Catholic described it, "[T]he Gregorian was to the Church what West Point was to the Army. The 'Greg' was, and still is, I suppose, the premier school for clerics."[67] Its influence was perpetuated not only by graduates dominating the hierarchy, including nearly all recent popes, but largely through its graduates who took up teaching. By the late 1960s, 230 of 280 American bishops were alumni, as were 7 of 10 North American cardinals. Half of American archbishops also studied in Rome.[68]

Among Latin American bishops, most with advanced education had completed their studies in Rome. This is definitely the case in Mexico. For example, the majority of the founding professors at Mexico's own Pontifical University in 1895 were graduates.[69] Although half of Mexico's bishops taught, among those attending the Gregorian University, nearly two-thirds returned from Rome to make seminary teaching their careers.

Latin America became interested in having its priests attend the Gregorian after a Chilean monsignor visited the region in the mid-19th century, recommending that the Vatican establish a Latin American College at the Gregorian University named after Pope Pius IX, hence the Colegio Pio Latino América was born. The idea of sending Mexican priests to Rome, however, increased in popularity after state persecution in the 1920s.[70] In fact, many bishops estimated that, by the late 1930s, Mexico accounted for nearly half of all Latin American priests attending the university.

The Gregorian University plays a special role among priests who later became bishops. Having credentials as a graduate of the Gregorian, while not essential, immensely improves one's chances of becoming a bishop. By 1945, nearly half (45 percent) of all Mexican bishops were graduates.[71] In fact, it is clear from recent bishops that the path to becoming a bishop was much faster for Gregorian graduates than any other seminary graduate in or outside of Mexico. Although half of all bishops in our sample graduated from the Gregorian University, of the few bishops who reached their post less than 15 years after ordination, three-quarters were Gregorian alumni. The relationship between the Gregorian University and becoming a bishop is well understood in Mexico. As the rector of the Colegio Pio Latino América jokingly told a Mexican priest many years ago, "To be a bishop in Mexico you need to be baptized, you need to be confirmed, and you need to be a graduate of the Colegio Pio Latino América. You can dispense with the first two but not the last one."[72] Although most priests are carefully selected to attend seminary in Rome, and such an educational opportunity is considered a plum, in rare cases selection may be accidental.[73]

The Colegio Pio Latino América is not an educational institution or a college within a university; rather it is a regional dormitory that for more than a century has housed Latin American priests. Each prospective priest from Latin America, including Mexico, attends different schools at the Gregorian University based on his specialty and interests. It is the residential college, however, which provides an important, unifying socializing environment, bringing together many priests from Latin America.

The Gregorian University's influence is largely curricular. Most priests who have passed through its classrooms remember the rigidity of its theological education. Theodore Hesburgh, former president of Notre Dame and a lifelong educator, describes it well:

> The teaching was rigid and unimaginative and almost rote: the syllabus and instruction methods had not changed, I think, from the way things were done when they started the university in 1558. Each major subject was boiled down to fifteen propositions, and at the end of each course you had to defend any one of those fifteen theses that

the examining professor picked at random. . . . And yet, as rigid and old-fashioned as the Gregorian was, it provided me with good, intellectual discipline and a wonderful grounding in classical scholastic philosophy and theology.[74]

To scholars, this education meant that young priests received a narrow view of papal authority, which in turn affected their future views as priests and bishops toward the pope, their unwillingness to question his authority, the source of his views, and the importance of hierarchy.[75] Others view the Gregorian curriculum, which is extremely demanding and controlled by Jesuits, as focused heavily on administration compared to other Roman institutions operated by Franciscans and Dominicans.[76]

For the many Mexican priests who graduated from the Gregorian University while residing in the Colegio Pio Latino América, the experience was formative. In the first place, coming in contact with numerous priests from Latin America, many of whom were later to lead their own hierarchies, separated them from their peers in Mexico. Mexican bishops repeatedly refer to close friendships developed among Latin American clergy. Future Mexican bishops from various dioceses also came to know each other.[77] Second, many future bishops believe that living in a major center of European Christianity also provided a context special to their socialization.[78] Hesburgh's own recollections correspond strongly with those of Mexican bishops; indeed, they could easily have been written by his Mexican counterparts. He found his formation in Syracuse, New York, and at Notre Dame "provincial" compared to the "international" flavor at the Gregorian and actually learned Spanish from a fellow Mexican student.[79]

For Mexicans who remained at the Gregorian University during World War II, unable to return to Mexico, it took on a different tone. Approximately 100 Mexicans had almost no communication with their homeland during the war. This increased their reliance on international influences and decreased the impact of Mexican experiences. Third, although the curriculum can be described as traditional, many priests considered the western cultural opening, compared to that found in Mexico, to be extraordinary. Rosendo Huesca believes it was his experience at the Gregorian that sparked his interest in psychology, which he later studied at Fordham University in the Bronx. He also believes that his interest in the strength and influence of Catholic minorities, exemplified by English experiences, stems from his education in Rome.[80] Other bishops who have drawn comparisons to their seminary training in Mexico offer various adjectives to describe the differences: rich, different, broad, and diverse. For other bishops, the proximity of their exposure to the Catholic Church, the Pope, and the Vatican stood out. In short, they experienced the larger environment of Catholicism within the context of Rome.[81]

By the 1960s, even the Gregorian University was subject to the currents sweeping Rome after the Vatican II Concilium. For those students attending the university during this period, the study of theology changed. Many describe it as an extraordinary era, as they witnessed new influences on their dogma and institutions.[82] Bishop Ricardo Guízar Díaz, who attended the Gregorian University during the 1950s and 1960s, describes it as two different eras, pre- and postconcilium.[83]

Some of the most important consequences of receiving an education at the Gregorian University were altered in 1963 when Mexico created the Colegio México to replace the Colegio Pio Latino América. Thus, instead of living with many other Latin American priests, Mexicans began residing in their own dormitory. The reasons for this change are debated. A number of priests believe the hierarchy created the Mexican college because they were afraid Latin American students would influence Mexicans with radical, liberation theology philosophy.[84] This does explain, to some extent, why Catholic currents throughout Latin America have not generated similar consequences among Mexican clergy, who remained isolated from their peers. Bishop Méndez Arceo, for example, who did not believe in this liberation theology explanation, nevertheless concluded that earlier levels of communication with Latin Americans were eliminated. The former prefect of studies at the Colegio Pio Latino América, Rubén Murillo, also considers the Colegio México's creation a great loss in establishing significant friendships among future priests and bishops throughout the region. Others have suggested that it was founded to counteract Jesuit influence at the Colegio Pio Latino América.[85] The traditional explanation is that Mexicans constituted the largest number of Latin American students, generally half of the student body, and therefore needed their own residence hall.

Conclusions

Educational choices and experiences have figured significantly in the future careers of priests and bishops. The importance of advanced education among the Church hierarchy is illustrated by the role it plays in the career choices of priests who become Mexican bishops. It would be expected that those priests who work their way up the appropriate Church administrative hierarchy, in this case higher education, would be in a stronger position to advance into the episcopate. In other closed institutional structures, such as the Mexican officer corps, similar patterns exist between higher education and internal career choices.

Mexican bishops, however, are more likely to have taught in their respective diocesan seminaries than to have performed any other task. The universality of this experience demonstrates not only the importance of seminary education in priests' formation but also the value the episcopate places on teaching as an intellectual, administrative, and experiential credential in assessing future qualities of potential bishops.

As is true among other leadership groups in Mexico, Latin America, and elsewhere in the world, where priests attend school is often determinative of their values, career emphasis in the priesthood, and success in becoming a bishop. The Catholic Church, unlike other autonomous institutional elites, provides a sizable number of educational choices that it funds and staffs. Nevertheless, several domestic institutions have stood out in graduating future bishops: Morelia and Guadalajara. It is obvious from the figures cited above that these two institutions' credentials are highly valued and that priests may make significant contacts among teaching staff and administrators.

Mexican bishops have also passed through two other significant educational experiences: Rome and New Mexico. Similar to their secular, political counterparts, future bishops have traveled abroad for advanced religious and philosophical education. But unlike Mexican politicians, bishops have obtained this education at primarily two institutions, institutions the Church controls. On the other hand, a Roman education at the Gregorian University serves to bring priests together with their most prominent counterparts from the outside Catholic world. The establishment of the Colegio México has reduced considerably these personal and intellectual contacts and is likely to have important future consequences on Mexican Catholic ideology.

Many Mexican clergy also have shared a unique educational experience, a product of historical circumstances, in attending the Montezuma seminary in the United States, the only interdiocesan seminary, in effect a *national* Mexican seminary, to have existed. Early generations of graduates formed in this foreign environment produced a significant number of bishops, many of whom played critical roles in the ideological currents of the 1960s.

Clerical educational patterns in Mexico have remained quite constant in the latter half of this century. But as the backgrounds of younger bishops illustrate, several significant changes are apparent, changes having consequences for episcopate leadership and attitudes. Among the most important of these patterns is a recent decline in teaching careers in favor of a heavier emphasis on pastoral experiences. These experiences are critical in drawing priests closer to their parishioners and in making future Church leaders more aware of laypersons' problems.

A second recent development among bishops' educational trends is that larger numbers are remaining in Mexico to complete their seminary education. This has important consequences for the Mexican episcopate's receptivity to currents of thought circulating in Rome and in emphasizing the organic priest as the major source of Church leadership. It is also likely to contribute to a more nationally oriented, rather than internationally predisposed, bishop.

Accompanying this last trend is the reversal of a long-standing and increasing trend of obtaining higher education at the doctoral level. Mexican bishops, in their selection of future peers, are not stressing this previous pattern. Instead, priests are completing basic theological education and activating their careers more quickly than in the past. This may be due to the general pressures created by an aging clergy. It is bound to have some effect on episcopal receptivity to intellectual issues. In the future, the intellectual diversity that the Catholic hierarchy provides its priests will be more dependent on diocesan differences than on national and international experiences.

NOTES

1. See Roderic Ai Camp, *Mexico's Leaders: Their Education and Recruitment* (Tucson: University of Arizona Press, 1980), and *Recruitment across Two Centuries: Mexico, 1884–1993* (Austin: University of Texas Press, 1995).

2. Roderic Ai Camp, *Entrepreneurs and Politics in Twentieth Century Mexico* (New York: Oxford University Press, 1989), 220.

3. Roderic Ai Camp, *Generals in the Palacio: The Military in Modern Mexico* (New York: Oxford University Press, 1992).

4. Manuel R. González Ramírez, *La Iglesia mexicana en cifras* (Mexico City, 1969), 119.

5. Thomas G. Sanders, "The Chilean Episcopate," *American Universities Field Staff Reports* 15, no. 3 (August 1968): 14.

6. Daniel H. Levine, *Religion and Politics in Latin America: The Catholic Church in Venezuela and Colombia* (Princeton: Princeton University Press, 1981), 100–101.

7. This became an important issue in the designation of José Luis Dibildox as bishop of the new Tarahumara diocese, an individual with no rural or missionary experiences and no time in the Tarahumara prelature. Manuel Robles and Rodrigo Vera, "Prigione, acusado de entorpecer la paz en Chiapas y de desplazar a los Jesuitas en la Tarahumara," *Proceso,* January 24, 1994, 30–35.

8. Personal interview with Bishop José Melgoza Osorio, Nezahualcóyotl Diocese, Nezahualcóyotl, México, May 27, 1987.

9. Take for example Mario de Gasperín, who on the surface appears to represent the classic track of the educated *generalist,* as professor, prefect of discipline, and prefect of studies of the Jalapa seminary. "I returned to the Jalapa seminary from Rome as a professor, a task I performed for 20 years. Five of those years I served in a barrio as a parish priest [San Antonio de Padua, Jalapa], and 14 years in another parish [San José, Jalapa]. I carried out my teaching tasks in the morning, and from 4 to 10 in the afternoon I served as a parish priest. Believe me, I was very influenced by what I saw in these parishes. When Oscar Lewis's book *[The Children of Sánchez]* came out, I not only agreed with it, but I thought he didn't report half of the reality I witnessed." Personal interview, Querétaro Diocese, Querétaro, Querétaro, July 12, 1993.

10. Personal interview with Father Antonio Roqueñi, Mexico Archdiocese, Mexico City, July 14, 1993.

11. Personal interview with Manuel Samaniego Barriga, Bishop of Cuautitlán, Cuautitlán Diocese, Cuautitlán, México, February 13, 1991. Another example of this is the career of Adolfo Hernández Hurtado, who at 38 was one of the youngest priests in decades to be selected as a bishop. After serving as a parish priest for 14 years from 1943 through 1957, he became the first bishop of Tapachula, Chiapas. Personal interview, Guadalajara Diocese, Guadalajara, Jalisco, July 7, 1993.

12. Personal interview with Javier Navarro Rodríguez, auxiliary bishop of Guadalajara, Guadalajara Diocese, Guadalajara, Jalisco, July 8, 1993.

13. *Documentación e Información Católica* 13 (April 1985): 315.

14. The percentage is higher among U.S. Catholic priests. Only one in seven priests received his entire elementary education in public schools. See Joseph H. Fichter, *Religion as an Occupation: A Study in the Sociology of Professions* (Terre Haute, Ind.: University of Notre Dame Press, 1961), 39.

15. Conferencia del Episcopado Mexicano, "Sagrada Congregación para la Educación Católica," *Documentación e Información Católica* 14 (December 1986), 876–903.

16. See Bishop Jorge Martínez Martínez's autobiography for a reference to this activity. *Memorias y reflexiones de un obispo* (Mexico City: Editorial Villicaña, 1986), 27.

17. Daniel H. Levine, *Religion and Politics in Latin America: The Catholic Church in Venezuela and Colombia* (Princeton: Princeton University Press, 1981), 103.

18. Gustavo Pérez Ramírez and Yván Labelle, *El problema sacerdotal en América La-*

tina (Madrid: FERES, 1964), 93. Some unusual cases exist of priests and even bishops entering the priesthood as older adults, as is increasingly the case in the United States. For example, Andrés Estrada Jasso entered the San Luis Potosí seminary at age 13 in 1930 but left in 1940 and moved to Monterrey, where he married, had a family, and taught at a university. After his wife died in 1985, he returned to the seminary and was ordained in 1988. Personal interview by Scott Pentzer and Meg Mitchell with Andrés Estrada Jasso, San Luis Potosí Diocese, San Luis Potosí, San Luis Potosí, July 13, 1993.

19. Enrique Luengo, "Los párrocos: una visión," unpublished manuscript, Department of Social and Political Sciences, Ibero-American University, December 1989, 42.

20. Daniel H. Levine, *Religion and Politics in Latin America,* 101–102.

21. This may be an important trend for other reasons, too. One of the concerns expressed by some bishops is that the Church is too focused on advanced education, thereby creating an elite clergy. One bishop recalls the archbishop of Guadalajara sending out his most well educated priests to serve in small, rural parishes, solely to preserve their sense of humility. Personal interview with Bishop José Melgoza Osorio.

22. For some excellent data on recent, broad trends in politicians' education, see Alfonso Galindo, "Education of Mexican Government Officials," *Statistical Abstract of Latin America* (Los Angeles: UCLA Latin American Center, 1990), 30: 565–599.

23. Thomas Reese, *A Flock of Shepherds: The National Conference of Catholic Bishops* (Kansas City, Mo.: Sheed & Ward, 1992), 3–4.

24. José Ignacio Dávila Garibi, *El v. episcopado mexicano en el año jubilar guadalupano* (Mexico, 1945), 71–76. Garibi also discovered that all bishops who had taught or served in seminary administrative posts were graduates of the same seminaries.

25. Enrique Luengo, "Los párrocos, una visión," 46.

26. Ibid., 49.

27. Thomas Sanders points out the fact that the Chilean bishops felt that their lack of exposure to new currents in their pre-Vatican II Chilean education limited their vision. "The Chilean Episcopate," 14.

28. Dennis M. Hanratty, "Change and Conflict in the Contemporary Mexican Catholic Church," unpublished Ph.D. dissertation, Duke University, 1980, 286.

29. Personal interview with Bishop Adolfo Hernández Hurtado, Guadalajara Archdiocese, Guadalajara, Jalisco, July 7, 1993.

30. Manuel R. González Ramírez, *La iglesia mexicana en cifras,* 121.

31. Personal interview with Bishop Raúl Vera López, Ciudad Altamirano Diocese, Guerrero, Mexico City, May 3, 1992.

32. Personal interview with Father Antonio Roqueñi Ornelas.

33. Personal interview with Raúl Padilla, rector of the University of Guadalajara, Guadalajara, Jalisco, July 8, 1993.

34. Enrique Luengo, "Los párrocos: una visión," 37.

35. Claude Pomerlau, "The Catholic Church in Mexico and Its Changing Relationship to Society and the State," unpublished manuscript, December 1980, 10.

36. Martalena Negrete, *Relaciones entre la iglesia y el estado en México, 1930–1940* (Mexico City: El Colegio de México, 1988), 296–297.

37. Oscar González et al., "Batallas en el reino de este mundo," *Nexos,* no. 78 (June 1984): 27; Claude Pomerlau, "Cambios en el liderazgo y la crisis de autoridad en el catolicismo mexicano," in *Religión y política en México,* Martín de la Rosa et al., eds. (Mexico City: Siglo XXI, 1985), 255, citing Luis Núñez and Félix Palencia, *Seminarios y seminaristas de México en 1973* (Chihuahua: privately published, 1974).

38. Claude Pomerlau, "The Catholic Church in Mexico and Its Changing Relationship to the State," Chapter 3, 36.

39. Claude Pomerlau, "Cambios en el liderazgo y la crisis de autoridad en el catolicismo mexicano," 252.

40. Personal interview with Luis Narro Rodríguez, director of the Center of Educational Studies, Mexico City, June 28, 1989.

41. Personal interviews with Ricardo Cuellar Romo, Mexican Episcopate, Mexico Archdiocese, Mexico City, May 25, 1987, and Guillermo Schulenburg, abbot of the Basilica of Guadalupe, Mexico Archdiocese, Mexico City, February 18, 1991.

42. Ivan Vallier, *Catholicism, Social Control, and Modernization in Latin America* (Englewood Cliffs, N.J.: Prentice-Hall, 1970), 100.

43. For example, in 1952, four of the instructors at the Morelia seminary were Manuel Pérez Gil González, Manuel Castro Ruiz, Victoriano Alvarez Teña, and José de Jesús Tirado Pedraza, all of whom became bishops. See *Directorio de la Iglesia en México* (Mexico City: Buena Prensa, 1952), 108–109.

44. Fausto Zerón Medina, who studied in the archives in Rome, examined the Mary Brothers seminary in Guadalajara, where he discovered that instructions involving their goals and methods in the 19th century were essentially the same as those he received as a student there in the 1950s. Personal interview, Mexico City, May 29, 1987.

45. Claude Pomerlau, "The Catholic Church in Mexico and Its Changing Relationship to Society and the State," Chapter 3, 25.

46. Martalena Negrete, *Relaciones entre la iglesia y el estado en Mexico,* 296–297.

47. Personal interview by Scott Pentzer with Rafael Ramírez Díaz, abbot of the Basilica of Guanajuato, Guanajuato Diocese, Guanajuato, Guanajuato, July 9, 1993.

48. Personal interview with Archbishop Manuel Pérez Gil, Tlanepantla Diocese, Tlanepantla, México, February 18, 1991.

49. Personal interview with Cardinal Juan Jesús Posadas Ocampo, Guadalajara Archdiocese, Mexican Episcopate, Mexico City, February 20, 1991.

50. Personal interview by Scott Pentzer and Meg Mitchell with Father Tranquilino Romero.

51. Personal interview with Father Antonio García Montaño, member of the Passion Order, Mexico Archdiocese, Mexico City, February 15, 1991. Although no data is available on attrition, 78 percent of the higher seminaries provided data in a 1990 survey that indicates a substantial increase in enrollment since 1982, averaging 50 percent by 1987. *Documentación e Información Católica* 19 (October 24, 1991): 652–664.

52. Enrique Luengo, "Los párrocos: una visión," 21.

53. Personal interview with Manuel Hinojosa Ortiz, Mexico City, June 1, 1988.

54. Personal interview with Fausto Zerón Medina.

55. *Cambio,* May 15, 1989, 39; Conferencia del Episcopado Mexicano, *Directorio eclesiástico, 1984–1985,* 29; Oscar González et al., "Batallas en el reino de esto mundo," 21; Raúl Macín, "Los protestantes mexicanos: un voto tradicional," in *La sucesión presidencial en 1988,* by Abraham Nuncio, ed. (Mexico City: Grijalbo, 1988), n.p.; *Enciclopedia de México,* 13:7442–7443; *Proceso,* October 3, 1977, 24.

56. Martaelena Negrete, *Relaciones entre la iglesia y el estado en México, 1930–1940,* 301.

57. Luis Medina Ascensio, *Historia del Seminario de Montezuma, sus precedentes, fundación y consolidación, 1910–1953* (Mexico City: Editorial Jus, 1962), 152–153, 189, 202; Manuel González Ramírez, *La Iglesia mexicana en cifras,* 130.

58. Manuel González Ramírez, *La Iglesia mexicana en cifras,* 131; Luis Medina Ascensio, *Historia del Seminario de Montezuma,* 192.

59. Personal interview with Bishop Manuel Pérez Gil.

60. José Macías, *Montezuma en sus exalumnos, 1937–1962* (Mexico City, 1962), 83–

84; Antonio García Montaño, "Los obispos mexicanos de la segunda mitad del siglo xx," unpublished paper, 1992, n.p.

61. José Macías, *Montezuma en sus exalumnos*, 101–112.

62. Personal interview with Bishop Manuel Pérez Gil.

63. Personal interview with Bishop Rafael Muñoz, Aguascalientes Diocese, Mexico City, July 15, 1993.

64. Personal interview with Bishop Magin Camarino Torreblanca Reyes, Texcoco Diocese, Texcoco, México, July 12, 1993.

65. Personal interview with José Alvarez Franco, Tateposco, Tonala, Jalisco, July 7, 1993.

66. Howard T. Sanks, *Authority in the Church: A Study in Changing Paradigms* (Missoula, Mont.: Scholar's Press, 1974), 3.

67. Theodore M. Hesburgh, *God, Country, Notre Dame* (New York: Fawcett, 1990), 33.

68. Thomas Reese, *Archbishop: Inside the Power Structure of the American Catholic Church* (New York: Harper and Row, 1989), 78.

69. Manuel Olimón Nolasco, *Tensiones y acercamientos, la iglesia y el estado en la historia del pueblo mexicano* (Mexico City: Instituto Mexicano de Doctrina Social Cristiana, 1990), 29.

70. Personal interview with Bishop Francisco Aguilera González, Mexico Archdiocese, Mexico City, June 1, 1987.

71. José Ignacio Dávila Garibi, *El v. episcopado mexicano en el año jubilar guadalupano*, 83–84.

72. Personal interview with Manuel Concha Malo, Mexico Archdiocese, Mexico City, June 21, 1989.

73. Samuel Ruiz's education there is a case in point. The person who was chosen to go could not leave because his military service papers were not in order, so Ruiz was asked to replace him. Personal interview with Bishop Samuel Ruiz, San Cristóbal de las Casas Diocese, Lago de Guadalupe, Cuautitlán, México, April 30, 1992.

74. Theodore M. Hesburgh, *God, Country, Notre Dame*, 33.

75. Howard T. Sanks, *Authority in the Church*, 4, 112.

76. Personal interview with José Rogelio Alvarez, Mexico City, February 15, 1991.

77. Ricardo Guizar Díaz, bishop of Atlacomulco, who attended the Gregorian University from 1950 through 1960, counted five other bishops in his class—two from Latin America and three from Mexico: Abelardo Alvarado Alcántara, auxiliary bishop of Mexico City; Juan Sandoval Iñiquez, bishop of Ciudad Juárez; and Javier Lozano Barragán, bishop of Zacatecas. Personal interview, Atlacomulco Diocese, Atlacomulco, México, June 28, 1994.

78. Personal interviews with Bishop José Melgoza Osorio, Mexico Archdiocese, Mexico City, May 27, 1987, and Bishop Samuel Ruiz.

79. Theodore Hesburgh, *God, Country, Notre Dame*, 30–31.

80. Personal interview with Archbishop Rosendo Huesca, Puebla Diocese, Puebla, Puebla, July 16, 1993.

81. Personal interviews with Bishop Luis Mena, Mexico Archdiocese, Mexico City, July 13, 1993, and Bishop Mario de Gasperín.

82. Personal interview by Scott Pentzer and Meg Mitchell with Father Salvador Juan Villapando, San Luis Potosí Diocese, San Luis Potosí, San Luis Potosí, July 12, 1993.

83. Personal interview with Bishop Ricardo Guízar Díaz.

84. Personal interviews with Father Rafael Tapia, Father Abelardo Hernández, and Father Humberto Vargas, Puebla Archdiocese, Puebla, Puebla, July 16, 1993.

85. Martín de la Rosa, "Iglesia y sociedad en el México de hoy," in *Religión y política en México,* Martín de la Rosa and Charles A. Reilly, eds. (Mexico City: Siglo XXI, 1985), 284.

8

Who Are the Bishops?

Consequences of Family and Place

A ll leadership groups in Mexico share certain characteristics that set them apart from the general population. The most tangible differences between elites and masses can be measured according to their geographic, social, and economic origins. Priests who become bishops are not representative of priests as a whole, nor are they representative of the Mexican population when measured according to these variables. Nevertheless, these distinctions are worth identifying because they may have significant consequences for the careers of future priests and their road to success as bishops and, more important, they may contrast substantially with those of other leadership groups, particularly political and military, linking bishops to the Mexican populations in ways that other groups do not share.

Consequences of Birth

As I have suggested in an analysis of Mexican political leadership over time, regionalism has played a critical role in the representativeness of national politicians and in the locus of their recruitment. The most striking feature of place of birth in the backgrounds of Mexican political leaders for the last half century is the phenomenal growth of Mexico City, the nation's capital, which now accounts for approximately 20 percent of the population. The capital, however, is heavily overrepresented among national politicians, who in the 1990s come from the Federal District in figures twice that amount. Among younger leaders in the federal government, nearly two-thirds are capital city natives.

Regionalism provides an equally striking pattern for the 20th-century Catholic leadership, yet its geographic distortions are quite different from those of politicians, consequently having different results on the composition of the Church hierarchy. As this chapter will demonstrate, the geographic differences that set Church and political leadership apart also have consequences for their values and behavior and on their potential linkages to the citizenry in general.

Over time, the argument can be made that West Central Mexico (Michoacán, Guanajuato, México, and Morelos) is to the clergy what the Federal District was to Mexican politicians. The expansion of the Federal District, accompanied by the centralization of Mexican political leadership, evolved into the nerve center of politics and the locus of future political recruitment. The Catholic Church, however, with its institutional reputation for centralization, drew its careerists from a broader provincial, yet historically significant, base.

The data in Table 8-1 suggest that West Central Mexico has long produced a disproportionate share of bishops. Among the older bishops, born before the Revolution of 1910, who have guided the Church since the 1960s, more than one-third came from these states, accounting for only 21 percent of the general population in 1910, the census closest to the average birth date of our sample. Yet as the population of the West Central region declined, the region maintained its importance as the birthplace of bishops and produced nearly 45 percent of all Mexican bishops born after 1920.

As leadership groups institutionalize, they tend to establish structural patterns along geographic lines that contribute to formal and informal recruitment channels, and these patterns are slow to alter. Mexican priests, although they have not been well examined, come disproportionately from the same region. According to Antonio García Montaño, large numbers of priests, nuns, and brothers come from three important states: Guanajuato, Jalisco, and Michoacán.[1] The historical explanation for this shares parallels with that of politicians and, to a lesser extent, the officer corps. Religious resources such as buildings, dioceses, seminaries, and other religiously oriented activities were concentrated in the West Central and Western regions of Mexico. In fact, as one scholar has argued, "until recently,

Table 8-1. Birthplaces of Bishops, by Generation

Year of Birth	West Central	West	East Central	North	Gulf	South	Federal District	Foreign
Bishops								
Pre-1899	38%	44%	13%	0%	0%	6%	0%	0%
1900–1909	38	31	15	0	8	0	8	0
1910–1919	30	19	22	15	0	7	7	0
1920–1929	34	23	11	9	3	9	11	0
1930–	49	21	9	4	9	2	4	2
Average	39	25	13	9	4	5	7	1
Other Elites								
Politicians	13	15	15	15	13	9	19	1
Generals	9	14	15	18	15	9	19	0
General Population								
1910 Census	21	16	22	11	14	12	5	
1950 Census	17	14	18	15	13	12	12	

Sources: The data in this and all other tables referring to bishops are based on a nearly complete sample of individuals who headed Mexican dioceses from 1960 through 1995. The sample totals 138. Data for politicians comes from Roderic Ai Camp, *Political Recruitment across Two Centuries: Mexico 1884–1991* (Austin: University of Texas Press, 1995), based on a subsample of 2,003 national political figures. Figures do not add up to 100 because of rounding.

wide areas of the country were divided into dioceses so large that they remained unmanageable and isolated."[2]

If we examine the geographic composition of the episcopate at several points in time during the scope of our survey, we discover that in 1969, of the 78 active bishops, 23 (30 percent) were from Michoacán, 22 (28 percent) from Jalisco, 5 (6 percent) from Puebla, and 4 (5 percent) from Guanajuato. Only one bishop was born in Mexico City. By diocese, the Church institutional boundaries within which a potential priest first enters the seminary and is claimed as a disciple, the distribution was further exaggerated: 27 from Morelia (Michoacán), 24 from Guadalajara (Jalisco), and 8 from Puebla (Puebla)—in sum, 59 or three-quarters of all bishops.[3] Twenty years later, in 1989, of 106 bishops, 20 (19 percent) were from Michoacán, 17 (16 percent) were from Jalisco, 15 (14 percent) were from Guanajuato, and 11 (10 percent) were from the Federal District, suggesting little change in the domination of the three West Central and Western states but a striking increase in Mexico City as a birthplace among bishops.

The Federal District is strongly underrepresented in the backgrounds of bishops not only compared to the birthplaces of the general population but also compared to the birthplaces of mexican priests, accounting for 15 percent of priests and 25 percent of nuns in the 1980s. This can be explained by the fact that most priests from Mexico City (93 percent) are not diocesan clergy but are members of religious orders (39 percent) or have other institutional affiliations (54 percent). However, religious orders account for only a small percentage of all priests and bishops in Mexico, but they are concentrated in the capital, as are 88 percent and 68 percent of male and female religious institutes, respectively.[4]

The data in Table 8-1 also suggest the comparative underrepresentation of the Church hierarchy from numerous regions when contrasted with political and military elites. The weakness of the Church hierarchy is apparent in the East Central, Gulf, and North. To some extent, the northern distribution can be explained by its frontier mentality and recent history, with a lower level of Church presence and a strong 20th-century heritage associated with the anticlerical leadership of the Mexican Revolution. Although Porfirio Díaz produced a dominant northern political generation, the revolutionaries continued that bias well into the 20th century, a pattern that potentially could have been reinstated in 1994 by Sonoran Luis Donaldo Colosio's candidacy as president had he not been assassinated. The Gulf's position can also be explained somewhat by a thinner Church presence historically and, more recently, by the extreme suppression of religion in the state of Tabasco during the 1930s, vividly portrayed in Graham Greene's *Power and the Glory.*

Where Church leadership origins are weak, especially the Federal District, other Mexican elites are strong, not only politicians and generals but also intellectuals and leading capitalists. This broad geographic imbalance has additional geographic implications for urban and rural as well as nationwide patterns. Other than the differences apparent in the capital, the single most striking contrast among the three leadership groups occurs in the West Central region, where the Church doubles its representation compared to the population in general, while the officer corps underrepresents it at approximately the same level.

West Central Mexico was the heart of the Cristero rebellion in Mexico, a movement involving large numbers of committed Catholic laypersons and some lower clergy. As demonstrated elsewhere, future clergy and priests were very much influenced by this movement in the late 1920s, a movement reinforcing their desires to remain religiously active and pursue priestly vocations. In fact, of the Mexican bishops about whom we have information, nearly one-fifth indicated direct experience with the Cristero rebellion, either impacting on their childhood and their parents' lives, their ability to obtain a seminary education, or, in rare cases, their active involvement in the rebellion. One out of three bishops affected by the Cristero movement was born in West Central Mexico. At the same time, these deeply religious areas created a culture rejecting the military as a desirable career, given the belief that the military, as the civil authorities' enforcement arm, was responsible for killing friends and relatives associated with the movement.

Mexican clergy strongly believe that geography continues to play a significant role in the formation of future priests and bishops. In explaining the influence of three seminaries (Morelia, Michoacán; León, Guanajuato; and Guadalajara, Jalisco) in the early 1990s, the late Cardinal Juan Jesús Posadas Ocampo of Guadalajara suggested that "the reason for the domination of these schools is that the regions in which they are located have been very religious. The colonial inheritance has remained very important in these regions in religious terms and has continued to produce considerable interest in the Catholic Church."[5]

Among the dioceses that exhibit these qualities, none is more influential or prestigious than that of the archdiocese of Morelia, Michoacán. The Morelia archdiocese is to Catholic clergy (bishops especially) what Mexico City is to politicians: a place where future leaders are brought together to be educated and formed in a shared culture. Bishop Manuel Samaniego Barriga, a native of Pangamacutiro, Michoacán, who attended seminary in Morelia and performed his first priestly duties as vicar in a Morelia parish, describes briefly the depth of its religious heritage:

> I believe that the archdiocese of Morelia has had an extended tradition of being extremely religious and in its long history has produced many notable religious figures, including Morelos, Hidalgo, and of course the first Mexican bishop, very famous in religious history, Zummáraga. Also during the Reform they were extremely strong, producing important figures during the civil wars. Therefore, anyone who is the least bit religious thinks of Morelia in strong religious terms. At the time I was there the seminary produced other figures who were not my classmates but were teachers, including a bishop of Querétaro and Archbishop Martínez of Morelia.[6]

Not only does religious history and the Church's institutional presence flavor an environment favorable to a religious career, but a larger peer group generates a psychological catalyst for making such a professional choice. Some clergy have pointed to the significance of individual towns, rather than dioceses or states, as disproportionate sources of prominent Church leaders.[7] For example, Cotija, described as a small gateway town into the mountainous region of Michoacán, has produced numerous bishops.[8] Bishop Raúl Vera of Ciudad Altamirano, Guerrero, describes his hometown of Acambaro, Guanajuato, in the heart of the West Central region, as strongly influenced by evangelical Catholicism, a term rarely heard in Mexico, and home to numerous priests. Two members of his father's family joined the Franciscans, and three became nuns.[9]

Examinations of other elite Mexicans' birthplaces also suggest that geographic location considerably affects institutional careers and upward mobility within their respective bureaucracies. If a subset of archbishops and cardinals is separated from all other Mexican bishops, comparisons can be drawn from this more select group within the general Church hierarchy. West Central birthplaces continue to be overly represented among this group, but not in percentages significantly higher than among all bishops. Interestingly, although the South and East Central regions are underrepresented among the birthplaces of all bishops, they are strongly overrepresented, with 19 percent (South) and 15 percent (East Central) among the highest levels of the episcopate, suggesting the initial advantages of being born in the West Central and West are not necessarily translated into more successful careers within the Church. On the other hand, it becomes equally apparent that coming from Mexico City is not associated with career success in the Church, which not only is underrepresented among bishops but is practically missing altogether among the elite hierarchy's birthplaces.

Background data on birthplaces of bishops and archbishops also suggest another pattern within certain dioceses. The West, second only to the West Central region in the level of overrepresentation in bishops' backgrounds, is sorely underrepresented among elite bishops, declining from 27 percent of bishops' birthplaces to only 15 percent of those of archbishops and cardinals. Guadalajara, the single most important archdiocese outside of Mexico City, is the religious center in the West. Yet bishops themselves complain vociferously that the Vatican imposes outsiders, clergy born and educated outside the diocese, on Guadalajara, breeding considerable resentment among both priests and bishops native to Jalisco. This assertion is strongly borne out in the data.

Being born in certain regions may have hindered the careers of some bishops at the very top of the hierarchy. Among politicians, the explanation for this is that birthplace often determines where one attends school and the discipline in which an individual majors. Location and professional career choice have positively affected Mexican political success. Earlier in the century, attendance at the National University (UNAM) and a major in law were tied strongly to career achievement; more recently, attendance at private schools, such as the Autonomous Technological Institute of Mexico (ITAM), and a major in economics have become increasingly significant.

Among clergy, therefore, one would expect priests from regions weakest in producing bishops to have the fewest career opportunities. However, this is not the case. In terms of the pace of career achievement, bishops born in the South and North, two regions traditionally underrepresented among all bishops, have advanced most rapidly. While only 13 percent of all bishops achieved their posts in fewer than 15 years after they were ordained (typically at age 24–25), twice that percentage from both of these regions were on a fast promotion track. This can be explained largely by the rapid expansion of dioceses in these regions and, consequently, by increased opportunities for talented priests, selected from an artificially small pool of priests from these regions, to reach positions of great responsibility in their 40s. In contrast, bishops having the slowest upward mobility, requiring 26 or more years to reach that position, are from Mexico City in percentages twice the national average among all other bishops. This can be explained in large part by structural conditions, too, in which Mexico City proper is a single large archdiocese, where the cardinal archbishop is aided by auxiliary bishops. These auxiliary divisions do not develop the same level of religious institutional and educational structures associated with more traditional, single-bishop dioceses.[10]

A direct consequence of regionalism and a significant feature of the Mexican episcopate that sets it apart from most other prominent leadership groups are the geographic roots it retains within its governing structures. Mexican politicians have lost this provincial flavor by directing power and recruitment to the capital. Although popular mythology views the Church as a centralized hierarchy, the reality is quite different. Each diocese is essentially autonomous, and the bishop does not answer to any national leader, archbishop or cardinal, but only to the Pope in Rome. One way to determine the degree to which bishops make their way as leaders in their own dioceses is to compile figures for those priests who actually end up leading their own diocese. In Mexico, such priests account for 38 percent of all bishops. This pattern changed among older bishops. Of those governing dioceses in the 1960s who were born before the turn of the century, only 6 percent served in their own native diocese compared to 44 percent born after 1900. Again, those regions traditionally underrepresented in Mexican bishops' backgrounds are more likely to promote their own recruits, in this case, the North and the Gulf, where three out of four bishops are homegrown.

One of the significant peculiarities of Mexican clergy, a feature distinguishing them from all other elite groups in Mexico, is their overwhelming training and formation in their diocese of origin or at the leading seminary within their region of birth. This pattern contradicts the general one for educated Mexicans. As one scholar of higher education argued: "Between the end of the Revolution and 1940, the [Federal] District maintained and probably increased its dominance of the manpower resources of the nation. Capacity in middle and higher education was even more heavily concentrated in the capital city in these years than in later ones, and it is unlikely that a large percentage of the graduates settled elsewhere."[11] This was definitely true of Mexican politicians from the provinces educated in Mexico City, most of whom remained in the capital. Even as of the mid-1960s, when most of Mexico's current leadership was educated, higher education throughout Latin America was still a capital city phenomenon.[12]

Mexico's bishops, unlike its politicians and generals, are educated in multiple institutions, the majority of which are located in the provinces, not Mexico City. In fact, among future bishops, those who attend the Mexico City seminary, one of the more important institutions, are primarily from other regions. The reverse is true elsewhere in Mexico. For example, all graduates from the Tridentino Morelia seminary who became bishops were from the West Central region, as were Monterrey seminarians from the North. Three-quarters of the Guadalajara and two-thirds of the Palafoxian seminary graduates in Puebla were from their respective regions. One can reverse these figures to demonstrate that among all bishops from the West, West Central, East Central, and North, more than half attended the primary higher seminary within their region of birth.

Place of birth not only determines where individuals attend school, even at higher levels of education, but also affects the discipline selected, at least among politicians. For example, Peter McDonough found this to be true of leaders in Brazil, where growing up in the interior limited their educational horizons, "with the result that their choice of university specialization turns out to be traditional in comparison with the paths followed by their peers from Rio and São Paulo."[13] The same pattern occurs among Mexican politicians. For example, if they come from Mexico City, they are much more likely to select economics than their provincial peers.

The economic development of the provinces and the lack of educational institutions do not affect Mexican bishops in the same way they influence politicians' educational choices. The Catholic Church, unlike the Mexican government, builds into its recruitment process an educational standard that all priests must meet; in short, they must graduate from seminary before being ordained. Consequently priests receive a minimum level of higher education. Many bishops, however, tend to receive higher levels of education, nearly half obtaining Ph.D.s in theology and philosophy. No relationship exists between a future bishop's birthplace and access to higher education. In fact, bishops born in Mexico City have the lowest levels of higher education. In contrast, their political colleagues from Mexico City reach the highest levels.

The Catholic Church, as an integral institution, shares more in common with the Mexican military than it does with politicians. Similar to the military, it created its own educational institutions, and once it asks a person to consider the priesthood, financial considerations and geography have little bearing on the individual's educational future. Unlike the military, however, which recruits a disproportionate percentage of future officers from the Federal District, the Church has decentralized its educational and recruitment institutions, thus downplaying the importance of any one region or diocese.

Given peculiar historical circumstances over which the Church had no control, geography did affect Mexican priests' educational locations, especially during the 1930s and 1940s. Many future bishops, who otherwise might have remained in Mexico to be educated in Mexican seminaries, as noted in the previous chapters, instead received their training abroad, either at the Montezuma seminary in New Mexico or the Gregorian University in Rome. Not surprisingly, those regions most affected by religious suppression and the Cristero rebellion sent their priests to the Montezuma seminary. The West Central region accounted for the largest percentage of future priests educated at this seminary, graduating one-fifth of Mexican bishops since the 1960s. Those regions sending the fewest future bishops to the seminary were the East Central and the North, where religious tolerance was more favorable. World War II also increased attendance at Montezuma, substituting for the Gregorian University, but its impact would have applied equally to all regions. Although half of all bishops traveled to the Gregorian University to obtain higher training beyond the seminary level, Mexican priests born in the East Central region were more likely to receive their education in Rome than any other geographic group.

One of the arguments that can be made about the Catholic hierarchy's links with the Mexican population, distinguishing it from the political, military, and especially intellectual leadership, is its maintenance of strong local roots. No other elites in Mexico can claim such close ties between where they work and their own geographic, familial origins as those in the Catholic hierarchy. The Church's structure encouraged this regional, grassroots pattern, both through the shape of the diocese and through the major and minor seminaries spread throughout the republic. In fact, in his study of priests, Enrique Luengo demonstrates that rank-and-file clergy are less representative of their home base than are bishops. In an examination of different parishes in Chihuahua (North), México (West Central), Guanajuato (West Central), and Mexico City, Luengo discovered a range in priests' birthplaces in their parishes' home state from a high of 75 percent in Chihuahua to a low of 23 percent in Mexico City, with an average of exactly one out of three, comparable but slightly lower than the 38 percent figure for bishops.[14]

Enrique Krauze suggested in the mid-1980s that the Mexican episcopate was opening up its structure by selecting bishops with roots in their dioceses. He described it as a new episcopate, a regional episcopate, seeking a different modus vivendi with the state.[15] The fact is, however, over 90 percent of all bishops since the 1960s have worked in their diocese of origin and more than 40 percent of the bishops ended up administering their native diocese. If any geographic pattern exists, it may well be the reverse, at least among priests. Manuel González Ramírez reported that only 6 percent of priests in 1968 resided outside their diocese of origin, generally in the North or Center, and 84 percent of all priests working outside their diocese of origin could be found in the Mexico City archdiocese.[16] As the number of dioceses expanded by 30 percent in that period, the Church found itself forced to draw both priests and bishops from many other regions.

Recent regional recruitment patterns of Mexican priests and bishops suggest several possible consequences. In the first place, like top political figures, both priests and bishops have fewer direct links with their parishes than in earlier eras. The lack of such linkages may make communication more difficult between leadership and constituencies. Yet bishops have far stronger ties to the communities they govern than do politicians. In the second place, bishops begin their careers in their local dioceses, not in Mexico City, where most successful national politicians initiate their careers. Among politicians, generals, and intellectuals, the only group that stresses this initial provincial experience is the officer corps, in which recent graduates from the Heroic Military College typically are sent as young lieutenants to military zone commands, somewhat comparable to large dioceses or political states.

Regardless of where bishops end up, they have spent their careers in the provinces, not in one central city or region. More important, bishops who move to a region eventually take on the contextual perspective of their diocese, often absorbing the flavor of their local constituents. The advantage of moving bishops around is that they have a much deeper perspective of different regional problems based on local issues. It also makes them more sympathetic to the problems of other bishops, even when they disagree with their colleagues' particular pastoral strategy or focus.

The stronger grassroots experiences of Mexican bishops compared to other leadership groups is reinforced by the autonomy and decentralized structure of the Church nationally. The national influence on bishops does not come from the cardinal archbishop in Mexico City but rather from the council of bishops, the episcopate, which is essentially a democratic, legislative body of equals. Although the episcopate issues recommendations only, the voices of every diocese and larger pastoral regions are represented in those decisions rather than having to rely on a national elite sitting in Mexico City to interpret the needs of the provinces.

Some scholars have argued that place of birth, especially in Third World cultures, may well affect values, especially if they are from the provinces and rural settings. Military analysts such as Morris Janowitz, for example, have made such an argument.[17] Although it is extremely difficult to categorize bishops by their ideological preferences, especially since they vary considerably depending on which aspects of their values are being assessed, some observations can be made about their posture on a more socially and politically active role for the Church. On this issue alone, approximately two-thirds are moderate, and the remaining one-third are divided nearly equally between progressives and traditionalists. However, when their regional origins are identified, it becomes apparent that the progressives come disproportionately from three regions in descending order of significance: South, North, and the Federal District.

Bishops born in the South, given its special problems, are much more likely to be progressive. The conditions found in the highlands of Chiapas, which have strongly attracted the sympathy of Bishop Samuel Ruiz, are common to Oaxaca and Guerrero, two other states in this region, Mexico's poorest economically and socially. Although the North is often perceived as religiously conservative, its proximity to the United States, its higher levels of economic development, and its support for opposition parties produced an environment favorable to a more activist posture on political matters. Finally, the Federal District, with its extreme examples of urban poverty and highly contentious elections among a sophisticated citizenry, exposes future priests and bishops to progressive and contradictory influences.

Regionalism as a geographic variable is not necessarily the most important influence on elite careers or on their formation. In many societies, which regionally might be fairly homogeneous, the strongest dichotomy is rural versus urban. In many respects, Mexico falls into this category; urban and rural cultural differences are more pronounced, for example, than those found between West and East Central regions.[18] These differences in urban and rural backgrounds have become increasingly pronounced as Mexican society has urbanized, and its elites, economic, intellectual, political, and military, have become nearly universally urban in origin.

The Church's leadership, however, stands out among all Mexican groups as an exception to these patterns. As the data in Table 8-2 demonstrate, bishops, unlike any other group of Mexican leaders, have strong rural roots historically, making

Table 8-2. Origins of Mexican Bishops

Year of Birth	Rural	Urban
Pre-1900	69%	31%
1900–1909	69	31
1910–1919	59	41
1920–1929	49	51
1930–	47	53
Average	54	46

clergy more representative of the Mexican population. More than half of the bishops serving Mexican dioceses in the last 30 years count rural communities (fewer than 5,000 people) as their birthplace.[19] Bishops, of course, are a product of the rank-and-file clergy. As one bishop suggested, "Most clergy come from smaller communities and many from rural areas. There aren't many indigenous clergy in Mexico because the spiritual conversion of these indigenous groups is lacking and because they have not had the educational abilities allowing them the possibility of becoming priests."[20]

The strength of bishops' rural roots may also be part of an interesting trend identified by Enrique Luengo. In his survey of selected parishes and dioceses in the 1980s, he discovered that priests disproportionately were coming increasingly from rural or semiurban areas to help urban populations. In fact, only 13 percent of the priests he interviewed ended up leaving urban parishes to minister to parishioners in rural parishes. Luengo also noted that half of all priests end up in parishes having better social-economic conditions than those in which they were born.[21] Although we cannot judge the economic and social characteristics of parishes where bishops served, our data measured whether or not Mexican bishops served in rural parishes sometime during their careers. In fact, one-third of the bishops served in rural parishes, and of those, they were more likely to have been born in a rural setting. Priests who grew up in rural areas and who later became bishops disproportionately either sought or were assigned to rural, pastoral tasks compared to their urban-born peers.

Mexican priests and bishops are not alone in their rural origins. Of the seminary students studying in South and Central America in the 1960s, approximately two-fifths came from rural communities. Only 7 percent of seminary students claimed hometowns with populations of half a million or more.[22] Brazilian bishops historically have strong rural roots since more than two-thirds were from small villages and towns.[23] Although the Mexican pattern since 1910 gradually favors urban centers, the percentage of bishops today from rural Mexico is representative of the population as a whole. In contrast, among politicians in the Carlos Salinas administration (1988–1994), only 6 percent were born in rural communities.

People with urban backgrounds can associate more easily with successful elites, giving them access to the credentials necessary to enter the elite and accelerating their upward mobility or success along a specific career track. For example, on only six occasions have urban-born national politicians received less education than their rural counterparts, none of these occurring after 1932. Since the 1930s, urban-born politicians were twice as likely as their rural-born peers to go beyond the preparatory school level. Among bishops, however, the differences between rural- and urban-born priests are moderated by the educational structure, the decentralization of the Church's seminary system, and student support once they are enrolled. Thus, no perceptible differences can be found among those bishops who become archbishops and cardinals on the basis of birthplace alone.

The important mediating effects of the Church's educational system on rural/ urban origins can be seen in the relationship between bishops' educational achievements and their place of birth. Among bishops, the best educated are those who receive multiple Ph.D.s, generally in canon law and theology. In fact, although slightly over half of all bishops come from rural origins, 71 percent of those with more than one Ph.D. were born in rural locales. Usually, rural products are also disadvantaged because they tend to be disproportionately overrepresented among the working class, having the least access to educational and career opportunities. Although rural-born bishops more often had working-class parents, these figures are not significantly different from those of their urban-born colleagues.

Rural/urban backgrounds do have a significant influence on the Church hierarchy in Mexico, even if they do not affect the rapidity of priests' rise within the institution nor their access to the credentials most typical of priests who become bishops. A priest's background, at least among those who become bishops, does affect his choice of career within the Church. If an attempt is made to classify the careers of priests up to the time they actually are appointed bishops, as suggested in the previous chapter, four categories are most typical: pastoral, teaching, local administration, and national administration. Most future bishops pursue seminary teaching and administrative careers, as the data in Table 8-3 reveal. The remaining half are divided roughly between pastoral pursuits and administration. Although one-fourth of all bishops have made pastoral service their primary career activity, twice as many of these bishops came from rural rather than urban birthplaces. A rural upbringing is more likely to influence a priest to pursue strongly a career track in serving parishes directly rather than following a more intellectual and administrative course.

Interestingly, birthplace is also associated with another career track: administration. On the local level, where most church administrative careers occur, the distribution of future bishops' birthplaces is just the reverse of that found among priests primarily in the pastoral field. It is difficult to ascertain with any certainty why urban-born priests are disproportionately represented in Church administra-

Table 8-3. Origins and Church Careers of
Mexican Bishops

Church Career	Rural	Urban
Pastoral	33%	16%
Seminary	51	57
Local administration	11	24
National administration	5	3

tion. One explanation is that, given the fact that the diocese typically is located in an urban center in fairly sizable Mexican cities, urban-born priests, in their personal formation, are more at home functioning socially in that setting and interacting with sophisticated peers in urban political, intellectual, and economic communities.

A bishop's place of birth not only is related to his long-term career patterns, but also can be linked to his initial assignments after returning to the diocese, usually the diocese in which he began his seminary education. Over the long run, teaching is the most widely followed career path to becoming a bishop, and place of birth is not tied to that choice. But an examination of the future bishop's *first position* indicates that a disproportionate number start out as seminary teachers or administrators. Urban-born priests end up in these posts one-third more frequently than those from rural backgrounds. This can be explained by the fact that a larger percentage of future bishops from rural backgrounds generally serve as parish priests, often in rural parishes. Such assignments make it difficult, if not impossible, to teach simultaneously. Most seminary instructors perform other duties, including those of parish priests, but in the diocese in which the seminary is located.

The Influence of Social Origins

The most controversial background variable, which most interests social scientists, is social origin. Social origins are thought to be important for a variety of reasons. Many students of political elites have sought to prove a link between social class and specific ideological values. Others believe that elites, because they tend to come disproportionately from certain social backgrounds, lose touch with the citizenry. Still others argue that specific social backgrounds, and parents' occupational choices, may be very influential in determining their children's careers.

Mexican clergy themselves believe that their class origins are important. Their views often correspond, interestingly, to those of social analysts. Most Mexican priests agree that their social background tends to be from working and lower middle classes, setting Mexico apart from some other Latin American countries. One bishop explained why a priest's social circumstances might be relevant:

> I think this is true, perhaps because poor environments create a sort of spiritual service toward other poor people. That is, people understand conditions and they can relate to them more easily than someone from a different social background. In one sense, this is an advantage, because this ties the common people together with the clergy. In another sense, it's a disadvantage because, as you know, many times people who come from such social class backgrounds, once they rise into positions of more prestige or authority, try to forget their past, and they don't think of themselves any longer as being equal to the people from whom they come.[24]

Not only do some clergy believe social class experiences can strongly affect a person's ability to relate to different social classes, but they also probably affect their career choices. As one priest frankly admitted, as an individual "from a poor social background, I am not a priest who would be very capable practicing in

Polanco [a wealthy commercial and residential section in Mexico City]. I think the difference between the social background of a priest and the constituency he deals with could create many difficult problems because most priests are from lower-middle- or lower-class backgrounds."[25] Some priests suggest that bishops come disproportionately from middle-class backgrounds compared to priests as a whole. In other words, elite clergy, those who rise highest on the Church institutional ladder, are a more selective group. This argument has parallels with the officer corps.

In Mexico, the officer corps also has been described as lower middle class, but some officers suggest that those who actually complete higher military training, specifically the Higher War College, tend to be from the middle class, and that officers from working-class origins wash out in much larger numbers. It is not due to their ability but to the fact that their spouses find it difficult to adjust socially to the demands of their rank.[26] Other priests argue that social class origins have little to do with success in the hierarchy and that in Mexico one cannot speak in terms of higher, lower, and middle clergy socially because the vast majority of priests are from the middle and lower classes.[27]

Social background data is the most difficult to obtain on any elite group, and bishops are no exception. Although such information has been acquired for one-fifth of the bishops in the sample, the empirical data, however tentative, conform closely to priests' and bishops' own observations: slightly more than half of all bishops come from working-class families, one-third from middle-class origins, and a small group (fewer than 10 percent) from upper-class parents. The backgrounds of Mexican bishops correspond to data on Latin American priests in general, the majority of whom come from parents who were small farmers, artisans, and small businesspeople. Two-thirds of all seminary students in Latin America in the 1960s were on full fellowships, an economic indicator of their working-class origins.[28] A study of seminary students in the United States found that two-thirds of the students, on the basis of family income, were lower middle class, and 13 percent were lower class.[29] Greeley noted that Catholic priests in the United States come from somewhat higher social class backgrounds than typical American Catholics, a description that would be accurate of Mexican priests.[30] On the whole, however, most scholars of U.S. Catholic clergy describe them as highly representative of the Catholic population.[31]

Mexican bishops share much more in common socially with their U.S. counterparts than they do with bishops in some countries in South America. For example, in 1947, not a single Catholic bishop in the United States was the son of a college graduate, a figure that increased to only 5 percent 10 years later. Only 20 percent of U.S. seminary students in the 1960s were the sons of college graduates. In a more recent study of American bishops, most were found to be the children of working-class parents and had strong memories of the Depression and the New Deal. Only 11 percent had fathers who were college graduates, and two-thirds came from homes where the father did not graduate from high school.[32] The social origins of American archbishops differed little from that of bishops.[33]

In Brazil and Chile, the social origins of bishops differ substantially from those of their Mexican peers. Historically, in the earlier part of the 20th century, Brazil recruited a much larger portion of its church leaders from wealthy families, indeed, from established families of the imperial aristocracy.[34] In Chile, even in the late 20th century, this pattern remained unchanged. Although the middle class was well represented among Chilean bishops, a substantial number were from aristocratic families and fewer than 10 percent could claim working-class origins.[35] Mexican clergy are aware of these social differences. For example, one priest pointed to the case of Chile, arguing that the different social origins of Mexican priests reinforce a traditional bond between common people and their priests, even if they might be suspicious of the Church as an institution.[36]

It has been argued that class origins affect the status of Catholic clergy in Mexico. One scholar suggests that religious clergy (members of orders) are more prestigious because they tend to recruit more heavily from middle and upper classes. he concludes that "diocesan (secular) clergy, most of whom come from the lower class, have less influence within the church than their religious colleagues."[37] While it may be true that religious clergy dominate certain intellectual activities, they certainly do not exercise a significant influence in the Mexican episcopate. They account for a tiny percentage of Mexican bishops, in numbers comparable or smaller to their percentage among all clergy.

What is interesting about the data for Mexican bishops is that instead of becoming increasingly middle class in origin, along with the Mexican population, their working-class backgrounds have increased. Priests, like other professional groups, sometimes initiate a profession as a means of gaining upward social mobility. The clergy is one of the few professional occupations in Mexico where that is still a real possibility; indeed, upward mobility was achieved by over half of the Church's leaders. Father Pascual Torres Escobedo, for example, described himself as coming from a "ranchito" near Fresnillo, Zacatecas, the son of a small farmer, who did not admire priests. Yet his mother insisted that he obtain an education, and his only means was to attend seminary. By the time he was 14 or 15, he knew he wanted to become a priest.[38]

The Catholic Church provides other opportunities for the extreme poor, not in the strict sense of upward social mobility, but in developing their talents to the fullest. Father Antonio García describes his intellectual accomplishments and his expanded world view, while purposely committing himself to economic conditions not much different from his origins:

> I came from a very small town in the mountains of Michoacán. My parents were peasants, and we had very little contact with the outside world. By the time I was 11 years old, I had received only three years of primary education. I was very fortunate

Table 8-4. Social Origins of Mexican Bishops

Year of Birth	Working Class	Middle Class	Upper Class
Pre-1900	0%	33%	67%
1900–1919	44	56	0
1920–	73	20	7
Average	56	33	11

to meet a nun who helped send me to Mexico City to go to school. At the lower seminary, I studied day and night in order to catch up on all of the education I missed. I did my preparatory studies at the seminary and then I was sent to Italy for two years where I studied social communications. I joined the Order of the Passion, an Italian group which takes a vow of poverty.[39]

There have been recent Mexican Church leaders who have pursued extremely modest lives. José Salazar López, cardinal of Guadalajara in the 1970s, lived in a tiny room with almost no furniture, dressing in such simple clothes that on one occasion he was refused admission into the College of Cardinals in Rome because the guards did not believe he was a cardinal.

The Catholic Church seeks out the poor as a spiritual savior. In saving a person's soul, it occasionally recruits a priest, as in the case of Father Pedro, who serves in the diocese of San Cristóbal de las Casas, Chiapas. Father Pedro's father worked for the Mérida, Yucatán, city government, and his mother sold food on the street to make ends meet. They were extremely poor, and in high school, he began associating with a group involved in drugs and petty theft. In his third year in high school, he began to attend Church, something he had not done before, and became involved with a group of religiously motivated young people. This decision changed his life. He and several of these friends attended seminary and went into the priesthood.[40]

Mexican bishops do not appear to be significantly different in social composition from priests, although probably a larger percentage are from the middle class. Nevertheless, bishops also come from the most popular classes, including peasants. Bishop Mario de Gasperín, of Italian immigrant origin, proudly describes his modest origins:

My grandparents were from Northern Italy, from a town near Padua, with a strong Catholic tradition. They came as campesinos at the time of Porfirio Díaz. In my youth, I worked as a campesino. My family's history is one of losing their land, first in the Revolution, then again during the agrarian reforms, and finally during World War II, during which time my parents were placed in a concentration camp. It was a very difficult life for us, but I look back now and think it probably saved my parents, or at least my father's life, since had he been in Italy, he would have fought and probably died in the war.[41]

The observations of priests and bishops and the data in Table 8-4 reinforce the view that many individuals of modest means enter the priesthood and rise to the highest positions in the Church. But among bishops, can it be asserted that their class origins have an effect on their careers within the Church and on the pace with which they rise up the hierarchy? Fewer than half of all bishops obtain education beyond that of a basic seminary degree. Yet of those bishops who obtain only seminary educations, about equal to the percentage of bishops who come from the working class, an overwhelming 86 percent come from working-class parents. In contrast, among those bishops who obtain higher educations, measured by doctorates, middle- and upper-class bishops account for nearly 90 percent of the graduates, although only 42 percent of bishops come from such social origins.

Clearly, class origins determine educational achievement within the Church leadership. The priests' financial condition is not the determining variable since the Church supports their studies abroad. A more likely explanation is that young priests from middle- and upper-class backgrounds may have a stronger proclivity for intellectual pursuits. It is well known that family environment enhances the educational skills of most students; thus, in the initial preparatory and seminary education, priests from middle-class or more sophisticated backgrounds are better prepared to cope with academic demands.

This pattern is supported by the fact that bishops from lower-class origins are less likely to have taught in seminaries than their more socially privileged peers. More than eight out of 10 bishops actually teach, but of those who do not teach, half again as many are from working-class origins. This is important to a priest's career since teaching is the most common career path to becoming a bishop. Archbishop Manuel Pérez Gil, a professor and administrator at the Morelia seminary, a leading institution, and former head of the episcopate's education and culture committee, came from a highly privileged background:

> I was born in Morelia, and my father was a successful lawyer, a notary public who served in various public offices, including justice of the Michoacán state supreme court. His name was Francisco Pérez Gil Ortiz. My grandfather was also a lawyer, a government official for many years. He directed the university, later became the rector of the Colegio de San Nicolás, and taught there for many years. He also served as secretary of government of the state and twice as interim governor. My great-grandfather was Antonio Pérez Gil, governor of the state. My mother was the daughter of a very wealthy landowner who had haciendas in many parts of the hot country, the Balsas region.[42]

Most bishops and priests, when discussing their social origins, typically identify themselves as coming from the middle social strata, generally the lower middle or the working class. They commonly stress the view, however, that if they are from the middle class, it is a certain kind of "typical" Mexican provincial middle class. As one bishop described it: "What I mean by middle class is something more significant than income. Basically we are middle class from large families; we generally come from the provinces, also from smaller towns, and these middle-class families have very strong moral qualities and a cohesive family environment. Even when the income is lower than what we might describe as typical, these qualities still apply. It isn't a question of income, but values."[43]

Priests who came from very modest circumstances have not felt the social pressures described by Mexican political figures who gained an opportunity to enter the ranks of academic preparatory programs composed largely of middle- and upper-class students. Some of these future leaders felt lost in this social environment and were relieved to be taken under the wing of a sympathetic professor, often from similar social circumstances. In contrast to future politicians, however, the number of priests from working-class backgrounds is so great that typically they have "never felt any difference coming from a lower-class background."[44]

Priests' social origins do not affect their choice of broad tracks within the Catholic Church. However, the small minority of priests from wealthy backgrounds who become bishops achieve those positions at a faster pace. About half of all priests who become bishops do so fewer than 20 years after they are ordained. No differences can be discerned among priests from working- or middle-class backgrounds. But among priests from wealthy origins, all reached their positions as bishops in less than 20 years.

It might be expected that priests from certain social circumstances would be more likely to choose specific assignments during their careers or even to identify with broad ideological wings within the Catholic episcopate, however subjective the determination of those categories. In reality, bishops from fortunate social circumstances are not any less likely to have served in a rural parish, nor are bishops from modest circumstances any more likely to have experienced such service than their wealthier peers. However, it is significant to note that whereas half of all bishops served as parish priests, the standard assignment among all rank-and-file diocesan priests, it is true for two-thirds of bishops from working-class families compared to only one-third from middle- and upper-class families. Thus, social class does favor somewhat the career choices of some bishops. A priest's social origins, contrary to popular mythology, also does not seem to determine which of the wings (progressive, moderate, or traditional) with which he is identified. A priest's assignment to a specific diocese and the social composition of that diocese appear to be more important determinants of a bishop's values.

Other family background characteristics may be more important in determining a priest's values or his career success. In the case of Mexican military officers and political leaders, it is common to find a parent who was a successful military or civilian leader. In fact, being politically active not only promotes an interest in politics but also endows an individual with certain experiences and skills that enhance a political career. Likewise, a disproportionate percentage of military officers are the children of active duty or retired officers, and an even higher percentage of those who reach the rank of general come from military families. Priests and nuns, of course, would not share these same characteristics since faithfulness to their vows prevents them from marrying and raising a family.

Priests' connections to religious families can be measured by something other than parents. Instead, it is suggestive to compare priests who were known to have uncles and aunts or brothers and sisters who were priests and nuns. This variable, as distinct from social class, does have stronger implications for future bishops and for the presence of other background variables. For example, as suggested previously, one of the determining historical experiences of the generation of bishops appointed in the 1960s was their childhood contact with the Cristero rebellion. Although nearly 20 percent of bishops were affected in some direct way by the Cristero movement, more than twice that number, 44 percent, were related to priests and nuns personally affected by this seminal, religious-political event. The composition of a priest's family, therefore, may well expose him to specific religious experiences or expose him more intensely or in different ways compared to families without such religious affiliations.

These familial connections can also be translated into priestly values. Although one out of three priests is known to have close relatives who were priests or nuns, the figure is much higher for those identified with the traditional wing of the Mexican episcopate. This is not surprising since individuals with long family traditions within an institution often tend to be the repositories of the organization's basic values, wanting to conserve their antecedents' beliefs.

The degree to which bishops have religious relatives, however, does not affect their career choices within the Catholic Church. Such familial ties, however, differ according to the pace of the priest's career rise and, even more significantly, according to whether or not he moves to a plane higher than that of bishop. A small number of bishops are appointed with fewer than 15 years experience. Twice as many of these come from families with priests and nuns as do priests following a more typical chronology to becoming bishops. This suggests that knowing clergy, in some cases even bishops, well prior to entering the priesthood has been helpful to a priest's career. The same pattern can be found among archbishops and cardinals. Although only one-third of all bishops have such familial backgrounds, the highest-ranking figures in the episcopate report such backgrounds 57 percent of the time, again suggesting the advantages of personal connections to other, generally older clergy.

Conclusions

Mexican bishops are characterized by numerous background qualities of place, social origin, and family often not found among other elite groups. The fact that Mexican bishops differ from other leadership groups in Mexico, in particular national politicians who are most threatened by Church leadership, is politically significant. These differences have many possible consequences for church-state relations, especially for the potential role of the Church as a social and political actor outside its traditional pastoral tasks.

Among the distinguishing variables pointed to in the previous analysis, one of the most important qualities is the degree to which Mexican bishops are products of their place of origin, indeed are formed and trained there by the institution they serve. This quality tells us not only something about the bishop's character but also something about the nature of the institution he represents. As the composition of Mexican bishops suggests, the Catholic Church structurally is decentralized within Mexico. Not only does the autonomy of each diocese affect the pattern of recruitment and the life experiences of bishops and priests, but also the composition of those priests and bishops, in turn, reinforces the institutional structures' biases.

Mexican bishops draw on deep roots of their constituencies and parishes. Even though they are often assigned dioceses far from their original birthplaces, nearly all have served at length in their home dioceses, developing a strong understanding of the needs of provincial Mexico, regardless of region. It is critical to keep in mind that provincial Mexico generally provides the catalyst for major political change and/or violence in the 20th century, as the guerrilla movement in Chiapas in January 1994 illustrates. Mexican bishops, unlike their political counterparts, do not centralize their training, formation, or education; rather, they draw on a broad set of geographic experiences, even if their geographic origins overrepresents certain regions.

The centralization of Mexican political authority is a serious weakness in Mexican political culture and in governing.[45] Mexican political leadership reflects this centralization, taking on homogeneous, geographically narrow experiences, and thus weakening political leaders' hands-on knowledge about diverse provincial issues and values. These geographic and urban biases produce considerable resentment in the neglected provinces and are an important variable in strengthening opposition political groups.[46]

Originally, Mexican politicians were products of their region, identifying strongly with local and provincial interests. Many of these regions counted influential universities, established by the Church, as training grounds for political leaders. Why then did the Church retain a traditional, provincial bias, while political leaders pursued an increasingly centralized national path?

The hierarchical structure of the Church may well be an advantage in its evolution. As political issues became broadly based and leadership needed to focus on national versus local problems, Mexico City grew in importance. After independence, Mexico City, as the political capital, no longer shared power with Spain or the Spanish Crown. Politicians centralized power in Mexico City to control the provinces and impose broad policy preferences. The Church, however, retained an international link with Rome. Given the relationship between national bishops and the Pope, a proclivity toward religious centralization in Mexico City was unnecessary. Rather, regional distribution patterns among priests and hierarchy were established in those regions where the Church carried out its proselytizing most heavily, creating the greatest number of parishes and institutions.

Today, not only do bishops originate from many diverse provinces, but also they remain in the provinces throughout their entire careers, never moving vertically but occasionally moving laterally, as if they were governors of more than one state. These multiple opportunities allow bishops to compare directly the experiences of one region to those of another and to enrich their skills and knowledge of Mexico on the local level. Bishops who have served in different dioceses are quick to point out contrasts characterizing these differing constituencies.

Not only are Mexican bishops products of provincial backgrounds and experiences, but also they personally better represent rural regions, the "forgotten Mexico," than any other group. They also better represent the social origins of Mexico's present population, which remains working class. It is no accident that various bishops in Oaxaca, Chiapas, and some of the vast rural pastoral regions have become the spokespersons for the rural poor and indigenous peoples. The nature of their social origins does not mean that Mexican bishops necessarily become the exclusive representatives of these same interests, but they clearly have the potential for better understanding these concerns and for having some personal linkages to populations representing these viewpoints.

Bishops, therefore, have the ability to represent the demands of Mexico's least articulate constituencies, those constituencies where political parties are weakly developed. This does not mean that bishops desire to perform this role, but if political leadership continues to demonstrate an ignorance of rural and provincial problems or a desire to neglect those issues, bishops are the most likely leaders in the short run to fill that political vacuum.

Data on the composition of bishops suggest that the Church is also vulnerable to certain biases in its leadership's background qualities. Some pitfalls of geographic domination from the West and West Central regions within the Catholic episcopate await the Church. Although the hierarchy's regional biases are far more diverse than the comparable political leadership's, such geographic distortions do breed resentment, especially when bishops from outside a diocese are appointed to a diocese producing a disproportionate number of qualified priests. The policy of selecting bishops will have to weigh the benefits of a "local" bishop against the benefits of an "outside" bishop who views problems with a fresh, locally unbiased vision.

NOTES

1. Antonio García Montaño, "Los obispos mexicanos de la segunda mitad del siglo xx," unpublished paper, 1992.

2. Claude Pomerlau, "The Catholic Church in Mexico and Its Changing Relationship to Society and the State," unpublished Ph.D. dissertation, University of Notre Dame, 1980, 10.

3. Manuel González Ramírez, *La Iglesia mexicana en cifras* (Mexico City, 1969), 80–81.

4. Oscar Aguilar and Enrique Luengo, "Iglesia y gobierno en el D.F.," in *D.F.: gobierno y sociedad civil*, Pablo González Casanova, ed. (Mexico City: El Caballito, 1987), Table 20.

5. Personal interview with Cardinal Juan José Posadas Ocampo, cardinal of Guadalajara, Mexico City, February 20, 1991.

6. Personal interview with Bishop Manuel Samaniego Barriga, Cuautitlán Diocese, Cuautitlán, México, February 13, 1991.

7. Some sources believe that popular mythology about communities is sometimes incorrect. Gabriel Zaid, a leading Mexican intellectual and Monterrey native, suggests that many Mexicans believe Monterrey, a major northern, industrial center and Mexico's third largest city, is the epitome of capitalism and Catholicism. He argues, however, that "in the last century Monterrey was a very strong, active Masonic center. For example, just examine the names of some of the leading entrepreneurs from that area of the country, names like Virgilio Garza, or Platon, which, of course, are names reflective of an anti-Christian origin. Monterrey, in my opinion, has never been a strong Catholic city." Of course, one can make the argument that popular impressions are far more significant than historic reality. Nevertheless, the data on regional birthplaces reinforces Zaid's interpretation.

8. Personal interview with Father Antonio García Montaño and José Rogelio Alvarez, Mexico City, February 15, 1993. For example, Antonio Guízar Valencia, archbishop of Chihuahua, 1958–1969, and Luis Guízar Barragán, bishop of Saltillo, 1955–1975, both came from this small community. Among Mexican politicians of comparable generations, Atlacomulco, México, is such a community, having given birth to several distinguished national figures who also governed their home state, including Alfredo del Mazo Vélez and Isidro Fabela Alfaro.

9. Personal interview with Bishop Raúl Vera López, Ciudad Altamirano Diocese, Guerrero, Mexico City, May 3, 1992.

10. With the retirement of Cardinal Corripio of the Mexico Archdiocese in late 1994, the Vatican plans to consider the opportunity to divide up the capital into multiple dioceses.

11. Charles N. Myers, *Education and National Development in Mexico* (Princeton: Princeton University Press, 1965), 112.

12. Arthur Liebman, Kenneth Walker, and Myron Glazer, *Latin American University Students: A Six Nation Study* (Cambridge: Harvard University Press, 1972), 40, concludes that "[i]n 50 percent of the countries more than three-quarters of the students attended the principal university of that country, located in the capital. In over 85 percent of the countries, one-third or more of the students attended the country's major university located in the capital, while many of the remaining students attended other universities in the same city." A detailed portrait of the Mexican pattern can be found in David E. Lorey, *The University System and Economic Development in Mexico since 1929* (Stanford: Stanford University Press, 1993).

13. Peter McDonough, *Power and Ideology in Brazil* (Princeton: Princeton University Press, 1981), 68.

14. Enrique Luengo, "Los párrocos: una visión," unpublished manuscript, Department of Social and Political Sciences, Ibero-American University, December 1989, based on a preliminary examination of 153 parish priests, 27–28, published as "Percepción política de los párrocos en México," in *Religiosidad y política en México*, Carlos Martínez Assad, ed. (Mexico City: Ibero-American University, 1992), 199–239.

15. Enrique Krauze, "Chihuahua, ida y vuelta," *Vuelta* no. 115 (June 1986): 37.

16. Manuel González Ramírez, *La iglesia mexicana en cifras*, 103–104.

17. See Morris Janowitz, *The Military in the Development of New Nations* (Chicago: University of Chicago Press, 1964), 58; George Kourvetaris and Betty Dobratz, *Social Origins and Political Orientations of Officer Corps in a World Perspective* (Denver: Graduate School of International Studies, University of Denver, 1973), 11.

18. See Octavio Paz's exploration of this issue, *The Other Mexico: Critique of the Pyramid* (New York: Grove Press, 1972).

19. Daniel H. Levine found a similar pattern among bishops in Venezuela and Colombia, where 64 and 50 percent, respectively, came from small towns. *Religion and Politics in Latin America: The Catholic Church in Venezuela and Colombia* (Princeton: Princeton University Press, 1981), 102.

20. Personal interview with Bishop Francisco Aguilera González, auxiliary bishop of the Archdiocese of Mexico City, June 1, 1987.

21. Enrique Luengo, "Los párrocos: una visión," 32–33.

22. Gustavo Pérez Ramírez and Yván Labelle, *El problema sacerdotal en América Latina* (Madrid: FERES, 1964), 66–67. This work is the most comprehensive sociological analysis of priests in Latin America.

23. Sergio Miceli, *A Elite Eclesiástica Brasileira* (Rio de Janeiro: Editora Bertrand Brasil, 1988), 84.

24. Personal interview with Bishop José Melgoza Osorio, Ciudad Nezahualcóyotl Diocese, Ciudad Nezahualcóyotl, México, May 27, 1987, who oversaw the single largest area of urban poverty in Mexico.

25. Personal interview with with Antonio García Montaño.

26. Roderic Ai Camp, *Generals in the Palacio: The Military in Modern Mexico* (New York: Oxford University Press, 1992), 123–126.

27. Personal interview with Samuel Morín Suárez, secretary to the bishop of Toluca, Toluca Diocese, Toluca, México, June 9, 1988.

28. Gustavo Pérez Ramírez and Yván Labelle, *El problema sacerdotal en América Latina*, 88.

29. Joseph H. Fichter, *Religion as an Occupation: A Study in the Sociology of Professions* (Terre Haute, Ind.: University of Notre Dame Press, 1961), 63, 79. The parents of

U.S. Catholic priests typically were in service and unskilled, crafts and operative, clerical and sales, and managerial positions.

30. Andrew M. Greeley, *Priests in the United States: Reflections on a Survey* (New York: Doubleday, 1972), 17.

31. Gerhard Lenski, *The Religious Factor: A Sociological Study of Religion's Impact on Politics and Family Life* (Garden City, N.Y.: Doubleday, 1963), 258.

32. Thomas Reese, *A Flock of Shepherds: The National Conference of Catholic Bishops* (Kansas City, Mo.: Sheed and Ward, 1992), 1–2.

33. Thomas Reese, *Archbishop: Inside the Power Structure of the American Catholic Church* (New York: Harper and Row, 1989), 77.

34. Sergio Miceli, *A Elite Eclesiástica Brasileira,* 86.

35. Thomas G. Sanders, "The Chilean Episcopate," *American Universities Field Staff Reports* 15, no. 3 (August 1968): 14.

36. Interview by Scott Pentzer and Meg Mitchell with Father Jesús López Larra de Castañeda, Zacatecas Diocese, Zacatecas, Zacatecas, July 19, 1993.

37. Claude Pomerleau, "The Changing Church in Mexico and Its Challenge to the State," *Review of Politics* 43, no. 4 (October 1981): 550.

38. Interview by Scott Pentzer and Meg Mitchell with Father Pascual Torres Escobedo, Zacatecas Diocese, Zacatecas, Zacatecas, July 19, 1993.

39. Personal interview with Antonio García Montaño.

40. Interview by Shannan Mattiace with Father Pedro, San Cristóbal de las Casas Diocese, San Cristóbal de las Casas, Chiapas, April 12, 1988.

41. Personal interview with Bishop Mario de Gasperín, Querétaro Diocese, Querétaro, Querétaro, July 12, 1993.

42. Personal interview with Archbishop Manuel Pérez Gil, Tlanepantla Diocese, Tlanepantla, México, February 18, 1991.

43. Personal interview with Bishop Abelardo Alcántara, Mexico Archdiocese, Mexico City, June 2, 1987.

44. Personal interview with Antonio García Montaño.

45. Some of the consequences of this are developed in my "Province versus the Center: Democratizing Mexico's Political Culture," in *Democracy in Latin America,* Phil Kelly, ed. (forthcoming, 1997).

46. See, for example, the argument concerning northern Mexico in Edward J. Williams, "The Resurgent North and Contemporary Mexican Regionalism," *Mexican Studies* 6, no. 2 (Summer 1990): 299–323.

9

Church-State Interlocks

Informal Relations

No single interest group in Mexico can claim to have had a historical importance exceeding that of the Catholic Church in both the 19th and 20th centuries. Yet despite its significance, including the Church's influence on the Mexican
populace, linkages between clergy and politicians and the Church and the state
have been weak, informal, and founded on mutual ignorance.

Politicians and clergy alike are quick to identify and criticize their own ignorance. Most prominent leaders within each camp suggest that their lack of substantive knowledge about the other and the institutions they represent extends back to
their respective childhoods, to the familial milieu in which each was raised. As
one bishop suggested: "The explanation for the public officials' lack of knowledge
about the Church can be explained by the fact that those interested in public
careers at a very young age gradually move away from their contact with and
knowledge of the Church. The higher up people go within the government, the
more they fear that they will be seen in some way as connected to the Church." [1]
Politicians themselves believe that they are more ignorant of Church affairs than
are clergy of their activities. As one former government official explained, politicians typically are not exposed to consistent Catholic values in their homes. [2]
These deficiencies in religious preparation may well lead to serious policy consequences. One intellectual with strong ties to both political and religious institutions
described such results:

> I have been asked constantly for advice in the last few months by my preparatory
> school companions in the Chamber of Deputies, both from the PRI and the PRD.
> They are anticipating a debate in the near future on the issue of formal relations
> between the Vatican See and the State. I would describe their knowledge of church
> history and background with the state as abysmally ignorant. [3]

Church officials are no less critical of their own peers. They believe they, too,
lack a cultural preparation about politicians and political life. Similar to Alvarez,
they are convinced it leads to misinformation and misunderstandings about secular

institutions. As a leading church official in the Federal District argues, the most serious misconception resulting from such ignorance is that "politicians think the clergy are political in their sense, and the clergy believe politicians are not religious in their sense."[4]

Gaps in knowledge on the part of politicians and clergy are accentuated by their lack of social and familial ties. Although other important groups, such as the officer corps and prominent entrepreneurs, share some of these characteristics, they are not nearly as exaggerated. Most bishops suggest that little social contact occurs between the political leadership and the clergy, especially openly, as illustrated by Adolfo Suárez Rivera, president of the Mexican episcopate, who exclaimed after being invited to dine in Los Pinos with President Salinas, "We entered through the front door!"[5] At lower levels, social contact between politicians and clergy is based on the relationship between the politician and his parish priest. This relationship is typically described as sacramental, not personal, in nature, suggesting that a politician would have the local priest marry his children in Church or perform other religious ceremonies but would not get together with the priest to discuss important social and political issues.

Personal Linkages: Social, Familial, and Educational

Because social linkages between the two groups are so weak and structural relationships, as will be demonstrated, are so informal, personal ties become a significant vehicle for enhancing institutional channels. As one Church official noted, anticipating possible constitutional changes in church-state relations, they "will come about because of the way the relationship presently exists, through personal friendships."[6] Strong personal ties also facilitate helpful relations among alleged political antagonists. A personal anecdote reveals some potential implications:

> There is much more that meets the eye in the relationship between the Church and the state. This is where friendship becomes a very important means of facilitating relationships that have significant policy consequences. For example, I was recently asked to attend a special ceremony to replace the remains of Vasco de Quiroga and begin a process of beatification for sainthood. Many prominent Church leaders were going to attend, and I was invited to a sumptuous meal. When I asked the person who invited me who was sponsoring the dinner, he told me it was the head of Mexican Masonry. Can you imagine the national president of the Mexican Masons paying for a dinner for the sainthood of a Catholic figure?[7]

These personal linkages are essential to higher officials, especially presidents. Some Church officials have alleged that prominent politicians and higher clergy often are related.[8] Some prominent political families are even descendants of priests, such as the Justo Sierra family.[9] Such links, if widespread, would have profound implications for church-state relations and religion in Mexico. They tend to be exceptional, however, rather than typical, otherwise both groups would not coexist in an environment where they remained largely ignorant of the other's behavior and institutional values.

The common pattern is one where top officials rely on lifelong friends or establish important relationships through other family members with Church leaders. For example, President Luis Echeverría is a prototype of the Liberal, Mexican politician, having married outside of the Church. His wife comes from a strongly anticlerical political family in Jalisco. On the other hand, one of Echeverría's aunts founded and served as superior of the Espíritu Santo Congregation and another joined the Daughters of Mary Immaculate of Guadalupe order. Echeverría educated his children in the Jesuit-operated Ibero-American University and maintained close personal ties to Bishop Sergio Méndez Arceo.[10] President José López Portillo also was willing to forego Liberal rhetoric, having joined Bishop Rafael García of Tabasco while wearing the presidential sash, to officiate at a Mass for his mother.[11]

Generally speaking, most Mexican politicians establish personal linkages to the Church through secular individuals in the political world who are related to important clergy or who grew up in familial environments where such contacts were normal. The classic example of such a successful politician is Agustín Téllez Cruz, son of a state superior court justice. Like several other prominent Mexican political figures, including novelist Agustín Yáñez, Téllez Cruz joined the Mexican Catholic Youth Association. His son Carlos married Paulina Martínez, daughter of Jorge Martínez Gómez del Campo, Mexico's key figure linking the Pope to Presidents Echeverría and López Portillo, in a ceremony performed by Pope John Paul II.[12] President Salinas selected Téllez Cruz to represent him at the Vatican two years before formal relations were established in 1992. The separation between the clergy and politicians is such that only on the rarest of occasions in Mexico will an ex-priest become a successful politician or a politician become a priest.[13]

If ties between the Catholic Church and the government are tenuous at best, a widespread belief exists in Mexico that the PRI's long-standing opponent, the National Action Party, is a Church ally. Not only is this a widely shared perception on the part of the general population, but the PRI's leaders believe it to be the case. They also claim close ties between the Church and private sector groups, Televisa, and bankers.[14] Leading entrepreneurs, some of whom have played important roles in PAN, also maintain personal friendships among bishops, priests, and nuns. Yet as one student of business families concluded, most private sector leaders "are strangely unwilling for their own sons or daughters to enter religious orders."[15]

The alleged connection between the National Action Party and the Catholic Church stems from two historical patterns. In the first place, Catholic Christian philosophy, similar in content to that found throughout Latin America's Christian Democratic movement, exerted an important intellectual influence on PAN ideology in the 1950s and 1960s.[16] The second explanation for the persistence of this myth is that many presidents of PAN during its early years were top leaders of the Catholic Association of Mexican Youth (ACJM).[17] Abel Vicencio Tovar, a former leader of both organizations, explains:

> You must remember that in the old days the ACJM was not a spiritual organization that stressed a message of faith but an interest group fighting in favor of practical

issues. Some of us in that organization transferred our loyalty to PAN, believing it would be the ideal vehicle for our political efforts. The Catholic hierarchy cut off their support for ACJM a long time ago, perhaps because of government pressure, and although the ACJM still exists, it hasn't had an active political role since the 1960s.[18]

A third explanation for the alleged link between Catholics and PAN stems from PRI propagandists' efforts to popularize such an alliance. Given the postrevolutionary, Liberal, anticlerical doctrine's influence, visible associations with the Church would be the political kiss of death.[19] PAN also was recognized as a legitimate opposition party because it would be advantageous to the political elite to include moderate Catholic dissidents and other factions of the "Right" in a political party.[20]

A fourth reason for the connection between the two is that PAN often supported policies favorable to the Church, specifically those reforming constitutional articles restricting religious freedoms and religion in education. Finally, as Vicencio Tovar himself suggests, many committed Catholics in the past joined PAN in the belief that "only though PAN will the Church regain its position in society."[21] Nevertheless, as the data in chapter 5 illustrate, PAN does not attract proportionately more Catholic voters than the PRI.

Despite the fact that at different periods in the party's history PAN shared with the Catholic Church some of its goals, no evidence of any concrete linkage, financial or otherwise, exists between the Church and the party, at least since 1958.[22] Nevertheless, Mexican scholars continue to claim a substantive link between the Church and PAN without any concrete evidence.[23] These scholars tend to subscribe to a broader linkage between Church and party based on individual incidents and to assume incorrectly that the Church is somehow acting as a unified institution in partisan political matters. Evidence does exist of individual bishops from the North and the Bajío region explicitly supporting PAN.[24] But as Soledad Loaeza suggests, although individual members of the hierarchy and clergy are sympathetic to PAN, their attitude is ambiguous when it comes to supporting PAN or collaborating with political authorities.[25]

In reality, little connection exists between PAN and the Catholic Church in partisan political matters. In the first place, as David Bailey discovered many years ago, the hierarchy correctly believed it could influence government policy more readily and effectively through its own efforts and channels rather than through PAN.[26] Second, as Abel Vicencio Tovar explains, during his days in Catholic Action he had close relations with many priests as friends and advisers. In political life, however, he has almost no contact with clergy, suggesting "that the Church does not want these ties with PAN, and we don't want them with the Church."[27] Although individual bishops have indicated a favorable posture toward PAN, many publicly have denounced partisan positions, criticizing their peers, including Cardinal Corripio, for alleged statements sympathetic to PAN.[28] Others widely denounced PAN presidential candidate Manuel Clouthier's call for civil resistance in 1988.[29]

Much of the political scholarship on PAN and the Church fails to recognize the fact that priests, like Mexicans in general, are divided in their political preferences, supporting a wide spectrum of parties, including the left-of-center PRD. Heberto Castillo, a former PRD leader and presidential candidate in 1988, argues that considerable contact exists among PRD politicians and priests.[30] It is the PRD's policy that each of its candidates meet with local priests and Jewish and Protestant representatives.[31] Enrique Luengo's study of priests clearly demonstrates many priests' sympathies with the PRD.[32] In fact, top PRI officials have noted that the PRD, more so than the PRI, has initiated the greatest contact with the Church since 1989. They also readily admit that PAN won the Chihuahua gubernatorial election in 1992 without relying on the Church.[33]

In recent years PAN, just as the PRD, typically relies on personal contacts with individual clergy, especially through their former professors from such institutions as the Ibero-American University. For example, Manuel Clouthier was the diocesan president of the Christian Family Movement, one of the most important lay organizations associated with the Catholic Church.[34] The difference between PAN on one hand and the PRD and PRI on the other is that their range of contacts between politicians and clergy extends deeper and broader, and individual PAN candidates are more likely to have been steeped in a stronger Catholic familial upbringing than the typical politician from the other two parties. Such differences could facilitate contacts between PAN and Church leadership; they do not, however, guarantee PAN a special place among the episcopate or support, financial or otherwise, from the Church.

Politicians generally have not been able to rely on familial relationships or social contacts to increase extensively their ties to Catholic clergy. The most important possible sites of contact between the two groups, which potentially could alter the cultural-religious barriers between secular and religious Mexicans, are educational institutions. The educational system potentially could affect church-state relations on two fronts. First, Catholic schools, as would be the case in any educational system, are extremely important agents of political socialization.[35] Furthermore, although religiously operated schools are prohibited from teaching religion or using unofficial texts in the classroom, the government is lax in its enforcement of these provisions, and schools, at least in the Federal District, supplement official textbooks "with books more in line with the Church's point of view, start school days with prayers, offer classes in ethics and morals, invite priests periodically to lecture, and encourage students to go to church."[36] Indeed, religious orders within the Catholic Church, notably the Jesuits, previously entertained a goal of educating leaders who pursued activities in all realms of society, including politics, and would be in a position to mold other individuals.[37] Education is likely to exercise such an effect given the fact that Mexican politicians are strongly influenced in the formation of their values and in establishing critical career contacts in public schools.[38]

In order to assess the potential for private Catholic schools to exercise a similar influence, it is essential to understand their impact on the overall educational structure in Mexico. By 1990, student enrollment in Catholic schools reached 11 percent of the university population and nearly double that for preparatory programs (see Table 9-1).[39] Many prominent religious schools were founded in the early 1940s under Manuel Avila Camacho's administration's religious tolerance.[40] By

Table 9-1. Student Enrollment in Mexican Schools

Educational Level	Public	Catholic	Private
Preschool	92%	6%	2%
Primary	94	5	1
Vocational	32	61	7
Middle school	92	6	2
High school	77	16	7
Preparatory	65	19	16
Teacher training	68	22	10
University	86	11	3

Source: *Excélsior*, April 24, 1990, 43A, estimates for the 1989 school year.

1991, the Church controlled more than 3,500 institutions at all levels. The fact that Catholic schools are educating one-fifth of all teachers in Mexico also has implications for future student socialization patterns.

Although Catholic schools at the preparatory and university levels (13 universities in the 1990s) have continued to increase, a contrary pattern achieved some prominence in the 1970s. The Jesuits, the most influential Catholic order in education, began to abandon formal school and their goal of training future leaders, believing they could better use their resources to help the poor directly rather than train an elite who would be sympathetic to the plight of the underclass in Latin America and Mexico. Since Jesuit schools accounted for more than 400,000 alumni in Mexico in 1990, their posture toward formal education is critical. Other teaching orders, including the Sacred Heart Sisters, the Ursulines, and the Missionary Sisters of St. Theresa, also shifted to this strategy. Among these orders, however, only the Jesuits educate future politicians. One of the schools they decided to close in 1973 was the Instituto Patria, with 6,000 living alumni.[41] The Instituto Patria was one of Mexico's largest Catholic preparatory institutions, but it was not among the most influential in educating future Mexican politicians and intellectuals, although its graduates included Genaro Borrego, a former president of the National Executive Committee of the PRI; Fernando Solana, secretary of foreign relations, 1988–1994; and Fernando Baeza Melendez, congressman and governor of Chihuahua.

The growth in Catholic schools since the 1940s does not imply automatically that Mexicans from secular Liberal backgrounds attended in large numbers. In fact, a definite change occurred in educational patterns among the last three political generations. A member of the oldest generation, Adrián Lajous Martínez, describes them:

In the 1920s, many elite Mexicans sent their children to public school, and they did so because of a strong conviction that public schools were important to Mexico's future. For example, Public Secondary School No. 2 in the Federal District educated many of Mexico's future politicians of my generation [including Presidents Luis Echeverría and José López Portillo]. Today, no one from the middle or upper middle classes would ever send their kids to such an institution. It just wouldn't happen . . . with the exception that some of these people still send their children to the National

University for reasons of prestige and tradition, but even this is becoming less and less common. . . .

That generation of postrevolutionary Liberals has died, the generation who believed in the value of public education. My generation has taken over, and it has been more interested in what it can accomplish for itself than what it can accomplish for Mexico. And we of course have now been replaced by a younger generation.[42]

Other politicians from this generation are equally critical of their peers, believing that the majority of public officials today are sending their children to religiously operated schools for their secondary and preparatory education and that their decision to do so contradicts their public statements about education, damaging public schools' prestige.

The generation of Miguel de la Madrid, who himself attended Catholic schools, became the first to attend Catholic schools in larger numbers. For example, in the 1940s, Porfirio Muñoz Ledo attended the Brothers of Mary primary school on a government scholarship. He recalls very positive relationships with the priests who were his teachers. He also attended the Centro Universitario Mexicano (more popularly called CUM), a Brothers of Mary preparatory institution graduating numerous political figures.[43] Miguel Alemán, Jr., son of President Alemán, also graduated from the same preparatory school. Alemán attended La Sagrada Familia primary school in Jalapa, which couldn't legally exist (religious schools were formally banned in Veracruz during this era), changing its name to the secular Susana Fantana (the mother of Christopher Columbus) school to survive.[44] Other CUM graduates include Manuel Bartlett, de la Madrid's secretary of government, a crucial figure in church-state relations; Alfredo del Mazo, another major precandidate for the 1988 PRI presidential nomination; Mario Moya Palencia, secretary of government under Luis Echeverría; and Miguel Mancera, director of the Bank of Mexico under de la Madrid, Salinas, and Ernesto Zedillo.

Other Catholic schools have produced important Mexican political figures, including La Salle, which counts Miguel de la Madrid and PRI leader Humberto Lugo Gil among its graduates; Cristóbal Colón, which also includes de la Madrid and former PRI president, Adolfo Lugo Verduzco, as alumni; the Colegio Francés Morelos, which includes President Luis Echeverría and Hugo Margáin, former treasury secretary, as alumni; and the Colegio México, all of which are located in Mexico City.[45]

These schools also reinforce a certain social environment, given the fact that few students from working-class backgrounds can attend private institutions, secular or parochial. Exceptional cases of students like Muñoz Ledo who receive scholarships exist, but most graduates are from upper- and middle-class families. Specifically, only 14 percent come from working-class families, and 47 and 21 percent, respectively, from middle- and upper-class backgrounds.[46] The director of secondary education under Manuel Avila Camacho (1941–1945) recognized the problem of educational access half a century ago. As he revealed:

I established a rule that in private schools in Mexico, which were always taking upper social classes as their students, they should admit 5 percent of their students from lower-class Mexicans who couldn't afford to send their children to these institutions.

They had to accept this decision. One day, a representative of all the private schools, a Jesuit, came to see me. He wanted to deal with me as a practicing Catholic, rather than as a public official. I explained the rationale for my decision to him. He complained about my decision. He argued that children who were from poor backgrounds have different customs, habits, poor clothes—all of which affects the discipline in their schools. I argued that the people from these upper social classes needed to get to know these ordinary Mexicans, to make friends, so that they would learn something from their more fortunate, wealthier student companions, and these students would learn something from them. I suggested to him that when Mexicans take communion, we don't distinguish between rich and poor, so why should we distinguish between them in education. The priest turned red, was extremely embarrassed, and had nothing else to say to me about this matter.[47]

At the university level, the most important institutions have been the Jesuit-run Ibero-American University and the Pan American Institute for Higher Management operated by Opus Dei. Both of these institutions are important because they have brought together Mexican entrepreneurial and political figures. No evidence exists to suggest, however, that graduates of either of these institutions were influenced by their instructors' religious ideology.[48]

Most politicians are sending their children to private schools, and many of these to private, Catholic institutions. They justify their decisions, as do many Americans, with the rationale that the quality of Mexican public schools has declined. Politicians believe, however, that the graduates of these institutions have not yet translated ideas linked to their educational formation into policies. They argue that their numbers would have to be much greater before they influence policy outcomes. However, reforms instituted under Salinas changed the ambience for future policies affecting church-state relations, encountering sympathy among the younger generation of politicians who were products of religious schooling.

National and Local Structural Relations

Personal ties between politicians and higher level clergy, which politicians individually use to communicate concerns to the Catholic Church, have extended to and superseded institutional relationships. Knowledgeable Mexican religious scholars have actually described the institutional ties as a "personal relationship."[49] Prior to recognition of the Catholic Church in 1992, the Mexican government relied on two personal vehicles to provide an informal framework for working relations with the Church: personal contacts, with no official institutional status, and individual presidents. In the 1970s and 1980s, "the church hierarchy has for the most part agreed to play according to the informal rules of the game. . . . No formulas exist to define the relationship between the church's institutions and the society. Institutional relationships depend as much on precedents and personalities relating to particular issues as on the overall requirements of stability."[50]

The relationship between church and state at the national level is complicated by the fact that government officials like to deal with it as a monolithic institution.

Indeed, most believe the Church in Mexico has a single leader. Few politicians understand the autonomy of individual bishops and dioceses and the consequences for Church policy, even as it relates to the state. As one prominent brother and student of religion suggested, even as the 1980s came to a close, Mexicans continued to deal with a church-state relationship in mythical terms. Younger leaders find it difficult to understand a second complicating characteristic: the difference between the Vatican-state relationship, and the Mexican church-state relationship.[51]

A third element placing obstacles in the path of the relationship extends back to politicians and clergy lacking similar cultural-religious developmental experiences in their early formation. This difference led to a serious problem in communication: a dissimilar vocabulary. As Ricardo Cuellar Romo, secretary of the episcopate, argued, "Sometimes, I think that the real problem in the communication between Church and the state is that we are not using the same language. Without an identical basis or platform of communication, we understand the same concept completely differently."[52]

The latter point is one that characterizes the relationship of the state to other important Mexican groups. For example, Mexican entrepreneurs, who have more in common with politicians than do clergy, also have difficulties in communicating to the state—difficulties that they, too, attribute to different vocabulary and conceptual definitions.[53] These differences in language also have reinforced their isolation from one another as individuals.

Since the 1970s, several key individuals have played significant roles in maintaining and improving church-state relations on a personal level as representatives of their respective institutions. One of the actors captures the informality and happenstance of how the Mexican government maintains its most important interest group relationship:

> One day, a friend of mine who worked for President Echeverría came to see me. He was in the area of church-state relations and indicated he would like having me come to work for him. Later, however, he decided to go to the United States and suggested I go see someone else about this position. I wasn't that interested at the time, but after several weeks, belatedly I decided to go interview with the person whose name he had given me. I didn't know this individual at all, and I went for an interview at the Cooperative Workers Bank, under the directorship of Jorge Martínez Gómez del Campo. His responsibility, other than directing the bank, was to handle all relations between the government, the Church, and the Vatican. There were just the two of us and several assistants. The government does not have any formal department for dealing with the Church [before 1992], and it was done completely informally by us. We handled all the correspondence between the government and the Catholic Church as well as the Vatican, including personal correspondence between the president and the Pope. One of the reasons why I was given this job was because of my contacts with the Church. Since my schooling in Guadalajara, I knew the archbishop, and I had developed a very close relationship with him, almost familial in nature.[54]

Fausto Zerón-Medina and Jorge Martínez Gómez del Campo handled church-state relations initially for President Echeverría and then for President José López

Portillo. Echeverría placed considerable trust in these two individuals, allowing them to write position papers that he presented, without previewing, to the Vatican. Other officials in his administration solicited criticisms and information on issues involving the Church. During these administrations, the cardinal of the archdiocese of Mexico, Miguel Dario Miranda, maintained direct relations with the president. After Miranda retired in 1977, he was replaced by Cardinal Corripio, who had neither the talents nor inclination to sustain this type of top-level, personal relationship. Since 1978, from the Church's side, the Vatican delegate, Girolamo Prigione, seized the responsibility as the major communication link between the hierarchy, the Vatican, and the Mexican government.

Prigione altered the pattern under Echeverría and the first years of López Portillo's administration, making it clear to López Portillo that he did not want any intermediaries between himself and the president, thus alienating Jorge Martínez del Campo. Prigione exercised tremendous influence over church-state relations since his arrival in 1978, building a spacious home for entertaining key political figures. With Martínez del Campo's departure, the linkage from the government's point of view became even more informal and decentralized. Nicéforo Guerrero Reynoso, a department head in the secretariat of government in the 1970s, became director general of federal property in the secretariat of urbanization and ecology, where one of his primary responsibilities was church-state relations, especially legal conflicts.[55] The informal decentralization of governmental responsibility for different aspects of the relationship made it difficult for clergy to know to whom they should be addressing their problems. Prior to 1970, the secretary of government directly handled most church-state issues.

Depending on the administration, individual secretaries or other officials in the government secretariat played important roles in facilitating communication between the Church and government. Recently, either these individuals took the initiative to establish important links with the hierarchy, or Prigione, a crafty judge of influential political figures, personally established a social relationship. Prigione cultivated, among other figures, General Miguel Angel Godínez, José López Portillo's presidential chief of staff and the military zone commander of Chiapas during the uprising of the Zapatista Army of National Liberation.[56] He also established a very close personal relationship with Manuel Bartlett, Miguel de la Madrid's secretary of government and a front-runner for the 1988 PRI presidential nomination.[57] Under President Salinas, Prigione continued excellent relations with Fernando Gutiérrez Barrios, who replaced Bartlett but whom Prigione had known since 1982.[58] Church officials also felt comfortable dealing with his subsecretary of government, Jorge Carrillo Olea.[59]

The history of church-state relations in Mexico since the Revolution is replete with examples of extraofficial and below-the-surface relations between individuals in both institutions. But according to many clergy, the Church always felt uncomfortable with this type of informal relationship, believing it to be on the "receiving end."[60] One of the reasons higher clergy hoped for constitutional reform was to clearly institutionalize links between church and state. In 1992, with the achievement of such reforms, the Salinas administration created a new director general of religious affairs within the secretariat of government, headed by the experienced Nicéforo Guerrero Reynoso.

Local and State Linkages: Presaging New National Patterns?

An examination of the structural and personal linkages between church and state at the national level compared to similar patterns at the state and local level reveals similar sources of contact but a substantially different depth of personal exchanges. The relationship at the local level differs in that each diocese, or each pastoral region consisting of various bishops, is composed of multiple individual and personal relationships. Contrary to Mexican perceptions of the Church, individual dioceses typically ignore the national institutional hierarchy's directives and instead rely on direct and indirect, formal and informal, and legal and illegal relations.[61]

Interviews with numerous priests and bishops, however, suggest that on the whole, relations both prior to and after the constitutional reforms were excellent. Bishops who are willing to discuss their relationships with state authorities explain that it depends largely on the individual governor's personality, not on the tenor of national church-state relations. As a former bishop of Zacatecas suggested:

> I see the relationship as very ambiguous. There are periods of tension and periods where the relationship is quite close. . . . For example, my relations in Zacatecas were excellent with the then governor. I found him to be a very serious man, interested in helping the welfare of the people of his state. We worked very closely together to assist poor people. I believe to this day he was a good man, but that his state did not receive many resources. He did something very unusual for that time, he invited me both times to his state of the union address in 1971 and 1972, which I can tell you was very rare in those days, and of course I wore civilian clothes, not my black garb. [The first presidential invitation to the clergy to attend a state of the union address did not occur until Salinas became president.] I believe that suggests how he felt about me and our relationship.[62]

Most governors and bishops reported very positive relationships. Some of these individuals had more extensive social ties with each other, similar to Bishop Rovalo; others were less frequent in their social contact but equally respectful. In fact, friendships were strong enough between bishops and governors in some cases that a bishop went to bat politically for a governor. The most unusual case reported in interviews for this book is that of Sonoran governor Armando Briebich, who became embroiled in a national political dispute with President Echeverría. Carlos Quintero Arce, the archbishop of Hermosillo, Sonora's capital, is fondly remembered by Briebich because he remained strongly supportive of the governor's position, even to the extent of holding a Mass to support him.[63]

Although constitutional violations have been permitted for decades, they are much more likely to be allowed, on more than a personal basis, at the state rather than the national level. For example, just north of the capital, in the state of Querétaro, 36 bishops, 200 priests, and 35,000 faithful attended an open ceremony in the La Corregidora football stadium with the permission of Governor Mariano Palacios Alcocer.[64] The bishop of Querétaro during this era, Mario Gasperín Gasperín, always has felt respectfully treated by civil authorities and has been able to confront local and state authorities on any matter in frank terms, without alienating his secular peers. He described similar conditions as bishop of Tuxpan, Veracruz. In a comparable situation in the state of México, a governor also granted permission to Church authorities to have a huge Mass in the public football stadium.[65] In this case, however, the Communist Party found out about the prospective celebration and pressured the national secretary of government to intervene and prohibit the event, which is constitutionally banned. Nevertheless, typically, their relations were positive, as former governor Alfredo del Mazo asserts, recalling only one small incident with any of the bishops during his administration. The bishop of Toluca announced publicly that the state was badly administered. Taking this as an insult, the governor canceled his next meeting with the bishop and sent his secretary general to respond to the bishop's criticisms. After that, he noted, they had no more difficulties.[66]

Perhaps the only factor that worked against good relations at the state level, except in those situations where a governor came from a strongly anticlerical background, is that some older bishops raised during the Cristero era tended to be distrustful. Magín C. Torreblanca, bishop of Texcoco, México, who grew up during the 1920s and 1930s and was raised by an uncle, the bishop of San Cristóbal de la Casas, Chiapas, and Puebla, Puebla, believes such a background could affect a bishop's personal relationships. He describes his own relationships with the governor and mayor as good.[67] Bishops typically appear to have more frequent contact with the governor and state authorities than they do with local officials or the mayor.[68] One scholar even suggested that certain bishops were held in such high regard by state authorities that they were consulted in the selection of official party candidates.[69] If that was the case, it was rare and has not continued into the present.

Nicéforo Guerrero, who often handled governmental disputes with the Church, even at the local and state level, argues that numerous cases exist of extraordinarily close relations between governors and bishops. Individuals with such ties meet regularly for lunch, using their resources and efforts to resolve issues in which both the Church and state share mutual interests. When the state government becomes involved in a dispute to which the Church is a party, typically it involves the state secretary general of government (similar to a lieutenant governor), unless the issue is of extreme importance.[70]

State authorities, specifically secretaries general, sometimes are involved in disputes between clergy, not between the Church and secular authorities. In recent years, the most frequent disputes complicating church-state relations are between Catholics and Protestants, especially in rural villages. In earlier eras, however, they often involved conflicts among Catholics. For example, Manuel Hinojosa Ortiz, who served as secretary general of government in Michoacán, a traditional, Catholic stronghold, became involved in such a dispute when the mayor of a small village complained that the village had loaned its patron saint to a neighboring community, but that this town now refused to return the saint. Although Hinojosa did not want to become involved in a purely spiritual matter, the mayor explained that his village planned to march to the other community to seize the saint by force.

Using informal personal ties typical of clergy-politician relations, Hinojosa asked a well-connected friend to explain the situation to the appropriate bishop. He, too, refused to intervene because the village came under the territorial control of a religious order, not his diocese. Hinojosa then sent a representative of his own to the leader of the offending village, explaining the impending attack, emphasizing that many villagers would die but implying that the leader would be the first to die. He wanted to leave it to leader's imagination that this was a government threat. This implied threat was effective, and the leader returned the saint the following day.[71]

Even closer relations tend to characterize church and state at the local level because of the esteem with which local communities hold their priests. Priests often are deeply involved in local activities. As suggested earlier, outside of family, schoolteachers and priests command the greatest confidence among the Mexican populace. Priests are active in community affairs, and for many years, they have participated in local secular activities. Two-fifths of all priests claim to have regular contact with civil authorities—specifically, 10 percent with a representative of the secretariat of government (national), 16 percent with local and federal legislators, and 5 percent with governors.[72] For example, a priest from the state of México who described governmental relations as cordial reports that in the 1980s he belonged to the Toluca City Council's cultural committee in the state capital. He received numerous invitations to official government events and small gifts, including new books, from the government, contributed an article on the Church in Toluca for a government publication, and regularly attended social events with politicians.[73]

Priests report that the most common request from local and state government authorities generally involves social and educational assistance. More than half of all priests interviewed in the Luengo study report such requests. Many priests appear to be purposely recruited by local secular institutions, or at least into organizations affiliated with such institutions, as a means of linking governmental and religious representatives together.[74] This is quite common in the arena of social and educational assistance. Allan Metz reports: "[S]upposedly lay *patronatos* (charitable foundations) received parish support for medical services and educational programs where government facilities proved to be lacking. Since the church is constitutionally prohibited from directly engaging in secular matters [before 1992], priests form 'civic groups with lay boards of officers.' Therefore, the church offers services to the state while simultaneously extending its own influence."[75] Such linkages are not confined to those between government officials and the clergy. Within the PRD, a minority of activists identify strongly with the concepts of liberation theology, and they provide an important bridge to the progressive sector of the Church, especially in those dioceses or parishes where ecclesiastical base communities are common.[76]

In the Federal District, the seat of the national government, the relationship is more complex because it houses the episcopate, a national council of bishops, local bishops subsumed under the archdiocese of Mexico, one of Mexico's two cardinals, the symbolic leader of the Catholic Church, and the papal nuncio, the Pope's official representative. An excellent illustration of the complexity of local-national church-state relations can be found in an incident involving a pro-life protest against the display of art at the Museum of Modern Art in Chapultepec Park. Interestingly, it has been alleged that the cardinal used the pro-life group to protest against the show, informing them of the exhibit. However, the pro-life protesters, instead of directing their complaint to the secretariat of government, the logical agency, sent letters to the secretariat of national defense. The Church and its allies eventually succeeded in having the museum director fired.[77] Although this incident involved a diverse number of actors, local and national, relations typically are very positive. A student of the Federal District concludes that most relations there occur on two levels: bureaucratic, essentially gaining permission to hold religious events, and informal, clergy and politicians requesting favors of each other in the form of religious ceremonies or solving a priest's problems in his capacity as an ordinary citizen.[78]

Presidential Friendships

Naturally, the most significant element in establishing the tone of church-state relations is the president. Mexican presidents relate to the Church on a personal and informal level, similar to national and state politicians.[79] In fact, when presidents built their political careers at the state level, coming from the provinces, it was often their personal ties to a local bishop that provided the initial link to good relations with the hierarchy. The last president to have been born and raised in the provinces was Gustavo Díaz Ordaz (1964–1970), who developed a close personal friendship with the bishop of Puebla, Octaviano Márquez y Toriz. Díaz Ordaz was rector of the University of Puebla and secretary general of government at the time Márquez y Toriz was a professor and spiritual director of the Palafoxian seminary. Their friendship was so strong that the president actually gave him a new car each year of his administration.[80]

Díaz Ordaz's successor, Luis Echeverría, broadened presidential ties with the Catholic Church. As indicated above, he selected Jorge Martínez Gómez del Campo, who he met while serving as *oficial mayor* of the secretariat of public education in the mid-1950s, to represent him in important church-state matters. Martínez Gómez del Campo was involved in the parents' educational association, where he impressed Echeverría. They maintained their friendship during the ensuing years.[81] During Echeverría's campaign, the president initiated a pattern replicated by each of his successors, making contact with each individual bishop.[82] Echeverría recalls numerous conversations with clergy, contacts that he began as secretary of government under Díaz Ordaz.[83]

Fausto Zerón-Medina, who worked directly under Martínez Gómez del Campo, described church relations with Echeverría as cordial and communications as "absolutely open." He emphasized that it was the president who "made possible direct communication between the episcopate and himself, as well as all of his important collaborators in the cabinet. For example, to show you how he dealt with the Catholic Church, we initiated a reform of some of the laws dealing with education during his administration, and he gave this proposed reform directly to the clergy for their opinion. Later, after they had an opportunity to analyze the proposed revisions, the government met with the clergy, including the secretary of education, Porfirio Muñoz Ledo."[84] Echeverría further incorporated the clergy into the policy process, even including them in cabinet meetings involving discussions of regional problems.[85] The Church confirms this level of exchange. Bishop Genaro Alamilla, secretary general of the Mexican episcopate for nine years, recalled numerous meetings with government authorities that were "somewhat hidden, secret, and mysterious," typically in private homes. The Church in turn strengthened its ties with the administration, often using the abbot of the Basilica of the Virgin of Guadalupe, Guillermo Schulenburg, as a channel of communication.[86] In fact, when Schulenburg went to the government with a request to help rebuild the basilica, Mexico's most popular religious shrine, the president was delighted to help, seeing it as satisfying popular demands rather than as a purely spiritual place.[87]

Not only did Echeverría improve the decision-making process concerning religious matters, but he paid attention to smaller matters of courtesy, offering the hierarchy significant political information. Specifically, several hours before the announcement of José López Portillo as the PRI's presidential candidate, he called in Martínez Gómez del Campo, asking him to "tell 'our friend,' " referring to Cardinal Miranda, that the candidate would be López Portillo. He did this to show church leadership and the cardinal his respect for the Church."[88] In this particular case, however, Cardinal Miranda lacked the political sophistication to understand the information conveyed to him. When Martínez Gómez del Campo suggested that the president wanted the cardinal to send his greetings to the candidate, Miranda allegedly replied, "OK, but why should I? I don't know him."[89]

Echeverría was not content to do this solely within Mexico with the national hierarchy. He sent his subsecretary of government properties, Pedro Moctezuma Díaz Infante, as his personal representative to the cardinal's consecration. Because Moctezuma, an architect, was the person most responsible for the restoration and protection of Church buildings, his presence in Rome opened up additional channels of communication with the hierarchy. When an earthquake occurred during his administration, Echeverría ordered Church buildings to be the first to be reconstructed. Echeverría belied a public image of having traditional relations with the Church, but insiders describe his relations with the Church as the closest in many decades.[90]

Echeverría established a specific, close relationship with a single bishop, similar to his predecessor. On June 9, 1970, Bishop Sergio Méndez Arceo sent a letter to the PRI presidential candidate, as well as to Efraín González Morfín, PAN's candidate. His correspondence, which became known as the "letter of Anenecuilco," was a pioneer statement on abuses in church-state relations.[91] Echeverría was impressed with Méndez Arceo's forthrightness and attempted in his own manner to improve relations on a personal and institutional level. Their relationship was such that Méndez Arceo became the first bishop since the Revolution to visit Los Pinos, the presidential residence, on a regular basis.[92] Both men shared similar populist ideas.

Soledad Loaeza has suggested that Echeverría improved relations with the Church due to a desire to use popular religion as a means of reformulating the grassroots basis of the regime.[93] This is surely the case. The president established a program called Acción Concertada in the last year of his administration. He told Martínez Gómez del Campo that he was not opposed to the religious faith of the Mexican people, but that he wanted to incorporate the clergy's social influence into government programs. Acción Concertada had this in mind—to involve lower and higher clergy in social, economic, and moral programs.[94] Although never implemented, it suggested the degree to which the relationship had improved and the willingness of the president to make pragmatic use of Church influence and prestige.

José López Portillo incorporated the intent of this program into his own presidential campaign strategy, visiting 40 bishops from October 1975 to June 1976. He definitely altered his personal relations with Catholic clergy. In his public life, up to the time he became the PRI candidate, he never had consulted with clergy about social problems.[95] In his conversation with Bishop Pablo Rovalo Ascué of Zacatecas, the candidate raised the issue of Church ownership of real estate. This subject came to occupy an important place in later discussions.[96] López Portillo came from a familial background with dual religious-Liberal influences. His mother was a fervent Catholic, but the president himself was not a believer.[97] His administration was fraught with political and economic crises; nevertheless, his relations with the Church were cordial. Unlike his two predecessors, López Portillo did not establish personal links to an individual bishop; rather, he relied more heavily on his ties to the Vatican delegate, Girolamo Prigione. Consequently, López Portillo distanced himself from Martínez Gómez del Campo, whose contacts were extensive throughout the Mexican hierarchy, and both Gómez del Campo and Zerón-Medina resigned their positions.

Despite these internal upheavals and López Portillo's public image as a firm traditional Liberal, he allowed Pope John Paul II to visit Mexico in 1979, violating some constitutional provisions. Porfirio Muñoz Ledo, who had served as his secretary of public education and was then ambassador to the United Nations, urged the president to allow the Pope to come without establishing formal relations.[98] Loaeza considers the invitation to be a personal decision of the president.[99] Although the president's posture during the visit could only be described as "correct," his family met with the Pope, suggesting a separation between his public and private lives.[100] Too much should not be attributed to this distinction since it does not imply a different personal philosophy on the part of the president but rather his response to family members. The Pope, in his public statements, basically supported the Mexican government, calling on priests to concentrate on spiritual, not worldly, matters.

When Miguel de la Madrid became the PRI's candidate for president he, too, as had his two predecessors, initiated relations with the clergy. His political career and lack of extensive contacts with clergy are typical of his generation. His own account of this illustrates why personal ties are crucial to institutional communication:

Before I became president, I did have a reason to know certain clergy, mainly ordinary parish priests, especially because of family matters, and in school. But I never had close relations with the religious hierarchy, and this was never common among other politicians I knew. When I became secretary of programming and budgeting, and needed to organize a new census, I developed relations with the hierarchy, especially with Cardinal Corripio, to obtain their collaboration. I wanted them to be supportive of the census, and even to help us, and they were happy to do so. But I really came to know the clergy as a candidate for president, especially the bishops, because we had many talks, and I exchanged views with them and we developed a rather cordial relationship. . . . As president, I did have informal conversations with several small groups or individuals about various problems, and they listened to my point of view and I to their's.[101]

De la Madrid, however, firmly changed the structural relationship between the Church and state. Although all requests from the Church on religious matters came through the secretariat of government, the agency responsible for day-to-day problem solving, de la Madrid reinforced López Portillo's decision to rely on the Vatican delegate. He told the Vatican he would not select a personal representative.[102] The president's reliance on Prigione, while extremely helpful to Vatican-state relations, complicated domestic church-state relations, again because bishops are autonomous and because the episcopate is not necessarily in sync with the views of the Vatican delegate. Prigione skillfully strengthened his relations with the president, often giving private Masses at his residence for the president's wife, a devout Catholic.

Prigione developed extremely close social and working ties with Bartlett, who professed to Prigione the traditional Liberal views most public figures hold but stressed the pragmatic necessities of the relationship. The linkage between Prigione and Bartlett reached such a level of cooperation that Prigione manipulated secular authorities to reinforce his own ideological biases against the Mexican hierarchy. As part of a long-term strategy, Prigione encouraged the replacement of progressive bishops with individuals more sympathetic to his and the Vatican's position on pastoral issues, a position that brought Prigione into conflict with various progressive bishops, the cardinal archbishop of Mexico, and even on occasion the episcopate. Arturo Lona Reyes, a much reviled bishop for his orientation toward the poor in Tehuantepec, complained that during the de la Madrid administration, Manuel Bartlett, through Prigione, accused Lona on numerous occasions of being a Marxist guerrilla.[103] Bishop Manuel Talamás Camandari of Ciudad Juárez, a veteran of the Second Vatican Concilium, recalled numerous meetings with de la Madrid's cabinet, including Bartlett, who he described as preoccupied with the Church's potential influence on public opinion.[104]

Prigione described the tone of President de la Madrid's relationship with the Church as one of greater freedom, allowing the Church to speak out more openly than in the past. The president also took into account Church views and wanted the Church to be informed of government policies. Prigione reported a meeting in May 1987, between the secretary of government, Manuel Bartlett, the secretary of the treasury, Ignacio Petriciolli, and 12 bishops and archbishops, during which they discussed political-economic policies. He argued that such meetings encouraged a dialogue between government and the Church. He was equally adamant in suggesting that given the public relationship between church and state, neither the Church nor the government could inform the press of their meeting.[105] Overall, Prigione characterized relations between de la Madrid and the Church as a "common-law marriage." Although he saw them as cordial, he insisted that they must change and that the government must face new realities. At the end of the de la Madrid administration, long before any sense of an impending change in the relationship was to occur under President Salinas, Prigione remained optimistic about the future relationship, believing he was planting the seeds of change among the present leadership and that younger politicians would share a more open view of the Church, a prescient outlook.

Numerous tensions between church and state characterized de la Madrid's tenure as president; nevertheless, Church leaders believed de la Madrid wanted to improve the relationship, at least at a personal if not an institutional level. A Mexico City bishop explains why:

> The government looks for the same relation with the Church that it has with the people in general. It does it more on a personal than on an institutional level. The reason why it doesn't institutionalize this relationship is that legally it doesn't recognize us, and it wouldn't want to contribute in any way to changing this status. Politicians and technocrats both maintain relations with the Church, often very good friendships with individual priests and with all levels of clergy. The government and the party understand that the Church could serve as a useful bridge to the people, and they are sensitive to the potential role we can play.[106]

Although some scholars have described de la Madrid's public posture toward the Church as cold, the Church began an effort on its own initiative, led by Cardinal Corripio, to strengthen the relationship.[107] As the late Cardinal Posadas, who was close to Prigione and a leader in the episcopate, concluded, President de la Madrid, despite his public image, made it possible to bring both institutions closer together because of his own personal orientation.[108]

When Carlos Salinas de Gortari became the PRI presidential candidate in the fall of 1987, there was nothing in his personal, religious background to suggest that he felt a particularly strong, positive association with Catholicism. Although he was baptized, confirmed, and married within the Catholic Church, he was not a practicing Catholic.[109] As a candidate, he established cordial relations with Mexico's bishops, meeting with all but two of the active episcopate during his campaign. Ironically, the episcopate itself, in an internal document, viewed Salinas as a "disciple and descendant of Reyes Heroles," a public figure of the post-1970s era whose anticlericalism could be described as rabid, and declared that Salinas shared the worst of Reyes Heroles's beliefs—those belonging to the socialist generation of Francois Miterrand's French government.[110]

Salinas, by being the first president to invite several representatives of the episcopate to his inauguration, symbolically announced a new direction regarding church-state relations, adding concrete evidence to the gesture when he indicated in his state of the union address that church-state relations needed modernizing. One of his severest critics, Porfirio Muñoz Ledo, believes Salinas shifted the relationship from a personal to an institutional level because he understood the value of religion to Mexican culture. He also believes the president incorporated the Catholic Church, specifically the Vatican delegate, into the composition of a new political alliance.[111]

After six months of his administration, the clergy were already struck by Salinas's level of personal contacts, including numerous luncheons with the hierarchy to discuss issues of mutual interest. Many considered it to be a remarkable change in the level of collegiality between politicians and the clergy.[112] Nevertheless, these secret, personal encounters "provoked a division in the breast of the Church," since many bishops did not trust the government's promises.[113]

By 1990, Salinas reinstituted Echeverría's concept of appointing a personal representative, selecting Agustín Téllez Cruz for the position. However, his appointment differed considerably from that of Echeverría, for although he relied on a government figure with familial, clerical ties, he made it public, designating Téllez Cruz as his personal emissary to the Vatican. The Vatican, in turn, strengthened Prigione's position, giving him comparable status as its personal representative to Salinas. Salinas reinforced the personal linkage between both men, installing a direct telephone line to the president at the apostolic delegate's official residence.[114] Prigione continued to enjoy a strong personal friendship with Salinas's first two secretaries of government, Francisco Gutiérrez Barrios and Patrocinio González Garrido, through early 1994.

Conclusions

When leadership groups in a society are compartmentalized on the basis of their social origins, familial values, and educational socialization—relying heavily on popular mythology for their knowledge of each other's goals, values, and attitudes—it creates difficulties for institutional relations and for understanding the functions performed by organizational structures representing respective leadership groups. One of the most important consequences of politicians' ignorance about clergy and, to a lesser extent, clergy's ignorance about politicians for effective communication is that they accentuate the need for greater reliance on social and personal links. Personal linkages were substitutes for formal institutional linkages prior to 1992 but at a cost of clear lines of communication, especially politicians' misunderstanding of individual clergy's motivations as representative of the motivations of all bishops.

Mexican politicians for many decades have relied on relatives or friends boasting special ties to the Church or clergy in making important policy decisions and communications. These linkages are tenuous and inconsistent at best, varying from one presidential administration to the next. The selectiveness and capriciousness of personal ties subject the government and individual presidents to greater possibilities for misreading the Church based on the level and breadth of knowledge enjoyed by an individual contact. In other words, all of the biases and limitations of one or two individuals are incorporated into what the government knows and understands about a large complex institution. Such reliance is risky at best, without considering the difficulties it creates for clergy, at all levels, to communicate effectively with the state.

Mexico's popular mythology maintains that the National Action Party has special ties to the clergy and to Catholicism. Whereas it is true that Panista leaders have not hidden their religious beliefs or the youthful origins in Catholic families, once in pursuit of political careers, they have shed most of their religious ties. The Catholic Church, whether the episcopate or the clergy, shares no special links to PAN politicians or the party. PAN politicians, on the other hand, while having been influenced by social Christian thought, have not sought out a special relationship with the Church. Individual clergy may well be partisan supporters of PAN, just as they are of the PRI, the PRD, and other parties.

Elite Catholic schools, primarily in Mexico City, have educated many political leaders from both PAN and the PRI. Although their education at parochial schools may have made especially younger politicians more understanding of or sympathetic to religion and Catholicism, their formation in these environments has not led to increased contacts between future politicians and bishops. Such schools do not produce future members of the episcopate because few bishops come from Mexico City, and clergy typically come from a social extraction different from those Mexicans who can afford to enroll in such schools. Local and regional politicians, on the other hand, are more likely to have shared educational experiences in provincial capitals.

These differing educational, social, and cultural experiences produce consequences other than ignorance about each other's orientation and interests. These differences also lead to a much more fundamental basis of miscommunication: distinct cultural vocabularies. Clergy, just as entrepreneurs, face some of the same issues in relating institutionally to the state, believing that they understand individual issues with the same clarity as their political counterparts. Instead, they are often talking past one another because they are using the same language but with distinct definitions.

Structural relations between church and state are informed by personal and informal relations, as is often the case with other groups linked to the Mexican state. Typically, in the last two decades, the government used unofficial agencies or representatives in the federal bureaucracy to sustain church relations. Individual presidents flavored not only the relationship's direction but also the means of establishing communication, which varied in quality and tone from one administration to the next. A significant consequence of relying on presidential prerogatives to make such choices is further centralization of executive power, increasing the probability of inconsistency in important institutional relationships.

Local patterns appear to be quite similar. But the smaller geographic size and the more comparable functional status of a diocesan bishop and a state governor have facilitated a more positive relationship. Although such relations can change at the whim of an individual governor or bishop, bishops and former governors typically report cordial relations. They have been freer of the federal government's rhetoric, built into the constitution, to openly ignore constitutional violations, indeed, to aid and abet in those violations by granting specific permission to the Church for activities contravening the law. Governors and mayors have their ears closer to the local populace, which is both religious and Catholic. Relations, as well as personal ties, are more frequent, broader, and inclined toward the social plane, thus establishing a basis for better, if not formal, linkages.

NOTES

1. Personal interview with Bishop Abelardo Alvarado Alcántara, Mexico Archdiocese, Mexico City, June 2, 1987.

2. Personal interview with Sealtiel Alatriste, descendant of a distinguished Liberal family, Mexico City, June 3, 1988.

3. Personal interview with José Rogelio Alvarez, Mexico City, February 15, 1991.

4. Personal interview with Father Guillermo Schulenburg, abbot of the Basilica of Guadalupe, Mexico Archdiocese, Mexico City, February 18, 1991.

5. Allan Metz, "Mexican Church-State Relations under President Carlos Salinas de Gortari," *Journal of Church and State* 34, no. 1 (Winter 1992): 116.

6. Personal interview with Father Samuel Morín Suárez, secretary to the bishop, Toluca Diocese, Toluca, México, June 9, 1988.

7. Personal interview with José Rogelio Alvarez.

8. As related to the late David C. Bailey by Father Francisco Aguilera, later a bishop, Mexico Archdiocese, Mexico City, August 4, 1976.

9. Antonio Jáquez has alleged that the family of Edmundo Sánchez Cano, governor of Oaxaca, descended from priests. "Sacerdotes que dejaron su ministerio exponen la 'sinrazón' del celibato," *Proceso,* April 9, 1990, 22.

10. Francisco Suárez Farias, *Elite, tecnocracia y movilidad política en México* (Mexico City: Universidad Autónomo Metropolitana-Xochimilco, 1991), 121.

11. Oscar Hinojosa, "Dejarán de ser en la noche los encuentros con funcionarios mexicanos: Prigione," *Proceso,* December 12, 1988, 10.

12. *Proceso,* February 19, 1990, 10–13.

13. The only known case I could find at the national level is that of Higinio Vázquez Santana, *oficial mayor* of the secretariat of public education in 1931, who also reached the rank of brigade general in the Mexican Army. He left public life in the 1930s, enrolled in the Montezuma seminary in 1941 at the age of 57, and was ordained two years later. In his youth, he had studied in Rome and had attended the Guadalajara seminary with classmate José Garibi, who later became cardinal. See José López Escalera, *Diccionario biográfico y de historia de México* (Mexico City: Editorial del Magistrado, 1964), 1130. In the Salinas administration, Luis Benavides, a central figure in national, technical education, also in the secretariat of public education, joined the Brothers of Mary, serving as vice-provincial of the central region, the order's second most important post, and teaching at the CUM. He left the order in the 1970s. *Proceso,* December 17, 1990, 25.

14. Partido Revolucionario Institucional, "Memorandum sobre las relaciones estado-iglesia católica," November 1988, unpublished manuscript, 20.

15. Larissa Adler Lomnitz and Marisol Pérez-Lizaur, *A Mexican Elite Family, 1820–1980* (Princeton: Princeton University Press, 1987), 204.

16. Eventually, a split occurred between the more liberal, Catholic social wing of the party and the conservative, northern business wing, leading to PAN's failure to agree on a presidential candidate in 1976. See George Philip, *The Presidency in Mexican Politics* (New York: St. Martin's, 1992), 106. By the late 1980s, however, a convergence of interests occurred among the business community, progressive Catholics, and secular leadership

within PAN, part of a larger movement involving additional groups in Latin America. See Paul E. Sigmund, "From Corporatism to Neo-Liberalism?: The Transformation of the Idea of Subsidiarity in Catholic Social Thought in Latin America," paper presented at the National Latin American Studies Association, Los Angeles, September 1992, 12. In the 1990s, Mexico's more progressive businessmen, represented by Coparmex leadership, argued that Christian socialism was the best path for Mexico's future and a vehicle for political participation. Roberto Blancarte, *El poder salinismo e la iglesia católica, una nueva convivencia?* (Mexico City: Grijalbo, 1991), 122.

17. Soledad Loaeza, "Derecha y democracia en el cambio político mexicano: 1982–1988," *Foro Internacional* 30, no. 4 (April–June 1990): 649. As Loaeza correctly argued, this influence did not indicate that PAN depended on the Catholic Church.

18. Personal interview with Abel Vicencio Tovar, former PAN president and legislative leader, Mexico City, July 13, 1993.

19. James F. Creagan, "Minority Political Parties in Mexico: Their Role in a One-Party System," unpublished Ph.D. dissertation, University of Virginia, 1965, 119.

20. Laura Nuzzi O'Shaughnessy, "Opposition in an Authoritarian Regime: The Incorporation and Institutionalization of the Mexican National Action Party (PAN)," unpublished Ph.D. dissertation, Indiana University, 1979, 94.

21. James F. Creagan, "Minority Political Parties in Mexico," 151.

22. Ibid., 120.

23. For example, see Soledad Loaeza, "The Role of the Right in Political Change in Mexico, 1982–1988," in *The Right and Democracy in Latin America,* Douglas A. Chalmers et al., eds. (New York: Praeger, 1992), 134, which states that the Catholic Church backed the National Action Party in dismantling the PRI's electoral hegemony from 1982 to 1988.

24. Bernardo Barranco Villafan and Raquel Pastor Escobar, "La presencia de la iglesia católica en el proceso de sucesión presidencial 1988," *Análisis Sociales* no. 2 (1988): 54.

25. Soledad Loaeza, "The Role of the Right in Political Change in Mexico, 1982–1988," 131.

26. Personal interview by David C. Bailey with Father Tom O'Rourke, Mexico Archdiocese, Mexico City, July 21, 1976.

27. Personal interview with Abel Vicencio Tovar. Vicente Fox, the PAN governor of Guanajuato and a likely presidential contender in 1999, has stated publicly that the Church hierarchy provided little assistance to PAN candidates. See George Grayson, *The Church in Contemporary Mexico* (Washington: CSIS, 1992), 43.

28. Bernardo Barranco Villafan and Raquel Pastor Escobar, *Jearquía católica y modernización política en México* (Mexico City: Palabra Ediciones, Centro Antonio de Montesinos, 1989), 50.

29. Bernardo Barranco Villafan and Raquel Pastor Escobar, "La presencia de la iglesia católica en el proceso de sucesión presidencial 1988," 54.

30. Personal interview with Heberto Castillo, Mexico City, July 12, 1993.

31. Personal interview with Ricardo Pascoe, secretary of communications, PRD, Mexico City, May 5, 1992. As Pascoe suggests, although many priests may not sympathize with the PRD, their relations have been very positive.

32. Porfirio Muñoz Ledo, a former PRI president and president of the PRD since 1992, describes his campaign experiences in Guanajuato, a traditional Catholic state and PAN stronghold, where he encountered open, sensitive, socially oriented, and nondogmatic priests devoted to helping their parishioners. He found that among the two dozen priests he met, those who supported PAN were in the minority. Personal interview, Mexico City, February 21, 1991.

33. Personal interview with Senator Miguel Alemán, secretary of finances of the CEN of the PRI, Mexico City, July 30, 1992.

34. José Luis Gaona Vega, "Los candidatos presidenciales tras el apoyo de obispos," *Punto,* June 27, 1988, 12.

35. Otto Granados Roldán, governor of Guanajuato, has made such an assertion in "La iglesia Católica mexicana como grupo de presión," in *Cuadernos de Humanidades,* no. 17 (Mexico City: UNAM, Departamento de Humanidades, 1981), 28. Also see José Luis Sierra Villarreal et al., *Política y poder en Yucatán* (Mérida: Academia Yucatanese de Ciencias y Artes, 1986), 238, which asserts that the Legionnaires of Christ's University of Mayab in Yucatán socializes students in traditional and conservative values at the highest levels.

36. Susan Eckstein, "Politicos and Priests: The Iron Law of Oligarchy and Interorganizational Relations," *Comparative Politics* 9 (July 1977): 472. Soledad Loaeza also considers it surprising that while the state restricted the Church's access to the education of workers and peasants, it left open opportunities for the Church to "socialize the essential groups in the reproduction of the state itself, the middle classes and the bourgeoisie who could pay for this education." "La rebelión de la Iglesia," *Nexos,* June 1984, 13.

37. Susana Rodríguez, "Ayer alumnos, hoy dirigentes," *Mira,* August 22, 1990, 17.

38. See Roderic Ai Camp, *Recruitment across Two Centuries: Mexico, 1884–1991* (Austin: University of Texas Press, 1995), Chapter 4, and *The Making of a Government: The Socialization of Politicians in Modern Mexico* (Tucson: University of Arizona Press, 1984).

39. For other data, see Nashiki Gómez and Martín de Jesús Díaz Vázquez, "Educación e iglesias," in "Política," *El Nacional,* April 16, 1991, 8–9; Soledad Loaeza, "La Iglesia católica mexicana y el reformismo autoritario," *Foro Internacional* 25, no. 2 (October–December 1984): 142; *Sonorense,* May 6, 1990, 2; and *Proceso,* February 19, 1990, 14.

40. Oscar Hinojosa and Rodrigo Vera, "Política de dos caras ante el problema religioso," *Proceso,* August 14, 1989, 19.

41. Susana Rodríguez, "Ayer alumnos, hoy dirigentes," 19; Claude Pomerlau, "The Catholic Church in Mexico and Its Changing Relationship to Society and the State," unpublished manuscript, December 1980, Chapter 6, 14.

42. Personal interview with Adrián Martínez Lajous, Mexico City, June 2, 1988.

43. Personal interview with Porfirio Muñoz Ledo.

44. Personal interview with Miguel Alemán, Jr.

45. Homero Campa and Rodrigo Vera, "Los colegios religioso, trampolín al poder público," *Proceso,* July 20, 1987, 6–7; *Proceso,* December 17, 1990, 25.

46. George Grayson, *The Church in Contemporary Mexico* (Washington: CSIS, 1992), 44.

47. Personal interview with Antonio Armendáriz, Mexico City, June 1, 1988. Armendáriz, a contemporary of President Miguel Alemán, came from extremely modest circumstances and believed strongly that his good fortune in receiving a higher education determined his future.

48. Manuel Buendía, *La Santa Madre* (Mexico City: Océano, 1985), 52–58; Oscar Hinojosa, "El Opus Dei, a la conquista de la dirección civil," *Proceso,* June 9, 1980, 18; Oscar Hinojosa, "El Opus Dei avanza del poder en México," *Proceso,* May 30, 1983, 11–12.

49. Personal interview with Father Carlos Escandon Domínguez, Mexico City, May 25, 1987.

50. Claude Pomerlau, "The Changing Church in Mexico and Its Challenge to the State," *Review of Politics* 43, no. 4 (October 1981): 549. A classic example during this period is

the cooperation between government and church officials at the highest levels, who met secretly to review the required textbooks provided by federal agencies. They edited certain passages and solved other problems brought to light by parents' groups. David C. Bailey, "The Church since 1940," in *Twentieth Century Mexico*, W. Dirk Raat and William H. Beezley, eds. (Lincoln: University of Nebraska Press, 1986), 238. Father Faustino Cervantes told Bailey in a 1976 interview that he wrote the essay on philosophy used by public normal schools and that 80 percent of the changes in recent textbooks were his work. Mexico Archdiocese, Mexico City, August 2, 1976.

51. Personal interview with Father Luis Narro Rodríguez, director of the Center of Educational Studies, Mexico City, June 28, 1989.

52. Personal interview with Father Ricardo Cuellar Romo, Mexican Episcopate, Mexico Archdiocese, Mexico City, May 25, 1987.

53. Roderic Ai Camp, *Entrepreneurs and the State in Twentieth-Century Mexico* (New York: Oxford University Press, 1989), 51–52.

54. Personal interview with Fausto Zerón-Medina, Mexico City, May 29, 1987.

55. Personal interview with Nicéforo Guerrero Reynoso, Secretariat of Urbanization and Ecology, Mexico City, June 19, 1989.

56. Prigione's ties to Godínez, quite unusual between the Church and the military, may offer an additional explanation as to why Prigione constantly interfered with Bishop Samuel Ruiz's role in the Chiapan diocese under Godínez's military command, to the extent that he tried to have the Pope remove Ruiz. Oscar Hinojosa, "Dejarán de ser en la noche los encuentros con funcionarios mexicanos," 10.

57. *Unomásuno*, December 13, 1988, 9.

58. *Unomásuno*, December 12, 1988, 5.

59. Ibid. Carrillo Olea had a long career in government security matters and was also a product of military academy education, with ties to the military leadership, an important, unique link for the Church.

60. Personal interview with Father Reuben Murillo, Ibero-American University, Mexico City, June 20, 1989.

61. Allan Metz, "Church-State Relations in Contemporary Mexico, 1968–1988," in *The Religions Challenge to the State*, Matthew C. Moen and Lowell S. Gustafson, eds. (Philadelphia: Temple University Press, 1992), 110. Ivan Vallier also suggests that the Church at the diocesan level often enters into short-term "contracts" with non-Church groups or agencies to lend legitimacy to a policy or to serve as added lines of defense against a real or imagined enemy. *Catholicism, Social Control, and Modernization in Latin America* (Englewood Cliffs, N.J.: Prentice-Hall, 1970), 33.

62. Personal interview with Bishop José Pablo Rovalo, Episcopal Vicariate, Mexico Diocese, Mexico City, February 21, 1991.

63. Personal interview with Carlos Armando Briebich, Mexico City, August 5, 1992. Briebich was forced by the president to resign.

64. Rodrigo Vera, "Prigione, a un paso de culminar su misión de trece años," *Proceso*, March 11, 1991, 8. Interestingly, Palacios Alcocer later played a significant role in writing the government's version of the church-state constitutional reforms.

65. Personal interview with Bishop Mario de Gasperín, Querétaro Diocese, Querétaro, Querétaro, July 12, 1993.

66. Personal interview with Alfredo del Mazo, Mexico City, February 15, 1991.

67. Personal interview with Bishop Magín C. Torreblanca Reyes, Texcoco Diocese, Texcoco, México, July 12, 1993.

68. Personal interview with Bishop Manuel Samaniego Barriga, Cuautitlán Diocese, Cuautitlán, México, February 13, 1991.

69. David C. Bailey, "The Church since 1940," 238. I found no evidence of this in the 1980s or 1990s.

70. Personal interview with Nicéforo Guerrero Reynoso.

71. Personal interview with Manuel Hinojosa Ortiz, Mexico City, June 1, 1988.

72. Enrique Luengo, "Los párrocos: una visión," unpublished manuscript, Department of Social and Political Sciences, Ibero-American University, 1989, 69–71.

73. Personal interview with Father Enrique Reyna Carrillo, Church of Our Lady of the Unprotected, Toluca Diocese, Toluca, México, June 9, 1988.

74. Susan Eckstein, "Politicos and Priests," 469.

75. Allan Metz, "Mexican Church-State Relations under President Carlos Salinas de Gortari," 111.

76. Bernardo Barranco Villafan and Raquel Pastor Escobar, "La presencia de la iglesia católica en el proceso de sucesión presidencial 1988," 54.

77. Shepard Barbash, "Religion to the Rescue," *Mexico Journal*, March 14, 1988, 26.

78. Oscar Aguilar and Enrique Luengo, "Iglesia y gobierno en el D.F.," *D.F.: gobierno y sociedad civil*, Pablo González Casanova, ed. (Mexico City: El Caballito, 1987), 13.

79. For a prominent politician's in-a-nutshell summary of presidential church-state relations, see Alfonso Martínez Domínguez's comments in Pedro Alisedo, "En México hay que componer muchas cosas, menos la Iglesia, que is la verdad," *Proceso*, May 14, 1990, 11.

80. Personal interview with Fausto Zerón-Medina.

81. Ibid. Also see Oscar Hinojosa, "Dejarán de ser en la noche los encuentros con funcionarios mexicanos," 9, who considered Fausto Zerón-Medina an influential figure. Soledad Loaeza also considered Martínez Gómez del Campo the most important single link between ecclesiastical and government authorities, although he exaggerated the time span. "La Iglesia católica mexicana y el reformismo autoritario," 153.

82. Father Miguel Concha Malo, unpublished manuscript, n.p. Concha is a student of church-state relations and longtime confidant of the late Bishop Sergio Méndez Arceo. Also see Oscar Aguilar and Ismael Martínez, "La Iglesia católica mexicana como factor de riesgo para la estabilidad del sistema político mexicano," unpublished paper, May 1987, 8.

83. Personal interview with President Luis Echeverría Alvarez, Mexico City, August 2, 1992.

84. Personal interview with Fausto Zerón-Medina, May 29, 1987.

85. Oscar Hinojosa, "Dejarán de ser en la noche los encuentros con funcionarios mexicanos," 9.

86. George Grayson, *The Church in Contemporary Mexico*, 54.

87. This is the view of Schulemburg himself. See Homero Campa, "El Abad de la Basílica de Guadalupe se retira, tras de su derrota ante Corripio," *Proceso*, December 10, 1990, 21.

88. Personal interview with Fausto Zerón-Medina.

89. Oscar Hinojosa, "Dejarán de ser en la noche los encuentros con funcionarios mexicanos," 9–10.

90. Personal interview with Fausto Zerón-Medina. This augured well for the relation to the Church of Zedillo's first government secretary, Esteban Moctezuma Barragán, since he was Pedro's son.

91. Personal interview with Manuel Concha Malo.

92. Personal interview with José Rogelio Alvarez.

93. Soledad Loaeza, "La Iglesia católica mexicana y el reformismo autoritario," 156.

94. *Proceso*, February 19, 1990, 11; Emilio Hernández, "Echeverría impuso a José López Portillo su plan de Alianza con la Iglesia," *Proceso*, May 27, 1985, 6.

95. Personal interview with President José López Portillo, February 19, 1991.

96. Emilio Hernández, "Echeverría impulsó a José López Portillo su plan Alianza con la Iglesia," 8.

97. Personal interview with Sealtiel Alatriste, López Portillo's boss early in his public career, Mexico City, June 3, 1988.

98. Personal interview with Porfirio Muñoz Ledo.

99. Soledad Loaeza, "La Iglesia católica mexicana y el reformismo autoritario," 139.

100. Silvia M. Bénard Calva, "Espejos encontrados: México siempre fiel?," *Religiosidad y política en México,* Carlos Martínez Assad, ed. (Mexico City: Ibero-American University, 1992), 194.

101. Personal interview with President Miguel de la Madrid, Mexico City, February 22, 1991.

102. Ibid.

103. Oscar Hinojosa, "Prigione, enlace de Bartlett para reprender a obispos críticos," *Proceso,* August 18, 1986, 8.

104. "Política," *El Nacional,* May 10, 1990, 22.

105. Personal interview with the Vatican delegate, Girolamo Prigione, Apostolic Residence, Mexico Archdiocese, Mexico City, June 2, 1987.

106. Personal interview with Bishop Francisco Aguilera González, Mexico Archdiocese, Mexico City, June 1, 1987.

107. Manuel Olimón Nolasco, *Tensiones y acercamientos, la iglesia y el estado en la historia del pueblo mexicano* (Mexico City: Instituto Mexicano de Doctrina Social Cristiana, 1990), 67; Oscar González et al., "Batallas en el reino de este mundo," *Nexos,* no. 78 (June 1984): 20.

108. Personal interview with Cardinal Juan José Posadas Ocampo, Archdiocese of Guadalajara, Mexican Episcopate, Mexico City, February 20, 1991.

109. Allan Metz, "Mexican Church-State Relations under President Carlos Salinas," 114.

110. Bernardo Barranco and Raquel Pastor, "La presencia de la iglesia católica en el proceso de sucesión presidencial 1988," 40.

111. Personal interview with Porfirio Muñoz Ledo.

112. Personal interview with Father Ernesto Domínguez Quiroga, Mexico City, June 13, 1989.

113. Rodrigo Vera, "En secreto, negociaciones entre funcionarios públicos y herarcas católicos," *Proceso,* August 7, 1989, 8.

114. George W. Grayson, *The Church in Contemporary Mexico,* 37.

Structure and Decision Making

International and National Actors

The Catholic Church can be likened to an international corporation consisting of local and regional franchises. These franchises play by the organization's general rules, but independent CEOs, bishops, make most decisions and implement policy choices. The Catholic Church's structure is complicated by the fact that it incorporates international and national actors at many levels, it draws on diverse forms of funding, it recruits rank-and-file clergy from different nationalities, and its clergy are divided into two categories.

The Church consists of a clear hierarchical structure, although one that exercises less influence than is commonly assumed. The Pope, who can be described as the cardinal of the Catholic Church, is essentially the bishop of the archdiocese of Rome. The difference between the Pope and any ordinary bishop is in the composition of his diocese and the process by which he is selected. The Pope's diocese consists of cardinals rather than rank-and-file clergy. Ironically, the archbishop of the Roman diocese, the Pope, is the only bishop in the Catholic Church elected by his peers, a collective body of cardinals.[1]

The cardinals, as members of the diocese of Rome, are incorporated into a College of Cardinals. They are divided into two groups: residential bishops, who, like Cardinal Ernesto Corripio, remain in the dioceses they govern (in Corripio's case, the archdiocese of Mexico in the capital), and nonresidential cardinals, who are expected to live in Rome, filling posts in the Roman Curia, the papal administration. Church leadership in Rome maintains itself by filling vacancies in the College of Cardinals, expanding its membership to meet the demands of a growing Church.[2] Cardinals obtain their prestige not because they exercise any more influence over their diocese, or that of the neighboring bishop, but because they are eligible to become the next Pope, and because collectively only they vote for a Pope.

The Roman Curia is essentially the Pope's personal administrative staff, a sort of combined executive office building and cabinet, where a cardinal heads each agency or department. Unlike a traditional, political bureaucracy, which receives its power through legislation, the Curia's only authority is drawn directly from the Pope, acting as his personal assistant.[3] It is important to understand the Curia's status because the Pope, as the ultimate bishop, can, if he wishes, interact with any individual clergy without passing through another intermediary.

Nevertheless, like any large organization, individuals given the authority to implement decisions often take on the organization's institutional interests, interpreting them through their own personal biases.[4] The Curia exercises power and influence because it conveys the Pope's values and goals on a more mundane and practical level, it provides the Pope with information and advice, and it influences his personnel decisions, specifically the selection of cardinals, who will select the Pope's successor from their peers, and bishops, the pool from which cardinals are drawn.

It is crucial to understand the Catholic Church's international structure because many domestic characteristics are linked to these institutional patterns. Edward Cleary argues that few analyses of the Latin American Church consider the transnational character of Roman Catholicism. He identifies three sets of formal links between the Latin American Church and the Vatican. First, as we suggested, individual bishops are interrelated to the Pope through the Curia in Rome; second, the Conference of Latin American Bishops (CELAM), a regional body of bishops, forges strong ties with Rome through the Pontifical Commission for Latin America; and third, papal nuncios represent the Vatican in each country through the Curia's secretariat of state.[5]

Intervention or Nonintervention: The Papal Nuncio

The influence of the Vatican delegate[6] in a specific country depends on many variables other than assigned mission. Among the variables that play a role are the size of the Catholic constituency, the location of the country, the longevity of the papal nuncio in his post, the attitude of the population toward Rome, and, of course, the individual nuncio's skill. In Mexico, Girolamo Prigione, the delegate during most of the period on which this book focuses and the only Vatican representative to attract the attention of scholars and journalists in many decades, operates from an advantageous position in several respects. First, despite historical tensions between the Catholic Church and the Mexican government, most Mexicans in the 1990s placed considerable confidence in the Vatican, more so than did Latin Americans, North Americans, or Spaniards.[7] Prigione, assigned to Mexico in 1976, served as a delegate three times longer than his predecessors, who, according to George Grayson, typically did not speak Spanish or interest themselves in Mexican Church affairs.[8]

The responsibility of the Vatican is to take a broad, universal view of religious matters since it represents the "whole" Church, not a geographic region. The Vatican's bias, therefore, is to achieve a certain level of unity among the bishops, the titular representatives of individual dioceses. The Vatican delegate is critical to accomplishing unification, becoming integral to episcopal decision making. In

Mexico, Prigione's arrival coincided with the emergence of a more integrated and active council of bishops.

Two countervailing forces came together in Mexico during the late 1970s and early 1980s. The first of these, a stronger Mexican Conference of Bishops (CEM), enhanced Prigione's influence. Indeed, its greater visibility may well have been a by-product of Prigione's influence. The second structural development at the national level relates to the growth of pastoral regions, cooperative arrangements among bishops organized geographically on the basis of shared diocesan social and economic variables. These regional divisions strengthened the hand of individual bishops, creating natural allies focusing on shared problems and perspectives and at the same time reinforcing differences the papal nuncio strived to overcome. As a secretary general of the Mexican Conference of Bishops argues, "He can't generalize about the situation in Mexico because of the variation in problems from one diocese to the next."[9] According to member bishops of the most progressive pastoral region, the Pacific South, Prigione formulated and applied a long-term strategy to weaken, divide, and eventually eliminate their orientation.[10] Even if that were not the case, Prigione, or any Vatican delegate, likely would view Mexican Catholicism differently from any individual bishop.[11]

In general terms, informal activities of nuncios often have exceeded their assigned responsibilities. In Latin America, the wider the range of responsibilities taken on by the nuncio, the greater the numbers of domestic clergy who resent their intrusions.[12] As Luigi Einaudi explains, nuncios have no independent authority over other bishops. He does suggest, however, that in smaller, isolated countries, depending on particular situations, a nuncio's role can be quite significant.[13]

When conflicts occur between the papal nuncio, a bishop representing the Pope, and diocesan bishops, who reside in their countries of origin, both can appeal to the Pope, their only legal superior. Theoretically, both share equal status and influence. In practice, since the papal nuncio and the diocesan bishops must send their appeals through the Curia in Rome, the papal nuncio often has an advantage because he has more contacts inside the Roman bureaucracy or friends at court.[14] This is not always the case because individual bishops may also have contacts within the Curia. A bishop's activity outside of Mexico as a member of regional or international Catholic committees or organizations or advanced education at the Gregorian University serves as an essential personal tie in international and national Church politics. These linkages give bishops greater or lesser access to cardinals in the Vatican administration and to the Pope.

Prigione has interjected his influence on Mexican religious matters to a degree unmatched in recent political history. He has operated at several levels, most importantly among bishops. Prigione's long-term task in Mexico was to reestablish church-state relations, specifically, diplomatic recognition of the Vatican, to revise the constitutional provisions restricting Church behavior, most importantly those involving legal recognition of the Church, and to moderate ideological differences within the hierarchy by influencing the choice of new bishops.

Prigione has a well-deserved reputation as a controversial figure in Mexican religious and political affairs. Mexican clergy view him from various perspectives, adding to his notorious stature. Bishops of all persuasions, including those who admire Prigione's accomplishments, readily admit that he has generated resentment among their peers. There are those who believe that in spite of criticism of his intervention in domestic church-state matters, he has the hierarchy's respect. A bishop in this category who is objective about Prigione's accomplishments believes that these tensions emanate

> from the emotional and ideological attitudes of the bishops. The nuncio of course is strongly on the right and is very much against liberation theology. Those bishops who might be described as a bit leftist are emotionally against him, even though some of the things he has accomplished are good. . . . His problem is that he is too strong; essentially, he has exceeded his authority.[15]

In the public eye, however, and among other bishops, Prigione's reputation is tarnished. The head of the CEM, Sergio Obeso Rivera, as early as de la Madrid's administration, had to declare to reporters that Prigione was not the leader of Mexican bishops who were not in the service of the Vatican, exclaiming that the "internal life of the country has nothing to do with him."[16] While Obeso Rivera's strong defense is understandable given Mexicans' misconceptions about Church structures, it ignores the nuncio's actual role, as distinct from his theoretical, de jure role. As one highly placed priest exclaimed with great emotion, "The bishops have complete autonomy in Mexico, *but they are not exercising it*. Instead, they are allowing Prigione to represent them" (emphasis added).[17] Indeed, Prigione increased contact between the episcopate leadership, specifically the president and the secretary general of the Mexican Conference of Bishops, and government officials.[18] Lower clergy, perhaps more sensitive to nationalism, are extremely critical of Prigione. Some bishops reportedly use in private a phrase circulating among laypersons during the 1990s, "PRIgione," to illustrate their perception of his government collaborationist strategy.[19]

The crucial question is, however, why are Mexican bishops passive and/or subordinate to the papal nuncio? Mexico is not an isolated, small Catholic country of the type described by Enaudi. Prigione's influence over the bishops has been explained as a consequence of the level of discipline within the Church hierarchy and their lack of self-respect. As a critic charges: "Look, why was Posadas [the murdered cardinal] at the Guadalajara airport to pick up Prigione—he was a cardinal, a prince of the Church. How is it possible that someone of Posadas's stature, of which only a few hundred exist in the world, would meet the Vatican delegate at the airport, an individual without comparable rank?"[20]

Even his severest critics credit Prigione with successfully changing the church-state relationship in 1992. From a government expert's point of view, Prigione succeeded because of his relationship with the Pope, established through excellent personal relations with the Vatican secretary of state, Cardinal Agustin Casarola.[21] A second explanation is that Prigione accomplished this change with the bishops' permission, although he has totally abused their relationship. He is characterized as politically able, operating in a highly centralized fashion similar to Salinas. He succeeded in his task because the bishops, as a consequence of internal divisions, likely would not have accomplished such changes alone.[22]

Prigione also generated heavy criticism from bishops for other reasons. One of his severest critics, Bishop Arturo Lona Reyes, accuses Prigione of "behaving like a diplomat, an ambassador preoccupied with church-state relations," who represents only the Pope instead of voicing the needs of the Mexican people, the task of a Christian and residential bishop.[23] In short, Prigione represents the international not the national Church's interests and the Pope's activist posture. The severest criticism of Prigione, however, is reserved for his interference in domestic, internal Church matters involving purely Mexican religious problems and church-government disputes. As one diplomat remarked to George Grayson: "Prigione breaks all the rules in intervening in domestic Mexican affairs. If Negroponte [U.S. ambassador to Mexico] were half as intrusive as Prigione he would be PGN'd [declared persona non grata]."[24] A concrete example explains the resentment of Mexican clergy, high and low:

> The bishop of Zamora, Michoacán, changed the parish priest of San José de Gracia as part of a normal reassignment, which the priest himself desired. But some very wealthy people in the Federal District who were from San José de Gracia wanted this priest to remain. They pressured Prigione to intervene, and he complied, writing a letter to the bishop without knowing anything about the situation. The presbyteriat responded, saying they appreciated his suggestions, but that this was a matter for the bishop, and he had made his decision.[25]

What is most significant is not that Prigione was unable to alter the outcome of the bishop's decision, but that he attempted to do so in the first place, interfering in a matter unquestionably the bishop's responsibility. The influence the papal nuncio has come to exercise places special pressures on Mexico's bishops. His interference also suggests Prigione's lack of sensitivity to his role and his relationship to the hierarchy. His influence finally backfired among the bishops, who in their October 1994 episcopal conference in Cuernavaca elected a moderate progressive, Sergio Obeso Rivera of Jalapa, as their head; provided clear support for Bishop Samuel Ruiz; and selected a new spokesperson, Abelardo Alvarado Alcántara, to replace Luis Reynoso, a close friend of Prigione's.[26]

Prigione's aggressive and undiplomatic posture also interjects him as a third party directly into church-state matters involving the episcopate and government officials. Mexican government officials enhanced Prigione's position because they misunderstood the Church's decision-making structure and, as is true of their own internal process, favor an approach focusing on a single, dominant figure. Ironically, an excellent illustration of this can be found in Chiapas at least a year and a half before the Zapatista Army of National Liberation initiated its attack in January 1994. As Ricardo Pascoe revealed: "Samuel Ruiz was telling me that they [the government] wanted to negotiate the problems with the Chiapas peasants through Prigione. The government wanted to use this approach because this is how they operate internally. They are thinking in terms of their particular political logic and structure."[27]

Prigione also seduced the government into purely internal Church matters, manipulating public officials to achieve his own personal ends. For example, Bishop Lona Reyes met with the secretary of government, Manuel Bartlett, and the subsecretary of government, Fernando Elías Calles, on at least four occasions during the de la Madrid administration, three times at Prigione's residence rather than at the government secretariat.[28]

The tensions between Prigione and the bishops collectively appear less intense than those between the Vatican delegate and Ernesto Corripio, the cardinal archbishop primate of Mexico. According to some knowledgeable observers, Corripio retained his influence with individual bishops, but Prigione maintained stronger links to the episcopate.[29] Corripio did not have the political clout Prigione could bring to bear in the Vatican. Every time they took opposite sides on an issue, Prigione was victorious. Prigione outmaneuvered the cardinal in his relations with government officials primarily because Corripio raised problems, whereas Prigione was at the forefront of resolving outstanding issues (from the government's point of view). The government likes Prigione because his strategy is to negotiate, their favored approach.[30]

Corripio also has faced some prominent political issues within his diocese, notably a conflict with Guillermo Schulenburg over the autonomy of the Basilica of Guadalupe. Schulenburg, director of the shrine since 1963, hoped to convert the Basilica into a separate diocese, which Corripio opposed for financial and political reasons. It is the primary religious attraction in the archdiocese and in all of Mexico. Prigione became deeply involved in the conflict before the episcopate rejected the proposal.[31]

The Vatican delegate not only has alienated clergy but also has raised politicians' ire inside and outside government. As a leading political figure concludes:

> The Vatican delegate's presence is deadly for the Church. It has caused many problems for the clergy, and he has played an extremely improper role. I think he has abused his functions as a Vatican delegate. He wants to succeed along his own lines here, and I have warned friends in the Vatican about his controversial role. In my opinion, he is the first delegate to assume this kind of role in Mexico, and it has been most unfortunate. I don't think we need someone from the outside to deal with church-state relations.[32]

A senator, who is also the president of the Federation of Masonic Lodges in the Valley of Mexico, asked that Prigione be declared persona non grata for his constant interference in Mexican internal affairs, as did the leadership of the Authentic Party of the Mexican Revolution. Prigione further alienated government officials when, immediately following the reestablishment of formal Vatican relations, he requested recognition as dean of the foreign diplomatic corps, counting his prior years served in Mexico as the delegate.[33]

National Structures: Linking the Dioceses to the Episcopate

In Roman Catholicism, the hierarchical structure of the Church is the bearer of the sacred power Jesus Christ committed to his apostles. What distinguishes Catholicism from most other Christian faiths is the nature of the hierarchical power derived from the apostles.[34] The importance of hierarchy in the Latin American Catholic Church is reinforced by historical experience and by church-state relationships in the colonial period. Church scholars have described the institution as undergoing few changes, characterizing it as "decentralized, extremely uncoordinated in its regional and diocesan activities, and structurally awkward. The Church emerged as a series of isolated ecclesiastical units, each one focused almost exclusively on its local, immediate situation."[35] Not only is this level of decentralization significant in understanding the decision-making process within the Catholic Church, but as Vallier hypothesized more than two decades ago, it may well explain the Church's traditional focus. He argued that the Church's structural decentralization, involving scattered, segmented organizations, created a dependency on traditional secular structures and behavior.[36] Furthermore, as secular states modernized, the Catholic structure made no explicit provision for the modern nation-state within the Church's organizational framework.[37] In the Mexican case, these structural inadequacies adversely affected parochial and diocesan institutional development.

Until 1962, most Latin American bishops experienced isolation from each other and from the larger church organization. Only rarely did bishops meet within their own countries and then only in special circumstances.[38] Beginning in the 1960s, regional structural developments reduced their isolation, and this change had consequences for dogma and religious rituals. Most North Americans are unaware of the Latin American Church's organizational weakness in contrast to the long-standing National Council of Bishops in the United States.[39] The increased collegiality of bishops was a significant by-product of Vatican II.[40] Instead of relying only on individual dioceses, which remain the basic hierarchical structure of the Church, a plethora of national and regional organizations emerged, drawing clergy from diverse geographic origins. This cross-fertilization increased communication within the Church.[41] Even in the late 1970s, the Mexican Catholic hierarchy remained reluctant to encourage national coordination and cooperation between hierarchy, clergy, and laypersons. The increase in extradiocesan episcopal conferences in Mexico and elsewhere influenced bishops' social and moral posture.[42] When spiritual values are expressed by individual bishops, or by the Pope as leader of the Catholic Church, it is difficult to identify them with national attitudes. When the bishops speak collectively, as in the CEM, it gives their attitudes greater national weight and legitimacy.[43]

Of the structural changes that have bridged Mexican diocesan boundaries, the establishment of pastoral regions is by far the most important in the eyes of bishops.[44] Pastoral regions have functioned in two structural capacities: to cooperate and speak with a single voice for the needs of a geographic area and to bring the whole episcopate together to speak with a unified national voice. Regional representatives, as detailed below, are incorporated into an executive council of the Mexican episcopate.

Structural relations with the state can also affect Church behavior. In Argentina, for example, as was true under the original Church-Crown patronate agreement, the state exercised some economic control, paying part of priests' salaries and educational expenses. These characteristics, among others, influenced the Argentina Church's behavior religiously and politically under military rule in the 1970s.[45] Mexico's Church, of course, is strongly separated from the state financially and bureaucratically, establishing its domestic autonomy. It is confronted by one small consequence of recent Mexican religious history: the existence of the Mexican Apostolic Catholic Church, a creature of President Plutarco Elías Calles's radical anticlerical policies. Calles attempted to create a schismatic Church, hoping to split the Mexican Catholic Church and secularize its control. A single bishop, with half a dozen or so parishes, still heads such a church in the archdiocese of Mexico.[46]

By 1990, Mexico's formal organizational structure included 15 archdioceses (incorporating 13 auxiliary bishops), 55 dioceses (with 3 assistant bishops), and 7 special territories. The Mexican Council of Bishops (episcopate) counted 92 bishops, 16 bishops emeriti, and the Vatican delegate.[47] Mexico, with one of the largest Catholic populations, has a small number of bishops per capita. In 1962, Mexico boasted 65 bishops for a population of 33 million, yet Argentina had 66 bishops for only 23 million people, Brazil had 204 bishops for 61 million people, and Colombia had 52 bishops for only 14 million people.[48] As Bishop Sergio Méndez Arceo argued, the strength of the Brazilian Church resides in the number and diversity of its dioceses. He believed Mexico required more dioceses, at least 80 additional bishops, to provide better representation of different viewpoints within the episcopate.[49] A student of the Chilean episcopate also has argued that its small size and frequent meetings gave it a progressive character and image distinguishing it from other Latin American clerical hierarchies.[50] Although the number of parishes doubled between World War II and the mid-1970s and Mexico added more dioceses from 1957 to 1975 than all of the dioceses established in the previous 450 years (34), Mexico's population nearly doubled every two decades during the same period.[51] During the 1960s and 1970s, Mexico's ordination of new priests was sufficient to adequately maintain a constant supply of clergy. The most important dioceses, based on the number of ordinations, were Guadalajara, Morelia, México, Puebla, and Zamora.[52]

In the 1990s, the secretariat of government reported 34,131 churches scattered through 6,070 parishes.[53] The number of churches and parishes continues to grow, but the number of priests, while not declining in absolute numbers, is declining in relation to the population. From 1980 to 1990, the number of priests grew from 10,195 to 10,330, only 1.3 percent, while the population increased nearly 18 percent.[54] In Latin America, there are approximately two priests for every 10,000 Catholics. In the United States, however, there are five times as many priests per capita, or 10 per 10,000 Catholics.[55] Of the slightly more than 10,000 priests in Mexico, 72 percent are diocesan versus 28 percent religious.[56] There are also 22 priests practicing in Mexico without official Church recognition.[57] The consequence of these low ratios of dioceses and priests to the population of faithful is that the Church is not ministering effectively to its flock, especially in rural areas, parishioners share a less positive view of their bishops and priests, and priests protest their bishops' actions more frequently.[58]

The relatively small size of the Mexican clergy and hierarchy may be another element contributing to the perception of the Church as a homogeneous institution. Mexican bishops differ not so much on their goals but on how they should be achieved. This image of the Church as a homogeneous body has plagued it throughout its governmental relationship. It has been suggested, for example, that if Mexico's presidents had understood in the 1920s that episcopal leadership did not necessarily represent the Church as an institution, the Cristiada could have been avoided altogether.[59]

The single most important institution within the Mexican Catholic hierarchy is the Conference of Mexican Bishops (CEM). The CEM was established in 1935, taking on its present name in 1953. Its goals are to study and to resolve pastoral issues, to promote the best means for solving Mexican social and economic problems, and to identify the most effective activities of clergy, religious, and laypersons. The ultimate authority of this organization is the plenary assembly, which normally meets twice a year.[60] Plenary sessions were not held consistently until 1966. Mexico's CEM follows a pattern occurring elsewhere in the Catholic world. The Second Vatican Council encouraged national episcopal conferences and planning to achieve greater communication among bishops.[61]

Many observers believe that, since the late 1960s, episcopal conferences have exercised a significant influence on the Church's development in Mexico. Undoubtedly this is the case. Nevertheless, CEM policy statements, particularly those marking a strong departure from past experiences, rarely are put into practice.[62] In Mexico and elsewhere in the region, the majority of bishops are not intellectually oriented and do not make an active effort to apply the policy statements, effectively blocking institutional and theological renewal at the diocesan level.[63]

The CEM consists of five institutions: the presidential council, the permanent episcopal council, the general secretariat, the pastoral regions, and the episcopal committees. The top executive body of the CEM is a presidential council of six bishops elected by the full assembly. Although the statutes require only that the president be a bishop, in fact only archbishops have served. Informal requirements of the post, which can be ascertained from those who have filled the presidency, include a reputation as an ideological moderate.[64] Recent presidents were Archbishop Adolfo Suárez Rivera of Monterrey, Nuevo León, 1989–1994; Archbishop Sergio Obeso Rivera of Jalapa, Veracruz, 1983–1988 and 1994–1997; Cardinal Ernesto Corripio Ahumada of Mexico, 1968–1973 and 1979–1982; and Cardinal José Salazar López of Guadalajara, 1973–1979.[65]

The permanent council, lower in rank than its presidential counterpart, subsumes the presidential council among a larger body of 15 representatives from Mexico's pastoral regions. This council meets at least four times yearly. It is responsible for ensuring the implementation and continuity of CEM objectives. It is far more influential than the smaller presidential body, effectively functioning as an executive council of the large plenary assembly, often called on to make decisions in crisis situations.[66]

Long-term policy making, however, is the responsibility of the plenary assembly, which meets twice a year. Although all bishops may participate in the assembly, only active bishops can vote. The assembly considers various issues important to the Church and often adopts statements from the appropriate committee as general policy.[67] Sometimes the atmosphere of these meetings can be tense. As one participant noted in his memoirs, although assembly sessions are not likely to change participants' minds, they do shed more light on the subject at hand.[68]

The assembly also plays a decisive role in selecting its leadership and establishing the tone of the episcopate. The CEM secretary general obtains potential nominees from the representatives of the pastoral regions, passing on recommendations with an assessment of each nominee's support to the permanent council, which then presents its slate of nominees to the full assembly.[69]

The CEM assembly, presidency, councils, and committees have no formal authority within the Mexican Catholic Church. Once again, it is essential to stress each individual bishop's autonomy. Nevertheless, scholars assert correctly that even without formal authority, this body and its president have influenced the global direction of the Mexican Church, and certain policy patterns are associated with individual CEM presidents.[70] Archbishop Manuel Pérez Gil, secretary general of the CEM immediately prior to constitutional changes in church-state relations, assessed its influence:

> The CEM as a conference has absolutely no influence. Nevertheless, when all of the bishops come together each year, it provides a forum for very frank communication on the problems all of us are facing, including the pastoral regions. . . . In the CEM there exists a strong sense of unity, which I witnessed as secretary general of this organization from 1988 to 1991. I believe there exists a strong continuity in values within the CEM and a strong sense of unity among the bishops despite the differences that appear in the press and elsewhere.[71]

Bishops who are identified as mavericks within the Church agree that a high level of respect for their differing postures exists within the CEM, and that they in turn give it equal respect.[72]

There are 19 episcopal committees, divided into four categories: religious doctrine, evangelical agents, pastoral issues, and special services. According to Claude Pomerlau, the most controversial of these committees are those on doctrine and faith, social ministry, Indians, evangelization, and catechesis.[73] Each committee is presided over by a bishop and several of his colleagues' assistants, drawing on a staff of knowledgeable clergy and experts. Religious scholars often influence episcopal policy through contributions to committee reports and documents.[74] Members of these committees and all other councils and committees are elected by their peers for three-year terms.

In the early history of the CEM, two original episcopal agencies, the Social Secretariat and the National Center for Social Communication, developed into influential voices favoring progressive social change. The hierarchy, as late as 1968, perceived the first of these, which published numerous articles, books, and pamphlets dealing with Mexican society, as the intellectual center of the Church on social questions. For a brief period, it became linked to the CEM Commission on Social Pastorals, headed by Adalberto Almeida Merino, influencing policy statements on social development. The Social Secretariat's increasingly radical posture, including its declaration on July 31, 1970, that bishops were not authentic representatives of the faithful because they were selected by Rome, ended its official status.[75] The National Center for Social Communication, originally founded to provide religious news, also charted an autonomous direction. In 1968, after its staff supported students and political prisoners from the student movement, the hierarchy withdrew its recognition. Some bishops, including the then president of the Lay Apostate Committee, labeled the staff Marxist infiltrators.[76]

The CEM's evolution has consequences for the role of the Vatican delegate in Church matters and for the relationship between the Church and political leadership. Mexico's top public figures, for their part, believe a strong tension exists between the bishops and the Vatican delegate. As President Miguel de la Madrid observes, "The bishops want to keep the authority of the Catholic Church in the hands of Mexicans, and they don't like the way the Vatican Delegate is involving himself in various Church matters. . . . Although most bishops respect him, they have different attitudes about the role he should play."[77]

Mexican bishops see the Vatican delegate's primary responsibility as maintaining external relations between Rome and the state. They agree with President de la Madrid's assessment that Prigione is too involved in internal Church matters. It is apparent that increasing tensions between the CEM and the Vatican delegate have led to bishops' increasing efforts to strengthen their position, to guarantee their autonomy, and to establish and maintain constant, direct communications with Rome, bypassing Prigione.[78] Tensions between the Vatican delegate and the CEM also have complicated relations with the government, which, similar to the Vatican delegate himself, prefers dealing with a centralized hierarchy, not a cluster of autonomous bishops. The state, however, recognized the advantage of such tensions in an internal document, noting that it could deal with both parties, playing them off against one another.[79]

Prigione's high profile and involvement in both internal and external affairs add to the public's ignorance of Church structures, requiring the Vatican delegate's vigorous public explanation and defense of his role in establishing new relations with Mexico. Prigione was particularly annoyed with Bishop Genaro Alamilla, often an episcopate spokesperson to the media. As an exasperated Prigione explained to the press:

> I repeat that the negotiation is in charge of the apostolic delegate. Each bishop speaks for his diocese. The Episcopate speaks through the voice of its president at the bishops' request. Monsignor Genaro Alamilla is not the voice of the episcopate. He speaks for himself. The official channel of the Vatican is the apostolic delegate. The Conference of Mexican Bishops consists of equals. The president, and the only person authorized to express the bishops' judgment, is the archbishop of Monterrey, Adolfo Suárez Rivera.[80]

On policy issues involving the episcopate, Prigione demonstrated his success in obtaining the CEM's support for his negotiating position in reestablishing relations between the Vatican and the government. Most bishops prior to 1992 did not consider formal relations a significant issue and, in fact, wanted to separate it from other more pressing domestic issues involving the status of clergy and the Church in Mexico.[81] Nevertheless, with the support of Mexican allies in the episcopate, Prigione succeeded in persuading the majority of bishops by 1990 to demand constitutional changes as the price of renewed diplomatic relations.[82] On other issues, essentially internal Mexican religious matters, Prigione has found himself on the losing end. For example, he associated himself with Abbot Schulenburg's request to separate the Basilica of Guadalupe from the Mexico archdiocese. Cardinal Corripio, leading the opposition to this position, succeeded in defeating it overwhelmingly in an episcopal vote.[83]

Tensions between the Vatican delegate and the Mexican episcopate continued after the reestablishment of church-state relations in 1992. Prigione continued his involvement in controversial domestic matters, including an attempt to remove the outspoken bishop of San Cristóbal de las Casas, Samuel Ruiz, who countered the delegate's machinations with the Vatican and governmental authorities by becoming, in early 1994, the mediator between Chiapan rebels and the government.[84] Several prominent clergy, including Antonio Roqueñi, made public their requests to Prigione to resign his post and leave Mexico.[85] At least two cases exist of the Mexican episcopate desiring to remove a Vatican delegate. If they wish to implement such a change, they must make a formal request to Rome. In both previous situations, the episcopate met with success. Although many clergy believe Prigione's fortunes with the Vatican have declined, they consider such a request unlikely given the number of bishops who remain personally loyal.[86]

The final structural variable crossing diocesan boundaries in Catholic life, operating on both national and international levels, is the presence of religious orders. Throughout Latin America, members of male and female religious orders have contributed significantly, and in some policy arenas overwhelmingly, to Catholicism. Their involvement in Catholic institutional structures has, at first glance, an immediate potential for generating dissent among clerical ranks. Given their own institutional prerogatives and their linkages to the Pope, religious orders complicate institutional and hierarchical arrangements in the national Church, expanding domestic and international influences. Furthermore, some analysts have suggested that, at least in the case of Mexico, a high level of respect exists for religious orders because many Mexicans readily identify with their concrete achievements, especially in parochial education.[87]

Religious-order priests provided Catholicism's foundation in Latin America during the conquest and colonization. But the explanation for a resurgence of their influence in the late 20th century stems from Pope John XXIII's request in the early 1960s that religious orders send 10 percent of their members to Latin America. Although they never met this quota, thousands of religious priests and sisters left Europe and the United States to work there.[88] Mexico remains apart from the rest of Latin America, as with so many other religious characteristics, in its lower percentages of religious-order priests. During the Revolution, orders accounted for 16 percent of the priests in Mexico, and nearly double that (28 percent) in Latin America. Yet by World War II, Mexico's percentage of religious priests remained essentially static (17 percent), whereas Latin America's increased rapidly to nearly half of all priests (47 percent). By the 1960s, Mexico's figures had risen to 20 percent, the lowest percentage of religious-order priests in Latin America. (Colombia was the next lowest with 40 percent.) The average throughout Latin America was 51 percent, and excluding Mexico, the figures were even higher.[89]

By the mid-1980s, religious-order priests accounted for approximately 29 percent of all Mexican clergy. Although they belonged to 44 different orders, the most important were Jesuits, 383; Misioneros del Espíritú Santo, 227; Franciscans (Saint Francis), 163; Franciscans (Saint Evangeline), 134; Franciscans (Saint Paul), 124; and Agustinians (Saint Nicholas), 117. Religious-order priests were most strongly represented in the dioceses of Mexico (66 percent), Tuxtepec (57 percent), San Cristóbal de las Casas, Chiapas (52 percent), and Netzahualcóyotl, México (51 percent).[90] Most were involved in teaching and parish activities.[91] Enrique Luengo reports that the number of religious priests is on the rise in the 1990s, and the number of diocesan priests is declining.[92] The orders' composition also has changed in the last three decades, from higher levels of foreign priests (Spanish and American) to mostly Mexican-born.[93] According to some bishops, one explanation for their lack of influence in Mexico is the fact that foreigners dominate their ranks.[94]

Structural differences between the organization of religious orders and diocesan clergy have important consequences for their relations to each other and outside groups. Religious-order priests differ from diocesan priests in that they tend to live in communities directed by a residential superior. In reality, however, similar to most diocesan priests, many Mexicans live with their families or in the local parish, not with their peers.[95] The head of the religious order, a superior general, typically resides in Rome. Ultimately, each member of a religious order is responsible to the Pope. However, in their day-to-day pastoral work, religious priests are responsible to their local bishops. In other areas, however, they can be more independent, although this varies from one order and location to the next. This higher level of autonomy, in general, grants them greater opportunities to pursue strategies different from those of the diocesan bishop.[96] For example, members of the Jesuit order agree that the initiative for most of their activities in any particular diocese derives from their religious community, not from the bishop.[97] Some analysts also have speculated that bishops from religious orders may have greater authority over members of their own order than would a secular bishop.[98]

Structurally, orders differ from diocesan priests' institutions in two other ways. The basic institutional structure for a diocesan priest, detailed in the following chapter, is the diocese. But religious-order priests and brothers belong to international or regional communities extending well beyond local boundaries. This has led scholars to argue that the diocesan Church's strongest bond is among the local parish, patron saints, and the faithful, whereas religious orders, given their transnational communities, pose greater threats to secular nationalism.[99] The other distinction is largely financial. Religious orders are typically better funded, have autonomous sources of income, and, most important, take care of their members when they are ill or incapacitated.

Sharp divisions between religious and secular Catholic priests existed historically, especially in the colonial era. In recent decades, the potential for such conflicts stems from several conditions. Religious-order members often initiate new parochial schools, especially in urban centers, after which they turn over functioning institutions to their secular counterparts. This pattern, however, unlike a similar colonial mission strategy, has not generated distrust or resentment.[100] More important, distrust may have more to do with differing social origins. As one priest argues, religious orders, because of their vows and, often, an emphasis on intellectual achievements, tend to be more selective than diocesan institutions. As a consequence, a higher percentage of their members come from middle- and occasionally upper-middle-class backgrounds and from larger communities. Diocesan priests, who typically come from smaller provincial communities and from lower-middle-class origins, reflect somewhat different values and orientations.[101] These social differences often generate cultural barriers, social prejudices, and jealousies.[102] Finally, the communities' financial condition and religious-order members' greater economic autonomy have spawned some resentment on the part of diocesan priests.[103]

Older bishops and priests believe tensions between the two groups have existed in the past but have improved markedly. Mexican clergy attribute their unity to several peculiarly Mexican circumstances. In the first place, the repression of the Church in the 1920s and 1930s drew Mexican clergy closer together, regardless of their institutional status. Second, the smaller representation of foreigners among religious orders creates a pool of clergy who share greater similarities than is the case elsewhere in the region. The archbishop of Yucatán, for example, suggests this is true in his diocese, despite the presence of progressive Maryknoll priests and nuns, many from the United States.[104] Priests and religious-order members from all ideological persuasions, as well as bishops and the Vatican delegate, find the relationship between the two groups harmonious. A recent study, based on a series of interviews with Yucatán and Chiapas priests, reached the same conclusion.[105]

The religious orders' hierarchy, vaguely analogous to the CEM, has witnessed conflicts on important policy issues. Religious orders are represented by a governing board of the National Conference of Religious Institutes of Mexico (CIRM). The CIRM disagreed with the CEM recently over the issue of reestablishing church-state relations. In a letter to the CEM, the CIRM's governing board criticized its efforts to alter these relations, arguing that the Church was becoming a legitimizing agent for the state, a view expressed by numerous diocesan clergy, and that the CEM failed to promote any discussion of its strategy among the laity and the rank-and-file clergy.[106]

Extranational Influences, Finances, and Personnel

An additional structural factor that influences the Catholic Church and its relationship to the state is its financial autonomy. The economic development of a society generally affects the relationship between important groups and the state. This has been particularly true, for example, of intellectuals and their relationship to the government in Third World cultures, including Latin American and Mexico.[107] As suggested above, some Latin American Catholic churches retain a financial linkage to the state, especially in the realm of religiously controlled education. Insufficient attention has been paid in the literature to Church sources of funding. This linkage, in terms of general Church policies, specifically educational programs, generates obstacles to the Church's implementation of goals independent of the state.[108]

Because of Mexico's overall level of economic development and the size of its population living in poverty, the Church is confronted with far more problems and tasks than it has resources to handle. The lack of economic development also affects parishioners' ties to their religion. Mexicans who migrate to the United States, even temporarily, are more easily attracted to Protestant sects. This has occurred in Zacatecas.[109] If the hierarchy understands this linkage between economic development, migration, and Protestantism, then it would be even more disposed to cooperate with the government in achieving economic growth.

Within the Church itself, the most significant reflection of its difficult economic situation is the financial insecurity of its priests and parishes. Most of Mexico's parishes have depended on individual benefactors to supplement internal Church resources. Church reliance on these individual benefactors, however, shares the same risks as Church dependence on the state. When many parishes attempted to introduce some of the more progressive features of Vatican II in the late 1960s and early 1970s, their benefactors abandoned them.[110]

Surprisingly, many of Mexico's priests are themselves in a precarious financial situation. When a priest from a poor home is ordained and receives a parish, he often will take his parents or other members of his family along. For example, no priest in the archdiocese of Mexico has a set salary; they have to make it on their own. Their incomes range from substantial to barely enough to survive, encouraging some priests to run their parishes like businesses, charging fees for private services.[111] Naturally, high fees produce resentment from their constituents. Other priests who are more imaginative attempt to find additional sources of income for their parishes. Most priests, however, lack sufficient funds to carry out their parishes' required activities. Jacques Chaveriat, a French-born priest who operates a center in Mexico City helping priests work with marginal people, provides financial assistance to approximately 15 percent of the dioceses. This assistance includes providing care for priests who become ill or physically incapacitated. A troubling consequence of impoverished priests is their constant fixation on finances to the detriment of other important concerns. As Chaveriat also confirms, many priests, most of whom are from lower-middle-class backgrounds, face a rough retirement since neither their families nor the Church provides for them.[112]

According to Nicéforo Guerrero, who was responsible for overseeing Church financial matters under government supervision, Catholic revenues come from two primary sources. The first is money collected from the parish. For example, in the case of the Mexico archdiocese, the main source of income is the tithe. Parishes also receive many donations from the business community, and these can be substantial. The other source of income is from the hierarchy itself, which is well compensated.[113] Interestingly, the Vatican considers the Mexican Church to be sufficiently self-supporting to send funds to Rome.[114] This has not always been the case. Pope Paul VI explained to Eduardo Bustamante, a former secretary of government properties, that the true enemy of Mexico's Catholic Church was the economy. He believed that the Church was unable to carry out its mission because it lacked appropriate resources, giving examples of building projects the Church could not afford that would provide for Mexican spiritual and physical needs. He even admitted to Bustamante that the government had been very helpful in maintaining Church buildings, doing a better job in saving these structures from disrepair than the Church could do with its inadequate financial resources.[115] The Salinas administration carried on this tradition, introducing a pilot program in Veracruz to remodel and construct churches and housing for priests with Solidarity (Pronasol) funds.[116] In reality, few dioceses or shrines provide any funds to the Vatican, including the Basilica of Guadalupe.[117]

The Mexican Catholic Church, given its historical relationship, retains few financial linkages to the state. The state has subsidized the Church by not charging property taxes, theoretically difficult prior to 1992 since the Church had no legal status and could not own real estate. Because the Church does not receive direct government subsidies and because private donations, however generous, are inadequate, the hierarchy has sought out funds from abroad.

In numerous Latin American countries, external linkages have made the Catholic Church financially dependent on major industrialized countries, whose governments generally have sought to maintain the status quo.[118] Typically, however, churches receive assistance from private foundations whose interests (to promote change) rarely correspond with those of their governments. Mexico's Church, compared to the rest of Latin America, receives relatively little outside funding. According to the episcopate, although Mexico is one of the two largest Catholic countries in Latin America, it ranked lowest in the amount of funds received from outside sources. Ricardo Cuellar Romo, secretary of the episcopate, explains why:

> One of the reasons why we have received so little help is that we haven't asked for much, and this stems from the fact they we have a great deal of pride in wanting to use our resources, rather than depending on international organizations. We also are very discreet in Mexico. For example, clergy from other countries have commented on the modesty of the episcopal building. We don't believe in using resources that way. When we ask for help from international organizations, we always provide a certain percentage for the project so that we do not become totally dependent.[119]

The Catholic Church's modest, physical furnishings are a product not only of its limited financial resources but also of its historical relationship with the government since the 1920s, when discreetness became tantamount to survival. More important, Mexican bishops are very nationalistic, and their nationalism is reflected in their external relations, especially toward the United States, in much the same way that politicians express their nationalism. The Mexican government never has taken advantage of U.S. economic or military foreign aid programs at levels found elsewhere in Latin America.

In spite of its nationalistic sentiments, the Church has borrowed funds from numerous private institutions.[120] Germany is the most important source of Catholic assistance, followed by the Netherlands, Canada, France, and the United States. According to one religious scholar, even Mexico's individual dioceses have requested aid from abroad.[121] Funding comes primarily from two types of institutions: secular (such as the Ford Foundation) and Catholic (associated with foreign episcopates).[122] Receiving outside funds can have a determinative influence on the Church's autonomy and policy direction only if the lender restricts their use or if the Church can obtain funds for a specific use only from external sources. In other words, if churches cannot acquire resources to pursue radical departures from traditional policies, they are not likely to accomplish such changes. It is not accidental that Brazil, which probably receives the highest level of outside funds, relying heavily on foreign priests, pioneered the ecclesiastical base community movement.

Bishops, regardless of ideological posture, agree that monies that come to them through international channels are provided without any strings attached. Bishops and priests with firsthand knowledge of such gifts report no cases in which funds from Europe, Canada, or the United States have restrictions. For example, the World Council of Churches never placed any restrictions on its gifts.[123] Mexico's Vatican delegate also confirms this assessment.[124] Bishops from diverse ideological postures within the Mexican episcopate also are able to obtain foreign monies.[125]

Mexican nationalism and a bishop's ideological posture, however, can have potential or real consequences for diocesan policies. Sergio Méndez Arceo, described earlier as a controversial pioneer in introducing social tenets of Mexican liberation theology, made an extraordinary confession: "I decided not to take any outside funds because I feared that the government would accuse me of receiving help from abroad, putting me in an awkward situation because of my support for progressive activities. This may not have been the best decision in the long run, but I couldn't take the risk because of the liberal programs I had initiated."[126] Although bishops never felt any fear of being manipulated by foreign sources, some bishops, given special circumstances, believed the government might well use nationalistic rhetoric against them.

International influences potentially affect the Catholic Church as a national actor in three ways. First, its structural, institutional links are embedded into a larger, international organization in Rome. Second, it also retains financial linkages to external sources, Catholic and non-Catholic alike. Third, national Catholic churches are linked as religious allies on spiritual and religious issues to other countries and their dioceses. They also share ties through foreign nationals who serve, often in lifelong capacities, the needs of parishioners in Mexico. These multiple linkages help explain why analysts in the early 1970s foresaw the Church playing a role in expanding the dialogue in general United States–Latin American relations.[127]

Given Mexico's proximity to the United States and the presence of a powerful Catholic hierarchy in the United States, a special relationship might be expected to evolve between the two hierarchies. Of the 49 million Catholics in the United States, 27 percent are Hispanics, and one-fifth of those are Mexican in origin. In the mid-1980s, the United States counted 17 Hispanic bishops among its 350-member episcopate.[128] The North American hierarchy evidences a long historical interest in the fate of Mexico's Catholics. At the high point of Church repression during the Cristiada, it issued over one million copies of a "Pastoral Letter of the Catholic Episcopate of the United States on the Religious Situation in Mexico," defending Mexico's Church.[129] In fact, historians believe that if the American Catholic community had not denounced Mexico's religious policies, especially through the National Catholic Welfare Conference, it is unlikely that the U.S.

State Department would have pressured Mexico's government to solve its differences with the Church.[130] On the other hand, the United States also served as a major source of anti-Catholic sentiment in Mexico, providing a strong Masonic influence contributing strongly to Liberal positions on church and state in the 19th century.[131]

In a more recent historical context, some analysts have suggested the potential for an alliance among progressive Latin American and U.S. bishops, both of whom criticized North American capitalism's negative consequences.[132] Although such a union is not likely in the Mexican case, it is worth emphasizing that the Mexican hierarchy, when it is most unified, is least likely to be influenced by or desire an alliance with external allies.

Some observers, including prominent Mexican politicians, believe the linkage between the United States and the Catholic Church goes well beyond Catholic laypersons in one country being concerned about the religious freedom of fellow laity south of the border. President José López Portillo, who views the Church from a politician's traditional, Liberal posture, offers such an interpretation:

The Catholic Church, by definition, is imbued with the responsibility for universal matters. It has always had to make concessions to nationalism. . . . I think the Catholic Church now wants to reestablish some of its previous power. I have this theory that there is a coincidence of North American and Church interests on an international level, and that the two have an important influence. I believe the North American influence has a lot in common with the Catholic Church's religious mobilization.[133]

The U.S. Catholic hierarchy long has maintained personal ties with Mexican counterparts, especially along the border. For example, the archbishop of San Antonio attended Archbishop Suárez Rivera's consecration ceremonies in Monterrey in 1984.[134] More important, however, the two hierarchies have cooperated on policy issues of mutual interest. For example, as early as 1974, bishops from both countries met in El Paso, Texas, to determine policies to assist Mexican immigrants to the United States.[135] As their shared interests intensified, so have pressures for more formal collaboration between the two episcopates. Since 1982, a Mexican/United States Border Bishops Commission has met ad hoc, desiring to establish a permanent, working commission.[136] Cooperation extends to lower levels among numerous charitable programs and in all geographic dioceses. Mérida, Yucatán, for example, has an exchange program with the diocese of Erie, Michigan, which has sent medical teams and other volunteers to provide health care and libraries in rural parishes.[137]

The potential linkages between the Mexican and U.S. Catholic episcopates have drawn the Mexican hierarchy into two important policy arenas: foreign debt and the North American Free Trade Agreement. Interestingly, in an unusual twist to its relationship with the state, the Catholic hierarchy involved itself in the debt issue at the request of the Mexican government. Mexican officials hoped to capitalize on their strongly shared sense of nationalism. According to *Proceso,* the Church became involved in this critical foreign policy issue in the fall of 1988.[138] In the spring of 1989, Pedro Aspe Armella, Mexico's treasury secretary, sent his assistant secretary to ask the Church's help in tempering U.S. demands on debt repayment. Later that summer, U.S. and Mexican bishops collaborated on a joint letter to President George Bush, informing the president that "as pastors we are deeply anguished by the devastating effects of the debt on real people, especially the world's poor, who had no voice in creating the debt and received minimal benefit from it. . . . Still, Mexico . . . has not been able to reduce its debt; on the contrary, the debt has grown. In addition the very effort is strangling the economy."[139] Among those who signed the letter were the president of the National Conference of Catholic Bishops, North American bishops from Boston, San Antonio, Columbus, and Salt Lake City; Mexico's president of the CEM, Archbishop Suárez Rivera; and Cardinal Corripio. The bishops met again in the fall of 1990 and early in 1991 in the United States.[140] The United States National Conference of Catholic Bishops made it clear in its fall 1989 statement that it believed the debt threatened democratic development, that Mexico's repayment entailed great social costs, and that political considerations should be paramount in deciding the debtor nation's ability to pay.[141] The Catholic hierarchies of both countries, through similar positions and collaborative efforts, aided Mexican government efforts to renegotiate the terms of the debt. In return, the government rewarded the Church financially.[142]

Contrary to its efforts to help the government when Church and government interests in helping ordinary Mexicans coincided, the Church pursued an entirely different tack on a free trade agreement. The United States Catholic Conference met on May 9, 1991, to discuss the NAFTA initiative, inviting seven bishops from each country. The focus of the meeting, addressed by Carla Hills, chief U.S. negotiator, was its probable effects on the poor. The CEM executive council and several North American bishops met again the following week in Mexico City. After discussion, the CEM responded to specific questions from Archbishop Daniel Pilarczyk, president of the United States Catholic Conference. In a letter to the archbishop dated May 18, 1991, the CEM urged him to keep in mind the human consequences of such an agreement. The letter writers also conceded to the archbishop that they believed such an agreement, in the long run, might contribute positively to democratic participation.[143] Other bishops, identified with the progressive wing of the Church, voiced even stronger social concerns about NAFTA and the "pernicious effect it may have on the inner relationship and cohesion of civil society and more concretely, on the living and working conditions of the impoverished majorities who are excluded from the new modernizing market."[144] Both the episcopate's president and the social pastoral committee expressed similar public reservations in 1992 and 1993, squarely criticizing the impending agreement.

The presence of foreign clergy also exposes Mexico's Church to international influences. Throughout Latin America, foreign-born priests have exercised a formative influence on pastoral issues, on the clergy's progressive orientation, and on Church activism, especially in the 1970s and 1980s. Some scholars have argued that differences also exist among foreign clergy, describing American priests as "doers" who work in rural and slum areas and Europeans as having a stronger intellectual bent, making them more likely to be involved in Church politics.[145]

The potential that foreign sources will affect the Catholic Church's behavior and structure occurs at two levels. Just as selected priests and future bishops described the impact of experiences abroad, typically at the Gregorian University, as bringing them in contact with priests from other countries as well as with a European milieu, an important minority of Mexican priests volunteer for foreign missions. In 1980, 7 percent, or approximately 700 priests, were serving abroad.[146] Among bishops, if we discount their educational experiences, only a tiny percentage obtained direct experience in Latin America, usually serving with regional organizations, not as parish missionaries. A second form of contact between foreign and domestic priests occurs through the Mexican seminary system. According to Nicéforo Guerrero, who at one time was responsible for approving immigration papers of foreign priests, their numbers are small in a given year, but over longer periods their numbers are substantial. Many Latin American priests come to Mexico to obtain their seminary education.[147] Thus, they come in contact with other seminary students rather than directly affecting fellow priests. Many other priests come to teach in the seminary and enter Mexico legally. Most of these teachers are French in origin.

Foreign priests residing in Mexican dioceses and among religious orders have the greatest potential for influencing the clergy. Mexico has been unique among Latin American countries for its small percentage of foreign-born priests. In fact, in the early 1970s it had the highest percentage of native-born priests in Latin America, and all bishops but one were born in Mexico.[148] In 1963, 371 Spanish, 56 American, and 33 European priests resided in Mexico. In 1989, requests from priests for permission to enter Mexico came primarily from Spain, Italy, Colombia, and the United States.[149] Of the 1,400 clergy in the Mexico Archdiocese in 1976, 75–80 were foreign missionaries. In the last three decades, the percentage of Mexican priests has remained relatively constant, from 84 percent in 1963 (of the foreigners, 53 percent were Spanish, 22 percent were Italian, 17 percent were American or Latin American, and 9 percent were European) to 93 percent of diocesan priests in 1989.[150] Regular orders in Mexico today, as is true elsewhere in Latin America, have higher percentages of foreign-born priests, but in 1971 they were only 13 percent, fewer than diocesan priests. The uniqueness of the Mexican situation is explained by the fact that constitutionally priests must be Mexican by birth. The regulatory laws prescribe that the secretariat of government fix the number of foreign priests.[151] Although the constitution had been violated prior to 1992, as was true of most other religiously related provisions, it encouraged a much stronger reliance on organic clergy.

Mexico fell behind in its per capita priest-to-population ratio as a consequence of its heavier reliance on native-born priests. On the other hand, this self-sufficiency favored an emphasis on the priesthood as a vocation to a degree not found elsewhere in Latin America.[152] The smaller numbers of foreign-born priests among Mexican clergy also make the Church less susceptible to threats against deporting priests who fall afoul of civil authorities, a situation faced by Bishop Samuel Ruiz, whose diocese and state have high levels of regular order and foreign priests and nuns.[153]

The most important consequence of foreign-born priests within the clergy is a potential to divide Church ranks, a weakness that could be exploited by both the institution and the state. Mexico has a long history, extending back to the colonial period, of conflicts between Spanish and native-born Mexicans in all sectors of society, including the clergy and political leadership. Favoritism shown to peninsular-born Spaniards created serious resentment among native-born Mexicans of Spanish and mestizo origins. Indeed, it was a major source of disgruntlement leading to New Spain's independence.

Interestingly, a legacy of these conflicts remained in Mexico well into the 20th century, at least until the early 1970s. A public figure, an adviser to President Cárdenas, recalls a revealing anecdote from the late 1930s:

> One day, many years ago, General Cárdenas asked me to read a letter he had received from a priest. The priest explained that he understood that Cárdenas was not a believer nor a practicing Catholic, but that he was a good Mexican and a nationalist. He felt that Cárdenas would be interested in protecting the interests of all Mexicans. The reason he was writing was to complain that Mexican priests were being mistreated by the Church hierarchy by being sent to the worst parishes, particularly smaller, rural villages, while Spanish priests were receiving preferred parishes. He wanted the president to intervene in this situation.[154]

Bailey discovered in his interviews in the mid-1970s that some priests still believed bad feelings between Spanish and Mexican clergy existed.

My interviews with diocesan priests, members of religious orders, and bishops revealed no conflicts among foreign and domestic priests, including Spaniards and other nationalities, in the late 1980s and 1990s. Although some clergy did agree that some of the Latin American priests or members of orders, specifically the Maryknolls, were more liberal in their theological posture than the average Mexican priests, they perceived no important ideological differences or influences attributable to foreign clergy. A native of Chiapas, where the highest percentage of foreign priests in Mexico reside, describes the typical experience: "There are foreign priests in Chiapas, but generally speaking they don't behave any differently than other secular priests; they integrate themselves in their job and diocese, they don't try to impose or implant something totally new. There is no clash between foreign and diocesan priests."[155]

A final source of foreign influence, one that has introduced strong linkages among clergy, the private sector, and the government, is the paraecclesiastical order, Opus Dei. As a leading analyst of this organization suggests, it can best be described as a "modern" type of Catholic order, modeled after the traditional religious orders. Opus Dei is not a typical, religious order in that most of its members are laypersons, not priests. The vast majority of individuals who have joined Opus Dei worldwide are young professionals and advanced students, typically from traditional Catholic middle-class families characterized by strong religious values. Although three membership categories in Opus Dei exist, nearly one-third of its members correspond most closely to other religious orders. These individuals donate their secular earnings to residential communities, undertake vows of celibacy and obedience, and study to become Catholic priests, although few are ordained. Laypersons, women and men alike, make up 98 percent of Opus Dei's membership.[156]

Opus Dei also differs from other religious orders, with the exception of the Jesuits, in that its legal status since 1979 allows it to report directly to the Vatican and the episcopate, not the individual diocesan bishop.[157] Opus Dei has attracted much attention in the media and in popular culture for its alleged secrecy. Those analysts who paint Opus Dei as a subversive organization seem out of touch with reality.[158] Opus Dei never has hidden its primary goal: to place its members in positions of influence and power in society. The secrecy surrounding Opus Dei is purely an effort to set it apart from other groups and create an attractive aura among committed Catholics.

Opus Dei was founded in Spain in the 1930s and came to Mexico in 1949. Today, 7,250 Opus Dei members (10 percent of worldwide membership) reside in Mexico.[159] Although these numbers far exceed members of all other male, Mexican religious orders, they include only 65 priests, one-third of whom reside in the Federal District.[160] In 1970, Opus Dei began amplifying its activities, representing Catholicism's conservative wing.[161] In Mexico, Opus Dei's strongest links with society occur through the private sector. Individual businessmen who associate with Opus Dei exercise tremendous influence in the private sector and in government.[162] Its ties to Mexico's Catholic hierarchy, however, are tenuous. In its earlier days, Cardinal Garibi y Rivera of Guadalajara supported the order, and some analysts alleged that ties to Opus Dei might prove useful in climbing the ladder to bishop.[163] No evidence exists to support such claims.

What is evident about Opus Dei's influence is its involvement in education. In a sense, Opus Dei members substituted for the Jesuits when the latter decided to move away from educating elites, precisely the group Opus Dei wishes to socialize.[164] It has established schools at all educational levels, but its most prominent Mexican institution is the Pan American Institute of Higher Management (IPADE), funded by a prominent group of businessmen and directed by an Opus Dei priest. IPADE has graduated numerous influential businessmen and public sector elites, but these alumni are not actual members of Opus Dei.[165] Its influence on church-state relations, therefore, is indirect.

Conclusions

Multiple variables, both domestic and foreign, influence decision making within the Mexican Catholic Church and complicate its relations with outside institutions, including the government. In particular, international actors may lessen or accentuate tensions already existing between domestic clerical and political actors. The degree to which domestic Church policies, represented by the collective episcopate, are in sync with the Vatican not only depends on attitudes of the faithful and the beliefs of the clergy, compared to those of a sitting Pope, but also may be affected by the views of the Vatican delegate. The degree to which influential members of the episcopate have "friends" in the Vatican may determine their ability to convey strongly a point of view differing from the delegate or at least a point of view shared by many members of the episcopate.

In Mexico's case, contrary to the experience of most Catholic countries of comparable size, the Vatican delegate who helped to engineer new church-state relations exercised an unusual and significant role in Church decision making. Not only did he affect the importance of church-state relations in the overall agenda of issues concerning the Mexican episcopate, but he sought to improve Church relations at the price (according to many Mexican clergy) of episcopal sovereignty and autonomy. Mexico's Vatican delegate used his diplomatic and political skills to skillfully manipulate both the state and the hierarchy in strengthening the Vatican's position, but not necessarily the Mexican episcopate's position. His ability to exercise such power has depended to some degree on the bishops' passive behavior and, perhaps more importantly, on the political leadership's misperception that Church policy is determined by a highly centralized executive authority, namely the cardinal archbishop of Mexico and the Vatican delegate.

Individual bishops, who, as we have seen, are extremely autonomous, have strengthened their posture nationally through the implementation of pastoral regions. These regions, which are incorporated within the formal episcopal hierarchy, have produced a level of closeness and cooperation among bishops who share similar pastoral conditions. This has encouraged bishops to develop closer personal and ideological ties and greater respect for wide differences among various dioceses, differences most bishops clearly appreciate. On the other hand, by accentuating these differences and collectively allocating legitimacy to individual bishops, these regions reinforce attitudinal divisions, with potential political or ideological consequences, within the hierarchy.

The Mexican episcopate (CEM) has become a stronger voice in the affairs of bishops. It has accomplished for all bishops what pastoral regions have provided to smaller groups. Nevertheless, despite a much more active posture and a willingness to take frequent public positions on controversial social and economic issues, the CEM has exercised a limited influence on Mexican clerical issues. One of the most important limitations can be explained by a conflict of interest between the Vatican and its representative and the CEM and its collective membership. Many of the bishops, especially through 1992, placed much greater emphasis on practical issues than on international, structural issues involving church and state.

A structural characteristic that also crosses national and international institutional boundaries, having a tremendous impact in Latin America, is the degree to which a clergy counts foreign-born priests in its midst. In Mexico, as we have seen, the peculiar Church political history led to stringent conditions that discouraged the immigration of foreign priests to a degree not found elsewhere in the region. The small numbers of priests probably have contributed to the progressive wing's more modest representation and to greater homogeneity among the clergy.

A built-in feature of the Mexican clergy, as is true elsewhere in the region, is the presence of religious orders, which also cross national and international boundaries and provide fertile ground for potential institutional divisions. While Mexico has seen such divisions in the past, religious orders have not contributed significantly to such differences in the last two decades. Although they are often the source of foreign priests, the small numbers of foreigners limits the potential for divisive consequences.

Mexico, as we have seen, also has produced a more autonomous Church without direct financial links to the government. Although it often seeks and receives funding from abroad, these funds appear to be given without any strings. The ability of the Church to operate independently of the state, especially in financial terms, strengthens its ability as an institution to serve its constituency's interests, especially if it confronts the state's position.

The Church further strengthened its position through personal and institutional linkages with the U.S. Catholic hierarchy, notably along the border, but elsewhere, including the South, as well. The Church is willing to use its ties to the United States to express a position independent of the Mexican government, or it may also help the government improve its international position vis-à-vis the United States on important domestic, economic issues. Regardless of how the Church is involved, its actions demonstrate that it is a significant, complex actor in Mexican affairs, and that if the situation demands that it perform secular assignments in the interest of the laity, especially the poor, Church leadership is willing to accept such a task.

NOTES

1. John L. McKenzie, *The Roman Catholic Church* (New York: Holt, Rinehart, 1969), 32–33.

2. Ibid., 5.

3. Ibid., 17–18.

4. Brian Smith, "Religion and Social Change: Classical Theories and New Formulations in the Content of Recent Developments in Latin America," *Latin American Research Review* 10 (1975): 22.

5. Edward L. Cleary, *Crisis and Change: The Church in Latin America Today* (Maryknoll: Orbis Books, 1985), 13.

6. Prigione was given the title Vatican delegate for most of his tenure because Mexico did not have formal relations with the Vatican. This term is used interchangeable with papal nuncio, the official diplomatic title given to a Vatican ambassador.

7. Mori de México, "Encuesta Semanal," November 27, 1992.

8. George Grayson, *The Church in Contemporary Mexico* (Washington: CSIS, 1992), 35.

9. Personal interview with Archbishop Manuel Pérez Gil, Tlanepantla Diocese, Tlanepantla, México, February 18, 1991.

10. Grupo Consultor Interdisciplinario, "Carta de política mexicana, las relaciones estado-iglesias," February 21, 1992, 9.

11. For example, see José Luis Gaona Vega's statement that Prigione has "a view of the Church distinct from some northern bishops." "La designación de Sandoval Iñiguez fue hecha por 'manos extrañas a la región," *Punto,* March 21, 1988, 11.

12. Edward L. Cleary, *Crisis and Change: The Church in Latin America Today,* 15.

13. *Latin American Institutional Development: The Changing Catholic Church,* Luigi Einaudi, ed. (Santa Monica, Calif.: Rand Corporation, 1969), 13.

14. Ibid., 13.

15. Personal interview with Archbishop Rosendo Huesca, Puebla Archdiocese, Puebla, Puebla, July 16, 1993.

16. Oscar Hinojosa, "La misión evangélica ordena dejar la sacristía, afirma Obeso Rivera," *Proceso*, September 8, 1986, 13.

17. Personal interview with Father Antonio Roqueñi, director of international relations, Archdiocese of Mexico, Mexico City, July 14, 1993.

18. George Grayson, *The Church in Contemporary Mexico*, 37.

19. Personal interview with Mariclaire Acosta, president of the Comisión Mexicana de Defensa y Promoción de los Derechos Humanos, August 3, 1992.

20. Personal interview, Mexican priest, Mexico Archdiocese, Mexico City.

21. Personal interview with Manuel Carrillo Poblano, adviser to the subsecretary of government in charge of church affairs, Mexico City, August 4, 1992.

22. Personal interview with Antonio Roqueñi.

23. *El Nacional*, March 24, 1990, 7.

24. George Grayson, *The Church in Contemporary Mexico*, 37.

25. Personal interview with a Mexican bishop, July 1993.

26. *National Catholic Reporter*, November 11, 1994, 11.

27. Personal interview with Ricardo Pascoe, secretary of communications, PRD, Mexico City, May 5, 1992.

28. Oscar Hinojosa, "Prigione, enlace de Bartlett para reprender a obispos críticos," *Proceso*, August 18, 1986, 8. It is interesting to note that Elías Calles is the grandson of President Calles (1924–1928), Mexico's most anti-Church president in this century.

29. Personal interview with Arturo Nuñez Jiménez, subsecretary of government in charge of church affairs, Mexico City, February 12, 1993.

30. Personal interview with Manuel Carrillo Poblano, adviser to the subsecretary of government in charge of church affairs, Mexico City, August 4, 1992.

31. For background, see *El Nacional*, May 5, 1990, 8, and Rodrigo Vera, "Dinero, historia y política, puntos clave en la posible conversión de la basilica en diócesis: Schulenburg," *Proceso*, June 3, 1991, 14–15. It is possible that the archdiocese may be divided after Corripio's retirement.

32. Personal interview, Mexico City, 1991. Cuauhtémoc Cárdenas, the PRD's presidential candidate, believes Prigione generated numerous conflicts within the Church through his constant interference. Personal interview with Cuauhtémoc Cárdenas, Mexico City, May 6, 1992.

33. Marta Eugenia García Ugarte, "Las posiciones políticas de la jearquía católica, efectos en la cultura religiosa mexicana," *Religiosidad y política en México*, Carlos Martínez Assad, ed. (Mexico City: Ibero-American University, 1992), 108; *El Nacional*, March 27, 1990, n.p.; personal interview with Arturo Nuñez Jiménez.

34. John L. McKenzie, *The Roman Catholic Church*, 3.

35. Ivan Vallier, "Religious Elites, Differentiations, and Developments in Roman Catholicism," *Elites in Latin America*, Seymour Martin Lipset, ed. (New York: Oxford University Press, 1968), 192–193.

36. Ivan Vallier, *Catholicism, Social Control, and Modernization in Latin America* (Englewood Cliffs, N.J.: Prentice-Hall, 1970), 41.

37. *Latin American Institutional Development*, 9.

38. Edward L. Cleary, *Crisis and Change: The Church in Latin American Today*, 28.

39. Ibid., 11.

40. As Vikram Chand concluded, "Episcopal collegiality both stimulated greater national and international coordination between bishops and promoted the decentralization of Church authority at all levels." "Democracy in Mexico: The Politics of the State of Chihuahua in National Perspective," unpublished Ph.D. dissertation, Harvard University, May 1991, 203.

41. Ivan Vallier, "Religious Elites, Differentiations, and Developments in Roman Catholicism," 201.

42. Claude Pomerlau, "The Catholic Church in Mexico and Its Changing Relationship to Society and the State," unpublished manuscript, 1980, 7, 9–10.

43. Ivan Vallier, *Catholicism, Social Control, and Modernization in Latin America,* 88.

44. Personal interview with Raúl Vera López, bishop of Ciudad Altamirano, Mexico Archdiocese, Mexico City, May 3, 1992.

45. For additional influences, see Margaret E. Crahan's fascinating interpretations in "Church and State in Latin America: Assassinating Some Old and New Stereotypes," *Daedalus* 120, no. 3 (Summer 1991): 144.

46. Personal interview with Arturo Nuñez Jiménez, February 12, 1993.

47. Conferencia del Episcopado Mexicano, *Directorio, 1989–1991* (Mexico City: CEM, 1989), 86–88.

48. Ivan Labelle and Adriana Estrada, *Latin America: Socio-Religious Data (Catholicism),* vol. 2 (Mexico: Center of Intercultural Formation, 1964), 82.

49. Personal interview with Bishop Sergio Méndez Arceo, Mexico Archdiocese, Mexico City, June 21, 1989.

50. Thomas G. Sanders, "The Chilean Episcopate," *American Universities Field Staff Reports* 15, no. 3 (August 1968): 5.

51. Otto Granados Roldán, "La iglesia Católica mexicana como grupo de presión," *Cuadernos de Humanidades,* no. 17 (Mexico: UNAM, Departamento de Humanidades, 1981), 34; Oscar Hinojosa, "Dejarán de ser en la noche los encuentros con funcionarios mexicanos: Prigione," *Proceso,* December 12, 1988, 9.

52. *Directorio eclesiástico de la república mexicana,* 14th ed., (Mexico: Curia del Arzobispo de México, 1985), 1:1047.

53. Secretaria de Gobernación, Dirección General de Gobierno, "Catalogo Nacional de Cultos Religiosos en México," unpublished manuscript, 1991, 9.

54. Manuel Carrillo Poblano, "Jerarquía católica mexicana," *Este País,* June 1991, 13.

55. Anthony J. Gill, "Rendering unto Caesar?: Religious Competition and Catholic Political Strategy in Latin America," paper presented at the Latin American Studies Association, Los Angeles, September 1992, 7.

56. Dennis Goulet, "The Mexican Church: Into the Public Arena," *America,* April 8, 1989, 320.

57. *Proceso,* June 20, 1988, 20–23.

58. Thomas Reese, *Archbishop: Inside the Power Structure of the American Catholic Church* (New York: Harper and Row, 1989), 64.

59. Personal interview with José Rogelio Alvarez, Mexico City, February 15, 1991.

60. Antonio García Montaño, "Los obispos mexicanos de la segunda mitad del siglo xx," unpublished manuscript, n.p.; Conferencia del Episcopado Mexicano, *Directorio, 1986–1988* (Mexico City: CEM, 1986), n.p.

61. Daniel H. Levine, *Religion and Politics in Latin America: The Catholic Church in Venezuela and Colombia* (Princeton: Princeton University Press, 1981), 9.

62. Claude Pomerlau, "The Catholic Church in Mexico and Its Changing Relationship to Society and the State," 11.

63. *Latin American Institutional Development: The Changing Catholic Church,* 43.

64. George Grayson, *The Church in Contemporary Mexico,* 26.

65. Antonio García Montaño, "Los obispos mexicanos de la segunda mitad del siglo xx." Prior presidents were Archbishop Octaviano Márquez y Toriz, Puebla, 1953–1959, 1963–1967, and Cardinal José Garibi Rivera, 1960–1962.

66. George Grayson, *The Church in Contemporary Mexico,* 25–28.

67. For example, Father Jesús Vergara, who has published works on church-state relations in Mexico, was asked by the episcopate to prepare a position paper on election fraud. The bishops reserved the right to make a moral judgment on the issue of fraud after reading his paper, but in the end, they discarded his recommendations, making no statement at all. Personal interview, Mexico City, June 29, 1989.

68. Jorge Martínez Martínez, *Memorias y reflexiones de un obispo* (Mexico City: Editorial Villicaña, 1986), 134.

69. George Grayson, *The Church in Contemporary Mexico*, 26.

70. Patricia Arias et al., *Radiografía de la iglesia católica en México* (Mexico City: UNAM, 1981), 97.

71. Personal interview with Archbishop Manuel Pérez Gil.

72. Oscar Hinojosa, "Prigione, enlace de Bartlett para reprender a obispos críticos," 8.

73. Claude Pomerlau, "The Catholic Church in Mexico and Its Changing Relationship to Society and the State," Chapter 3, 8.

74. For example, some members of the Instituto Mexicano de Doctrina Social Cristiano, founded in 1983 to study, teach, and research social Christian doctrine, advise the hierarchy. *El Nacional,* July 8, 1992, 11.

75. Dennis M. Hanratty, "Change and Conflict in the Contemporary Mexican Catholic Church," unpublished Ph.D. dissertation, Duke University, 1980, 25, 148; Patricia Arias et al., *Radiografía de la iglesia católica en México,* 46–47.

76. Martín de la Rosa, "La Iglesia católica en México, del Vaticano II a la CELAM III," *Cuadernos Políticos* 19 (January–March 1979); 96; Claude Pomerlau, "The Catholic Church in Mexico and Its Changing Relationship to Society and the State," Chapter 3, 11.

77. Personal interview with President Miguel de la Madrid, Mexico City, February 22, 1991.

78. Personal interview with Luis Narro Rodríguez, director of the Center of Educational Studies, Mexico City, June 28, 1989.

79. Partido Revolucionario Institucional, "Memorandum sobre las relaciones estado-iglesia católica," unpublished manuscript, November 1988, 35.

80. *Unomásuno,* December 13, 1989, 9.

81. Numerous interviews with bishops, 1987–1992, and personal interview with Roberto Blancarte, Mexico City, February 20, 1991.

82. George Grayson, *The Church in Contemporary Mexico,* 32.

83. Homero Campa, "El Abad de la Basílica de Guadalupe se retira, tras de su derrota ante Corripio," *Proceso,* December 10, 1990, 21.

84. The immediate catalyst of Prigione's efforts began on August 6, 1993, when Ruiz sent a letter to the Pope denouncing election vices, centralized control, corruption, and Salinas's neoliberal policies. On October 26, 1993, Prigione called Ruiz, claiming that on the instructions of Bernardin Gantin, prefect of the Vatican Congregation of Bishops, he was asking him to resign. The Mexican secretariat of government also sought his resignation through Prigione. Prigione's actions led to a series of events, outlined in Francisco Gómez Maza's "Represión disfrazada de disciplina religiosa en el caso Ruiz," *El Financiero,* November 7, 1993, 21.

85. For published details, see interview with Roqueñi, in Arturo Cano, "Los nuncios no duran tanto," "Enfoque," *La Reforma,* January 20, 1994, 12–13, and María Eugenia Mondragón, "Disputas dividen a representantes espirutuales," *El Financiero,* October 4, 1994, 38.

86. Personal interview with Father Jesús Vergara, Mexico City, June 29, 1989.

87. Personal interview with Nicéforo Guerrero, director general real estate, Secretariat of Urbanization and Ecology, Mexico City, June 19, 1989.

88. Edward L. Cleary, *Crisis and Change: The Church in Latin America,* 9.

89. Ivan Labelle and Adriana Estrada, *Latin America: Socio-Religious Data (Catholicism),* 86, 146.

90. *Directorio eclesiástico de la república mexicana,* 7: 475, 1049.

91. Manuel R. González Ramírez, *La Iglesia mexicana en cifras* (Mexico City, 1969), 160.

92. Enrique Luengo, "Los párrocos: una visión," unpublished manuscript, Department of Social and Political Sciences, Ibero-American University, December 1989, 24.

93. Personal interview with Bishop Jorge Martínez Martínez, Mexico Archdiocese, Mexico City, May 28, 1987.

94. Personal interview with Bishop Raúl Vera, the first Mexican from the Dominican order to serve as a bishop in 130 years.

95. Personal interview with former sister Martha Musi, Mexico City, June 1, 1988.

96. Personal interview with Bishop Sergio Méndez Arceo.

97. Personal interview with former president of the Ibero-American University, Ernesto Menenses Morales, Mexico City, June 6, 1988.

98. *Latin American Institutional Development: The Changing Catholic Church,* 14.

99. Claude Pomerlau, "The Catholic Church in Mexico and Its Changing Relationship to Society and the State," Chapter 3, 4.

100. Personal interview with Father Jacques Chaveriat, Mexico Archdiocese, Mexico City, June 8, 1988.

101. Personal interview with Father Ernesto Menenses Morales, June 6, 1988.

102. The same situation can be found within the officer corps, particularly among those who graduate from the Higher War College. See Roderic Ai Camp, *Generals in the Palacio: The Military in Modern Mexico* (New York: Oxford University Press, 1992), 124.

103. Personal interview with Luis Bazdresch, Ibero-American University, Mexico City, June 20, 1989.

104. Interview between Shannan Mattiace and Archbishop Manuel Castro Ruiz, Mérida Archdiocese, Mérida, Mexico, August 21, 1989.

105. Shannan Mattiace, "The Social Role of the Mexican Catholic Church: The Case of the Yucatán Base Community," senior honors thesis, Central University of Iowa, 1990, 40.

106. Carlos Marín, "La Iglesia, en riesgo de privatizarse, advierten las órdenes religiosas," *Proceso,* February 24, 1992, 11–12; Grupo Consultor Interdisciplinario, "Carta de política mexicana, la relación estado-iglesia, nuevos espacios para conflictos," March 6, 1992, 5. The CEM denounced the statement as false and unjust.

107. Roderic Ai Camp, *Intellectuals and the State in Twentieth-Century Mexico* (Austin: University of Texas Press, 1985), 57.

108. Brian Smith, "Religion and Social Change: Classical Theories and New Formulations in the Content of Recent Developments in Latin America," 19.

109. Lucía Alonso Reyes, "Función social de la iglesia en Zacatecas," *Memorias, segundo informe de investigación sobre el estado de Zacatecas* (Zacatecas, 1989), 192.

110. Interview by David C. Bailey with Father Tom O'Rourke, Archdiocese of Mexico, Mexico City, July 21, 1976.

111. Interview by David C. Bailey with José Martín Rivera, Curia, Archdiocese of Mexico, Mexico City, August 3, 1976.

112. Personal interview with Father Jacques Chaveriat.

113. Personal interview with Nicéforo Guerrero Reynoso, director of religious affairs, Secretariat of Government, Mexico City, June 19, 1989.

114. Otto Granados Roldán, "La iglesia católica mexicana como grupo de presión," 38.

115. Personal interview with Eduardo Bustamante, Mexico City, May 29, 1987.

116. Manuel Robles, "Fondos de Pronasol para remodelar y construir templos y hasta casas para sacerdotes," *Proceso,* June 3, 1991, 12–13.

117. Rodrigo Vera, "Dinero, historia y política, puntos clave en la posible conversión de la Basílica en diócesis: Schulenburg," 15.

118. Cornelia Butler Flora and Rosario Bello, "The Impact of the Catholic Church on National Level Change in Latin America," *Journal of Church and State* 31, no. 3 (Autumn 1989): 530.

119. Personal interview with Ricardo Cuellar Romo.

120. For example, Mexico received $7 million from the Foundation for Community Assistance, a coordinating institution for the episcopates of the United States, France, Holland, Switzerland, Italy, Germany, and Luxembourg, which focuses on aid to the Catholic Church in health, housing, education, and employment among the poor. *Punto,* September 15, 1986, 11.

121. Personal interview with Luis Bazdresch, Ibero-American University, Mexico City, June 20, 1989.

122. Personal interview with Father Jesús Vergara.

123. Personal interview with Fathers Manuel Concha Malo, Luis Bazdresch, and Jesús Vergara.

124. Personal interview with Girolamo Prigione.

125. Oscar Hinojosa, "Prigione, enlace de Bartlett para reprender a obispos críticos," 8, cites the case of Bishop Lona, who, although he worked for several years to obtain assistance, received a large grant from a Dutch foundation to develop cooperatives in his diocese.

126. Personal interview with Bishop Sergio Méndez Arceo.

127. John B. Housley, "The Role of the Churches in U.S.–Latin American Relations," in *Prospects for Latin America,* David S. Smith., ed. (New York: International Fellows Policy Series, Columbia University, 1970), 28.

128. Lawrence J. Mosqueda, *Chicanos, Catholicism, and Political Ideology* (Lanham, Md.: University Press of America, 1986), 140.

129. Committee of the American Episcopate, "Pastoral Letter of the Catholic Episcopate of the United States on the Religious Situation in Mexico," December 1926.

130. Douglas J. Slawson, "The National Conference Welfare Conference and the Church-State Conflict in Mexico, 1925–1929," *Americas* 47 (July 1990): 93.

131. Personal interview with Gabriel Zaid, Mexico City, June 7, 1988.

132. Ken Serbin, "Latin America's Catholic Church: Religious Rivalries and the North-South Divide," *North-South Issues* 2, no. 1 (1993): 6.

133. Personal interview with President José López Portillo, Mexico City, February 19, 1991.

134. *La Jornada,* November 17, 1988, 4.

135. *Documentación e Información Católica* 2, no. 41 (1974): 425–426.

136. United States Catholic Conference, Report, March 18, 1990, n.p.

137. Personal interview by Shannan Mattiace with Father Avila, Mérida Archdiocese, Mérida, Yucatán, August 17, 1989.

138. *Proceso,* January 29, 1990, 12. This is not the first case of the Church taking a nationalistic posture in a foreign policy issue, albeit without U.S. episcopal cooperation. The CEM passed a formal declaration on May 1, 1938, urging Catholics to contribute to payment of Mexico's debt resulting from the petroleum nationalization. See Roberto Blancarte, *Iglesia y estado en México, seis décadas de acomodo y de conciliación imposible* (Mexico City: IMCSC, 1990), 18–19.

139. United States National Conference of Catholic Bishops, "Relieving Third World Debt: A Call for Co-Responsibility, Justice, and Solidarity," September 27, 1989, 4.

140. United States Catholic Conference, Press Release, July 12, 1989, n.p. Among the Mexican bishops who attended were Archbishop Adolfo Suárez, Bishop Abelardo Alvarado, Cardinal Ernesto Corripio, Archbishop Manuel Pérez Gil, and Emilio Berlie, bishop of Tijuana. See United States Catholic Conference, "Churches Responding to the Debt Crisis," Seminar on the Mexican Debt Crisis, January 25–26, 1990, 1–6.

141. United States National Conference of Catholic Bishops, "Relieving Third World Debt," 7, 11, 13.

142. After the U.S. Treasury approved a debt-for-equity swap program, the Mexican government authorized Church participation in the scheme to the tune of $6 million. Jesuit Enrique González Torres served as the Church's broker, and foreign donors to Mexican Church ventures bought discounted Mexican debt from creditor banks, then donated the debt paper to the Catholic-affiliated Foundation for Assistance to the Community, which traded it back to the government for hard cash. By June 1991, $110 million had been exchanged in this manner. Michael Tangeman, *Mexico at the Crossroads: Politics, the Church, and the Poor* (Maryknoll: Orbis, 1994), 129, 146. I am indebted to Luis Rubio for first bringing this to my attention. Personal interview, Mexico City, February 13, 1991.

143. United States Catholic Conference, "Report of International Justice and Peace Department," April 2, 1992, n.p.

144. "Public Opinion and the FTA Negotiations: Citizen Alternatives," open letter to participants in the International Forum, Zacatecas, Mexico, October 25–27, 1991.

145. *Latin American Institutional Development: The Changing Catholic Church,* 69.

146. Claude Pomerlau, "The Catholic Church in Mexico and Its Changing Relationship to Society and the State," Chapter 3, n. 37.

147. Personal interview with Nicéforo Guerrero.

148. David B. Barrett, *World Christian Encyclopedia* (New York: Oxford University Press, 1982), 488.

149. Enrique Luengo, "Los párrocos: una visión," 29–30.

150. Manuel R. González Ramírez, *La Iglesia mexicana en cifras,* 164–165.

151. *Ley reglamentaria del artículo 130 de la constitución federal* (Mexico, 1988), 400.

152. Michael Elmer, "The Mexican Church," *The Tablet* 233 (January 1979): 76.

153. The government expelled three foreign priests in June 1995 and impeded the return of five other clergy attending missions abroad. These actions prompted a response from the Council of Mexican Bishops praising Ruiz and the work of foreign priests and nuns and asking the secretary of government to desist from such actions. Inter-Press Service, October 14, 1995. Enrique Luengo, "Los párrocos: una visión," 72, also cites such a case.

154. Personal interview with Manuel Hinojosa Ortiz.

155. Personal interview by Shannan Mattiace with Father Felipe Vendura, Carranza, Mexico, August 15, 1989.

156. José V. Casanova, "The First Secular Institute: The Opus Dei as a Religious Movement-Organization," *Annual Review of the Social Sciences of Religion* 6 (1982): 259.

157. Víctor Gabriel Muro González, "Iglesia y movimientos sociales en México, 1977–1982, los casos de Ciudad Juárez y el Istmo de Tehuantepec," unpublished Ph.D. dissertation, El Colegio de México, August 1991, 426.

158. John Creighton, "The Autonomous Kingdoms of Opus Dei," *Humanist* 47 (March–April 1987): 13.

159. *El Nacional,* June 8, 1992, 5.

160. *Directorio eclesiástico de la república mexicana,* 1:55; Oscar Aguilar and Enrique

Luengo, "Iglesia y gobierno en el D.F.," in *D.F.: Gobierno y sociedad civil*, Pablo González Casanova, ed. (Mexico: El Caballito, 1987), Table 10.

161. Soledad Loaeza, "La Iglesia católica mexicana y el reformismo autoritario," *Foro Internacional* 25, no. 2 (October–December 1984): 150–151.

162. Oscar Hinojosa, "El Opus Dei, a la conquista de la dirección civil," *Proceso*, June 9, 1980, 16.

163. Alicia Olivera de Bonfil, "La Iglesia en México, 1926–1970," in *Contemporary Mexico: Papers of the IV International Congress of Mexican History*, James W. Wilkie et al., eds. (Los Angeles: UCLA, Latin American Center, 1976), 314; *Punto*, March 16, 1987, 10.

164. Soledad Loaeza, "Continuity and Change in the Mexican Catholic Church," in *Church and Politics in Latin America*, Dermot Keogh, ed. (New York: St. Martin's Press, 1990), 291.

165. Manuel Buendía, *La Santa Madre* (Mexico City: Océano, 1985), 50, 177; Oscar Hinojosa, "El Opus Dei, a la conquista de la dirección civil," 15–17; George Grayson, *The Church in Contemporary Mexico*, 44–46.

11

Structure and Decision Making

The Bishop in His Diocese

This book has argued that the diocese is the basic unit of the Catholic Church's hierarchical structure and that parishes are the building blocks of the dioceses. To better understand formal and informal relationships among the most important local clerical actors, it is useful to identify the typical diocesan institutions and those who direct them. As is the case of any institution, personnel labels are used loosely, often conveying mistaken associations and influence.

Essentially, two types of diocesan priests compose rank-and-file members of the bishop's or archbishop's staff. The parish priest, *cura* or *párroco* in Mexico, is in charge of or associated with a specific church and the faithful within the parish boundaries. In larger parishes, priests or vicars are assigned to parish priests as assistants. In some cases, more than one church exists in a parish; the individuals assigned to these affiliated churches are simply called priests or *sacerdotes*.[1]

A presbyterial council exists in each diocese to help the bishop confront pastoral problems. Council members are called canons. Each individual bishop determines the function and organization of the presbyterial council, which consists of priests. He may use the priests to test his proposals, to obtain their advice, or to promote his pastoral policies throughout the diocese.

Governing the Diocese: The Autonomous Bishop

The most important figure in the diocese is, of course, the bishop. Bishops deserve a much closer examination in Mexico and elsewhere in the region because although canon law prescribes their powers and responsibilities, few popular or scholarly analyses exist of how power actually is exercised.[2] Bishops are divided into four categories. Not all bishops govern geographic territories (dioceses). Many priests selected as bishops, having no diocese of their own, are assigned a geographic place name of a diocese that no longer exists. The typical bishop (first type) can be described as a residential administrator, indicating his status in charge of a diocese, a territorial assignment.[3] Other bishops, without a formal diocese (second type), typically function as auxiliary bishops to residential bishops until a diocese becomes available. Some, however, serve their entire tenure as bishops in an auxiliary capacity. Two types of auxiliary bishops exist, and the distinction is important. There are coadjutors, auxiliary bishops with rights of succession to the diocese in which they are assisting, and regular auxiliaries, who may or may not replace an incumbent bishop.[4] A third type of bishop is also in charge of a geographic location, typically rural and underdeveloped, often including a missionary territory. These are referred to as vicariates. Within the vicariate are territorial prelatures (fourth type) assigned to specific religious orders, such as the Franciscans in Nayarit. The bishops from these prelatures are selected from within the corresponding order.

The episcopate recognizes a fifth category, emeritus bishops. In Mexico, at the beginning of the decade, 16 individuals claimed such status. As suggested in the analysis of the CEM, emeritus bishops may attend national episcopate meetings and participate in discussions. They may not, however, vote on episcopal policy statements. According to one emeritus bishop, only two to three retired bishops actually attend these sessions in Mexico.[5] Bishops retain active status until age 75, after which they must resign. The Pope, however, may reject their resignation. For example, Genaro Alamillo Arteaga, a close confidant of Cardinal Corripio and one of his auxiliaries from 1980, resigned his post as bishop at age 75 in 1989 but remained an active member of the CEM as president of the Social Communications Committee. Blancarte argues he was useful to the episcopate in this position because he had nothing to lose and would speak frankly.[6] He became noted for his bluntness as an episcopate spokesperson. If a resignation is accepted, which is typically the case, the bishop obtains emeritus status. An important consequence of an elderly retirement age among bishops is that most serve several decades in a given diocese, resulting in their institutional authority becoming identified with the individual officeholder.[7]

Bishops require the assistance of other priests. This is especially true among the oldest, largest, and most populated archdioceses. Bishops in these larger dioceses must appoint a chancellor who no longer needs to be a priest. He is responsible for the archives and for preparing certain canonical documents.[8] The most important task a bishop can assign to his auxiliary bishop or a priest is that of vicar general, who may receive substantial powers as the bishop's executive officer in administrative and pastoral matters. Each diocese has an administrative office, the chancery, similar to that of the Roman curia, which handles normal administrative tasks.[9]

The physical buildings associated with a Mexican diocese and its administrative personnel are modest. Levine found this to be the case in South America.[10] Bishops typically live simply, operate with minimal staffs, in some cases just a Sister, and are readily available to their constituencies.[11] Bishops are granted executive, legislative, and judicial powers in their respective dioceses. Canon law requires them to exercise executive authority personally, but they may delegate other responsibilities to their vicar. A residential bishop must reside in his diocese, may not be absent for more than one month, and must make a personal report to the Pope every five years.[12]

The other individual who may play an important role in the diocese is the bishop's secretary, who is granted no special rights under canon law. The secretary functions as chief of staff, both as a source of information and as the bishop's adviser. The secretary's influence depends largely on the individual holding the post and on the level of trust he shares with his boss.[13]

It is important to clarify that archbishops do not rank above bishops, although often greater prestige is associated with their dioceses. Because an archbishop may have one or more auxiliary bishops, he does supervise nonresidential bishops. Under canon law, similar to bishops, the archbishop is responsible only for his archdiocese. Cardinals are selected from among archbishops. Of the two types (residential and nonresidential cardinals), only the first resides in Mexico. The Mexican archdioceses that have been selected as deserving a cardinal are the archdiocese of Mexico (Mexico's most important archdiocese) in the capital city and Guadalajara and Monterrey, in Mexico's second and third largest cities. The cardinal of Guadalajara, however, was murdered in May 1993 and replaced by a new archbishop, who became a cardinal in late 1994. The cardinal of the archdiocese of Mexico, as discussed earlier, may exercise more or less national influence depending on his personal skills and inclinations. Mexico's cardinal is expected to take an interest in national matters given the fact that one-fifth of the population resides in the extended Federal District metropolitan area and that it is the seat of economic, intellectual, and political power.[14] As of 1989, Cardinal Corripio required 7 auxiliary bishops. Some of these auxiliaries previously headed residential dioceses elsewhere in Mexico, often successfully. Others left their original dioceses after a controversial tenure for reassignment to the Mexico archdiocese. Auxiliaries who prove themselves in their first post in the Mexico archdiocese are promoted to a residential diocese outside Mexico City.[15]

Juridically, bishops and archbishops exercise considerable authority. Specifically, Aguilar cites 52 powers, including removing ecclesiastical officials, designating priests as seminary professors and directors, granting leaves to clergy, and giving priests permission to be politically active.[16] For example, when Luengo carried out his study of Mexican priests, he sought permission from the appropriate bishops. They responded in three ways: accepting or rejecting his request, leaving it up to each priest, or deciding on it jointly with their priests.[17] In addition to these formal powers, a bishop's influence in his own diocese depends greatly on his interpersonal skills, his relations to priests, and his respect for the laity. A bishop may even manage to place some restrictions on religious orders in his diocese even though they are not subject to him directly for most activities.[18] As one priest suggests, his degree of autonomy depends on the bishop's relationship to the Pope, the ideology of his diocese, and if the bishop's assignment is merely a stepping-stone to another diocese.[19]

Bishops themselves describe their decision-making authority as autonomous. As one bishop expressed it:

I know that my immediate superior is the Pope, and this obviously affects my ability to make decisions. However, because of the problems in my diocese, I have to take into consideration the recommendations of the Mexican episcopate, but those recommendations are not a requirement. I give even greater consideration to the pastoral group, a body of seven dioceses in our pastoral region who meet every two months to discuss mutual problems and solutions.[20]

A bishop, compared to a Mexican state governor, exercises far more autonomy in his diocese than does his secular counterpart.[21] One of the reasons why bishops have so much discretionary influence is that they combine executive, legislative, and judicial authority. Basically, the primary restriction on their authority relates to fiscal matters.[22] Yet bishops differ considerably in how they exercise their decision-making powers.

Most bishops believe they are part of a collegial structure. The level to which they extend that collegiality to decision making depends on the bishop's individual attitudes.[23] Sergio Méndez Arceo represented one extreme, a bishop who believed rank-and-file clergy should be involved in all significant decisions, including selecting new bishops. Méndez Arceo complained, shortly before his death, that the Mexican episcopate as a whole was not willing to listen to lower clergy and showed little concern for top-down decision making.[24] This pattern also was apparent in the United States in the 1970s, where Greeley reported that the episcopate did not seem inclined to support specific changes in the power structure.[25]

As Bishop Raúl Vera López argues, however, today broad pastoral responsibilities require extensive efforts. Although bishops retain sufficient autonomy to carry out these tasks, they need assistance at many levels. According to one study, the most successful American bishops are those who select their staffs based on competence and personality, delegating responsibilities to their chosen representatives. Such bishops are well informed about their dioceses and rarely intervene to resolve a dispute.[26] As Pomerlau suggests and Mexican clergy confirm, a bishop's degree of autonomy transforms conflict on various questions into personality and loyalty issues.[27]

Bishops receive considerable powers, and many exercise them fully, but cases exist where bishops have lost some autonomy. According to one interpretation, Cardinal Corripio's lack of leadership, or perhaps his coincidence of interests with the Vatican delegate, Girolamo Prigione, permitted the papal nuncio to intervene in selected dioceses. For example, Archbishop Bartolomé Carrasco Briseño of Oaxaca was not able to enforce celibacy among a large number of priests in his poor, southern diocese. The Vatican delegate recommended a coadjutor bishop who received control over the priests, effectively giving him power over the diocese's day-to-day operations.[28] Although the Vatican delegate considerably reduced the archbishop's authority, he could not have done so without the archbishop's permission. Those bishops who remain adamantly opposed to Prigione's philosophy or who wish to assure themselves of complete autonomy refuse to accept auxiliary bishops. However, a bishop can, as demonstrated below, specify precisely the powers to be assigned an auxiliary bishop.

Theoretically, few characteristics are built into the Church's structure that encourage the bishop to be responsive to their parishioners' needs. It is important to consider that progressive bishops do not necessarily govern progressive dioceses.[29] Mexican Catholics typically see their bishops as pastors of Christ. In the Tijuana diocese in 1970, the laity defined the bishop's role first as a pastor of the people of God and only second as an administrator. Nearly two decades later, following a new survey, the majority still viewed their bishop this way.[30]

Choosing a Successor: Who Selects the Bishop?

The most important single decision affecting a diocese is choosing the bishop. Given Mexican bishops' longevity, this may determine policies and decisions for decades to come. Canon laws specify that a bishop exhibit strong moral, human, and religious qualities, be at least 35 years of age, perform the duties of a priest for five years, and be college-educated in either theology, canon law, or religious literature. In the long run, bishops or their confidants select the priests who form the pool from which their replacements are chosen. Priests sent to study at the Gregorian University in Rome typically become part of this group.

According to Mexican clergy, those selected as future potential bishops also share certain informal qualities or at least are perceived to have them. First, they must possess strong moral qualities. Second, they must demonstrate considerable intellectual capacity. Third, they should exhibit strong interpersonal skills, the ability to govern a group of people, and the talent to manage finances. Finally, they seek an individual, as one archbishop expressed it, who knows "when to and when not to change."[31] Bishops do not personally select all of their future peers. Recommendations often are made by the bishops' closest aides. The process at this stage is informal, open, and competitive. Future priests and bishops also are selected on the basis of their behavior, including their obedience and discipline to the Church and Church authority and their attitude toward God.[32]

When a bishop is asked specifically to recommend a priest to become bishop, he tends to select, as indicated earlier, individuals serving in close proximity.[33] In other words, he tends to recommend administrative types, particularly seminary teachers and staff. It should be remembered, however, that in Mexico, "administrative" priests often perform all other tasks associated with a typical parish priest. Mexico's dioceses are understaffed, and clergy perform as jacks of all trades. When a bishop selects assistants, his choices depend greatly on his perception of their personal loyalty. As Reese argues, bishops seek out team players who will defend the boss's decision in public, even if they disagree in private.[34] Mexican priests who convey critical, outspoken images do not become bishops.[35]

Priests can become residential diocesan bishops through two broad tracks—either as auxiliaries, with or without rights of succession, or directly from their posts as priests. In the United States, three-quarters of all bishops served first as auxiliaries. However, only 10 percent of the auxiliaries succeeded to posts in their same diocese after serving as auxiliaries, suggesting rights of succession are not common.[36] In Mexico, serving as an auxiliary bishop has not been as important a career track for becoming a diocesan bishop since only 40 percent served in this capacity since the late 1960s. However, it is apparent that their numbers are increasing in the last decade.

The appointment pattern among auxiliary bishops in the United States offers some interesting parallels with those found in Mexico, differing in certain respects from the process for promotion directly to bishop. In the U.S. model, it is the responsibility of the diocesan bishop to draw up a list of three names, a *ternus* or *terna*, and submit it to the papal nuncio.[37] The nuncio makes his own investigation of these priests, sending along his personal recommendations to the Vatican. This process assumes that the bishop himself can best choose an assistant. However, as Reese reports, there are good reasons not to allow a bishop to make the choice because "often times they are rubber stamps to his own ecclesiology and his own vision of the church, whether that is in one direction or the other."[38] Interestingly, the same charge made in Mexico, that in recent years auxiliaries are imposed on some bishops, is also common in the United States. Yet as is the case in Mexico, a bishop must consent to or request an auxiliary in the first place. A difference does exist between the United States and Mexico in this process. According to the American papal nuncio in the late 1980s, if a bishop did not concur with Rome's choice, the result was a stalemate.[39]

According to canon law, a bishop does not have the right to appoint an auxiliary, only the ability to request one. Mexican bishops and clergy believe that the incumbent bishop does not have a preponderant voice in the decision, as is the case in the United States. Most observers argue that in the last two decades Mexico's Vatican delegate exercised the greatest influence in the selection of auxiliary bishops.[40] Sources typically cite the examples of the dioceses of Oaxaca, Oaxaca; Ciudad Juárez, Chihuahua; and Chihuahua, Chihuahua, where in each case Prigione used an auxiliary bishop with rights of succession to alter the diocese's ideological flavor.[41] Ciudad Juárez's bishop, Manuel Talamás Camandari, complained openly about the process, informing the media that it was inappropriate for a bishop "to be designated by hands foreign to the regional reality," and that it was lamentable that no attention was paid to the diocese's priests, who requested a different auxiliary. Unlike the archbishop of Oaxaca, Talamás clearly specified his auxiliary's duties, stating, "I will continue to make the decisions; he will be subordinate to me; my autonomy will continue unaffected. In case the adjutor bishop has an opinion different from mine, mine will prevail."[42]

Bishops' selection process in Mexico and the United States shares many of the same characteristics found in the designation of auxiliaries. The process can be divided into three components: the role of bishops, the importance of the papal nuncio, and the influence of the Vatican. Initially, bishops play the most important role. Bishops may propose names individually, again suggesting a *terna*, or they also may suggest names collectively at regular episcopal conferences. Some bishops suggest that this process occurs as often as once a year in Mexico.[43] Names of individual priests can be passed on directly to the Vatican or, as is more typically the case, forwarded to the Vatican through the delegate.[44] Furthermore, when a bishop visits the Pope every five years, he identifies priests with the potential to become bishops. The most successful priests on these lists are individuals with a strong mentor—a bishop, the Vatican delegate, or a friend in the Roman Curia. It is not a position for which priests campaign.

Bishops, however, may use a second alternative, accepted under canon law, to make their recommendations. Historically, the Church permitted the selection of a bishop through consultation, either among the episcopacy or among priests in the diocese. These bodies might recommend a single candidate, effectively electing a bishop. These "elected" bishops require the Pope's approval. Some dioceses in Germany and Switzerland enjoy this procedure as a regular practice.[45] Interestingly, however, the origins of the *terna* system can be traced back to Ireland, where priests played the decisive role in the selection process, submitting candidates' names to Rome. Ironically, under the Irish system, when diocesan clergy exercised a voice in the nomination process, they typically selected a senior priest, one unlikely to advocate innovation. They also favored local over outside candidates.[46] According to Reese, the Vatican opposes group consultations on the grounds, which may be well founded, that such meetings could be divisive, lead to politicking, and generate pressure group activities.[47] In Mexico, collective consultation within the diocese is neither common nor successful. The only bishop who openly seems to have attempted a decentralized approach to succession was the late Sergio Méndez Arceo. Shortly before retiring, he convoked a presbyterate of all priests in his diocese, which recommended three outstanding candidates. None of them became the new bishop because, according to insiders, the Vatican delegate wanted to put an end to the bishop's active support of ecclesiastical base communities.[48]

The second actor in the designation process is the Vatican delegate. The degree to which the delegate is actually involved in selecting a new bishop depends on his posture and influence in the Vatican. Under canon law, the papal nuncio may make his own nominations, different from those of the bishop. Theoretically, the Pope can appoint any priest, including an individual not on the nuncio's or the bishop's lists. But as the U.S. papal nuncio indicated to Reese, in the North American experience, the successful priest is always on someone's list.[49] The role of the nuncio is not confined to providing a list of names, whether his, the bishop's, or a combination, but to explain the candidates' qualities to the Vatican and to interpret the larger setting in a specific diocese. It is this task, as well as how the individual delegate conceptualizes it, that has produced so much controversy in Mexico and elsewhere in the Catholic world.[50] According to official Vatican instructions, papal delegates are responsible for instituting the information-gathering process in the selection process. In the United States, the delegate sends a confidential questionnaire on each candidate to people who know him.[51] Their supervision of the process itself gives them a decided edge in interjecting personal recommendations.[52]

Observers of the selection process, who extend beyond the Church, all agree that Mexico's Vatican delegate intervenes strongly in the selection process, affecting the outcome of the designations. A number of accusations have been leveled against Girolamo Prigione, setting him apart from his predecessors, among them that he consults a narrower constituency than his predecessors, thus reinforcing his own biases.

Second, critics charge that Prigione has allowed an ideological litmus test rather than a priest's inherent qualities to influence his recommendations. According to observers, of the more than 30 new bishops over whose selection he presided since 1978, the majority represent a conservative line.[53] Naturally, those who favor an opposing ideological posture respond critically to his choices, especially since his replacements number nearly half of the active episcopate. A more widespread criticism is the issue of quality, echoing a claim that some of these bishops do not enjoy support in their own dioceses.[54] Prigione readily admits his role in the selection process, considering it his most important responsibility. He claims, however, that he has not selected conservatives nor radicals but moderates, bishops who will be "a unifying factor in their diocese, not a source of friction and discord."[55] The empirical evidence that something is amiss ideologically, however, is apparent. Earlier, this book provided data on the diocesan or seminary origins of Mexico's bishops, which over time have exaggerated the contributions of several leading schools and regions. Yet many of the younger, first-time bishops under Prigione come from two conservative dioceses or seminaries, León and Durango.[56] In fact, between 1980 and 1992, eight bishops, those of Tulancingo, Hidalgo; Huejutla, Hidalgo; Mazatlán, Sinaloa; León, Guanajuato; Campeche, Campeche (later the coadjutor of Oaxaca); Mexicali, Baja California; Tehuacán, Puebla; and Tacámbaro, Michoacán, came from these dioceses and/or seminaries, suggesting an entirely new departure from the dominant patterns. Since neither seminary has ever been mentioned by a single priest or bishop as a leading institution, intellectual/educational quality is not a variable.

Third, Prigione also has been accused of imposing candidates from outside the diocese. It is this issue, more than any other, that alienates large numbers of clergy, high and low. It is not so much a question of whether the priest is from the immediate diocese at the moment of his selection but whether he originates from the diocese, is familiar with its problems, and has ties to other clergy. Critics charge that Prigione recommends outsiders, as in the case of Guadalajara's new archbishop in 1987, Juan Jesús Posadas, because it gives him greater control. Archbishop Rosendo Huesca, a friend of Prigione, offers a convincing and different view of the delegate's motivations, especially in selecting auxiliary bishops:

> This situation has a long history in the Church. There are Vatican delegates who prefer solutions that are local or native. My own designation falls into this category. Other delegates believe an outsider is the only one who can bring change to a diocese, so he doesn't like to select a local. Personally, I don't believe this, and I think it is a bad idea. I and other bishops have spoken to Prigione about our views on this issue. But he says no, he doesn't want another local person in these dioceses. This is his bias. Because of our close relationship, if I asked for an auxiliary bishop, he would give me a local out of respect, but he wouldn't like it.[57]

Given Huesca's relationship to Prigione, this explanation suggests that it is not just a question of the linkage between ideological orientation and place of origin but a belief that "new blood" or change in other dimensions of a bishop's tasks are best accomplished, from the delegate's viewpoint, through the appointment of an outsider.

The third actor in the process is, of course, the Vatican Curia. Delegates' reports on potential candidates are sent to the Congregation of Bishops. A staff member, a single priest, handles all of the reports from Latin America, excluding Brazil. If an individual recommended for another post is already a bishop, only staff members become involved in making the recommendation to the Pope. If a priest is being promoted to bishop, the full congregation considers the recommendations. An individual cardinal, or presenter, is chosen by the undersecretary of the congregation and summarizes and presents the full picture to other members. Finally, the prefect, in charge of the congregation's selection process, takes the delegate's, the congregation's, and his own recommendation before an audience with the Pope, who determines the final choice. According to insiders among American bishops, the congregation's choice, which, of course, may coincide with the Vatican delegate's, is overwhelmingly accepted by the Pope.[58] It is apparent from this process that the Vatican delegate has a larger voice than that of the incumbent bishop, and that the delegate, not the bishop, is more likely to have a friend in the congregation or know its prefect. Some claims have been put forth that the Mexican government might be a hidden actor in this process, but absolutely no evidence exists to support such an assertion.[59]

Priest and Bishop: Dissension in the Ranks?

No institution with a bureaucratic hierarchy can claim to function without tensions. Numerous variables exacerbate natural tensions that exist among administrators and rank-and-file members of an organization. Among the most important of these, often serving as catalysts for conflict, include introducing new institutional policies affecting goals or procedures; substantially increasing new personnel, who through age or experience have different socializing experiences from those of the incumbent staff; appointing a strong-willed administrator whose views are out of sync with his organization; and selecting an administrator insensitive to or ineffective in interpersonal skills.

The primary problem affecting bishop-priest relations in Mexico and elsewhere focuses on communication. Priests and bishops perceive the level of communication and their respective roles in the decision-making process differently. In the United States, where decision making is likely to be somewhat more decentralized, approximately half of all bishops believed priests should exercise considerable power in the diocese. About the same percentage of bishops agreed that priests do have such influence. Among priests, only 10 percent more than bishops thought they should receive such powers, but only one out of four priests actually believed they exercised such influence.[60] In Chile, on the other hand, 70 percent of the priests and bishops Brian Smith interviewed in the late 1970s favored a centralized model of decision making, allocating most authority to bishops.[61]

In the Luengo survey of Mexican priests, most suggested that regular communication occurred, nearly half describing it as frequent. One-fifth of all priests, however, said communication occurred only when necessary, suggesting no established modes of communication structures were functioning, and only two-fifths of the bishops initiated requests for information and input from their priests.[62] This survey data is a much fairer indicator of actual attitudes since outside observers typically agree that while the majority of priests accept the official Church philosophy of the moment, many do so not out of conviction but from pragmatism to avoid conflict.[63]

Bishops, like any other administrators, encounter difficulties in dealing with groups of individuals. Many priests, given an intellectual bent, believe priests can be a difficult lot to influence. Mexican priests illustrate this view with their own derogatory saying: "To give advice to a priest is the same as giving injections to a corpse."[64] Nevertheless, either a lack of communication or an all-too-clear ideological agenda led to many conflicts by the late 1970s and early 1980s, as Vatican II's patina began wearing thin and reactions set in against the most innovative elements of liberation theology.[65] Claude Pomerlau concluded that fully one-third of all dioceses faced serious, internal conflicts during this period.[66] Numerous conflicts in the 1970s have been well documented by Patricia Arias, including an extraordinary case in Aguascalientes lasting nearly six years.[67]

Priests vary from diocese to diocese in their assessments of bishops. Some consider their individual bishop to be quite domineering or authoritarian, as appears to be the case in Zamora, Michoacán.[68] Popular and even academic perceptions, however, reinforce the belief that only those bishops and archbishops who tow a conservative or traditional line are authoritarian. I would argue that a more sensible and revealing interpretation centers not on the bishop's real or perceived pastoral values but on the level of respect and autonomy he grants to his priests and the degree to which he establishes communication links. In other words, process takes precedence over ideology.

José Melgoza Osorio participated in the concilium in Rome in 1962, returning to Mexico to hold numerous seminars on Vatican II concepts. Yet Melgoza, who served as bishop of Ciudad Valles in San Luis Potosí and later as bishop of Nezahualcóyotl, Mexico's fastest growing concentration of urban, marginal people, energetically rejected Marxist influences. Melgoza is a bishop who seeks unity by imposing homogeneity, which he describes unabashedly in the following terms:

> Even in pursuing these difficult problems I have never agreed with the marriage of Marxism and religion. I had problems with the priests in the diocese who wanted to use this radical approach, and I persuaded them to leave my diocese, some of whom are now working in Nicaragua. For me, my first job was to educate my priests, and this included many priests who came from the provinces who, because of their own education and formation, had a variety of ideas. I tried to teach them what I considered this diocese's problems, and secondly, I attempted to create a sense of community and fraternity among all the priests. I do think we achieved this fairly well, although not 100 percent, through regular meetings and group discussions.[69]

Other bishops have sought a positive working relationship with their priests by granting them autonomy in process but enforcing a general framework of spiritual and pastoral goals. José Pablo Rovalo Azcué, who became bishop of Zacatecas, transferred his priestly experiences to his attitudes as bishop. As he suggested, "When you are a priest, you are dependent upon the bishop because he basically establishes the guidelines from which you work. I developed a close relationship with my bishop, so I felt very free to do things in my parish. I always followed my own techniques." When Rovalo became bishop, he recalled that "I always established some general guidelines, but I didn't tell them [priests] how to carry out those efforts."[70] Historians of the Zacatecas church confirm Rovalo's own recollections, suggesting that he and Adalberto Almeida Merino, another Vatican II veteran who preceded him in the diocese during most of the 1960s, "encouraged or at a minimum permitted the expression of some progressive positions. . . . Rovalo introduced dialogue and consultation, permitting priests greater participation in decisions concerning the diocese."[71] His immediate successor, Rafael Muñoz Núñez, a centrist, opposed this progressive philosophy, and many priests and seminarians left the vocation. Priests may also change dioceses, as they did under Bishop Melgoza, but typically priest and bishop try to resolve their differences. Besides, as McKenzie suggests, a priest becomes a marked man in the place to which he transfers.[72]

Today, the Zacatecas diocese is categorized as conservative, yet the bishop, Javier Lozano Barragán, has earned the respect of his most progressive priest, self-described as the "black sheep" in the diocese. He believes he is widely accepted by fellow priests despite his "heterodoxy." More important, while characterizing his bishop as strict, he maintains a good rapport with him, describing him as both a father and a brother who has given him and other priests expanded opportunities to discover themselves, to expand their formal education, and to function without the rancor generated by economic differences since all priests are paid out of a common fund.[73]

A third approach is that pursued by Archbishop Rosendo Huesca, who, as suggested above, is reputed to be a religious conservative. But as is so often the case among adept administrators, personal ideological biases, even within the scope of an institution's traditional philosophic position, do not necessarily translate into an exclusionary, arbitrary administrator. Again, let Huesca speak for himself:

> My attitude toward my priests is to respect Vatican II provisions. I have divided the diocese into six districts. Each month, I meet with the six councils representing these districts. They are responsible for electing their own representatives. Every two months, I meet with these representatives too. Generally, I do consult with them. I believe I have a good relationship with my priests. Only in isolated cases have I had conflicts with them. I try to give them sufficient autonomy, and they prefer to participate actively in diocese affairs. I don't have any ideological blocks because that would prevent their involvement. Yes, we do share a diversity of views, but these views are tolerable to all.[74]

The key to Huesca's success is the establishment and actual use of mediating structures between bishop and priest. Perhaps even more important is how he personally treats each priest. Father Rafael Tapia, a disciple of liberation theology, initiated base communities in the Puebla archdiocese. Even though Huesca was not particularly keen on the idea, he gave Tapia complete autonomy to implement the program, saying it was part of Vatican II and if it benefited his parishioners, he would permit it. Tapia and other priests I interviewed in the diocese, despite their policy disagreements, respected him greatly, characterizing him as "kind," "sweet," and "respectful."[75]

The most publicized, radical change in a diocese's leadership was the transition between Bishop Sergio Méndez Arceo, the leading progressive of the 1960s and 1970s, and his successor, Juan Jesús Posadas Ocampo, eventually cardinal archbishop of Guadalajara. Outside observers and some progressive priests within the diocese describe the changed environment as decisive, curtailing an experimental era. Yet a priest's ability to survive radical changes and even to take on greater responsibilities also depends on the priest's interpersonal skills and respect for the bishop. Father José Mendoza Carrillo, a native of Yautepec, Morelos, and a graduate of the Montezuma seminary, pursued an extraordinarily unique, unorthodox career under Méndez Arceo, teaching in a *public* secondary school in Cuautla and becoming active in the teachers' union movement. When Posadas became bishop, he did not prohibit Mendoza from teaching but increased his other responsibilities, forcing him to leave secondary teaching to direct the diocesan seminary. Under the current bishop, whose reputation is allegedly more conservative than Posadas, Mendoza directs *La Gaceta Diocesana* and sometimes acts as a diocesan auditor or intervenor for the bishop.[76]

The bishop's personal qualities, then, as is so often the case with natural leaders, can mediate tension-producing deficiencies in a centralized, hierarchical decision-making structure. Nevertheless, some bishops recognize that many of these potential conflicts could be eliminated or moderated, excepting human failings, if the structures themselves were improved. Such bishops formally have proposed institutional changes to facilitate increased communication and collaboration among bishops, clergy, and laity.[77] Many priests, similar to their perceptive peers in the episcopate, advocate alterations within the parish, attempting to improve Church-to-laity communication, which more than half of all priests cite as the reason the Church's message fails to reach parishioners.[78]

The problems that priest and bishop face are not, of course, solely tied to the bishop's administrative style but also relate to the parish structure. The parish evolved as the basic local unit over a period of 1,000 years. It introduces a territorial rigidity limiting flexibility in assigning personnel and churches to those areas of greatest demand. As Edward Cleary notes, evangelicals in Mexico and Latin America have no such limitations.[79] The parish structure, in combination with a proportionally declining population of priests, strains the Mexican Church's resources. Mexican dioceses exist where the ratio of priests to the population is now lower than during the high point of state religious persecution in the 1920s and 1930s.[80] In some rural regions, including Chiapas, churches are organized into pastoral zones, not parishes, producing significant consequences. Many priests in these large territories have resorted to training laypersons to perform some of the sacramental and leadership tasks traditionally assumed by clergy.[81]

Priests spend most of their time educating parishioners in their religious faith and supporting Christian lay groups. Catechism and youth groups are common in three-quarters of all parishes, whereas Catholic Action organizations and both Christian family movements and base ecclesiastical communities are found in 33 and 25 percent of parishes, respectively. Only 5 percent of a priest's time is spent on human and social development.[82]

Although parish priests allegedly devote a minor amount of their day to social and human problems, they are perceived in a positive light by laity, other clergy, and elite secular Mexicans who often distinguish them from their episcopal peers. Characteristics ascribed to priests include their strong identity with parish communities, their modesty, their cooperativeness with each other, and their pragmatism.[83] Adrián Lajous Martínez, who maintains a highly critical view of Catholicism, served as president of Mexico's Family Planning Association, which opposes Church policy on birth control. He discovered after dozens of conversations with women that priests, contrary to the Pope's stated policy on birth control, a point of conflict between laity and the Church, were sympathetic to their dilemma, advising them that it was a matter of personal conscience.[84]

Divisions in the Church: Origins, Tendencies, and Consequences

One of the issues attracting analysts' attention is the level of ideological heterogeneity within the clergy. The degree to which these differences are real rather than apparent not only influences the Church's institutional unity but also establishes conditions affecting its relationship with the state. The literature both inside and outside of Mexico focuses on three common themes applicable to the Mexican case. In the first place, socioeconomic differences play a significant role.[85] These differences are drawn from two sources: the social makeup of the clergy itself and the pronounced socioeconomic differences between various dioceses. Many observers argue that the rank-and-file clergy in Mexico, as a whole, represent more modest origins and a stronger provincial perspective than does the episcopate, even though the latter is extracted from the same pool of men.[86] Politicians who have dealt directly with the episcopate also believe that the intellectual range of bishops, based on their level of education and knowledge, explains their heterogeneity.[87]

A second source of differences involves the relationship between the church and external actors, specifically the Vatican, the role of the Vatican delegate, and the presence of foreign priests.[88] An influential delegate, advocating an agenda different from the episcopate, can exacerbate divisions existing naturally. For example, it is clear that Girolamo Prigione's first priority was Vatican-state relations, an issue far from the minds of most Mexican bishops and clergy.[89] The impact of outside influence at the top is complemented by innovations introduced by priests and nuns from abroad.[90] Although these influences are strongly reduced in Mexico because of foreign clergy's limited presence, some impact undoubtedly occurs. In fact, elsewhere in Latin America, David Mutchler argues that foreign education alone provides a significant source of disagreement.[91]

Finally, national developmental patterns and political situations of a given society accentuate change and force institutions to take new positions.[92] Vallier pointed out two decades ago that the Catholic Church, as part of a broad Latin

American trend, was moving away from its local and regional origins to a more integrated, national model.[93] This is reflected in Mexico institutionally in the strengthening of the episcopate. Politically, President Salinas's decision to alter church-state relations after more than 70 years provoked different responses among the clergy, especially the episcopate, responses that also varied according to generational experiences, another variable promoting diversity.

Most observers of the Mexican Catholic Church, and clergy themselves, tend to lump the episcopate into three broad ideological groups: left, center, and right (or radical, moderate, and conservative). Labels are very dangerous to use, and they rarely capture the complexity of an individual bishop's point of view. Bishops take a pronounced, public position on an issue that places them in one category, while believing and practicing a philosophy that places them in another. The most comprehensive and accurate categorization available is that offered by Eduardo Sota, whose use of the word "tendency" is also more apt.[94]

- *Vatican Tendency*—A group of bishops, represented by Girolamo Prigione, who advocate the interests and objectives, both spiritual and political, of the Vatican. According to some analysts, fewer than 10 bishops actually have supported this tendency, which until 1992 included reestablishment of Vatican-state relations.

- *Spiritual Mission Tendency*—Bishops who favor this tendency believe strongly that the primary mission of the Church is spiritual; consequently they have no interest in political matters. However, they will speak out if they believe the religious (spiritual) rights of Catholics are violated.

- *Chihuahua Tendency*—This group, which takes its name from the actions of the northern bishops in 1986, is willing to openly fight for political rights, electoral integrity, and democratic change, believing it a moral obligation and essential to the welfare of its parishioners. It also favored the Church's legal recognition, since its members believed it was essential to their ability to make pronouncements on secular issues affecting the laity. However, they are not, for the most part, progressive on other pastoral and spiritual issues. They include Carlos Quintero Arce of Hermosillo, Luis Reynoso of Cuernavaca, Alfredo Torres Romero of Toluca, and Genaro Alamilla of Mexico.[95]

- *Southern Tendency*—They draw their orientation and leadership from bishops in the Pacific-South region who are strongly sympathetic to the Church of the Poor, particularly to the problems of peasants and indigenous Mexicans. They support social, structural changes as a means of alleviating their parishioners' poverty and exploitation. Although they share some similarities with the northern group, specifically concerning their willingness to speak out, their focus is on social-economic issues, not electoral politics. They combine some of the characteristics found in Vallier's pastor and pluralist categories. Bishops identified with this tendency include Samuel Ruiz of San Cristóbal de las Casas, Manuel Talamás of Ciudad Juárez, Arturo Lona of Tehuantepec, and Bartolomé Carrasco of Oaxaca.[96] Although they typically are identified as disciples of the late Sergio Méndez Arceo, Blancarte argues this is misleading, classifying Méndez Arceo as the only true radical bishop of his generation.[97] It is probably more accurate to describe these bishops, in Méndez Arceo's own words, as sympathetic to the social philosophy spelled out in "Injustice in Mexico," the Mexican episcopal document of 1971.[98]

- *Silent Majority Tendency*—This is the largest group, composing nearly three-quarters of all bishops, who rarely offer any public statements, making it difficult to assess their actual ideological postures. Most would be moderates, and some who are traditionalists fall into this category. The moderates who do speak out from the leadership of the CEM include Cardinal Corripio, Adolfo Suárez, and Sergio Obeso Rivera. Perhaps a better term is the equilibrium tendency.[99]

The Catholic hierarchy is the first to admit the existence of such divisions. Even the head of the episcopate's doctrine of faith committee has made public the strong tensions dividing bishops on theological matters.[100] However, he and other clergy argue that these differences are healthy and important to the Church's growth. As one priest expressed it:

> I consider this to be a wonderful richness within the Church. For example, a conservative group is more interested in the development of the individual. Another group exists that is more interested in the community, the condition of people. It is fair to say that in certain respects they are not actually opposed to each other but serve as a balance to each other in the Church's tasks. I think these differences are necessary for the health of the Church because a Church that has only one vision of promoting a single institutional mission would not be positive.[101]

A very strong tendency exists within the Catholic hierarchy to temper these divisions, or at least their consequences. Bishops argue that outside communities, including the media, exaggerate these differences in Mexico. Thomas Sanders, who studied the Catholic Church throughout Latin America, offers support for this view. He suggests that despite the undeniable existence of divisions with the Church, "it is erroneous to regard bishops as eager to promote political cleavage and conflict. Bishops are a distinct type of institutional leadership or elite who, despite their differences on many matters, are motivated in the final analysis by Catholic religious values and committed to preserving the religious unity of the Church. Like the Pope, they symbolize that Church unity within their geographical jurisdictions or dioceses."[102]

A similar pattern and a desire to correct this impression from bishops of various ideological tendencies can be detected in the Mexican case. As a moderate bishop who served on several important CEM committees explained, he never had witnessed "any serious conflict, based either on policy or on personalities at CEM conferences, despite what the papers have said."[103] Even Mexico's most controversial bishop, Samuel Ruiz, who has earned the ire of the Vatican delegate, made a passionate argument for institutional unity: "I don't see myself as exceptional [ideologically speaking]. I see all of us belonging to an institution that has a long history. We are all part of that history. It is the media that stresses these 'ideological' differences, not those of us in the Church. *I repeat, we are all part of the same institution*" (emphasis added).[104]

This does not mean, however, that bishops publicly will come to the defense of their more radical peers. Arturo Lona Reyes, outspoken bishop of Tehuantepec, who has been accused of being a murderer and a guerrilla, admitted that few of his fellow bishops defend him against these charges. Instead, an archbishop advised him to tone down his declarations to avoid problems.[105]

Tensions exist between the national leadership of the CEM, who attempt to maintain a pleasant working relationship with the state by using behind-the-scenes negotiations, and local bishops, who are faced with difficult problems in their dioceses, giving low priority to any effect their actions may have on national relations. As David Bailey concluded several decades ago: "[T]here is a lack of cohesion in the episcopate, much of it due to Mexico's regionalism; most bishops are jealous of their autonomy, and believe that they are the best judges of how to handle matters in their own diocese, whether the issues be education, social action, or political relations."[106]

Conclusions

The evolution of the diocese as the central structural unit of bishops' power and influence produces multiple consequences for the Catholic Church and for the church's relations with other institutions. The diocese can be seen as both a strength and a weakness, as would any decentralized unit in a larger organization. By nature, large, well-established bureaucracies tend to be conserving, not unchanging but evolving slowly and incrementally. Mexico's Catholic hierarchy is large enough to incorporate many points of view. By the hierarchy's own admission, the structural division of the Church into dioceses along geographic and social boundaries contributes decisively to bishops' socializing experiences and pastoral orientations.

Often, the nature of an issue and its timing determine these differences, exacerbated by the diocesan structure. Contrary to popular opinion, bishops are frequently ahead of priests in their social postures. This was illustrated clearly in Chihuahua in the 1970s, where Bishops Adalberto Almeida and Manuel Talamás attempted to introduce some of the concepts of liberation theology, including renovating the seminary curriculum. Their attempts were resoundingly defeated by a conservative, staunchly opposed clergy.[107]

The Church, unlike most multinational companies, does not have central corporate headquarters in Mexico, or even for that matter in Rome, through which its executives, bishops, archbishops, and cardinals must pass. Naturally, the Church does provide a strong set of institutional beliefs, or if you will, a corporate culture. Although the Pope voices these values, they are tempered and flavored by bishops' experiences in their local dioceses. The ideological mandates of international and national institutions do not appear to be the most important forces for change within the Church. Instead, personnel selection processes largely determine the episcopate's spiritual and pastoral direction.

Structures take on a significant influence in the Mexican episcopate through the role assigned to and defined by the Vatican's representative. During the last two decades, Girolamo Prigione, Mexico's papal nuncio, has wielded an extraordinary influence over the episcopate, not as a policeman of Catholic religious beliefs but as a well-heard voice in selecting future bishops. Indeed, Prigione's influence will be felt in the hierarchy for years to come, long after he leaves Mexico. On the other hand, reaction to the delegate's intervention has led to strengthening regional and national institutions representing the Mexican hierarchy and an increasing rejection of his implicit or explicit policies.

Allan Metz makes a convincing argument that the Mexican Church depends heavily on the Vatican, and that such dependency can present problems for the Church in its relationship to the state. He suggests that these problems have not arisen because the state and the Vatican generally have seen eye to eye on fundamental issues. If the Church's loyalty to the Vatican produced a conflict with the state, the Mexican Church would choose the Vatican.[108] Under normal circumstances, Metz's conclusion is correct. But it can be argued that the Vatican's understanding of the Mexican Church relies too heavily on its delegate's interpretation. If an issue arose that compromised bishops' nationalism, casting the Vatican on the opposing side, it is quite probable that the bishops would stand independent of the Vatican, if not necessarily with the state.

The Vatican delegate's motives for making specific personnel recommendations are hotly debated. It is clear, however, that he is selecting moderate traditionalists, expanding the potential, at least at an ideological level, for homogeneity among the episcopate. The episcopate itself has moved in a centrist direction as a compromise between the progressive and traditional wings. In fact, the choice of Ernesto Corripio as CEM head in the late 1970s was classified as a compromise choice between the two extreme wings.[109] Although Prigione succeeded in having Cardinal Corripio in the Mexico archdiocese replaced on June 16, 1995 by Norberto Rivera (well-known for his opposition to base community organizations and liberation theology) and identified with mainstream Vatican views, he alienated the majority of the 1,800 priests in Mexico City who had recommended other candidates.[110] Prigione's recent appointees from Durango and León interject a new, potentially divisive pattern in episcopal leadership, distorting long-term patterns in geographic and educational recruitment.

Decentralized, autonomous diocesan structures, when they convey an image of weakness and dissension, affect Church relations with outside institutions. The state, when it clearly understands the origins of these weakness, can exploit them to its own advantage.[111] The state, on the other hand, relying on authoritarian solutions for most of its political problems, seeks out single actors to resolve church-state disputes. It does not want to communicate with a collective body. Although the logical figure to whom the state should address its queries and complaints is the president of the CEM, it has relied almost exclusively on the Vatican delegate since 1977 to coordinate its relations with the Church. The state's reliance reinforces the Vatican delegate's position. The state's choice also opens it up to the problem of dealing with a group unrepresentative of the episcopate's actual interests.[112]

The state's misunderstanding of the Church's decentralized structure has generated new tensions. Its alliance with the Vatican delegate, in some cases against local bishops, such as Samuel Ruiz, has opened up the government to deserved criticism, encouraging a backlash among the hierarchy. Many members of the hierarchy also are concerned about what they believe to be the delegate's excessive influence and the CEM's weakness vis-à-vis the Vatican's representative.

Problems generated by the structural relationships between the Vatican and the diocese are repeated between the diocese and the parish. The bishops' strength, their almost complete autonomy from any national and international institutional authority, explains their tendency to be authoritarian. Even bishops with a strong commitment to social change and increased laity and priest participation in the decision-making process can themselves become authoritarian in the defense of their prerogatives.[113]

The centralization of authority, even when it occurs at various structural levels, promotes communication problems; Mexican priests identify it as the primary administrative source of problems in their parishes. Nevertheless, progressive bishops do not have a monopoly on effective communication or even on the goodwill of their priests. As is true within most large organizations, the individual executive's skill is crucial in determining administrative effectiveness. Various bishops have demonstrated a capacity for tolerance and effective communication amid ideological differences with some of their priests.

Mexico's Catholic Church cannot be understood, either in terms of its leadership or its rank-and-file clergy, without examining it at the local level. The image it conveys as a national, unified institution is misleading. The Church is a complex organization of local and regional voices most concerned about the issues and personalities in their dioceses, not in the episcopate or the Vatican.

NOTES

1. "Organización actual de la Iglesia Católica," unpublished manuscript, n.d., n.p.

2. Thomas Reese, *Archbishop: Inside the Power Structure of the American Catholic Church* (New York: Harper and Row, 1989), vi.

3. Manuel Carrillo Poblano, "Jerarquía católica mexicana," *Este País*, June 1991, 15; John L. McKenzie, *The Roman Catholic Church* (New York: Holt, Rinehart, 1969), 41.

4. Antonio García Montaño, "Los obispos mexicanos de la segunda mitad del siglo xx," unpublished manuscript, n.d., 11.

5. "Política," *El Nacional*, May 10, 1990, 23.

6. Roberto Blancarte, *El poder salinismo e iglesia católica, una nueva convivencia?* (Mexico City: Grijalbo, 1991), 289.

7. Claude Pomerlau, "Cambios en el liderazgo y la crisis de autoridad en el catolicismo mexicano," in *Religión y política en México*, Martín de la Rosa et al., eds. (Mexico City: Siglo XXI, 1985), 251.

8. Thomas Reese, *Archbishop*, 59.

9. John L. McKenzie, *The Roman Catholic Church*, 53.

10. Daniel H. Levine, *Religion and Politics in Latin America: The Catholic Church in Venezuela and Colombia* (Princeton: Princeton University Press, 1981), 107.

11. Based on my visits to 30 dioceses from 1987 through 1995.

12. Antonio García Montaño, "Los obispos mexicanos de la segunda mitad del siglo xx," 10.

13. John L. McKenzie, *The Roman Catholic Church*, 54.

14. George Grayson, *The Church in Contemporary Mexico* (Washington: CSIS, 1992), 29.

15. For example, Ricardo Watty Urquidi, born in San Diego, California, joined the order of the Misioneros del Espíritu Santo, receiving his first assignment in the archdiocese as the parish priest of San Marcos, Mexicaltezingo, Federal District, in 1971. He became an auxiliary bishop to Cardinal Corripio in 1980 and, after a decade of service, became at age 52 bishop of Nuevo Laredo. For career details, see *Cambio*, May 15, 1989, 40.

16. Oscar Aguilar and Enrique Luengo, "Iglesia y gobierno en el D.F.," in *D.F.: gobierno y sociedad civil*, Pablo González Casanova, ed. (Mexico City: El Caballito, 1987), 198.

17. Enrique Luengo, "Los párrocos: una visión," unpublished manuscript, Department of Social and Political Sciences, Ibero-American University, December 1989. Subsequently, a broader, published version, focusing on politics, appeared in Eduardo Sota García and Enrique Luengo González, *Entre la conciencia y la obediencia: la opinión del clero sobre la política en México* (Mexico City: Ibero-American University, 1994).

18. Luigi Einaudi, ed., *Latin American Institutional Development: The Changing Catholic Church* (Santa Monica, Calif.: Rand Corporation, 1969), 14.

19. Personal interview with Father Baltazar López, parish priest, Cuernavaca Diocese, Cuernavaca, Morelos, June 3, 1988.

20. Personal interview with Bishop Manuel Samaniego Barriga, Cuautitlán Diocese, Cuautitlán, México, February 13, 1991.

21. Personal interview with Jean Meyer, Mexico City, June 21, 1989. Some politicians have argued, with good reason, that bishops are highly autonomous in religious matters, but when they move into the arena of political issues (prior to 1992), the Vatican delegate, or even a powerful parishioner, can exert a hidden but more influential role. Personal interview with Manuel Hinojosa Ortiz, Mexico City, June 1, 1988.

22. Thomas Reese, *Archbishop*, 58.

23. Personal interview with Bishop Raúl Vera López, Ciudad Altamirano Diocese, Guerrero, Mexico City, May 3, 1992.

24. Personal interview with Bishop Sergio Méndez Arceo, Mexico City, June 21, 1989.

25. Specifically, Greeley wrote: "Bishops, on the other hand, are willing to admit theoretically that there is a need for greater decentralization of power, but they do not seem to be inclined to support many specific changes in the power structure. They are by and large inclined to think that the present practical distribution of power is ideal." Andrew M. Greeley, *Priests in the United States: Reflections on a Survey* (New York: Doubleday, 1972), 104.

26. John L. McKenzie, *The Roman Catholic Church*, 56.

27. Claude Pomerlau, "Cambios en el liderazgo y la crisis de autoridad en el catolicismo mexicano," 252.

28. Bartolomé Carrasco personally requested help from the Vatican over the issue of celibacy. However, the individual recommended by Prigione, and sent by the Vatican, changed the ideological line favored by the bishop. This revision generated considerable conflict in the diocese between conservatives and progressives, causing a group of priests

to travel to Mexico City to meet with Prigione. *El Nacional,* March 24, 1990, 7; *Proceso,* March 12, 1990, 20; George Grayson, *The Church in Contemporary Mexico,* 25.

29. Ivan Vallier, *Catholicism, Social Control, and Modernization in Latin America* (Englewood Cliffs, N.J.: Prentice-Hall, 1970), 100, citing a 12-diocese study of France, Chile, and the United States.

30. Catholic Church, Diocese of Tijuana, *Plan pastoral, 1989–1994, hacia una iglesia nueva* (Tijuana: La Diocese, 1989), 103, 233, based on a survey of 22,000 parishioners.

31. Personal interview with Archbishop Manuel Pérez Gil, Tlanepantla Archdiocese, Tlanepantla, México, February 18, 1991.

32. Personal interview with Fausto Zerón Medina, Mexico City, May 27, 1987.

33. For example, see Thomas Reese's statement that in the United States, "[i]t is not surprising that chancellors, secretaries to bishops, and seminary rectors have a better chance of getting nominated at province meetings than the pastor of a rural parish. They are better known to bishops." *Archbishop,* 6.

34. Thomas Reese, *A Flock of Shepherds: The National Conference of Catholic Bishops* (Kansas City, Mo.: Sheed and Ward, 1992), 5.

35. Personal interview with Father Salvador Tello Robles, Madre de Dios Parish, Guadalajara Archdiocese, Guadalajara, Jalisco, Mexico, July 6, 1993.

36. Thomas Reese, *Archbishop,* 27, 47.

37. Bishop Sergio Méndez Arceo recalled a case of a Mexican bishop recommending only a single candidate before the tenure of Girolamo Prigione, essentially assuring his choice. Personal interview.

38. Thomas Reese, *Archbishop,* 14–15, 17.

39. Nevertheless, a student of the U.S. selection process concluded that while it is customary for the bishop to select a priest he prefers, there "is nothing to prevent the Holy See from appointing a coadjutor (or auxiliary) against the will of the resident bishop." See John T. Finnegan, "The Present Canonical Practice in the Catholic Church," in *The Choosing of Bishops,* William W. Bassett, ed. (Hartford, Conn.: The Canon Law Society of America, 1971), 93.

40. Personal interview with Juan Bazdresch, Ibero-American University, Mexico City, June 20, 1989; personal interview with Roberto Blancarte, Mexico City, February 20, 1991; personal interview with Luis Narro Rodríguez, Center of Educational Studies, Mexico City, June 28, 1989.

41. Rodrigo Vera, "La jerarquía en combate contra seguidores de Méndez Arceo y su obra en Morelos," *Proceso,* April 3, 1989, 18.

42. José Luis Gaona Vega, "La designación de Sandoval Iñiguez fue hecha por 'manos extrañas a la región,'" *Punto,* March 21, 1988, 11.

43. Personal interview with Archbishop Manuel Pérez Gil.

44. According to canon law, as of September 1, 1970, each individual bishop referred to in Article 1, paragraph 2, has "the right to propose candidates directly to the Holy See." William H. Bassett, *The Choosing of Bishops* (Hartford, Conn.: The Canon Law Society of America, 1971), 104.

45. John T. Finnegan, "The Present Canonical Practice in the Catholic Church," 91.

46. Robert Trisco, "The Variety of Procedures in Modern History," in *The Choosing of Bishops,* William W. Bassett, ed. (Hartford, Conn.: The Canon Law Society of America, 1971), 38–40.

47. Thomas Reese, *Archbishop,* 4.

48. Personal interview with José Rogelio Alvarez and Father Antonio García Montaño, Mexico City, February 15, 1991.

49. Thomas Reese, *Archbishop,* 9.

50. Luigi Einaudi, however, argues that the diocesan structure, and not the decision-making process itself, is what provides for political and religious diversity leading to the political and theological controversies. *Latin American Institutional Development,* 10.

51. Thomas Reese, *Archbishop,* 31.

52. John T. Finnegan, "The Present Canonical Practice in the Catholic Church," 101, citing *On Papal Diplomats,* June 24, 1969.

53. Rodrigo Vera, "La jerarquía en combate contra seguidores de Méndez Arceo y su obra en Morelos," 19. An often-cited case is that of Juan José Posadas, who became Mexico's second cardinal after becoming archbishop of Guadalajara. He was Prigione's original choice to replace Sergio Méndez Arceo in Cuernavaca. See Oscar Aguilar and Enrique Luengo, "Iglesia y gobierno en el D.F.," 15. He also has been accused of intervening in the selection of religious order leaders. According to Roberto Blancarte, he prevented Sister Manuela Charría from becoming secretary general of the Latin American Confederation of Religious (CLAR). *El poder salinismo e iglesia católica, una nueva convivencia?,* 254.

54. Personal interview with Fathers Rafael Tapia, Abelardo Hernández, and Humberto Vargas, Archdiocese of Puebla, Puebla, Puebla, July 16, 1993.

55. George Grayson, *The Church in Contemporary Mexico,* 35.

56. I am indebted to Rodrigo Vera, "La jerarquía en combate contra seguidores de Méndez Arceo y su obra en Morelos," 19, for suggesting the existence of such a pattern.

57. Personal interview with Archbishop Rosendo Huesca, Puebla Archdiocese, Puebla, Puebla, July 16, 1993.

58. Thomas Reese, *Archbishop,* 43.

59. Aurora Berdejo Arvizu, "Los obispos violentan la constitución," *Excélsior,* April 11, 1991, 34.

60. Andrew M. Greeley, *Priests in the United States,* 105–106.

61. Brian H. Smith, *The Church and Politics in Chile: Challenges to Modern Catholicism* (Princeton: Princeton University Press, 1982), 41.

62. Enrique Luengo, "Los párrocos, una visión," 65.

63. Lucía Alonso Reyes, "Función social de la iglesia en Zacatecas," *Memorias, segundo informe de investigación sobre el estado de Zacatecas* (Zacatecas, 1989), 180.

64. Jorge Martínez, *Memorias y reflexiones de un obispo* (Mexico City: Editorial Villicaña, 1986), 21.

65. The most extreme claim I found of a conflict between priest and bishop is that of Father Rafael Isaías Cachú Torres, who claims that Bishop José Melgoza Osorio of the Nezahualcóyotl Diocese in the State of México tried to have him murdered and also that he was beaten by another priest, all because he denounced corruption within the Church. The Church officially suspended him in 1988. *El Nacional,* April 6, 1991, n.p.

66. Claude Pomerlau, "Cambios en el liderazgo y la crisis de autoridad en el catolicismo mexicano," 249.

67. Patricia Arias et al., *Radiografía de la iglesia católica en México* (Mexico City: UNAM, 1981), 33–39, most fully develops the case of Aguascalientes, where an authoritarian bishop intensified a public dispute between himself and his priests, forcing the Vatican delegate to send an inspector. Although never publicized, a coadjutor auxiliary bishop, Alfredo Torres, administered the diocese for more than a year from 1975 to 1976, after the bishop, Salvador Quezada Limón, was removed. Quezada returned in December 1976, but Torres remained as the administrator until 1980, when he became bishop of Toluca.

68. Personal interview with Jean Meyer, Mexico City, June 21, 1989.

69. Personal interview with Bishop José Melgoza Osorio, Nezahualcóyotl Diocese, Nezahualcóyotl, México, May 27, 1987.

70. Personal interview with Bishop José Pablo Rovalo, Episcopal Vicariate, Fifth Zone, Mexico Archdiocese, February 21, 1991.

71. Lucía Alonso Reyes, "Función social de la iglesia en Zacatecas," 180–181.

72. John L. McKenzie, *The Roman Catholic Church,* 64.

73. Personal interview by Scott Pentzer and Meg Mitchell with Father Pascual Torres Escobedo, Zacatecas Diocese, Zacatecas, Zacatecas, July 19, 1993.

74. Personal interview with Archbishop Rosendo Huesca.

75. Personal interviews with Fathers Rafael Tapia, Abelardo Hernández, and Humberto Vargas.

76. Personal interview by Scott Pentzer with Father José Mendoza Carrillo, Cuernavaca Diocese, Cuernavaca, Morelos, July 30, 1993.

77. Manuel Talamás did so, but the proposal was rejected by the CEM. Patricia Arías et al., *Radiografía de la iglesia católica en México,* 41.

78. Enrique Luengo, "Los párrocos: una visión," 66.

79. Edward L. Cleary, "Politics and Religion—Crisis, Constraints, and Restructuring," in *Conflict and Competition: The Latin American Church in a Changing Environment,* Edward L. Cleary and Hannah Stewart-Gambino, eds. (Boulder, Colo.: Lynne Rienner, 1992), 217.

80. Claude Pomerlau, "The Catholic Church in Mexico and Its Changing Relationship to Society and the State," unpublished manuscript, December 1980, Chapter 3, 6. For evidence of the decline in the 1920s and 1930s, see James W. Wilkie, "Statistical Indicators of the Impact of National Revolution on the Catholic Church in Mexico, 1910–1967," *Journal of Church and State* 12, no. 1 (Winter 1970): 98.

81. Shannan Mattiace, "The Social Role of the Mexican Catholic Church: The Case of the Yucatán Base Community," senior honors thesis, Central University of Iowa, 1990, 22, 39.

82. Enrique Luengo, "Los párrocos, una visión," 59; José María Díaz Mozaz and Vicente J. Sastre, "Una encuesta de opinión al clero mexicano, aproximación a la realidad socio-religiosa mexicana," *Vida Pastoral* 2, no. 11 (August 1976): 17.

83. Personal interview with Father Jesús Vergara, Mexico City, June 29, 1989.

84. Personal interview with Adrián Lajous Martínez, Mexico City, June 2, 1988.

85. Guadalupe Baez, "En la Iglesia hay divisiones teológicas," *Unomásuno,* June 27, 1990, 3.

86. Marta Eugenia García Ugarte, "Las posiciones políticas de la jeararquía católica, efectos en la cultura religiosa mexicana," in *Religiosidad y política en México,* Carlos Martínez Assad, ed. (Mexico City: Ibero-American University, 1992), 68–69.

87. Personal interview with Alfredo del Mazo, Mexico City, February 15, 1991.

88. *El Nacional,* April 29, 1990, 15.

89. Personal interview with Arturo Núñez Jiménez, former subsecretary of government (in charge of church-state affairs), Mexico City, February 12, 1993.

90. Brian H. Smith, "Religion and Social Change: Classical Theories and New Formulations in the Content of Recent Developments in Latin America," *Latin American Research Review* 10 (1975): 19.

91. David Mutchler, *The Church as a Political Factor in Latin America* (New York: Praeger, 1971), 211–212.

92. Scott Mainwaring, *The Catholic Church and Politics in Brazil, 1916–1985* (Stanford: Stanford University Press, 1986), 237–238.

93. Ivan Vallier, "Religious Elites, Differentiations, and Developments in Roman Catholicism," in *Elites in Latin America,* Seymour Martin Lipset, ed. (New York: Oxford University Press, 1968), 197.

94. Eduardo E. Sota García, "La percepción social y política de los párrocos del estado de México," M.A. thesis, Ibero-American University, January 1992, n.p. For a government analyst's point of view, see Manuel Carrillo Poblano, "La iglesia católica hoy," unpublished manuscript, 1994.

95. Cindy Anders, "No Power, No Glory," *Proceso,* June 15, 1989, 19.

96. Oscar González et al., "Batallas en el reino de este mundo," *Nexos* no. 78 (June 1984): 24; Obispos de la Región Pacífico Sur, *Evangelio y bienes temporales* (Oaxaca: Catedral de Santa María de la Asunción, 1985), 2–3; Partido Institucional Revolucionario, "Memorandum sobre las relaciones estado-iglesia católica," unpublished manuscript, November 1988, 7; Oscar Aguilar and Enrique Luengo, "Iglesia y gobierno en el D.F.," 13.

97. Personal interview with Roberto Blancarte, Mexico City, February 20, 1991.

98. Personal interview with Bishop Sergio Méndez Arceo.

99. Personal interview with the secretary to the bishop of Toluca, Samuel Morín Suárez, Toluca Diocese, Toluca, México, June 9, 1988; Dennis M. Hanratty, "The Church," in *Prospects for Mexico,* George W. Grayson, ed. (Washington: Center for the Study of Foreign Affairs, 1988), 117; Miguel Angel Rivera, "Soy una tercera corriente dentro la Iglesia: la equilibradora," *Proceso,* October 3, 1977, 24; Dennis Goulet, "The Mexican Church: Into the Public Arena," *America,* April 9, 1989, 321–322.

100. Guadalupe Baez, "En la Iglesia hay divisiones teológicas," 3.

101. Personal interview with Father Jacques Chaveriat, Mexico Archdiocese, Mexico City, June 8, 1988.

102. Thomas G. Sanders, "The Chilean Episcopate," *American Universities Field Staff Reports* 15, no. 3 (August 1968): 2.

103. Personal interview with Bishop Manuel Samaniego Barriga.

104. Personal interview with Bishop Samuel Ruiz, San Cristóbal de las Casas Diocese, Chiapas, Lago de Guadalupe, Cuautitlán, México, April 30, 1992.

105. Carlos Fazio, "El episcopado, contra 'la desinformación' oficial sobre sus actividades," *Proceso,* September 1, 1986, 14; Rodrigo Vera, "La visita del Papa a Salinas, arranque de las nuevas relaciones," *Proceso,* January 1, 1990, 11.

106. David C. Bailey, unpublished essay, n.d., n.p.

107. Vikram Khub Chand, "Politics, Institutions, and Democracy in Mexico: The Politics of the State of Chihuahua in National Perspective," unpublished Ph.D. dissertation, Harvard University, May 1991, 223.

108. Allan Metz, "Church-State Relations in Contemporary Mexico, 1968–1988," in *The Religious Challenge to the State,* Matthew C. Moen and Lowell S. Gustafson, eds. (Philadelphia: Temple University Press, 1992), 113.

109. Soledad Loaeza, "La Iglesia católica mexicana y el reformismo autoritario," *Foro Internacional* 25, no. 2 (October–December 1984): 151.

110. Prigione owes his remarkable success in imposing his choice of bishops in large part to his close relationship to Cardinal Angelo Sodano, Vatican secretary of state, who comes from the same region of Italy as Prigione and attended seminary with him. The priests voted for Sergio Obeso Rivera, twice head of the Mexican Council of Bishops; Abelardo Alvarado Alcántara, auxiliary bishop of the archdiocese and former rector of the Mexico seminary; Ricardo Watty Urquidi, bishop of Nuevo León and former auxiliary bishop of Mexico; and Luis Morales Reyes from the Torreón diocese. Prigione's candidates included the bishops of Tijuana, Cuernavaca, and Zacatecas, all of whom were more visible than Norberto Rivera. Rivera closed the Regional Seminary of the Southeast in the state of Puebla, which in 1990 was the largest seminary favoring liberation theology tenets. *Proceso,* June 19, 1995, 30; Eduardo Molina y Vedia, "Appointment of Cardinal Marks Advances for the Conservative Sector," *InterPress Service,* June 23, 1995.

111. As Dennis Goulet suggests, the provincialization of church activism makes it possible for the government to deploy its arsenal of weapons to control or confine such activism. "The Mexican Church: Into the Public Arena," 322.

112. Federico Reyes Heroles also makes this point in an interview with Rafael Rodríguez Castañeda. "La relación con el Papa riesgoso acto pragmático en busca de popularidad," *Proceso,* February 26, 1990, 14.

113. For example, Dennis Hanratty cites a case in Torreón in 1976 of a supporter of liberation theology who strongly attacked the Catholic left when it challenged his control over the diocese. "Change and Conflict in the Contemporary Mexican Catholic Church," unpublished Ph.D. dissertation, Duke University, 1980, 15.

12

The Church Viewed through
Political and Clerical Lenses

Mexico passed through one of the most economically and politically dynamic stages of its development in the 1980s and 1990s. The Catholic Church and Catholicism were witnesses to, and active ingredients in, ongoing alterations in Mexican society. It is fortuitous that field research for this project began at this juncture, especially since no one would have predicted a newly formalized relationship between church and state in the mid-1980s.

The literature on church-state relations and on the Catholic Church's potential political or social role in the region ignores the combined views of actual actors in the relationship—politicians and clergy—a serious methodological flaw. It is also important to integrate rank-and-file clergy's interpretations with those of the episcopate, not only to understand frontline troops' attitudes on implementing Catholic doctrine but also to comprehend the future direction of Church leadership drawn from this community of priests. Furthermore, an occasional interpretation of prominent intellectuals is included since much of what the Church does or can bestow on society is cultural in scope, and intellectuals have contributed heavily to the secular environment governing Mexican church-state relations.

The views of the Catholic episcopate and rank-and-file clergy are particularly important because, as Daniel Levine argues, their perceptions and self-images of the institutional Church and its religious doctrine "determine the direction, intensity, and style of action that members undertake. It is the stuff of which commitments and martyrs are made."[1] It is also the case, as Levine suggests, that religion generally shapes behavior in the daily life of the community. Implicit political messages, associated with religious traditions, may also be transmitted through the latent political culture, including attitudes toward authority.[2] Although, as we have seen, many politicians reject strong Catholic influences in their upbringing in the strict spiritual sense, they are affected indirectly by Catholic and secular cultural influences.

Throughout this work, the focus implicitly and explicitly is on the relationship between religion and politics, or the broader pastoral role the Church might play, willing or unwillingly, in Mexican society. The implicit connections between religion and politics in the general culture suggest that a long-standing relationship exists. As Levine aptly concludes, the existence of such a relationship is not new; rather, it is worth exploring the new forms and ideas that this relationship takes in Latin America or Mexico.[3]

It is also important to point out a major difference between bishops and politicians in Mexico, a difference reinforced in these interviews. Most members of the Catholic hierarchy have adjusted to Mexico's secular constitutional system, and they speak its language.[4] Indeed, an irony of Mexican life is that clergy recognized the legitimacy of the constitution well before the 1992 reforms, but politicians, as one scholar argued, were obliged to ignore it to survive.[5] In short, most clergy accepted the society and state in which they operated, whereas many politicians, especially up to 1992, did not fully accept the Church, ignoring its institutional role. President Echeverría confirms this interpretation, confessing, "I am inclined to believe that we established and valued a modus vivendi between Church and State without really understanding what the Church was all about."[6] It has even been suggested that the word "clerical" in the Mexican political vocabulary is a pejorative term applied to clergy who abandon their strictly moral and spiritual tasks to intervene in politics.[7]

As indicated in the chapter on linkages between clergy and public figures, one of the reasons why politicians remain more ignorant of the Church is their general lack of social contact with clergy. Another explanation, however, is confined to the secular community, specifically politicians. Given Mexico's historical experience, including the suppression of the Catholic Church in the 1920s and 1930s, Mexicans created social customs to avoid religiously oriented conversations. As Adrián Lajous reflected: "What's very interesting is that when we have social gatherings and breakfasts together, even with people I know very well, we basically don't discuss religion. Religion is a very personal matter in Mexico, and it can be an extremely conflictual subject, so we don't bring it up. It's not even a subject you discuss with your friends, because it's not in good taste to do so."[8]

During the decade from 1985 to 1995, I posed several questions to the various communities selected for interviews. These questions included what type of role the Catholic Church was playing or should be playing; what political role, if any, it should engage in; and up through 1992, how the formal relationship between church and state should be altered, and if it should not, why not? Furthermore, I also asked both politicians and clergy how they viewed each other; that is, whether they differed in the goals each sought for society.

How Politicians View the Catholic Church

President Echeverría, who in the 1970s informally contributed to increased contact between the state and the Catholic Church, expresses a very deep understanding and respect for religion and its contributions to Mexican culture. He believes them to be significant, and he has a specific vision of Mexican Catholicism:

What the Church is in essence, true of many religions, is an institution focusing on societal morality and on an afterlife that can be achieved through salvation. They established the norms of conduct, a system of Judeo-Christian ethics. Their project of social behavior was transferred into education, all ultimately for eternal salvation. In contrast to pre-Christian societies, Christians have always shown more concern, authentic or not, for the poor. They always have been focused on the family, especially on human relations within the family. . . .

The Church lives with political and economic power, but Christianity is for the poor. Its preoccupation should be with the less fortunate, to be Christian. I think it does have a basic social role that stems from its historic bases.[9]

The president's view of the Church goes a long way in explaining his relationship to Bishop Sergio Méndez Arceo, as well as the populist economic policies he implemented during his administration.

A second view of the Church, much more widespread among public figures, stresses its role as a builder of human values rather than as an advocate of the interests of less fortunate Mexicans. Politicians who support this perspective go beyond the spiritual benefits religion may offer, stressing two fundamental elements: ethics and equality. The first and most important Church task in their eyes is to "develop a set of rituals, or of behavior, so that you have a set of values on how to behave during life's major crises or changes. . . . They ultimately affect personal behavior, and collectively the behavior of society. . . . I think, in Mexico, that the Church can establish a set of ethical values for personal and social conduct more rapidly, and more effectively, than any other institution."[10]

Many politicians see an ethical deficiency in societal norms affecting behavior in all sectors. They argue that the Church could help to develop ethical principles that would affect social responsibility among workers, employers, and public servants. They cite examples of economic and political ethics that led to abuses in salaries and corruption. To these politicians, the issue of election impartiality relies on a foundation of political ethics. They believe the Church has a responsibility to teach actively these principles through the pulpit and pastoral letters.

Julio Faesler, a prominent figure in Mexican public life in the 1970s and 1980s, left politics to encourage the development of nongovernmental civic and human rights organizations. He makes a convincing case for the Church in eliminating the distinction between private and public morality, believing the two are inextricably bound:

Morality covers all aspects of a person's behavior. Integrity has to apply to all activities of a person. Children are accustomed to seeing the effects of corruption creep into their own homes. A fundamental morality must exist. This concept of two moralities, public and private, is a false dichotomy that interferes with the morality of a person's behavior. For example, look at the irony of Calles's dying and confessing to a Jesuit priest on his deathbed or a public official going to Church for his daughter's wedding. I think the Church now can play a more important role in helping to bridge the two behaviors, public and private.[11]

Another politician, from an older generation, who also believes the Church's role in forming values is essential, stresses the promotion of love and equality, strongly maintaining that in its educational role, the Church will, through teaching social equality, promote mutual respect, including that between clergy and public officials.[12] In fact, clarifying and increasing the sophistication of such values are seen in a positive light, even to the extent that they would prevent elites, including politicians, from manipulating the population for their own ends.

It can be argued in the Mexican case that the intense conflict between church and state and the Liberal victory impeded and retarded the Catholic Church's cultural role since the mid-19th century. In other words, it has concentrated on family and family issues to avoid deeper involvement in secular moral questions. However, a broader moral issue that has raised its head in Mexico is that of drugs and corruption, a problem found in many societal institutions, including government. Many politicians, including Miguel Alemán, Jr., believe the Church has a role to play in breaking the vicious cycle of drugs and corruption.[13] Examples already have been cited, including pastoral statements about military drug-related corruption, propelling the Church into the political arena.

When politicians are questioned more specifically about a broader social and political Church role, differences become more intense, especially among political figures associated with the government or Institutional Revolutionary Party and those leading the opposition parties, PAN and the PRD. One politician suggested that the Church has a tendency to involve itself in social and political issues because its traditional role, within Mexico's history, is one of dissidence. The Church is a focus for organized dissent.[14]

Most Mexican politicians, even those who in their youth were influenced favorably by Marxism, generally see the value of faith, especially in their personal formation.[15] Those who do not believe the Church should perform any political function tend to link their posture to a belief that the Church has not contributed positively to social integration. Most of the older generation are in agreement in condemning active Church involvement in politics. Nevertheless, some of these same politicians, who also favored constitutional reforms, accept the Church's role in assisting the state when it benefits the interests of the people and Mexico as a whole. For example, they view the Church's contributions to the debt negotiations favorably.[16]

Analysts have suggested that the Catholic Church is naturally inclined to play a mediating role in society because reconciliation as a public policy corresponds to Christian values of love and forgiveness. They argue that bishops are more likely to recognize the moral relativism of opposing political forces.[17] Mexican politicians with a more jaundiced view of the Catholic Church are not convinced that the public has sought it out to express their views to the government, but rather that clergy have taken the initiative in "making the demands of their constituents their business, rather than their constituents making their demands the Church's business."[18] As one public figure who is religious concluded, priests should provide lots of advice and express social views to their parishioners, but they should not do this in an active way, nor become "a lawyer for the people."[19] Politicians in this category believe the Church should limit its activities to spiritual matters, avoiding all involvement in partisan actions.[20]

Yet many politicians willingly recognize that the government, not the Church, generated conditions favoring Church involvement. They argue that since the government has not decentralized de facto authority to other branches, specifically the judicial branch, the ordinary person has little recourse for having their demands heard.[21] Public figures who support this posture believe the Church has a responsibility to take a position on fair elections, to condemn political corruption, and to advise the government on social and economic issues. They believe the Church can pursue such a strategy without stepping over the bounds of political neutrality, defending itself on the grounds that these are issues of political morality, not party politics.

Contrary to what might be expected, opposition party leaders, especially the left, support an activist perspective.[22] Heberto Castillo, who ran as a presidential candidate in 1988 but withdrew in favor of Cuauhtémoc Cárdenas and later joined the PRD, spent time in jail after the 1968 student movement, where he became friends with a priest, witnessing firsthand the Church's progressive wing. He believes the Church played an important role in unifying people from different political parties in favor of political change. He argues that the Church publicly should defend human rights and that both priests and laypersons should exercise their rights of expression and peaceful demonstration.[23]

PAN leaders do not take as radical a view as Heberto Castillo. Although they believe the Church should involve itself in public disputes on some issues, it should not become what one figure described as a "confrontational interest group."[24] They too believe the Church should promote Christian values, illuminating them for other, secular institutions. They argue that the Church should have the liberty to teach people religious values in cultural institutions, including schools and the mass media. As is true of all politicians, the Church should not involve itself in a partisan manner on any issue.

Politicians view Catholic clergy, both priests and bishops, somewhat differently from the institution itself. Some politicians see very little difference between clergy and their political peers in terms of values. They see individual human qualities as more influential than formal religious training or background. Based on personal experience, they cite many individual cases of secular individuals strongly interested in human social welfare and Catholic priests who demonstrate little concern for others.

Other politicians, while admitting the existence of exceptional, unflattering, clerical behavior, return to the issue of social responsibility, arguing that public figures as a whole are not well prepared and trained in this fundamental human value. They believe that social responsibility is not yet part of the political culture and that too many politicians are working for their own interests rather than serving the populace.[25] Instead, they suggest that one of the fundamental tenets of Catholicism is to help others, a value they believe is ingrained among priests.

Another view is that politicians and clergy differ on the emphasis they give to certain common goals. Politicians believe both groups favor modernizing society. But one difference some of them point to is their belief that politicians are pushing more strongly for the interjection of international influences.[26] They also believe that clergy, like them, wish to see the welfare of society improve. The difference is that politicians concentrate on the physical, whereas priests tend to focus on the spiritual and psychological, well-being of the population. Miguel Alemán, Jr., makes the point that you cannot have fraternity without liberty and equality. In short, politicians tend to focus on improving a Mexican's standard of living in order to achieve other fundamental humanistic and political goals.[27]

When confronted with the issue of whether or not the church-state relationship should change, generational factors sometimes, but not always, play a role. Many politicians believe that reforms that permit the Church to express itself openly on various issues are integral to the political opening occurring in society. They believe that a new national consensus, incorporating the Church, is essential in deciding Mexico's future direction.[28] Like the majority of Mexican people, prominent politicians favored voting rights for priests, although priests widely violated the constitution and voted prior to 1992. Politicians, from both the PRI and the opposition, viewed such rights as essential to the democratization process.[29] They also supported changes in the constitution because "we are proposing a democratic society in Mexico in which the law and the reality should coincide" and therefore the relationship should be transparent.[30]

Other politicians, such as President Miguel de la Madrid, saw the existing relationship as sufficiently positive, both from the clergy's and the politicians' viewpoint, believing changes should occur only gradually and incrementally. He told the Vatican delegate that although he thought the Church's role should be more important, it would be extremely difficult as president to implement changes given existing pressures.[31] De la Madrid believed that once Mexico developed a widespread consensus, one he had not yet witnessed, then they could make the changes. Even if reforms were introduced, the president did not favor altering basic constitutional principles, including Church property rights.[32]

President José López Portillo, similar to de la Madrid, believed that the risks of making constitutional changes far outweighed the potential gains. He, too, specifically opposed legalizing Church ownership of real property. He also disputed the liberalization of the constitution because he concluded that "the clergy has a tendency to participate, without voting, from the pulpit. It is also evident, for historical reasons, that it will tend to be more on the side of political right than the left, or the center right. Also, with the tradition of Masonry, this will produce a conflict between certain groups in society and the Church."[33]

Large numbers of politicians continued to oppose constitutional changes, not just because of the risks they might entail if implemented but essentially because they were true believers in the original Liberal principles. These political leaders are sincere in their beliefs that 19th-century Liberal ideas on separation of church and state have validity today. They refer to the bitter experiences of the past as a rationale for leaving constitutional provisions untouched. Some even argued that a legalized Church would destroy Mexico's political equilibrium.[34]

How Bishops View the Church's Role

For the analyst, it is important to measure the beliefs of a leadership group by its actions. Yet actions alone are not an accurate measure of beliefs. Levine notes

that the radical language in Church documents and public statements differs substantially from the roles and actions to which the episcopate is willing to commit
the Church.[35] As has been argued throughout this work, clergy are a heterogeneous bunch, and this is equally true when it comes to assessing their proper role
as members of an institution. Catholic ecclesiologies (theologies on the nature of
the Church) are often at odds with each other when referring to the Church's
character, its involvement in secular issues, and its moral responsibility to the
laity.[36] Bishops themselves are not unaware that their own perception of their
institution's broader role is strongly dependent on world and Latin American political developments, on economic and social relationships, on geopolitical forces,
and on Cold War forces prior to the 1990s.[37] According to one observer, at the
beginning of the 1970s, a bishop (implicitly the institutional Church) played at
least two important roles: first, as a moral guarantor of religious values in society,
preventing the state from weakening those attitudes; and second, as a socioethical
spokesperson, assisting the formation of an underlying value consensus.[38] The
episcopate formally stated their task:

> Our mission as bishops is, essentially and fundamentally, one of illumination and educa-
> tion of believers' conscience, helping them to perceive the exigencies and responsibili-
> ties of their faith in their personal lives, in their human activities, and in their relation-
> ships and compromises, which changing circumstances have imposed on them.[39]

How does the formal task, specified in Church documents, reflect bishops'
views in reality? Most Mexican bishops would consider the development of the
faith and, most important, its responsibilities a fundamental task. Some bishops
define it more narrowly; others more broadly. A number of bishops have com-
mented on their evangelical role. Some of these same bishops, however, suggest
that while sustaining faith is their primary mission, the methods for accomplishing
it have changed.[40] Others place this evangelical mission in a more institutionally
selfish context, arguing that the Catholic Church faces tremendous competition
from evangelical Protestant sects and that, therefore, it must take this task more
seriously. Bishops readily admit that while conserving religious faith is essential
at all levels of society, including clergy themselves, they need to develop a
stronger sense of faith and of conscience.[41] Bishops do not confine these spiritual
mores to the laity's individual psyches but argue for "developing a sense of coordination between religious beliefs and the way people actually live," corresponding quite closely with their "official" mission statement.[42]

Bishops who most firmly conceptualize the Church's role as a strengthening of
faith and evangelism nevertheless see these tasks as thrusting the Church across
other boundaries. Most broadly, the episcopate has talked about the Church's formation of values. In fact, they do not see the state's task as dictating values but as
guaranteeing them within the legal system.[43] Bishops who believe in the informal
educating role of the Church recognize that it must perform social tasks. As one
bishop suggests, "I would especially note the importance of education and the
Church's role in this, not so much in the formal sense, but in the development of
a personal culture and a set of values for each Mexican. We need to conserve
these values, to improve on them, and to develop them."[44]

The narrowest interpretation bishops give to the specific values that are part of their evangelical task is a sense of love and respect for each other.[45] Those bishops who support such a view argue that the Church provides a cultural matrix for Mexicans, indeed, that its influence is central to their culture, an interpretation with which most intellectual observers would agree. They do not see this cultural task as competing with the state but rather as projecting the "reign of God" across Mexico.[46]

Most bishops also recognize that even their spiritual tasks often draw them into temporal activities. Conceptually, a number of bishops believe that you cannot separate religious from pastoral functions. As Bishop Francisco Aguilera González perceptively concludes:

> The Christian faith in the Church has as a primary objective, an essential objective, to give a sense of definition to our existence, our lives, and to make us live valuable human lives. I think that you can't just talk about spiritual perfection as a goal of religion, but you must talk about temporal conditions, too. All of the religious people, regardless of whether they are bishops or ordinary priests, have to look at the situation in this way.[47]

Bishops are quick to point out that the source of these temporal activities is typically not the clergy but lay activists, influenced by the clergy's original evangelical roles. As one bishop insists, "I want to stress again that it is the responsibility of laypeople, based on their Christian beliefs, and not the Church leadership, to carry out this function."[48]

The Church, as a framer of societal morality, actively determines a culture's conscience and sense of social responsibility. References to love, liberty, and sense of conscience frequently are repeated among bishops. Bishops see the situation of their dioceses as heavily challenged by poverty and social ills. As one archbishop described his view:

> To me, we really need to make great strides in improving the quality of human life. We need to develop more organizations that will help the people both in their religious education and in improving their standard of living. I think in almost all dioceses there is a strong effort to try to create better conditions for all Mexicans.[49]

For many bishops, not just members of the progressive wing, the Church's spiritual voice, in the formation of both religious and secular values, speaks to providing a better life. Some conceptualize this task in terms of improved living conditions in their diocese. Others focus on changing the mental capacities of the faithful, seeing informal education as performing a transcendental role. For example, they define the Church as

> trying to revitalize people in all of these aspects; to make them organize themselves in such a way that they can teach themselves how to raise the questions that are necessary to improve their lives and to bring about an improvement in their lives by removing the sort of patronizing relationship they have had with certain institutions.[50]

Such a change introduces long-term repercussions not only on citizen-state relations but also on citizens' relationship with the Church itself. For clergy who identify more closely with the progressive wing, the Church should take a further step in defining its sense of social responsibility, encouraging greater access to communication, stimulating Mexicans to be active participants in their society, and supporting the development of organizations, such as labor unions, whose goals support the working classes' improved welfare.[51]

Still other bishops, not identified with any homogeneous, ideological tendency within the Church, see its informal educational task as strengthening civic responsibility. As one bishop lamented before the 1994 presidential election, when voter turnout reached extraordinarily low levels, "It is difficult to persuade Mexicans to be involved. We face a serious deficiency in civic responsibilities."[52] Those who advocate civic educational tasks distinguish between party politics and society's social and civic well-being. Even Girolamo Prigione, the Vatican delegate, recognizes the need to educate Mexicans about their obligations and to do so immediately since it involves a long, tortuous path.[53] John Paul II lectured Mexican bishops on their duty to speak out on social and ethical issues, "even if it meant telling political leaders how to act."[54]

Finally, there are those clergy among the episcopate who envision formal education as a major Church responsibility. They believe the Church has a responsibility to educate schoolchildren, to form teachers, and to improve the preparation of priests.[55]

Few bishops in response to these questions argued for an exclusionary institutional task or suggested that their primary task should replace those their colleagues preferred. Instead, they opted to stress one of several alternatives, all of which repeatedly were identified. One of the most significant limitations on the Church's ability to carry out its spiritual and secular educational tasks can be explained by its relationship to the largely secular intellectual community. As one bishop who favored a focus on poverty, education, and a stronger sense of faith concluded, the Church is "not doing this in close association with lay intellectuals in Mexico. We don't have any influence at an intellectual level as Catholics."[56]

When bishops are questioned more explicitly on the role, if any, the Church plays in politics, the diversity of their responses increases. The strongest linkage between the episcopate's position and the Church's role in politics is the changing tenor of the times. As we have noted, the bishops have offered evaluative statements about Mexican political conditions. For example, in November 1988 at the episcopal conference in Guadalajara, the bishops pointed to the people's lack of confidence in the governmental system due to electoral fraud, corruption, centralism, and bureaucratic ineptitude.[57] The episcopate also has made it clear that it has a moral responsibility to denounce any actions, government or otherwise, that violate the basic tenets of Christianity.[58] This includes condemning corruption and poor public sector management. An analysis of 260 episcopal documents from the 1980s—55 percent of which referred to political and social topics, 27 percent to ethical problems (abortion being the most common), and 14 percent to economic themes—illustrates the episcopate's concern with broad social and political issues.[59]

To obtain an "official view" of the episcopate, although not specifically that of the Conference of Mexican Bishops, it is worth summarizing several points in a pastoral document entitled "Pastoral Instruction on the Political Dimensions of Faith," written by Adolfo Suárez Rivera, the CEM's president in the 1990s. Many bishops referred to this document as instructive of the Church's stated posture on its political role and how it views Mexico's larger political-social context. The document states:

- Excessive concentration of authority in the federal executive branch and among state executives is seriously detrimental to legislative and judicial powers.

- Absolute control of the electoral process by the party/government reduces pluralism and civic responsibility.

- Enthronement of a single party during the last 60 years thanks to organizational corporatism leads to abuse of power.[60]

Suárez Rivera went on to establish the Church's position on political participation, arguing that faith involves the totality of life and influences all personal dimensions, including politics. In this sense, people are political, and politics cannot be separated from faith. Mexicans are responsible before God, including their political, social, and economic views and activities. Christ, argues Archbishop Suárez Rivera, was not neutral or uncritical politically, behaving as a political subject in attitude, words, and deeds.

In February through April 1987, the archdiocese of Chihuahua, which provided the catalyst for the confrontation between the Church and the government after the fraudulent state elections of 1986, offered a series of workshops on Catholics and democracy. Adalberto Almeida y Merino requested that each parish establish such activities the previous November. In these workshops, priests dealt with the following topics: the actual situation and aspirations of Mexicans, the extent and limits of Church intervention, diverse forms of government, the Church and democracy, achieving integral democracy, and education for democracy. In the teaching materials it provided, the Church cited the Medellín and Puebla conferences. These documents are critical of governmental failures, provide discussion of diverse forms of government, and identify democratic institutions, including popular suffrage, representative government, separation of powers, and legal guarantees of fundamental liberties.[61]

Throughout the 1980s, Church pastoral documents cited numerous criticisms of the developmental model and the political system, the same criticisms addressed by Mexican intellectuals and foreign analysts.[62] The Vatican, as represented by Prigione, did not contradict the episcopate's views on civic responsibility, supporting the bishops in their demands that Mexicans exercise their rights to participate politically.[63] The bishops, as they did on several occasions under Salinas, even took public stances on economic policy issues. For example, the majority of bishops opposed the Economic Solidarity Pact, not because of its substance but because of the undemocratic and unrepresentative manner in which it was formulated.[64]

The underlying prejudices of Mexican bishops favor a strong posture on increasing democratic behavior and a moral responsibility to encourage civic education, including making Mexicans aware of the importance of understanding and exercising their democratic rights. Bishops come at this Church role from a variety of angles, but the end results are the same. Nevertheless, it is worth illustrating some of these viewpoints to illuminate how clergy conceptualize the Church and therefore its role.

> If you think of it [the Church] as a large community, then it has to intervene in these social and political issues. It has no choice. To speak of politics at its moral level, then definitely the Church must always be involved. Always. If you're talking about politics in a much larger context, then we can never be involved in defending parties or candidates or telling people how to vote.[65]

> It would be a mistake for us if we substituted for the laity in political activities. But the Church has always had the capability to exercise, and should exercise, a moral influence.[66]

> The Church continues to create [values] and educate people and it has the right, indeed the responsibility, to judge the acts of all Mexican citizens as part of this larger environment. It has an obligation to make moral judgments, but not in its own interests, which would be wrong of us to do, but in the interests of the people. I think the bishops in northern Mexico are correct in their position that the Church has taken in these affairs.[67]

Mexican bishops envision their "political" role as a subsidiary responsibility to the primary tasks of setting a moral compass and contributing to a sense of social and civic responsibility. For example, Bishop Javier Lozano Barragán, a highly respected moderate and president of the episcopate's religious doctrine committee, clearly recognizes that a fundamental weakness in Mexican political culture is intolerance of opposing views, arguing that Mexicans confuse unity with uniformity.[68] The Church has a responsibility, in bishops' minds, to help obviate such perceptions. Bishops also believe that politicians often misconstrue the motives of clergy performing these necessary tasks, viewing priests as wanting to become involved in politics—defined in terms of partisan support for parties and candidates—or in the decision-making process.

The definition of "political" is by the very nature of politics ambiguous. As the former head of the CEM suggested, "To remain silent is to participate, because all human actions are political, including omissions."[69] Bishops who take a narrow view of political involvement believe that such priests are serving only part of their community.[70] The most adamant bishops, who sometimes appear to step over the boundaries of politics into partisanship, explain their posture in civic terms. Manuel Talamás best expresses this view: "On whose authority can someone tell me not to participate in politics? The ultimate objective of our participation in politics is to do so with human character in order to assist the helpless. My interest in the triumph of PAN is to insure that democracy really exists."[71] A minority of church leaders are optimistic that the boundaries between what is and is not political are becoming clearer. As one priest bluntly stated, "We do not have to become politicians to carry out our various pastoral tasks."[72]

A number of bishops, including some progressives, see political education, and especially public postures on electoral fraud, as secondary issues to a much more fundamental moral code. These individuals focus very strongly on human dignity as an essential quality. They believe the political issues are superficial compared to human qualities they describe as necessary for Mexico's development. Respect for other human beings underlies all other behavior, political and otherwise.[73] This is a distinction that Ivan Vallier developed several decades ago in trying to separate the Church's socioethical and political role. He argued that a difference exists between bishops who articulate values of social justice, freedom from oppression, and love for one's neighbor and those who emphasize redistribution of wealth, radical modes of change, and an end to political repression. He describes them as two different levels of articulation, the first representing a value system based on religious principles and the second endorsing a set of political strategies.[74] It is easy to distinguish between freedom from oppression and redistribution of wealth on a continuum of values versus policy, but it seems impossible to separate love for one's neighbor from calling for an end to political repression. One naturally follows from the other. Such a posture could hardly be described as a political strategy. In short, Vallier's distinctions are helpful on some issues but not on others.

A more useful distinction attempts to measure bishops' and priests' actual involvement as implementers of temporal values or policies as distinct from purveyors of values. According to Levine, *activism* involves Church personnel directly in social and political conflict, whereas *activation* concerns evangelizing the faithful and providing them with a spiritual inspiration to be carried over into temporal activities. Essentially, it is up to laity to take up the values or principles offered by Catholic priests and apply those to society.[75] It can be argued in the Mexican case that most bishops would strongly support the activation alternative. Although most bishops would like to avoid activism, many permit their priests to be so engaged. Some observers believe, however, that Mexican bishops attempt to distinguish between political and social activism, discouraging the former and encouraging or permitting the latter.[76]

When the Church hierarchy is asked specifically to compare its goals with those of Mexico's politicians, some interesting distinctions, several fundamental to understanding the relationship between the two, arise. Many bishops are skeptical that politicians truly want to serve society. They provide many examples, all supporting the view that government serves many interests but not necessarily the people's. Interestingly, clergy have not argued that their values somehow differ from politicians'. Instead, they believe their goals, purposes, and intentions differ. Culturally, they do identify some obstacles. One of the issues apparent in an examination of state-intellectual relations in Mexico is that of language. Do representatives of both groups speak the same language, use the same vocabulary?[77] Some clergy believe differences do exist that obfuscate their ability to understand each other. For example, one bishop suggested that clergy often use the term "bien comun," a term equivalent to the well-being or general welfare of the community. They claim, however, that since the National Action Party uses this term frequently in its political rhetoric, that PRIistas imply a linkage between clergy and PAN.[78]

The problem of language involves politicians and clergy in political disputes.

As one bishop lamented, "We don't want power, we only want justice. But a politician would not understand this desire very clearly."[79] For these bishops, the losers are not the Church or the government but the ordinary Mexican. The conceptual obstacles to their communication are lessened by most clergy's belief that mutual respect from each institution has improved markedly in recent years, promoting a positive environment supportive of better relations. Clergy believe that respect and an ability to sit down and negotiate differences are more important in overcoming potential conflicts than are any fundamental differences in values.

It was probably this mutual respect that encouraged clergy to favor legal changes in church-state relations, anticipating the 1992 constitutional reforms. Bishops frequently made the argument that the present generation of clergy, or politicians for that matter, should not be blamed for historic mistakes. As Girolamo Prigione admits, "The Church committed many errors in the past, and we are paying for these today. We are like a family, and like any family, we have our faults. We need desperately to create a dialogue with the government in order to resolve and avoid these differences. We have to live for the present."[80]

A second major justification for changing the relationship, expressed by many sectors of society, is the tremendous gap between legal theory and practical reality. Surprisingly, most bishops personally found the situation tolerable because they could function independently of the laws, generally without retribution. Nevertheless, they viewed the damage caused by the theory-practice gap as significant. This is most eloquently expressed by Bishop Samaniego Barriga, who described his feelings this way:

> When this [legal relationship] changes, if indeed it does, I'm sure I will feel strange because I have grown up my entire life with this dual reality. I think Mexico is damaging itself by living under this double standard, the life of reality versus the life of constitutional theory. There is an expression that is used, and I don't remember who said it, but it goes something like this: there are many things that deserve respect, but the thing that deserves the most respect is reality. I think that by not conforming to reality, Mexico has hurt the soul and spirit of both individual priests and the nation as a whole.[81]

Finally, most bishops cared more about changing the legal position of the Church as an institutional force in society than about changing their own status. The late Cardinal Posadas argued that the Church could carry out the functions described above more effectively if it was given a juridical personality, and therefore the right to own property, including its seminaries, churches, and other facilities.[82] Catholic bishops never sought this recognition for their church alone but for all churches, believing these legal rights to be subsumed under the larger issue of human rights in general.

Priests and the Church: Views of the Rank and File

The views of priests on the pastoral and political role of the Catholic Church are also essential to include. They provide the perspective of the typical clergy, those who form the pool from which future bishops are selected. Their views are often in sync with those of their parishioners, at least in the case of the United States.[83] Based on studies of industrial nations outside of Mexico, priests are generally more socially activist and liberal than are Catholic laity but more conservative than their bishops.[84] Neither of these qualities necessarily apply to Mexican priests, and only the latter relationship is examined. Finally, it is essential to keep in mind differences between expressed beliefs and practical actions. One should not conclude that Mexican priests act in a "progressive" manner, but they express these views in interviews. Eduardo Sota, a primary investigator in the Luengo survey, discovered at the end of many individual interviews that priests readily admitted that the questions made them think of what they should have done versus what they had done.

Not surprisingly, Catholic priests' choices of important Church missions correspond to bishops' selections. Nevertheless, while priests' views tend to reinforce the hierarchy's, they emphasize specific elements or conceptualize the same missions somewhat differently. For example, most priests agree that the evangelical role is an essential Church task. Many priests see it as being performed in a broad fashion. Some priests have argued that the Church provides additional mechanisms for expanding the laity's faith through its hospitals and private schools.[85] Mexican priests universally are concerned about the laity's spiritual condition because they describe their faith as "fragile." They attribute it to a lack of literacy and education among the poor, their failure to provide a sound religious education, and insufficient contact between priest and laity.[86]

Many priests believe the Church has a responsibility to explain evangelization more clearly to Catholics. They recognize the difficulty of confronting popular religious beliefs that have been melded indiscriminately with Catholic Christian principles.[87] These priests believe strongly that the Church is failing in its primary religious mission if it does not improve the level of Christianity among the populace. Clergy who recognize the low levels of education among a sizable portion of the populace attach an important qualifying role to their spiritual tasks. As Ernesto Menenses Morales, a Jesuit and lifelong educator explains, "One task which it [the Church] has is what I would describe as a civilizing function, because there are many Indian villages. . . . The second task is to evangelize these people, which in my opinion you can't do until you complete the first task."[88]

As in the case of many bishops, progressives and moderates alike, a number of priests believe greater emphasis should be placed on the needs of the poor. Yet some clergy see this as a task to be incorporated within its broader evangelical mission.[89] They also believe the future of Christianity in Mexico is threatened if it ignores this task, believing that the Church is a significant moral leader. However, the strength of its moral position relies heavily on its defense of the average Mexican's interests.[90] The most radical priests believe that the Church is a bridge between God and the people, but that the hierarchy, because it does not share a view favorable to the interests of the poor, fails to stress this approach. As Jalisco Father José Alvarez Franco argues, "The Church is hierarchical, but Jesus never supported this type of structure."[91]

The other task on which priests are typically unified, similar to bishops, is the

Church's mission in forming and disseminating basic values. As one priest argued, the Church cannot confine itself to spiritual development alone but must become involved in the development of human values.[92] The Church's goal, in the clergy's opinion, is that human beings should follow Christ in all of their temporal activities. Ricardo Cuellar Romo, a well-educated priest who worked for the CEM, eloquently expresses this mission:

> The Church plays a role in supporting the values that our people use as a means of self-identity. The Church is a source of the national conscience, but at the same time it represents an institution that attempts to serve the temporal realities in social and political affairs and to create a form of harmonic progress. Without losing the Mexican people's historic identity, we try to improve their values in terms of integrity, justice, truth, etc., which are the soul of the people, but in the case of Mexico, these values have been severely battered and repressed by many of our social and political experiences.[93]

Among the values that clergy repeatedly raise are self-worth, human dignity, and defining a place for oneself within the larger societal context.

Mexican clergy believe that changing people's values, moral and secular, is an extremely difficult task. Some of these priests see this mission as far more problematic than evangelizing the populace. They point further to the failure of secular and religious educational institutions to instruct Mexicans in basic values, even suggesting that the Church should collaborate with the state in order to accomplish such a goal. Priests interviewed in the mid-1970s offered the same interpretation, that schools were not producing true Christians.[94] More broadly stated, clergy advocate that the Church should develop human resources as it develops people religiously, and that these two tasks should not be separated.

The most important social role referred to among Catholic priests is their need to create a fundamental sense of consciousness, or social responsibility, about the country's problems.[95] They think of a social consciousness as integral to Catholic faith. While some believe this should favor the marginal population, others stress that this should never become an exclusionary approach. Those willing to be self-critical openly admit that both clergy and public officials are often lacking in the necessary skills and knowledge to resolve many of the problems a social consciousness would raise. They argue further that the Church has an intellectual task to improve future priests' seminary training. They link changes in human and intellectual development to changes in society. Priests also believe that they, as representatives of the Church, have a special task to perform, especially because they are typically seen as the most influential figure in villages and small towns.[96] They also conceptualize their social tasks somewhat differently from bishops, noting that the Church as an institution and religion as a cultural ingredient are essential to the life of the ordinary Mexican.[97] In this sense, on a day-to-day basis, the Church automatically is involved in social activities.

Within a social realm, probably the most important mission the Church has tackled and priests believe it should aggressively pursue is improving social morality or justice, specifically respect for individual human rights. As one priest noted, the main task of the Church is to defend human rights not protected by the constitution. The degree of commitment and success with which it has performed this task has given the Church institutional credibility. Some clergy worry that the Church will absorb greater responsibility for institutional credibility given their view that most Mexicans hold secular institutions in low esteem.

Contrary to the view that Mexican priests are politically conservative, they share diverse intellectual interests while expressing considerable consensus on broad political concerns. Surprisingly, in the Luengo survey, two-thirds of the clergy read *Proceso,* Mexico's most important critical, independent, left-of-center weekly. Fewer than one-fourth read Mexico's two leading intellectual monthlies, *Vuelta* and *Nexos.* At the time Luengo's survey was taken, more than nine out of 10 priests believed that Mexico's political and economic situation would eventually produce conflict, such as the Chiapan rebellion, leading to the demise of social peace. The same overwhelming percentage of priests also believed the hierarchy must work to promote Church social doctrines contrary to government policies. They also recognized that government officials would object to priests assuming such a critical posture and that politicians feared any type of Church social pastoralism. The vast majority of priests also believe the Church is worried about electoral fraud.[98]

Given these perceptions, priests' attitudes toward Church political involvement are interesting. Numerous interviews with priests clearly suggest that they believe it is the laity who will change society, who will alter those structures contributing to economic and social woes. Many clergy suggest that the Church has no direct responsibility for instituting such changes, but that these changes will ultimately occur without its direct involvement. Instead, they argue that the Church's political role is indirect, that it provides educational programs and human resources to develop people's sense of responsibility, leading them to become politically and socially active.

Similar to bishops, priests universally denounce any Church involvement in partisan politics, specifically, a preference for a political party. As one priest explained, "If anyone were to come and ask me about a political candidate, I would say that any individual who advocated justice would be a good candidate, but that you would have to choose between such candidates because the Church can't make the choice for you. We can describe positive goals, but we can't decide who should achieve them."[99]

One of the positive goals that priests do agree on is their role in encouraging civic responsibility, notably, as was true in the case of Mexican bishops, encouraging people to vote and to understand their obligations as citizens.[100] Priests also argued that they should register to vote as an example to their parishioners, but that democratization per se lay with the people.[101]

Clergy link the Catholic Church's political mission, or responsibility, to its broader human rights mission. They argue that it cannot remain isolated because individual human rights are so clearly expressed in Christian doctrine. The Church does have a responsibility, in the priests' view, to represent its parishioners' desires and to defend them against aggression, even if the perpetrator is the state. Priests expect that they, or their bishops, will have to make increasing public pronouncements about various political situations. They understand, similar to bishops, that their motives will be misinterpreted, especially by the government. Other clergy also suggest that bishops are fearful of taking the Church in this direction because they are unsure of its consequences.

The most extreme position is taken by priests who believe there is no such thing as an apolitical priest or bishop. A veteran priest, officially suspended since 1983 for his political involvement but practicing without Church sanction, explained: "The majority of the time my pastoral tendency was to involve myself with political groups on the left. This bothered the hierarchy. I founded two student fronts that also alienated the bishops. . . . Those who say nothing about politics form part of the population who remain silent and do nothing. . . . They [the hierarchy] should never be partisan, and use the Church for other purposes, but they need to speak out." [102]

Other priests suggest the Church's political task is to encourage a participatory posture among the general populace, not expressed solely through voting. These clergy conclude that the Church indirectly exercises a "political" role by encouraging parishioners to be actively involved in many lay and religious organizations that develop decision-making skills and in local, civic structures, including parish councils.

The constitutional reforms proposed by the Salinas administration did not find an important place in the agenda of the typical parish priest. Most priests interviewed in the Luengo study wanted legal status for the Church, and an equal number, four-fifths of all priests, actually believed legal status would improve the Church's defense of social doctrine and values. [103] On the issue most relevant to priests, their right to vote, priests as a whole were not adamant about obtaining it although they believed it was a basic human right. A primary explanation for this attitude is that priests who wanted to participate politically already were voting. [104] Other priests argued that changing the law would not alter attitudes among educated Mexicans anyway, suggesting they had few strong incentives to see the reforms implemented. [105]

Other priests were more concerned about how legal changes might affect their ability to convey basic moral values, deemed an essential task, through education. In short, they believed the restrictive constitutional provisions regarding religious education limited the Church's influence in teaching essential family values. Some priests also believed the laws should be altered not because it would significantly change church-state behavior, but because it would eliminate the legal basis for the state to persecute the Church. One priest admitted that some of his peers might well oppose such changes for selfish reasons. If the Church obtained legal status, it would undergo fiscal scrutiny as a taxable corporation subject to government audits. According to one source, parish priests often plead poverty when it comes time to contribute to diocesan projects. In short, the bishop has to accept their word, without any financial evidence. A new legal status would require priests to keep accounting data, information also available to the bishop. [106]

Misunderstandings and tensions between politicians and clergy will continue into the future regardless of President Salinas's reforms. Rank-and-file clergy, as is true of the hierarchy, identify essential differences between themselves and government officials. Similar to bishops, they believe that politicians understand very little about the Church and about what clergy do. They argue that numerous politicians who are closely tied to the Masons retain interpretations of the Church that border on 19th-century myths. As one priest frankly complained about a politician friend, "He constantly speaks to me about various activities in politics, but he never asks me, nor does he understand, anything about my career within the Church." [107] On the other hand, he points out, priests are required to study politics in seminary in order to comprehend the Mexican reality.

Father Samuel Morín Suárez, who has a sophisticated understanding of church-state issues, further argues that the conflict between church and state is not institutional but personal. He suggests that it is not that the institutions are opposed to one another, but rather that their personal representatives, at given points in time, moderate or exaggerate their differences. He believes the primary explanation for these problems is that the two groups understand little about each other, and therefore they find it difficult to establish a dialogue.

Priests and bishops both praise politicians for their strong sense of nationalism. Indeed, they argue that politicians and clergy share this sentiment. Many priests and bishops alike define politicians' primary task as improving Mexico's social and economic conditions. Priests distinguish themselves from politicians in terms of their motivations. For example, they point to the personal economic interests of government officials. They admit that such concerns motivate some priests as well but, in general, consider such characterizations as exceptional. [108] Clergy point to the modest economic circumstances of most priests. As one individual concluded, "I can't think of one person who I've known who has used his religious position to improve the condition of his own life." [109] Many priests distinguish clergy from politicians on the issue of corruption, believing it to have contaminated politicians more widely, and at higher levels, than among priests. They believe politicians in Mexico fail to distinguish between their personal and public lives.

Many priests do not identify major differences between clergy and politicians in terms of their goals; rather, they see more important distinctions in their methodology. As one priest expressed this sentiment: "I think we all agree on similar ends, but not on the means for how these should be achieved. I would say that the state's methods are eminently positivist, but that the Church's methods are tied more to an emphasis on faith, or on theology. . . . Some clergy forget this, and want to become the new leaders of society. But this is not our function. We are here to represent society, not to lead it." [110]

Another major distinction between public figures and clergy, from the point of view of priests, stems from a different chronological perspective. Mexican priests believe they are organizing society to achieve transcendental, as distinct from short-term, goals, and therefore they emphasize important values having long-lasting consequences. [111] Priests argue that they differ from politicians because they have a well-defined, underlying philosophy that provides a foundation for their temporal values and goals. Their primary task as clergy is to teach other Mexicans these values. Politicians, on the other hand, must solve basic societal problems. Priests have the responsibility to socialize society in these Christian values, indirectly influencing problem solving, but have no direct responsibility for actively solving such issues.

The views politicians and clergy have about each other and their respective roles explain numerous tensions or potential conflicts characterizing their relationship. Their insights about each other suggest that their future relationship may encounter difficulties, although these are likely to come about initially through difficult contextual problems, such as an extreme economic downturn and deferred or too rapid political change. These differences in perceptions between and among clergy and politicians suggest some fundamental obstacles to mediating such pressures.

It is clear that many politicians and most clergy see the Church's universal task as one of formulating values. They perceive such values as formative to individual Mexicans and to society collectively. The values most often referred to by both groups incorporate fundamental Christian Catholic principles, including love, respect, equality, and basic human rights. Differences of interpretation exist within the clergy as to how these values might be implemented. However, even when most priests agree on basic social tasks, they suggest when comparing their roles to politicians' that it is laypersons and politicians who must provide the leadership to solve societal problems. Their role is to make people aware of societal issues, to sensitize the population to particular concerns, and to educate people on how they can voice their concerns and contribute solutions.

This task alone potentially promotes conflict between the church and state, especially when many politicians believe clergy are not responding to societal demands but rather are making their own personal concerns those of the population. Politicians' views on this religious task are changing. A number of politicians accept a larger Church social role and even are willing to collaborate with the Church on mutually beneficial public policies.

Perhaps the single value most likely to promote disagreement among clergy and politicians is the issue of social responsibility. Interestingly, this a fundamental, missing value among Mexican private sector leaders. The Church, it seems, has adopted this value by default. This is not to imply that many politicians do not take social responsibility seriously. Nevertheless, the clergy has placed this issue at the forefront of Catholicism's tasks in Mexico, whether in pursuit of political, economic, or social goals. The degree of emphasis the Church allocates to this issue, and the way in which it interprets its institutional responsibility, engenders conflicts or disputes with secular authorities.

The other characteristic that distinguishes politicians from clergy is clergy's emphasis on spiritual matters. Politicians agree with clergy that their focus on these issues separates them from politicians. Yet these same spiritual concerns, founded on basic societal values, can also generate divisive differences between the two groups. It is not the spiritual concerns themselves that are problematic, but the values on which they are constructed. These values can be interpreted in many fashions, and it is their implementation that poses the greatest potential conflict between the two leadership groups.

In the secular world, the potential for confrontation between Mexico's church and state other than in electoral politics appears most clearly in their educational tasks. The primary question is teaching and development of basic values, of which formal education is merely a vehicle. Bishops and clergy recognize such tasks can involve them more deeply in secular matters. They rely heavily on the argument that it is the lay person they teach who must provide the necessary leadership to implement these values, not the clergy.

As long as clergy function to determine a sensitive, social conscience, to provide the parameters of social responsibility, and to develop basic moral outlines of Mexican values, they will find themselves confronting tensions with the secular world in general and the political world in particular. These tensions are exacerbated by the fact that within the Church, individually and institutionally, divisions exist as to the degree of its commitment to and conceptualization of the Church's social tasks. Even the Pope has not shied away from a sense of social responsibility.

The evidence from Mexican pastoral documents and recent episcopate declarations establishes unequivocally the Church's desire to play a responsible civic role and to identify the serious political and social weaknesses of government and society. The episcopate repeated these concerns forcefully and clearly in October 1994, shortly after the presidential elections. The Church, acting as an expressive conscience of the people, will confront contrary secular social and political expectations.

Finally, clergy view their differences with politicians as stemming from differences in language, in conceptualization, and in their ability to communicate rather than from fundamental differences in values. This is a significant point, and although difficult to change, these differences can be moderated. Much more social exchange needs to occur among politicians and clergy, and politicians especially require a deeper understanding of clergy, the Church as an institution, and religion. Some of the castelike features that separate Mexico's military from its civilian leadership produce similar consequences for government-Church relationships. A significant goal of priests and bishops is national unity, developing a sense of mutual respect in society. Their deep commitment to this goal is likely to reinforce the Church's role as a mediator, a task it attempted to perform in Chiapas.[112] The Church sees this task in a sophisticated light, however, understanding that it needs to provide a firm foundation on which to construct a permanent mediating mentality among the leadership and the population. Since mediation and peaceful negotiation are the cornerstones of Church values and behavior, they will mark the Church's approach in dealing with the state into the 21st century.

NOTES

1. Daniel H. Levine, *Religion and Politics in Latin America: The Catholic Church in Venezuela and Colombia* (Princeton: Princeton University Press, 1981), 54, 13. Levine also cautioned, and correctly, that "bishops feel a special obligation to preserve the institution itself as a source of continuity and a focus of shared values and loyalties over time and space. The way they do this depends on their images of the church and of religion

itself, and cannot be simply deduced from their 'politics' *tout court*." "Religion and Politics: Drawing Lines, Understanding Change," *Latin American Research Review* 20, no. 1 (1985): 189.

2. Kenneth D. Wald, D. E. Owen, and S. D. Hill, Jr., "Churches as Political Communities," *American Political Science Review* 82, no. 2 (June 1988): 533.

3. Daniel H. Levine, *Religion and Political Conflict in Latin America* (Chapel Hill: University of North Carolina Press, 1986), 17.

4. Philip E. Hammond, "The Conditions for Civil Religion: A Comparison of the United States and Mexico," in *Varieties of Civil Religion,* Robert W. Bella and Philip E. Hammond, eds. (New York: Harper and Row, 1980), 59.

5. Claude Pomerlau, "Religion and Values in the Formation of Modern Mexico: Some Economic and Political Considerations," in *Global Economics and Religion,* J. Finn, ed. (New Brunswick, N.J.: Transaction Books, 1983), 152.

6. Personal interview with President Luis Echeverría, Mexico City, August 2, 1992.

7. Leonor Ludlow, "Tensiones y presiones en las relaciones entre estado e iglesia," in *17 angulos de un sexsenio,* Germán Pérez, ed. (Mexico City: Plaza y Valdes, 1987), 385.

8. Personal interview with Adrián Lajous Martínez, Mexico City, June 2, 1988.

9. Personal interview with President Luis Echeverría.

10. Personal interview with Pedro Daniel Martínez García, Mexico City, May 27, 1985.

11. Personal interview with Julio Faesler, president of the Acuerdo Nacional para la Democracia (ACUDE), Mexico City, February 12, 1993. Antonio Armendáriz claimed that "I don't know any politician in all my years of public life whose wife hasn't actively practiced Catholic religious beliefs, and it is probable that the men have been active Catholics as well. Or another way to express it is, I can't recall any deceased politician that I've known who was not buried within the Catholic Church." Personal interview, Mexico City, June 1, 1988.

12. Personal interview with Antonio Armendáriz.

13. Personal interview with Senator Miguel Alemán, Jr., Mexico City, July 30, 1992.

14. Personal interview with Ricardo Pascoe, communications secretary, PRD, Mexico City, May 5, 1992.

15. Personal interview with Alejandro Spíndola, Mexico City, July 31, 1992.

16. Personal interview with Emilio Alanis Patiño, Mexico City, July 31, 1992.

17. Thomas G. Sanders, "The Politics of Catholicism in Latin America," *Journal of Inter-American Studies and World Affairs* 24, no. 2 (May 1982): 257.

18. Personal interview with Adrián Lajous Martínez.

19. Personal interview with Carlos Mainero, Mexico City, August 4, 1992.

20. Personal interview with Congressman Agustín Basave, Mexico City, August 4, 1992.

21. Personal interview with Pedro Daniel García Martínez.

22. This is particularly striking considering Bernardo Barranco Villafan and Raquel Pastor Escobar believe that the left generally demonstrates little knowledge about the Church or religion in Mexico. *Jerarquía católica y modernización política en México* (Mexico City: Palabra Ediciones, Centro Antonio De Montesinos, 1989), 44.

23. Personal interview with Heberto Castillo, Mexico City, July 12, 1993.

24. Personal interview with former PAN president, Abel Vicencio Tovar, Mexico City, July 13, 1993.

25. Personal interview with Seatiel Alatriste, Mexico City, June 1, 1988.

26. Personal interview with Carlos Armando Briebich, Mexico City, August 5, 1992.

27. Personal interview with Miguel Alemán, Jr. The argument can be made that even if these views more closely represent their rhetoric than their substance, they still illustrate differing perceptual and substantive interpretations.

28. Personal interview with Ricardo Pascoe.

29. Personal interview with Alfredo del Mazo, precandidate for the PRI presidential nomination in 1988, Mexico City, February 15, 1991.

30. Personal interview with Porfirio Muñoz Ledo, president of the PRD, Mexico City, February 21, 1991.

31. Personal interview with Archbishop Girolamo Prigione, Vatican Delegate, Mexico Archdiocese, Mexico City, June 2, 1987.

32. Personal interview with President Miguel de la Madrid, Mexico City, February 22, 1991.

33. Personal interview with President José López Portillo, Mexico City, February 19, 1991.

34. Personal interview with Congressman Juan José Rodríguez Pratts, Mexico City, June 8, 1988.

35. Daniel H. Levine, *Religion and Politics in Latin America*, 10.

36. Brian Smith, "Religion and Social Change: Classical Theories and New Formulations in the Content of Recent Developments in Latin America," *Latin American Research Review* 10 (1975): 12.

37. Jorge Martínez, *Memorias y reflexiones de un obispo* (Mexico City: Editorial Villicaña, 1986), 29.

38. Ivan Vallier, *Catholicism, Social Control, and Modernization in Latin America* (Englewood Cliffs, N.J.: Prentice-Hall, 1970), 87.

39. "Carta pastoral del episcopado mexicano sobre el desarrollo e integración del país," March 26, 1968, reprinted from *Christus* (1968): 390, 397.

40. Personal interview with Bishop Javier Navarro Rodríguez, Guadalajara Archdiocese, Guadalajara, Jalisco, July 8, 1993.

41. One bishop who took the posture that the faith needed reinforcing remarked that the Virgin of Guadalupe was the secret of their faith, which is reflected in the saying that 90 percent of Mexicans are Catholic, but 99 percent are Guadalupanos. Personal interview with Bishop Adolfo Hernández Hurtado, Guadalajara Diocese, Guadalajara, Jalisco, July 7, 1993.

42. Personal interview with Bishop José Melgoza Osorio, Nezahualcóyotl Diocese, Nezahualcóyotl, México, May 27, 1987.

43. Conferencia del Episcopado Mexicano, *Presencia de la iglesia en el mundo de la educación en México, instrucción pastoral* (Mexico City: CEM, 1988), 31.

44. Personal interview with Bishop Abelardo Alvarado Alcántara, Mexico Archdiocese, Mexico City, June 2, 1987.

45. Personal interview with Bishop Ramón Godínez, secretary general of the CEM, Mexico Archdiocese, Mexico City, July 16, 1993.

46. Personal interview with Bishop Mario de Gasperín, Querétaro Diocese, Querétaro, Querétaro, July 12, 1993.

47. Personal interview with Bishop Francisco Aguilera González, Mexico Archdiocese, Mexico City, June 1, 1987.

48. Personal interview with Bishop Jorge Martínez, Mexico Archdiocese, Mexico City, May 28, 1987.

49. Personal interview with Archbishop Manuel Pérez Gil, Tlanepantla Archdiocese, Tlanepantla, México, February 18, 1991.

50. Personal interview with Bishop Francisco Aguilera González.

51. Personal interview with Bishop Raúl Vera, Ciudad Altamirano Diocese, Guerrero, Mexico City, May 3, 1992.

52. Personal interview with Bishop Luis Mena, Mexico Archdiocese, Mexico City, July 13, 1993.

53. Personal interview with Archbishop Girolamo Prigione.

54. *New York Times*, May 12, 1990, n.p.

55. Personal interview with Cardinal Juan Jesús Posadas Ocampo, Guadalajara Diocese, Mexico City, February 20, 1991.

56. Personal interview with Archbishop Rosendo Huesca, Puebla Archdiocese, Puebla, Puebla, July 16, 1993.

57. *Proceso*, November 28, 1988, 18.

58. Dennis M. Hanratty, "The Church," in *Prospects for Mexico*, George Grayson, ed. (Washington: Center for the Study of Foreign Affairs, U.S. Department of State, 1988), 118.

59. Bernardo Barranco Villafan and Raquel Pastor Escobar, *Jerarquía católica y modernización política en México*, 23–24.

60. Adolfo Suárez Rivera, "Instrucción pastoral sobre la dimensión política de la fe," Archdioceses of Monterrey, Monterrey, Nuevo León, March 1987, 6, 9, 17, 23.

61. *Documentación e Información Católica* 15 (January 22, 1987): 31, 37; (January 8, 1987): 4; (January 22, 1987): 29; (January 29, 1987): 53–58; (February 12, 1987): 101, 109.

62. A decade earlier, in 1971, Mexican bishops in Rome actually laid part of the blame for Mexico's economic and social injustice at their own feet in the pastoral report entitled "Justice in Mexico." Dennis Goulet, "The Mexican Church: Into the Public Arena," *America* 160, no. 13 (April 8, 1989): 318.

63. Enrique Garza Ramírez, ed., *Nuevo León* (Monterrey: Universidad Autónomo de Nuevo León, 1985), 102.

64. Oscar González et al., "Batallas en el reino de este mundo," *Nexos*, no. 78 (June 1984): 19.

65. Personal interview with Bishop Jorge Martínez.

66. Personal interview with Bishop Raúl Vera.

67. Personal interview with Bishop Francisco Aguilera González.

68. Guadalupe Báez, "Maniqueísmo político, lo que priva en México," *Unomásuno*, September 30, 1990, n.p.

69. Oscar Hinojosa, "La misión evangélica ordena dejar la sacristía, afirma Obeso Rivera," *Proceso*, September 8, 1986, 11.

70. Miguel Angel Rivera, "Soy una tercera corriente dentro la Iglesia: la equilibradora," *Proceso*, October 3, 1977, 24.

71. Oscar González et al., "Batallas en el reino de este mundo," 26.

72. Personal interview with Abbot Guillermo Schulenburg, Basilica of Guadalupe, Mexico Archdiocese, Mexico City, February 18, 1991.

73. Personal interview with Bishop José Pablo Rovalo, Mexico Archdiocese, Mexico City, February 21, 1991.

74. Ivan Vallier, *Catholicism, Social Control, and Modernization in Latin America*, 87–88.

75. Daniel H. Levine, "Church Elites in Venezuela and Colombia: Context, Background and Beliefs," *Latin American Research Review* 14, no. 1 (1979): 62.

76. Dennis M. Hanratty, "Change and Conflict in the Contemporary Mexican Catholic Church," unpublished Ph.D. dissertation, Duke University, 1980, 14.

77. Roderic Ai Camp, *Intellectuals and the State in Twentieth-Century Mexico* (Austin: University of Texas Press, 1985), 19.

78. Personal interview with Bishop Abelardo Alvarado Alcántara.

79. Personal interview with Bishop José Melgoza Osorio.

80. Personal interview with Archbishop Girolamo Prigione.

81. Personal interview with Bishop Manuel Samaniego Barriga, Cuautitlán Diocese, Cuautitlán, México, February 13, 1991.

82. Personal interview with Cardinal Juan Jesús Posadas Osorio. As Genaro Alamilla Arteaga, spokesperson for the episcopate, expressed it, "The Church is not a ghost, it is a universal reality in a country." Adolfo Sánchez Rebolledo, "Los motivos de la Iglesia, entrevista con Genaro Alamilla Arteaga," *Nexos* no. 141 (September 1989): 25.

83. David C. Leege and Joseph Gremillion, *The People, Their Pastors, and the Church: Viewpoints on Church Policies and Positions* (Terre Haute, Ind.: University of Notre Dame Study of Catholic Parish Life, Report no. 7, 1986), 4.

84. James Davison Hunter, "Religious Elites in Advanced Industrial Society," *Comparative Studies in Society and History* 29 (April 1987): 365.

85. Personal interview with Father Servando García, Acatlán de Juárez Parish, Guadalajara Diocese, Jalisco, July 6, 1993.

86. Personal interview with Father Alberto Aguirre, Seminary of the State of México, Toluca Diocese, Toluca, México, June 9, 1988.

87. Personal interview with Father Fernando Glagoaga, Church of Our Lady of the Unprotected, Toluca Diocese, Toluca, México, June 9, 1988.

88. Personal interview with Father Ernesto Menenses Morales, Mexico City, June 6, 1988.

89. Personal interview with Father Ernesto Domínguez Quiroga, Mexico City, June 13, 1989.

90. Personal interview with Father Jesús Vergara, Mexico City, June 29, 1989.

91. Personal interview with Father José Alvarez Franco, Tateposco, Tonala, Jalisco, July 7, 1993.

92. Personal interview with Father Samuel Morín Suárez, Toluca Diocese, Toluca, México, June 9, 1988.

93. Personal interview with Father Ricardo Cuellar Romo, Mexican Episcopate, Mexico Archdiocese, Mexico City, May 25, 1987.

94. Interview between David C. Bailey with Father Carlos Talavera, director of the Social Secretariat, Mexico Archdiocese, Mexico City, August 21, 1976.

95. Personal interview with Father Reuben Murillo, Ibero-American University, Mexico City, June 20, 1989.

96. Personal interview between Shannan Mattiace and Father Kent, Cottolengo, Yucatán, March 28, 1988.

97. Personal interview by Shannan Mattiace with a parish priest, Santiago Parish, Mérida Archdiocese, Mérida, Yucatán, March 28, 1988.

98. Enrique Luengo González, "Los párrocos: una visión," unpublished manuscript, Department of Social and Political Sciences, Ibero-American University, December 1989, 74, 87, 94.

99. Personal interview with Father Luis Gamino Botello, Precious Blood of Christ Church, Mexico Archdiocese, Mexico City, June 10, 1988.

100. Personal interview by Scott Pentzer and Meg Mitchell with Father Ochoa Aguilar, San Luis Potosí Diocese, San Luis Potosí, July 14, 1993.

101. Personal interview by Scott Pentzer with Father José Mendoza Carrillo, Cuernavaca Diocese, Cuernavaca, Morelos, July 30, 1993.

102. Personal interview with Father José Alvarez Franco.

103. Enrique Luengo González, "Los párrocos: una visión," 81.

104. Personal interview with Father Luis Gamino Botello.

105. Father Samuel Morín Suárez argued that if priests ended up casting their ballots publicly, it would do more damage than good by dividing rather than unifying Mexicans. Personal interview.

106. Personal interview by Scott Pentzer with Father José Mendoza Carrillo.

107. Personal interview with Father Samuel Morín Suárez.

108. Personal interview with Father Antonio Roqueñi, Mexico Archdiocese, Mexico City, July 14, 1993.

109. Personal interview with Father Ernesto Menenses Morales.

110. Personal interview with Father Carlos Escandon Domínguez, Mexico City, May 25, 1987.

111. Personal interview with Father Jacques Chaveriat, Mexico Archdiocese, Mexico City, June 8, 1988.

112. Personal interview with Miguel Alvarez, Mexico City, October 9, 1994.

Appendix: Mexican Bishops

Diocese and Ecclesiastical Region	Bishop	Years in Office
Acapulco, Guerrero, 1958 Acapulco (archdiocese since 1983)	*José Pilar Quezada Valdés* * *Rafael Bello Ruiz*	1959–1976 1976–1995
Aguascalientes, Aguascalientes, 1899 Guadalajara	José María de Jesús Portugal y Serratos Ignacio Valdespino y Díaz José de Jesús López y González *Salvador Quezada Limón* *Rafael Muñoz Núñez*	1902–1912 1913–1928 1930–1950 1951–1984 1984–1995
Apatzingán, Michoacán, 1962 Morelia	*Victoriano Alvarez y Tena* *José Fernández Arteaga* *Miguel Patiño Velázquez* (MSF)	1962–1974 1974–1980 1980–1995
Atlacomulco, México, 1984 Mexico	*Ricardo Guízar Díaz*	1984–1995
Autlán, Jalisco, 1961 Guadalajara	*Miguel González Ibarra* *José Maclovio Vázquez Silo* *Lázaro Pérez Jiménez*	1961–1969 1969–1991 1991–1995
Campeche, Campeche, 1885 Yucatán	Francisco Plancarte y Navarrete Rómulo Betancourt y Torres Francisco de P. Mendoza y Herrera Jaime de Anesagasti y Llamas Vicente Castellanos Núnez Francisco María González Arias Luis Guizar y Barragán Alberto Mendoza y Bedolla *Jesús García Ayala* *Héctor González Martínez* *Carlos Suárez Cázares*	1896–1898 1900–1901 1905–1909 1909–1910 1912–1921 1922–1931 1932–1938 1939–1967 1967–1982 1982–1987 1988–1994

Diocese and Ecclesiastical Region	Bishop	Years in Office
Celaya, Guanajuato, 1974 San Luis Potosi	*Victorino Alvarez Teña*	1974–1987
	Jesús Humberto Velázquez Garay	1987–1995
Chetumal, Quintana Roo, 1970 (Prelatura)	Jorge Bernal Vargas (LC)	1974–1995
Chihuahua, Chihuahua, 1891 Chihuahua (archdiocese since 1959)	José de Jesús Ortiz y Rodríguez	1893–1901
	Nicolás Pérez Gavilán	1902–1919
	Antonio Guizar Valencia	1921–1958
	Antonio Guizar Valencia (archbishop)	1959–1969
	Adalberto Almeida Merino	1969–1991
	José Fernández Arteaga	1991–1995
Chilapa, Guerrero, 1866 Acapulco	Buenaventura Portillo y Tejeda (OFM)	1882–1889
	Ramón Ibarra y González	1890–1902
	Homobono Anaya y Gutiérrez	1902–1906
	Francisco María Campos y Angeles	1907–1923
	José Guadalupe Ortiz y López	1923–1926
	Leopoldo Díaz y Escudero	1930–1955
	Alfonso Toríz Cobian	1956–1958
	Fidel Cortés Pérez	1959–1982
	José María Hernández González	1983–1988
	Efrén Ramos Salazar	1990–1995
Ciudad Altamirano, Guerrero, 1965 Acapulco	*Juan Navarro Ramírez*	1965–1970
	Manuel Samaniego Barriga	1971–1980
	José Lizares Estrada	1980–1987
	Raúl Vera López (OP)	1987–1995
Ciudad Guzmán, Jalisco, 1972 Guadalajara	*Leobardo Viera Contreras*	1972–1977
	Serafín Vázquez Elizalde	1978–1995
Ciudad Juárez, Chihuahua, 1957 Chihuahua	*Manuel Talamas Camandari*	1957–1992
	Juan Sandoval Iñiquez	1992–1994
	Renato Ascencio León	1994–1995
Ciudad Lázaro Cárdenas, Michoacán, 1985 Acapulco	*Jesús Sahagún de la Parra*	1985–1992
	Salvador Flores Huerta	1992–1995
Ciudad Nezahualcóyotl, México, 1979 Tlalnepantla	*José Melgoza Osorio*	1979–1988
	José María Hernández González	1988–1995
Ciudad Obregón, Sonora, 1960 Hermosillo	José Soledad Torres y Castañeda	1960–1966
	Miguel González Ibarra	1967–1982
	Luis Reynoso Cervantes	1982–1987
	Vicente García Bernal	1988–1995
Ciudad Valles, San Luis Potosí, 1961 Monterrey	*Carlos Quintero Arce*	1961–1966
	José Melgoza Osorio	1970–1979

Diocese and Ecclesiastical Region	Bishop	Years in Office
	Juvencio González Alvarez	1980–1994
	José Galván Galindo	1994–1995
Ciudad Victoria, Tamaulipas, 1964 Monterrey	*Alfonso Hinojosa Berrones*	1974–1985
	Raymundo López Mateos (OFM)	1985–1995
Coatzacoalcos, Veracruz, 1984 Jalapa	*Carlos Talavera Ramírez*	1984–1995
Colima, Colima, 1881 Guadalajara	Francisco Melitón Vargas y Gutiérrez	1883–1888
	Francisco de Paula Díaz Montes	1889–1891
	Atenogenes Silva Alvarez y Tostado	1892–1900
	Jose Amador Velasco Peña	1903–1949
	Ignacio de Alba Hernández	1949–1967
	Leobardo Viera Contreras	1967–1972
	Rogelio Sánchez González	1972–1981
	José Fernández Arteaga	1981–1988
	Gilberto Valbuena Sánchez	1988–1995
Cuautitlán, México, 1979 Tlalnepantla	*Manuel Samaniego Barriga*	1979–1995
Cuernavaca, Morelos, 1891 Mexico	Fortino Hipólito Vera y Talonia	1894–1898
	Francisco Plancarte y Navarrete	1898–1911
	Manuel Fulcheri y Pietrasanta	1912–1922
	Francisco Uranga y Saenz	1927–1930
	Francisco Maria González Aras	1931–1946
	Alfonso Espino y Silva	1947–1951
	Sergio Méndez Arceo	1952–1982
	Juan Jesús Posadas Ocampo	1982–1987
	Luis Cervantes Reynoso	1987–1995
Culiacán, Sinaloa, 1891 Durango	*Lino Aquirre y García*	1959–1969
	Luis Rojas Mena	1969–1993
	Benjamín Jiménez Hernández	1993–1995
Durango, Durango, 1620 Durango (archdiocese since 1891)	J. Vicente Salinas Infanzon	1869–1894
	J. Vicente Salinas Infanzon (archbishop)	1894–1895
	Santiago de Zubiría y Manzanera	1895–1909
	Francisco Mendoza y Herrera	1912–1923
	José María González Valencia	1924–1959
	Lucio Torreblanca y Tapia	1959–1961
	Antonio López Aviña	1961–1993
	José Trinidad Medel Pérez	1993–1995
El Nayar, Nayarit, 1962 (Prelatura)	Manuel Romero Arvizu (OFM)	1962–[?]
	Antonio Pérez Sánchez	[?]–1995

Diocese and Ecclesiastical Region	Bishop	Years in Office
El Salto, Durango, 1968 (Prelatura)	Francisco Medina Ramírez (OCD)	1968–1982
	Manuel Mireles Vaquera	1982–1995
Guadalajara, Jalisco, 1548 Guadalajara (archdiocese since 1864)	Pedro Loza	1869–1898
	Jacinto López y Romo	1900
	José de Jesús Ortiz	1902–1912
	Francisco Orozco y Jiménez	1913–1936
	José Garibi Rivera	1936–1969
	José Salazar López	1970–1987
	Juan Jesús Posadas Ocampo	1987–1993
	Juan Sandoval Iñiquez	1993–1995
Hermosillo, Sonora, 1963 Hermosillo (archdiocese since 1964, formerly 1779 Sonora)	Jesús María Rico Santoyo	1884
	Herculano López de la Mora	1887–1902
	Ignacio Valdespino y Díaz	1902–1913
	Juan María Navarrete Guerrero	1919–1964
	Juan María Navarrete Guerrero (archbishop)	1964–1968
	Carlos Quintero Arce	1968–1995
Huajuapan de León, Oaxaca, 1903 Puebla	*José López Lara*	1968–1981
	J. Jesús Aquilera Rodríquez	1982–1990
	Felipe Padilla Cardona	1992–1995
Huautla, Oaxaca, 1973 (Prelatura)	Hermenegildo Ramírez Sánchez (MJ)	1975–1995
Huejutla, Hidalgo, 1922 Puebla	José de Jesús Manríquez y Zárate	1923–1939
	Manuel J. Yerena y Camarena	1940–1963
	Bartolome Carrasco	1963–1967
	Serafín Vázquez Elizalde	1969–1978
	Juan de Dios Caballero Reyes	1978–1994
	Salvador Martínez Pérez	1994–1995
Jalapa, Veracruz, 1863 Jalapa (archdiocese since 1951)	Ignacio Suárez Peredo Bezares	1887–1894
	Joaquín Arcadio Pegaza	1895–1919
	Rafael Guizar Valencia	1919–1938
	Manuel Pío López Estrada	1939–1951
	Manuel Pío López Estrada (archbishop)	1951–1968
	Emilio Abascal Salmerón	1968–1979
	Sergio Obeso Rivera	1979–1995
La Paz, Baja California del Sur, 1988 (Prelatura, 1952)	Braulio Rafael León Villegas	1990–1995
León, Guanajuato, 1864 San Luis Potosí	Tomás Barón Morales	1883–1898
	Santiago de la Garza Zambrano	1898–1900
	Leopoldo Ruiz de Flores	1900–1907
	José Mora y del Río	1907–1908
	Emeterio Valverde Téllez	1909–1948

Diocese and Ecclesiastical Region	Bishop	Years in Office
	Manuel Martín del Campo y Padilla	1948–1965
	Anselmo Zarza Bernal	1966–1992
	Rafael García González	1992–1995
Linares, Nuevo León, 1962 Monterrey	*Anselmo Zarza Bernal*	1962–1966
	Antonio Sahagún López	1966–1974
	Rafael Gallardo García	1974–1988
	Ramón Calderón Batres	1988–1995
Madera, Chihuahua, 1994 (Prelatura, 1966)	*Renato Ascencio Léon*	1988–1994
Matamoros, Tamaulipas, 1959 Monterrey	*Estanislao Alcaraz Figueroa*	1959–1968
	Sabás Magaña García	1969–1991
	Francisco Javier Chavolla Ramos	1991–1995
Mazatlán, Sinaloa, 1959 Durango	*Miguel García Franco*	1959–1980
	Rafael Barraza Sánchez	1980–1995
Mexicali, Baja California, 1966 Hermosillo	*Manuel Pérez Gil González*	1966–1984
	José Ulises Macías Salcedo	1984–1995
México, Mexico City, 1530 Mexico (archdiocese since 1547)	Pelagio Antonio de Labastida y Dávalos	1863–1891
	Próspero María Alarcón y Sánchez	1892–1908
	José Mora y del Río	1909–1928
	Pascual Díaz Barreto (SJ)	1929–1936
	Luis María Martínez y Rodríguez	1937–1956
	Miguel Dario Miranda y Gómez (cardinal)	1956–1977
	Ernesto Corripio Ahumada (cardinal)	1977–1995
	Norberto Rivera Carrera	
	Auxiliary Bishops by Zone:	
	1. *Genaro Arteaga Alamilla*	1980–1992
	2. *Ricardo Watty Urquidi*	1980–1990
	3. *José Pablo Rovalo Azcué*	1980–1985
	Abelardo Alvarado Alcántara	1985–1994
	4. *Luis Mena Arroyo*	1979–1994
	5. *Javier Lozano Barragán*	1979–1984
	José Pablo Rovalo Azcué	1985–1990
	6. *Francisco María Aguilera González*	1979–1994
	7. *Francisco Orozco Lomelín*	1952–1990
	8. *Jorge Martínez Martínez*	1971–1993
Mixes, Oaxaca, 1965 (Prelatura)	Braulio Sánchez Fuentes (SDB)	1970–1995

Diocese and Ecclesiastical Region	Bishop	Years in Office
Monterrey, Nuevo León, 1777 Monterrey (archdiocese since 1899)	Jacinto López Romo	1886–1899
	Jacinto López Romo (archbishop)	1899
	Santiago de la Garza Zambrano	1900–1907
	Leopoldo Ruiz y Flores	1907–1911
	Francisco Plancarte y Navarrete	1912–1920
	Juan de Herrera y Piña	1921–1927
	José Guadalupe Ortíz y López	1930–1940
	Guillemo Trischler y Córdoba	1941–1952
	Alfonso Espino y Silva	1952–1976
	J. de Jesús Tirado Pedraza	1976–1983
	Adolfo Suárez Rivera	1983–1995
Morelia, Michoacán, 1536 Michoacan (archdiocese since 1863)	Leopoldo Ruíz y Flores	1912–1941
	Luis María Altamirano y Bulnes	1941–1972
	Estanislao Alcaraz Figueroa (archbishop)	1972–1995
Nezahualcóyotl, México, 1979 Tlanepantla	*José Melgoza Osorio*	1979–1989
	José María Hernández González	1989–1995
Nueva Casas Grandes, Chihuahua, 1977 (Prelatura)	Hilario Chávez Hoya (MNM)	1977–1995
Nuevo Laredo, Tamaulipas, 1990 Monterrey	*Ricardo Watty Urquidi* (M.Sp.S.)	1990–1995
Oaxaca, Oaxaca, 1535 Oaxaca (archdiocese since 1892)	Vicente Fermín Márquez Carrizosa	1869–1887
	Eulogio Gillow y Závala	1887–1892
	Eulogio Gillow y Závala (archbishop)	1892–1922
	José Otón Núñez y Zárate	1922–1941
	Fortino Gómez León	1942–1967
	Ernesto Corripio Ahumada	1967–1976
	Bartólome Carasco Briseño	1976–1994
	Héctor González Martínez	1994–1995
Papantla, Teziutlán, Puebla, 1923 Jalapa	Nicolás Corona y Corona	1923–1950
	Luis G. Cabrera Cruz	1951–1958
	Alfonso Sánchez Tinoco	1959–1970
	Sergio Obeso Rivera	1971–1974
	Genaro Alamilla Arteaga	1974–1980
	Lorenzo Cárdenas Aregullín	1980–1995
Parras, Chihuahua, 1992 Chihuahua	José Andrés Corral Arredondo	1992–1995
Puebla, Puebla, 1525 Puebla (archdiocese since 1904)	Francisco de Paula Vera	1880–1884
	José María Mora y Daza	1885–1887
	José del Refugio Guerra y Alva	1888
	Francisco Melitón Vargas	1888–1896

Diocese and Ecclesiastical Region	Bishop	Years in Office
	Perfecto Amezquita y Gutiérrez	1897–1900
	Ramón Ibarra y González	1902–1904
	Ramón Ibarra y González (arch-bishop)	1904–1917
	Enrique Sánchez y Paredes	1919–1923
	Pedro Vera y Zuria	1924–1944
	Ignacio Márquez y Toriz	1945–1950
	Octaviano Márquez y Toriz	1951–1971
	Ernesto Corripio y Ahumada	1976–1977
	Rosendo Huesca Pacheco	1977–1995
Querétaro, Querétaro, 1863 San Luis Potosí	Rafael Sábas Camacho García	1885–1908
	Manuel Rivera Múñoz	1908–1914
	Francisco Banegas Galván	1919–1932
	Marciano Tinajero Estrada	1933–1957
	Alfonso Toriz Cobián	1958–1987
	Mario de Gasperín Gasperín	1987–1995
Saltillo, Coahuila, 1893 Monterrey	Santiago Garza Zambrano	1893–1898
	José María de Jesús Portugal (OFM)	1898–1902
	Jesús María Echavarría y Aguirre	1905–1955
	Luis Guizar Barragán	1955–1975
	Francisco Villalobos Padilla	1975–1995
San Andrés Tuxtla, Veracruz, 1959 Jalapa	Jesús Villarreal y Fierro	1959–1968
	Arturo A. Szymanski Ramírez	1968–1969
	Guillermo Ranzahuer González	1969–1995
San Cristóbal de las Casas, Chiapas, 1541 Oaxaca	Mariano Luque y Ayerdi	1882–1901
	Francisco Orozco y Jiménez	1902–1912
	Maximino Ruíz y Flores	1913–1919
	Gerardo Anaya	1920–1942
	Lucio Torreblanca	1944–1957
	Samuel Ruiz García	1960–1995
San Juan de los Lagos, Jalisco, 1972 Guadalajara	*Francisco Javier Nuño Guerrero*	1972–1981
	José López Lara	1981–1987
	J. Trinidad Sepúlveda Ruíz	1987–1995
San Luis Potosí, San Luis Potosí, 1855 San Luis Potosí	Ignacio Montes de Oca y Obregón	1884–1921
	Miguel de la Mora	1922–1930
	Guillermo Tritscheler y Córdoba	1931–1941
	Gerardo Anaya y Diez de Bonilla	1941–1958
	Luis Cabrera Cruz	1958–1968
	Estanislao Alcaraz Figueroa	1968–1972
	Ezequiel Perea Sánchez	1972–1988
	Arturo A. Szymanski Ramírez	1988–1995
Tabasco, Villahermosa, Tabasco, 1882 Yucatán	Agustín de la J. Torres Hernández (CM)	1882–1885

Diocese and Ecclesiastical Region	Bishop	Years in Office
	Perfecto Amezquita Gutiérrez (CM)	1896
	Francisco M. Campos Angeles	1898–1907
	Leonardo Castellanos y Castellanos	1908–1912
	Antonio Hernández y Rodríguez	1913–1922
	Pascual Díaz Barreto (SJ)	1923–1929
	Vicente Camacho y Moya	1930–1943
	José de Jesús Angulo del Valle y Navarro	1943–1966
	Antonio Hernández Gallegos	1967–1973
	Rafael García González	1974–1992
	Florencio Olvera Ochoa	1992–1995
Tacámbaro, Michoacán, 1920 Morelia	Leopoldo Lara y Torres	1921–1933
	Manuel Pío López y Estrada	1934–1939
	Abraham Martínez Betancourt	1940–1979
	Luis Morales Reyes	1979–1985
	Alberto Suárez Inda	1985–1995
Tampico, Tamaulipas, 1871 Monterrey	Eduardo Sánchez Camacho	1880–1896
	Filemón Fierro y Terán	1897–1905
	José de Jesús Guzmán y Sánchez	1910–1914
	José Guadalupe Ortiz y López	1919–1923
	Serafín Amora y González	1923–1955
	Ernesto Corripio Ahumada	1956–1967
	Arturo A. Szymanski Ramírez	1968–1988
	Rafael Gallardo García (OSA)	1988–1995
Tapachula, Chiapas, 1958 Oaxaca	*Adolfo Hernández Hurtado*	1958–1970
	Bartolomé Carrasco	1971–1976
	Juevenal Porcayo Uribe	1976–1983
	Luis Miguel Cantón Marín	1984–1991
	Felipe Arizmendi Esquivel	1991–1995
Tarahumara, 1994 Chihuahua	*José Diboldox Martínez*	1994–1995
Tehuacán, Puebla, 1962 Puebla	*Rafael Ayala y Ayala*	1962–1985
	Norberto Rivera Carrera	1985–1995
Tehuantepec, Oaxaca, 1891 Oaxaca	José Mora y del Río	1893–1901
	Carlos de J. Mejía Laguna	1903–1907
	Ignacio Placencia y Moreira	1908–1922
	Jenaro Méndez del Río	1923–1933
	Jesús Villarreal y Fierro	1933–1959
	José de Jesús Alba Palacios	1959–1971
	Arturo Lona Reyes	1971–1995
Tepic, Nayarit, 1891 Guadalajara	Ignacio Díaz Macedo	1893–1905
	Andrés Segura y Domínguez	1906–1918

Diocese and Ecclesiastical Region	Bishop	Years in Office
	Manuel Azpeitia Palomar	1919–1935
	Anastasio Hurtado y Robles	1936–1971
	Adolfo Suárez Rivera	1971–1980
	Alfonso Humberto Robles Cota	1981–1995
Texcoco, México, 1960 Mexico	Francisco Ferreira Arreola	1960–1977
	Magín Torreblanca Reyes	1978–1995
Tijuana, Baja California, 1964 Hermosillo	*Alfredo Galindo Mendoza*	1964–1969
	Juan Jesús Posadas Ocampo	1970–1982
	Emilio Berlié Belaunzarán	1983–1995
Tlalnepantla, México, 1964 Tlalnepantla (archdiocese 1989)	Felipe de Jesús Cueto González (OFM)	1964–1980
	Adolfo Suárez Rivera	1980–1984
	Manuel Pérez-Gil González	1984–1995
Tlapa, Guerrero, 1992 Acapulco	Alejo Zavala Castro	1992–1995
Tlaxcala, Tlaxcala, 1959 Puebla	*Luis Munive Escobar*	1959–1995
Toluca, México, 1950 Mexico	*Arturo Velez Martínez*	1951–1980
	Alfredo Torres Romero	1980–1995
Torreón, Coahuila, 1958 Durango	*Fernando Romo Gutiérrez*	1958–1994
	Luis Morales Reyes	1994–1995
Tula, Hidalgo, 1961 Mexico	*Jesús Sahagún de la Parra*	1961–1986
	José Trinidad Medel Pérez	1986–1993
	Octavio Villegas Aguilar	1994–1995
Tulancingo, Hidalgo, 1864 Hidalgo	Agustín de Jesús Torres Hernández (CM)	1885–1889
	José María Armas Rosales	1891–1898
	Maximiano Reynoso de Corral	1899–1902
	José Mora y del Río	1902–1907
	Juan de J. Herrera y Piña	1907–1921
	Vicente Castellanos Núñez	1921–1932
	Luis M. Altamirano y Bulnes	1933–1937
	Miguel Dario Miranda y Gómez	1937–1955
	Adalberto Almeida Merino	1956–1962
	José Esaúl Robles	1962–1974
	Pedro Aranda-Díaz Muñoz	1975–1995
Tuxpan, Veracruz, 1963 Jalapa	*Ignacio Lehonor Arroyo*	*1963–1982*
	Mario de Gasperín Gasperín	*1983–1989*
	Luis Gabriel Cuara Mendez	*1989–1995*
Tuxtepec, Oaxaca, 1979 Oaxaca	*Jesús Castillo Rentería* (MNM)	1979–1995

Diocese and Ecclesiastical Region	Bishop	Years in Office
Tuxtla Gutiérrez, Chiapas, 1964 Oaxaca	*José Trinidad Sepúlveda Ruiz de Velasco*	1965–1988
	Felipe Aguirre Franco	1988–1995
Veracruz, Veracruz, 1963 Jalapa	*José Guadalupe Padilla Lozano*	1963–1995
Yucatán, Mérida, Yucatán, 1561 Yucatán (archdiocese since 1906)	Leandro Rodríguez de la Gala	1869–1887
	Cresencio Carrillo y Ancona	1887–1897
	José Guadalupe Alba Franco (OFM)	1899
	Martín Tritschler y Córdoba	1900–1942
	Fernando Ruiz Solorzano	1944–1969
	Manuel Castro Ruiz	1969–1995
Zacatecas, Zacatecas, 1863 Guadalajara	José María del Refugio Guerra y Alba	1873–1888
	Buenaventura de María Portillo (friar)	1889–1899
	José Guadalupe de Jesús Alva (friar)	1900–1910
	Miguel María de la Mora y de la Mora	1911–1922
	Ignacio Placencia y Moreira	1923–1951
	Francisco Javier Nuño	1951–1954
	Antonio López Aviña	1955–1961
	Adalberto Almeida y Merino	1962–1969
	José Pablo Robalo Azcue	1970–1972
	Rafael Muñoz Núñez	1972–1984
	Javier Lozano Barragán	1984–1995
Zamora, Michoacán, 1863 Morelia	*José G. Anaya*	1947–1967
	José Salazar López	1967–1970
	José Esaúl Robles Jiménez	1970–1993
	Carlos Suárez Cázeres	1994–1995

*The names of bishops included in the data bank for the tables in this book are italicized.

Bibliographic Essay

Religion and religion and politics offer a vast array of literature that explores the institutional Catholic Church as well as the issues of religion and society generally. To understand the Church's role in the Latin American context, no better place exists to start than the work of Daniel H. Levine, who provides an evolving theoretical argument sensitive to the linkages between politics and religion while at the same time recognizing the special qualities that religion poses for the social scientist. His comparative study, *Religions and Politics in Latin America: The Catholic Church in Venezuela and Colombia* (Princeton: Princeton University Press, 1981), lays out some essential arguments that are followed up in, among other articles, his "Religion and Politics: Dimensions of Renewal," *Thought* 59, no. 233 (June 1984): 117–135, and "From Church and State to Religion and Politics and Back Again," *World Affairs* 150 (Fall 1987): 93–108. Two other country-specific works of great value are Scott Mainwaring, *The Catholic Church and Politics in Brazil, 1916–1985* (Stanford: Stanford University Press, 1986), and Brian H. Smith, *The Church and Politics in Chile: Challenges to Modern Catholicism* (Princeton: Princeton University Press, 1982). Two additional general works are equally important to the broad picture: Edward L. Cleary's *Crisis and Change: The Church in Latin America Today* (Maryknoll: Orbis Books, 1985), and his excellent coedited work with Hannah Stewart-Gambino, *Conflict and Competition: The Latin American Church in a Changing Environment* (Boulder, Colo.: Lynne Rienner, 1992), especially Cleary's chapter "Politics and Religion—Crisis, Constraints, and Restructuring," 197–221. A path-breaking work for its time and still highly relevant to contemporary research is Ivan Vallier, *Catholicism, Social Control, and Modernization in Latin America* (Englewood Cliffs, N.J.: Prentice-Hall, 1970). The other general works from this same period are David Mutchler, *The Church as a Political Factor in Latin America* (New York: Praeger, 1971), and Thomas G. Sanders, "The Politics of Catholicism in Latin America," *Journal of Inter-American Studies and World Affairs* 24 (May 1982): 241–258. Finally, Margaret Crahan provides fresh insights in her overview of church-state relations in the 1990s, "Church and State in Latin America: Assassinating Some Old and New Stereotypes," *Daedalus* 120, no. 3 (Summer 1991): 131–158, as do Cornelia Butler Flora and Rosario Bello in "The Impact of the Catholic Church on National Level Change in Latin America," *Journal of Church and State* 31, no. 3 (Autumn 1989): 527–542.

Among the most useful non–Latin American literature on religion and politics are Gerhard Lenski, *The Religious Factor: A Sociological Study of Religion's Impact on Politics and Family Life* (Garden City, N.Y.: Doubleday, 1963); Philip E. Hammond, "The Conditions for Civil Religion: A Comparison of the United States and Mexico," in *Varieties of*

Civil Religion, Robert W. Bella and Philip E. Hammond, eds. (New York: Harper and Row, 1980), 40–85; and perhaps the broadest, most international portrait, Eric O. Hanson, *The Catholic Church in World Politics* (Princeton: Princeton University Press, 1987). Some major theoretical reinterpretations can also be found in Kenneth Wald, Dennis E. Owen, and Samuel S. Hills, "Political Cohesion in Churches," *Journal of Politics* 52, no. 1 (February 1990): 197–215, and "Churches as Political Communities," *American Political Science Review* 82, no. 2 (June 1988): 531–548, as well as Robert Wuthnow, "Understanding Religion and Politics," *Daedalus* 20, no. 3 (Summer 1991): 1–19. Similar insights from the Latin American case can be drawn from Michael Fleet and Brian Smith's innovative "Rethinking Catholicism and Politics in Latin America," paper presented at the Latin American Studies Association, Miami, 1989.

The historical pattern in Mexican church-state relations specifically offers a much stronger literature than the recent, post-1968 era. The strongest research in this field covering the decades since 1930 is that of Roberto Blancarte, whose publications, based on a Ph.D. dissertation at the Sorbonne, can be found in *Historia de la iglesia católica en México* (Mexico City: Fondo de Cultura Económica, 1992), and, for the 1988–1992 period, *El poder salinismo e iglesia católica, una nueva convivencia?* (Mexico City: Grijalbo, 1991). Blancarte also provides an excellent critical interpretation of the historical literature since 1929 in "La iglesia católica en México desde 1929: Introducción crítica a la producción historiográfica (1968–1988)," *Cristianismo y Sociedad*, no. 101 (1989): 27–42. Ralph Carleton Beals, "Bureaucratic Change in the Mexican Catholic Church, 1926–1950," Ph.D. dissertation, University of California, Berkeley, 1966, also provides a helpful historical picture, as does Peter L. Reich's "Mexico's Hidden Revolution: The Catholic Church in Politics since 1929," Ph.D. dissertation, University of California, Los Angeles, 1991, which offers significant insights into the 1930s, and Elwood Rufus Gotshall, "Catholicism and Catholic Action in Mexico, 1929–41," Ph.D. dissertation, University of Pittsburgh, 1970, which captures its linkages to a socially and politically active laity. The international, historical perspective is well explored in Servando Ortoll's "Catholic Organizations in Mexico's National Politics and International Diplomacy (1926–1942)," Ph.D. dissertation, Columbia University, 1986. Essential to understanding some of the historical, structural issues is Karl Schmitt, "Church and State in Mexico: A Corporatist Relationship," *The Americas* 40 (January 1984): 349–376. An essential primary source is *DIC, Documentación e Información Católica*, which republishes many of the pastoral letters and documents from individual dioceses and from the Council of Mexican Bishops. It covers the last two decades.

North American scholars began to consider the contemporary Mexican Church more seriously in the 1980s, during which time several important works were completed. Among the most significant are Claude Pomerlau, "The Changing Church in Mexico and Its Challenge to the State," *Review of Politics* 43, no. 4 (October 1981): 540–559; Dennis M. Hanratty, "Change and Conflict in the Contemporary Mexican Catholic Church," Ph.D. dissertation, Duke University, 1980, "The Political Role of the Mexican Catholic Church: Contemporary Issues," *Thought* 59 (June 1984): 164–182, and "Church-State Relations in Mexico in the 1980s," *Thought* 63 (1988): 207–223; and Dennis Goulet, "The Mexican Church: Into the Public Arena," *America* 160 (April 8, 1989): 318–322. George Grayson provides an update through the Salinas period in his *The Church in Contemporary Mexico* (Washington: CSIS, 1992), as does Allan Metz in "Church-State Relations in Contemporary Mexico, 1968–1988," in *The Religious Challenge to the State*, Matthew C. Moen and Lowell S. Gustafson, eds. (Philadelphia: Temple University Press, 1992), 102–128, and "Mexican Church-State Relations under President Carlos Salinas de Gortari," *Journal of Church and State* 34 (Winter 1992): 111–130. In Mexico, the most comprehensive work is that of Martín de la Rosa and Charles A. Reilly, eds., *Religión y política en México* (Mexico City: Siglo XXI, 1985), and Carlos Martínez Assad, ed., *Religiosidad y política en México* (Mexico City: Ibero-American University, 1992). Two insightful views of the changing relationship in 1992 are available in Grupo Consultor Interdisciplinario, "Carta de política Mexicana, las relaciones estado-iglesias," February 21, 1992, and Instituto Mexicano de Estrategias, "Relaciones estado-iglesia, nuevo marco jurídico," Reporte Ejecutivo, December 31, 1992.

In addition, a number of scholars have begun to explore the potential and actual role of the Church in Mexican politics, specifically in the area of electoral politics and political liberalization. Among the most important efforts in this area is that of Soledad Loaeza. Although she clearly takes an anticlerical, partisan view and her arguments are repeated verbatim in different citations, her interpretations are insightful. Among the most helpful are "La Iglesia católica mexicana y el reformismo autoritario," *Foro Internacional* 25, no. 2 (October–December 1984): 138–165; "La Iglesia y la democracia en México," *Revista Mexicana de Socioloqia* 47, no. 1 (January–March 1985): 161–168; and "Continuity and Change in the Mexican Catholic Church," in *Church and Politics in Latin America*, Dermot Keogh, ed. (New York: St. Martin's, 1990), 272–298. Bernardo Barranco Villafan and Raquel Pastor Escobar, *Jerarquía católica y modernización política en México* (Mexico City: Palabra Ediciones, 1989), and Silvia Marcela Bénard, "The Relationship between Church and State in Mexico: An Analysis of the Pope's Visit in 1979," M.A. thesis, University of Texas, Austin, 1986, are also insightful. One of the finest studies of the Church's political role in the context of interest group literature is Otto Granados Roldán, *La Iglesia católica mexicana como grupo de presión* (Mexico City: Humanidades, UNAM, 1981). The best case studies are two Ph.D. dissertations examining Chihuahua, where the Catholic Church played a significant and overt role in election matters in the mid-1980s: Vikram Khub Chand, "Politicization, Institutions, and Democratization in Mexico: The Politics of the State of Chihuahua in National Perspective," Harvard University, 1991, and Silvia Marcela Bénard, "Struggling for a Democratic Future: Political Change in Chihuahua, 1983–1992," University of Texas, Austin, 1994. Two additional case studies, prior to 1982, are equally useful: Yolanda Padilla Rangel, *Con la iglesia hemostopado, catolicismo y sociedád en Aguascalientes, un conflicto de los años 70's* (Aguascalientes: Instituto Cultural, 1991), and Víctor Gabriel Muro González, "Iglesia y movimientos sociales en México, los casos de ciudad Juárez y el istmo de Tehuantepec," Ph.D. dissertation, Colegio de México, 1991.

Church involvement in human rights and social issues has been well covered in Latin America and, relatively speaking, in Mexico. A broad perspective can be found in Brian H. Smith, "Church and Human Rights in Latin America," *Journal of Inter-American Studies and World Affairs* 21 (February 1979): 89–128, and "Religion and Social Change: Classical Theories and New Formulations in the Context of Recent Developments in Latin America," *Latin American Research Review* 10 (1975): 3–34; and Carolyn Cook Dipboye, "The Roman Catholic Church and the Political Structure for Human Rights in Latin America, 1968–1980," *Journal of Church and State* 24 (Autumn 1982): 497–524.

A voluminous literature exists on liberation theology in Latin America, although it does not cover Mexico extensively because of the lesser role of liberation theology in Mexico. A useful orientation to the major arguments in the literature can be found in Daniel H. Levine, "Assessing the Impacts of Liberation Theology in Latin America," *Review of Politics* 50 (1988): 241–263; Michael Dodson, "The Christian Left in Latin American Politics," *Journal of Inter-American Studies and World Affairs* 21 (February 1979): 45–68; John H. Yoder, "The Wider Setting of 'Liberation Theology,' " *Review of Politics* 50 (1988): 285–296; and Frederick Sontag, "Liberation Theology and Its View of Political Violence," *Jour-*

nal of Church and State 31 (Spring 1989): 269–286. On CEBs, see W. E. Hewitt, "Christian Base Communities (CEBS): Structure, Orientation, and Sociopolitical Thrust," *Thought* 63, no. 249 (June 1988): 162–175, and Thomas C. Bruneau, "Basic Christian Communities in Latin American: Their Nature and Significance, Especially in Brazil," in *Churches and Politics in Latin America,* Daniel Levine, ed. (Beverly Hills: Sage Publications, 1980). The most comprehensive work on Mexico can be found in Martín de la Rosa and Thomas Reilly, *Religion e política en México,* cited above, as well as in Miguel Concha Malo, "Tensiones entre la religión de pueblo y las CEB's en México con sectores de la jearquía: Implicaciones eclesiologicas," *Ciencia Tomista* 114 (May–August 1987): 287–310, and Matilde Gastalver and Lino F. Salas, *Las comunidades eclesiales de base y el movimiento popular en México* (Mexico City: Ibero-American University, 1983). In English, the best work available is Michael Tangeman, *Mexico at the Crossroads: Politics, the Church, and the Poor* (Maryknoll: Orbis Books, 1994).

Very little work has been done, with the exception of some pioneer research among a handful of Mexican and North American scholars, on religious values, religiosity, and partisanship. An essential starting place for some of the issues raised in the field generally, outside of Mexico, is Kenneth D. Wald, *Religion and Politics in the United States* (New York: St. Martin's, 1987); Andrew Greeley, *The Catholic Myth: The Behavior and Belief of American Catholics* (New York: Collier Books, 1990); David C. Leege, M. R. Welch, and T. A. Trozzolo, "Religiosity, Church Social Teaching, and Socio-Political Attitudes," *Review of Religious Research* 28 (1986): 118–128; Michael Welch and David Leege, "Religious Predictors of Catholic Parishioners' Socio-political Attitudes: Devotional Style, Closeness to God, Imagery, and Agenetic/Communal Religious Identity," *Journal for the Scientific Study of Religion* 27 (December 1988): 536–552; and David C. Leege and Joseph Gremillion, *The People, Their Pastors, and the Church: Viewpoints on Church Policies and Positions,* Notre Dame Study of Catholic Parish Life, Report no. 7 (Terre Haute, Ind.: University of Notre Dame, 1986). The Mexican Church, specifically the Diocese of Tijuana, contributes data from 22,000 parish respondents in *Plan pastoral, 1989–1994, hacia una iglesia nueva* (Tijuana, 1989). For a comparative evaluation of Catholic and Protestant religious values in Central America, see Andrew Stein, "Religion and Mass Politics in Central America," paper presented at the New England Council of Latin Americanists, Boston University, 1992, and, on Chile, Timothy J. Steigena and Kenneth M. Coleman, "Protestantism and Politics in Chile: 1972–1991," paper presented at the same conference.

In Mexico, several broad cultural surveys include invaluable data on religion. The most useful comparatively is that of the World Values Survey, available from the University of Michigan and other major survey research centers, as well as the data in Alberto Hernández Medina et al., eds., *Como somos los mexicanos* (Mexico City: Centro de Estudios Educativos, 1987), and Enrique Alduncin, *Los valores de los mexicanos* (Mexico City: Fomento Cultural Banamex, 1986), and *Los valores de los mexicanos, México en tiempo de cambio* (Mexico City: Fomento Cultural Banamex, 1991). Miguel Basáñez conducted numerous polls for my research, some of which have been published, in part, in *Este País,* in other periodicals, or are reported in chapter 5, note 20. Enrique Luengo's study of Ibero-American University students can be found in "La religiosidad de los estudiantes de la UIA," *Umbral XXI,* no. 9 (Summer 1992): 39–45, which is available in much greater detail in his *La religión y los jóvenes de México: el desgaste de una relación?* (Mexico City: Ibero-American University, 1993), based on his Ph.D. dissertation. General comparisons of cultural values among students are available in the excellent study, including data from Colombia, by Rogelio Díaz-Guerrero and Lorand B. Szalay, *Understanding Mexicans and Americans: Cultural Perspectives in Conflict* (New York: Plenum Press, 1991). The pioneers among North American scholars are Kenneth Coleman and Charles Davis. See

Charles Davis, "Religion and Partisan Loyalty: The Case of Catholic Workers in Mexico," *Western Political Quarterly* 45 (March 1992): 275–290, and with Kenneth M. Coleman, "Discontinuous Educational Experiences and Political and Religious Nonconformity in Authoritarian Regimes: Mexico," *Social Science Quarterly* 58, no. 3 (December 1977): 489–497. The Church itself conducted a comprehensive study of 14,000 Catholics in Comisión Episcopal para el Apostolado de los Laicos, *Qué piensan los laicos mexicanos del sínodo '87* (Mexico City: CEM, 1986). For a more subjective view, see Claude Pomerlau, "Religion and Values in the Formation of Modern Mexico: Some Economic and Political Considerations," in *Global Economics and Religion*, J. Finn, ed. (New Brunswick, N.J.: Transaction Books, 1983), 143–160.

Although it seems extraordinary, the least examined topics of Catholicism in Latin America are the rank-and-file troops of the Catholic Church, its priests. Most of what can be learned about priests has to be undertaken through interviews by the enterprising researcher. Two broad studies from which some comparisons can be drawn are available: Joseph H. Fichter, *Religion as an Occupation: A Study in the Sociology of Professions* (Terre Haute, Ind.: University of Notre Dame, 1961), and Andrew Greeley's excellent sociological work, *Priests in the United States: Reflections on a Survey* (New York: Doubleday, 1971). Some statistical data on priests in Latin America can be found in Gustavo Pérez Ramírez and Yván Labelle, *El problema sacerdotal en América Latina* (Madrid: FERES, 1964). Works focused on an earlier period elsewhere in Latin America for higher clergy only are Sergio Miceli, *A elite eclesiástica brasileira* (Rio de Janeiro: Editora Bertrand Brasil, 1988), and Thomas G. Sanders's brief "The Chilean Episcopate," *American Universities Field Staff Reports* 15, no. 3 (August 1968). Daniel Levine includes a comparative chapter on Venezuelan and Colombian bishops in his previously cited *Religion and Politics in Latin America*. For Mexico, only one study exists, based on a large cooperative project at Ibero-American University headed by Enrique Luengo, available in "Percepción política de los párrocos en México," in *Religiosidad y política en México*, Carlos Martínez Assad, ed. (Mexico City: Ibero-American University, 1992), 199–239. A broader version is available in a master's thesis by one of the student participants, Eduardo Sota García: "La percepción social y política de los párrocos del estado de México," Ibero-American University, 1992. A published version, focusing on politics, is available in Eduardo Sota García and Enrique Luengo, *Entre la conciencia y la obediencia: La opinión del clero sobre la política en México* (Mexico City: Ibero-American University, 1994). Some general background data on priests are also available in the now dated Manuel González Ramírez, *La iglesia mexicana en cifras* (Mexico City, 1969), and the privately published work of Luis Núñez and Félix Palencia, *Seminarios y seminaristas de México en 1973* (Chihuahua, 1974). A survey of 234 priests from all regions is also presented in José María Díaz Mozaz and Vicente J. Sastre, "Una encuesta de opinión al clero mexicano, aproximación a la realidad socio-religiosa mexicana," *Vida Pastoral* 2, no. 1 (August 1976): 13–24. Some basic data are available from the Conferencia del Episcopado Mexicano's regularly published *Directorio Eclesiástico*. Biographical information is very difficult to obtain, and the most useful sources are the *Enciclopedia de México* and individual issues of the *Documentación e Información Católica*, but only for bishops and other high-ranking clergy. Antonio García Montaño provides unpublished biographical information in his paper "Los obispos mexicanos de la segunda mitad del siglo xx" (1992). Some very interesting information about the educational experiences of priests and bishops can be gleaned from Luis Medina Ascensio's excellent in-depth explorations of the Montezuma seminary in New Mexico, *Historia del Seminario de Montezuma, sus precedentes, fundación y consolidación, 1910–1953* (Mexico City: Editorial Jus, 1962), and *Montezuma íntimo, su escenario, su gente, su vida* (Mexico City: Editorial Jus, 1962), and José Macías's more detailed work about its alumni, *Montezuma en sus exalumnos, 1937–1962* (Mexico City, 1962), which lists all of the graduates alphabetically and by class. Theodore M. Hesburgh, *God, Country, Notre Dame* (New York: Fawcett, 1990), provides some brief insights into the Gregorian University experience.

The institutional experiences within the Catholic Church, the transitions it is undergoing, and important information about the decision-making process have been explored more fully outside of Latin America, especially in Thomas Reese, *Archbishop: Inside the Power Structure of the American Catholic Church* (New York: Harper and Row, 1989), and *A Flock of Shepherds: The National Conference of Catholic Bishops* (Kansas City, Mo.: Sheed and Ward, 1992); John L. McKenzie, *The Roman Catholic Church* (New York: Holt, Rinehart, 1969), especially 1–123, which provides the most detailed description of church structure; and Howard T. Sanks, *Authority in the Church: A Study in Changing Paradigms* (Missoula, Mont.: Scholar's Press, 1974). For Latin America generally, a good place to start for an institutional analysis is Luigi Einaudi, ed., *Latin American Institutional Development: The Changing Catholic Church* (Santa Monica, Calif.: Rand Corporation, 1969). For Mexico, the only work that focuses more directly on decision making at the diocese level, and on the relationship to the government, is that of Oscar Aguilar and Enrique Luengo, "Iglesia y gobierno en el D.F.," in *D.F.: gobierno y sociedad civil,* Pablo González Casanova, ed. (Mexico City: El Caballito, 1987).

Although there have been many allegations of a relationship between the Catholic Church and the National Action Party in Mexico, little substantive evidence and analysis of such a relationship exist. The best work is focused on the parties, not the Church, with only tangential references to the Church. In addition to the works recommended above on electoral politics, they include Soledad Loaeza, "Derecha y democracia en el cambio político mexicano: 1982–1988," *Foro Internacional* 30 (April–June 1990): 631–658; Laura Nuzzi O'Shaughnessy, "Opposition in an Authoritarian Regime: The Incorporation and Institutionalization of the Mexican National Action Party (PAN)," Ph.D. dissertation, Indiana University, 1979; James F. Creagan, "Minority Political Parties in Mexico: Their Role in a One-Party System," Ph.D. dissertation, University of Virginia, 1965; and Bernardo Barranco Villafan and Raquel Pastor Escobar, "La presencia de la iglesia católica en el proceso de sucesión presidencial 1988," *Análisis Sociales* no. 2 (1988): 42–61. The only study that examines the connection between priests and the PRI at the local level is Susan Eckstein, "Politicos and Priests: The Iron Law of Oligarchy and Inter-organizational Relations," *Comparative Politics* 9 (July 1977): 463–481. The case studies by Vikram Khub Chand and Silvia Bénard, mentioned above, also add important insights concerning church-party relations. Numerous case studies that examine conflicts between the Church and the state, and their consequences, can be found in Patricia Arias et al., *Radiografía de la iglesia católica en México* (Mexico City: UNAM, 1981). The historic impact of the Catholic Church on PAN is most thoroughly examined in Donald Mabry, *Mexico's Acción Nacional: A Catholic Alternative to Revolution* (Syracuse: Syracuse University Press, 1973), and David C. Bailey, "The Church since 1940," in *Twentieth Century Mexico,* William H. Beezley and W. Dirk Raat, eds. (Lincoln: University of Nebraska Press, 1986), 236–242. *Proceso,* the Mexican weekly, has paid the closest attention to this relationship of any periodical in Mexico, especially in Rodrigo Vera's articles.

Most of the information on decision making within the Catholic Church in Mexico comes, given the lack of published studies, from personal interviews with the actors themselves—bishops, priests, and local politicians. As far as internal church matters are concerned, particularly the bishop succession process, an important theoretical understanding of canon law is available in John T. Finnegan, "The Present Canonical Practice in the Catholic Church," in *The Choosing of Bishops,* William W. Bassett, ed. (Hartford, Conn.:

The Canon Law Society of America, 1971), 85–102. For insights into the actual practice in the United States, see Thomas Reese's *Archbishop.* Individual cases at the diocese level are presented by Rodrigo Vera in *Proceso,* and José Luis Gaona Vega in *Punto.* Gaona Vega has covered the Church for many years and has made his entire collection of articles available. The ideological conflicts among Mexico's bishops are dealt with in considerable detail in Marta Eugenia García Ugarte, "Las posiciones políticas de la jerarquía católica, efectos en la cultura religiosa mexicana," in *Religiosidad y política en México,* Carlos Martínez Assad, ed. (Mexico City: Ibero-American University, 1992), 61–116.

Basically, one can search in vain for views of national politicians on the Catholic Church and Catholicism or views of the church hierarchy on national, secular leadership. No comparative literature is available from which to borrow. Instead, I relied initially on my own work on group-state relations and the literature on which that research was based to suggest some possible patterns in the Mexican case. On entrepreneurial, military, and intellectual relations to the state, see my *Entrepreneurs and Politics in Twentieth-Century Mexico* (New York: Oxford University Press, 1989); *Generals in the Palace: The Military in Modern Mexico* (New York: Oxford University Press, 1992); and *Intellectuals and the State in Twentieth-Century Mexico* (Austin: University of Texas Press, 1985), which provide guidance and some insights into relationships peculiar to Mexico. A study that explores how religious elites view their own roles in society is James Davison Hunter, "Religious Elites in Advanced Industrial Society," *Comparative Studies in Society and History* 29 (April 1987): 360–374. Other specific works helpful to understanding the general relationship include Leonor Ludlow, "Tensiones y presiones en las relaciones entre estado e iglesia," in *17 angulos de un sexsenio,* Germán Pérez, ed. (Mexico City: Plaza y Valdes, 1987), 385–398, and Manuel Olimón Nolasco, *Tensiones y acercamientos, la iglesia y el estado en la historia del pueblo mexicano* (Mexico City: Instituto Mexicano de Doctrina Social Cristiana, 1990). The only firsthand account representing a government point of view is the Institutional Revolutionary Party, "Memorandum sobre las relaciones estado-iglesia católica," November 1988. The Church, unlike the state, has left a written record of its views on the state in general, and the elites in particular, in the multitude of Mexican episcopate publications and pastoral letters, often reported, as suggested above, in complete detail in *Información e Documentación Católica.* Although these are too numerous to cite, it is essential to peruse *Sociedad civil y sociedad religiosa* (Mexico City: Libreria Parroquial de Claveria, 1985); Adolfo Suárez Rivera, *Instrucción pastoral sobre la dimensión político de la fe* (Monterrey: Archbishopric of Monterrey, March 1987); and *Compromiso cristiano ante las opciones sociales y la política* (Mexico City: Edición de Senal, 1973), for the recent Mexican hierarchy's historical perspective within the larger Church context.

Index

Abortion
  laity's views on, 122
Acción Católica de la Juventud Mexicana
    (ACJM)
  linking Church to PAN, 57
Acosta Urquidi, Mariclare
  family roots of, 143
  on violence in Guerrero, 100 n. 26
Aguascalientes
  important case study of bishop, 279 n.
    67
Aguilera González, Francisco María
  comment on family influence, 136–137
  spiritual and temporal tasks intertwined,
    290
Alemán, Miguel
  conciliation pattern, 28–29
Almeida, Alberto
  civic education project, 292
  confrontation with Manuel Bartlett, 65
  dealings with Vatican delegate, 65
  role in Chihuahua electoral fraud, 64
  social pastoral statement, 68
  support for progressive positions, 77 n.
    137
Alvarado Alcántara, Abelardo
  seminary influence on, 146
Anticlericalism
  consequences of bishops steeped in, 213
  in the historical context, 24
  impact on liberation theology, 88
Archbishops
  relation to bishops, 261

Argentina
  economic control of Church in, 234
Arias, Patricia
  study of Aguascalientes, 279 n. 67
Armendáriz, Antonio
  access to education, 208–209
Article 343
  CEM's position on, 67
  restrictions on priests in 1987 electoral
    code, 67
Atheists
  important differences, 124
  political views of, 123
Auxiliary bishops
  appointment pattern among, 264
  canon law on, 264
  priests who become, 263–264
  in the United States, 264
Avila Camacho, Manuel
  climate of administration, 28
  "I am a believer" declaration, 28

Bailey, David C.
  on Catholic literature, 9
  on PAN connection to Church, 205
  on textbooks, 224–225 n. 50
Bartlett, Manuel
  role in 1986 Chihuahua election fraud,
    64
  ties to Girolamo Prigione, 211, 218
Basáñez, Miguel
  polls on religion, 127 n. 20

Basave, Agustín
    family religious influences, 142
Base ecclesiastical communities (CEBs)
    bishops' support for, 91–92
    CEM's position toward, 93
    focus of, 92
    impact on women, 91
    influence on Protestantism, 96
    operation of, 92–93
    prohibitions against, 93
    resistance to, 93
    role of, 90
    source of conflict with state, 98
Bazdresch, Juan
    on family influences, 138
Bennett, Douglas, 5
Birthplace
    consequences for politicians, 180
    differences among groups, 182, 185
    effects on bishops' careers, 184, 190
    effects on educational choices, 186,
        190
    Federal District's importance, 182, 185
    hinders careers, 184, 190
    impact on discipline choices, 186
    importance of, 197
    influence on initial assignment, 191
    most important among bishops, 181–182
    rural versus urban, 189
    underrepresented regions, 182
    West Central Mexico's importance, 181
    West's importance, 184
Bishops
    admit ideological divisions, 273
    attendance at Gregorian University, 171,
        174
    attendance at Vatican II, 85
    attitudes toward partisanship, 125
    birthplaces, 181–185, 189
    careers in provinces, 187
    changing career patterns, 155
    choice of, 263–265
    chronology of, 309
    consequences of birthplace for, 180
    criticism of election fraud, 125
    decision-making, 262
    development of faith role, 289
    early careers, 155
    early identification of, 165
    educational trends, 174

    emeritus, 260
    formation in diocese of origin, 185
    four common career categories, 156
    friendships at seminaries, 166
    geographic biases, 199
    geographic origins, 13, 185–191, 199
    identification of social origins, 195
    importance of personal qualities, 270
    importance of teaching, 173
    importance of views, 283
    influenced by priests in career choice,
        144
    initial career assignments, 157
    juridical authority, 261
    level of advanced education, 159
    moral values of Church, 289
    need for closer analysis, 259
    opinion of partisan politics, 54
    priests' support for, 274
    reason they cannot ignore fraud, 69
    recruitment patterns among, 187
    relationship between birthplace and
        education, 190
    reservations toward CEBs, 94
    residence at Colegio Pio Latino
        América, 171
    restrictions on authority, 262
    role in Catholic structure, 228
    rural representation, 198
    school attendance, 158, 173
    secular education of, 162
    seminaries where educated, 160, 174
    social origins, 191–195
    support for CEBs, 92
    teaching experiences of, 159, 165
    type of degrees, 159
    types, 260
    urban background influence among,
        189
    views of Church political roles, 291
    views of Church role, 288–295
    where educated, 160, 174
Briebich, Armando
    view of relations with Church, 212
Butler Flora, Cornelia
    on clergy, 12

Cardinals
    College of, 228
    role in Catholic structure, 228, 161

Career tracks
  family environment's role in, 136
  generalist, 156
  major categories of reasons for choice
    of, 136
  priests, 15–16
  specialists, 157
Carpizo, Jorge
  encouraged Church activism on human
    rights, 82
Carrasco, Bartolomé
  help from Vatican, 277 n. 28
Carrillo Poblano, Manuel
  on consequence of reforms, 40
Castillo, Heberto
  childhood, 140
Catholic Church
  actual role, 51
  autonomous actor, 12, 251
  builder of human values, 285
  and business, 63, 210
  central education center, 159
  communication problems with
    politicians, 210
  connection to PAN, 204
  cultural role retarded, 286
  decentralized structure, 9, 13, 197–198
  direct political role, 126
  dogma, 50
  educational commonalities with military,
    186
  educational linkages to population, 6,
    286
  financial autonomy of, 241
  formal structure, 125
  hierarchical structure, 198
  human rights posture in 1970s, 80
  identification with state, 8
  increasing participation, 6
  informality of ties to politicians, 210
  as interest group, 202
  interest group activity, 12
  internal conflicts, 35
  international structure, 229
  local roots, 187–188
  nationalism, 243
  outside funding, 243
  parishes, 235
  physical modesty, 243
  political role, 51

  population's support for, 112–113
  position on temporal power, 51
  property taxes on, 243
  reasons for remaining independent of
    state, 70
  reflecting societal concerns, 52
  seminaries operated by, 160
  social role of, 297
  sources of funding, 242
  state financial support for, 243
  strength, 8
  structure, 228, 275
  teaches civic responsibility, 15
  teachings on abortion, 50
  tenuous ties to government, 204
  World Council of Churches support for,
    244
Catholicism, Mexican
  differences with United States, 4
  esteem for, 14
  impact on political culture, 5
  importance in Mexico, 4, 113
  influence ranked, 7
  limited influence, 8
  monopoly on religion, 25
  obstacles to influence, 7
  origins of statist values, 5
  political influence, 112
  sources of influence, 6
  young people's, 111
Catholics
  conceptualization of God, 112
  education of Mexican, 8
  favor Church discussion of problems,
    123
  on individual rights, 118
  opposed to Church indoctrination, 122
  percentage in Mexico, 111
  political preferences of, 120
  on redefining Church's social role,
    123
  rejection of Church political role, 119
  on role of Church in secular affairs,
    118
  social views, 117
  support for PAN, 120–121
  views of bishops, 263
  views of church-state history, 117
  views of Vatican relations, 118
CEBs. *See* base ecclesiastical communities

CELAM. *See* Conference of Latin
American Bishops
CEM. *See* Conference of Mexican Bishops
Centralization of Church
misperceptions, 26
Centro Universitario Mexicano
education of prominent Mexicans, 208
Chand, Vikran Khub
experiences of Chihuahua bishops with
Vatican II, 76 n. 111
Chaveriat, Jacques
on priests' financial situation, 242
Chiapas rebellion
clerical involvement in, 41
Chihuahua
archdiocese civic education project, 292
bishops' published statement, 66
electoral fraud in 1986, 58, 64
local bishops' pamphlet on, 64
outside support of bishops from, 64
political ramifications, 67
repercussions of bishops' statement on,
66
role of Manuel Bartlett in, 64
Washington Post statement, 66
Chihuahua tendency
defined, 272
Chile
bishops' career patterns, 155
bishops' social origins, 193
Christian Democracy
influence in PAN, 29, 58
Civic responsibility
Catholic teachings on, 15
Cleary, Edward
limits on evangelicals, 270
Clergy
as actors, 12
credentialing process, 154
differences between lower and higher,
25
ignorance of politicians, 202
importance of Cristero rebellion among,
146–147
pastoral tasks, 155
victims of human rights abuses, 84
Colegio México
consequences of living at, 173
Colegio Pio Latino América
description of, 171

importance to bishops, 171
reasons Mexicans left, 173
Conference of Latin American Bishops
(CELAM), Puebla, 1979
bishops' involvement in, 30
differences with Medellín, 30
impact on base communities, 90
position on social justice, 68
reunion's impact, 30
seminal event, 29
Vatican II's effects on, 86
Conference of Mexican Bishops (CEM)
assembly functions, 237
committees, 237
criticisms of development, 292
criticisms of participation, 61
democratization posture, 62, 293
on distribution of wealth, 68
episcopal agencies, 237
evolution of, 238
on foreign debt, 68–69
foundation of, 236
human rights position, 81, 83
importance, 250
institutions, 236
interest in PAN, 293
involvement in fraud issue, 63
lack of conflict within, 273
on liberty, 70 n. 6
long-term policies, 236
meeting with Jorge Carpizo, 82
National Center for Social
Communication, 237–238
perception of fraud, 62
permanent council of, 236
politics defined, 293
position on right to vote, 61
position toward CEBs, 93
public's ignorance of role, 238
reactions to constitutional reforms, 37–
38
on respect for human beings, 294
Social Secretariat, 237
statement on free elections, 61
support for Girolamo Prigione, 238
support for political candidates, 69
tempers ideological divisions, 273
view of Church political role, 291–
292
view of Vatican delegate, 238

Conflict between church and state
  Church human rights role as source,
    83
  Church moral influence as source, 52
Constitution, 1917
  antecedent of 1992 reforms, 35
  anti-Church provisions, 26
  consequences on culture, 27
  violations on state level, 213
Constitutional reforms
  Article 3, 36
  basic principles of, 35
  bylaws, 35–36
  Church initiation of, 33
  congressional role in, 35
  criticisms of bishops, 38–39
  decision-making process of, 34–35
  fiscal consequences, 39
  internal conflicts' impact on, 35
  law of religious associations and public
    cults, 36
  negotiations of, 34
  political legitimacy and, 33
  presidential motivations for, 32
  primary changes, 37
  Protestant view of, 40
  public opinion's impact on, 33
  reactions to, 37–38
  reviving Church interest in politics, 40
  role of Carlos Salinas de Gortari, 31
  role of secretariat of government, 35
  theory and reality, 34
  and Vatican relations, 37
Corripio Ahumada, Ernesto
  distribution of pamphlets on Marxism,
    59
  effort to strengthen state ties, 219
  reasons Mexicans lack political interests,
    75 n. 98
Cristero War
  bishops' personal experiences in, 146,
    196
  compared to politicians' revolutionary
    experiences, 147
  and differences with Latin America, 27
  influence on formation of priests, 146,
    148
  unique heritage of, 28
Cuba
  consequences for Catholicism, 29

Cuellar Romo, Ricardo
  explains lack of outside funds, 243
Curia
  administrative power, 229
  influence on bishop selection process,
    267
  source of bishops, 158
  structure, 228

Davis, Charles
  religious involvement, 130 n. 55
Debt, foreign
  bishops' posture on, 245
  collaboration of Mexican and U.S.
    bishops on, 246
Decision-making theory, 17
De la Madrid, Miguel
  on bishops' position in Chihuahua, 58
  changed structure of church-state
    relationship, 218
  family religious environment, 138–139
  generation's attendance at private
    schools, 208
  importance of personal ties, 218
  reason for delaying church-state reforms,
    45 n. 60, 288
  reason for wanting to improve relations
    between church and state, 219
  relations with clergy, 217
  reliance on Prigione, 219
Democratic Electoral Movement (MED),
    60
Democratization
  position of CEM, 62
Díaz, Porfirio
  pattern of church-state relations, 25
Díaz Ordaz, Gustavo
  personal relationship with bishop, 43 n.
    41, 215
Diocese
  autonomy of, 185
  basic unit of Catholic Church, 259
  bishops as product of, 13, 185
  evolution of importance, 274
  impact of pastoral regions, 234
  isolation in Church structure, 234
  limitations of, 270
  modesty of buildings, 260
  Morelia, 183
  types of diocesan priests, 259

Drogus, Carol Ann
  Catholicism and religious beliefs, 128 n.
    29

Earthquake, Mexico City, 1985
  impact on Church prestige, 31
Echeverría, Luis
  courtesy to religious leaders, 216
  example of personal ties to clergy, 204
  family influences, 139
  pattern of relationship with Church,
    215–216
  relationship with Jorge Martínez Gómez
    del Campo, 215
  relationship with Sergio Méndez Arceo,
    216, 285
  view of Catholic Church, 284
Education
  American bishops', 159–160
  bishops', 154, 159, 173
  Catholic Church's structure of, 159
  Catholic school graduates, 208
  Catholic student population, 206–207
  changing trends in bishops', 174
  Church's task defined, 291
  clerical patterns, 174
  consequences of seminary, 16
  elite ties to Church, 6
  enrollment figures, 207
  impact on politicians, 145
  importance in becoming a bishop, 156,
    173
  importance in career choice, 145
  increase in Catholic levels of, 207
  influence on liberalism, 207
  influence on religiosity, 114–115
  Instituto Patria, 207
  potential influence on church-state ties,
    206
  social environment of Catholic schools,
    208
Election of 1988
  Church involvement in allegations of
    fraud, 63
  human rights violations during, 80
  religiosity and voting in, 121
Electoral fraud
  bishops' criticism of, 125

Chihuahua in 1986, 58, 64–66
  and partisan politics, 60
  right to vote, 60
  source of conflict between church and
    state, 58
Electoral reforms
  influence on church-state relation, 31
Elite theories
  on features of leadership, 13

Faesler, Julio
  on Church role in morality, 285
Faith
  bishops' view of Church's role in, 289
Family characteristics
  importance in determining priest's
    career, 196
Family religious beliefs
  impact on future priests and politicians,
    149
Federal District
  church-state relations in, 215
Fichter, Joseph H.
  survey of U.S. priests and brothers, 135
Fleet, Michael
  on rank-and-file Catholics, 114
Foreign clergy
  effects on Church behavior, 247
  exposure of Mexico to international
    influences, 246
  lack of impact, 248
  most important consequences of, 247–
    248
  numbers of, 247
  presence in Mexico, 246–247
  President Cárdenas's involvement with,
    248
  sources of, 247
Fuentes, Carlos, 4

García, Antonio
  social origins, 193–194
Gasperín Gasperín, Mario de
  modest social origins, 194
  pastoral career, 175
Gaudium et Spes, 85
Gender
  role in religiosity, 114

Geography
  role in laity's view of Church
    participation, 119
  role in religiosity, 115–116
González Guevara, Rodolfo
  description of family religious
    influences, 140–141
GRACE scale, 112
Greeley, Andrew
  on Catholic view of God, 112
  on priests' reasons for career choice, 136
Gregorian University, Rome
  American graduates, 170
  bishops' attendance at, 161, 171
  Colegio México, 173
  Colegio Pio Latino América, 171
  content of education at, 171–172
  decline in attendance, 161
  formative experience, 172
  impact on bishops' careers, 171
  influence, 170
  Latin American interest in, 171
  Vatican II influences at, 172
  during World War II, 172
Guerrero, Nicéforo
  on Church revenues, 242
  on good relations between governors and
    bishops, 213
  on importance of *mayordomo,* 26
Guízar Díaz, Ricardo
  experiences at Gregorian University, 172

Hinojosa Ortiz, Manuel
  example of conflict among Catholics,
    213–214
Historical context
  absorbed through socialization, 11
  alliance between church and state, 24
  anticlericalism, 24
  effect on careers, 146
  as formative agent, 149
  hostility toward Church, 10–11
  impact on theory, 10
  importance of Cristero rebellion, 146
  after independence, 25
  influence on liberation theology, 88
  liberalism in, 25
  premise of, 11
  pre-1910 themes in, 24

Huerta, Victoriano
  Church support for, 27
Huesca Pacheco, Rosendo
  attitude toward priests, 269
  example of seminary contacts, 166
  explains selection of outsider bishops,
    266
Human rights
  bishops' criticism of, 125
  Catholic Church's posture in 1970s, 80
  clergy as victims of abuse, 84
  elections of 1988, 80
  first attention to, 79
  impact of 1917 Constitution on, 80
  Mexican record on, 79
  Pro Vida role in, 84
  Puebla conference's influence on, 80
  religious orders' role in, 81
  source of church conflict with state, 98

Ibero-American University
  and ties between PAN and Church,
    206
Ideological divisions
  among bishops, 271
  sources of differences, 271
  tendencies, 272–273
Ideology
  of Latin American Catholicism, 18
Income
  influence on religiosity, 115
Informal channels
  between church and state, 17
  national patterns, 17
Institutional context
  Catholic Church, 14
Institutional Revolutionary Party (PRI)
  alleged Church support for, 60
  popularizes PAN ties to Church, 205
  priests' opposition to, 59
Instituto Patria
  educates political elites, 207

Jardi, Teresa
  death threats to, 82
Jesuits
  role in elite education, 206

Kinship
  importance in religious careers, 143, 197
  religious relatives, 143
Klesner, Joseph
  regionalism and religious voting, 122
Krauze, Enrique
  recognition of bishops' local roots, 187

Laity
  Church attendance by, 114
  Church's potential to influence, 109
  neglected in research, 110
  perception of priests, 271
  potential influence of, 109
  types, 114
  views on abortion, 122
Lajous Martínez, Adrián
  on birth control, 271
  on Catholic education, 207
Language
  differences between clergy's and
    politicians' vocabulary, 294
  political disputes emerging from
    differences in, 295
Law of Religious Associations and Public
    Cults
  contents, 36
Leadership
  Catholic selection process, 16
Levine, Daniel
  activism and activation, 294
  establishment politics, 3
  school attendance of bishops, 158
  student movement's effects, 30
  views of clergy, 283
Liberalism
  heritage of in priests' background, 138
  impact on Miguel de la Madrid's
    upbringing, 139
  influence on Church's political role,
    119–120
  influence on socialization, 11
  intertwined with Catholicism, 149
  premise, 11
  principles, 25
  retarded Church cultural role, 286
  socializing influences of, 124–125
Liberation theology
  bishops' opposition to, 89

changes introduced in Mexico, 86
conceptualization, 88–89
consequences for Mexico, 86–87
effect on indigenous practices, 87
impact on decentralization, 86
impact on laity, 87
influence among Mexican clergy, 86
influence on seminary education, 87
Marxism in, 89
Pope's condemnation of, 90
reasons for limited effects in Mexico,
    87–88
Literature
  ignores views of major actors, 283
Loaeza, Soledad
  reason for Echeverría improving Church
    relations, 217
  on support for parties, 72 n. 33
Lomnitz, Larissa, 5
Lona Reyes, Arturo
  relationship with other bishops, 274
López Mateos, Adolfo
  Protestant wife, 107 n. 152
López Portillo, José
  family influences in upbringing, 139–
    140, 217
  on linkages between U.S. and Mexican
    bishops, 245
  personal relations with clergy, 217
  reliance on Prigione, 217
  risks of changing Church relationship,
    288
  visit of Pope, 217
Lozano Barragán, Javier
  respect of priests for, 269
Luengo, Enrique
  permission from bishops to carry out
    study of priests, 261
  requests of local government to priests,
    214
  school attendance of priests, 158

Mainwaring, Scott
  on Church morality, 15
Márquez y Toriz, Octaviano
  friendship with President Gustavo Díaz
    Ordaz, 215
Martínez Báez, Antonio
  upbringing in Michoacán, 141

Martínez del Campo, Jorge
  key figure in Church relationship to
    presidents, 211
Marxism
  Church position on, 59
Masses
  potential partisan influence of, 109
Mayordomo
  importance of, 26
Medina Plascencia, Carlos
  mixing religion and politics, 52
Melgoza Osorio, José
  generalist, 156
  imposition of unity in diocese, 268
Méndez Arceo, Sergio
  change in leadership of diocese, 270
  consequences of nationalism, 244
  "Letter of Anenecuilco," 52
  position on Marxism, 59
  priests' decision-making role, 262
  relationship to Luis Echeverría, 216
  role in CEBs, 91
Methodists
  support for human rights, 81
Methodology
  religion and politics, 3
Metz, Allan
  Church services to the state, 214
Mexican Apostolic Catholic Church
  existence of, 235
Mexican Democratic Party (PDM)
  Catholic support for, 58
  members' support for Church political
    role, 119
Meyer, Jean
  on Cristero War heritage, 28
Moctezuma Díaz Infante, Pedro
  Echeverría's representative, 216
Montezuma seminary, New Mexico
  bishops' attendance at, 161, 168
  curriculum, 170
  graduates who became bishops, 169
  graduation rate at, 167
  history, 166–167
  importance as recruitment center, 168
  justification for, 161
  limitations of influence, 168
  original class at, 166
  peculiarity of to Mexico, 166

reason for closing, 170
  revival of ideas, 168
  stronger ties to U.S. episcopate, 168
Morality
  bishops' shaping of, 53
  influence on decision making, 15
Morelia archdiocese
  central importance to bishops, 183
Morín Suárez, Samuel
  personal conflict between church and
    state, 300
Muñoz, Rafael
  recollections of Montezuma seminary,
    170
Muñoz Ledo, Porfirio
  on Archbishop Almeida, 76 n. 114
  campaign experiences, 223 n. 32
Mutchler, David
  on foreign education, 271

National Action Party (PAN)
  ACJM connection to Catholic Church,
    204
  benefits from religious identification, 56
  bishops' dislike for, 60
  Catholic voting for, 29, 121
  Christian socialism's influence in, 222 n.
    16
  Church identification with, 56
  impact on laity, 110
  lack of connection to Church, 205
  linkages to Church, 57, 204–205
  mythology about, 221
  pressure on reforms, 46 n. 71
  supporters, 121
  support for Church, 57, 287
National Center for Social Communication
  student movement of 1968, 237–238
  voice for progressive change, 237
North American Free Trade Agreement
    (NAFTA)
  bishops' posture on, 245
  U.S. bishops' opposition to, 246

Opus Dei
  description, 248
  differences from other orders, 249
  history, 249
  influence in education, 249

Opus Dei (*continued*)
  Pan American Institute of Higher
    Management (IPADE), 249

Papal nuncio
  CEM's role in enhancing influence of,
    230
  contacts with Curia, 230
  differing agenda of, 18
  impact on church-state relationship, 17,
    250
  influence on ideological divisions, 271
  informal activities of, 230
  motives in appointing bishops, 275
  Prigione's assignment as, 230
  selection of bishops, 265–267
  variables in influence of, 229
Participation, 6
Partido Católico Nacional, 27
Partisan politics
  actual Church involvement in, 56
  against PRI, 59
  Church identification with PAN, 56–57
  Church posture toward, 54
  clergy's attitudes toward, 56
  critics of Church in, 54
  episcopate's opinion on, 54
  increase since 1979, 57
  laity's role in, 55
Party of the Democratic Revolution (PRD)
  support for Catholic Church, 287
  sympathies for liberation theology, 214
Pascoe, Ricardo
  description of family religious
    influences, 141
Pastoral regions
  importance for dioceses, 234, 250
Pérez Gil, Manuel
  assesses CEM influence, 237
  friendships at Montezuma seminary, 169
  recollections of seminary education, 164
  teaching career, 195
Personal linkages
  essential to presidents, 203
  example of Agustín Téllez Cruz, 204
  lifelong ties of politicians, 204
  negative consequences of, 220
  as substitute for formal institutions, 220
  weakness of between politicians and
    clergy, 203

Personal revelations
  bishops' recollections of, 148–149
  reason for joining priesthood, 148
Political model
  deficiencies in, 12
Political system
  declining legitimacy of, 31
Politicians
  advocates of Church ethical values, 285
  belief that Church should avoid partisan
    matters, 286
  children in private schools, 209
  differences with clergy, 287
  education, 154
  examples of personal linkages to clergy,
    204
  exposure to Catholic values, 202
  government generated Church
    involvement, 287
  ignorance of clergy, 202, 284
  informality of ties to clergy, 210
  lack of social ties to clergy, 203
  major difference with bishops, 284
  opposition's support for Church, 287
  opposition to changing relationship with
    Church, 288
  on social responsibility issue, 287
  on value of faith, 286
  view clergy as different from institution,
    287
  views of Catholic Church, 284–288
  views on changes in church-state
    relationship, 288
Posadas Ocampo, Juan Jesús
  assassination of, 101 n. 47
  changes in Cuernavaca diocese, 270
  favored juridical personality for Church,
    295
  seminary completion figures of
    generation, 164
Premises, 11–17
Presidents
  friendships among clergy, 215
Priests
  age of at career choice, 135
  becoming bishops, 263
  career tracks of, 15, 155
  Church's mission according to, 296–297
  contact with government officials, 214
  denunciation of partisan politics, 298

differences with politicians, 302
educational satisfaction, 163
education of, 16
emphasis on external actors in career
   choice, 136
evangelizing role of Church, 296
family environment, 136
financial condition, 242
first-time positions, 156
grandparents' beliefs, 137–138
human rights mission of Church, 298
individual ties to PAN, 206
interest in political affairs, 52
laity's view of, 271
leadership abilities of, 16
level of religious kinship among, 143
level of respect for, 7, 113
national unity goals, 302
needs of poor, 296
numbers, 235
parents' religious beliefs, 137
party identification, 57
pastoral experiences, 156
perceptions of laity, 7
as political candidates, 57
political intolerance among, 53
political tasks of Church, 299
praise for politicians' nationalism, 300
problems of theory and reality, 55
progressive views, 298
reasons for joining clergy, 135
relations with bishops, 268
school attendance, 158
significance of peers to, 144
sympathies of for PAN, 57, 206
sympathies of for PRD, 206
transcendental goals, 300
views of rank and file, 295–302
Prigione, Girolamo
   admits errors of Church, 295
   alienation of Federal District priests,
      275
   alienation of government officials, 233
   altered relations with Mexican
      presidents, 211
   CEM's support for, 238
   changed relations with Vatican, 231
   clergy's criticism of, 231
   conflict with Ernesto Corripio Ahumada,
      233

   controversial reputation, 230–231
   description of Miguel de la Madrid's
      relations to Church, 218
   ignored needs of Mexican people, 232
   imposition of outsider bishops, 266
   interference in Chiapas, 232, 239
   intervention in Church internal affairs,
      232
   long-term strategy, 230
   optimism about future relationship, 219
   on partisan politics, 55
   on priests' families, 137
   reason for success, 281 n. 110
   relationship with Manuel Bartlett, 218
   replacement of progressive bishops,
      218
   role in Chihuahua declaration, 65
   selection of bishops, 265–267
   tarnished reputation of, 231
   tensions generated by, 231, 239
   unmatched influence of, 230
Pro-life groups
   human rights role, 84–85
   influence on voting, 85
   Museum of Modern Art incident, 215
Protestants
   bishops' view of, 95–96
   Catholic clergy's view of, 95
   conflicts with Catholics, 95
   conversions to, 94
   differences with Catholics, 96–97
   evangelical, 95
   expansion of political actors, 97
   growth of, 94
   importance in Mexico, 4
   influence on politicians' upbringing, 141
   nationalism and, 98
   political impact of, 96
   potential influence of, 97
   significance as an issue, 97
   view of reforms, 40

Recruitment
   patterns among bishops, 187
Recruitment theory
   facilitates understanding of Church, 18
Reese, Thomas
   and bishops' education in the United
      States, 159

Regionalism
  differences between bishops and
    politicians, 180
  as geographic variable, 188
  importance of clergy's roots, 185, 187
  role in Church structure, 234
  rural versus urban, 189
Relationship between bishops and priests
  assessment of by priests, 268
  bishops' administrative style, 269
  difficulties in, 268
  level of communication, 267–268
  personal qualities of bishops, 269–270
  primary problem in, 267
Relationship between government and
    Church
  Armando Briebich's view of, 212
  centralization of communication's effects
    on, 276
  example of Zacatecas, 212
  in Federal District, 214
  governors' views of, 21
  local linkages, 212, 214
  presidential friendships, 215
  state's misunderstanding of Church
    structure, 276
Relationship between religion and politics
  focus of study, 283–284
Religion
  impact on values, 50
  secular role in Mexico, 4
Religion and politics
  examinations of, 3
  interest in Mexican, 3
Religiosity
  impact on political values, 116
  impact on change, 117
  influence on voting, 120
Religious beliefs
  of Mexican population, 5
Religious intensity
  correlation with voting, 122
  determinants of, 113
  partisanship and, 121
Religious-order priests
  changing composition of, 240
  divisions with diocesan priests, 240–
    241
  foreign presence among, 241
  hierarchy of, 241

historic contributions, 239
influence, 250
international linkages, 240
most important, 240
numbers in Mexico, 239–240
role in human rights, 81
social differences with diocesan priests,
  241
source of education, 163
structural differences with diocesan
  priests, 240
Religious scholars
  work on Mexico, 14
Religious values
  belief in Christianity, 111
  Catholic, 111
  exploration of, 11
  importance in Mexican culture, 111
Religious workers
  consequences for religion, 8
  growth of, 7
Rerum Novarum, 27
Research on Church
  difficulties, 9
Revolution of 1910
  return to 19th-century theme, 26
Reyes Heroles, Federico
  on Carlos Salinas's motivations, 32
Reyes Heroles, Jesús
  reaction to Pope's visit, 44 n. 55
Reynoso Cervantes, Luis
  specialist, 157
Rivera Carrera, Norberto
  criticism of neo-Liberalism, 78 n. 146
Roqueñi, Antonio
  classic example of secular education,
    162
  specialist, 157
Rovalo, José Pablo
  granting autonomy to priests, 268–269
  parents' influence, 138
Ruiz García, Samuel
  argument for unity, 273–274
  defense of indigenous rights, 92
  description of, 105 n. 123
  human rights efforts, 81
  leader in liberation theology, 92
  parents, 137
  Prigione's attempt to remove, 254 n. 84
  role in CEBs, 91

Salazar López, José
  modest life, 194
Salinas de Gortari, Carlos
  appointed personal representative to
    Vatican, 220
  Church in modernization program, 110
  Church perception of as presidential
    candidate, 219
  established cordial relations with
    Church, 219
  institutionalized relationship with
    Church, 220
  invitation of bishops to inauguration, 31
  motivations for reforms, 32–34
  provoked different responses from
    clergy, 272
Samaniego Barriga, Manuel
  gap between theory and reality, 295
  on Morelia archdiocese, 183
  pastoralist, 157
Schulenburg, Guillermo
  communication channel to president, 216
Second Concilium of Bishops. *See* Vatican
  II
Secretariat of Government
  reaction to reforms, 38
Secularism
  increasing growth in Mexico, 4
Selection process
  auxiliary bishops, 264–265
  bishops, 265–266
  papal delegate's influence over bishops',
    265–266
Seminaries
  bishops' access to, 158–159
  completion rates, 165
  curriculum, 163
  declining class size, 165
  differences among, 163
  duration of attendance at, 158
  education of bishops, 160
  impact of persecution on, 164
  important, 163
  Montezuma, 161
  philosophy, 162
  priests' age of attendance at, 145–146
  purpose, 162
  rectors who became bishops, 167
  satisfaction with, 163
  socialization at, 162

source of future bishops, 155
source of future friendships among
  bishops, 166
Silent majority tendency
  defined, 273
Smith, Brian
  on rank-and-file Catholics, 114
Social justice
  Church role in formulating, 53
  Church's posture on, 67
  pastoral statements on, 68
Social mobilization, 6
Socialization
  historical experiences, 11
Social origins
  of bishops, 193–195
  bishops' self-identification, 195
  commonalities between U.S. and
    Mexican bishops, 192
  difficulties in obtaining data on, 192
  effects on career choices, 196
  effects on priests' attitudes, 192
  importance to clergy, 191, 197
  of Latin American bishops, 192
  middle class, 193
  of military, 192
  relation to bishops' education, 194
  relation to teaching, 195
  social pressures of, 195
  upward mobility's relation to, 193
  working class, 193
Southern tendency
  defined, 272
Spiritual mission tendency
  defined, 272
Spiritual voice
  bishops' view of Church's, 290
Statist values, 5
Stein, Andrew
  on differences between Catholics and
    Protestants, 133 n. 89
Stewart-Gambino, Hannah
  on survey research's importance, 127
Structures
  Church hierarchical, 234
  informal links between clergy and state,
    209, 221
  Ivan Vallier on importance of, 234
  local linkages between clergy and state,
    212, 221

Structures (*continued*)
    national-level complications, 209–210,
        233
    politicians' misunderstanding of Church,
        210
Student movement of 1968
    human rights response to, 80
    influence on clergy's attitudes, 80
    Mexican episcopate reaction to, 30
    schism within the Church, 30
    turning point in church-state relations,
        29
Suárez Rivera, Adolfo
    invitation to Los Pinos, 203
    on political participation, 51
    statement on Church's political role, 292

Talamás Calamandari, Manuel
    directed laity voting, 125
Téllez Cruz, Agustín
    religious ties of, 204
Theoretical arguments
    decision making, 17
    framework of, 9
    importance of empirical findings for, 124
    importance of history in, 10
    institutional explorations, 8
    Latin American case, 9
    spiritual qualities considered in, 10
    state theory, 9
Torreblanca, Magín C.
    effects of Cristero background, 213

Universal Declaration of Human Rights,
        United Nations
    Article 4, 99
U.S. bishops
    influence in Mexico, 251
    interest in Mexico, 244
    José López Portillo on alliance with
        Mexico, 245
    personal ties to Mexico, 245
    policy issues linked, 245
    potential alliance with Mexican bishops,
        245

Vallier, Ivan
    on Church structure, 234
    on national development patterns, 271

Values
    bishops' views on, 290
    of Catholicism, 5
    defined, 290
    differing views on bishops', 294
    dual track, 22 n. 47
    emphasis on spiritual matters, 301
    priests and politicians in agreement, 301
    priests' views of, 297, 299
    shaping of moral, 53
    similarities between priests and bishops
        concerning, 297
    teaching of, 302
Vatican
    bishop selection process, 267
    complicating church-state relations, 10
    distinguishing role, 17
    misunderstanding of Mexican
        episcopate, 275
    reestablishing relations, 37
    role in Chihuahua in 1986, 65
Vatican tendency
    ideological group, 272
Vatican II
    bishops' view of, 86
    Gaudium et Spes, 85
    history's effect on, 86
    Mexican bishops' attendance at, 85
    origins of ideas presented at, 85
    reasons for limited influence in Mexico,
        88–89
Vázquez Santana, Higinio
    example of politician who became a
        priest, 222 n. 4
Vera López, Raúl
    on bishops' need for assistance, 262
Vergara, Jesús
    position paper on election fraud, 254
Vicar general
    importance to diocese, 260
Vicencio Tovar, Abel
    ACJM ties, 204–205
    on constitutional reforms, 39
    family religious influences, 140
Violence
    Church opposition to, 53
    impact on Mexican formation, 150
Voluntary organizations
    membership in, 6

Voting
  Church encouragement for, 62
  separate Church vote, 62

Wald, Kenneth
  on local church, 13
Watty Urquidi, Ricardo
  religious-order priest, 277 n. 15
West Central Mexico
  heart of Cristero rebellion, 183
  source of bishops, 181

Zaid, Gabriel
  family's religious values, 143
  Monterrey's Catholicism, 199 n. 7
Zerón Medina, Fausto
  describes Echeverría's relationship to
    Church, 215–216
  informality of ties between church and
    state, 210
  key figure in link between church and
    state, 142
  President Echeverría's trust in, 211

BX 1428.2 .C27 1997
Camp, Roderic Ai.
Crossing swords
    90041

DATE DUE

AUG 0 5 2002			

VILLA JULIE COLLEGE LIBRARY
STEVENSON, MD 21153